"Ted Bell was our national school bell, ringing in a new era of commitment to excellence . . . He found *A Nation At Risk*. He leaves behind a nation on the move. No man could have a greater legacy."

Richard W. Riley, U.S. Secretary of Education

RECLAIMING OUR NATION AT RISK

LESSONS LEARNED:
REFORMING OUR PUBLIC SCHOOLS

Kent Lloyd and Diane Ramsey
with *Terrel H. Bell*

Copyright © 1998 by The Terrel H. Bell KNOWLEDGE NETWORK for
Education Reform

Library of Congress Cataloging-in-Publication Data

Lloyd, Kent (1931) and Diane Ramsey (1940)
RECLAIMING OUR NATION AT RISK. Lessons Learned: Reforming Our Public
Schools.
Includes bibliographical references
Education—United States—Reform. 2. Education—United States—Public
Schools. 3. Education change—United States. 4. Education—Research. 5. Educa-
tion—Charter Schools. 6. Education—Character Education. 7. Education—Family
Involvement. 8. Education—Academic Standards. 9. Education—Public Engage-
ment.

ISBN 0-9634636-3-2

1 3 5 7 9 10 6 4 2
Advanced Printing, April 1997
Second Printing, May 1997
Third Printing, September 1997
Fourth Printing, February 1998

RECLAIMING OUR NATION AT RISK

Lessons Learned: Reforming Our Public Schools

by Kent Lloyd and Diane Ramsey with Terrel H. Bell

Chapter 13. PARENT ENGAGEMENT
Saturday afternoon, March 22

Chapter 14. EMPOWERING YOUR COMMUNITY SCHOOL, PART I
Saturday morning, April 19

PREFACE

Half of our children face a lifetime of despair and poverty because we are failing to prepare them with high-quality academic and character education. This preventable "cancer of ignorance" is the most significant moral issue of our time! In 1983, a landmark report, *A Nation At Risk*, called our attention to the decline of educational achievement among high school graduates—and the sobering consequences of poverty, discrimination, ill-health and violence. Heroic school reformers, including teachers, administrators, parents and community leaders, have fought hard to reverse the "rising tide of mediocrity that threatens our very future as a Nation and a people." Yet the students who were in kindergarten in 1983 have now graduated from high school. Only half of these are enrolled in college or are working at well-paid jobs. The other half are in low-skill, low-paying jobs, unemployed, on welfare, or in prison—all part of an expanding underclass maintained at growing public expense.

As a nation, we cannot continue to turn deaf ears to the cries of our disadvantaged white and minority children. Countless reports, conferences, national and state summit meetings warn of personal, economic, and political calamities. Each child is valuable in our democracy. Educators and caring adults must work together to create responsible, viable learning communities for all children and for those who help them to succeed. Valiant grassroots efforts are at work to transform our public schools, but they are not moving fast enough. Many citizens in neighborhoods across America are struggling with the painful reality that they must drastically transform their schools—or public education will be lost. *We believe that a quality elementary education is the best and least expensive affirmative action program.*

This report approaches school reform by focusing on the "good news." We interviewed 44 nationally-recognized school reformers and education leaders about the most effective ways of reforming failing urban and suburban elementary schools. A pioneering school reformer, John Goodlad, told us, the authors, that reform scholars usually talk only to each other in their professional journals, technical reports and newsletters. He challenged us to find a more effective way of translating the school reform message to those who must carry it out. To present our findings, we created a fictional School Board that appoints a Citizens' Commission on Reform of Jefferson Elementary School. Our interviewees appear as distinguished "guests" before this fictional Citizens' Commission. Our interview data, along with information from the articles and books of interviewees, is presented as their "testimonies" during Commission Hearings. Commission members are composites of real people we have met while working with hundreds of similar citizen and educational groups over the past 30 years. The dialogue of these characters dramatizes the often conflicting attitudes and views of many Americans on the vexing subject of school reform. The dialogue is intertwined with issues of race and class that complicate and enrich public discourse in our democracy today. Although we do not agree with all that is said by the fictional Commission members, we have tried to represent their opinions accurately and fairly.

RECLAIMING OUR NATION AT RISK describes the "good news" of school reform all across America today. This guide to grassroots reform does not "re-invent the wheel," but identifies 20 successful school reform models and 35 "best practices" in 15 states and 18 cities. They show that we now know how to deliver high-quality education to all children, especially those "at risk." We now know these children can learn as well as middle-class children when given an equal opportunity to do so by knowledge-able, skilled and dedicated teachers and by committed, informed parents.

The conclusions and recommendations of the Citizens' Commission reconcile the "best practice" reform ideas that are being implemented in America today. We hope that policymakers, media people, educators, active parents and interested citizens will appreciate our view of this moral challenge. This resource book makes nine unique contributions to carrying out successful school reform to benefit all our children by:

1) describing *successful reform models and best practices* now being implemented throughout the nation as reported by the 44 reformers and educational leaders whom we interviewed;

2) reporting *valuable lessons learned* about how to reform community elementary schools;

3) modeling the actual *public engagement process* that every school must go through to carry out successful whole-school reform, thereby reconnecting parents with their neighborhood schools;

4) identifying the *eight essential components* for a successful whole-school reform model, including challenging academic standards, character education, professional staff development, school support services, technology support, parent and community engagement, student assessment and adult accountability, and school reform councils;

5) providing an *inventory questionnaire* for assessing local elementary schools against a high-performance model school;

6) showing how a *representative school-site team*—Citizens' Commission—undertakes a *reform discovery journey* together to design a *blueprint* or *reform package* that will meet the unique needs of their own elementary school;

7) exploding *seven common education myths* that block genuine reform;

8) demonstrating how *in-district independent public schools* can work effectively —with leadership from local school board members, superintendents, principals, teachers, parents and community leaders—to provide quality education for all our children; and

9) illustrating how parents and teachers can create *responsible family and classroom learning cultures.*

Other essential lessons were learned from our sample of successful reform pioneers and educational leaders. Almost without exception, successful reform comes only when the local school site is fully empowered. Authority and accountability must be transferred from the centralized, heavily regulated school district to a representative, school-based reform council of informed and committed teacher, parent and community representatives directed by a skilled, experienced principal-educator. In short, successful reform whole-school reform requires public engagement—parent and community representatives working together as equals with professional educators.

We believe this comprehensive study will become a useful source book to guide citizens in communities across the country in reforming public schools at all levels. We have focused on elementary schools to illustrate the public engagement process because they are less complex than middle and high schools. We have also tried to stretch beyond traditional concerns of public educators by presenting wider economic, social, political and cultural perspectives on why school reform is so essential to all Americans.

This manuscript is the work of many people. We thank our 44 guest reformers and national education leaders, our dedicated staff and consultants, and our focus groups for their reactions. We thank our distinguished reviewers who read and offered helpful feedback: Wayne Burnette, Tom Boysen, Maria Casillas, Christopher Cross, Stuart Gothold, Sven Groennings, Nathaniel Jackson, and our senior editor, Mary Lythgoe Bradford, who made a special contribution. We thank our private foundation sponsors—Kellogg, Freddie Mac, and Hewlett—for major assistance in supporting this reform study. We also thank Exxon, Ford Motor, MCI, Rockefeller, Rockwell, and Union Carbide for their earlier contributions. Without these supporters, this project could not have been undertaken and shared with the American people. As authors, we take sole responsibility for the final report and recommendations.

We are grateful for the counsel and encouragement of our co-author, Terrel H. Bell, father of *A Nation At Risk* and former U.S. Secretary of Education. He made major contributions to this study before his untimely death in 1996. In our opinion, this distinguished educator and courageous reform hero represented everything that makes quality education for all our children the "noblest work of man." To him we dedicate this work—Ted's final school reform report.

Introduction
THE CRISIS AT JEFFERSON ELEMENTARY SCHOOL
Friday, August 29

School Board President Jack Clayton parked his BMW in his reserved space in front of the County School District offices. This short meeting at 10:00 a.m. would be difficult and perhaps nasty—but long overdue. He moved briskly up the steps into the old building that had served as the home of the County School District for almost 50 years. Jack reached the elevators and greeted two young women with coffee cups and donuts. They smiled but didn't seem to know that he was the most important "dude" around here—except perhaps for Dr. Thomas Dooley, who had been the county superintendent for the past five years.

Maybe Dooley's been around here too long! If he was doing his job, I wouldn't have to be here today delivering my bad news, he thought.

He hurried down the hall to room 512, the big corner office marked, Dr. Thomas Dooley, Superintendent. Joannie was, as usual, at the reception desk answering telephones. When she looked up and recognized Jack, she flashed her brilliant smile.

With her enthusiasm, maybe she should be in this meeting today, Jack thought. *Maybe I could just leave her a memo for Tom and disappear. There's Mary Katherine, Tom's special assistant. She's really good.*

The superintendent's door seemed to magically open as he approached, and Jack went in. They did "the weather's too damn hot and humid for August" routine, and moved to sit at the low round table overlooking the park. Jack noticed that Tom was nervous and impatient, not quite the usual "in charge" cool professional.

"Tom," said Jack, "the full Board has met to review the failing situation at Jefferson Elementary. As we all know, the state superintendent has placed Jefferson on the reconstitution list. It will soon be taken over by the state to be reorganized or closed by this time next school year. This is damn embarrassing to the district. I'm not blaming you exactly, but now we have to go begging to the state capitol for more time. You know that Governor Scott is running for re-election. He's got a "get tough on world-class education standards" policy. We know he's for saving the taxpayers' money by advocating home schooling and private vouchers. His new pit bull, right-wing Secretary of Education Jim Collins, is hellbent to beat up and embarrass us all."

"You got that right, Jack," Tom said, "but Scott and Collins don't know what we're facing. Scott and his right-wing Republican legislature are starving us to death. Hell, no state budget increases for education in two years! What can we do about this, Jack? It looks like it's out of our hands."

"We have a plan, Tom. But to be successful, we need to work together. We have to put up a united front when we negotiate with the Governor and his Secretary of Education. First, we write a letter to the Governor signed by me as President of the School Board and you as Superintendent. I will also brief John Lyons, our State Senator, and my buddy, Cole Green, the Gov's special assistant. Our letter will propose that the state allow us to clean up our own mess by appointing an independent Citizens' Commission. The new Commission will take an objective look at just how badly Jefferson is performing and will try to determine the cause. Is it the disadvantaged kids or the welfare families in the public housing projects? Is it the drug dealers? Maybe it's the union protecting the system's rejects— poor and inexperienced teachers—no one else wants? Maybe it's our burned out principal? Whatever it is, we have a problem and someone has to find a solution. We need a 'silver bullet.'

"Tom, we're bankrupt and the Governor knows it," Jack said. "The district is going down and we can't protect your job if we don't have a reform plan. Three Board members want to fire your butt over this and hire a new superintendent. All they need is one more for a majority vote. That would buy us another year, but then we're right back where we started from. Worse, I get to face hostile parents every School Board meeting, and I have to make the same lame excuses. We look like we don't know what the hell we're doing!"

Dooley looked pale but listened with rapt attention. Jack went on: "Back to our letter to the Governor. We'll propose a Citizens' Reform Commission for Jefferson Elementary School. The new Commission will assess the situation. They'll take their time and write a report with recommendations on how we can turn this 'turkey' around. This could be our own little *A Nation At Risk* report with a plan for saving Jefferson over the next three years. We can all be heroes! Who knows, maybe we'll even help the poor kids for a change."

Dooley shook his head and asked, "Do you really think it'll work?"

"Well, it won't work without a strong reform commission made up of respected teachers, parents and community leaders. We'll also need outside consultants who can be trusted to keep everybody honest and on track. And, Tom, whatever they come up with—and we'd better pray they come up with a miracle—you and my Board better smile sweetly and give them anything they want. The Governor, the media dogs and the parents will be watching. Are you with us?"

"Wait just a damn minute, Jack! You say you have the Board's authority to propose this 'hairbrain' scheme? You want to turn over the assessment and reorganization of the worst school in the district to a bunch of outside amateurs? Classroom teachers and parents have no experience in reforming anything, let alone Jefferson Elementary School?"

"Tom, everybody knows that so-called reform reports just end up on the shelf. If you don't agree to this 'hairbrain' scheme, as you call it, I can't save your dumb-ass job. You'll be fired next Thursday night at the Board meeting because I'll provide the fourth vote. Am I getting your attention? We're not going through another year of shuffling the chairs on the Titanic—we've already hit the iceberg and a lot of people are going overboard without lifeboats. This includes the superintendent, the principal, teachers, classified and district staff. Today you get to decide. Next week it's out of your hands. In November half our Board face re-election. Unless we start damage control now, the state takes us over with headlines in *The Washington Post*. Am I getting through to you? It's over, we blew it. Time has run out!"

Tom's face went ashen. Suddenly he wasn't the same arrogant top dog. Jack had sent the spear right through Tom's heart. Tom would have to save face. *I'll have to get word out to my national network that I'm unhappy with the*

Board and my contract, Tom thought. *I need a better district where it's warm in the winter in Florida or California.*

"Okay, Jack. I'm in. What do you want me to do?"

"Sign the letter I'm preparing for the Governor. I want you to help me select the members of the new Reform Commission. Then promise me you'll back off and not try to influence their findings in any way. Just smile when they're appointed and tell the press how happy you are. Say you're looking forward to this citizen's report with recommendations for saving Jefferson Elementary School. Ain't democracy wonderful?"

"But, Jack, I've...we've...got to have some control or this could become a 'runaway' Commission. We can staff it from my office. I can get Bill Johnson, my assistant superintendent for curriculum, to act as executive director. We can appoint some teachers who owe us, and some friendly parents. It shouldn't take long to get a standard reform report recommending more money and more parent involvement. Then we'll retire Jefferson's principal, Mrs. Olive Carter, with an early buyout, shuffle some teachers, appoint a new parent association and give them something to chew on. Keep them busy. This is a piece of cake!"

"Tom, you're not listening!" Jack said impatiently. "This is not just window dressing. This new School Reform Commission will be completely independent from your office—period. If I hear that you are trying to influence their investigations in any way, I'll personally recommend that you be sacked before your contract expires next July. Are we clear about this!"

"Okay, okay Jack, have it your way," Tom said as he slumped in his chair. "But you can't trust an independent commission to come up with real solutions. In the last 10 years, our whole central office staff of professional educators hasn't been able to turn this sorry mess around!"

"Well, we're going to try," said Jack. "I'm asking Ramon Gonzales, vice-chair of the County Board of Education, to chair the new Reform Commission. He's smart and he's Hispanic. He's also the only one who isn't facing re-election next November. We need a woman vice chair. We're looking for the best principal in our district—someone who's independent, smart and credible with the Board and the other principals. Who do you think fits that description?"

"I have one principal that fits those specs," Tom said. "But she would never take leave from Lawndale Elementary School to take this assignment.

It'd tarnish her image and kill a promising career as a superintendent. By the way, she's Korean."

"Are you talking about Kim Su Young? asked Jack. "How long has she been a principal?"

"About seven years. She was at Moffit Elementary before I transferred her to Lawndale. But she'll never agree to this."

"She doesn't have to transfer to be vice-chair," Jack said. "It'll require ten Saturdays over the next year, and it's a voluntary commission. It could be a real resumé builder. I will also need four teachers, four parents and two community representatives, preferably a business leader and someone from the volunteer sector, like health or the churches. How about Paul Christopher as the business guy? He's a new face, and he was president of his Kiwanis club last year. He's been active in the Chamber's task force on education!"

"Do you think he'd play?" asked Tom.

"Won't know 'til I ask him," said Jack. "He's ambitious. He wants to run for the School Board. Belonging to this Commission would bring him higher county visibility. So how about the volunteer community? Has anyone been an agitator lately? We don't want to be accused of loading up the Commission with our patsies."

"There's only one person that fits your description," said Tom, "Sister Christina Peterson. She's the former Catholic nun who heads Community Interfaith. That group makes people nervous when they protest public housing conditions. We could look good by giving the local churches a chance, too. Sister Christina is respected by the parish priests, ministers and rabbis. In fact, the community youth love her too."

"How about the teachers at Jefferson?" asked Jack. "We need four with the right profile—minority, racial, ethnic, gender and age. We don't want to get fried by some union nut running to the Office of Civil Rights. We need to select a new teacher, an older teacher and two other very respected ones. Check with your people at Jefferson. Be sure to brief the principal about the new Commission. Tell her we need her enthusiasm and support. She could retire as a hero next year if we don't have to close Jefferson down.

Jack went on. "I'll also talk with Jenny Worth, president of Jefferson's parent group, and John Stokes, our district Title I director. They can tell us which parents they've worked with who are respected by the community. We must avoid parent 'terrorists' on either the religious right or liberal left. I feel like we're choosing a jury. We'd better pick a representative group of respected members that can get the job done without anyone questioning their fairness or their integrity. From now on this is a 'no-contact sport.' No communication with the Commission members by you or your staff. I'll talk with the Board about a 'no contact-no comment' policy until the Commission makes its report next June. If the Board likes what they come up with, we can go with it. Otherwise we can 'deep six' the report like we usually do. Nobody expects these reform studies to go anywhere!" *In any case, Tom will be long gone, and we can pass this mess to a new superintendent. That will take the heat off the Board,* thought Jack.

"I guess you're right," Tom said.

"The last point is we have to hire Commission consultants who know plenty about school reform. They can provide our cover, and they can act as Commission facilitators. I'll check with my friends in the training business. We need an effective team—a man and a woman—who can relate well with the members and let the Commission make up its own mind. The Commission will need to hear from the best experts in the country if they are to come up with a credible report. Being this close to Washington, D.C., we'll be working in a national media fish bowl. Above all, we've got to look credible!

"I'll need your names by close of business Monday, so we can interview by Wednesday," Jack said. "I'll get cracking too. I'll call the Gov's office and work up the letter. I'll fax it out Monday morning with your signature. I want to announce the appointment of this new Commission by next Wednesday night's Board meeting. We've got to spend that meeting on proposed amendments to the district's budget."

Jack left the superintendent's office much relieved. *Tom may be slow to act,* thought Jack, *but he'll defend his turf 'til death. He'll go along, take his time, and get the word out to his national network for another superintendency for next year. He has no choice. God help us! Are we really going to appoint a Citizens' Reform Commission that works?* Jack bounded down the stairs of the old district office, slid into his car and drove to his insurance office at Ballston Towers. *This had better work,* he thought.

****

Cole Green sat at his desk in the Governor's office skimming through the new state education budget numbers. He was preparing to brief Governor Scott before Tuesday's press conference.

Last month's press conference announcing Jim Collins as state superintendent went well, thought Cole. *It got the media attention away from the embarrassing nationwide story that the state had not accepted Goals 2000 money to help communities plan for local school improvement. Governor Scott had just about run out of fed-bashing excuses. The charge is sounding hollow that the U.S. Department of Education is trying to play federal School Board and control local schools with new regulations. Reporters keep quoting back congressional language stating that the federal money can only be used for local planning and decisions on how to improve neighborhood schools. Maybe Collins can figure a face-saving way out of this one and take the heat off the Governor. We've got to get voter attention off education and onto the state re-election campaign.*

The buzzer sounded, and Cole picked up his phone to speak with Jack Clayton. "Jack, old buddy, why aren't you out golfing on this great Friday afternoon? How's the insurance business? I was talking with the Governor about you just yesterday. We're planning a big fundraising dinner in late September for his re-election campaign. Scott hopes you'll serve on the committee "

"Cole, I hear you, but right now I need a favor from the Governor," said Jack. "As you know, for the second year, Jefferson Elementary, one of our disadvantaged schools, failed to come up to speed on our state performance testing program. The legislation mandates that the state will take over the school and either close it down or reorganize it—sort of like a bankruptcy thing. Hell, you can have this political turkey if you want it. I can see the 6:00 p.m. news now: parents protesting in the streets at the Governor's fundraising dinner. The Governor, in front of the press, trying to explain how he's going to help their children when the state closes Jefferson down. Scott's opponent, Gary Hatfield, will have a field-day. It'll make a nice media picture: The Governor stands against increasing the state school budget with his latest publicity stunt—turning down Goals 2000 funds that could actually provide more federal money for high-poverty schools like Jefferson. It's not exactly going to win votes. By the way, why doesn't the Gov turn down that awful federal Title I money? And while he's at it, he could offend the special ed parents by turning down their federal funding."

"Jack, I get the picture. This is a disaster waiting to happen. I told the

Governor that we have to stop talking about education. He's already got the home schoolers, the Catholic school parents and the wealthy private schoolers. The national and state polls show that voters place quality education for their children as the number one issue. And we're not on the right side by advocating vouchers that take more money away from public schools where we've been cutting budgets. We can't get elected without picking up the parent vote."

"Cole, get this: Governor Scott is a big advocate of local control. How's it going to look if he has the state close Jefferson, a predominantly minority, disadvantaged elementary school. It would force the minority kids to be bused across town to a wealthy, White neighborhood school. This will hardly play well in state and national media? It also makes our county schools look bad and embarrasses my School Board in front of our voters. I can hardly then go to my business friends and start raising funds for the Governor's re-election campaign. He'll be painted as the bad guy.

"Here's my plan. You need to give me a green light by Tuesday noon. By then, you'll have our written request signed by me and the School Super Dr. Dooley. I'll count on you to grease the skids with Collins after you have the Gov's blessing. Don't screw us over on this one, Cole. It's a top priority with a time-sensitive window. We've got a lot of work to do by Board meeting time next Wednesday night. Can I count on you?"

"Jack, I agree. You can count on me," said Cole.

****

Jack Clayton gaveled the County School Board meeting to order on Wednesday, September 4 at 7:30 p.m. It was a larger than usual audience of about 200, with camera crews and what looked like reporters—just waiting for their 11:00 news stories. After the pledge of alliance and the reading of previous Board meeting minutes, Jack reviewed the night's agenda. "Ladies and gentlemen, before we take up proposed amendments to the district's budget tonight, we have an exciting announcement," Jack said. "It's one that will show that local school boards can be an important part of school reform in communities throughout the nation. The Governor believes that local challenges are best solved by the citizens closest to the problem. Consistent with that view, he has granted authority to the County School Board to act for the state in appointing the new Jefferson Elementary School Reform Commission. This new Citizens' Commission will be independent of this Board and of all other district officials. It is charged with conducting a thorough investigation of Jefferson. It will recommend a plan for its reform and renewal using necessary community, private, state and federal resources. The Commission will report back its findings and recommendations to the Board of Education not later than June 18, 1997."

"During this school year, the independent Commission will conduct an in-depth assessment, will search for new reform strategies, and will identify best practices to recommend to our Board. Jefferson Elementary will continue to operate under the supervision of Dr. Tom Dooley and his staff. They will assist the principal, Mrs. Olive Carter, and the teachers and staff who now serve there. Jefferson will not be shut down or taken over by the state this year."

"What happens a year from now will depend on the new Commission's report and reform plan. We hope their proposals will save Jefferson Elementary School and its children. And that once again, it will take its place as one of the leading elementary schools in the county. It has a distinguished past and we look forward to an even more distinguished future. We have dedicated and talented students, educators, parents and community leaders who can help us show that democracy can work to solve even our most demanding challenges.

"Now let me introduce our distinguished Commission. Please hold your applause until all 12 are standing. These citizens from the community have agreed to serve as volunteers for over 100 hours each—at least ten Saturdays during the coming year. I will first introduce the chair and vice-chair of the Commission. Ramon Gonzales, who is serving as vice president of the County School Board, will be chair. Mrs. Kim Su Young, principal of Lawndale Elementary School, will serve as vice chair. They will also continue in their current assignments.

"Our teacher representatives are Delores Williams, first grade; Tamar Espinosa, third grade; Kathie Sorensen, fifth grade; and Ted Alexander, sixth grade. Our parent representatives are Maria Morales, Lenora Brown, Deborah Cohen, and Dale Jones. Our community representatives are Sister Christina Peterson of Community Interfaith and Paul Christopher, owner and partner with Christopher and Larsen, Insurance, Inc. Paul also serves as president of the Ballston Kiwanis Service Club. Consultants from a non-profit education reform group will provide services to the Commission. This new Citizens' Commission will hold public hearings beginning on Saturday, September 21, from 8:00 a.m. until 5:00 p.m. at the Jefferson Elementary School."

The group remained standing as the audience applauded.

"We appreciate your willingness to serve our community over the next year," Jack said. "We wish you God's speed in carrying out this important assignment!"

****

Chapter 1
BEGINNING THE 'DISCOVERY JOURNEY'

Saturday morning, September 21

Maria Morales opened the door of their '85 Chevy car, and kissed her husband, Miguel. She gave him instructions for taking the two boys to soccer practice, their oldest daughter Tonya to her babysitting job, and Elena to her music lesson. Maria could see that Miguel was trying to be a good sport. Tending the children before for his extra part-time job at 6:00 p.m. was not making him very happy, especially after their late Friday night party!

And what am I doing at this school on Saturday at 7:50 anyway? At least I'm early and there's no snide comment about always being late…that it's part of the culture. I don't know what I can contribute to this new reform Commission—but all my neighbors are impressed with the story and picture in the Patriot. Now I'm a celebrity—my five minutes of fame. Who are these other Commission members? I'll bet they're all well educated—at least college graduates. And me with a high school diploma. I'm the only one who attended Jefferson in the '60s, when it was a pretty good school. Now it's the school that the state wants to close for poor performance! How embarrassing! We had such great teachers then. I wonder what happened? Better get inside to the library. Hope it's air conditioned.

"Welcome to the first official Hearing and meeting of the Jefferson Citizens' Commission on School Reform. My name is Ramon Gonzales, I will be serving as chair of our new Commission. We will introduce the 12 citizen members, and our consultants, in a few minutes. We also welcome you parents and community representatives—don't see any media here. You Commissioners who have just joined us, please take your seats around our tables. They're arranged in a square so we can all see each other. I'm glad to see each of you this morning right on time and looking eager. You men

1

may want to take off your ties and jackets. Even with these fans, it feels a bit warm for suits in here today. We want you to be comfortable. My apologies for not getting the word out. From now on, our dress on Saturdays will be casual. May I introduce Mrs. Kim Su Young, principal at Lawndale Elementary School, who will serve as vice chair of our Commission. She will read our Commission's official charge or mandate from the County Board of Education."

Mission of the Citizens' Commission on Jefferson Elementary School Reform

"Thank you, Mr. Gonzales. Ladies and Gentlemen of the Commission. I'm pleased to serve as your vice chair. Our mandate reads: 'To the Chair, Vice Chair and Members of the Jefferson Citizens' Commission on School Reform: Your mission is to produce a short written document that reports your findings and recommendations publicly to the County Board of Education by June 18. After careful review of proven school reform practices in other elementary schools throughout the nation, you are to make an assessment of conditions in the Jefferson Elementary School, determine the causes for the poor performance of students attending that school, and make recommendations on how the County Board and its Superintendent can take whatever actions are necessary to provide a quality education for all students in the Jefferson attendance area.

'The School District has provided a modest operating budget to hold official hearings and other Commission meetings and to bring in nationally-recognized experts in public school reform to present their experience and recommendations.

'Your two consultant-facilitators represent an independent source of knowledge about national research on school reform. They have practical experience working with reform groups to conduct assessments and hearings, intergroup and interpersonal experience in helping Commission members explore conflicting views and reconcile them, and expertise in helping your Commission to develop findings and recommendations for your final report to the Board. You can look to them for their experience and knowledge of how to get this project accomplished on time.

'You have nine months to accomplish your mission. You are expected to meet together one Saturday each month. Information about student or teacher performance will be provided to you at your Commission Hearings. Your Chair and Vice Chair will organize the agenda for each hearing after consulting with the professional team each week. We expect the final report to be the product of careful study, and, if possible, the considered consensus of the entire Commission. Your final report to the Commission on June 18 will be a public meeting open to all citizens and the media. You deserve the thanks of the children and families of Jefferson Elementary School and all County citizens for your voluntary community service. Good luck on your mission. The County School Board. President, Jack Clayton, September 21, 1996.'

"Mr. Gonzales, this is the legal mandate of the Jefferson Citizens' Commission on School Reform."

"Thank you, Mrs. Kim Su Young. I would now like to hand out a list of proposed Rules of the Game that will guide our Commission hearings and discussions during the next nine months. They are meant to help us be as efficient and effective as possible in the time we spend together and to build and maintain trust and respect with each other and as a group. In some ways, we are like a jury trying to arrive at a verdict. We then recommend a just sentence or program for rehabilitation to save not only a community school but the futures of thousands of students who will attend that school. Please read carefully the eight Commission Guidelines found on page 2 in your notebook. I will take questions when you've finished. By the way, you may want to take notes for your own personal use and reflections. The notebooks at your tables have references and background materials. I'll read our guidelines aloud with you:

1. **Participate fully**. All citizen Commissioners are equal team members. We are expected to assess Jefferson Elementary's performance and to identify best reform practices for our final report of recommendations for change and improvement;

2. **Keep open minds**. We all have or will form our own opinions about this school. As an official Commission, we must begin with an open mind and conduct an objective search for why this school is failing and what can be done to turn it around. Over the next nine months, we will hear testimony and weigh all the evidence;

3. **Compare best practices**. Our investigation will be informed by testimony of the leading national experts in school reform, by research findings, and by views of parents and teachers on our Commission;

4. **Anticipate disagreements**. During our Hearings and discussions, it is expected that members of the Commission will disagree. Only by open and honest discussion, respect for different views, debate and careful deliberation can we expect to explore the objective evidence and discover answers for our final report;

5. **Work for group consensus**. Commission members will develop and reconcile our findings, conclusions and recommendations while respecting all views and working for real group consensus in our policy decisions;

6. **Expect consultant-facilitators to take leadership roles**. Consultants will take the lead in organizing the presentation of topics and facilitating our joint discovery process. They will help us resolve these differences—and there will be many—by agitating us to stay honest with each other even when we would prefer to hide or avoid the encounter. We believe that the open democratic dialogue will help produce a joint report that will be a far more valuable document than any single expert, individual Commissioner or consultant could produce alone;

7. **Attend all Commission Hearings and meetings**. We will meet for 10 Saturdays from 8:00 a.m. to 5:00 p.m. monthly here at Jefferson. If you have any questions, you can call the Chair or Vice Chair. You have the telephone numbers listed in your materials. We expect you to arrange your travel and other obligations so as to attend the full-day of Saturday meetings; and

8. **Meet all Commission responsibilities**. Each member is expected to fully participate in each Saturday Hearing for the full time we are in session and to review the assigned reading materials in preparation for each Hearing. The estimated total volunteer time each Commission member is expected to invest in this project is about 100 hours. We recognize that this is a major sacrifice for you, your family and your other obligations—but we believe that the educational and community service experience will be worth the sacrifice. We will work hard and not waste your time.

"Do you have any questions about these Commission Guidelines or Rules?" asked Ramon Gonzales. He saw Dale Jones hesitantly raise his hand. "Yes, Mr. Jones?"

"I have a back problem that bothers me when I sit for very long," said Dale. "Can I get up and stretch from time to time?"

"Of course," said Ray. "By next month's Hearing we'll have more comfortable chairs. We'll also schedule breaks for stretching, making calls, getting drinks, using restrooms, whatever." He saw Mrs. Brown shift uneasily in her chair. "Mrs. Brown?"

"You kind of answered my question. I just need to call my sister and check on my kids to see that everything's all right. Where's a phone I can use?"

"We'll see that the office is open so anyone can use the phone during breaks or lunch. Mrs. Cohen, you have a question?"

"Yes," said Debbie, "I'm a working mom, an attorney with two kids. Could we trim these hearings by having working lunches, and then quit at 3 o'clock? It's hard to get personal business done in one less Saturday each month."

Well, Ms. highfalutin, workin' mom, Lenora thought. *Are you too busy to spend a full Saturday with us common folk. At least you can pay for a babysitter. I have to beg my sister to take care of my kids, then I get to pay back takin' care of hers. What'd I get myself into?*

"Appreciate your time deficit, Mrs. Cohen," Ramon said. "But, our consultants say this is the most effective model and will save time in the long run. We'll start and quit on time. If we can do our work in fewer Saturdays, hey, I'm all for it."

"If there are no more questions on how we'll work together, we'll take a vote. All those who can vote to adopt our Commission guidelines, please raise your hand. Opposed? The vote is unanimous for adopting the Rules. We'll break now and reassemble at 9:30 to introduce our fellow Commissioners. We have coffee, juices and fresh fruit for refreshments. Enjoy!"

****

Introducing Citizens' Commission Members

Ramon stood as the group took their seats. "I'd like to introduce our two consultants who will be working with us this year, Mrs. Wendy Swenson and Dr. Nathaniel Johnson. Wendy, I understand you're starting off. The time is yours."

"Thank you, Ray. Nate and I will be your facilitators. Since we must work together for the next year, we're taking time to share our backgrounds. It's important that we learn to know, respect and trust each other. It'll make our work faster, more enjoyable and less stressful. Between now and noon when we break for lunch, we want to get a better idea of who you are. We'll introduce ourselves using the Tombstone exercise, not to be morbid, but to get better acquainted. Tell us some basic information like your age, education, profession, hobbies, family status, children and their ages. You might share your political and religious affiliation, but that's optional. Just helps us understand where you are coming from. And you might share why you accepted the invitation to become a member of this Citizens' Commission. You have about five minutes to introduce yourself to the group. Let's rotate clockwise around the table. Nate will be our timer and will give a signal to help keep us on track. Who'd like to begin?"

Dale Jones bristled. *Is she crazy? I'm not about to open up in front of these strangers. Looks like we're in for some '60s style 'touchy-feely' stuff. I'll just hang back and let these clowns make fools of themselves.*

"I'll start off," Paul said nervously. "My name is Paul Christopher. My tombstone reads: Here lies Paul who valued his time with his family most of all and wanted to be a good father and husband. He was a successful insurance executive and community leader. He was 42. My wife Julia and I have four children—two boys and two girls—ranging in age from 13 to 7. I'm president of the Kiwanis Club this year, and we're Episcopalians. Not much time for hobbies, but I still love golf and play tennis weekly. I like to water ski. I have an MBA from the University of Virginia. I accepted a position on this Citizens' Commission because I want to do something important for kids. If we do a good job, we could be a model for school reform, not just in this county, but across the whole country."

"I guess I'm next. Here lies Deborah Cohen. I'm Debbie to my friends, a 36-year old, single Jewish woman with two children, David 14 and Heather 11. I was raised in West Los Angeles, the daughter of a UCLA history professor. I'm a trial lawyer, a graduate of USC Law School. I moved to the D.C. area in 1979 and worked briefly in President Carter's Justice Department. When Carter lost to Reagan in 1980, I went into partnership with a colleague at Justice and we've been defending clients ever since. I was divorced five years ago and am raising my two children alone. I've been a PTA president at David's middle school. This is Heather's last year at

Jefferson, then we're out of here. It's a terrible school now! But I'm still trying to hang on to our public school system.

"I'm serving on this Citizens' Commission because something must be done about Jefferson. Teachers and parents can't do anything alone. When Jack Clayton said this Commission could pull off something historic and just maybe make a difference—it seemed worth the gamble of a 100 hours. So I'm here, but not to waste time!"

Deborah's one tough cookie, thought Paul. *I wonder how her two children survive her type-A behavior. Can't imagine her as a mother of young children.*

"I'm next. My name is Delores Williams, and I have taught first grade at Jefferson for seven years. I like teaching these children. I don't know why politicians are making such a big deal about this school. If they'd give us the money we need for supplies and teacher aides, we could get along just fine. But that's another story.

"Here lies Delores. She's 42. She was a good wife to her husband, Michael, and a good mother. Jennifer, age 15, went to Jefferson. Violet is 10 and goes here now. She was committed to teaching all children to think well of themselves and to read by the time they finish first grade! I'm a Baptist. As a working mom, I don't have time for hobbies except the church choir. The jury's still out for me on what this Commission is really up to. But we need to cut through the bull and really do what's good for the kids."

"Hey, Ms. Williams," Lenora Brown said. "It's hard for me to call you Delores after all these years of callin' you Ms. Williams. My kids loved you as a first grade teacher. I'll always owe you. We think you're the greatest!" *She's a Black sister I'm proud of,* thought Lenora.

"Well, let's see. Here lies Lenora Brown. She was a good mother and a born-again Christian. But I don't go to my Pentecostal Church much anymore. I went to Jefferson Elementary and I'm proud of it! I still think the School Board's jerkin' us around with this Commission. It's just an excuse not to spend more money like they do in those high-class schools in north county! I'm an unemployed high school graduate right now. I'm 28, a single parent with three beautiful little girls who go to Jefferson. The best job I ever had was Head Start aide. That was before I went through my messy divorce and 'hit the bottle.' But I'm okay now. I'm surprised I'd be asked to be on this Commission. But I love my girls and want 'em to get a good education and that's why I'm here. As for politics, I think all politicians are crooks and voting is a waste of time."

Now there's a real winner. How in hell was she appointed to this Commission? What can a welfare mom who was probably pregnant at 15 possibly contribute? Kind of cute and spunky though. I guess someone has to represent the lower-class parents of Jefferson, thought Debbie.

A slender, greying man spoke. "I'm Ted Alexander. I've taught sixth grade at Jefferson for the past 11 years. Before that, I taught at two other schools in this county. I'll retire in three years, but I'm real concerned at how Jefferson has changed these past 10 years. I've got some strong opinions on what went wrong, but I guess we'll get to that later. My epitaph reads: Here lies Ted Alexander, a hippie refugee from the '60s. He was a teacher who wanted to make a difference. I'm still a real live liberal Democrat, but we don't have courageous leaders like Jack Kennedy anymore.

"My wife Lilly and I have two grown children and five grandchildren. The families live in California and Vermont. I worry about the education of my grandchildren. I just hope the public schools will survive this fascist Republican Congress, these conservative crazies in the state capitol, and the greedy corporate leaders who are ripping off our environment. I don't belong to any organized religion. I've dabbled in new age meditation. I think they're on to something we lost. My new hobby is the internet, and I love spending time on my computer most nights. I was appointed to this Commission because I have lots of experience teaching sixth graders. I think I can help come up with some ideas. "

Yeah, I'll bet you can. It's a '60s flower child turned public school teacher and he's protected by the union. They all are. That's why we have the worst public education system in the modern world. We're spending money up the gazoo! I can't wait to hear your recommendations. Probably you'll want to give the teachers a raise and throw more money at the problem. If the teachers would do their damn job in the first place, we wouldn't be here, Paul thought.

"I'll jump in here," said Kim Su Young. "As you know, I've been principal at Lawndale Elementary for the past seven years. The main reason I volunteered to join this Citizens' Commission is that I've spent the past 22 years as a public school teacher and principal. I'm frustrated with what's happening to children in poor schools like Jefferson. In my seven years as a principal in this County, the School Board has never done much of anything. Now they're forced into taking some action. Maybe we'll have a chance to make history.

"My epitaph says, here lies Kim Su Young, 45-years old, a Korean American whose father, a former military officer, was sent to the Korean embassy in Washington, D.C. in 1962. When he retired, we stayed in Maryland. I became a United States citizen and continued my schooling at the University of Maryland. I have a B.A. and M.A. in education and began my teaching in third grade. American education has been good to me. Now it's a blessing to my own two daughters, ages 8 and 10. I feel that I must give back something to those students at Jefferson who are experiencing what Jonathan Kozol calls 'death at an early age.' I'm angry that a nation as rich as America treats its innocent children like this. My hobbies are reading and gourmet cooking. My husband and I also like to travel abroad at least once each year. I go to the Presbyterian Church. I vote for the best candidate. I was a moderate George Bush Republican."

I'm impressed by this serious no-nonsense woman! She knows who she is and what she's about, thought Nate Johnson. *I wonder if there are many principals like her in the district? And being Asian, she knows about world-class education standards. Koreans are very disciplined. She could be chair of this Commission. Ray Gonzales will have trouble keeping up with her!*

Dale Jones took his turn. "Hear lies Dale, 29, white male, conservative Republican and a Rush Limbaugh disciple who voted for Ross Perot in '92. I'm a born-again Baptist and active in the Christian Coalition. I've been waiting for the government to come up with a school voucher plan so I can afford to take my three children out of Jefferson Elementary and enroll them in the nearest Christian school. Hell, we're among the last Whites here. My wife, Sally, is even talking about home schooling, and she isn't a college graduate, so I don't know if she could pull it off when they get older. We're plenty anxious about our children's future.

"I've never been a great student—I played lots of sports—but now I'm finding out the hard way that union jobs are gone and about the only ones left are low-wage service jobs. I could hardly read my diploma even though I had a solid 'C' average. I've discovered that the high school teachers at Washington-Lee where I graduated lied to me. Right now, I'm driving a cab. I guess you could call me an angry White male whose being discriminated against. My hobbies? Can't afford to take much time off from my cabbie job. I do like to go fishing and bowling when I can. I also play softball with my Baptist church league all summer on Tuesday nights."

Maria Morales thought, *maybe I'm not the only low-income parent here. Dale seems like a nice guy—but he's through at 29. He's a high school jock without a decent education and already feeling the heat of competition. What a life! I feel sorry for him.*

"Here lies Tamar Espinosa, 26, a new third grade teacher at Jefferson. I'm a single mom with one child. Mary will start kindergarten next year. I'm a Catholic but I believe in public schools, and so I became a teacher after graduating from George Mason University in June '94. I'm a widow. My husband was killed three years ago in a car accident. This left me to finish school. I loved my first year, but I'm depressed by the terrible conditions and the helplessness that teachers and parents seem to feel. Politically I am an independent, but I like President Clinton's support for education. We need the federal programs. We could not survive at Jefferson without money from Title I, bilingual education and school lunches. My dream is to become a principal of a world-class elementary school where teachers and parents believe that all children can achieve high standards. I might even like to be U.S. Secretary of Education some day. This is America and anything's possible!

She went on. "The reason I agreed to serve on this Commission is that I want to learn all about how our school can be reformed. When the Chairman of the County Board of Education, Jack Clayton, asked if I would serve, I said I would if he was serious about backing us and not trying to water down our recommendations. I'm excited about hearing from the 'biggies' in school reform and learning what has happened since *A Nation At Risk* in 1983. I read about these people in graduate school. This will be like a high-powered graduate seminar. I can't wait."

Did someone say idealism is dead, thought Kim. *What a refreshing young teacher. But she's naïve too! A few years in these horrible urban schools and she will be ready to move on. I'm glad she's with us, tho'. She'll keep us all on our toes.*

The next speaker was Sister Christina Peterson. "I'm with Community Interfaith. On my tombstone, I'd put: Here lies a former Catholic nun who has found her calling as a community organizer. I'm 51-years old, a liberal Democrat who believes in social action. I want to help the poor to learn the skills to help themselves in a system that's rigged against them. At Interfaith, we work with parish priests, ministers and rabbis in involving members of their congregations in rebuilding neighborhood institutions like public housing projects, health clinics and schools. We also work with youth leaders in Boy and Girl Scouts and Big Brothers. I was raised in Chicago, where I entered the convent. I graduated from Loyola University in philosophy. I worked with Saul Alinsky as a community organizer. I moved here in 1976, and I've been active in this community ever since.

"I'm a member of this Citizens' Commission because I believe we can do some sacred work here. It's the right opportunity for service. Something tells me we may also have been blessed with the right combination of people."

Oh, oh, Ramon Gonzales thought. *Now we have a Commission conscience! A nun at that. But she is not your stereotype sister. She doesn't take herself too seriously. She seems to know her way around, and it will be good to have a religious perspective.*

It was finally Maria Morales' turn. "Here lies Maria. She was a 42-year-old Latina, a practicing Catholic, and a mother of four wonderful children—Raul 12, Juan 10, Tonya 8, and Elena 6. I was born in northern Mexico and came to Los Angeles when I was 10. I married Miguel when I was 16. He works for the General Services Administration, and he was transferred to Washington D.C. in 1984. All of my children have been to Jefferson. So I am an active parent in our children's education. I'm also helping with Jefferson's Title I program as a reading tutor. Besides taking care of my family, including my mother and aunt, I'm active in the parent organization at Jefferson. I don't have time for hobbies. I vote and help out at the polling booths on election day—and I'm a Democrat.

"I'm flattered to be asked to join this Commission. It's about time something was done. This is a once in a lifetime chance to change the education system and start meeting the needs of our kids. My children's future depends on what we do here. I am determined that this Commission does not become a front for the Board of Education. I don't know exactly what to do yet—but I will know in a few months. I want serious change at Jefferson!"

Debbie was impressed. *Whoa! This woman is serious and tough. She means business. It goes to show you that you can't judge the character by appearances. She looks like an uneducated, lower-class, Mexican mother who goes daily to mass and blindly follows the parish priest. But Maria is a survivor with courage who loves and defends her kids. These Commission women are surprisingly strong and outspoken.*

"Good morning," said Kathie Sorensen. "I am 36. I teach fifth grade at Jefferson Elementary. I hope my epitaph reads: Here lies Kathie. She was a great mother of three children, a loving wife and a good teacher who made a difference. She was also a strong Mormon woman who believes in giving Christian service to her family, friends and fellow community members. My hobbies are working each week with teenage girls in our church. I'm also getting a Master's Degree in education. My husband Bill and I usually vote for moderate Republicans when we can find them. It's scary to watch the conservative crazies trying to take over the party and attack public education. They want to take taxpayer money for private vouchers, home and private schooling for the wealthy.

"I agreed to serve on this Commission because I hope we can come up with a plan to save Jefferson Elementary from the poor performance of many fellow teachers and the lack of parental interest. I'm worried that whatever we come up with will not be put into place by our Board of Education. Sorry Mr. Gonzales, but you must understand that we are sick and tired of being neglected. Jefferson children face a lifetime of poverty and pain because we adults have failed them. I know I'm getting on my soapbox, but this Commission had better be for real or I'm going to work to replace our Board of Education with people who can make a difference. We need the resources to do what must be done for these children now. But, I've said enough."

It was finally Ramon Gonzales' turn, and he was ready. "You know me. I'm 38. I'm chair of this Citizens' Commission and vice chair of the County Board of Education. I hear you Kathie! And I want to make it perfectly clear (was it Nixon who used to say that?) that I would not have accepted this assignment unless I felt that I have the support of the Board. As an independent Commission, we have full authority to make serious recommendations, within reason and certain budget constraints. The Board recognizes that they have been negligent and that the superintendent's office has not cleared up the mess at Jefferson. The state has forced us to act sooner than we would have on our own. But, now, we can move ahead. This Commission has the right and the responsibility to lead the way! But, I don't plan to be part of a whitewash report.

"We've failed the children of Jefferson and violated the trust of their parents. We must start a brand new ball game. I know that championship teams first must train and get prepared to play before they can hope to win. Our enemies are selfish special interests who benefit from the status quo. We'll have to show through our Commission work that average American citizens can make grassroots democracy work to benefit the children of this community. This Commission can get the job done. I admit that I was not enthusiastic about taking time to make these long introductions of Commission members. But, now I see that it's been a valuable use of our time. As we get better acquainted with each other, we can learn to work together and negotiate differences. We need to come up with a powerful report by next June.

"Here's a little background: I'm Hispanic, age 38. I've been married to a wonderful wife, Marianne, for the past 15 years. We've been blessed with two beautiful daughters who attend Jefferson School. You can see I have a strong personal interest in this Commission's reform report. I was trained at UCLA in English and the University of Yale law school. My specialty is civil rights law. I am a moderate Democrat who believes in the rule of law. Change and reform can take place within this system if we practice democracy. My hobbies are U.S. history, especially the southwestern part of the country. I used to play soccer in college and tried out for the U.S. Olympic team in 1974. Now I spend my spare time on Board of Education business. I'm excited to be here today!"

Kim Su Young was surprised. *I'm impressed with his anger and his commitment. I expected the same 'ol, same 'ol political whitewash. Well, we'll see. It's only the first morning. Everyone's happy to talk about themselves. Wait 'til the disagreements come up.*

"I'll introduce myself," said Wendy Swenson. "I'm 31-years old, married, with no children, yet. I was a Peace Corp volunteer after Dartmouth where I majored in American history. I went to Bolivia, and returned to take a master's degree at Brattleboro, Vermont in community organizing. I took postgraduate training from Ernesto Cortes, the master of community organizing. He's Southwest Director of the Industrial Areas Foundation in Austin, Texas, and he'll be testifying before us. I just moved here and now work as a lead organizer with County Interfaith, assigned to social service agencies. My hobbies are bicycling, skiing, and rock climbing with my husband, John.

"I am here because Ernie Cortes asked me if I'd be interested in working on this project. After a week's training with Nate, here I am. From your introductions, I'm excited to get to know you better. I can see some potential clashes of views and personalities. But, hey, this is America."

Nate had been attentive to Wendy and the others. "I've been unusually quiet for me. My name is Nate Johnson. I don't ever want to read my tombstone—but I certainly have been learning a great deal from listening to people introduce themselves from this exercise, so here goes: Here lies Nate Johnson, a loving husband and father of two children, now grown. I've been an educator all my life. I started as a high school science teacher in the Los Angeles City Schools and as intergroup relations director for the school district in Inglewood, California. I've owned a private proprietary trade school. I've been a community college instructor and counselor, and I'm now a community college trustee. I have a M.A. and a Ph.D. in Leadership and Human Behavior.

"I've also worked with the Los Angeles Police Commission training officers and with the *Center for Leadership Development* where I taught postdoctoral leadership training seminars for minority educators under a Rockefeller grant. I've seen education at all levels and from all sides in urban America. I don't much like what I see. My hobbies are tending grandchildren. I'm doing volunteer leadership training and counseling for my large Crenshaw Community Christian Church. I'm here because I think this Commission can actually reform Jefferson. I'll give it my best shot. Of course, after you've made your report—the real struggle with the education bureaucracy begins. So let's get started."

What a team Wendy and Nate make! I'm impressed, Paul thought. *Wendy is a good-looking blonde who is sharp and confident, especially for just being 31. Seems to know her business. And Nate—a big black dude with a deep bass voice! I wouldn't want to tangle with him in a dark alley. He looks like he was a leader of the Los Angeles Crips gang or something. Man, he's been around the block a few times, and now he teaches leadership at a church? He can't be for real. Still, they make a great contrast. Seem to complement each other. I guess we'll find out.*

Wendy stood and said, "Thank you, Nate, and all 12 of you. It's noon and time for our lunch break. A buffet lunch will be available for the Commissioners in the school cafeteria just down the hall to the right. Tables have been set up for four people each. We ask that you sit with the three other people randomly assigned to your table as listed on our agenda sheets. The purpose of this lunch together is to get better acquainted. Plan on getting some exercise by walking outside after you eat. Be back in this room by 1:00 p.m. sharp."

The audience of parents and a few teachers had dwindled to about 15 people. Kathryn Jones was taking careful notes to report back to her Christian Coalition group. She would go outside and down the street to the mall for lunch. She could telephone from there without being overheard.

****

Chapter 2
MODERN SCHOOL REFORM AND
STUDENT ACHIEVEMENT
Saturday afternoon, September 21

After lunch, Ray welcomed them back. "I hope you enjoyed the food and are getting better acquainted. Well, take a good look around. Some of you will become trusted friends before we're through next June. Now, I'm going to turn the time over to Nate to lead our discussion. We Commission members may want to start keeping a brief journal on what we're going to hear about the last fourteen years of school reform."

Nate Johnson stood. "Back in April 1983, *A Nation At Risk* issued this prophetic warning: 'Our once unchallenged preeminence is being overtaken by competitors throughout the world...the educational foundations of our society are presently being eroded by a rising tide of mediocrity that threatens our very future as a Nation and a people.' For the first time in our history, 'the educational skills of one generation...will not even approach those of their parents.' The Commission called for raising high school graduation requirements, higher teacher salaries, and incentives for attracting gifted students into the teaching profession. We must harness knowledge of the humanities to science and technology if the latter are to remain relevant."[1]

Paul Christopher raised his hand. "I was here in 1983 when Ronald Reagan was President. I read about the release and national publicity that Secretary of Education Bell and David Gardner, chair of the National Commission on Excellence, generated by this landmark report."

"Yes, Paul," said Nate, "*A Nation At Risk* was electrifying. Not since Sputnik in 1957 has attention been so riveted on public education. The report was a brief, harsh, but realistic assessment. It focused on American high

schools and their unprepared graduates. The 12 million copies disseminated nationwide fueled a debate on public education. In a May 1983 Gallup
Poll, American taxpayers expressed their willingness to support increased
funding for education. Just after the Commission's report, there came a
blizzard of more than 200 reform studies. They defined the mission of education as serving the student and the national interest. Commissions, task
forces, scholars, foundations and associations decided to take advantage of
the national mood to leverage reform. Each delivered a bleak assessment
of public schools. Over the next 12 months, the reform movement gained
momentum among all sectors of the public."

Modern School Reform in America

Nate continued. "After 14 years of national school reform by a few courageous educators, parents and community leaders, the overall academic
achievement by American students today is no better than it was in the
early 1970s, although we now educate far more disadvantaged students.
Many students are learning facts and information, but they are unable to
comprehend their meaning. Perhaps that wouldn't be such a big deal if the
world hadn't changed. But the demands of employment are much higher
today. **Fifty percent of high school graduates are unprepared for the challenges of our new global knowledge economy, to support a family or become responsible citizens.** The National Assessment of Education Progress
(NAEP) reports consistently poor or average performance by American students, when compared with other students in modern nations, in mathematics, science, geography, history, civics, literature, writing and reading
skills and the arts."

"What in the hell has this country been doing since 1983?" asked Dale
Jones. "I thought you said that the country was all excited about school
reform. I heard that George Bush met with the governors in 1989 and solved
the problem. I didn't know it was this bad," said Dale, shaking his head. "I
heard on the radio that 50% of our high school graduates can't hold a job in
today's automobile factories."

Nate nodded and said, "Before we can answer your question, Dale, let's
look at the way school reformers have tried to improve student performance.
During the past 14 years, there have been three phases or waves of school
reform at the local, state and national levels. We need to understand these
waves so our Commission can learn from those reformers about what works
and why.[2] We also need to learn what doesn't work."

The First Wave of Reform—Governors Respond. "The first wave of reform flowed from the state house rather than the school house or the home. The catalyst of change came from outside the education community. Governors took a leadership role. Reforms were low-cost, easily understood, quickly implemented, and highly visible. Using the state bureaucracy with its top-down, centralized authority, elected officials advocated an agenda for action that was largely regulatory—laws, mandates and detailed rule-making. This was meant to pressure educators for school reform. They were going to change components of the existing system incrementally. Governors took advantage of increased revenues from higher taxes, which they spent on education.

"Reform reports attracted new allies and education became a hot political campaign topic in the 1980s and into the 1990s. Governors established reform commissions and sponsored comprehensive reform packages. They advocated legislative and regulatory changes, and state-based higher academic standards. Some of them earned the title of education governors. Three of these were Bill Clinton of Arkansas, Richard Riley of South Carolina and Lamar Alexander of Tennessee."

"That's impressive," said Tamar Espinosa, the third grade teacher. "You mean these three actually knew each other and worked together on state reform in the 1980s? Now one is President, one is U.S. Secretary of Education, and the other one was Secretary under President Bush."

"Yes," said Nate. "The primary reform goal was that all students achieve excellence or at least increase their learning significantly. The most popular strategy required students to meet higher standards. Many states required teenagers to pass standardized achievement tests in order to graduate. Additional academic courses were often required, but diluted in content and rigor. Other strategies were constructing performance standards for moving to the next grade or maintaining a certain grade-point average for participating on athletic teams. They upgraded curriculum in five basic subjects—English, mathematics, history, science and geography. Reformers tried to revitalize the teaching profession by testing to requalify teachers, basing salaries on performance, and creating career ladders. They even developed 11-month contracts and alternative credentialing.

"Governors believed that the easiest and least expensive reforms to mandate were accountability mechanisms such as testing and assessment. Business leaders saw education and training as the key to improving productivity, standards of living and competitiveness.

"The National Governor's Association (NGA) wrote a five-year strategy in 1986 called *Time for Results.* This long-term reform agenda set up task forces to examine such critical issues as classroom technology and teacher certification. It stated, 'Better schools mean better jobs…To meet stiff competition from workers in the rest of the world, we must educate ourselves and our children as we never have before.'"[3]

Debbie Cohen interrupted, "But, Nate, it's only right that governors should take the lead in school reform since education is supposed to be funded by the state. We spend 35% to over 50% of our state budgets on education."

"Debbie, that's right. States and local governments finance about 89% of total public education operations. But most states have constitutional restrictions against deficit spending. This means that when state revenues go down, funds for public education go down. For example, just when most reforms were getting underway, the severe recession of 1991 to 1993 forced governors to cut back state funds for education. And another thing, when state tax money is limited, funds are taken from schools to spend on new prison facilities and welfare."

"Where were the educators during this first phase of national reform?" Paul asked. "Sounds like it was led by the Governors."

The Second Wave of Reform—Educators Respond. "Paul, the second wave was led by educators," said Nate. "Throughout the late '70s and early '80s, we'd been studying effective schools. Successful schools had strong leadership by principals and teachers who were flexible, innovative, and committed to their work and their students. They had unified visions of the ideal school and high expectations for all students. They had a positive school climate with instruction tied to assessment.[4]

"Later, improvements focused on genuine parent involvement to help counter the tendency of educators to marginalize parents or to keep them out. Successful programs had external collaborators who brought outside intervention reforms to individual schools.

"By 1986 the restructuring movement focused on the local school site. It shifted some decision-making authority from top down to bottom up. Reformers decentralized to completely reorganize the instructional procedures. They focused on strategies like public school choice, teachers and their working conditions, and business/industry partnerships."

"But did anything happen because of these demonstration projects?" Ray asked.

"Yes, the reform pioneers initiated changes in all kinds of schools with all kinds of students. The Accelerated Schools Project was led by Henry Levin at Stanford University. It began operating in 140 schools in 16 states and showed that, under proper conditions, at-risk students could learn as rapidly as their White, middle-class counterparts. The Coalition of Essential Schools, led by Theodore Sizer at Brown University, identified nine learning principles and was operating in 125 schools. James Comer at Yale University worked in 165 schools with minority, inner-city students and their parents. His developmental program helped them bridge the cultural differences between home and school. Mortimer Adler inspired the Paideia project in 200 schools across the country. It combined a broad core curriculum with ways of teaching that help students learn to think critically.

"Another restructuring strategy that educators used was to mandate improvements in the skills and performance of teachers in their classrooms. They tried to attract more capable people, especially minorities, into teaching by proposing high-status programs, special scholarships and loan forgiveness. They also raised standards for teacher education, set new licensing qualifications, and improved subject-matter knowledge of future teachers. Educators even sought alternative certification paths to recruit other college graduates into teaching, modestly higher pay based on performance and career ladders for teachers.

"Another important reform strategy was local business and industry partnerships. They identified entry points, developed vocational curricula and loaned personnel to schools. Their growing concern for disadvantaged children resulted in initiatives on preschool programs and expanded Head Start programs. They also tried to coordinate health, nutrition and educational services into multi-service community schools."

"Nate, why don't you talk about what the conservatives did for local school reform in the late '80s? We wanted private school vouchers that would give parents a choice. Why aren't you talking about these initiatives?" Dale asked.

"I was going to cover that later, Dale," Nate replied. "But briefly stated, conservatives want to involve parents as consumers through private school choice. They argue that people should have a choice in a democracy, and that children learn better when enrolled in schools they want to attend. They contend that good schools attract more students and resources. This forces other schools to make changes that would attract more customers. This approach appealed to democratic and market-choice supporters and emphasized the parental role."

"Nate," Dale interrupted again, "most educators can't reform schools because they're lazy and don't know what the hell they're doing! Just give me a voucher and I'll find a cheap Christian school to send my kids to. If enough parents pull out of the public schools, the bad ones will close and the good ones will get better."

"Dale, we want to save the debate on vouchers for another Saturday," said Nate. "Today we're just overviewing the reform activities that were actually tried by different public or education leaders. In this second wave, school reformers also tried to counter the top down, political and business strategy of the easy fix. Some 1980s reformers made impressive headway with their demonstration models and generated great enthusiasm. But their programs were frequently contradictory and highly fragmented. They were poorly implemented and often abandoned. They involved only a small number of school districts and selected schools. They also rarely moved beyond the demonstration stage, so they had little impact. Most reforms failed because of their cosmetic nature and their lack of additional public resources. Reforms failed because parents believed that someone else's school was doing poorly, not theirs. Some critics compared the students of today favorably with those 20 and 50 years ago, without considering the new demands of a global knowledge economy. Many thought that low student achievement was limited to inner-city, minority students, in spite of growing evidence that at least half of America's students were performing poorly—those from families of all income or class levels in both public and private schools."

"Nate, get serious," said Debbie. "Educators will always protect their fellow teachers and principals from real change. That's what frustrated President Bush and the governors."

"You're partly right, Debbie. Reform always moves slowly. This frustrates our state and national political leaders. President Bush, a Republican who believed that education was largely a state and local matter, did realize that our failure to reform schools at the local and state level had major implications on our nation's economy. He began to see our difficulty in getting skilled manpower to run our armed forces. Our rising crime and drug rates don't stop at the state line, but spill out and affect other states, even those with good education systems."

"That's right, Nate," said Kim Su Young. "Even with all the activity of leading governors in the first wave and educational reformers in the second, the results were still fragmented, limited and uneven. This is especially true when compared with the national education systems of other modern nations. What was the third reform wave about?"

The Third Wave—National Policy Makers Respond. "The third wave," Nate continued, "is characterized by national leadership. We pick up the story again in September 1989, in Charlottesville, Virginia where the first education president, Thomas Jefferson, lived. President George Bush called for a two-day summit with the nation's governors. The conference was to discuss the clear linkage between America's education crises and our declining economic competitiveness. The President, the nation's governors, cabinet members, White House staff and other aides were there.

"Participants worked on a process for setting national education goals modeled after the ones designed by the Southern Governors' Association. They agreed to make regulatory and legislative changes that would make the use of federal funds more flexible and accountable. They agreed to restructure the education system state by state and to make annual progress reports. The summit helped to shape future educational change by committing governors to the creation of national performance goals, especially in math and science. They decided to leave implementation up to the states and local communities and to hold educators accountable.

"Some governors asked for clarification on the federal role in education. They discussed having a national report card to allow comparisons among students, schools, states and countries. They recommended increased federal support for early-childhood education programs, particularly Head Start."

"Wait a minute, Nate!" said Paul. "I thought national goals were a Clinton invention meant to force federal regulation on our local schools. You mean it was started by a Republican president and some Republican governors? They first called for national education goals?"

"Well, Paul, by January 1990, the National Governors Association Task Force on Education, together with members of the White House staff, recommended six National Education Goals for the year 2000. But the problem was that four significant groups were left out of the Charlottesville goal-setting process:

- parents who are the primary consumers of education for their children;

- business leaders who hire high school and college graduates;

- educators who are required to educate our students; and

- members of Congress who translate presidential proposals into legislation and budget priorities.

"This failure to build a broad coalition proved fatal to President Bush's plan to enact national goals into federal legislation. He was unable to become the 'education president' who carried out national education reform because Congress would not pass his education programs."

"Well, what happened to President Bush's National Education Goals?" Kathie asked.

"In April 1991, President Bush got together with his new Secretary of Education Lamar Alexander and unveiled America 2000. It was supposed to end the decline in academic achievement and the stalemate in national education reform and to identify schooling practices that needed to be changed. Its objective was to produce world-class students who would be competitive workers in the new global economy. It clearly advocated a limited federal role in education. It called for 'better and more accountable schools' based on world-class standards, with national examinations to measure student achievement. It also advocated better preparation and development of teachers. It recommended a definite timetable to establish national standards and assessments in the core subjects, but opposed a national curriculum. Before his defeat in 1992, President Bush was able to increase funding for Head Start, but no significant new education legislation was enacted."

"I thought that Lamar Alexander was against national education goals and standards and testing," said Paul. "In fact, he was against any federal education role, including the federal Department of Education. Am I right?"

"Well, I can't speak for Lamar Alexander," said Nate. "But as U.S. Secretary of Education, the record shows that he advocated many federal programs he now opposes.

"But Nate, I thought we had national education goals," Kathie said.

"Yes, we do. But they emerged in stages and have caused a lot of controversy. In July 1990, the Bush White House and the National Governors Association jointly agreed to form the National Education Goals Panel."*

"In 1992 Clinton was campaigning for the Presidency on his record as an education governor. After taking office in 1993, he appointed former South Carolina Governor Richard Riley as Secretary of Education. The President and his new Secretary were then successful in passing the most comprehensive federal legislation since President Lyndon Johnson in 1964. Goals 2000 is the keystone of this reform package.

"The new law used the same six national goals adopted by Bush and the governors. Congress added two new goals to the original six. One recognized the need for stronger teacher education and professional development. The second spelled out the importance of parent involvement. Goals 2000 was passed by a bipartisan Congress and signed into law by President Clinton on March 31, 1994. Please follow me on your handout while I read the eight National Education Goals:

Goal 1: By the year 2000, all children in America will start school ready to learn.

Goal 2: By the year 2000, the high school graduation rate will increase to at least 90%.

Goal 3: By the year 2000, all students will leave grades 4, 8, and 12 having demonstrated competency over challenging subject matter including

---

* In 1994, under President Clinton's leadership, the Educate America Act was passed forming the Goals Panel, an independent agency of the executive branch. It is charged with the responsibility of supporting system-wide reform. Its purpose is to monitor national and state progress toward the national goals, to report progress every year, and to recommend improvements for assessing goals. The Goals Panel is also charged with building a national consensus for education improvement. It is supposed to identify promising reform strategies and recommend actions for federal, state and local governments. It also works to establish a system of academic standards and assessments. The Panel issues an annual report showing state and national progress in reaching national targets.

English, mathematics, science, foreign languages, civics and government, economics, arts, history, and geography, and every school in America will ensure that all students learn to use their minds well, so they may be prepared for responsible citizenship, further learning, and productive employment in our Nation's modern economy.

Goal 4: By the year 2000, the Nation's teaching force will have access to programs for the continued improvement of their professional skills and the opportunity to acquire the knowledge and skills needed to instruct and prepare all American students for the next century.

Goal 6: By the year 2000, every adult American will be literate and will possess the knowledge and skills necessary to compete in a global economy and exercise the rights and responsibilities of citizenship.

Goal 7: By the year 2000, every school in the United States will be free of drugs, violence, and the unauthorized presence of firearms and alcohol and will offer a disciplined environment conducive to learning.

Goal 8: By the year 2000, every school will promote partnerships that will increase parental involvement and participation in promoting the social, emotional, and academic growth of children.

"Just a damn minute, Nate!" Dale Jones sounded angry! "Goals 2000 is a federal, socialist trick to control local schools. That's why some governors stood up to Clinton's education secretary and refused to accept Goals 2000 money with its federal 'strings' attached."

"Dale, there are no federal strings with the money. We'll have an opportunity later in our Hearing schedule to explore the role of the federal government in some detail. But it will interest you to know that when Congress enacted Goals 2000 legislation, they addressed the very problem you fear.

"This is the actual wording: 'Nothing in this Act shall be construed to authorize an officer or employee of the Federal Government to mandate, direct, or control a State, local educational agency, or school's curriculum, program of instruction…Congress reaffirms that the responsibility for control of education is reserved to the States and local school systems.' The primary goal of the *GOALS 2000: Educate America Act* is to encourage local community-based actions that meet pressing educational needs, help more students achieve to higher standards, increase parental participation, and improve teaching."[5]

"In the first year, four states declined Goals 2000 funds. But this federal program was to help state officials plan, design and carry out assessments of their own version of challenging academic standards for students at grades 4, 8 and 12. Today, all states have now accepted Goals 2000 funds for planning grants and are improving state academic requirements in math, science, history, geography, English, foreign language and arts education.

"National standards in history and literature were criticized so much that they were sent back to their designers for further refinement. They've now been improved and re-released."*

"Well, I didn't know that. But I'm still suspicious of the feds," said Dale.

"I disagree with Dale completely," Debbie interjected. "I've worked for the Justice Department and I know where this country would be without a strong federal role in law enforcement. For the first time, I'm reading these national education goals and wondering what the fuss is all about. Who could possibly be against these goals for all America's children? They may be a little too ambitious—the year 2000 is just around the corner. How are we coming on achieving these goals?"

"We'll review that progress later this afternoon, Debbie. Let me summarize by saying that the U.S. Department of Education and several private national foundations began supporting professional academic associations and research centers in their development of national academic curriculum standards. These included the subjects of science, history, arts, civics, geography and English. As early as 1989, the National Council of Teachers of Mathematics announced new mathematics standards. They're now training classroom teachers for these new math standards.

"Well," said Ted, "I understand that the Department of Defense schools are already adapting academic curriculum to meet national goals, and they are testing for performance. Before we began reducing the size of our Armed Forces, this federal school system was like the 13ᵗʰ largest school district in the United States. I know this because my son and his family are stationed in Germany. I have two grandchildren in those schools."

"I'm glad you brought that up, Ted," said Nate. "The Department of Defense operates schools for the families of service personnel in Europe

---

* History standards were revised and re-released in April 1996 to the applause of Diane Ravitch and national columnist George Will. The Council for Basic Education played a critical role in assembling two distinguished panels of historians to review the standards.

and Asia. Very early it identified academic standards and implementation targets and then assessed progress toward reaching those goals. Its pioneering work has shown that connecting educational goals and standards to educational results can be done—for all America's students. They do it by involving the parents and by emphasizing performance-based education."

"Let's go on now and talk about the new Republican Congress which was elected in 1994. The newly elected legislators were angry about federal regulations in education, so they targeted for elimination the Department of Education and its programs. Many were elected with the support of the Christian Coalition and frustrated parents. During the first year of the Gingrich-led revolt against domestic programs, conservative members of Congress attacked Goals 2000 and tried to cut federal education programs and budgets.

"In direct response to this strategy, on April 5, 1995, a bipartisan *National Education Summit* called for support of world-class education standards. It was convened by U.S. Secretary of Education Richard Riley, former U.S. Secretary Terrel H. Bell, and U.S. Senator James Jeffords, Chairman of the Senate Subcommittee on Education. One hundred fifty national business, policy, education, parent and community leaders gathered in Washington D.C. to participate in **Key to the Future: National Summit on World-Class Education for All America's Children.** The Summit was telecast to 11 sites where over 600 regional leaders were conducting mini-summits. Speakers, panels and small group discussions focused on the need for world-class academic standards as a national school reform strategy. They also called for all community leaders and parents to participate in programs that reform neighborhood schools."

"I'm confused," Maria said. "I heard on the TV that a national summit on raising national academic standards was held in New York in 1996."

"Yes, Maria. Another national summit was called in March 1996 by Governor Tommy Thompson, chairman of the National Governors Association, and Louis Gerstner, chairman of IBM. It focused on raising national academic standards and rapidly introducing technology into schools. That summit was held at the IBM conference center in Palisades, New York."

"I guess now it's my turn to get confused," said Kim Su Young. "I understand your review of the first three waves of school reform. What I don't understand is where this Commission fits in the picture. We aren't a group of Governors working at the state level. And we aren't a group of educators working within the school at the local level. And we aren't working at the national level. That takes care of three waves (see *Figure 2.1 Four Waves of National Public School Reform*). Is there a fourth wave of reform?"

The Fourth Wave—Grassroots Public Engagement. "Excellent question, Kim. Yes, we're just entering a **fourth wave—grassroots public engagement—a nationwide, school-site, community-based, reform movement driven by parents, teachers, and citizens.** After 14 years of school reform all over the United States, and despite the work of thousands of dedicated reformers—including governors, business leaders, presidents and educators—fewer Americans are saying that public schools are doing a good job. More of them are saying they have little or no confidence in the public schools. If you want statistics, some 62% of Americans believe that the education children are receiving is 'fair, poor or very poor.'[6] They feel helpless about their own local schools. When asked how important a problem the quality of public education is for this country, 69% of those responding in a national survey said it was one of the most important.[7] Another recent study of public attitudes toward public schools in California found that citizens see the connection between improved schools and quality of life. Improving schools came out ahead of other sensitive issues like environment, taxes, and crime. The survey also discovered that Californians believe that public schools can improve over the next decade and that more money should be spent. They believe that schools should teach civic responsibility, and they should provide additional services to poor children like health and dental care.[8]

Nate continued. "Research during the last 30 years has shown that family involvement in education is critical to a child's success in school! So it's ironic that parents have been systematically excluded from schools by many teachers they are trying to support. *U.S. News and World Report* recently found that lack of parent involvement is the most serious problem in getting the schools back on track. To counter this, U.S. Secretary of Education Richard Riley has sponsored a parent initiative. In 1994 President Clinton and the Congress enacted legislation that created parent participation as a new National Education Goal.

"In successful school reform, the teacher is a partner with the parent. Some study findings about teachers are troubling, however. Public Agenda

Figure 2.1
FOUR WAVES OF PUBLIC EDUCATION REFORM

Strategies	1st Wave	2nd Wave	3rd Wave	4th Wave
Policy Document	*A Nation At Risk* 1983	Effective Schools Literature 1979-86	National Education Goals 2000 1994	State Charters District Charters 1996+
Change Leverage	Top Down Mass Production	Bottom Up Individualized Learning	National Academic Standards/ Assessments	Public Engagement Accountability
Unit of Change	State Regulations	Local School Site	School Districts & High-Poverty Schools	School Site District Office Learning Cultures
Leadership	Education Gov's State Legislators & Employers	Professional Educators; Business/School Partnerships	President, Congress National Assoc.; Business, Family/ School Partnerships	Principals, Teacher/Parent/ Student Partnership
Primary Funding	State Taxes	Local Property Taxces	State Equalizing Tax Support Base	State Taxes for Independent School Site
Organization Base	State Governor State Office of Education & School District	Local Schools	National: Federal/ Prof. Assoc. & Foundations	Independent School-Site Council
Technology	Computers in Schools	Computer Labs	Interactive Networks, Internet, Voice Mail	Classroom Computers CD Roms
Outcome	Raised State Acad. Stds. & Grad. Req.	Improved Classroom Learning Process	Local School Ref. Improved Student Performance	Create Demand Public School Choice
Students Impacted	Reform States Top 50%	Pilot Demonstration Schools	Targeted to All Children, & to Disadv. Children	All Students
Summary	**Policymakers Demanding Educator Accountability**	**Education Service Providers Enabling Students to Learn**	**Goals, Standards, Assessment Driven**	**Public Engagement Ownership Accountability**

states, 'Far from being strong advocates for high-level learning in their own fields, they [teachers] seem to downplay the importance of the very subjects they teach.' Only 26% of American teachers, compared to 93% of Japanese teachers, believe that academic achievement results from serious study, *not from inherent ability*. This means that 74% actually believe that academic achievement is the result of being born smart, not that all students are capable of reaching high academic standards! Many teachers resent the standards movement and perceive it as an indictment of their failures. By the way, most teachers are overburdened and haven't had time to get retrained in how to teach these new challenging standards.

"Teachers aren't the only ones who are frustrated. The public, which includes new members of Congress, teachers and parents, is poorly informed about school reform in our country. One sign of frustration is the voucher movement. A second is the rapidly growing charter schools movement. A third is the revolt against nationwide academic standards. A fourth is sharply partisan debates over family values.[9]

"I think I know where you're heading, Nate," said Ray. "I see the appointment of the Jefferson Citizens' School Reform Commission as an example of **the fourth wave—a public engagement strategy to bring about grassroots reform.** Informed and active parents, educators and community leaders must send a common cultural message to our students. This message is that success in life depends a great deal on gaining knowledge and skills. We must inform all interested parents and teachers about school reform and what they can do to improve their own *family and classroom learning cultures*. If we don't work together in school reform, we will continue to waste America's most precious resources—our children."

"Thanks, Nate, for the great overview of modern school reform," said Ray. "I simply had no idea how much was going on and how our Jefferson Citizens' Commission fits into the national picture. We will look dumb if we don't explore what other reformers have tried to do without looking at the whole school reform picture.

"Before we turn to our next topic, which is student achievement," said Nate, "and our first guest, let's take a short refreshment break. See you back here in 15 minutes."

****

Wendy Swenson welcomed the group back. "Our challenge in school reform today is to get the attention of the public, the policymakers, and corporate leaders. Most of us are used to hearing about the bad news of schools. Too many crises compete for our attention. Most national leaders in America today are men, and men have traditionally been insensitive to America's education challenges because they see education as women's work. They prefer to spend their competitive energies making money or exercising power.

"Since *A Nation At Risk* came out, have our schools improved? How many and which groups of children are succeeding in these schools today? Probably very few of us know how our Jefferson students compare with students across the country in terms of academic performance. We need this information before we can find a solution.

Lost Generations: Academic Achievement of American Students[10]

"We need a background briefing on American educational performance today. Please turn to the material for today's Hearing. We'll focus on academic achievement of American students. We'll start by reviewing reports of the National Education Goals Panel* and also reports by the U.S. Department of Education.

"The Third National Education Goal states: '**By the year 2000, all students will leave grades 4, 8, and 12 having demonstrated competency over challenging subject matter including English, mathematics, science, foreign languages, civics and government, economics, arts, history and geography, and every school in America will ensure that all students learn to use their minds well, so they may be prepared for responsible citizenship, further learning, and productive employment in our Nation's modern economy.'**

"The American public is beginning to understand that all children must be given the chance to earn a world-class education if they are to become successful, prosperous, contributing citizens. As we review this information, keep in mind that our student population has been constantly changing since the 1970s. Unlike most other modern nations, we have been educating increasing numbers of disadvantaged Whites, minorities, immigrants,

---

* The Goals Panel, an independent, bipartisan agency, is not part of the U.S. Department of Education. The Panel's membership consists of eight governors, two administration officials, four members of Congress, and four state legislators.

and children with disabilities. For example, Hispanic students in public schools doubled from 11% to 22% between 1973 and 1993. Students with disabilities are now almost 12% of the total student body.

"Most other nations do not face this massive challenge. For example, elementary and secondary enrollment in the 1995-96 school year reached almost 51 million students—45 million in public schools and 5.6 million in private schools.[11] Nine out of every ten students in the U.S. attend public schools. In 1992 the American population (25- to 34-year olds) that graduated from high school was 84%, compared with 90% in Germany, 89% in Japan, and 82% in England. We have nearly three million classroom teachers (1.8 million of them in elementary schools). Our elementary public school classrooms average 19.1 pupils for each teacher. The average public school teacher salary for a nine-month contract is about $38,000 and about $25,000 for new entering teachers. Last year, we had nearly 112,000 schools in America—85,400 public and 26,100 private ones. And in 1994-95, public elementary and secondary schools spent $244 billion, with 11.5% of that total coming from federal funds. In some high-poverty schools, however, estimated federal assistance reaches as much as 35%."

"The 1995 Goals Panel Report shows that our nation is not even halfway to meeting our National Education Goals by the year 2000. The good news is that between 1982 and 1992, high school students improved dramatically in earning the recommended credits, from 13% to 47%. Among minority students, Asian Americans take a stronger course curriculum than Whites."

Wendy took a deep breath and continued. "The bad news is that **today only one of two American youths between the ages of 19 and 24 has the knowledge to become a productive worker or succeed in college, and also become a responsible parent, an informed consumer and an accountable citizen** (see Figure 2.2 *An American Catastrophe: The Knowledge Gap).*"[12]

"Wendy! said Debbie. "I find that figure—one out of two youngsters being really functionally illiterate—to be unbelievable! If this is true, this nation is in deep trouble. We might as well move to Canada or Europe."

"Debbie, we've arrived at these estimates from several sources," said Wendy. "The most obvious was the recent National Assessment of Educational Progress (NAEP) study of adult literacy. The study found that less than half of young adults (18- to 24-year olds) could pass literacy tests requiring them to do such things as read maps, take a bus, make correct change

Figure 2.2

AN AMERICAN CATASTROPHE: THE KNOWLEDGE GAP

Only one of two young adults is developing the values, knowledge and skills to succeed in college, to hold a productive job and to participate responsibly in family and community life.

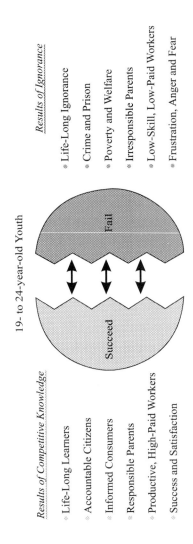

19- to 24-year-old Youth

Results of Competitive Knowledge

* Life-Long Learners
* Accountable Citizens
* Informed Consumers
* Responsible Parents
* Productive, High-Paid Workers
* Success and Satisfaction

Results of Ignorance

* Life-Long Ignorance
* Crime and Prison
* Poverty and Welfare
* Irresponsible Parents
* Low-Skill, Low-Paid Workers
* Frustration, Anger and Fear

Source: The Terrel H. Bell Knowledge Network for Education Reform (1997)

or read directions for completing work tasks. This means that more than half are unable to function effectively in modern life and work. When we add knowledge of geography, math, or advanced reading and analytical skills, the one-out-of-two is very much in line.[13]* Remember this is not a generation as well educated as 1950s high school graduates who were taught by a generation of 1930s-educated teachers. Back then only about 39% of our population graduated, but they were relatively better educated than most of our high school graduates today. After WWII most high school dropouts and graduates alike could find good union jobs in the booming industrial economy. But today students don't even get the basic survival skills to hold a good job or go to college. The survival skills in our complex modern world are far more demanding."

"I told you those teachers at Washington and Lee High School lied to me!" said Dale. "Today there are no good union manufacturing jobs, only piss-poor, low-wage service jobs like driving a cab or flipping burgers. I feel cheated no matter how hard I work. I can't feed my family, and I can't buy a home. I'd be better off on welfare!"

Hey, red neck! thought Lenora. Then she spoke out! "You don't know nothin' about welfare, and tryin' to raise three kids. And now Governor Scott is trying to kick us Black mothers off welfare. My kids are hungry half the time, and I'm embarrassed to send them to school without decent clothes. It's not just Blacks that are getting screwed by this education system. Looks like you White boys are fixin' to have a pretty hard future, too."

Wendy continued. "Well, Dale, you and Lenora are examples of this community's failure to deliver your educational birthright." Wendy hammered away at the nation's failure to invest in children's education. She argued that underlying this neglect is a deep well-spring of prejudice that leads to discriminatory behavior against disadvantaged minorities and Whites.

---

*In the 1989 international study of Educational Testing Services, 61% of 17-year-old students could not read or understand relatively complicated material, such as that typically presented at the high school level. Nearly one-half appear to have limited mathematics skills and abilities that go little beyond adding, subtracting, and multiplying with whole numbers. More than one-half could not evaluate the procedures or results of a scientific study, and few included enough information in their written pieces to communicate their ideas effectively. Additionally, assessment results in other curriculum areas indicate that high school juniors have little sense of historical chronology, have not read much literature, and tend to be unfamiliar with the uses and potential applications of computers.

"We're uninformed—parents, especially fathers, beleaguered educators, and public officials. We tolerate today's relatively poor educational performance by children in most public schools. We can't sit on the sidelines anymore. Some people think the answer is to put their children in private schools or support private voucher plans. They avoid fixing the broken public school system. But remember, 9-out-of-10 children (90%) attend public schools. If we don't reform public schools, we're going to make things worse. American taxpayers pay less than citizens in most other advanced nations, and then we complain about it. Our political leaders haven't helped."

"We're smug about our outdated, bureaucratic state and local school systems. We finance only 180 school days per year—to support an outdated education system designed for the 19th century agricultural economy. Each year taxpayers in England fund their children for 192 days, in Germany for 210 days, in Israel 215 days, in Taiwan 222 days, in Japan for 243 days, and in China 251 days. Asian students, by the time they graduate from high school, have spent almost twice as much time in school as American students.[14] Yes, we have a national disaster in the making. Most of our competitors have national ministries of education, national curriculums and performance assessments to coordinate and ensure higher standards of performance. They fund and operate schools that turn out students whose academic achievements on average far exceed American students. Our students place about average or below in international comparisons, even though our best students are very competitive.

"In the area of adult literacy, we have almost four million adult Americans that cannot read, sign their names, or perform simple addition and subtraction. **Thirty million workers can scarcely read and write, and another 40 million lack the basic skills to get by in a technological and rapidly changing world.** Most young people experience a difficult transition from high school to work or college. Today, high school dropouts have inadequate skills, reduced productivity and a lower standard of living—condemning them to lives of borderline poverty. School dropouts seriously erode the nation's economic competitiveness. In 1991 unemployment rates for teenagers averaged around 16.4% for Whites, 22.9% for Hispanics, and 36.3% for African Americans. Prospects for high school graduates are not much better. **A high school diploma is not sufficient preparation to support a family in the global knowledge economy.**

"Illiteracy leads to poverty. We're spending over $200 billion annually in welfare payments, crime, job incompetence, lost tax revenues and remedial education—two-thirds the cost of national defense—because of illiteracy. By the year 2000, one out of three children will live in poverty. Teenagers with poor basic academic skills are *four* times more likely to live in poverty than teenagers with good skills. Children who experience poverty between the ages of 6 and 15 are **two to three times more likely** to become high school dropouts than those who are never poor.[15]

"In 1994, the most recent assessments, only 30% of fourth-grade students met the Goal Panel's performance standard in reading, about the same as in 1992. Among eighth graders, only 30% met the Panel's performance standard. **By the time students reached the twelfth grade and were ready for high school graduation, only 36%—a significant decrease from 1992— met the 'proficient' or 'advanced' reading levels required to find and hold a good job or go on to college.**[16] Minority students scored significantly lower relative to White students and did not improve their reading achievement between 1992 and 1994. Girls were slightly better readers than boys. But, there's some good news! In a 1991-92 international comparison, 9-year-old American students outperformed students in most other modern nations in assessments of narrative reading ability and 14-year-old students finished above Italy, West Germany and Spain in expository reading understanding."

"What's expository reading?" Lenora asked quietly, not sure she wanted to let everyone know she didn't understand. "And what are these levels, proficient and advanced?" Wendy didn't seem to hear her comment in her growing enthusiasm to share the information.

"In NAEP assessments of writing achievements by American students, the news was somewhat better. Over half of the fourth-grade students and three-fourths of the eighth-grade students could write well enough to produce relatively well-developed narrative, informative and persuasive papers. This encouraging snapshot of student writing is based on examinations of portfolios by a sample of students in 1992. **The bad news is that only 36% of eleventh graders could write complete sentences and only 2% were effective, coherent writers**.

"In 1994 approximately one-in-six fourth graders, one-in-seven eighth graders, and one-in-ten twelfth graders met the performance standards in

U.S. history. **Ninety percent of graduating seniors are functionally illiterate in understanding our country's history.** Minority students scored 8 to 18 points below White students in history achievement, while gaps between White and minority students decreased in higher grades.

"In 1994 assessments of geography achievement, approximately one-in-four students knew enough geography to pass the proficiency performance tests in grades four, eight and twelve. **Three-out-of-four American students are graduating with little working knowledge of geography.** Minority students placed even lower by 19 to 31 points.

"In mathematics achievement, we find that in 1996 only 21% of fourth graders, 24% of eighth graders and 16% of twelfth graders met the NAEP math proficiency standards. These scores are slightly better than those in 1992. **In grade twelve, five-out-of-six students preparing to graduate could not meet the mathematics proficiency level.** The gap in mathematics performance widened between Hispanic and White students in grade eight, and between Black and White students in grades four and eight. As White students improved, Black and Hispanic students fell farther behind.

"In 1991, 13-year-old Americans placed at the bottom in a six-nation comparison of life science, physical science, earth science and the nature of science. Our 9-year-old students placed above Canada, the Soviet Union and Spain and below South Korea and Taiwan. On international science assessments, however, the number of high school students taking biology, chemistry and physics classes nearly doubled (21.6%) during the decade—but this is not nearly enough to compete with students in other advanced nations.[17] In 1995 the Third International Mathematics and Science Study (TIMSS) was conducted. This study is the largest, most comprehensive, and most rigorous international comparison of education ever undertaken. It included 41 nations—one-half million students at five different grade levels.[18]

"In mathematics, U.S. eighth graders score below the international average of the 41 countries. The content taught in U.S. eighth-grade mathematics classes is at a seventh-grade level in comparison with other countries. Twenty seven nations scored above the U.S. in math—including Japan, France, and Canada—15 scored significantly better and 13 scored below.[19] The quality of mathematical content taught to American students is not as high as that taught to German and Japanese eighth graders. Only about 5%

of our best math students would qualify with the top 10% of the 41 countries' best students.

"U.S. eighth graders score above the international average in science— 16 countries were above and 24 scored below. Some 13% of our best science students would be included in the top 10% of the 41 countries' top students.

"A new study of science and math curriculum comparing 50 nations shows that American curriculum, textbooks and teachers try to cover too many math and science concepts and do so superficially.[20] U.S. eighth graders spend more class and homework time on math and science than German and Japanese students. German and Japanese teachers are better prepared than American teachers for their profession and receive better daily support for their teaching activities.

"One other indicator that helps place our students' performance in perspective is the number of students who take and pass Advance College Placement Tests. This indicator shows they are able to complete college-level academic studies. Between 1991 and 1995, although a still relatively low 5.7%, participation increased in areas such as English, mathematics, science and history. By contrast, almost 50% of high school students in France pass Advanced College Placement Tests. By the way, some of our disadvantaged students are prevented from taking these tests even when they are prepared because of the cost involved. Waivers should be provided."

Maria could hardly believe what she was hearing about how miserably American students as a whole are performing when compared with students in other modern nations. *I thought it was only Hispanic and Black kids but it's a lot of Anglo kids too. It looks like 25 million kids are not making it. They're headed toward lower skills and lives of poverty. Talk about a national tragedy! Americans are losing the war against ignorance. What can this Commission do about Jefferson?* thought Maria.

Wendy continued. "We have a recent report of what American teenagers really think about their schools.[21] Public Agenda, a group who conducted a national study of teen attitudes, came to several conclusions:

1. While most teenagers (88%) believe highly-educated people get a lot of respect in America and (96%) believe it is important to go to college, most view their high school experience as an exercise in the

art of 'getting by'—doing as little as possible to get the grades they need;

2. Most teenagers do not dislike their school. Three-out-of-four (78%) say they look forward to going to school each day, but there are too many disruptive students. Drugs and violence are not as serious a problem as their parents believe;

3. Teenagers agree that schools need to teach basic skills, computers, and values such as honesty and tolerance. They don't see any reason to study academic subjects such as history, science, and literature;

4. Most teenagers support the nationwide call for higher academic standards, which they think all students should have to meet. They don't believe most students are putting enough effort into their studies. Most students say that having to meet higher standards would make them work harder and learn more;

5. Teenagers say that a good teacher is the most influential adult in getting them to learn, but their parents monitor their homework;

6. Two-thirds of the teenagers interviewed said that they respond well to a teacher who challenges them to do better and learn more. Students respect teachers who are demanding and consistent, but would like them to be interesting and engaging;

7. Students complain of a lack of respect and civility in the public schools. They see the popular teenage culture as destructive—there's widespread cheating and obsession with clothes and looks;

8. Minority youngsters, particularly African-American teens, are more likely to consider a lack of order and discipline, along with poor teaching, as serious problems in their schools. African-American teens are more likely than White teens to say that subjects such as history, science, and math are important to learn, and a strong academic background is the chief component of future career success; and

9. Private school youngsters rate their schools, school experiences, teachers and classmates as outstanding. They report that drugs and violence, social promotion, and lack of challenge are relatively rare as compared with public school teens.

"In summary, what teenagers want from their public schools is more order in their schools and classrooms, more structure and self-discipline, and more teaching of ethical values, such as honesty and hard work. Does this picture of teenagers surprise you?"

"Wendy, I for one am very surprised by these findings," Ray said. "As a parent, I have assumed that it's only the parents and teachers that feel this way about the poor performance of our schools. And now you are saying that the teenagers feel like we do. I'm very surprised! Sounds like we all want reform in our public schools—not just the adults."

"Wendy," said Paul Christopher. "This is a lousy picture of American education you just painted. I can't believe we're doing so badly. I thought our poor education achievement was because we have so many minorities and immigrants. Are you saying it's this bad in suburban communities?"

"Well, Paul, not every school is failing. There are some exceptional schools in suburbs and even in the cities. I guess we could say the glass can be seen as half full as well as half empty. The top 20% of our students are very good indeed. They can hold their own with students in Asia or Europe. But our bottom 50% are not going to make it in our competitive global economy, unless we figure out how to wake up the public. In my judgment, this is the civil rights issue of the '90s. These figures represent real children. Their future lives are at stake!

"Lenora, you and Dale should not let your education be stopped. You feel you've been cheated by the public schools. The good news is that we have decent adult education programs. We have good community college systems and private technical training. You can supplement what you've already learned.

"But in all honesty, I'm discouraged," Wendy confessed. "The real message is we are falling short of achieving our National Education Goals. We don't have the public's attention. We need to enact these national goals as part of every state's progress. But it's just too slow.

"Now I want to introduce our first speaker, Mr. Ken Nelson, who is optimistic about our progress in education reform. He is executive director of the National Education Goals Panel—the group that publishes the report card each year on our national education achievements. Ken, welcome to our Citizens' Commission on Elementary School Reform. Would you begin by telling us what two or three lesson you've learned since you came to the Goals Panel? How can our Commission prepare for the challenges here at Jefferson?"

"Thank you, Wendy and Nate, Chairman Gonzales, and members of the Citizens' Commission. One lesson on school reform I have learned is that we have to work collaboratively. We need local participation with as many of the players as possible. You have to include everyone from the beginning—from planning to assessment. As the process unfolds, we must report progress to all parties, and we must get their periodic feedback.

"Right now, our education system is very rigid. I support the public schools, but I am a loving critic. I believe they have to change and have to be more accountable to the public. As a state policymaker, I used to say, if you don't bend, you will break. We're reaching the breaking point. But the good news is that some places in the country are doing very well. We're now entering the era of the 'educational consumer,' or people who are better informed. I'm optimistic that we can do it.

"Another lesson is that we [every community] have to be clear about what we want to do. We have to assess where we are now at the present time and develop a strategic plan to achieve those goals. Then we must report back to all parties how well we are doing. This is the goals process—the way to carry out school reform."

Christina raised her hand. "What are the unique contributions of the National Goals Panel to the school reform process?"

"We're committed to the reform process for the long run, not just for this decade or even the next decade. We don't have a 'quick fix,' nor even in one governor's term. People have to stay with it for the long haul. Second, the Goals Panel contributed a clear statement of measurable goals. So we think public accountability is necessary. This means that public schools have to be held accountable for their performance. A third Goals Panel contribution is that we've kept the National Education Goals in the public eye. The Goals Panel has governors, members of Congress and state legislators on it. This diverse group influences the National Governors Association, the Congress, and the National Conference of State Legislators and others. We also keep a high profile through the reports we issue—our 1996 Goals Report that we'll soon be releasing. It gives germane information for everyone, with state-by-state data. It's on the worldwide web, and it's available by request. Our annual report on progress towards the national goals became the subject of last spring's Governors' Conference."

Ray spoke up. "You know, Ken, there has been much controversy over the federal role. The National Goals Panel is a federal agency, but it has not attracted negative reactions like the U.S. Department of Education or Goals 2000. How do you explain this?"

"We're not part of the U.S. Department of Education. We report directly to Congress. School reform is a local issue. I myself focus on the states. I was a state legislator from Minnesota. I believe that's where the action is. Twelve of our 18 panel members are governors or state legislators. We believe that the standards must be generated at the state levels."

"Ken," said Kim Su Young, "your new panel report certainly supports the development of high academic standards. Can you describe for us a step-by-step approach that communities can carry out?"

"Yes, Kim. I'll hand this out and see what you think. It's taken from our new report that describes nine steps we believe will successfully involve parents and the public in setting higher standards:[22]

- **Step 1.** Build demand for standards and reform. Meetings should be held with all representatives of a community in order to provide information and build public support for higher academic standards.

- **Step 2.** Set high academic standards. The standards-setting process begins by gathering examples from other states and districts and professional groups who have already completed a great deal of outstanding work on academic standards. These should be adapted to the particular needs of the community and involve representative teachers, administrators, parents and community members in selecting new standards and holding community meetings to explain and build consensus.

- **Step 3.** Conduct an education inventory of your school system looking at test scores, course-taking patterns, and student and teacher absenteeism, discipline problems, etc.

- **Step 4.** Build community consensus through an honest public exchange of ideas about the performance of the public schools. Citizen committees should be organized and the case made to the greater community for establishing world-class standards, and a system that holds students and schools accountable for reaching them.

- **Step 5.** Reorganize for change. Setting the new academic standards is a necessary, but not sufficient, step to increase student achievement. The school system must be organized to achieve the objectives by introducing new curriculum, retraining teachers, assessing student progress and raising grade promotion and graduation requirements.

- **Step 6.** Develop new student assessments. New student assessments will have to be developed to measure student mastery of the essential knowledge and skills so that the standards and assessments can be aligned. Communities cannot hold their schools accountable without clear measures of progress.

- **Step 7.** Build staff capacity. Training new teachers and re-training experienced teachers and administrators should be an ongoing process to ensure that new standards will be taught effectively. Staff development activities should be focused on developing the new knowledge and skills essential to improving faculty performance.

- **Step 8.** Create an accountability system. An accountability system requires communities to measure and report student progress to the public regularly—just as the Goals Panel does annually to the nation.

- **Step 9.** Set checkpoints and make adjustments as needed. As new data on progress towards the improvement of public schools becomes available, continual negotiations must be made with many different parties in order to keep the school reform activities on target and to prevent entrenched interests from undermining the reform process.

"These steps are a framework for serious, long-lasting reform. I look forward to the report of the Citizens' Commission on Jefferson Elementary School Reform."

Wendy took the floor. "Thank you, Ken, for sharing your perspective. Keep up the great work!

"I'd like you to have another BEST PRACTICES example on Goal Line," said Wendy.[23]

BEST PRACTICES: GOAL LINE—
THE EDUCATION REFORM ONLINE NETWORK

In September 1992, the Coalition for Goals 2000 was founded to help Americans meet the National Education Goals by improving the teaching and learning in local communities across the country. This nonprofit corporation provides a framework, outside of government, within which grassroots citizens can learn what is working in education reform, who's doing it and where. The Coalition now engages 145 national organizations in education reform, making it possible for their state and local affiliates to assist local communities. It provides information and tools that help people become informed participants in local education reform.

GOAL LINE is an easy-to-use interactive computer network designed to increase the pace and scope of community efforts that improve education. To achieve this objective, it seeks to connect citizens and policy makers, from around the nation, by fostering conversations about education reform that leads to informed action.

GOAL LINE has been successfully piloted and now offers a national subscriber service. It has become a "meeting place" where Coalition Members and Communities can become part of a productive, national community striving for common goals. Its conference areas allow reformers to share with each other the programs working in their communities. It offers a comprehensive searchable database of more than 2000 exemplary programs and practices, organized around the Goals, that were selected with guidance from U.S. Departments of Education and Labor. Its Daily Updates provides the latest education reform news, in addition to disseminating information on what states are initiating, such as emerging content standards, or hard-to-find education reform resources, or publications, reports and conferences. It also has *The Daily Report Card* which digests local news media coverage of education reform.

In March 1995, the National Education Goals Panel selected **GOAL LINE** as its principal tool for disseminating information online to communities nationwide. GOAL LINE is located at The George Washington University in Washington, D.C.

Summary

"Now Nate will summarize some points made this afternoon," said Wendy.

"Let's get up and stretch," Nate said as he smiled and glanced at his notes. "**Modern school reform can be classified into four waves. First, governors introduced low-cost, top-down, state-wide reform that depends largely on regulatory laws and mandates. Students must meet higher academic standards in English, mathematics, history, science and geography before they can graduate. Second, educators worked from the bottom up. They organized school-based reforms in teaching and learning that were driven by strong principals and teachers who expected students and parents to share the responsibility for education. Third, the President joined with Congress and business leaders in defining education as a new national priority and enacted lofty education goals for all students. Fourth, our present wave of school reform is characterized by a nation-wide, school-site, community-based movement driven by parents, teachers, and citizens at the grassroots level. We are using field-tested whole-school change models dedicated to providing quality public educational opportunities for all America's students, with special focus on children who are disadvantaged.**

"We've described today the overall condition of public education. Nine out of ten Americans attend public schools. Our student population is constantly changing and growing—more minorities, more children with disabilities, more limited English speaking, more disadvantaged. The bottom line is that only half are being prepared for successful futures. This means that the fortunate half will soon be supporting the other half. No country will long survive that way.

"Today's more penetrating academic evaluations by the National Assessment of Educational Progress and the international academic measures are going beyond the limited I.Q. and multiple-choice testing procedures to reveal the depth of the challenge to all Americans. Assessments of academic progress reported relatively poor performance in every academic subject—reading, writing, mathematics, international assessments of math and science, history, geography and adult literacy.[24] Many American students are learning some facts and information but are unable to comprehend their meaning. We also reviewed a recent study by Public Agenda that shows that teenage students also feel like they are just 'getting by' and would like more challenging academic work, more discipline, more moral authority from teachers.

"Our first Commission guest, Ken Nelson, gave us his lessons in school reform. From the beginning, all community interest groups must be included. The community must be clear about what they intend to accomplish. There must be accountability for progress and regular reporting. He cited the contributions of the National Education Goals Panel to school reform—demonstrating that reform takes a long time. We must be patient. We must have measurable goals. We must keep school reform on the public agenda. Our Citizens' Commission, like The Goals Panel, broadly represents the public. Finally, Ken gave us nine steps to carry out the reform process that will be very helpful to us when we make our final recommendations for Jefferson.

"Perhaps the most troubling finding today was a warning from the Public Opinion surveys: The American public is withdrawing its support for public schools because they lack confidence that professional educators alone can improve public schools without including parents and community representatives as true partners in grassroots school reform. We call this public engagement."

Nate continued. "Today, we want to start a new practice as we break up. We have about 10 minutes left. Please bare with me. We take a one word 'temperature reading.' Think of one word that sums up your feelings about today's session. Let's start on my left and go around the room. Repeat your name and give us your one word."

"I'm Christina, and I'm excited."

"Paul, skeptical."

"I'm Tamar, and I'm challenged."

"I'm Kim, and I'm anticipating."

"Lenora—cautious."

"I'm Delores, and I'm overwhelmed."

"Maria—trusting."

"I'm Dale. I'm frustrated."

"Debbie—tentative."

"Kathie, and I'm impressed."

"Ray—engaged."

"Ted, and I'm tired."

"Wendy, appreciative."

"Nate, I guess I'm encouraged. Thanks a lot. You can see we're all in different places. But what a challenging group! As we now break up, please make a special effort to give everyone a warm handshake. Take care and see you next month!"

"Thank you, Nate," Ray said. "I believe we've made a good beginning. Thanks for participating with us on a Saturday. We appreciate your families for sharing you today. We also want to thank those in our audience for being with us. We'll hold these public Hearings every month, usually on the third Saturday. Everyone is welcome.

"Commissioners, bring your notebooks back with you next month, Saturday, October 26 at 8:00 a.m. and dress comfortably."

Chapter 3
PUBLIC SCHOOL CHOICE AND
DEMOCRATIC CIVIC CULTURE
Saturday morning, October 26

Ray drove east on Wilson Boulevard heading toward Jefferson Elementary School. It was 7:30 a.m. on Saturday morning and there was little traffic. *I can't wait to see how our consultants handle the topics of school choice and our democratic civic culture,* thought Ray. *I can already see tensions rising in the Commission. Dale is a follower of Rush Limbaugh. Paul is conservative too; he's educated, and a savvy businessman. Our minority parents are getting more sensitive to our discussions. Maria is a tough Hispanic woman who knows what she stands for. She'll blow this Commission sky high if we try to 'snow' her. Lenora is fearless, without much tact. But she's a natural leader. Among the minority teachers, Delores Williams is hard to read. She doesn't say much. She's watching Nate to see how things play out. I think she trusts him.*

Let's see…Tamar Espinosa is well-liked. She's a bright new teacher, but hasn't challenged anybody…yet. I wonder how these intergroup tensions will play out when we get to the bottom line of our negotiations? Kim Su Young is hard to read. She's a smart, cool customer—I wonder what she thinks of this game? We'd better come up with some real stuff here. Let's see…that leaves Debbie. She's very direct, a no-nonsense Jewish woman. Just waiting to pounce if we screw up. Kathie seems very competent. She's a great teacher. Glad my son is in her class. If all the teachers at Jefferson were that good, we would not be spending our Saturday meeting like this. I don't know where Ted's head is. He's laid back but clearly at home with the race/ethnic thing. He's having trouble with the younger women though— they treat him like a '60s antique. Christina is very interesting. She's a great team builder—not threatening—but very confident and comfortable in this group.

Last month's Hearing was fascinating. I've heard a lot about Deborah Meier and her New York City school. It sounds like Jefferson. I hope she has some answers for us. I've got to start acting more like an in-charge Chairman. Guess that'll be my role when we get down to hard negotiations over writing the report. How is this Commission possibly going to get a consensus report with so many different characters and points of view? But so far, so good. Nate and Wendy are laying a solid foundation.

There's Kim and Wendy just going up to the door. Let's see, it's 7:48. Just time to grab some coffee and a bagel. Got to watch my calories today 'cause I'm gaining a few pounds. I'll work out after I get home tonight.

"Please take your coffee or juice to your places," Ramon Gonzales, the chair, was speaking. "Let's begin our second Hearing of the Jefferson Elementary Citizens' Commission on School Reform. I hope everyone survived the past four weeks. The leaves are starting to turn and another colorful Fall is almost here. I hope you enjoyed your reading as much as I did. I feel like I'm in school again—and I'm looking forward to today's Commission Hearing and discussion.

"Last month we got a taste of what is ahead of us. Today we will begin gathering information from nationally-recognized school reformers that will help us put together our plan for reorganizing Jefferson Elementary School. Then we'll present our plan to the County School Board. You recall that Nate described the four waves of modern school reform last month. We finished the day looking at the achievement of American students with Ken Nelson, executive director of the National Education Goals Panel.

"Wendy, I understand that you will start and introduce our first guest."

"Thanks, Ray," said Wendy. "And thanks for the comfortable chairs. No wonder they call you the 'Chair...man!' Today we will hear from Deborah Meier, who has shown the world that disadvantaged children can be winners. They become winners when they are expected to learn and have competent teachers. By sharing Deborah's experience, this Commission can learn lessons that will help us change Jefferson Elementary and provide promising futures for all its students.

Public School Choice

"Our guest this morning," said Wendy, "has been teaching leadership and civic culture for over 24 years at the Central Park East Elementary and Secondary School in East Harlem in New York City. Deborah Meier was also the founder, and now the vice-president, of the Center for Collaborative Education in New York City, an affiliate of the National Coalition of Essential Schools. You'll be surprised by her story. Deborah, the time is yours."[1]

"Good morning. Your theme for today's Hearing—Public School Choice—is appropriate because choice is the heart of democracy. I firmly believe that the purpose of public schooling is to teach democracy. In fact, a national survey just last month reported that, in addition to teaching the basics, 86% said that preparing students for responsible citizenship is the most important purpose of the nation's schools.[2] Public schools can be grassroots community laboratories that put faces and names on people that we might otherwise see as mere statistics or categories. They can teach us how to conduct ourselves in public—for better or worse. The schools can train us for political conversations across divisions of race, class, religion and ideology. Both teachers and students must search for metaphors that bridge ideological, historical and personal differences. We cannot assume everyone will react the same way to the theory of evolution, the discovery of America, the Gulf War, or the value of certain lifestyle choices. Our differences complicate things, but dealing with the complicated is what training for good citizenship is all about. Ideas—or the ways we organize knowledge—are the medium of exchange in democratic life, just as money is in the marketplace. Democracy is based on our power to influence others by our public statements and actions as to what we want the future to look like. Democratic dialogue depends on people's ability to believe that money alone doesn't do *all* the talking."

Paul Christopher raised his hand. "But do kids have to learn about democracy in public school? Wouldn't a good private school do just as well? I know I'm getting pretty angry about our poor public school performance, especially in our inner cities and changing suburbs."

"One reason people are angry at public schools," Deborah said, "is that we've lost control over decisions affecting our communities. But if we abandon public schooling, we have lost one more vehicle for controlling our future. Privatizing removes schools from democratic control. Why bother to debate what direction we want the future to take if we no longer have a voice in what are arguably the most important institutions for shaping that future—our schools? Public school is one of the grassroots institutions that can be used to demonstrate how a community meets challenges and comes up with joint democratic solutions that benefit all families. We have a legitimate role in setting an agenda, not only for our own children, but for all children. It matters a lot whether the schools our children attend foster democratic or undemocratic values. That's not a private matter. If we abandon our system of common schools through apathy or privatization, we deprive everyone, not just the least advantaged, of the clash of ideas that will make us powerful."

Debbie Cohen had spotted a kindred spirit. She raised her hand. "Could you share how you put your thoughts on democratic schools into practice at Central Park East Elementary School? Was it anything like Jefferson Elementary?"

"The questions for those of us who began the experiment," said Debbie, "was how could the children at the bottom of America's social ladder use their schools to develop rather than stunt their intellectual potential? How could we provide the *least advantaged*, at public expense, with the opportunities that the *most advantaged* can buy privately for their own children? We saw children driven into dumbness by a failure to challenge their curiosity and to build on their natural drive toward competence. We had a few brave, well-situated officials who initiated imaginative public policy which allowed our school experience to happen. We had a small crew of teachers who were ready to take the risks and seize the opportunities. We developed specific reproducible ways of organizing schools and of getting teachers, students, and families to work together. We also had a group of families either desperate enough or eager enough to give it a chance. These policies allowed some form of faculty and student choice and far greater autonomy and self-governance than the system previously had. We also formed new partnerships with other community groups.

Dale Jones and Maria Morales raised their hands at the same time. "How in the world did this happen?" asked Maria. "You mean a school like Jefferson could be completely turned around like Central Park East? How did you do it?"

"In those early years," said Deborah, "we stumbled a lot over issues like personal autonomy and communal decision-making. We discovered that this democratic process was really time consuming. It was hard to argue among ourselves without frightening parents and raising doubts about our professionalism. We were trying to be authentic about what it actually took to manage and operate a real school under real circumstances. We couldn't blame our administrators or the district office. We were responsible for making it work or screwing it up. While we were learning the rules of the game, democratic decision-making was slow and frustrating, very inefficient and exhausting. But through the process, we gradually developed a new school culture of close bonds among students and teachers, mutual respect, and shared interests and goals. We built strong networks of human relationships based on trust.

"Our advisory system was the core. Every teacher or staff member advises 10 to 15 students for at least two years. They meet their students once a day for at least 45 minutes and discuss academic subjects, homework, plans for future education. They even talk about real life problems the students face such as homelessness, racism, violence, home life and relations with family members. Advisors become experts on each student they work with, and they follow them weekly to know how they are doing in and out of school."

"What role did the parents play in your new school" asked Dale.

"We developed close bonds with parents. We now have better attendance at our regular parent-teacher conferences—even though we're an inner-city school. This is because we've formed parent partnerships. These conferences include the student, parent and teacher or advisor, and they last at least a half-hour. Parents know what their children are expected to do in school and in their homework assignments."

"What is your curriculum for this new school?" asked Kathie. "And how are your teachers presenting it? Do they teach differently?"

"Our teachers are the ultimate decision makers over what goes on at Central Park East Elementary School. They are empowered to feel the intellectual excitement that's shared by their students. Our teachers are the experts and they are expected to share what they've learned with their students, who are novices. You don't go to tennis class in the summer and say to the tennis teacher, 'If you respect me, you'll assume I'm just as good a tennis player as you are.'" Deborah smiled as she let that idea sink in.

"We do not believe in tracking. All students are expected to learn at high levels—we call it 'critical habits of the mind.' This means they learn to examine evidence, make connections, and develop perspective. They learn to imagine alternatives and to see significance, rather than simply memorize masses of material. Teachers do not lecture, but are catalysts and coaches.

They help students with projects and discussions, and they relate education to the real world. We invite parents, business people and community leaders to observe what we do and give feedback so we can improve our 'work-in-progress.'"

Lenora raised her hand. "I think it's great that someone knows how to turn these public schools around. But it's also very depressing. Why don't we know about these 'breakthrough schools?' Where should we start?"

"We do know how to organize effective elementary and secondary schools," said Deborah. "But not in the delivery system we have now. Schools must be broken up into small communities, even if you have to organize many small schools within one larger school building. Next, everyone has to participate—teachers, students and parents—and they must have the simple democratic right to choose their public school and to take personal responsibility for it. Small schools allow teachers to take responsibility for creating a new learning culture that is challenging to all students. This must be without hindrance from red tape and district bureaucracies. Only by developing a democratic dialogue—the give and take necessary to demonstrate education—can true learning for students and teachers take place. To be successful, these schools must have independent budgets, staffing, scheduling, curriculum design and assessment.

"Small schools mean that the faculty will become accountable because their colleagues will come to know about their work and its impact on students. Small schools allow teachers and advisors to know the quality of work students are turning out. We have this in sports, drama and music clubs. Small schools are safer for students and teachers because everyone knows everyone else. They can forge bonds of respect and friendship and learn how to peacefully settle disputes. Small schools are laboratories where students can work with and learn to respect strong adults. These small schools must exhibit daily respect for everyone who works there. They should be interesting, exciting places of learning.

"At Central Park East, we have learned these lessons. The needs of each school culture are different. You can undertake your own reform journey. I've tried to give a sort of map for your journey in reforming Jefferson Elementary. Only by experiencing your own struggles can you actually reform the school's culture and watch student achievement soar. No reform guru can do it for you. Only when you pay the price by struggling with

BEST PRACTICES:
CENTRAL PARK EAST ELEMENTARY SCHOOL

Central Park East (CPE) is located in East Harlem. It is surrounded by battered public housing, sidewalk graffiti, iron-grill fences and padlocked storefronts. This New York City neighborhood is home to youth violence, gangs, arrests, teen pregnancies and AIDS. Dropping out of school is as common as graduating. The majority of CPE students are Latino and African-American although about 20-25% of the student body have always been White students who attend by choice. Over half of the students qualified for free lunches. Some 20% meet the state requirements for being labeled 'handicapped,' thus qualifying for special state funds. In 1974 when Deborah Meier was asked to became teacher-director of a new elementary school, test scores placed the district last out the 32 city districts. The school was to be housed in one wing of Public School 171.

"We began small with a few hundred students—kindergarten, first and second grades, and a few third graders," stated Ms. Meier. "We had no academic entrance qualifications and took all who said that this was what they wanted. We put all our resources into our classrooms. We rejected the progressive fad that children could acquire skills at their own pace, and individualism and active learning as ways of placating restless or angry kids. We thought adults had important things to teach children, not just to get out of their way. Our students all learn 'habits of the mind'— logic, perspective, making connections, being concrete, using evidence, building a case. We invited students—as young as four years old—to join parents and teachers for conferences at least twice each year to assess and celebrate the student's progress .

"For us, a democratic community was the nonnegotiable purpose of good schooling. We saw schools as laboratories of democracy for both children and teachers—with significant rights over their own workplace and collaboration between teachers and between teachers and parents. Perhaps the most important democratic principle was that of choice. We created the school as a school of choice—for teachers who taught there and for the students and their parents who attended. We insisted that parents (or grandparents, aunts, older siblings) visit before signing up, and we considered it our job to enlist their collaboration. Parents then applied in writing and explained why they chose CPE. We required at least one parent to promise to work closely with the school. We saw parents as crucial, but viewed their input as advisory. We all worked hard to build authentic forms of collaboration between the school and the family.

"Of the first seven graduating classes of CPE elementary school (1977-1984), 85% received regular diplomas and another 11% got GEDs or a total of 96%. This compares to roughly 50% citywide. Furthermore, two thirds of those who graduated from high school prior to the opening of our own secondary school had gone on to college. And the statistics held along race and class lines. In 1991, the Central Park East Secondary School topped this impressive showing. While some students moved and a few transferred, fewer than 5% of those who started with us in ninth grade dropped out along the way. And not only did the rest graduate with regular diplomas, but 90% went directly on to college and stayed there. These figures for 1991 have held up for each subsequent graduating class. And the graduates of 1994 outstripped their predecessors in quality of work achieved and colleges attended. We've gotten better and so have they.

"For most staff and many parents, well-wishers, and friends, the success of Central Park East is a dream come true. Our parents and alumni are, of course, our first line of defense. Later we adopted a lottery system that favors neighborhood students and siblings to limit the number of students that we were able to accommodate. We've found that our school-based democracy model works over and over again with different directors, with different staffs, and without extra funds. We look on our experience as a story not a perfect model to be copied because each school—teachers and parents—must start from scratch to build their own learning culture. It cannot be imported from some reform guru because if the people who must implement the changes—classroom teachers and parents—don't gain ownership by debating and gaining a testimony that changes must be made, then the reform will fail. "

reforms, will you begin to know what real public schools can do to build successful democratic communities. These communities will educate all children to become successful citizen leaders. It's an exciting journey. Good luck."

Wendy took over the discussion. "We want to thank you, Deborah, for your inspiring story. You've given us lots to think about. Good luck on replicating your experiences with Central Park East in your new assignment in Boston next Fall. Read her BEST PRACTICES example. We'll take a short break. Deborah will be available to answer questions."

****

Education and Democratic Civic Culture

After the break, Nate called the group to order, "Welcome back. Deborah Meier has shown us how principles of democracy can be applied to creating an effective public school. Many Americans like Deborah believe that the **main purpose of public education is to develop thoughtful and participating citizens.** According to this view, *teaching academic skills and preparing students for later employment are secondary to educating for democracy. By teaching democracy first, all participating children, regardless of background or disadvantaged circumstances, can learn the values, knowledge and skills to become leaders as life-long students, accountable citizens, responsible parents, informed consumers and productive workers."*

"Wait a minute, Nate," said Dale. "You're not going to give us this mumbo-jumbo liberal crap that public education for democracy is more important than preparing our kids to make a living? I don't want teachers spending time teaching democracy. This is a free country. Besides I listen to Rush Limbaugh every day, so I keep up with current events. I know what's going on with the Clintons and the other liberals."

"You're a piece of work, man," said Nate. "Does it ever occur to you that you're here today and able to complain because you live in a democracy? Democracy is working well enough that you are a member of this Commission and have an opportunity to help other children in this school get the kind of education you missed. If we can accomplish that much with our Commission, then 350 children, and thousands more who come through Jefferson in the future, will learn how to practice democracy, to become skilled leaders and to become productive workers.

"Dale forces us to revisit our democratic roots and ask why democracy is so important on this Citizens' Commission? It's a little like asking fish how they like the water. Fish take water for granted. It's a birthright. Ask new naturalized citizens how they feel about freedom and democracy, even with all our nation's problems. We can never improve our political system until we understand it first, then practice its principles. Only then can we teach democracy to our children who have never learned about it."

"Where did the idea of democracy come from? Why is it so important to teach our children today?" asked Dale.

"Well, it originated with the Greeks and Romans, who called for training virtuous citizens to create democratic states. It was the Englishman, John Locke, who translated modern democratic concepts for our American founding fathers. You probably already know, but let me just briefly review this history. Locke wrote about liberty and equality—the rights to life, liberty, and property; government by consensus; limited government; rule of law; importance of society over government; and the right of revolution.[3] The right of revolution means that people can revolt against a tyrannical government and proclaim the rights of free men to organize their own government. Using this concept, three founding fathers mobilized public opinion and justified the American Revolution: an immigrant from England named Thomas Paine published his *Common Sense* in January 1776; John Adams published his *Thoughts on Government* in April 1776; and Thomas Jefferson drafted the *Declaration of Independence* in July 1776, which contained the famous phrase 'life, liberty and the pursuit of happiness.'[4]

Lenora Brown spoke up. "During that time, my ancestors were in chains and not considered human enough even to vote. Why should my children learn this white man's history?"

"Good question, Lenora," said Nate. "African Americans became full citizens later in American history, just as women did. But let me return to the story of how it all started. It was the collection of political essays, entitled *The Federalist*, written by three more of our founders, James Madison, Alexander Hamilton and John Jay, that put forward the reasons for adopting a new representative form of democracy embodied in a federal constitution. *The Federalist* advocated good, free, republican, and constitutional government and the doctrine of judicial review. The United States then became the first modern democracy founded on universal principles of human equality, individual rights and popular consent.[5] While gradually accepted in principle, it took a tragic civil war with the Union united behind President Abraham Lincoln to make African-Americans free citizens. It took a constitutional amendment giving women voting rights, and a confrontational Civil Rights movement spearheaded by Martin Luther King, Jr.

to advance legal equality for all American citizens. Over the years, the American experiment with representative democracy has gradually spread around the world. A recent 20-year study of the rise of democracy at the community level in Italy concludes that four features are required for representative institutions to flourish: civic engagement; political equality; a sense of solidarity, trust, and tolerance; and dense networks of community social cooperation."[6]

"I have to object here, Nate," said Christina from Interfaith. "Just how do you square this idealistic view of democracy with what's happening in America today? We have growing homelessness, rising crime, rampant discrimination, declining standard of living, and not too long ago, the Savings and Loan rip-off. And let's not forget our Congress who've been bought with PAC money. I even hear that some Russian and Chinese leaders are saying they don't want our decadent popular culture exported to their countries."

"Yes, Christina, a lot of people think that American democracy has been betrayed. Our civic society has been eroded by the unregulated free market and the exploding bureaucratic welfare costs. In the United States today, a market-dominated society, which focuses mainly on property rights, profit margins and rule of law shows its best and worst features. Our government, originally organized to defend the public interest, has become captive of special-interest lobbies that gradually corrupt our democracy."

Dale nearly exploded. "Nate, you sound like a communist! We want unregulated free enterprise. That's the American way."

"Dale," said Paul quietly, "you're off base. Are you saying you want to eat polluted meat, fly on unsafe airplanes and live with your family next to a toxic waste dump? Federal regulations now prevent these abuses of the free market system. Some federal regulation is good."

Nate smiled and continued, "Many institutions have been shriveling up— our families, public schools, communities, friendship networks, voluntary associations and social movements. These are where people interact and negotiate with others and gradually develop into citizen leaders. Through this process, we develop the moral sensitivities to participate in representative democracy. It is the challenge we all face as citizens. Lincoln said that democracy is 'a government of the people, by the people, and for the people.'"

"As I look around the room, Nate, I realize that we represent different races, religions, professions, education," said Dale. "Is this what you mean by experiencing democracy in action?"

"That's right. Eventually marketplace greed and uncontrolled government entitlements will produce a backlash that can destroy both.[7] The major point is that only a civil society of informed and participating citizens— healthy enough to nourish individual worth and moral development—can counter-balance these two powerful forces. We know that people acquire the skills to participate in democracy through formal and informal education. If our public schools are not teaching the knowledge and skills of democratic leadership, then we'll get just what we deserve—a nation of barbarians. There'll be social warfare between racial and ethnic groups and destruction of our constitutional system! Some people think we are well on our way."

"Nate," Tamar Espinoza spoke up, "how did we get from the importance of teaching democracy to the need for public schools for all children?"

"Thomas Jefferson first proposed a system of public education 220 years ago. Public education was to seek out persons of 'worth and genius' from every condition of life and prepare them to defend representative democracy.[8] But I didn't realize that public education first started in 1647. The Massachusetts Bay Colony required towns and villages of 50 or more citizens to hire a school master who would teach all children reading and writing. Before the American republic was founded, householders in early towns taxed themselves for schools where all the young would be taught 'the laws of the land, and the principles of religion.' These comparatively prosperous settlers did not need schools for their own children who were sent to private academies or educated abroad. By establishing schools for all children, they served their self-interest. They feared that the ignorance of growing numbers of immigrants and poor children would endanger the ideals of self-government they'd brought from Europe, thus undermining their prosperity.[9]

"This sounds a lot like our situation today," said Paul. "The only difference is I haven't read about a taxpayer revolt over wanting to pay more taxes to strengthen public schools. Quite the opposite!

"Right on," said Nate. "Thomas Jefferson thought that the first priority for the civic culture is a system of universal public education. He believed that it should prepare everyone for citizenship and responsible leadership by developing their talents and abilities and by developing their capacity for full and intelligent participation in the democratic process. He emphasized that public education should be for all children, not just those from elite, wealthy families and groups, as was done in Europe. Jefferson argued that public education is essential to preserving democracy. It teaches individuals to understand and act out their inalienable rights and responsibilities as citizens. Maybe this sounds like a quaint idea today since most of us haven't had to sacrifice to enjoy our freedoms. Many of us haven't served in the armed forces defending our country against hostile enemies.[10]

"Educators and policymakers face two challenges: (1) educating to develop personal virtues of trustworthiness, autonomy, initiative, industry, identity, intimacy, and integrity; and (2) educating to preserve liberty and social justice—the very cultural values that make education for personal virtue possible in a moral society."

"What do you mean by moral society?" Lenora asked.

"Well, I'd say it's one that puts people first, and educates them for personal leadership and responsibility." Nate paused, "There can be no liberty, no equality, no social justice, and no stable free market system without democracy. Without public schools to bring us all together, representative democracy and free enterprise won't survive. Without public schools to bring us all together, we cannot build social capital.[11] In fact, it was Abraham Lincoln who described education as, 'the most important subject which we as a people can be engaged in.'"[12]*

Lenora was still agitated. "I'm Black and a single parent with three children. I can't wait for Mr. Jefferson's vision to come to pass. My kids, and their friends at Jefferson, need a good education now or they'll simply repeat my life and be thrown out on the dung heap!"

"You're exactly right, Lenora!" said Nate. "The challenge to our democracy is to prepare all citizens, even those who are disadvantaged, so they can fully participate in the economic, social and political life of the nation.[13]

---

*Horace Mann, one of the most influential American educators, frequently discussed this theme. In 1845, for example, he wrote: "As each citizen is to participate in the power of governing others, it is an essential preliminary that he should be imbued with a feeling for the wants, and a sense of the rights, of those whom he is chosen to govern…It becomes, then a momentous question, whether the children in our schools are educated in reference to themselves and their private interests only, or with a regard to the great social duties and prerogatives that await them . . .."

This is done best in our community institutions, like public schools. But, today, we are still sentencing disadvantaged students to underclass status. They will not have a chance to participate in middle-class American lifestyles. This is because we are failing to deal with two major sources of inequality—unequal funding and segregation.

"As you probably already know, the amount of funding for public schools is based on local property taxes. This means that schools in poor minority neighborhoods receive unequal funding. Per-pupil expenditures range from $2000 for a student in poor neighborhoods to more than $20,000 for a student in wealthy suburbs. This unjust tax system is being legally challenged and is slowly making its way through the courts. In the state of Kentucky, school financing was declared unconstitutional by the court five years ago. That state has now totally reformed their school system. The other source of inequality is segregation even though the Supreme Court overturned segregated schools in 1954. African-American and Hispanic-American students are still heavily concentrated in inner-city public schools where they've become the majority in the student body."

"Well just a minute, Nate," said Lenora. "Are you saying my children here at Jefferson Elementary don't get as much support as children in the north?"

"We're checking that out, Lenora. We will report back at a later Commission Hearing. But Jonathan Kozol has shown the effects of inadequate school funding, and it's depressing. He points out the lack of playgrounds, laboratory equipment, textbooks and computers in urban schools. He compares this condition with wealthier suburban schools, where resources are overflowing. They have comprehensive sports, arts and music programs, outstanding teachers and enriched academic opportunities. Some people say that money doesn't matter, but **school expenditures are directly associated with student achievement. Money buys highly-qualified teachers and smaller classes.** This was found to be true in a study of mathematics and reading achievements in New York City Schools. About 90% of achievement differences between minority and White students could be attributed to teacher experience and qualifications. Low-income, minority, and inner-city students have less-qualified teachers. They also have less access to science and math knowledge at school, fewer material resources, and less-engaging learning activities in their classrooms. [14]

"An unusual natural experiment happened in a public housing project in a Chicago suburb. A group of African-American students attended largely White and better-funded suburban schools. Compared to their peers with the same background (equivalent income and initial academic attainment) who went to inner-city schools, these students did far better. They were more likely to have the opportunity to take challenging courses, receive additional academic help, graduate on time, attend college and secure good jobs. **I think it's time to quit using race or class as an excuse for not educating both our minority and our disadvantaged White students?**"[15]

Dale sounded frustrated and confused. "But, Nate, I graduated from a pretty good suburban high school here. Famous people graduated from it. In the 1960s, it was one of the top high schools in the country. Even today they are well funded. It's not an inner-city school like those we played football against. What went wrong? As a high school graduate, I can't get a decent job."

"Well, it sounds like you were a victim of our ineffective factory-model school. That is the second major factor that twists our public schools away from Jefferson's vision—places where democracy would be taught to the children of all citizens. He saw public schools as the great equalizer. Let me give you a little background on this. During the early 19th century, America underwent rapid industrialization. Business used Fredrick Taylor's scientific management philosophy for greater productivity: one best way, one best system. Its impact on public education was to reproduce a factory-model school that served a business agenda. One early educator described the public education system as follows:

> Our schools are, in a sense, factories in which the raw materials [students] are to be shaped and fashioned into products to meet the various demands of life. The specifications for manufacturing come from the demands of 20th century civilization, and it is the business of the school to build its pupils to the specifications laid down. This demands good tools, specialized machinery, continuous measurements of production to see if it [meets] specifications....[16]

"I still don't see how this applies to me, Nate," said Dale.

"In the development of our modern public school, we lost the belief that the proper goal of education for all citizens in a democratic society is intellectual and character development. Instead, we developed a tracking system. Middle-class students were expected to be college material, so they were given college preparatory courses. Most minority or low-income students, like you Dale, were expected to go to work in factories as blue-collar employees or lower white-collar clerks. Their curriculum reflected less demanding and lower expectations. Teachers lectured and used low-level textbooks, and multiple-choice tests requiring only low-level cognitive skills. This approach created docile students who stayed out of trouble and received a good citizenship grade on their report cards. Letter grades had little meaning because they were based on the bell-shaped curve adopted from early intelligence testing. These students were tracked out of quality educational opportunities. Their chances for successful lives decreased when well-paying industrial jobs were gradually eliminated in the 1970s and '80s."

"Well, Nate, that's exactly what happened to me," said Dale. "Now I'm beginning to get the picture! I played football with friends who were treated differently in school. Now I see they were probably on the college prep track."

"The students whose parents and teachers planned for their college were provided with smaller classes, better teachers, honors and advanced college courses. They were expected to develop communication skills, like public speaking, discussion, and writing. The also learned problem solving, inquiry and analysis. Unless students have experience in practicing these skills in everyday life, they will be missing valuable preparation for real life after school. Otherwise, they can't become a life-long student, a responsible parent, an informed consumer, a productive worker and an accountable citizen in a working democracy."

"Nate," Maria asked, "it sounds like I got the same poor education as Dale and Lenora. Now I'm beginning to understand what you mean by the betrayal of democracy. It's going to happen again—to my children—if we don't make big changes now!"

"The challenge," Nate said, "is to develop a *responsible school learning culture* that fosters the knowledge and leadership skills we need to participate in a new constructive, multicultural democracy. A new curriculum would teach students how to make choices for their lives based on principles that benefit everyone in the larger community. According to this philosophy, students, along with their parents and teachers, would learn how to make politics like musicians make music. Just as it takes practice to play the piano, it takes knowledge and practice to learn the skills of democratic politics. For example, our founders constructed a Constitution for the nation in Philadelphia during the summer of 1787. Our civil rights leaders constructed a protest movement in the late 1950s and 1960s."

"The high school college prep classes I took in Southern California," said Debbie, "got me into UCLA. I majored in liberal arts with a history minor. This prepared me for going into law. Are you saying, Nate, that most disadvantaged and minority students are quietly tracked out of the opportunity to go on to college? That they're steered into dead-end jobs as early as middle school? That means our factory-model school is turning out rejects for today's world! That seems criminal."

Nate nodded his head. "Yes, the whole system is set up this way. It's not the fault of an individual teacher or school administrator. After World War II, the baby boom expanded schools rapidly. I was told that the Los Angeles City School District opened a new school each Monday morning for many years. Remember that most educators believed that getting through high school and holding a job was about all minority students and most White students could expect. Most students moved through schools like automobiles going through an assembly line, sitting passively through one class at a time.

"Today we need to develop a new sense of citizenship through civic education. That process shapes a political community into a larger public interest. Informed citizens must negotiate in every meaningful activity they undertake—at home, at school, at work and in religious and community associations. Students need to learn leadership skills for democratic participation. The practical reasoning necessary to do the right thing in the real world can be taught.[17] Can students of all ages learn to do this? Classrooms are the perfect laboratory to learn these leadership skills of inquiry, negotiation and social action. The word educate comes from the Latin *educare,* meaning to lead."

"Maybe I can contribute something here," said Kathie. "I used an unusual teaching method at the school where I taught in California before coming to Jefferson. My class decided to study the subject of homelessness. The class got fired up as they did the research. They went out into the community to interview public officials. Was that ever a learning experi-

BEST PRACTICES: EASTSHORE ELEMENTARY

Dear Dad,

You asked me to relate to you the details of the homeless project that I did with my fifth-grade class a few years ago. It all started with a book that I found called *The Kid's Guide to SOCIAL ACTION*,[19] which outlined a process that kids could use to create change in their communities. We began by brainstorming all the problems that they face in their communities. Interestingly enough, they were troubled by the homeless people they saw in other communities, in fact at first they were angry at them, seeing them as a nuisance. I thought this was an interesting attitude coming from students who, for the most part, were very well off. We decided to investigate the problem further by taking these steps:

1. The students gathered information from all the local agencies. They researched articles and learned as much as they could about the problem. They invited speakers into the classroom from these agencies, who were impressed with the depth of the kids' knowledge. The feelings of the kids began to change, and they wondered how much the community really knew about the problem.

2. The students designed a survey with facts about homelessness in Orange county and took the survey to the nearby shopping center. The hour and one half with the public taught them a lot about the ignorance of our community and made the students want to make a difference in this area. We established an organization called HOPIN, which stands for Helping Other People in Need. We organized into committees and elected officers. One of the students designed stationery with our emblem and we used it on all of our correspondence.

3. The students decided to focus on children. Their goals was to provide a birthday party for all of the children that were served by the Irvine Temporary Housing, a nonprofit organization that helped families in need. They worked with the volunteers to identify 10 children who belonged to families that had no home. The kids wanted to put together what they termed a "birthday in a box." The boxes include party goods, cake mixes, candles, presents,....everything they needed to provide a birthday party for

a child. The idea was that the shelter would take the box to the child around the time of their birthday, and the family could set up a great celebration. What they did lack was the money to put this all together.

4. The students decided to begin a letter writing campaign. They identified 100 companies in Irvine, and began to hand-write letters to each of these companies telling them of their project, and asking for any help they would like to give. In addition, we contacted the public TV station and asked for some air time to broadcast a performance that we put together. They graciously aired our class play about the homeless, and what having a home means to the kids in our class. They sang songs, recited poems and read essays, concluding with a dramatic presentation enacting the book, *Home Place.*

It was about this time that one of the students saw an article in the local paper, telling about how the city council was considering shutting down "Irvine Temporary Housing," due to budget constraints. This hit us really hard. We had worked so much with them and knew all the good that they were doing in the community. The students had toured their food bank and office facilities, and knew what a loss it would be to the community. We decided to go to the city council meeting and speak. Six students were chosen to represent the class. Their speeches were moving and passionate. They had a lot of knowledge and shared the results of the survey they conducted in Irvine, telling the City Council about the ignorance of the community on this issue. They shared the details about their project. By the end of the night, "Irvine Temporary Housing" was reinstated and the city council member promised to attend our performance latter in the month. A wonderful lesson in direct democracy for the students!

5. By now, the project was turning into this huge machine that was running on its own, and I was just trying to keep up. Letters and checks kept streaming in. Companies were extremely impressed with the students' letters. We had money and goods beyond our wildest dreams. The performance night was at hand. While running though our last dress rehearsal, we got a call from the Governor's office. At first the secretary hung up, chalking it up to

a prank call, then she came running into the classroom to get me on the phone. I remember asking the kids on my way to the office, "Does anyone know why the governor would want to talk to me?" Joey Rubin sheepishly raised his hand and told me that he wrote the governor and told him about our project and had invited him to our program that night. The call told us to expect a special letter tonight at 7:00 from the governor.

6. The evening of our performance, right at 7:00, a special courier came and delivered a letter of commendation to our Organization. It was a really exciting moment, and the students gave the performance of their lives! The television cameras were there and they broadcast it throughout Irvine. By the end of the night, we had raised over $3,000.

7. The students again broke into committees and took to the streets as they budgeted and shopped for each of the children, providing a huge "birthday in a box" for each one. The extra money was used to pay rent on three different apartments for three families in need for one month. The money, which continued to come in, because the cable company continued to rebroadcast the performance, was donated to Irvine Temporary Housing.

8. I can't begin to tell you all that the students and I learned that year. I get teary-eyed just recounting it to you now. I learned a lot about the power of people, when they unite for good, even little people. These 10- and 11-year old students made a difference in their community and, most importantly, they learned that they could make a difference.

ence for all of us! It was a practical lesson in education for democracy! I brought along a short description of this project. Actually it's a letter I wrote to my father that I can hand out as an example."[18]

Nate spoke up. "Thank you, Kathie," said Nate. "That's a powerful example of what we're talking about. It's grassroots democracy. We also see students can develop intellectual skills with moral values. "

Summary

Nate looked very scholarly as he prepared to summarize the morning's presentations. "I'd like to begin by taking you back to Deborah Meier's discussion on education and civic culture. This may help us when we begin designing our final report in June. Deborah Meier made several powerful observations. Public schools can become the grassroots community laboratories for teaching America's children the principles of democracy. Public schools are the essential socializing force for children to learn about civic culture and become responsible citizens. Central Park East was an experiment in grassroots democracy that showed how dedicated teachers and parents could create a school culture with high levels of learning for all disadvantaged children. Disadvantaged children who are challenged to develop 'habits of the mind' can compete with any students and go on to receive educations that prepare them to work in good jobs for a civilized life. An essential factor in our success is that everyone—students, parents and teachers—has the right to choose a school for their public education. Each school, faculty and parent group must struggle together to create an effective school where children learn. There are no short cuts. The experiment takes time and focused energy.

"Because of its importance, our understanding of representative grassroots democracy will condition everything we do from now on in this Citizens' Commission! We made several points about schools and democracy. The main purpose of education in a democratic culture is to develop all children into thoughtful, participating citizens. The unique American heritage of representative democracy was a legacy from an Englishman, John Locke, who influenced our founders' ideas about natural liberty and equality of human beings: rights to life, liberty, property and the pursuit of happiness; limited government; rule of law; supremacy of society over government; and the right of revolution. By the Declaration of Independence, the amended Constitution and a painful Civil Rights Revolution spearheaded by Dr. Martin Luther King, Jr., all American citizens—men , women and minorities—have all the legal rights necessary for responsible citizenship.

"Effective teachers can use their classrooms and community projects to teach students the lessons of democracy and responsible citizenship. Unregulated free market forces and uncontrolled government entitlements to special interests groups have undermined democracy in America by gradually creating a growing disadvantaged underclass. Public education, first advocated by the founders, has been the path out of poverty and into economic prosperity, grassroots democracy and social freedom for most Americans. Discriminatory tax expenditures by states and urban centers have created 'savage inequalities' for inner-city and high-poverty schools—thus shattering the American Dream for one-out-of-two American children. And, finally, public school vouchers to pay private school tuition are not a serious or realistic solution to the public's neglect of quality education for America's 25 million disadvantaged children.

"With these heavy thoughts, it's time for lunch. Please remember to check your notebooks for your assigned lunch partners. We are hoping you can get better acquainted with other members of the Commission and discuss together what you have heard today. See you all back by 1:00 p.m." Nate was excited by the group's participation.

Chapter 4
PUBLIC CHARTER AND
INDEPENDENT PUBLIC SCHOOLS
Saturday afternoon, October 26

After lunch, the room buzzed with excitement as Commission members discussed the morning's topic among themselves. "If you'll turn to your notebooks," said Nate, "you'll see a special handout on private school vouchers. The voucher movement has been a major conservative strategy during the past 15 years. Conservatives want to use public funds for vouchers at private schools. Let's examine the arguments for vouchers in this educational Myth."

Charter Schools[1]

"This afternoon," said Nate, "we'll discuss the charter school movement, a public school choice alternative. We are pleased to have as our guest, Mr. Ted Kolderie, a highly-regarded public policy analyst at the Center for Policy Studies in Minneapolis. Mr. Kolderie has written a landmark paper on the charter school movement.[2] Could you tell us, Ted, what you mean by a charter school?"

"Nate, and members of the Citizens' Commission, I am pleased to describe this revolutionary public school movement. The charter schools are seeking to overcome bureaucratic resistance to systemic school reform. At present our K-12 system has about 15,000 school districts, with 85,000 public schools and 2.5 million teachers. The givens of the K-12 system—mandatory attendance, per-pupil financing, districting and exclusive franchise—guarantee customers, revenue, jobs and security to one organization within a geographic area. The state has given its assurance that the district will

MYTH: Giving public vouchers to parents for private school tuition will benefit transferring students; the resulting market competition will force public schools to improve.

Many conservatives are troubled about the "near-monopoly" public school system. They believe it is run by bureaucrats and union officials. Many also believe that the solution to improving education for both low-income and middle-income children is to provide "publicly-paid-for vouchers" that parents could use for tuition at private schools of their choice. In its report on educational reform, the Heritage Foundation concludes: "Transforming parents into education consumers will force the school to shape up or lose customers. It forces teachers and school administrators to improve instruction and toughen standards if they are to retain students—and with them funding.[3]

FINDING A: During the 1980s, many conservatives argued for school choice—public or private—to introduce market forces as a way of reforming public schools. Public educators initially rejected all forms of choice as a threat to financing public education. By the 1990s, the national debate on school choice shifted dramatically. The debate about public school choice is over. President Clinton, Secretary Riley and Al Shanker, president of The American Federation of Teachers (AFT), and most educators and public officials have called for public school choice, space permitting, as a way of strengthening public schools and involving parents in their children's education. Results have been mixed where public school choice has been tried.

Several states have experimented with *public school choice* in a variety of forms. The first is *district-wide* choice, which permits parents and students to select a public school *within* their home district, space permitting. Today, 17 states have passed laws creating some form of inter-district choice and most school districts allow within-district transfers for desegregating schools through busing, magnet schools, children with disabilities and hardships where parents request transfers for personal or academic reasons.

The second alternative is *statewide* choice. Minnesota has the oldest statewide choice model. In states where choice has been introduced, participation rates vary. By 1995-96, Minnesota had the highest rate (19%) among public school "choice" states.[4] Distance alone rules out school choice for millions of children unless transportation is provided. State-wide choice programs require significant administrative and financial support to be successful. They also tend to widen the gap between rich and poor districts.[5] Surveys conclude that the majority of public school parents appear satisfied with the education of their children and are not inclined to move them.

The third alternative is *private-school choice* involving vouchers that permits parents to send their children to private schools using public funds. In addition to Milwaukee, Wisconsin's small voucher plan, Ohio has recently approved a state voucher plan that provides $2,500 for up to 2,000 low-income students in Cleveland—*provided those low-income students don't transfer to suburban school districts.* (Of 1,864 students in the Cleveland program, 27% were already in private schools!)[6]

FINDING B: Most citizens favor choice for public schools but reject the market approach using public money for private school tuition. Evidence about the effectiveness of private-school choice, limited as it is, suggests that such a policy does not improve student achievement or stimulate school renewal. In Milwaukee, Wisconsin, in the first two years, an astonishing 40% of students who made the switch to private schools did not return the next year. Further, the standardized test scores of participating students have shown little or no improvement in reading and math and remain well below average in both.[7] Private schools in Milwaukee have no requirements to enroll students with disabilities or to be accountable for reporting academic achievement that public schools in that city must report.* The experiment has been limited to 7,000 students out of a student population of 98,000.[8]

Since 1988 England has experimented with school choice nationwide, supported by full public funding. Some conclusions are now emerging from recent research. First, there is no evidence that competition among schools leads to overall higher educational standards in either the schools receiving the students or the schools losing the students. In fact, schools

---

* A recent audit of private schools in the Milwaukee school-choice program by the Wisconsin Education Department has found that nearly a third of the schools exceeded enrollment limits set by state law. Both critics and advocates agree that more state oversight is needed. Two of the 17 participating schools have closed because of financial troubles related to state payment of $390,000 for students they did not enroll. Attempts to include religious schools were declared unconstitutional by the Wisconsin Supreme Court.

losing students also lost significant funding. With fewer funds, failing schools had to curtail their educational programs for the poor and minority students who remained trapped within them.

Second, although school choice is often heralded as a special help for working-class parents, the English experience shows that wealthier middle-class and professional parents are the chief beneficiaries. They have the resources to be more aggressive in getting their children into better schools. This strategy clearly advances the "aristocracy of wealth,"contrary to the value of equal opportunity advanced in serious democracies. Third, better schools, especially in inner cities, can recruit the most desirable students to fill their limited space.

Market reforms have led to an erosion of the education of children of the working-class—thus as an unequal two-tier school systems develops, class divisions increase. The choice system seems to work best for school officials not for parents, students, and employers. The school market is not like a true market in that space is rationed in good schools and demand rarely matches supply. The result often leads to confusion, frustration and disappointment among parents and students.[9] Al Shanker states: "Choice views education as a consumer good—as something that I, as a parent, buy for my children from some vendor…That goes against the tradition and values that have made our democracy the envy of the world. Education is a public good that communities have provided for all children because they are our future citizens.[10]

CONCLUSION. During the past decade, conservatives have mounted campaigns to persuade taxpayers to support a variety of voucher plans to pay partial costs for parents to enroll their children in private or religious schools. While of great symbolic value to frustrated conservative advocates, these plans have thus far proved to be of insignificant practical help for students in malfunctioning public schools. The two examples of voucher experiments are in Milwaukee, Wisconsin where 7,000 students and Cleveland, Ohio where 2,000 students attend private schools at partial public expense (out of the nation's 53,000 million students). The results of these experiments show that (1) educational quality in terms of higher student achievement has not improved for participating students; (2) poor financial accountability by participating schools is not an acceptable use of public funds; (3) attempts to extend public vouchers to religious schools has been ruled unconstitutional—a violation of Church and State—by the Wisconsin Supreme Court;[11] and (4) private schools have not opened enough schools to keep up with present demand—in Milwaukee, hundreds of voucher students remain on waiting lists.

Experience from England confirms the limited American experience in Milwaukee and Cleveland schools: the market model is *not* a good test of market forces because of the limitations of space (supply) for better schools, the inability to satisfy even those parents who could afford to make that choice (demand), and the public interest involved in providing all children with equal educational opportunities. Public officials who advocate draining public funds from public schools to subsidize both private and religious schools on the one hand, and middle-class and wealthy parents who now pay for their children's private schooling on the other hand, have an apparent conflict of interest. Proposals by advocates are veiled attempts to manipulate disadvantaged parents as pawns in this cynical game. These proposals tempt them with partial tuition vouchers worth about the same as tuition charged by parochial schools.

The challenge of reforming public schools is frustrating and discouraging for the one-out-two (25 million students) who need quality education now. Education is a political right, not a property right. The 14th Amendment guarantees that all Americans, including children, will be equally protected. Using scarce public education funds to advance private schooling is a diversionary tactic for an infinitesimal number of students while millions suffer, hardly qualifying as moral or political leadership.**

continue receiving money—basically everything it needs to succeed— **whether or not the students are performing up to a standard.**[12]

** The Republican candidate for President, on July 17-18, 1996, unveiled his education program to Catholic school audiences in Minneapolis and Milwaukee. He advocated giving cash scholarships of $1,000 for elementary school parents and $1500 for high schools parents to 5 million students, with half the money coming from the federal government and half from state governments. The net effect would be to transfer $62.5 billion annually from public education funding to private schools. Public schools, meanwhile, would loose $30 billion for the missing students (5 million students times an average of $6,000 ADA). An estimated 20 million educationally-disadvantaged students would still be left in troubled public schools even further impoverished from the drain on public funds.

"Before I launch into the very exciting charter school movement. Let me comment on the Commission theme for today—Public School Choice. Charter schools offer a real alternative to the present district-run school system if teachers and parents are willing to support it. The Gallup-Phi Delta Kappan Survey of 1993 makes very clear that the American public wants public school choice by a margin of 2 to 1. This opinion is even more widely held among Hispanics and African Americans, younger people, public school parents and women of all ages. It is also widely held by those in all occupational categories, lower-income levels, and urban and rural communities. [13]

"The governance arrangement of the present system has several serious limitations and consequences for improving individual school performance. **That is why we have made so little progress in school reform over the past decade.** Our school district system is unresponsive to state officials, local voters and parents. It creates an inequitable system because it is based on housing patterns that are stratified by income, social class and race. It's a system in which the reward structure pays off whether or not student learning improves. These are powerful disincentives. So it's not surprising that when districts are asked to achieve excellence, they respond with only a mere show of compliance. They may understand the message, **but they don't really know how to change.** When you think about it, our public education system runs directly counter to what businesses have learned. Incentives and competition create change. Bureaucratic structures with top-down, hierarchical management are being replaced by flatter organizations that are characterized by clear missions and high-performance goals. Businesses are learning that when front-line workers participate in decision making and accountability and are rewarded for results, they do better work.

"Public education has it all backwards. It is not smart to expect high performance from an institution or an individual in which the rewards are provided when they haven't achieved the mission. Why should an organization take risks, upset comfortable routines, or challenge powerful interests when they get rewarded anyway. This explains why good teachers and administrators can describe change, as well as the effort to put students first, as a risk. It explains why standards are not set for student and teacher performance, why performance is not measured, and why rewards are unrelated to performance. Senior teachers get to teach what they want to teach rather than what is most needed. Money spent for training is driven more by teachers' personal interests than by the school's needs. The system does not incorporate new technologies. And it explains why leadership does not intervene decisively when students are not learning. Why create controversy when rewards are provided anyway?

"Ted," said Paul, "I hear you saying that school districts have become maintenance organizations enforcing federal, state, and district regulations with no incentives for improving student performance."

"Yes, Paul, Albert Shanker said it best in 1991, 'Something has to be at stake. In other fields, your organization could fail. People [professionals] in these fields dislike change too. But they *have* to do it. We in education don't. Because for us nothing is at stake...We have got to deal with this question of consequences for adults. We do need something to happen that is truly revolutionary.' Governor Romer of Colorado described the essentials of this new strategy: 'We want to stay within the principles of public education. But we do have to have the ability to really change it.'"

"Mr. Kolderie," said Ted Alexander. "You sound like a conservative who doesn't really support public education. Am I right?"

"No, Mr. Alexander, quite the contrary. I believe in it, but the system and the educators are being paid with my tax dollars, so I think they should be held accountable. They should provide an educational experience that results in improved learning for all America's children, not just kids from upper middle-class families. I quarrel with the incentives that the system provides. Conventional school reform is not working fast enough to create serious change in our 15,000 school districts that benefits our students."

"You're a pretty tough critic of school reform, aren't you, Mr. Kolderie," Debbie said cautiously. "What do you think we should be doing? Will the charter school movement change the present system and still save public schooling?"

"We haven't approached school reform from the right perspective," Ted Kolderie said. "In spite of the heroic efforts of school reformers, committed educators and concerned parents, we've been trying to force improvement from the outside, and it can only come from the inside. Improvement has to be something the organization does on its own initiative, in its own interest, and using its own resources.

"The real question is: 'Why isn't the district doing these things now?' Superintendents and others are always talking about staff development, or parent involvement, or some new technology. There's something wrong with an institution that doesn't *do* what it thinks is the most important. There's something wrong with an institution when the things most critical to success—in this case, student achievement—are defined as extra work or are done only when someone outside provides extra resources.

"The state should make laws that required improvements in student achievement an imperative for local districts. This means creating new ways for parent and teacher groups to start and run local public schools without the supervision or veto of school boards and their superintendents.

"I've found eight essential parts to chartering. I've listed them in this handout:

1. The state says it's okay for more than one organization to offer public education in the community, and there are no limits (or at least very high ones) on the number of such schools that can be formed;

2. A charter school is a public school—not an elite academy that selects only special kids. It does not discriminate, and it observes basic rules of health and safety. It also follows civil rights laws and policies agreed upon by its public sponsor;

3. The school is an independent, legal entity and is not managed by the school districts; this makes site-management real not an illusion;

4. The charter removes the state education code and state and local regulations. This exchanges the district regulatory model for a performance model. The school is responsible for deciding how to meet performance targets. If the school does not meet the agreed-upon goals, their charter will not be renewed;

5. A charter can be combined with public school choice;

6. The state pays the school the same per-pupil expenditure as other public schools in the district;

7. Teachers decide their own working conditions. A charter school can have a few non-certified teachers without having to seek a waiver or alternative certification; and

8. The state lists questions the school/sponsor must answer to receive the charter. It does not dictate the regulatory answers.[14]

"Fifteen years of research on effective schools show similarities with best practices in top business organizations. Effective schools have a strong sense of commitment and purpose along with high expectations for academic achievement. There is an orderly and pleasant school climate, a strong emphasis on instruction and a regular assessment of achievement. This is accompanied by consistent efforts by home and school.

"Effective schools need two other conditions—complete autonomy balanced by full accountability. These are the exact opposite to what most public schools are doing today. Principals complain that state and district regulations have made them powerless. Therefore, they are not accountable."[15]

Ray's hand shot up. "Are charter schools just spinning off a few alternative schools so that aggressive parents and unhappy teachers can do their thing at public expense?"

"Thank you, Ray, for that question. The charter movement brings simple yet profound systems change that has ripple effects more important than establishing a few new model schools. The main idea is this: The state should withdraw the exclusive right to offer public education from the school districts. This change gives other qualified educators the opportunity to get a contract, called a charter, from the local school board or some other public body. They would then set up an autonomous performance-based public school that students could choose to attend without charge.

"When these charter schools are actually going, school districts that normally resist giving up their control will have to reconsider their traditional responsibilities. They'll have to move from regulatory to policy oversight and into technical assistance. This will encourage these nearly autonomous schools to manage themselves and to be accountable for improving student performance. These changes are actually happening because the incentive— the money—will be transferred from the district's budget to the autonomous charter schools that the board will not be able to control."

"Ted," Paul spoke up again, "I can see why school districts would resist the charter school movement if they're threatened with losing the money that comes with each student. For the first time since I joined this Commission, I'm hearing something that gives me hope. Maybe we can reform the public education system, if the incentive structure leverages change. This type of public enterprise zone would generate real competition. The people who stand to lose their monopoly status, like teacher unions and school boards, are fighting this movement, aren't they?"

"Well, yes and no. Many school boards and state teacher unions have opposed charter schools. But once the plan has been legislated, many former opponents support it. The National Education Association opened five charter schools in 1996. The American Federation of Teachers is cautiously embracing charter schools.[16] Several union leaders have explored the role of what's been called new 'high-performance unions' in school reform.[17] With the help of Governor Romer, Colorado has one of the strongest charter school laws. Randy Quinn, executive director of the Colorado School Board Association, points out that school boards are now contracting out services, like transportation, food, cleaning and maintenance. This means that school districts are already purchasers of educational services. So why not take the next logical step and purchase educational services from charter school contractors? Local school boards could provide start-up capital, technical assistance and planning. They could also provide liability and health insurance, personnel services, teacher retirement, and other legal and administrative support services.

"This would also help local school leaders concentrate their energy and creativity in providing quality learning opportunities for their students. When schools become more independent, they also become more accountable.[18] Charter schools will feel free to reach out for other resources—parents, school districts, universities, business and community associations.

"Where does that leave the school districts?" said Ray.

"School districts can reshape themselves to provide only those competitive services that the new public school market will demand. School district superintendents and board members can also provide educational auditing assistance. This will prepare schools for favorable accountability assessments—something like colleges and universities coming for accreditation. They can select among competitors for charter or alternative schools within their own district boundaries by encouraging responsible public enterprise to open up. This will help to phase out the negative parts of the public education bureaucracy and its regulations.[19]

"Outside Denver, in Jefferson County, Colorado, two pioneering charter schools have demonstrated the gradual conversion process that some school boards and superintendents experience. Jefferson Academy began as the project of a group of parents who hired a principal to run a conservative back-to-basics, strongly teacher-directed elementary school of 190 students. The second of Jefferson County's charters, a K-12 school organized by a group of teachers and parents, is a more liberal progressive school of 448 students. It features extensive personalization along with experimental learning, student decision-making and self-direction.

"Both schools encountered initial resistance by the local school board. They requested and obtained the right to operate free of local union contracts and free of board policies on curriculum, textbooks, staff selection, evaluation, pay scales and administrator certification requirements. The district has finally invited both schools to become alternative schools within the school district rather than separate charter schools. After seven years of inaction, these charter schools opened up the policies of Jefferson County School Board. Now the board actively seeks proposals for new alternative schools to function as options within the district system. The state of Colorado has been negotiating actively with local school districts to open up charter options. It has overruled one district to set up a state authorized charter school in Denver. Thus charter schools in Colorado, although modest in their beginnings, are spawning new connections that school reformers have called for as fundamental to restructuring the public education mainstream.[20]

"Minnesota passed the first charter school law in 1991. In the Forest Lake School District, after several years of petitioning their school board, parents were finally invited by the board of education to organize a Montessori school within the district."

"How big is the charter school movement, Mr. Kolderie?" asked Tamar.

"Since 1991 there are about 500 charter schools operating in 25 states.[21] However, 95% of these schools are in only eight states. These are Arizona, California, Colorado, Michigan, Minnesota, Massachusetts, New Hampshire, and Texas. * On September 22, 1995, at a charter school in San Diego, President Clinton announced the award of $5.5 million to nine states, plus two schools in New Mexico, even though it did not apply. The money is to encourage the establishment of new charter schools. Funding for the program grew to $18 million in 1996.

---

*In Washington, D.C., a new strong charter law was enacted by Congress in August 1996. The school board approved seven new charter schools. A separate new charter school board also has been established to approve charter schools in the district.

"About half of the 25 states have strong laws. Those with weak laws are, perhaps, worse off than states without any laws. Weak state laws usually reflect political compromises that destroy the chances for charter schools to be successful."

"Mr. Kolderie, what is the difference between strong and weak charter school laws?" Christina of Interfaith asked.

"Well, a strong law has a provision that allows a potential charter school to go around the local school board to some other public body to get its charter. In other words, if the local board objects, the sponsors could go to another group. Opponents of charter schools now publicly express their support, but they work to control the movement by asking policymakers to restrict charters to approval by local school boards. Without the option of going to an alternative public body for charter approval, sponsors are still under the veto power of the district's school board. If school boards will not negotiate in good faith, sponsors must have an alternative. So state charter laws are pseudo, weak or dead if the board has veto power over a chartering group's application. Right now, most districts have a monopoly and the veto power."

"Well, could you give us a good description of a charter school, Mr. Kolderie?" Dale asked.

"Well, they are small, with about 300 students, mostly younger ones. Especially in California, they try to innovate by using the latest technology. Enrollment appears to favor at-risk children.[22] Probably the most significant study of charter schools was done by the Hudson Institute. They reviewed 43 charter schools in seven states, and identified the characteristics of new charter schools. They are imaginative in their approaches; they attract terrific teachers; they have waiting lists that testify to the satisfaction of students and teachers; they have high parent involvement; and they often take troublesome and disadvantaged students from other neighboring schools.

"The trouble is that public charter schools receive less money than their counterpart public schools, but are expected to demonstrate higher student achievements. They are hampered by lack of cash flow, and lack of start-up and capital funds. They continue to face legal regulations that are supposed to be waived for autonomy and accountability, and they are often undermined by hostile district officials.[23]

"How do superintendents feel about charter schools?" asked Kim.

"Howard Fuller, the former superintendent of the Milwaukee schools, says that charter schools combine the best of choice and public-private partnerships. He champions charter schools for disadvantaged students to escape public education systems that are not accountable. 'Every day our kids are dying, as people continue to protect systems that are helping to intellectually destroy them ... In America there is a direct link between money and power. Let individual schools make the decisions about budget, personnel and curriculum. Parents must have the option to walk out of schools that are not educating their children.'[24] A county that wants to raise performance to meet high standards should convert its K-12 system into contract arrangements immediately.'"*

"This seems too good to be true, Ted," Paul said. " I'm very impressed with what you're saying about charter schools. They seem to have all the advantages I thought voucher plans do. The competition would force the monopoly school district to shape up its schools or lose money and students. But, unlike voucher plans, charter schools still keep most kids in public schools without draining tax money from the public schools. I am impressed that charter schools introduce a grassroots, entrepreneurial spirit into public schooling. Parents finally get to choose the school they think is right for their children without having to pay twice—once in taxes for public schools and a second time for private school tuition. But I'm worried about accountability for performance. How do we know they are measuring up?"[25]

"Dale, I hope this handout will answer most of your questions, before I begin my summary," said Nate. "Ted, as you can see by our response this afternoon, you've excited us all by your presentation. I for one had no idea that the charter school movement was exploding this quickly. You have given us much to ponder. Thank you for your contributions. I believe you will see your finger prints on the final Citizens' Commission Report."

"Thanks, Nate," said Ted Kolderie. "I've enjoyed appearing before this Commission. I believe the future of nationwide school reform is within our grasp. Charter schools are a bold new initiative that should be seriously considered."

---

*On February 10, 1997, the Duluth, Minnesota School Boart voted 9-0 to sponsor charter schools at two companies. They contracted with the Edison Project to provide educational services designed to improve student achievement.

BEST PRACTICES: CHARTER SCHOOL

Vaughn Next Century Learning Center is located in Pacoima, California, a low-income area where the harsh realities of everyday life in the barrio are clearly evident. Vaughn is a public charter school within the Los Angeles Unified School District. Family income averages about $15,000. Many families with five or six children live in small rental spaces, garages and trailers. Nearly all students (99.6%) qualify for free/reduced lunch. Of 1,142 students (pre K-5), 94.9% are Hispanics, with 87% classified as Limited-English-Proficient.

For over 40 years, low student achievement was the pattern in this "hopeless and helpless" school. Test scores were among the lowest in the state. Overcrowded conditions forced the school to adopt the first multi-track, year-round schedule at a time when the region provided only 163 instructional days. The principal resigned after anonymous death threats. Teacher turnover was high.

What happened to Vaughn Next Century in the last five years is an inspiring and powerful story. Dr. Yvonne Chan, the new principal, was determined to "turn the school around." In 1991 she implemented school-based management and began massive restructuring. Her energy and can-do attitude helped move needed innovations ahead in spite of obstacles. With California's education code over 6,000 pages, the school bureaucracy hindered reform efforts. Dr. Chan filed waivers for nearly every initiative, from fixing a broken window to taking a simple field trip.

In 1992 California enacted a charter school law allowing creation of autonomous public schools which could operate independently of a school board. "We were one of the first to apply for 'the waiver of all waivers,'" Dr. Chan explains. "The charter takes the handcuffs off the principal, the teachers and the parents—the people who know the kids best. In return, we are held responsible for how kids do."[26]

Vaughn Next Century was granted charter status in 1993 with a budget of $4.6 million. Chan revamped the spending, put services like payroll out for competitive bids and reorganized special education. At the end of the school year, with $1.2 million left, Vaughn's staff decided to use those funds for a 14-classroom complex, new computers, and an after-school soccer program. They hired more teachers to reach a total of 56 and reduced class sizes from a district average of 32 to 20 in grades 1 through 4.

The school has achieved dramatic success against tremendous odds. Student achievement has improved by 300% in reading and 220% in mathematics as measured by California Test of Basic Skills (CTBS) and the Aprenda Tests. Student attendance is at 99.49% with no suspensions. With teachers stressing language acceleration, student transitioning to English has increased by 108%. The mobility rate has been reduced from 71% to 27%. Parent satisfaction is indicated by active involvement, with volunteer hours reaching 9,000 last year. Today there's a student waiting list.

Several key factors associated with their charter status have contributed to their success. "Our school capacity has increased because of shared governance and commitment, visitor and media attention, and fiscal prudence that has brought more resources into our classrooms, including a computer for every four students." She has far more decision-making authority, including hiring and firing, than do principals working under union and district rules. Teachers work longer hours than they did before charter status, but they are paid more and given more authority. Teachers see themselves as leaders and owners of the school; all are accountable for student success. Each teacher serves on one of eight parent-teacher committees that meets weekly to make decisions as to how to run the school. For example, they eliminated the multi-track system and increased the instructional days to 200. Teachers are provided weekly preparation periods to plan and think together. They use instructional strategies that stress hands-on activities, teamwork, field learning, modeling and guided practice. Evaluation and supervision of all teachers is an ongoing process that includes mentors for new teachers. Their policy that students now wear school uniforms has eliminated competition to have "name brands" and helped to promote a sense of belonging on campus.

Summary

Nate began to summarize the afternoon's discussion. "**The private voucher movement comes from the public's frustration with the slow pace** of school reform and from a conservative belief that government should not be running local schools. Opponents of vouchers believe that tax dollars should not be given to wealthy parents who can afford the tuition for private schools, including religious schools. They also believe that taking scarce public tax dollars from public schools would make it even worse for middle-class and disadvantaged students who would be left behind. Perhaps even more costly to a democracy, students enrolling in private schools would not have the experience of going to school with children from all backgrounds. America's Founding Fathers advocated public schools so all our children could learn about and experience democracy.

"Private voucher advocates have demonstrated little interest in reforming public schools for those 50% of American students most at risk. Voucher programs have been around many years. They have yet to demonstrate that disadvantaged students would get a better education than they are currently receiving in public schools. In England, public vouchers for private schools have not had the impact advocates claim. They failed to force public schools to improve because of private school competition. Most private schools select only the very best middle-class and disadvantaged students. The private schools have not kept up with the demand, and they have not educated many children who are disadvantaged or have disabilities. Most states discriminate by unequal funding of public urban and rural schools. Public vouchers for private schools do not address the moral issue of our time, which is the need to provide quality education for all America's children.

"Turning now to charter schools, Ted Kolderie said that we must enact only strong charter laws in all states. When opposing interest groups effectively gut the legislation, we have essentially a dead or weak law, which is worse than no law. Critics then can say that charter schools don't work.

Nate continued. "Most charter schools are having trouble finding buildings, or capital and start up funds. Traditional school districts have already paid for their buildings by floating bonds at taxpayers expense. Charter schools don't now have the same legal authority to raise capital funds by selling bonds and must depend on school districts to give them space.

"Still we're amazed by the ingenuity of these charter pioneers. They're like start-up businesses. They must contract out services even before the state money actually arrives. Some banks are advancing start-up costs against expected state revenues. No strong national support group or technical assistance center provides help and coordination for the exploding network of activities and people.

"States, counties and local districts need to create good management and technical assistance procedures. Sophisticated assessment tools are needed. We need to set up ways to monitor charters before they get into trouble. The state should promptly close troubled charter schools before damage is done to students and before they lose their public funding. Ted believes the proper role for government is to promote equal educational opportunities for students while encouraging parents, educators and policymakers to organize and operate successful charter schools."

Wendy took over. "Thank you, Nate, for your remarks. Now I'd like to go around the group and have each of you give a one-sentence reaction to what we've heard today. Who'd like to start off?"

"I'll start off. I'm Paul and my mind is blown with the rise of the charter school movement. It's a way to reform public education by getting out from under the teacher unions and the district bureaucracy."

"I'm Ted. I like what I've heard about the new charter school movement."

"I'm impressed by what Deborah Meier told us," said Debbie. "Thanks for bringing her here today."

"Tamar. Deborah Meier makes me proud to be a teacher. Please thank her for me."

"I can second that," said Kathie. "Tell Deborah to keep up the great work."

Maria said, "This is a good day for Jefferson Elementary School, if we can pull it off."

"I'm Lenora and I've learned something special today. Here's a White woman who has saved minority children from lives of poverty and early death. I'm impressed."

Christina said, "I received inspiration and hope for our Citizens' Commission."

Dale was still angry about his education. "At least I understand what happened to me now. It was a good day."

"See, Dale, all this democracy stuff really isn't so bad after all. I'm delighted. I hate to put a damper on things, but reforms like these take miracle workers. Are the teachers here at Jefferson willing to work that hard?"

"My name is Kim. I'm encouraged by the questions I heard from Commission members today. I believe we're becoming a productive group."

"I have much to think about after this Hearing," said Delores. "Our guests Debbie and Ted were profound. I've had my eyes opened."

"Well, I too am overwhelmed at what we must do," said Ray. "But I'm encouraged!"

Wendy stood to close off the Hearing. "Once again I'm excited about our project. Today was outstanding for me. Please take a minute to shake hands or give a hug to everyone in the room before you leave. See you next month."

****

Chapter 5
NATIONAL ACADEMIC STANDARDS
AND CORE CURRICULUM
Saturday morning, November 23

Ted Alexander kissed his wife goodbye. He drove his '87 Toyota out of the driveway, resenting that another Saturday was to be sacrificed to the Citizens' Commission. *Don't they understand that Jefferson Elementary School is a hopeless place to work. It's physical plant is dilapidated—they'll find out soon enough. The principal, Olive Carter, and I go way back. But, hell, we're both just waiting to retire, so I'm not going to rock the boat. I sure don't want this Citizens' Commission checking up on achievement scores in my class—they're in the toilet every year. These kids try hard, but they can't get it together because of the poor homes they come from with their spaced-out parents. It's a waste of time.*

This reform business is just a political farce to get the Superintendent and the School Board off the hook. Hell, most of the board will stand for election this fall. They haven't done anything to impress the voters. I'm going to vote against every incumbent. I'm for term limits too. Maybe we can get some good union people to run for the Board, at least that will slow this county reform crap down. I'm counting on our superintendent, Dr. Dooley, to stall it out. Let the Commission fuss and pontificate with their final report. It'll be a one-day story. It'll just fade away like all school reform reports. Nate said things are even worse today than in 1983 when Bell and his national commission put out A Nation At Risk!

Ted pulled into the parking lot and slowly walked to the building.

Kim welcomed the group to the third Citizens' Commission Hearing. "Hope everyone is enjoying the last of our beautiful autumn leaves. Today, we have a great program. I'll turn the time over to Nate Johnson, who will introduce our first guest."

National Academic Standards

"Dr. Diane Ravitch is an educational historian at New York University. She is widely known and respected as a scholar and education critic. Her commentaries often appear in national journals and newspapers. She served in the Bush Administration as a presidential appointee in the U.S. Department of Education, where she was Assistant Secretary of Educational Research and Improvement. In 1995 she published the recognized work on national academic standards.[1] Diane, could you begin by summarizing the main issues in the debate on academic standards?"

"Thank you, Nate. I'm pleased to be here to discuss this critical topic. I believe it is the philosophical watershed issue of our day. The question is, do we intend to provide a first-rate education for all children, or are we content with our current low standards? Since the 1930s, we have watered down the curriculum and lowered our expectations. We have social studies instead of history, language arts instead of English. We have lax standards of grading, a laissez-faire attitude towards student misbehavior, and an absolute abhorrence of a well-defined academic curriculum. We even condone social promotion—moving students to the next grade when they haven't learned what's required.[2]

"Most elementary schools have practices that lead to 'dumbing down' the curriculum. This means the virtual elimination of good children's literature, history, science and mathematics—the challenging stuff that gets children excited and builds a solid foundation for future learning. The curriculum of 'expanding environments,' which emphasizes family and community, has replaced historical content, and language arts has replaced good literature. Found in virtually all public schools in the early grades, expanding environments contains no mythology, no legends, no hero tales, no biographies, no stories about great events in the life of our country or any other. This curriculum has no foundation in research—none whatsoever! When I conducted research on curriculum in the early grades, I checked my findings with a dozen leading scholars in the fields of cognitive psychology, child development, and curriculum theory. Not one knew of any research supporting the expanding environment approach. And not one defended it. Our children deserve better! They deserve real literature—poetry, myths, and biographies—not dumbed-down basal readers.[3]

"Dr. Ravitch," Kathie Sorenson interrupted. "I didn't go through a school of education for my undergraduate work. I majored in psychology and was hired right out of the university. I completed my credential while teaching my first year. In the past two years, I've been working on a master's degree in education, and I've found my program very challenging. But most of what I'm doing as a teacher I had to learn on my own. I certainly know many fellow teachers who do not have substantive academic knowledge. If they do, they are not sharing it with their classes. This year my district has asked me to learn about the new math standards curriculum and make presentations to other teachers and parents. This is a great approach to teaching math, but not all teachers are receptive. What is the reaction of the teaching profession to your charges that we're not using a challenging curriculum with high academic standards?"

"The response by many in the education field," Dr. Ravitch answered, "is to rationalize. They claim that the present curriculum simply requires more money and more time to demonstrate its effectiveness, even though we have been following the same pattern for decades. The net result is we continue doing what doesn't work and investing more money in it.

"What's becoming an embarrassment for our country, however, is the international math and science assessments. They show that America's students are not learning as much as students in other modern nations. But that doesn't seem to change public policy or major strategies in education. Many apologists are too busy defending the status quo and pointing out that the glass is half full. It is certainly half full across America. But in our urban centers, where half the students never even graduate, it's more than half empty. This is unacceptable."

"Wait a minute!" Maria Morales said. "Dr. Ravitch, are you saying that my children here at Jefferson are not receiving a good education because they don't get taught a curriculum with high academic standards? I thought all teachers were trained to teach high academic standards. I thought the district sent us the most effective teachers because we need even more help than those privileged middle-class schools."

"Inner city schools often get the least experienced teachers, teachers who have not been well trained in the subjects they are teaching. Teachers with seniority often transfer to what are perceived to be the very best schools with the best students. Of course, there are exceptional teachers who are dedicated and creative and are making a real difference in the lives of disadvantaged students. Urban education is in deep trouble because of inept big-city bureaucracies and the public's higher expectations for schools as compared to 50 years ago. It used to be that the public was neither surprised nor alarmed by the large numbers of young people who did not graduate from high school. They believed that progress was being made. For many years, public schools successfully integrated large numbers of immigrants and working-class children, preparing them for skilled and semi-skilled factory jobs at good wages. Some even went on to higher education.

"Today the factory model school is no longer adequate to prepare most students for the global economy where higher-order knowledge and skills are required. A large group of America's students are not being prepared for the world of work or for further education. When *A Nation At Risk* was published in 1983, it led to a national debate about the purpose of education and the best way to deliver that education to all children."

Paul Christopher raised his hand. "The picture you've painted for us today is a real eye-opener! I'm starting to feel like we've all been had! All of us—parents, employers and, maybe worst of all, teachers and students. What alternative do we have? I know that some urban schools are performing well. So I guess it can be done."

"What we need," Dr. Ravitch replied, "are schools that provide an excellent liberal arts education to all children. This means that they should be taught a strong core curriculum of history, literature, math, sciences, the arts and foreign languages. I want every child to have the same quality of education that the mayor and the superintendent of schools and the newspaper editor have had. I don't say that it will be easy, but we can't be satisfied with anything less. I believe that the school's mission is to uplift, teach, civilize and educate. Children arrive in school innocent, eager to learn, and full of potential. But they are not born wiser than their parents and teachers. Children learn by example, by experience and by instruction.

"Our goal should be how to improve all children's learning. Schools should be performance-based. They should be held accountable for results. We need to know whether or not children are learning. Standards and assessments should be required so we know what children are supposed to learn, and we have a valid way to determine whether or not children are learning, and to give parents accurate information about schools. Children have to understand that there are real consequences attached to their actions in school, like getting promoted, graduating or going to college. I believe that schools have a great deal to learn from sports and music. The great thing about sports and music is that you know you have to practice to improve your knowledge and skills if you want to succeed. You know that practice won't always be fun, and that the coach is the expert who shows you what standards of performance are required. Those who don't exert effort do not succeed."

"What's the difference between performance standards and content standards?" Dale asked.

"There are two kinds of standards. Content standards are what students should learn and what teachers should teach. Performance standards are how well you have to perform—or to demonstrate what you know—in order to qualify at basic, proficient or advanced levels. Letter grades like A, B, C or D represent a performance standard. Real-world feedback, based on an individual's effort and disciplined habits, builds self esteem and character.

"What we need now as an advanced society are national standards—not federal standards managed by the federal government. Today we have an informal national curriculum based on minimum competencies that are set forth in our tests and textbooks. We need high national standards, not our current low-level standards. In the real world, such subjects as math, science, and English demand knowledge that reflects very high international standards. These subjects can be taught effectively many different ways, but their fundamental principles are the same all over the world. We have to identify and teach these principles. Students who take advanced placement tests, like the SAT, the International Baccalaureate and the National Assessment of Educational Progress are expected to meet high standards in the major subject areas. These tests don't pretend there's Oregon math, New York science and Nebraska English.

"National standards are essential for equal opportunity and for excellence. We cannot avoid the issue. The only question is whether or not the standards will continue to be minimal or will be as challenging as the international standards used on our leading tests and by our top competitors. I'm encouraged, however, by the ongoing national debate on academic standards."

Debbie excitedly asked her next question. "Dr. Ravitch, can you tell us who has been developing the national academic standards? What role has the federal government taken?"

"Development of national academic standards is an academic and political exercise. The states are responsible, but they should find ways to collaborate so that their students meet international standards.[4] Some standards would be national; some would be state; some would be local. Business wants graduates who have been educated to a high national or international academic standard of knowledge and skill development. Our population is so mobile that we can't have one standard of achievement in Georgia, for example, and a completely different one in California. Georgia students may become adult workers in California or any other state and vice-versa. So we must have national standards of achievement that are recognized by students, parents and employers—perhaps even international or world-class, as we do for the Olympics. We must have standards for our rapidly developing global economy.

"This realization, although still not accepted by everyone, has led to a tacit partnership between the federal government, the academic associations, the large private foundations and the states. We know that it works because back in the 1980s, the National Council of Teachers of Mathematics began to develop the first national academic standards. By 1989 they had drafted math standards that are still being refined and are now being disseminated to individual classroom math teachers, thus bypassing complicated state and district bureaucracies. The development of these math standards was indirectly supported by the National Science Foundation and the U.S. Department of Education.

"When I was Assistant Secretary of the Office of Educational Research and Improvement in the U.S. Department of Education, the federal government funded development of voluntary national standards in every major academic area. For example, along with the National Endowment of the Arts, we funded development of arts education content standards. They were published in 1994 and included the visual arts, theater, dance, and music under the leadership of the Music Educators National Conference. Federal funds allowed The National Council for Geographic Education and the Association of American Geographers to develop and publish content standards. This work on geography standards received federal funds. The National Geographic Society lobbied for the inclusion of geography in the national goals. Also in 1994, the Center for Civic Education, which received federal funding, produced K-12 standards in civics and government which indicate the content to be learned and why it should be learned. These efforts produced constructive discussions with relatively little political controversy. Private foundation funds underwrote the development of economic standards by the National Council on Economic Education.

"History standards, however, became a political battleground. The U.S. Department of Education and the National Endowment for the Humanities awarded a contract to the National Center for History in the Schools at the University of California at Los Angeles. The group was to develop voluntary national standards for American and World History. When the group released a draft in 1994, they were charged with being excessively critical of the United States. The U.S. Senate reacted to public pressure by censuring the history standards. The vote was 99:1. The short-term effect was to undermine the whole national standards movement. Finally, the Council for Basic Education brought together two panels of historians. I was on one of these panels. We reviewed and recommended changes in the history standards.[5] UCLA adopted these suggestions and revised the history standards, which should be a guide for every district and state.[6] Because of the controversy, however, many states are backing away from history altogether. They are adopting bland social studies statements instead of real content standards. Virginia and California are two of the best states for history standards, but many others are very weak. My opinion is that the study of history must not be abandoned. It is far better to have controversy than ignorance.

"We are still trying to develop standards in the field of English. In 1996 the National Council of Teachers of English and the International Reading Association did produce standards. They were immediately criticized because they failed to define specific standards or provide lists of required reading. When a panel of peer reviewers said the effort would not lead to any real standards for teaching and learning English, Secretary Riley withdrew U.S. Department of Education funding support even before the standards were released."

Paul was puzzled. "So academic standards are developed with funding from the U.S. Department of Education, the National Science Foundation, the National Endowment for the Humanities, National Endowment of the Arts and the private national foundations. Right? How do the states adopt and integrate these standards into their curriculum?"

Dr. Ravitch paused a moment. "Well, people assume that once content and performance standards are designed, all the work has been done. That's only the first step. You might say, it's like deciding where you want to go before starting a trip. The proposed national academic standards must be integrated and balanced. Some are far too ambitious and voluminous. Other advanced nations have a central ministry of education to accomplish that task. In our country, the process must be carried out by states and localities, with the help of non-governmental organizations, which might include commercial developers of textbooks and assessments.

Dale said suspiciously. "Well, I've heard that the federal Department of Education has been controlling the academic standards development process. And I don't like them meddling with my kids' minds."

"Then, Dale, you'll be happy to know that the U.S. Department of Education does not write academic standards. It provides financial support for independent professional associations and provides grants to the states for developing their own content standards. As a political independent, I am encouraged by this work from all across the political spectrum to rally the nation around the need for challenging academic standards."

"Who can possibly be opposed to national academic standards?" Christina asked.

"Well, some people on both the left (especially in elite schools of education) and the right are opposed. The Christian Coalition is adamantly against any kind of national standards. These groups—on the right and the left—are afraid that the feds will control our local schools.

"Let's see just what the states are doing. The American Federation of Teachers, led by President Albert Shanker, has surveyed states to determine how well defined the academic standards are in math, science, English and social studies. Almost all 50 states and the District of Columbia, except Iowa and Wyoming, are strongly committed to standards-based reform. Only 15 states deserve passing grades for their efforts. Colorado, Virginia and Delaware are leading the way. The AFT has not yet attempted to assess the quality of the standards themselves or the assessment process and tools necessary to measure results.[7] The state standards in social studies and English that I have reviewed are far from world-class; in fact, most are very weak. We still have a long way to go to develop good academic standards."

Ted Alexander was fuming. *I knew we'd get this conservative party line! These education critics don't spend every day in the trenches the way I do. Our kids don't want to learn. Half their families are illegal immigrants. You just try and stand in front of a class of 30 kids all day, teaching them national academic standards? Give me a break! One more phony top-down, cheap school reform advanced by critics of public education to keep from spending tax money on minority kids! She did say that she was an independent who wants to educate all kids. I guess I'm confused about where she's coming from.*

Ray was delighted with the session and thought to himself. *Here I've always thought Diane Ravitch was a conservative who was not concerned about quality education for minority children. Was I wrong! She's a solid researcher and a dedicated educator. Where do these people come from? She's shown me why some public educators are not really educating our kids.*

Nate stood to conclude the session. "Thank you, Diane, for being with us and providing this valuable background on the national academic standards movement. Dr. Ravitch has agreed to stay and answer questions. For a contrary view, I direct your attention to our next education Myth. We'll now take a short break."

****

Core Curriculum

Wendy welcomed the group back. *She gives such energy,* thought Debbie. *I was that young and energetic once. But she'll get older, have kids, and get jaded.*

"It's my pleasure," Wendy said, "to introduce Dr. E.D. Hirsch, professor of English at the University of Virginia and president of the Core Knowledge Foundation in Charlottesville, Virginia. Dr. Hirsch is best known for his book, *Cultural Literacy.* Since its publication, he's become a much admired and sometimes controversial pioneer in the rediscovery of classic curriculum reading materials for elementary schools. In his new book, *The Schools We Need and Why We Don't Have Them,* Dr. Hirsch traces the historic failures of naturalistic educational philosophy that have guided our 20th century public education.[10] He compares this progressive philosophy with his own core curriculum approach. More than 200 schools in 37 states have voluntarily become Core Knowledge Schools. Let's get right to the point, Dr. Hirsch. Should Jefferson Elementary become a Core Knowledge School?"

"Thank you, Wendy. You do start with the bottom line. I understand Diane Ravitch was here earlier this morning. She presented background

MYTH: There is no crises in American public education. We face only a "manufactured crises" by public school reformers, politicians and corporate leaders.

Several respected educational researchers challenge the claim that public schools are in crises because of the marginal performance of American students over the past 25 years. David C. Berliner and Bruce J. Biddle, major spokesmen for this perspective, carefully examine the academic achievement scores of American students on "highly-suspect and superficial" SAT and other national tests, differentiating between White and disadvantaged students. They believe we should celebrate because overall student achievement levels have remained constant, despite the onslaught of poverty and unequal opportunities faced by increasing numbers of disadvantaged White and minority students. Few dispute this part of their rigorous analysis. They also point out the difficulties of comparing American students with foreign student populations (age, curriculum and sampling differences), and conclude that U.S. students are performing very well against their counterparts in competitor nations.

Berliner and Biddle identify four serious problems: (1) inadequate funding that plagues retched inner-city schools, (2) high poverty that envelopes minority students and their families, (3) racism that torments the nation, and (4) conservatives who "manufacture" today's national education crises as an excuse to abandon public schools. According to these authors, modern conservatives perpetrated the "fraud" of a public school crises—Reagan's Far Right cohorts, the Religious Right, and the neo-conservatives who influenced two Republican presidents and their advisors. Conservatives have convinced President Clinton, his Secretary of Education and appointees at the U.S. Department of Education that a genuine national education crisis exists. The conspiracy also includes corporate executives who hope to control the direction of education to benefit their business interests. Educators should not change their curriculum in response to growing public and private voices calling for national academic standards and state and local assessments of how effectively students are being schooled.

Berliner and Biddle argue that graduates will find plenty of jobs available for the expanding service and information economy in the nation's fastest growing occupations—paralegals, housekeepers, retail salespersons, cashiers and custodians. For every computer-programming job, there will be nine new jobs in these fastest growing categories. The number of janitors will be 1.5 times as many as lawyers, accountants, investment bankers, stockbrokers and computer-programmers combined.

FINDING A: Berliner and Biddle make several curious assumptions and interpretations of findings. While most students are performing at about the level of their counterparts 20 years ago, they assume that this level of performance is "good enough" in 1996. They fail to acknowledge, however, that all graduates face a rapidly changing multicultural society and knowledge-based global economy where high-paid industrial jobs are no longer available for high school dropouts or even graduates. The demands for advanced knowledge and skills in all occupations, including low-paid service jobs, are rapidly escalating to the point where breadwinners must acquire basic functional literacy—now defined as at least two years of postsecondary education—if they are to support a family above the poverty level. Low-wage, low-skill service jobs will continue to be filled by new immigrants, those seven out of 10 students who do not graduate from college, and by some college-educated, but low-skilled, individuals in various transitional stages.

Even these two authors acknowledge, "Most Americans will now have to shift occupations at least once, perhaps many more times, during their lifetimes. Our work force now requires more and more people who can assume higher-level skilled tasks and professional responsibilities, and this trend will continue...All of these changes mean that America needs citizens who are flexible, who embrace new ideas, who can reason well when faced with complex ideas, and who are capable of self-directed learning."[8] In the 1993 NAEP comprehensive adult literacy assessment of 18-24 year olds, only 52 percent have sufficient functional knowledge and skills to hold well-paying jobs.[9] Since most schools are, by default, educating half their students for low-wage, low-skill service jobs, most parents and their children, do not feel like celebrating victory. They do not look forward to having their children working in low-skill, low-wage jobs as life-long careers.

FINDING B. The 1994 NAEP assessments of proficient or advanced level found that only a small minority of American twelfth graders met proficiency levels in reading (34%); math (16% in 1992), history (11%), and geography (27%). The percentage of high school students passing Advanced Placement (AP) exams for college credit was 5.7%, more than double the number a decade ago. Meanwhile, over 50% of French students passed AP exams. The AP tests represent an international standard and reflects on the knowledge learned in high school. Student assessments of actual knowledge, not IQ or SAT tests is the bottom line. That many college bound students can take high school remedial work in college is hardly a testimony of the strength of our public education system. Analysis of test scores and their limitations is a helpful and necessary contribution. But as apologists for a stagnant public education system, Berliner and Biddle apparently miss the larger meaning of the educational policy "forest" for their methodological preoccupation with the "test score trees."

What qualifies as the genuine national education and moral "crisis" of our age, however, is the tragic mis-education of our disadvantaged White and minority students —many of whom face abject poverty with its attending dysfunctions of high crime, poor health, violence and drugs, and the "savage inequality" of inner-city school financial support. No one can defend today's education at these levels as providing the foundation for a high quality of life—life-long learners, accountable citizens, responsible parents and informed consumers as well as productive workers. Fortunately, growing numbers of parents, educators, employers, state and federal government leaders, and the general public disagree with Berliner and Biddle's conclusions about the "manufactured crisis."

material that compares the two models of classroom instruction—the progressive school culture that dominates the way schools of education train elementary classroom teachers, and the more classic culture, which I call the Core Knowledge Curriculum. **In my survey of research literature, I could not find one example of a carefully-controlled, longitudinal study of successfully implemented progressivist methods**.

"Now I'll go directly to what we mean by a Core Knowledge Curriculum. I believe that children from every ethnic and economic background should have access to a shared core of knowledge that is necessary to reading, understanding, and communicating. Our aim is to produce specific grade-by-grade guidelines. We've developed this after years of research, consultation, consensus-building, and field testing. We do not claim that other core approaches are not useful. No one has a lock on perfection. But we have made an impressive start!

Looking at his notes, he continued. "Our Core Knowledge guidelines are meant to constitute about 50% of a school's curriculum. The other half can be tailored to a district, school, or classroom. Our point is that a core of shared knowledge, grade-by-grade, is needed to achieve excellence and fairness. International studies show that *any* school that practices such a challenging and specific program will provide a more effective and fair education than one that lacks such commonality of content in each grade. High-performing systems in France, Sweden, Japan, and West Germany bear out this principle. It was our intent to test whether in rural, urban, and suburban settings of the United States we would find what other nations have already discovered."[11]

Delores Williams spoke up. "Dr. Hirsch, from what I've heard your work on cultural literacy glorifies White males from European cultures. That doesn't matter much to minority students who are poor."

"Thanks for being so direct, Mrs. Williams. Please call me Don. There is a widespread misunderstanding about core cultural knowledge. To illustrate the power of this approach for minority children who are disadvantaged, let me share our experience in two elementary schools. The Mohegan Public School in New York's South Bronx—the innermost part of the inner city—is surrounded by urban blight: trash, abandoned cars, crack houses. The students are mostly Latino or African American, all qualifying for free lunch.

"In January 1992, CBS Evening News devoted an Eye on America segment to the Mohegan School. Why did CBS focus on Mohegan? Because this school seemed an unlikely place for a low-cost, academically-solid program like Core Knowledge to succeed. Mohegan's talented principal, Jeffrey Litt, wrote to tell me that 'the richness of the curriculum' is of particular importance because, like 'most poverty-stricken and educationally under-served students, his students' experience was limited to remedial activities.' Since adopting the Core Knowledge curriculum, Mohegan's students are engaging in the integrated and coherent study of topics like Ancient Egypt, Greece, and Rome; the Industrial Revolution; limericks, haiku, and poetry; Rembrandt, Monet, and Michelangelo; Beethoven and Mozart. They also are studying the Underground Railroad; the Trail of Tears; *Brown v. Board of Education;* the Mexican Revolution; photosynthesis; medieval African empires; the Bill of Rights; ecosystems; women's suffrage; and the Harlem Renaissance.

It was Delores' turn to be surprised. "Are you saying, Dr. Hirsch, that you are including in your Core Curriculum the history, writings and experience of people of color and women, not just those of European White males?"

"Yes, our Core Curriculum represents all people. I believe that the education of children who are disadvantaged is the civil rights challenge of the 1990s. All children must be challenged to obtain *intellectual capital*—that's knowledge our multi-cultural society has found most useful. This is not limited to one group of people who are deemed to be superior. Knowledge is not just a matter of opinion or ethnic or racial pride. Some knowledge is more useful than other knowledge. I have never met a parent who didn't want the absolute-best education for his or her child. The Core Knowledge guidelines for elementary schools are far more specific than those issued by most school districts. For instance, instead of vague outcomes, such as first graders will be introduced to map skills, the geography section of the Core Knowledge *Sequence* says that first graders will learn the meaning of east, west, north, and south. They will be taught to locate on a map the equator, the Atlantic and Pacific Oceans, the seven continents, the United States, Mexico, Canada, and Central America.

"At the Mohegan School, we discovered that a school-wide core sequence enhances achievement *for all children*. Their disciplinary problems are down; teacher and student attendance is up; standardized tests scores are higher. Some teachers have even transferred their own children to the school! Some parents have taken their children out of private schools to send them to Mohegan. Schools across the nation are integrating Core Knowledge guidelines into their curriculums and reporting similar results."

Kathie Sorenson raised her hand. "I teach fifth grade at Jefferson. I want to know if students learn to go beyond memorizing facts. Will they learn to think?"

"Yes. Evelyn Hernandez, another fifth-grade teacher, told CBS News that Core Knowledge had tremendously increased the students' ability to question. In other words, **a coherent approach to specific content enhances students' critical and higher-order thinking skills**. I emphasize this point because some people object to teaching specific content. They suppose that critical thinking suffers when a teacher emphasizes mere information. Yet Core Knowledge teachers across the nation report that a coherent focus on content does lead to higher-order thinking skills. Trying to teach such skills directly is not as effective as teaching content in a way that motivates students to love it. As an added benefit, children acquire knowledge that is useful not just in next year's classroom but for the rest of their lives.

"Kathie, here are some of the research findings that show the correlation between a coherent, specific approach to knowledge and the development of higher-order skills. Learning can be fun, but it's still cumulative and sometimes arduous. Educators have always wanted to invent methods to streamline the time-consuming activity of learning. Back in the early Greek period, Proclus records an anecdote about an encounter between Euclid, the inventor of geometry, and King Ptolemy I of Egypt (276-196 B.C.). The King was impatiently trying to follow Euclid's *Elements* step by laborious step. Exasperated, the king demanded a faster, easier way to learn geometry—to which Euclid gave the famous, and still true, reply: 'There is no royal road to geometry.' Scientists have found that it takes repeated practice to forge new neural paths in our brains. Whether through unconscious play or conscious diligence, learning involves effort. There is no way around this.[12] Nothing can be reliably stored for recall without repetition. World class athletes or recognized professionals in every field come to know this simple rule.

"Even with computer technology, it's not easy to find short-cuts to learning. The human brain sets limits on the potential for educational innovation. We can't, for instance, put a faster chip in the human brain. It processes in thousandths rather than millionths of a second. We cannot change the fundamental, constructivist psychology of the learning process—we humans acquire new knowledge much as a tree acquires new leaves. The old leaves actively help nourish the new. The more old growth or prior knowledge we have, the faster new growth can occur, making learning an organic process in which knowledge builds upon knowledge.

"Well, you have a convert," said Kathie. "I know how angry I am when I inherit children from the fourth grade who still can't read or who can't do basic math or geography. I'd like to know what first through fourth grade teachers are suppose to be teaching. It would save about 30% of my time—that's what I'm now spending on remedial activities. Knowing what the sixth grade teacher expects to teach would help me be a better fifth grade teacher. In fact, surprise, I might even be held accountable if my students don't learn what I'm supposed to be teaching them. Excuse me for this speech, but I'm very excited by your approach."

"You're right, Kathie. **Modern classrooms require grade-by-grade shared knowledge**. We cannot effectively deliver completely individualized instruction. When an individual child gets what is being taught in a classroom, it's like someone finally getting the point of a joke. If you have the background knowledge, you'll get the joke. If you don't, you'll remain puzzled until somebody explains the knowledge-base that was taken for granted. A classroom of 25 to 35 children can move forward as a group only when all the children get the point. Studies that compare U.S. elementary schools to schools in countries with Core Knowledge systems disclose a striking difference in the structure of classroom activities. In the best performing classrooms, 80% of classroom time is constant discussion among students and between students and the teacher. By contrast, in the United States, over 50% of classroom time is spent with students in silent isolation.

"Behind this undue amount of 'alone time' in our schools is this theory: Every child is unique; therefore, every child should receive individually tailored instruction. This means that teachers need to be sensitive to each child's strengths and needs. The theory also reveals why good classroom teaching is difficult, and why a one-on-one tutorial is the most effective form of instruction. But modern education cannot be conducted as a one-on-one tutorial. Even in a country as affluent as the United States, instruction has to be carried out in classes of 25 to 35 pupils. For instance, in Dade County, Florida, the average class size for the early grades is 35. When a teacher gives individual attention to one child, 34 other pupils are left to fend for themselves. This is hardly a good trade-off, even if each child deserves individual attention. In California, they are reducing class size in K-3 to 20 students—a very expensive proposition.

"Progress has been slow in American elementary schools by international standards. **If an entire classroom must constantly pause while its lagging members acquire background knowledge that they should have gained in earlier grades, progress is bound to be slow.** For effective classroom instruction to take place, all class members must share enough common reference points for everyone to understand—even though they learn at different rates and respond to varied approaches. When this **commonality**

of knowledge is lacking, progress will be slow, especially when compared with systems that use a core curriculum."

"Are you saying our children here at Jefferson are slow?" Lenora Brown sounded insulted!

"Quite the contrary," answered Don Hirsch. "The myth that slight differences of intelligence make for vast differences in learning by low-income minority children is a cruel joke. White low-income children also perform very poorly when they have not been exposed to a challenging curriculum and good teachers. **Just as learning is cumulative so are learning deficits cumulative!** American students in the first grade are not far behind beginners in other developed nations. But as they move through the grade levels, their achievement falls further behind. This widening gap is the subject of one of the most important recent books on American education, *The Learning Gap,* by Stevenson and Stigler. This progressively widening gap closely parallels what happens within American elementary schools between advantaged and disadvantaged children. As the two groups progress from first to sixth grade, the achievement gap grows even larger and is almost never overcome.

"Hold on, Dr. Hirsch!" Tamar, the newest teacher, said. "You mean that year by year disadvantaged children are handicapped because they lose ground academically and because they attend high-poverty schools with a poor curriculum. They're given low expectations, the worst teachers, dilapidated buildings—and less money is spent on their education. Doesn't the Constitution say that all citizens are supposed to receive equal protection of the law against this kind of discrimination?"

"You are absolutely right, Tamar. In both cases, the widening gap represents the cumulative effect of learning deficits. Although a few talented and motivated children may overcome this handicap, most do not. The rift grows even wider in adult life. The basic causes of this permanent deficit, apart from motivational ones, are cognitive. That means learning builds upon learning, and lack of learning in the early grades builds up a cumulative negative effect.

"We know from large-scale longitudinal evidence, particularly from France, that this fateful gap between have and have-nots *can* be closed. But only one way to close it has been devised: to set forth explicit, year-by-year knowledge standards in early grades. These standards need to be known by all parties—educators, parents, and children. To reach this general level of excellence, such standards are requisites for home and school cooperation. But, equally, they are requisites in gaining fairness for the academic have-nots—the disadvantaged. Explicit year-by-year knowledge standards are necessary to enable schools in nations with strong elementary core curriculums to make up the knowledge deficits of children who are disadvantaged. Only by bridging this learning gap can disadvantaged White and minority children ever get equal educational opportunity. You're right, according to the 14th Amendment to the Constitution, which gives all citizens equal protection, many public schools are violating the law.

"But there is one more reason for every school to adopt a core curriculum. Americans have always been nomads, perhaps the most mobile people on the earth. Even more so today. I imagine that the students at Jefferson Elementary reflect this trend. Both urban or suburban schools often have 45% to 80% of students transferring in and out. Addressing this problem in the 1930s, one prominent educator said,

> The notion that each community must have a curriculum all its own is not only silly, but tragic. It neglects two important needs...the need of a democracy for many common elements in the culture of all the people [so that they] may discuss collective problems in terms that will convey common meanings...[and] the need of recognizing the American people simply will not 'stay put'...Under these conditions, failure to have a goodly measure of uniformity in school subjects and grade placement is a gross injustice...[13]

"High academic skill is based upon broad general knowledge. Someone once asked Boris Goldovsky how he could play the piano so brilliantly with such small hands. His reply was: 'Where in the world did you get the idea that we play the piano with our hands?'"

"It's the same with reading. We read with our eyes, but also with our minds. According to the epoch-making research of Thomas Sticht, by seventh grade, most children, even those who read badly, have already attained the technical proficiency they need. Their reading and their listening show the same rate and level of comprehension; thus the mechanics of reading are not the limiting factor. What is lacking in poor readers is a broad, reading vocabulary. Broad vocabulary means broad knowledge. To know a lot of words, you have to know a lot of things. Thus, broad general knowledge is an **essential** requisite to superior reading skill and is indirectly related to the skills that accompany it."

"Is that why we are told to read to our children every day?" Maria asked.

"Exactly. Superior reading skill is known to be highly correlated with most other academic skills, like writing, solving problems, and thinking critically. To concentrate on reading is to focus implicitly on a whole range of educational issues. It's sometimes claimed today, but not backed up with research, that knowledge changes so rapidly in our world that we should not get bogged down with mere information. And since information quickly becomes obsolete, it is more important to learn accessing skills (how to look things up or how to use a calculator) than to learn mere facts. However, psychological research doesn't support this claim.

"I received a letter from a head reference librarian that illustrates this point. He was a specialist in accessing knowledge. He was distressed because young people are being trained as reference specialists with so little general knowledge that they cannot effectively help the public access knowledge. His direct experience caused him to reject the theory that education is only the gaining of accessing skills. In fact, the opposite inference should be drawn from our fast-changing world. The fundamentals of science change very slowly; those of elementary math hardly at all. The famous names of geography and history (the 'leaves' of that knowledge tree) change faster (but not 'root' and 'branch' from year to year). A wide range of this stable, fundamental knowledge is the key to rapid adaptation and the learning of new skills. It is precisely because the needs of a modern economy are so changeable that one needs broad general knowledge in order to flourish. Only high literacy, which implies broad general knowledge, provides the flexibility to learn new things fast. The only known route to broad general knowledge for all is for a nation's schools to provide all students with a substantial, solid core of knowledge."

Lenora was getting angrier. "Wait a minute, Dr. Hirsch! Why haven't we been told this before? You mean that my babies don't learn this basic knowledge from our teachers and that's why they'll fall behind and eventually drop out? It's not because they're stupid or dumb, but because the school doesn't teach them the foundation knowledge all through school? If this is true, I want to sue someone's ass. I really feel betrayed. You're a teacher in this school, Delores. What do you say?"

"I don't know what to say, Lenora," said Delores. "I was trained to teach at the university in one way, and I've been teaching that way for seven years. I know these kids aren't learning much, but I thought it was because of our class sizes. We don't have teacher aides, and most of the children come from disadvantaged homes and parents that don't care or have little education themselves. I thought it might be because we don't have all the computers and modern equipment the wealthier White students do. How do other schools do it, Don?"

"The outside assessments of Core Curriculum Schools are just coming out," said Dr. Hirsch, "and they provide strong evidence that these schools are working. In San Antonio, Hawthorne Elementary showed significant increases in reading and mathematics on the 1994 Texas Assessment of Academic Skills.[14] In Maryland, a study of six Core Curriculum Schools will be published soon also showing increases in student academic achievement. But I'm not satisfied with our internal curricular assessments. We are turning to the question of quality control—what is the most effective delivery of the curriculum materials for each grade level and sequence.

"What we know now is that common content leads to higher school morale, as well as to better teaching and learning. At every Core Knowledge School, a sense of community and common purpose knits people together. Clear content guidelines encourage those who teach at the same grade level to collaborate. They create effective lesson plans and schoolwide activities together. A clear sense of purpose encourages cooperation among all grades. Because the Core Knowledge Sequence makes no requirements about how the specified knowledge should be presented, each school and each teacher have great scope for independence and creativity. Core Knowledge Schools have site-based governance, and their definite aims give a sense of communal purpose.

"How many of you on this Citizens' Commission are also parents?" asked Dr. Hirsch.

All but two raised their hands. "I could show you letters from frustrated parents who write and complain that they have no idea what their child will be learning during the year, and their principal is not able to tell them either. A mother of identical twins wrote that her children had been placed in different classrooms, and they were learning completely different things. Such incoherence is typical of elementary education in the United States today. It places enormous burdens on teachers. Students are so diverse

BEST PRACTICES: HAWTHORNE ELEMENTARY SCHOOL

Hawthorne Elementary School is one of 65 elementary schools in the San Antonio Independent School District (SAISD) of Texas. SAISD has a population of about 60,000 students, with Hawthorne itself serving 500 students in pre K-5. Its enrollment is 94 percent Hispanic (25 percent are Limited English Proficient (LEP) students), 2 percent Black, 3 percent White and 1 percent Asian. Nearly all students receive free or reduced lunches. Only 60% of its students are stable throughout the year, with 40% mobile or transient. The per pupil expenditure is approximately $4,900 annually—to the district average is $5,500.

It is not surprising that Hawthorne has been among the lowest achieving elementary schools in SAISD. In 1991, for example, Hawthorn ranked 41st among 65 district schools. As teachers became increasingly alarmed about their students' achievement levels, they realized that their curriculum defined only broad skills and objectives that resulted in great disparity between what students learned.

Teachers and administrators began searching for some core of specific content that they could agree on and teach at appropriate levels. They finally adopted the Core Knowledge Sequence, a content-based K-6 curriculum model based on ideas of Hirsch's *Cultural Literacy: What Every American Needs to Know*. The grade-by-grade model curriculum provides teachers with a program that all children can build upon year by year. This content includes literature, American and world civilization, science and technology, fine arts, and mathematics.

In the beginning, teachers and administrators formed a committee to discuss how Core Knowledge could be integrated into their existing curriculum. They found that change was not easy because so many were already comfortable with the teacher's editions and the units they'd taught in the past. But as they delved into Core Knowledge, as one teacher stated, "It is the integrated 'good stuff' that we all ought to be teaching."

It took many meetings for the committee to begin putting the specific content into monthly theme-based units. After much discussion—and "several confessions of our own ignorance about some topics"—the teachers came up with a "scope-and-sequence" centered around school-wide themes. With this rough plan, committee members called meetings with their grade levels and worked out remaining issues. Over the summer, teachers began to develop new units for nearly every month of the year. "It would have been overwhelming if we hadn't shared to the work," one teacher commented.

"I've never been more excited about teaching than I have been since using this program," she said. "But any doubts were eliminated when school began. Our questions were answered as our children's enthusiasm for learning skyrocketed! All students began to share enough common reference points to enable everyone to understand and learn, even though at differing rates and in response to varied approaches.

"I could see that when this commonality of knowledge is lacking, progress in learning is slow compared with systems using a core curriculum. Just as learning is cumulative, so are learning deficits. We'd seen the progressively widening gap between advantaged and disadvantaged children. Lack of learning in the early grades usually has, in comparative terms, a negatively cumulative effect. The only way to close this knowledge deficit is to set forth explicit, year-by-year knowledge standards in early grades, so that all educators, parents and children understand exactly what is being taught and what is to be mastered by all students."

Using data from the Texas Assessment of Academic Skills (TAAS), a revised criterion-referenced statewide testing program, the Hawthorne school has succeeded in raising achievement levels beyond the aggregate performance of other schools in the district with respect to reading. These findings support a central assumption of the Core Knowledge theory—that a sequenced curriculum will lead to steady increases in achievement, grade by grade. These findings also suggest that "schooling over time" with a curriculum-sequencing effect can overcome the negative influence of poverty and educational deprivation of children who enter school far below the academic standing of their more advantaged peers.

and so unevenly prepared at each grade level that teachers find it almost impossible to create learning communities. **The most significant diversity faced by our schools is not cultural diversity but, rather, diversity of aca-**

demic preparation.[15] To achieve excellence and fairness for all, an elementary school must have a coherent sequence of solid, specific content to follow!" Here is an example of one Core Knowledge School that made this work."

"Dr. Hirsch, Don, I'm a new third grade teacher at Jefferson," said Tamar. "How can we become a Core Knowledge School?"

"Tamar, the process of becoming a Core Knowledge School, the engagement process, is divided into three distinct phases—Consensus Building, Planning, and Implementing—that include seven steps. When you decide what you want to do, please get in touch with us. We'll get someone to come and make a presentation and answer your questions in detail. We feel that the Core Curriculum approach can reform American education. I've really enjoyed discussing this reform strategy with you. I wish you good luck in your mission. We'll all be watching for your report."

Wendy spoke up. "Thank you for meeting with us, Dr. Hirsch. You have given us much to think about as it applies to Jefferson Elementary School. Nate, could you present a summary of what we've heard about national academic standards from Dr. Ravitch and core curriculum from Dr. Hirsch?"

Summary

"Of course, Wendy, " Nate said. "We've had another power-packed Hearing today. **Dr. Diane Ravitch made several key points. Educational progressivism, now the tradition in public schools, has led to whole language reading, abhorrence of a well-defined academic curriculum, teaching social studies instead of history, and language arts instead of English. It has also led to social promotion, lax grading standards, and a laissez-faire attitude toward student misbehavior. This life-adjustment, child-centered curriculum has no foundation in research. It has produced a generation of children without the cultural literacy needed to survive and to prosper.**

"**The National Assessments of Educational Progress (NAEP) demonstrates that America's students are not learning at high levels, but this fact has no impact on public educational policy in this country. Parents should have the right to transfer their children from failing progressive schools to alternative schools, charter schools or private schools. Dr. Ravitch also emphasized that a quality education requires high national academic standards for all students. Our competitors are using interna-**

tionally-recognized academic standards to educate their students. The U.S. Department of Education and private foundations are providing funding for professional education groups and some states that are developing the challenging academic standards for math, science, arts education, geography, civics, economics, and history. These will eventually be adapted to classroom curricula.

"Don Hirsch believes that children from every ethnic and cultural background should learn a shared core of knowledge that facilitates understanding and communication. His Core Curriculum Foundation has designed an effective, standards-based academic curriculum for all elementary grades. Careful outside assessments show that his program dramatically raises achievement scores among students of all backgrounds, especially the disadvantaged. The Core Curriculum presents an integrated and grade-by-grade educational strategy that tells parents and teachers what should be learned in any given grade. High academic skill is based on the accumulation of broad general knowledge. Lastly, the Core Knowledge Foundation has a field-tested program that provides classroom curricula, books and materials to hundreds of rural, suburban and urban elementary schools throughout the United States."

Wendy smiled. "Thank you, Nate, for that great summary. It's time for lunch. Check your partner assignments. We'll see you back here at 1:00 p.m."

As the Commissioners broke for lunch, Kathryn Jones and a friend from the Christian Coalition approached Dr. E.D. Hirsch. They began an animated conversation about academic standards. After five minutes of intense discussion, Kathryn and her friend smiled, shook hands with Dr. Hirsch and left the building. They would return for the afternoon Hearing.

****

Chapter 6
COMPREHENSIVE SCHOOL REFORM
Saturday afternoon, November 23

After lunch, Wendy called the Commission to order. "I'd like to introduce our next guest.[1] John Anderson is president of New American Schools (NAS)—a non-profit, bipartisan, public-private partnership. NAS is a design-based, technical assistance organization that advances 'whole-school reform.' Its mission is to create and disseminate bold designs for high-quality, accountable schools that improve student achievement. Welcome to our Citizens' Commission Hearing, John. Could you start by telling us how New American Schools came into being?"

New American Schools

"Thank you, Wendy, and Citizens' Commission members. New American Schools was founded in 1991 by corporate and foundation leaders. Its broad mission is to create schools and districts capable of educating all students at high levels. We believe that all children can reach higher standards. Our founders laid out a plan to invest in high-quality school improvement designs that could help schools transform themselves into high-performance learning environments through whole-school reform. They used a venture capital model of investment: at each stage of development they examined the success of each design and continued to fund only those that demonstrated real potential for making schools work."

"How is this different from other reform approaches?" Debbie Cohen asked.

"Well, Debbie, the first thing that makes it different is the unprecedented commitment by prominent business and education leaders who wanted to make a substantial contribution to the improvement of American public education. Second, unlike many reforms which are add-on programs or isolated projects, the new American School designs aim to improve the whole school, from curricula and instruction to funding and community participation.

"When the organization was founded, we put out a Request for Proposals, called RFP in 'Washingtonese,' to all interested parties. It generated nearly 700 design submissions, each with a team representing education, business, community, universities, and social services. In June 1992, eleven of these Design Teams were selected to participate in Phase I, which was a year for developing the ideas into workable school-based programs. In June 1993, nine of these designs were selected for Phase II. Over the next two years, the nine Design Teams worked with 147 schools in 19 states. They field-tested their designs in partnership with teachers, administrators, parents, and students. In June 1995, seven New American Schools Design Teams were chosen to participate in Phase III. This phase is now testing our fundamental assumption: we can help large numbers of schools become high-performance learning environments by investing in the development of high-quality designs and in building school and district capacity to implement these designs."[2]

"What do these Design Teams do, Mr. Anderson?" Lenora asked.

"Our seven Design Teams use different methods, philosophies, and styles because we believe no single approach will succeed for all schools. Giving schools the opportunity and the responsibility to choose from a wide range of designs is fundamental to successful change. The designs provide a diversity of approaches that we believe most communities and schools will find compelling, and even exciting. They reflect our belief that reform of our nation's schools must be built on the actions of individual schools to transform themselves. With our assistance and support, they can become highly-effective learning environments capable of helping all students perform at high levels. Our mission lies in helping schools achieve this transformation. Each design offers schools a distinctive vision coupled with materials and assistance. Each permits considerable adaptation to fit a particular school culture and set of needs. As a school implements a design, it maintains an ongoing relationship with the Design Team. The school, not the Team, has ownership of the change process. The principles and vision of the design serve as a framework for change."

"How are these Design Teams funded?" asked Paul.

"NAS funded Phases I and II, the design and development phases. In Phase III or 'scale-up' phase, we have provided some core funding for Design Teams to support their transition to self sufficient organizations. Increasingly, however, a large share of design costs will be covered by fees-for-services paid by participating schools using funding from local, state, and federal programs. These teams are developing the capacity to market their designs and to provide ongoing technical assistance to increasingly more schools."

"What problems do you see to scaling-up? And how do you plan to make a big national impact using the seven Design Teams?" asked Ray.

"Well, let's first look at the importance of scaling-up. As we've considered our larger mission, it's apparent that a strategy focusing on only a handful of model schools would operate on the margins and benefit only a small number of children. These model schools would be the exception, not the rule.

"We've learned a lot from the large numbers of high-performance schools, inspired by and using New American Schools designs. Initially these schools were operating in environments where many barriers had to be overcome. We know that New American Schools' vision of high-performance schools can only be realized if a significant number of individual schools within a district change—a critical mass—and the policy and operating environment of the district change as well. Let's take a few examples. State and local policies often promote uniformity rather than diversity among schools in different communities. Many policies also promote regulations that fragment and diffuse reform efforts and work against strategic planning for improvement. Many schools lack the authority or flexibility to make decisions about their curriculum, staffing, schedules, budgets, and other fundamental aspects of schooling. In many cases, our nation's human services systems play an essential role in preparing children for learning and helping families support their children, but they too often work in isolation from the schools.

"Ray, we have four goals for achieving the New American Schools mission. First, we have to build a demand for better schools among the parents, teachers, business leaders, and communities. Second, we must meet that demand by making our designs, and others like them, available to large numbers of schools. Third, we must work with education, policy, business, and community leaders within school communities to create conditions that would support the transformation of these schools. Fourth, we must carefully document the process and measure the results. Then we must tell the story to the public."

"That's an ambitious agenda," said Paul. "Where are your schools operating?"

"In late 1994, New American Schools developed a process for selecting locations around the country to participate as partners in scale-up. We focused on a small number of school communities—states, districts, or groups of districts. We chose those that demonstrated the potential for widespread school improvement and for a supportive operating environment during the next five years. These states and districts serve as models for other communities across the country. After an intensive process of site visits, interviews, and proposal reviews, the ten school communities chosen to participate in the scale-up of NAS designs include: Cincinnati, Ohio; Dade County, Florida; Memphis, Tennessee; Philadelphia and Pittsburgh, Pennsylvania; San Antonio, Texas; and San Diego, California; selected districts in Kentucky and Maryland; and the Washington Alliance for Better Schools, which includes five districts in the Seattle area.

"Let me go over this short handout that describes the seven Design Teams participating in scale-up effort, as well as our two major partners:

- **ATLAS Communities** (based in Boston, Massachusetts) combines the work of Ted Sizer, James Comer, Howard Gardner, and the Educational Development Center. The design's goal is to create a unified, supportive school community of learners in each K through 12 feeder pattern which includes a curriculum based on deep exploration of essential questions, collaborative school governance, social service coordination, and parent involvement. ATLAS is now operating in 44 schools in Maryland, Memphis, Philadelphia, and Washington State.[3] (see Chapter 9 for a BEST PRACTICES Comer School—a key component of the ATLAS design).

- **Audrey Cohen College** (based in New York City) organizes curriculum and instruction around a single purpose each semester that focuses learning on student-directed projects and communication related to all aspects involving the larger community. Students demonstrate mastery of skills through an interdisciplinary project related to their purpose. Audrey Cohen College teams are working in 15 schools in Dade County, Florida, Memphis, San Diego, and Washington State. Here is a BEST PRACTICES handout.

BEST PRACTICES:
THE AUDREY COHEN COLLEGE DESIGN

Franklin Elementary School is in California's San Diego Unified School District. One of 114 elementary schools in the District, Franklin serves 620 students with a faculty of 26 teachers. The racial and ethnic composition of the student body is Hispanic (40%), Caucasian (23%), African American (19%), and Indochinese/Filipino/Asian (18%). Nearly 81% of these students receive free or reduced-price lunch. The average per pupil expenditure is $3,110.

Franklin Elementary is located in an ethnically-diverse residential area. Most children walk to this neighborhood school from their homes. Although mainly single-family dwellings, many are rentals. Even so, the student body is very stable, with 80% of the students remaining throughout the year. Some families decide to stay in the district so that their children can attend Franklin rather than send them to magnet or private schools. As one parent puts it, "I like Franklin because it gets the children involved more and gives a structure to the classrooms. It is very meaningful. My child is learning more in this school than any other school because of the focus of the System."

In 1993 Judith Brings, principal, and her faculty selected the Audrey Cohen College Design after researching different approaches to improving student achievement. They were impressed with **Purpose-Centered Education.** The Purpose contributes positively to the community or larger society. Every semester teachers and students address one of 24 pre-determined, enriching, developmentally-appropriate Purposes. For example, teachers and students use 'We Work for Good Health' as an overarching Purpose for one semester in the fourth grade.

They saw the **Constructive Action** component as a way students can learn to plan and implement a response to a challenge they identify in the community that relates to the semester's Purpose. During that term, in and outside the classroom, students develop knowledge and skills to help them address the challenge or problem and then assess their results. In the early grades, the Constructive Actions are group- rather than individual-oriented. Mrs. Brings notes that, with this collaborative approach, teachers together generate new, innovative thoughts, ideas, and strategies. The more experienced teachers mentor the newer ones. In turn, the students develop leadership, citizenship, organizational, and interpersonal skills as they learn how to set goals, solve problems, and plan. As one teacher comments, "My students are excited about making an impact and positive changes in their community. They really feel empowered."

Students take Dimension classes instead of taking classes by subject area. These classes focus learning on the semester's Purpose and integrate all required core subjects. This provides the opportunity for students to develop the knowledge and skills necessary for carrying out the semester's Purpose in the community or larger world. The five **Dimensions of Learning, Action, and Assessment**[sm] are consistent across the grades. They include the Purpose Dimension, Values and Ethics Dimension, Self and Others,[sm] Systems Dimension,[sm] and the Skills Dimension. [sm] Students examine perspectives from history, literature, philosophy, and government to help bring ethical considerations into decisions they make to achieve their Purposes. For example, in studying the values of environmental protection, they explore the shrinking rain forest and its impact on the quality of life.

Judith Brings is enthusiastic about other strengths of the Audrey Cohen College approach, stating that, "Its student-centered curriculum has students take charge of their own learning and assess their own work. They learn to work together as they analyze, plan, and implement a Constructive Action within the community. It also teaches students what a system is and how to work through it—knowledge that they will need for work and life." When asked about areas of improvement, Mrs. Brings mentions the need to avoid habit or repetition in Constructive Actions by adding new people to the "mix of old relationships" so that new thoughts and approaches are stimulated. She also is encouraging teachers to "let go further" so that students take charge of their own learning.

Students' Constructive Actions demonstrate "authentic performance" of what they have learned. In addition to self assessments, they also receive feedback from teachers. In evaluating the progress of their students, teachers use the College's checklist of essential Purpose Achievement Abilities [sm]. Both teachers and students benefit from unsolicited community feedback. Purpose speakers from the community, for example, frequently praise students' depth of learning, so evident from the informed questions they ask related to their Purposes.

Generally, teachers feel that students "seem more focused" because of the Purposes; even their "attendance is good." As one student puts it, "The new System is kind of hard but I like it very much. I like it because we learn more about other cultures and communities...It's not boring."

- **Co-NECT Schools** (based in Cambridge, Massachusetts) uses technology as a tool for learning and communication related to all aspects of a project-based and interdisciplinary curriculum. Students stay with the same teacher for at least two years. The design was developed by BBN Corporation, a high-technology company that helped develop the Internet. The Co-Nect design is being implemented in 36 school districts in Cincinnati, Dade County, Florida, Memphis, Philadelphia, and San Antonio. I have a handout for this one also.

BEST PRACTICES: THE Co-NECT SCHOOL DESIGN

Kilgour Elementary is a neighborhood school in an urban setting of Cincinnati, Ohio. It is one of 83 schools in the Cincinnati Public School District. Its 24 teachers serve 442 students, nearly half (47%) of whom receive free or reduced-price lunches. The student body is mostly White (53%) and Black (46%) with a few Asian (.6%) and Hispanic (.2%). The student/teacher ratio is 22:1 for kindergarten and 23:1 in regular classes of other grades. Average per pupil expenditure is $6,700.

Since it began in 1922, Kilgour Elementary has had a tradition of high academic achievement. In 1992 the U.S. Department of Education recognized Kilgour as a Blue Ribbon School of Excellence. Over the years, the school has developed several distinguishing features. Its teachers know each student and his/her contribution to Kilgour. Teachers are highly competent, dedicated to educating the "whole child," and carefully build a sense of comraderie that contributes to a close-knit, supportive school learning environment. The school stresses multicultural education so that students are informed and appreciative of their own and others' backgrounds, fosters active involvement of parents, and emphasizes giving to the neighborhood through community service projects. This practice has created strong support and involvement within the community.

Even with its fine record of academic achievements, in 1995 Mary Ronan, Kilgour's new principal, and her staff looked for a program that would help them continue challenging students to achieve at their highest levels of learning. "We were impressed that Co-NECT provides a comprehensive, technology-supported framework for school-wide restructuring," reflected Ms. Ronan.

They selected the Co-NECT design to revitalize teaching and learning with advanced technology and sustained professional development. Co-NECT focuses on significantly improving student achievement by integrating project-based learning, comprehensive assessment, cluster-based school organization, and the best available interactive technologies. Faculty representatives of each cluster serve on a school Design Team. Led by the principal, with input from parents and other community members, the team sets overall goals and monitors results.

Kilgour is just beginning its second year in the program. Students work not by themselves, but rather in groups taught by teachers in cross-disciplinary teams. The teacher role has shifted from the traditional "teacher-as-teller" to a participating facilitator and coach. Most students remain with the same teachers for more than one year. Also the curriculum, which focuses on authentic, interdisciplinary projects, seems to be meaningful and exciting to the students. In addition, the school has just been wired and computers have been installed in classrooms. As Co-NECT links subjects and people in and out of the school setting, it helps to create a total educational environment. One of the big advantages of Co-NECT, according to one teacher of 26 years, is "[a Co-NECT] consultant is available in school each month. We have almost immediate access to help…they seem as interested in the children as in having a successful project."

Kilgour's principal and faculty continue to search for effective ways of measuring student achievement. To eliminate the overemphasis on multiple-choice testing over the last 30 years, the Co-NECT design has involved teachers from the start of the program. They are trained to administer and score assessments of student progress by looking at a range of evaluations from standardized test scores, proficiency tests and promotion rates, to projects and portfolios. Kilgour students show significant gains. In 1995-96, for example, 83% of fourth graders passed proficiency tests in writing and math, 87% in reading, and 92% in citizenship. Of students taking the California Achievement Test, 80% tested above the national norm in mathematics (1994-95). They were especially proud of their National Chemistry Week winner in 1995.

The principal, teachers, and parents see students acquiring new skills and adopting new attitudes toward school and schoolwork. They report fewer student behavior problems and disciplinary incidents. Teachers see students assuming new responsibility for their own learning and taking ownership of the work. In the multi-grade classrooms, a feeling of support and family between students of different ages is developing. Younger students are learning more mature behavior and older students are adopting nurturing and mentoring relationships with younger students.

When asked how they could have improved the program, Ms. Ronan said, "by providing extensive staff inservice, particularly in the areas of multi-age and looping, before embarking on the overall restructuring." The teachers are highly trained and dedicated, boasting a 97% daily attendance rate. Parents at the school seem to think, as one parent puts it, that "Kilgour is a great place to learn and grow up." Some attribute part of this public school's success to the increase in parent involvement and to its PTA, which "has a great reputation for active involvement in the school." Volunteers share expertise with students, monitor computer labs, share resources, plan and implement field experiences, and help evaluate student projects. The forging of new community relationships has benefits that include partnerships with PNC Bank, our Partner-in-Education, and even schools abroad in "sister cities," such as Gifu, Japan, and Otjiwarongo, Namibia, Africa.

- **Expeditionary Learning Outward Bound** (based in Cambridge, Massachusetts) offers a curriculum centered around learning expeditions that develop intellectual and physical skills and character. The design is based on the principles of the Outward Bound program and offers a deep and focused curriculum, flexible scheduling, and multi-year student teacher assignments. Expeditionary

BEST PRACTICES: THE EXPEDITIONARY LEARNING OUTWARD BOUND DESIGN

Table Mound Elementary—"It's right for kids!"—is an "L-shaped," one-story school on the southwest side of Dubuque, Iowa. It is one of 12 elementary schools in the Dubuque Community School District. Officially opened in October 1960, Table Mound Elementary now serves 416 students, of whom 98% are Caucasian and 2% minority. Students travel from distant farms and nearby housing developments. Nearly 30% receive free or reduced-price lunches. The average per pupil expenditure is $5,000.

In May 1993, Table Mound became an Expeditionary Learning Outward Bound (ELOB) school, and divided into "learning communities" of several grades—K-2, 3-4 and 5-6. Today it is a leader among schools in the District and the tri-state area in Expeditionary Learning. Kris L. Hall, principal, said that Table Mound was drawn to this particular "break-the-mold" design for several reasons. First, it places equal value on students' character and intellectual development. Second, it recognizes the importance of creating a school culture that incorporates ELOB's ten design principles and key program components, such as Primacy of Self Discovery, Having Wonderful Ideas, Responsibility for Learning, Collaboration and Competition, Service and Compassion. Third, it sees learning as "an expedition into the unknown" and uses hands-on projects that call for intellectual inquiry, physical exploration, and community service to explore topics and themes. Fourth, it acknowledges many routes to learning. And, fifth, it assumes that all children can learn.

Like other Expeditionary Learning Outward Bound schools, Table Mound and its individual classrooms are structured with flexible sites, timetables, and student groupings. Students are not separated into "ability groups" by a tracking system. They work individually, in small groups, and in the larger group, drawing upon the strengths of a whole class. Students work with the same peers and team of teachers for more than one year. Students and their teachers are engaged in "field assignments," some of which take them outside the school building. As one third grader put it, "You don't just read things in books like female guppies are green. You go look at guppies or you raise some yourself."

Teachers are the driving force in the ELOB schools. Because they are the developers of curriculum, ELOB provides extensive professional development activities, such as summer planning institutes (5 to 10 days), summits for immersion in a discipline or topic (1 week), and Outward Bound wilderness courses. They share planning time, work collaboratively through team teaching, and participate in shared decision-making. They see their role as designers of Expeditionary Learning curricula and guides of learning expeditions, in addition to such initiatives as school/business partnerships and mentoring. Instead of working in isolation, they work closely with colleagues, family, and community members.

Learning expeditions are the major vehicle for teaching and learning in ELOB's Table Mound Elementary. Expeditions include one or more major projects and are characterized by active learning of academic content, different formats for assessment, extensive use of community resources (libraries, museums, experts), emphasis on character development and community service. The science topics range from insects, pond and plant life, to mammals and rockets. In discussing the exciting involvement of children in these expeditions, one teacher said, "As for my expedition on dinosaurs, my students absolutely 'ran with it!' They will be crushed when it is over. Their knowledge of this era could easily rival any adult's!" In social studies, expeditions focus on such topics as Native Americans, the Civil War and urban renewal. In a fourth grade expedition, *Have You Heard the News?*, students investigated the proposed budget cuts for education in their city. After researching the issues, students wrote letters to city council members and staged a mock hearing on the budget, taking the positions of various stakeholders. The superintendent even came to answer students' questions.

Since there are many routes to knowledge, Table Mound teachers have decided to have rigorous standards, set high-performance thresholds, and assess students' performance using portfolios, critique sessions, performance tasks, benchmarks, evaluation conferences, and self-evaluations. Many teachers involve parents and other community members in the review of portfolios, often at parent-teacher conferences. From 1993 to 1995, the Iowa Test of Basic Skills shows some improvements in reading and mathematics by fourth and fifth graders. A longitudinal evaluation of sixth graders (1992-95) shows slight improvement in reading and math.

Parent involvement is important to Table Mound Elementary. Since the introduction of ELOB, they have hundreds of parents enthusiastically participating. Parents are actively involved in classroom activities related to expeditions and student exhibitions and performances. A few are part of the School Improvement Council, a governing board that develops the school improvement plan. The school also has improved communication with parents about curricular goals and content. After moving from Dubuque, one parent wrote, "Learning will never have the same excitement, wonderment, or satisfaction that we experienced with expeditionary learning!"

Learning Outward Bound designs are now operating in 24 schools, including Cincinnati; Dade County, Florida; Maryland; Memphis; San Antonio; and Washington State. Here's another handout for you.

- **Modern Red Schoolhouse** (based in Indianapolis, Indiana) is a research-based design that helps all students achieve high standards through the development of standards-driven curriculum. The design employs traditional and performance-based assessments, and uses effective organizational patterns and professional development programs. It also implements effective community involvement strategies. Students master a rigorous curriculum designed to transmit a common culture, develop character, and promote the principles of democratic government. These elements of the traditional red schoolhouse are combined with a high level of flexibility in organizing instruction and deploying resources; use of innovative teaching methodologies; student groupings for continuous progress; and advanced technology as a learning and instructional management tool (see Chapter 5 for BEST PRACTICES example on a Hirsch Core Curriculum School).

- **The National Alliance for Restructuring Education** (based in Washington, D.C.) places school-level transformation in the context of broader systems change. States and districts working with the Alliance organize around broad principles of high performance and structure central offices and schools around high standards for students. The National Alliance is active in 129 schools in Kentucky, Pittsburgh, San Diego, and Washington State. I also have a BEST PRACTICES handout for you."

BEST PRACTICES: THE NATIONAL ALLIANCE FOR RESTRUCTURING EDUCATION DESIGN

Jackson Elementary is located at the top of a hill in Everett, a scenic suburb of Seattle, Washington. Originally built in 1948, Jackson was extensively remodeled and wired for technology four years ago. It overlooks Mt. Baker and Port Gardner Bay. Recent economic setbacks have brought change to the area. While it still retains pockets of affluence, the surrounding community encompasses low-income neighborhoods and several homeless shelters.

Everett School District serves 17,000 students in 24 schools. Jackson Elementary's 22 teachers and 37 staff service an average of 550 students, with another 250 who come and go throughout the year. Over half of the students (54%) qualify for free/reduced lunches. The student population is 82% Caucasian and 18% minority, including 6% Native American, 5% Hispanic, 4% African American, and 3% Pacific Islander.

In 1992 Washington state received a grant and selected Jackson Elementary as an Apple Classroom of Tomorrow (ACOT). Through the ACOT training, Jackson teachers were exposed to the "units of study" component conducted by the National Alliance for Restructuring Education. Linda Fisher, principal of Jackson for eight years, explained, "That [units of study] piece was difficult because we didn't know what standards were [at that time]. We didn't have state or district standards. We were struggling with 'what do we call a standard?' Things began to clear up when our district began to align everything for us. Now we have published documents for each grade level that align national, state, and district standards...state assessments are now being piloted."

The Alliance design has added structure that helped Jackson Elementary prioritize and integrate activities. It showed that systemic reform must proceed on more than just one front. Using the Alliance Design, Jackson organized its school structure around the five design tasks: standards and assessment, learning environments, community services and supports, public engagement, and high-performance management. They learned about high-performance management and site-based budgeting. "When money was released at the building level, we learned to juggle things as needed. We learned how to make group decisions and how to use our time as a staff differently—as a learning organization rather than a more traditional centralized administrative organization," said Ms. Fisher.

The District was impressed with the quality of training and began to access more Alliance trainers. In 1994 the National Alliance invited Jackson Elementary to be a demonstration site. Jackson's School Development Center (SDC) now trains teachers from around the country to integrate technology, "the catalyst for change," into the school program by connecting the teaching and learning to standards. The SCD learned the importance of getting principals to their Alliance training. "The more deeply involved the principals are, the better the model works when the teachers go back to the school," stated Ms. Fisher. Principals learned what the teachers' needs were going to be and how best to support them looking different—"going outside the box."

Every staff member is responsible for student learning. Everyone working at the school participates in their yearly staff retreat. Their team format—two to four people working together—has expanded. "It used to be that half a class would walk out with different specialists. Last year, we assigned each support person to a small teaching team. Now they don't go to 18 or 20 teachers, they only serve two to four teachers. We've tried to embed them inside the classroom instead of pulling out kids. They provide support in all basic skill areas not just reading or math. It's more integrated and exciting and is working well. You rarely see a classroom with only one adult anymore, which gives more support for kids and for teachers."

In discussing the challenges facing Jackson Elementary, Ms. Fisher stated, "We've a whole range of progress among our teachers…my philosophy has been to let people get on board at their own pace. When they're ready and we've provided the training [they'll begin to move]." Another targeted area is public engagement. "We're struggling to get two parents to participate on our site-based council. It's hard to consistently get parents from the at-risk population." Once they get parents and families at the school, they are trying to figure out what to tell them that would keep them coming—a dual purpose. The best motivation for getting parents and families to school seems to be good food or children performing. "At one exhibition on a unit of study, we had almost 100% attendance because the kids got so excited and got their parents there," said Ms. Fisher. "At our parent forums, 30 to 40% is usually a good turn-out."

The Alliance emphasis on measurements has helped the District increase their efforts, and regular benchmarking is occurring at different intervals, with direct assessments in third and fourth grades. As a building, Jackson sets performance goals. It is targeting an area of reading using an assessment tool called the Curriculum-based Measurement (CBM tool). "It's a tool to measure reading and math that can be easily and frequently administered. This year teachers want before and after testing to give them more regular data about what is lost over summer vacation." Each team also sets performance goals, especially for at-risk students. Last year they targeted specific kids and started probing weekly to identify their needs, what strategies were being used, and what the results were. The group met each week to learn how they could achieve greater progress.

- **Roots & Wings** (based in Baltimore, Maryland) builds upon the Success For All reading program developed by Bob Slavin and his colleagues at Johns Hopkins University. The elementary school design uses intensive instruction (including one-on-one tutoring and extended-day scheduling), an interdisciplinary science and social studies component, early childhood education, and family support services to help all students, regardless of background or challenges, perform at or above grade level. Roots and Wings is implementing its design model in New American Schools in Cincinnati; Dade County, Florida; Maryland; Memphis; San Antonio; and Washington State (see Chapter 10 for a BEST PRACTICES example of Slavin's Roots & Wings).

"Other reformers were asked to select one example of a "best practices" school using their program. I was asked to bring four examples from our seven Design Teams, and it was really hard selecting from among them.

Three other designs will be introduced at other Hearings by Dr. Slavin, the developer of the Roots and Wings design, Dr. Comer, one of the four principals associated with the ATLAS Communities Project, and the curriculum component of the Modern Red Schoolhouse design will be discussed by Dr. E.D.Hirsch. For more information on NAS and the seven Design Teams, you can also visit our Web site at www.naschools.org."

"Let me also just briefly mention our two main partners. First, **the Education Commission of the States (ECS)** is a non-profit organization based in Denver, Colorado. ECS assists governors, state legislators, state education officials, and others that develop policies to improve education. ECS helps the communications and public engagement aspects of the NAS effort, helps define policy barriers to school transformation, and enlists the support and involvement of state policymakers. ECS also plays an important role in helping to produce materials and disseminate information about the Design Teams nationwide through print, video, and electronic means.

"Second, the **RAND Corporation** has worked with NAS American Schools as a third-party evaluator and critical friend since the effort began. Working closely with the other partners and with schools implementing New American Schools designs, RAND will continue to provide feedback throughout the scale-up phase on the performance of the Design Teams and participating schools and districts. It will collect and analyze information that will help us publicly document the entire effort in a complete and accurate manner."

"What are some of the lessons you've learned in the past five years?" Paul asked. "I like this business-like approach to school reform."

"I think the first lesson," John replied, "is that there is no one formula. One size does not fit all. When we talk about changing schools and changing districts, we're finding that each has its own personality and its own culture. They can't be reformed without wanting to reform themselves and then seeking help. But they need options.

"Second, we've found that targeting an individual school for reform is not enough. You have to have systems of schools. We talk about critical mass. Schools can't do it alone. They have to have help from the districts in creating the right conditions for change.

"Third, we've found that, after an initial start-up phase, there's actually enough money in the system to do this. We don't need a massive infusion of new money. But we are talking about major rethinking of the way we spend the money. Schools must invest in transformation like businesses invest in promising ventures. This means you need to provide venture capital. It's working with school officials, who are beginning to see different ways categorical money can be spent for school change.

"Fourth, most schools not only need help from their districts, but they also need outside help in adapting these designs to their school culture. This is why NAS has supported the development of seven design-based organizations, each prepared to provide technical assistance to schools and districts. This will help them to adopt the best model and adapt it to their circumstances. This means that a significant portion (80%) of the school staff must be committed and take ownership before a team will even choose to focus its attention on improving that particular school.

"Fifth, reforms will only work if schools are committed enough to pay for it. Years of soft-money support reforms have not resulted in significant and sustained improvement. We will only work, therefore, in districts where schools are willing to pay for this assistance, and where the district is committing to involve at least 30% of its schools over the next five years.

"How are you assessing the programs so far?" asked Paul.

"RAND did a formative assessment of progress made during Phase II or the demonstration phase. They found that success of the NAS Design Teams varied according to school staffs' capability to implement the design, and to the team's readiness, choice of design and approach to development, and effectiveness in communicating the vision and specific implementation strategy. The teams also varied in their capacity to initially provide technical assistance. They've benefited from feedback on the demonstration phase, however, and are successfully moving forward in the scale-up phase.[4] Early evidence demonstrated that all seven Design Teams can and do result in improved teaching and learning environments and improved student performance. RAND will continue to evaluate and annually report on student results and implementation progress during the next four years."

"But what barriers in the schools did your Design Teams find?" asked Debbie.

"We identified several significant barriers to change in Phase II, Debbie. For example, professional development of teachers varied widely and was unfocused. The school culture sometimes clashed with that of the Design Team. Also schools and teams often were unable to address issues of public engagement that could threaten success of the reform initiative. We have learned that successful design implementation activities which lead to permanent changes in the culture of a school, require a new vision of professionalism in which teachers take greater responsibility for all school functions. **The key roles for the Design Teams, therefore, are to provide quality, focused professional training; to help establish critical information systems; to develop and support new forms of interaction between parents, teachers, and students; and to manage quality-control mechanisms for the delivery of high-quality curriculum and instruction."**

"What's your biggest challenge in working with schools?" Ray asked.

"Well, we know the question of how to hold schools accountable for improving student performance is perhaps the central issue facing reformers and policymakers. We've learned through our experience that school-level accountability must be coupled with school-level autonomy. Such autonomy involves:

- Substantial control over budgeting and spending within the school. An investment policy that earmarks funds for school transformation and renewal;

- Substantial power to hire, organize, and release staff. Focused designed-based support for ongoing professional development of teachers;

- Control over the curriculum and instructional strategies used in a school, as long as they are consistent with public standards for school performance. This means higher academic standards and a reliable and aligned system of assessment;

- Freedom to organize the school's schedule and teacher and student assignments;

- Freedom to extend performance standards beyond those that are required by the state;

- Substantial freedom to devise the specific means to show accountability to the community beyond those means required by the state or the district;

- Opportunities for students (and their parents) to choose to attend or leave the school, and

- A system to engage parents, teachers, and citizens in school improvement efforts; and

Paul liked what he heard. He egged John on. "These qualities of autonomy sound just like our discussion last month of the advantages of a charter school," Paul said.

Ray's hand went up. "John, these lessons you're learning about whole-school reform strategies are a great summary of what our Citizens' Commission has been hearing from national school reformers. They haven't been this comprehensive or clear about all the pieces, but I'm amazed at the extent of agreement around what is required for systemic reform. It seems that we know how to improve individual schools. It also seems that we run into barriers when we try to change individual schools without getting cooperation from higher authorities—the district, the state and the federal government. These regulatory bodies can shut down a successful reform that is well underway by regulating conditions counter to what is necessary to make reform successful. But how do you get agreement? How do you negotiate with the higher authorities or the school itself so that you don't get cut down just as you really get underway with your design activities?"

"Ray, you've asked a key question. I'm certain that all reformers believe they have the most effective model to carry out school improvement. But the big challenge is guaranteeing the support of the community, the parents, the school district superintendent and school board members, even when a majority of the teachers have voted to accept a specific design strategy. We have gradually moved to negotiating a written Memorandum of Understanding that defines the roles and expectations of all parties in the collaborative partnership to support sustained school improvement. This agreement is a catalyst to spark cooperation and consensus among all participating parties. This document of agreement describes the roles and expectations of all partners involved in the NAS effort and can be referred to when challenges arise. This agreement is required to move the vision forward and eventually change the culture of each school and the district as a whole. This is our experience!*

Wendy rose from her chair. "Thank you, John, for meeting with us. You have provided experiences and examples we need for our report on transforming Jefferson Elementary School. I'll turn the time back to Nate for our summary."

Summary

"Thank you, Wendy, **"Let me try to summarize the major points that John Anderson made. New American Schools is a nonprofit, private-public partnership that offers design-based, technical assistance. All children can reach higher levels of academic performance if we transform their schools into high-performance learning organizations. Seven new designs have been field-tested and selected because of their proven effectiveness at providing quality education programming for students across the United States. John also stressed that there is no one formula for school reform. Each school must find the approach that best fits its needs and environment. An individual school cannot be reformed long term without changing its supporting district system. Also schools must have the participation of a majority of teachers, administrators, policymakers, parents and community leaders in order to make necessary changes. Finally, schools should be held accountable for improved student achievement but they must be provided with management control over budgeting and spending, hiring and firing, organizing and training staff. They also need to manage decisions about curriculum and instructional strategies, scheduling and assignments (teacher and student), high-performance standards, school choice, and accountability standards. This comprehensive approach is often called whole-school reform."**

"Now," said Wendy, "let's share our reactions to what we've heard today. In your short summary sentence, just tell it like you feel it. Give your name."

"I'll start. I'm Ray. I'm really hopeful. We're hearing some very positive examples!"

"I'm Lenora, and this sure has been an education for me today!" she said.

"Dale. I'm beginning to think I should go back to school. This is exciting."

---

*U.S. Secretary Richard Riley, in his Fourth Annual State of American Education Address on February 18, 1997, in Atlanta, Georgia, cited New American Schools as, "…another powerful example of how change can take place. It has developed seven different, well conceived models of how to fix a failing school…That's public school choice at its best."

"I'm encouraged," said Debbie. "Some people do know how to educate disadvantaged children."

"I'm Paul. I'm impressed with what Hirsch and Anderson are doing. Keep up the good work!"

"Kim. I'm excited, but sobered about what it takes to turn a school around."

"My name is Delores. I can relate to these examples. I'm beginning to see how this could help us."

"Wendy. I'm envious of you teachers. What a great challenge!"

"I'm Kathie. I like what we've heard today."

"Ted. I'm skeptical. Guess I'm still doubtful."

"My name is Maria. I'm impatient to get started with these reforms at Jefferson."

Christina said, "I'm motivated and have high expectations for this Commission now."

"Tamar. I love this kind of day. This is why I'm a teacher. I want to make a difference in children's lives. I am deeply touched," she said.

"I'm Nate and I second all that's been said. Sometimes we stand on sacred ground with our guests who've come to testify. I salute some great and dedicated educators who are showing us the way. I'd like now to turn the time back to Ray."

"We've had another stimulating day," said Ray. "We meet next month on Saturday, December 14th. Do your holiday shopping early. We'll look at education and destructive behavior and consider another powerful strategy for reforming public schools—character education. Our guests will be Dr. Tom Lickona, director for the 4th and 5th Rs, from New York, Dr. B. David Brooks, president of the Thomas Jefferson Center for Character Education in Pasadena; and from Oakland, Dr. Eric Schaps, president of the Developmental Studies Center. Thanks also to our few stalwart community members who attended our public hearing today. See you all next month. Have a safe and happy holiday season."

Chapter 7
DESTRUCTIVE STUDENT AND CRIMINAL BEHAVIOR
Saturday morning, December 14

Christina Peterson lived alone. She was up early—habits learned long ago at the convent. After a small breakfast, she prepared to drive the short distance to Jefferson Elementary. *I'm looking forward to our discussion of character education today,* thought Christina. *I didn't know that educators had designed these value-based programs for schools. These ideas should have come from the faith communities. But I am glad educators are designing such impressive materials. Now we must start using them. So many parents need this training! I'm looking forward to another great day. This is my kind of education—it's about time we returned to basic values.*

At the same time, Dale Jones was leaving his house. The family was still sleeping as he got into his Chevy pickup. He drove six blocks to Jefferson Elementary and arrived at 7:50. Dale spotted members of the Commission driving up. Kim Su Young and Ray Gonzales walked in together. *How times have changed,* he thought. *I can't believe that just 30 years ago many of Jefferson's children would be attending a colored, segregated school. Black parents and teachers would not be on a Commission like this. Hell, there wouldn't be Latinos or Asians either. Yeah, times have changed. But I'll have to admit, these are caring people. And I'm really learning a lot. This character education stuff should be good. It's about time. I wish I'd been taught this when I was in school. Maybe my life would have been different....I guess I missed these values 'cause I don't go to church real often. But maybe it's not too late for my kids. I wonder what we'll do today—two guests from California. Now there's a state that's going downhill fast—immigrants and all that crime. I wonder what they could possibly say that would help us here at Jefferson?*

"Welcome to our fourth Hearing of the Citizens' Commission on Elementary School Reform," Ray said enthusiastically. We have a very exciting morning on a subject that we've heard much about from the media—destructive student and criminal behavior. This afternoon, we'll examine character education. How does our topic today relate to what our Commission is doing here at Jefferson? Now that everyone is here, I'll turn the time over to our facilitator, Wendy, to give us some answers."

"Thanks, Ray," she said. "To start off, I want to hand out our next MYTH. After today we'll never be the same. It will be a real eye-opener! We'll spend our morning looking at student misbehavior and crime and at the absence of character education programs in our schools and in many families.

Education and Destructive Student Behavior

Wendy pointed to the board. "The Seventh National Education Goal states: **'By the year 2000, every school in the United States will be free of drugs, violence, and the unauthorized presence of firearms and alcohol and will offer a disciplined environment conducive to learning.'**[1]

"I want to begin looking at destructive behavior by sharing data on **student use of drugs and alcohol.** Nearly all Americans (95%) say that drugs are a serious problem in this county. Smoking is the leading cause of early death among adults. We now know that nicotine is as addictive as heroin, and fewer than 20% are able to quit the first time they try. Most adults who smoke started as teenagers (89%). In fact, 70% of all children try cigarettes; 40% of them before high school.[2] Nearly a quarter of high school students smoke daily, and over 10% of seniors smoke 10 or more cigarettes per day. Three thousand teenagers start smoking every day, and a third of them will die prematurely. **That's the equivalent of three jumbo jet crashes everyday each year. This means that every 58 days, more American teenagers who smoke will die early than died in the Vietnam War.** And, of course, we know that smokers are 10 times as likely as nonsmokers to develop lung cancer and three times as likely to die at early ages from heart attack.

"Young people who use cigarettes are also more tempted to use other drugs. We know that current smokers are more likely to be heavy drinkers and illicit drug users than nonsmokers. A survey of tenth graders found that, between 1991 and 1994, those who reported using an illegal drug during the previous year increased from 24% to 33%. In 1994, one-out-of -four

MYTH: Media programming and advertising are harmless for our children.[3]

Mass media in the United States are a major influence in the life of each American. They consist of public and private network television, cable channels, records and tapes, newspapers, specialty newsletters, magazines and books. The most objectionable aspect of American television and film is violence, according to a large majority of respondents in eight nations. Eighty percent (80%) of Americans think television violence is "harmful," and 82% consider movies too violent.[4] Even television news gives too much attention to stories about violent crime say 57% of those surveyed.[5] This situation is especially alarming since the average child spends 30 to 35 hours a week before the TV set, and will witness 8000 television murders and another 100,000 acts of violence by completion of elementary school at age 11.[6] Parents (91%) and all adults (84%) believe that television programs should be rated.[7]

FINDING A: *Most electronic mass media—a dominant force that can mask our failures—are rapidly transforming millions of Americans into relatively ignorant and exploited people.*[8] Formal schooling competes poorly with our popular culture for the attention of our young people. Mass media promotes America's pop culture by communicating its message of immediate gratification daily into nearly every home, work and leisure place. The negative pop culture distorts who we are and who we should be, undermines our ability to deal constructively with life's challenges, rejects authority and resists attempts to hold behavior to standards.

Television shapes our values, attitudes and behavior as it glamorizes drugs and alcohol, sex and violence, wealth and materialism and reinforces pleasure-seeking and immediate gratification. We are constantly bombarded by cues about alcohol and drugs and the thrill of getting high. Yet research clearly shows that young people who use drugs are likely to drop out of school, to engage in premature and unprotected sexual activity and to commit crimes.

Advertisers use sexually irresponsible messages to sell entertainment and merchandise to younger and younger audiences. Sex is commercialized, depersonalized and separated from emotional involvement and commitment. It is little wonder that the United States has the highest teen pregnancy rate among the industrialized nations.

Most mass media is a seedbed for development of destructive habits. Television and video viewing are passive forms of entertainment. Excessive television watching (above two hours daily) distorts the learning process, reduces reading and is associated with a shrinking written vocabulary. The average 6- to 14-year-old child in America today, for example, uses 10,000 words as compared to children who used 25,000 words in 1945. As promoted by mass media, *America's pop culture of immediate gratification is sapping our resources, exploiting our citizens and creating a growing amoral, uneducated, unhealthy and unemployable underclass of Americans.*

FINDING B: *The link between media violence and increasingly violent social behavior is well documented.* The most comprehensive scientific assessment of television violence ever conducted finds that it poses substantial risks of harmful effects to viewers. The majority of programs on cable and network television contain violence, with one-out-of-four violent interactions involving the use of handguns. Premium cable channels present the highest percentage of violent programs (85%) and the greatest risk of harmful effects. Broadcast networks present violent programs less frequently (44%) than the industry norm (57%). Public broadcasting presents violent programs least often (18%). Movies, however, are 85% more likely than television to present violent scenes in a realistic setting.

Public alarm has led to several strategies to reduce the exposure of young people to these destructive influences. They have had mixed results. For example, "parental discretion" advisories, "PG-13" and "R" ratings have made programs and movies listed in a channel guide more attractive for boys, particularly those ages 10-14. For girls, the advisories have made programs less attractive. On behalf of police officers killed in the line of duty, law enforcement groups and conservative organizations across the country followed other strategies. They launched "stormy protests" over the heavy metal song, "Cop Killer," and used boycotts and threats to sue. Rapper Ice-T and record producer Time Warner Inc. agreed to stop selling the song. In an unusual move, the company recalled the album "Body Count" that contained the offensive song. Other groups who benefit from these sales, however, responded with emotionally intense charges of censorship.

One serious problem with most violent portrayals is their failure to show perpetrators of violent acts being punished or the negative consequences of their violent actions. In fact, some 47% of all violent conflicts on TV show no harm to victims, and 58% show no pain. Only a few programs (16%) show the long-term negative effects of violence, such as psychological, emotional or financial harm.

The scientific and public health fields generally agree that media violence has three primary harmful effects: learning aggressive attitudes and violent behaviors, becoming emotionally desensitized toward real world violence and its destructive consequences, and increasing fear of being attacked. The way violence is depicted in entertainment strongly influences the risk of such effects.[9] Children's viewing of television violence affects their development, increasing physical aggressiveness and violence.[10] In their early years, children are unable to distinguish between fantasy and reality. They are exposed to heroes who solve problems with violent action. By watching these role models, they see violence idealized. They begin associating it with love and goodness as well as with hate and hostility. As youth of all ages are exposed to more violence in the media today, they are committing more serious and violent crimes. Children's exposure to violence has a desensitizing and cumulative effect that carries over into adulthood.

FINDING C. Media messages, including a*dvertising, seriously undermine constructive values, attitudes and behavior of America's children.* Effective advertising can earn huge profits. Advertisers, therefore, carefully target their audiences to the sale of goods and services. In 1991, for example, corporations spent $130 billion on advertising, 50% more per capita than any other nation. Their marketing surveys show that the average post-adolescent spends 40 hours and $30 a week being entertained by non-print media, and that 60% of this growing audience of young adults do not read books. Their surveys also indicate that children ages 4 to 12 indirectly influence household budgets by an $8 billion expenditure annually. They now target about $500 million to reach children, five times what they spent a decade earlier. If the audience were to shrink by 1 %, the television industry alone would lose $250 million annually in advertising revenue. As a result, advertisers have increased dramatically the number of media messages to young people. The lucrative television linkup with different product lines has created a "need" in children to have certain fast foods, breakfast cereals, toys and athletic shoes.

FINDING D: *Mass media fails to report stories on public education or distorts them.* The activities of education—one of the nation's largest industries—are not reported by the media to parents and taxpayers.[11] Most media representatives are not literate about education as a complex institution in American life and how it relates to aspects of our society, such as economics or government. Only about a dozen of 3,500 network employees (1%) in both print and broadcast media work on education full time. Other evidence of this neglect of serious reporting and commentary on public education is provided by a study of air time for a 30-month period. It showed that only 350 of the 36,000 pieces (1%) on all subjects were devoted to education stories. Approximately 150 of these pieces had little to do with schools directly.

FINDING E: *Public Broadcasting Service (PBS) provides positive educational TV Programming.* While major TV networks show two or three hours each of 'back-to-school' specials, PBS and its member stations air 15 hours of education-related programming during the first week of September. PBS has daily series for preschoolers and older children, such as *Sesame Street* and *Mr. Rogers,* as well as shows, such as *Math: Who Needs It?* Public TV distributes more than 2,000 hours of instructional television (ITV) programming annually, specifically for classroom use, reaching 29 million K-12 students. Last year, President Clinton reached an agreement with major networks to provide three hours each week of children's programs. This year, commercial television networks have agreed to begin rating the contents of their shows for parental discretion like motion picture producers do.

said that someone had offered to sell or give them illegal drugs at school, and two-out-of-three said that they had used alcohol. A survey in 1995 showed that about 10 million current drinkers were under age 21. Although we don't have access to similar measures for elementary school students, we do have some evidence that sixth grade problem drinkers are on the rise.

"Next, let's look at **student and teacher victimization.** Every year nearly 3 million thefts and crimes occur on or near school campuses. This is almost 16,000 incidents per school day, with two-thirds of them considered violent crime—rape, robbery and assault. Even young children are afraid of being injured. For example, today 71% of children ages 7 to 10 worry that they might get shot or stabbed at school or home.[12] In 1991, four-out-of-ten tenth graders reported that during the pervious year they had been threatened or injured at school. By 1994 this had been reduced to nearly one-out-of-three. Between 1991 and 1994, the number of public school teachers who reported that a student from their school had threatened or physically attacked them during the previous year went from 10% to 15%—a significant 50% increase. A University of Michigan study reports that 9% of eighth graders carry a gun, knife, or club to school at least once a month. An estimated 270,000 guns go to school every day. When suburban high schoolers were surveyed, 20% endorsed shooting 'someone who has stolen something from you.'[13] In the decade between 1983 and 1993, the number of our young people (ages 1-19) who died from gunfire nearly doubled, reaching 5,737—a jump of 94.4 %. [14]

"Nate," said Debbie, "to put this in perspective, I read in *The Washington Post* that many Japanese feel the 'American disease' of guns is spreading to their country. They were alarmed that 17 people were killed by gunfire last year, about the same numbers as we have on a slow afternoon!"[15]

"That's a staggering comparison!" said Nate, "You mean 17 deaths in a whole year? What are we becoming in this country? Well, let's go on. In 1993 and 1994, Louis Harris and Associates surveyed American teachers, students and law enforcement officers about increasing violence and fears of violence in their schools.[16] The majority of teachers and law enforcement officers believe that major factors contributing to violence in public schools are lack of supervision at home, lack of family involvement in school, and exposure to violence in the mass media. In minority schools, however, a whopping 95% of teachers feel that lack of parental supervision is a major contributing factor. The study found that most public school teachers (77%) feel very safe in or around school. Fewer teachers (61%) feel safe when they have all or many minority students. Of the students, however, 50% feel safe and 40% feel somewhat safe. One third of the students have witnessed violent incidents in or around school often or sometimes. Among law enforcement officers, 44% feel that violence has increased.

"Another 1993 study of 729 school districts found that crime and violence in schools had reached epidemic proportions, with 82% of the districts polled having experienced violence in the previous five years. Crime was escalating even in rural and suburban areas that were previously considered much safer school environments.[17]

"Disruptions in class by students is another hot topic. Between 1992 and 1994, 17% of tenth graders reported that other students interfered with their own learning at least six times a week. During the same time period, by contrast, the number of secondary school teachers reporting that student misbehavior interfering with their teaching rose from 33% to 46%—a 24% increase.*[18]

"Cheating is another troublesome area. According to a national survey, 75% of high school students cheat on tests.**[19] Some 42% of male high-school respondents, and 31% of female respondents, said they had stolen something from a store within the previous 12 months. Nearly half of males and one-third of high school females said they would lie if necessary to get or keep a job.[20]

Nate asked, "What about disruptive student behavior in elementary schools? I'd like to hear from our teachers, Delores, Kathie, Tamar and Ted." Nate turned to them and said, "What is your experience?"

"I'll jump in," said Delores. "I teach first grade. My students don't seem to use drugs and alcohol by choice. But I will say I see more parents getting doctors to give their hyperactive children more ritalin. Some parents go too far! They don't seem to want to spend time with their children. And, of course, the kids act up more because they're anxious about not feeling loved and appreciated."

"I second that," Kathie said. "I teach fifth grade. I don't have a problem with students disrupting class to challenge my authority. It's not my students that have a drinking or alcohol problem…yet! It's many of their high strung, money-driven parents who are poor examples to their children. There is a dramatic rise in kids 'drugged out' on ritalin who may not be hyperactive. We now mainstream children with disabilities who may seriously disrupt classes. I have one student who is a Turette Syndrome child. About every 15 minutes, this child shouts out foul language. His mother

---

*The 83,000 students in the Long Beach District of California are among the public school systems to document success with a mandatory uniform policy. A school district study reports that assault and battery cases in grades K-8 dropped 34% in two years, fights dropped 51%, and suspensions dropped 32%.

**A majority of parents (82%) believe that all students complete their assignments when teachers give them homework. By contrast, only 4% of all students say that all their peers complete their homework.

doesn't know what to do, so she keeps him drugged most of the time. My appeals for help are simply not answered. I'm very frustrated because my principal won't back me up with the parents."

"I can relate to what Kathie is saying," said Ted, the sixth grade teacher. *Looks like we've hit a nerve with our teachers,* Ray Gonzales thought. "I also have at least one-fourth of my class that take some drugs to quiet them down," said Ted. "Parents don't seem to question the need for them—and certainly don't assume they can do anything at home to help their children calm down at school. Some home scenes are terrible places for children because of arguing, fighting and other abusive behavior. Parents who are fighting poverty, unemployment and divorce can't help but be uptight. But it carries over into my classroom.

"I'm spending more time counseling my kids about emotional conflicts at home. But I need some help with parents who themselves need counseling. They need to learn how to organize and run functional homes so that their children can have a shot at a good school experience before they start getting into gangs. More sixth grade kids are hiding pocket knives, and starting gang behavior. Gangs are starting as early as my sixth grade class— at recess and after school—especially with latch-key kids. We should provide after school programs to keep these kids off the streets until their parents get home. I notice more violence at recess by boys who are acting out their frustrations with other racial or ethnic group students. It's frightening to some of the less mature boys. They're distracted and afraid."

Tamar spoke up. "I'm a new teacher, just starting my second year. Nothing I learned in college prepared me for what I'm encountering each day in my third grade class. It's not illegal drugs that are the problem, just 'socially acceptable' prescription drugs given by parents. About six of my 32 students are, in some way, physically or learning disabled. I'm learning to live with this, although I could use some help from sensitive parents or teacher aides, which, of course, I don't have.

"My challenge is kids coming to school hungry without having had breakfast. Thank God for the federal school lunch program! But these kids also need medical care, and they aren't getting it here at school—or anywhere else. I can't teach children who are not healthy. Many also stay up late watching TV or don't have enough sleep because of crowded living conditions. They often act like zombies several days each week."

"Well, Ray, welcome to the world of the classroom teacher!" Kathie said. "We keep trying to tell you people on the Board of Education that tomorrow is here—in the trenches of our classrooms. It's our education war against ignorance. We don't have time to study this once a week or even once a month. We face this reality every day! And all we hear from the School Board is 'let's do a study on how we can cut waste and fraud so we don't have to raise property taxes.'"

"Yes, Kathie," Ray said, "I'm beginning to see what it's like from a teacher's point of view. I'm not discounting what you're saying. I guess that's why we're all here today—on this Commission. I hope we can get past the prejudices and 'silver-bullets' quick fixes."

Wendy cut in. "Before we go on, let me hand out a description of a young teacher's model for creatively handling disruptive classroom behavior. It shows the importance of starting where you are, being consistent and obtaining the principal's support."

I'm impressed with these teachers, Kim Su Young thought. *They're finally being asked for their opinions. They're very articulate! It's about time this Commission got some real information based on first-hand teaching experience.*

"Debbie, do you have a question or comment?" said Wendy.

"This subject of safe, drug free and nondisruptive schools," said Debbie, "is not just limited to high schools. As the *Three Strikes Discipline* example in our notebook shows, the problems are reaching down to grade schools. My children tell me that kids are carrying weapons to school because they're afraid. Here at Jefferson, we have a very destructive environment emerging. What will be next now that the middle-class parents are in flight from this neighborhood, especially now that Jefferson has been placed on the state's troubled school list? It could all fly apart while we're studying the big problems of national school reform!"

Wendy nodded. "You have a good issue, Debbie, but there's more. I'd like to go on now and discuss **school dropouts.** I've written the **Second National Education Goal** on the board: **'By the year 2000 the high school graduation rate will increase to at least 90%.** Elementary school education lays the foundation for all students—those who eventually graduate from high school and those who eventually dropout. **Dropouts make up half the heads of households on welfare and half the people in jail.** Dropouts earn an average of $12,800, about $6,000 less than high school graduates.

"Almost 40% of students who dropout either had a child or were expecting one. But get this—of all those who drop out, about 3% do so at or before the fourth grade, 20% drop out at or before the eighth grade, and 61% at or before the tenth grade. In 1993 the 'event rate' (that means those 15- to 24-year olds who leave tenth through twelfth grades in a given year) was 4.5%, representing 381,000 students. In 1970 the figure was 7%, so we're making some progress.

"But the real bottom line for judging school performance is the 'dropout status rate.' That means the percentage of 21- to 22-year olds who dropped out at some point in their school career and are without a high school diploma. The 1993 figure was 14%. While dropout rates differ between Whites, Blacks and Hispanics, Black graduation rates now almost equal White rates, but only 57% of Hispanics graduate.[21] (By the way, nearly one-half of all Hispanics ages 16-24 were born outside the U.S.). One-of-four inner-city districts had a dropout rate of 35%. Each year more than 750,000 adults take the General Education Development (GED) Tests, representing about one-in-seven high school completion rates. GED is a series of five tests in writing, social studies, science, interpreting literature and the arts, and mathematics.[22] Several corporations, including Chevron, Ford Motor, Coca-Cola, U.S. West, Bank of America, Burger King, and Kaiser Permanente have made dropout prevention a priority for their educational support activities.[23] Any questions at this point?

Wendy paused and looked around the room, "I'll go on then. One legacy of the sexual revolution is a highly-eroticized sexual environment. Growing up in this setting, many of America's children are preoccupied with sex in developmentally-distorted ways. They increasingly act out their sexual impulses. In the United States, in a 1992 study 54% of high school students say they have had sexual intercourse, including 61% of boys and 48% of girls. These figures do not show the most striking feature of the rising trend in sexual activity—that 40% of ninth graders have already had sex.[24] This is up from the 5% in 1970! By age 19, nearly 80% of young women and 86% of young men have had sexual intercourse. The number of sexually active teenage girls who report having multiple partners has risen from 38% in 1971 to nearly 60% by 1988.[25]

"During the past two decades, sexually-transmitted diseases (STD) have skyrocketed. **Each year 12 million people are infected, and two-out-of-three are under 25.** Once rare, Human Papilloma Virus is now the most common STD, infecting 38% of sexually-active females between the ages of 13 to 21. By age 18, more than 25% of girls and 16% of boys have suffered from sexual abuse, which reflects widespread sexual harassment and sexual corruption of children.[26]

"Today, **a million teenage girls get pregnant each year**—about half of them have abortions or miscarriages, and half have babies. Only 10% give their babies up for adoption.[27] This means that every year some 450,000 become unwed teen mothers—more than 15% are from middle-class homes. In 1965 the number of children born out of wedlock was 16.7%. By 1994, however, 46.4% of births, or almost half, were to unwed mothers.[28] And in some cities, 85% to 90% of babies were born to unwed teenagers.[29] The percentage of children born out of wedlock in 1994 represents the largest one-year increase since national figures have been kept.[30] Now what are some of the consequences? **When unmarried women have an illegitimate child before they reach 20 and do not finish high school, their children have a 79% chance of growing up in poverty**. By contrast, when women complete high school, marry and give birth after 20, their children have only an 8% chance.[31] To put this in perspective, between 1950 and 1994, the percentage children living in mother-only families climbed from 6% to 24%.[32]

"In 1980 New Jersey became the first state in the country to mandate comprehensive sex education, even in the primary grades. But since then, births to unwed teenage mothers in that state have risen from 67.6% to 84%. It appears that as sex education programs have become more solidly entrenched, the rate of sexual activity has exploded—although family breakdowns, changing norms, and media exposure all undermine social inhibitions about responsible sex.

"The model for comprehensive sex education, which originated in Sweden in the 1950s, is based on four assumptions. First, teenage sexual activity in inevitable. Second, educators should be value-neutral regarding sex. Third, schools should openly discuss sexual matters. Fourth, sex education should teach students about contraception. A 1986 Harris Poll found that **teens who took a comprehensive sex education course were** *significantly more likely* **to initiate sexual intercourse than teens whose sex education courses did not discuss contraceptives**.[33]

"There are two major approaches to sex education. The first—Abstinence, But—is widely used in today's schools; the second—Abstinence, No But— is rarely used. The Abstinence, But approach recognizes that the only safe sex is abstinence. Its supporters, however, believe that all students, many of whom may engage in sex as teenagers, need to be taught to practice safe sex through condom use. The statistics on illegitimate teenage sex show this approach has been disasterous!

"Abstinence, No Buts is openly ridiculed by critics. Yet advocates claim that it's a critical part of character education that promotes core ethical values.[34] This directive approach assumes (1) sexual abstinence is the *only* medically-safe and morally-responsible choice for unmarried teenagers; (2) condoms do not make premarital sex responsible because they don't make sex physically or emotionally safe, or ethically loving; and (3) the only truly safe sex is having sex *only* with a marriage partner who is having sex *only* with you. By avoiding intercourse until marriage, you will have a much greater chance of remaining healthy and able to have children.

"A senior policy analyst for the Guttmacher Institute, specializing in reproductive issues, stated that they haven't the faintest idea of how to prevent out-of-wedlock births.[35] Meanwhile, the U.S. Department of Health and Human Services is giving $20 million in grants to states that can show the most pronounced drop in out-of-wedlock births."

"But, Wendy, be serious. Nobody believes teenagers will practice abstinence!" Debbie said angrily. "You're not that much older than high school kids. Is this a serious strategy?"

"It's very controversial, Debbie. But it's a growing trend among some young people—especially those with strong religious values. Adopting abstinence is not only possible, but more and more student leaders are practicing it. When 24,000 students who were listed in Who's Who Among American High Schools were surveyed, permissiveness was in full bloom among young people.[36] The findings may surprise you:

- Eighty-three percent are active members of a religion and 71% attend services regularly;
- Nearly half don't drink and 88% have never smoked cigarettes;
- A vast majority (94%) never use drugs, including marijuana;
- Eighty percent do not think marijuana should be legalized and 90% would not use it if it was;
- Seventy-six percent have not had sexual intercourse;
- Some 87% favor a traditional marriage; and

- Fifty-two percent watch less than 10 hours of television per week.

"I think this finding about exceptional teenagers shows that some young people can and do practice responsible behavior. It's clearly connected to values and habits they acquire from somewhere," Wendy concluded.

Education for Responsible Behavior

"Now take a look at two BEST PRACTICES handouts while we take a refreshment break."

BEST PRACTICES: THREE STRIKES DISCIPLINE

Teaching at West Kerns Elementary in Salt Lake City, Utah, gave Cristine Hopkins insight into the violent world many students face. She was fortunate, however, since she wasn't injured when assaulted by a student. Another teacher wasn't so lucky. A student was held at gunpoint by another student on the playground when her sister wouldn't join a gang. But students weren't the only ones attacking. One student was traumatized after being assaulted by a parent in the hall. The principal, Dr. Donald G. Christensen, was held at gunpoint by a disgruntled parent. During the school year, he called the police about every other day. "Hello, Don, we'll be right over." Some students were violent, and many were disruptive.

During the beginning of the school year with her new fifth grade class, Mrs. Hopkins said, "Okay, students open your math books." A few students went to the back of the classroom, looking out the door to see if a friend might be "sluffing" in the hall. Some kept talking and others flipped paper frogs across their desks. Raising her voice, Mrs. Hopkins said, "You have until the count of three or I'll begin taking away minutes from your recess." Most of the class opened their books while others continued to disrupt. A few students looked as if they were considering her request. Finally, they opened their books and began to work.

Mrs. Hopkins reported that she spent 30 minutes teaching math and 15 minutes disciplining. This pattern continued every day. Traditional discipline techniques, like reasoning, pleading and threats, worked for only a few minutes. Students quickly resumed their own disruptive activities. "I understood the dysfunctional backgrounds of many of my students, but I also realized I couldn't correct their home or community problems. To be an effective teacher, I had to teach them appropriate classroom behavior."

Finally, frustrated but resolved to meet the challenge, Cristine Hopkins considered options for gaining control. She authored a method, known as *Three Strikes Discipline*, designed to eliminate moderate behaviors, such as defiance of authority, disrespectful or disorderly conduct, profanity/vulgarity or non-compliance. The next day, Mrs. Hopkins conferred with Dr. Christensen about her new plan. He pledged support. She implemented it immediately.[37]

When Mrs. Hopkins explained the particular classroom rule of no disruptions and its consequence if violated, most students marched to the Principal's office. They demanded to talk with him, arguing she had no right to discipline them for disrupting the class! Dr. Christensen listened and sent them back. Later when she sent students to the office, they were immediately assigned to a "time-out room" in a lower grade level where teachers and other students were told to ignore the student. Parents were notified that very day.

Cristine Hopkins was surprised at the success of *Three Strikes Discipline*. The method was 99% successful in preventing repeated disruptive behaviors. The first day she implemented the plan, 11 out of 28 students (39%) were suspended for repeated infractions of classroom rules. By the third day, 3 out of 28 students (11%) were suspended. After approximately two weeks, only one child was suspended for repeated disruptive behavior.

The method kept a behavior-disordered student functioning normally in Mrs. Hopkins classroom. Other teachers were constantly complaining about that student's vulgar, defiant and violent behavior. Yet he followed Cristine's classroom rules reasonably well. When there was an opening in a self-contained behavioral modification unit, this student's name and file were presented for placement. During the placement committee meeting, several comments were made about Cristine and her plan: "She's done all the right interventions that special education teachers are trained to use." "She can control this student, when the rest of the school can't." "Let's use Mrs. Hopkins' discipline plan as a model for our special education teachers to deal with students like him." " Even though she's a new teacher, it seems she has many more years of experience to be able to work with a student in this manner."

As a result of this recommendation, the principal developed a schoolwide plan. He reported the number of students sent to his office was "greatly reduced." The students seemed to be better behaved, and he was called to the classrooms less often. He recalls the number of violent incidences decreased by approximately 25% that year.

Mrs. Hopkins added a "master learning" component along with weekly mini-tests keyed to the instructional program. These tests provided feedback for ongoing monitoring and evaluation. The second component that she added was "integration of the curriculum into real-life experience." She established a mini-community (restaurant, bank, post office, businesses) where students eagerly applied their math and reading skills the last half hour of each day. By the end of the school year, her class "edged ahead" of the "gifted and talented" class in academic achievement.

BEST PRACTICES: BABY THINK IT OVER[38]

Teen pregnancy and parenting are major problems facing youth today. Each year there are one million teenage pregnancies, and half of these end in birth. Eighty three percent of the 500,000 who give birth are disadvantaged youth. Their disadvantages are compounded in terms of education and workforce experience. Future possibilities for a successful, satisfying life are severely limited by having and raising a baby. The baby's future too is often bleak.

Preventive strategies to help teens anticipate consequences of sexual behavior and the impact of a baby on their future have been largely ineffective. Such approaches as lectures and textbooks, even warnings by adults or other teens who have had first-hand experience with the challenges of teenage parenting, have failed to get the attention of most teenagers. Media messages that glamorize sex and peer pressures to experiment sexually are far more compelling motivators.

In 1996 a former NASA aerospace engineer in San Diego conceived of 'Baby Think It Over' as a teaching tool to provide teenagers with hands-on experience of the difficulties of parenting a newborn. Rick Jurmain, an inventor, has steadily improved the simulator, adding crying technology and an abuse detector. Another recent variation is the drug-dependent model, which is smaller and crankier than normal and trembles when it cries. Along with the baby simulator, Jurmain and his wife, Mary, have created a curriculum which teaches proper parenting skills and helps students calculate the cost of having and caring for a baby.

The cuddly, cute computerized doll can be 'set' to cry realistically at random intervals throughout the day and night. The doll's program can be set for "easy" or three cries until the baby is returned to class the following day or "difficult" with cries every hour or less. Its regular 'feedings' can only be given by the assigned student who inserts a keylike probe on a tamper-proof hospital bracelet into a probe on the baby's back for 35 minutes. The whole experience temporarily alters the lifestyle of a typical teenager in dramatic ways.

The students find it embarrassing to carry a baby around in public—to hangouts with friends, school basketball games, even other classes. But getting up in the night is far more exhausting than they anticipate and the baby's cry gradually becomes annoying. Sharin Frye liked feeding, holding, bathing the baby—having someone entirely depend on her. But when she had to get up at 2, 4 and 6 a.m., it 'made her real mad…During school, it would cry and I had to feed it….I couldn't wait to take it back.' Though she handled her five days and nights of parenting well, nights especially proved exhausting. Having a baby, at least for now, was just too much trouble.

Teachers of home economics, health and physical education, or family and consumer science have been searching for ways to convey the burdens of teen parenting for the teenager as well as the baby. One teacher has used two Baby Think It Over dolls in her elective classes in life-management skills and parenting and child development. She says that, in her 20 years of teaching, it is the 'most effective technique' she has seen in convincing students of the 'potential albatross' caring for a baby can be when they're not ready to make those sacrifices. Other teachers too are looking for ways to show the total responsibility of parenthood. In some high schools, the infant simulator program is required for both boys and girls. Several studies are being conducted to determine the effectiveness of this strategy for preventing teen pregnancies.

****

Education and Criminal Behavior

Commission members were in deep discussion about disruptive behavior at Jefferson when Nate said, "I know this morning was pretty heavy. We followed the statistics and saw the tragic waste of lives they represent. But until we understand the connection between disruptive behavior and educational achievement, we'll be unable or unwilling to solve these problems for the very children who will become tomorrow's statistics.

"Before we examine character education programs designed to counter disruptive student behavior, we have one more area to cover—criminal behavior that's linked to inadequate education. Even though adult crime has declined over the past five years, youth crime is steadily rising. Because many people have not learned to keep commitments or behave responsibly, we all pay the skyrocketing costs of what's called risk management—money for security personnel, surveillance technology and legal work.

"The United States is now number one in the world in terms of jailing its people, having passed both South Africa and Russia! Taking a closer look at the prison population, we find that **nearly one in four Black men (age 20 to 29) is under the control of the criminal justice system—in prison or jail, on probation or parole**. This is four times as many Black males as are incarcerated in South Africa.[39] Now what is the relationship between criminal behavior and education?"

"Nate, excuse me," said Debbie, "but before you get started, I read something interesting on prisons in the *Washington Post*. Our nation's new 'prison-industrial complex' is becoming a growth business that plays on the public's fear of crime. Since 1980 we've tripled our prison population. We now open almost three new prisons every week. We divert scarce state tax dollars from support of public schools to build and maintain new prisons. The average annual cost of building a cell to house one prisoner is $50,000. We spend another $21,000 just to keep him in jail each year and a whopping $1.5 million for life.[40] **The bottom line is that poorly-educated young men are the raw materials of our criminal justice system.** Yet American taxpayers spend far less on preparing them for productive work and good citizenship—only an average of $6000 each year to educate a young man or woman.

"That's sobering information, Debbie. Thanks for sharing it," Nate said. "Next, I call your attention to a handout in your notebook. It's a summary of the report, *Literacy Behind Prison Walls*.[41] Our objective here will be to get a feel for the background of individuals who are in U.S. jails. Is there a link between educational achievement and criminal behavior? We've all read estimates that 85% of juvenile delinquents have inadequate reading skills and 70% of prison inmates are functionally illiterate. First, let me explain that the 1991 National Literacy Act defined functional literacy as 'an individual's ability to read, write, and speak in English and compute and solve problems at levels of proficiency necessary to function on the job and in society, to achieve one's goals, and to develop one's knowledge and potential.' With that definition in mind, a comprehensive study—actually part of the 1993 National Adult Literacy Survey—carefully documents literacy levels of prisoners in our nation's state and federal prison system. It gives us a devastating, but highly descriptive, profile.

"Let's look at the American prison population in the 1990s. First, **90% of all prisoners are men, with 65% minority and 35% White. Assessments of average prose reading, documentary and quantitative skills show that 71% are functionally illiterate (levels one and two).** Eleven percent of prisoners report having learning disabilities, compared with only 3% of the general population. White inmates demonstrate higher average proficiencies than Black on all measures, and Black inmates score higher than Hispanic. In homes where English is not the first language, prisoners score significantly lower on literacy skills than where English is spoken (except for Asians). Inmates with lower levels of literacy are more likely to be unemployed prior to incarceration. If they are employed, they usually work in low-wage craft, service, labor, assembly, farming or fishing occupations. Also the literacy proficiencies of first-time and repeat offenders do not differ, and 77% of inmates are repeat offenders. This means that their **skills don't improve enough in prison to get them good jobs on the outside as an alternative lifestyle.**

"We know that parents' education is the single best predictor of children's eventual educational achievements. But for some reason, out of a total prison population of 765,651, more inmates (49%) report not having a high school diploma or GED than their parents (39%).

"Look at Table 7.1 in your notebook. It shows that Whites make up 76% of the general adult population, but as I said before, only 35% of the prison population. Over half of White prisoners (52%) score in the bottom two functionally-illiterate categories and have relatively poor educational preparation when compared to the general White population with dysfunctional literacy rates of 35%. Blacks are 11% of the adult population but 44% of the prison population. However, 81% of Black inmates score in the bottom two functionally-illiterate levels. Hispanics are 10% of the nation's adult population but 18% of inmates. Like Black inmates, 82% of Hispanics score at the bottom two levels of literacy. But Asians, who make up 2% of the general public, are only .5% of the inmates. Native Americans are 1% of the public but 2% of the prison population. Put another way, Whites who are better educated and score higher on functional literacy assessments are underrepresented in the prisons by 217%, but Asian Americans by an astounding 400%! Meanwhile Blacks are over represented by 400%; and Native Americans by 200%; and Hispanics by 180%.

"**There are 50,000 women in jail. The majority were high school dropouts unemployed at the time of their arrest.** Nearly 41% were African American, 34% were White and 25% Hispanic. Northwestern University studied women awaiting trial at the Cook County jail in Chicago. The crimes they committed were mostly nonviolent: 35% against property, such as shoplifting, 24% drug charges, 15% for prostitution or soliciting, and 10% for traffic offenses. More than 80% of incarcerated women suffered from at least one serious mental disorder. The most common psychiatric problems were clinical depression and substance abuse. One in three was a victim of rape or assault and has not received treatment. Nearly 80% had one child and more than a third had three or more children. Nearly 70% were dependent on drugs, alcohol or both.[42]

"These figures are absolutely astounding to me, Nate!" said Ray. "I still believe discrimination against minorities is a big piece of this picture...but I can't deny the relationship between low educational achievement and the number of prisoners who have low functional literacy levels. When the data is broken down by race and ethnic group, the reality is sobering. Can you believe the under representation of Asian Americans in the prison system? What's happening here? We've got to take a long look at the cultural values we carry. And we can't afford to go blindly on applying bandaids to our broken public school system that cripple half of our children. That

Table 7.1

CHARACTERISTICS OF PRISON INMATE POPULATIONS

BY MAJORITY/MINORITY GROUP STATUS

Inmates by Race/Ethnicity	% Adult General Population	% Adult Prison Population	Over/Under Represented	Combined Lowest Two Literacy Levels
White	76%	35%	-217%	52%
Black	11%	44%	+400%	81%*
Hispanic	10%	18%	+180%	82%*
Asian/Pacific Isl.	2%	.5%	-400%	-**
Native American	1%	2%	+200%	-**

*Represents a composite average of three proficiency levels on Prose, Document and Quantitative.

**No data reported. Nevertheless Asian Americans as a group are comparatively well educated, while Native American have historically as a group been less educationally prepared. Literacy scores are closely associated with formal education. Most high school and below achievers also tend to be proficient in the two lowest literacy levels which in turn is associated with low-wage occupations. The discrepancy between Hispanics (82%) and Blacks (81%) is not significant. What is astounding, however, is the incarceration rate of 44% for Blacks and 18% for Hispanics. This difference suggests a powerful force at work beyond literacy levels, such as possible discrimination by law enforcement officers and judges based on race (the preferred explanation of most Blacks), or a difference in cultural values held by different groups towards education, family and community.

amounts to about 75% of our minority children! If parents and teachers worked together, I think we can figure this out and prevent some of these destructive behavior patterns in childhood.

Summary

"This is a heavy discussion," Nate said. "There is a link between educational achievement and more serious crime. Is anyone feeling depressed yet? Let me ask members of the Commission to help summarize what we've heard thus far today. Try to relate these findings to our Jefferson Elementary School. We first looked at the Seventh National Education Goal: By the year 2000, every school in the United States will be free of drugs, violence, and the unauthorized presence of firearms and alcohol and will offer a disciplined environment conducive to learning. What struck you as most significant in all the trends?

"I thought drugs and alcohol was a problem at all the parties when I was going to high school," said Dale. **"Smoking was macho. But with all we've learned about the deadly effects of tobacco leading to cancer and heart disease and with most adults stopping, I just figured kids would give it up too. I was really surprised to learn that smoking is increasing among kids, about 3,000 take it up every day. These are the ones who are likely to die early from smoking. And I was shocked by the growing number of young serious drinkers, starting as early as sixth grade.** This is a war! And it looks like offers to sell illicit drugs to students on campus are climbing. Yes, this is a war and we better prepare a safe school here at Jefferson so our kids don't get started on smoking and drinking in grade school."

"I was surprised," said Tamar, **"to realize that both students and teachers are becoming victims of attacks. How can we stop students from bringing weapons to school? Half of the students and one-out-of-three teachers don't feel safe. If that's true at Jefferson, no wonder we lose good teachers."**

"I was struck," said Paul, **"by the agreement between the majority of law enforcement officers and teachers. Both groups feel that the major factors contributing to violence in public schools are lack of supervision at home, lack of family involvement in the schools, and exposure to violence in the mass media."**

Kathie spoke next, **"Student disruptions in class are increasing. Our discussion among Jefferson teachers suggests that 20% to 25% of students** are medicated, which interferes with learning in their classrooms. We must find other ways to curb this aggressive behavior."

Delores said, "I was kind of interested in the BEST PRACTICES: Three Strikes Disciplinary strategy. Sometimes a coordinated effort with the principal is all it takes to eliminate this waste of teacher and student time. No wonder we can't focus on educating our kids who want to be there. This best practice looks promising. I'm going to try it."

"I found out something I never knew today about kids who drop out of school," Kim said. "While overall we lose 14% of students at some point in their career, and 35% or more in many urban schools, I didn't realize we're losing kids in elementary school! This is shocking! I'm never going to let that happen again in my school. Now I wonder how many homeless children I'm missing?

"I'm Maria. I'm blown away by the rise in teen pregnancy and sexually transmitted diseases (SDT)! They've reached epidemic proportions among teenagers of all income groups. While this is a high school problem, what are we parents and teachers doing to prepare our elementary girls and boys to avoid these tragedies that so cripple our kids?"

"But Maria," Ted said. "I never knew the devastating impact of teenage pregnancy. Today, I learned that four out of five children of unmarried women under 20 who do not finish high school grow up in poverty. We better start talking to our boys too!"

"You have a question, Lenora?" Wendy asked.

"You know," said Lenora. "I was interested in those these teenagers havin' to take care of the baby doll for a week. That'll take all the romance out of havin' babies and runnin' away from home."

"I think you're right, Lenora," said Wendy.

"I was interested in the two models of sex education," said Debbie. "I didn't realize that the Abstinence, But model is so ineffective in preventing teenage STDs and pregnancy. I've never believed that the Abstinence, No-Buts model would work. But after today, I'm going to find out more about that one. I guess the habits and morals of top high school students impressed me. I want my daughter to know about this survey."

"I am ashamed to live in a country where the greatest number and percentage of its citizens are in jail," said Christina. "More than any other country, more than Russia and South Africa! What are we becoming? And nearly one-fourth of Black males in America are under control of the criminal justice system? This is a national scandal!"

"Can you believe," said Maria, "that 90% of prisoners are male, and only 10% are female. But what's really sobering news is that 70% or more are functionally illiterate. Blacks, Native Americans and Hispanics are greatly over represented as prisoners while Asians and Whites, especially those who are better educated, are greatly underrepresented. Why are some minorities ending up in jail and others ending up as engineers?"

"What a great job you've done summarizing," said Nate. "The information is alarming. I hope we can stop this from happening to the children at Jefferson. But now it's time for our lunch break. When we return, we'll interview our first guest, Dr. Thomas Lickona, a pioneer in character education. We'll see everybody back at 1:00 p.m. this afternoon."

****

Chapter 8
CHARACTER EDUCATION AND CITIZENSHIP
Saturday afternoon, December 14

"Welcome back," Wendy greeted the group. "This morning we examined the fruits of failure by families and schools to teach children a moral code required to become successful in any culture. We have looked at the increasing costs to public education of students who disrupt classroom teachers because they are bored or because they haven't the learning foundation required to move on to the next grade. We have also looked at our justice system and at the poor education of prisoners that has contributed to their anti-social behavior. Some educators are claiming that our failure to teach responsible values in public schools has resulted in destructive student behavior and more serious criminal behavior.

"Before introducing our first guest, I want to point out that several national surveys show a dramatic public consensus on the importance of teaching values. A Gallup poll, conducted for *Phi Delta Kappan,* showed that our citizens believe the following should be taught in our schools: honesty (97%); democracy (93%); acceptance of people of different races and ethnic backgrounds (93%); and caring for family and friends, moral courage; and the golden rule (90%). In another recent poll, the public cited drug abuse, lack of discipline and fighting/violence/gangs as the three most critical problems in our schools.[1] **Nearly everyone ranked the preparation of students to become responsible citizens as the most important purpose of public schools** (86% felt it was 'very important;' 12% 'quite important'), even above becoming economically self-sufficient. Also *U.S. News and World Report* carried the lead cover story, 'How to Raise A Moral Child: Let's Hear It for Honesty, Self-discipline and Empathy.'[2] It would be hard to imagine any stronger public mandate—schools should teach students core values. Teaching core values offers some hope of countering disruptive student behavior.

"It's interesting to note," Wendy continued, "that over half of the teachers surveyed say teaching values is more important than teaching academics. Nearly 10% say that teaching both is equally important! Almost eight-out-of-ten approve of teaching 'habits of good citizenship, such as voting and caring about the nation.'[3]

Character Education

"We have three guests who will discuss various aspects of character education. Dr. Thomas Lickona is director of the Center for the 4th and 5th Rs at the University of New York at Cortland. Tom, welcome to this Hearing of the Citizens' Commission on Jefferson Elementary School Reform. Could you begin with a short history of character education? Please define it and describe your approach."

"Thank you, Wendy, and members of the Citizens' Commission. I like what Theodore Roosevelt said, 'To educate a person in mind and not in morals is to educate a menace to society.' Your morning's discussion of student misbehavior and education and criminal behavior shows that our society is turning out more and more menaces.[4] I will argue today that parents and educators have failed to take seriously their responsibilities to teach moral or character education. Into this vacuum, a new immoral popular culture is encouraging this country to become the most violent of all industrialized nations.[5] It is also fast becoming one of the most sexually-decadent cultures.

"First, let me review the early history of character education. Until the 1950s, education had two great goals: to help people become smart and to help them become good—what the Greeks refer to as virtuous.[6] Our nation's first schools openly taught character education through discipline, teachers' example, and daily school curriculum. The Bible was the public school's source book for moral and religious instruction. Later in 1836, and for the next hundred years, McGuffey Readers were widely used in public schools (100 million copies sold). The popular readers contained favorite Biblical stories but added poems, exhortations, and heroic tales. While children practiced their reading or arithmetic, they also learned lessons about honesty, love of neighbor, kindness to animals, hard work, thriftiness, patriotism, and courage."

"Dr. Lickona, why don't we use the McGuffey readers in our schools today?" Christina Peterson asked.

"In the early part of the 1900s, the consensus supporting character education began to crumble under the onslaught of several powerful forces: Darwinism, logical positivism and personalism. Darwinism introduced the concept of evolution. Although a contribution to science, it led many people to question a fixed standard of morality. The philosophy of logical positivism separated hard, observable facts from values, which came to be considered as merely personal judgment. In the 1960s, a worldwide rise in personalism celebrated the worth, autonomy, and subjectivity of the person, emphasizing individual rights and freedom over responsibility. While correctly protesting societal oppression and injustice, it also de-legitimized moral authority. Finally, the swift rise of pluralism and multiculturalism in America rapidly secularized society and defined morality as a private matter based on personal opinion. By the 1970s, a new attempt at values education was introduced into the schools as 'values clarification.' The values clarification movement said: don't impose values but help students learn to choose their own. But it failed to distinguish between personal preferences and values that carry moral obligation, such as honesty and fairness."

"No wonder our society is going down the tubes!" Paul Christopher almost shouted. "What are we going to do about this situational ethics based on personal opinion?"

"In the 1990s, Paul, we're now seeing the beginnings of a new character education movement designed to counter situational ethics. This could restore good character to its historical place—the essential outcome of the school's moral enterprise. We don't know how many schools are catching on to moral or character education, but something significant is happening. In the early 1980s, the American Institute of Character Education in San Antonio, Texas produced early versions of curriculum materials for grades K-6. In July 1992, the Josephson Institute of Ethics called together more than 30 educational leaders representing state school boards, teacher unions, universities, ethics centers, youth organizations and religious groups. The institute published their six pillars of ethics and continued conducting surveys on the moral attitudes and behavior of students.[7] In March 1993, the Character Education Partnership was launched, headquartered in Alexandria, Virginia. It's a national coalition committed to putting character development at the top of the nation's educational agenda.[8] Just this past September, *Kappan* reported on its survey of 10,000 educators, who agreed on values critical to education—honesty, civility, equality, learning, freedom, and responsibility.[9] In the past few years, character education, a new field of research and practice, is suddenly booming."[10]

"Why now? What's behind this sudden national interest in character education?" Debbie asked. "Isn't this a cover for the Christian Right?"

"No, Debbie. The character education movement has the attention of serious scholars and educators from all persuasions—Christians, Jews, Moslems, and Buddhists, even secularists. Everyone is concerned about our slipping morality. I believe that most people see at least three causes of our cultural moral decline. First is the breakdown of the family, and the dramatic increase in single mothers who are cast into poverty with their children. Many critics have documented neglect of our children even as the country has become more prosperous. The number of children going into public schools with unprecedented emotional and behavioral problems is rising dangerously. These children are failing to achieve academically, getting pregnant, abusing drugs and alcohol, and getting in trouble with the law. Family disintegration, then, drives the character education movement in two ways. In order to conduct teaching and learning, schools have to teach the values kids aren't learning at home. Schools must also become caring moral communities that help children from dysfunctional homes focus on their work, control their anger, feel cared about, and become responsible students.

"The second cause is the troubling trends in youth character. Poor parenting, negative adult role models, the sex, violence, and materialism portrayed in mass media, and peer group pressure have all taken their toll on the character of our young people. I see several troubling trends: rising youth violence; increasing dishonesty (lying, cheating, and stealing); growing disrespect for authority; peer cruelty; bigotry on school campuses (from preschool through higher education); and ethical illiteracy. Other trends include declining work ethic and civic responsibility, increasing sexual immorality, self-centeredness, and self-destructive behavior. Let me just cite a few examples. The U.S. homicide rate for 15- to 24-year-old males is seven times higher than in Canada and 40 times higher than in Japan. The U.S. has one of the highest teenage pregnancy rates—Whites as well as Blacks— and the highest rates of teen abortion and drug use among young people in the developed world. Youth suicide has tripled in the past 25 years.[11] What is to be said about the morality of a modern society that permits this cannibalizing of its children?

"The third cause is that, given America's relatively rapid moral decline, some of us just may have been jolted out of our self-centered privatism and relativism. We are back searching for wisdom—that we share a basic morality, essential for our survival, and that adults must promote this morality by teaching the young, directly and indirectly. Most adults agree that such universal values as respect, responsibility, trustworthiness, fairness, caring and civic virtue must be acquired by all our young people if they are to become responsible adults. These values are not merely subjective, a matter of personal opinion. They have objective worth and a claim on our collective conscience as a society. *Not* teaching children these core ethical values is a grave failure of our age."

"Dr. Lickona, you've certainly made your point loud and clear,"Tamar spoke up. "I'm a new teacher. How do I start to grasp character education? How can we educators act responsibly when many families of the children we teach at Jefferson Elementary are not able to provide the moral education they'd like to?"

"To teach character education effectively," Tom answered, "we must understand that it encompasses three aspects of morality." He stepped to the whiteboard and wrote three words—cognitive (or thoughts), affective (or emotions), and behavioral (or actions). Then he said, "Good character consists of knowing the good, desiring the good, and doing the good. Schools must help children *understand* the core values, *adopt* or commit to them, and then *act upon* them. The cognitive side of character includes at least six moral qualities: perspective-taking, moral reasoning, thoughtful decision-making, and moral self-knowledge. The fifth quality is awareness of the moral dimensions of the situation. The sixth is knowing moral values and what they require of us in concrete cases. Full moral maturity and citizenship in a democratic society require these powers of rational moral thought.

"People can be very smart about right and wrong, but they may still choose the wrong. If moral education is merely intellectual, it misses the crucial emotional side of character , which serves as the bridge between judgment and action. The emotional side has at least the following qualities: conscience, which as been defined as the felt obligation to do what one judges to be right; self-respect; empathy; loving the good; self-control; and humility. Humility is a willingness both to recognize and correct our moral failings.

"At times, we know what we should do, and we feel strongly about it, yet we still fail to translate our judgment and feeling into effective moral behavior. Moral action draws upon three additional moral qualities: competence in such skills as listening, communicating, and cooperating; the will to mobilize our judgment and energy; and moral habit of responding to situations in a morally good way."

"How can this be translated to the school or classroom setting?" Kathie, the fifth grade teacher, wanted to know.

Kim looked at the teachers on the Commission. *They have to be sold on introducing character education into their daily classroom if this approach is going to fly. The parents and community members of the Commission look amazed— teachers actually taking the role of interested students. Of course, Ted looks bored,* she thought.

"Kathie, once we know the intellectual, emotional and behavioral guidelines for an effective character education program, then you can adopt a comprehensive approach for your school. This approach asks schools to see themselves through a moral lens; in fact, to consider that virtually everything that happens in the school affects the values and character of students. Then, plan to use all phases of classroom and school life as deliberate tools of character development. To maximize their moral clout, schools should develop a comprehensive, holistic approach. This means asking tough questions. Do present school practices support, neglect, or contradict its character education aims? For example, Kathie, here's a handout on classroom practice. This comprehensive approach to character education calls on the individual teacher to:

- **Act as caregiver, model, and mentor**, treating students with love and respect, setting a good example, supporting positive social behavior, and correcting hurtful actions through one-on-one guidance and whole-class discussion;

- **Create a moral community**, helping students know one another as persons, respect and care about one another, and feel valued membership in, and responsibility to, the group;

- **Practice moral discipline**, using the creation and enforcement of rules as opportunities to foster moral reasoning, voluntary compliance with rules, and a respect for others;

- **Create a democratic classroom environment**, involving students in decision making and the responsibility for making the classroom a good place to be and learn;

- **Teach values through the curriculum**, using the ethically-rich content of academic subjects as vehicles for teaching and examining moral questions;

- **Use cooperative learning** to develop students' appreciation of others, perspective taking, and ability to work with others toward common goals;

- **Develop the 'conscience of craft,'** fostering students' appreciation of learning, capacity for hard work, commitment to excellence, and sense of work as affecting the lives of others;

- **Encourage moral reflection** through reading, research, essay writing, journal keeping, discussion and debate; and

- **Teach conflict resolution**, so that students acquire the essential moral skills of solving conflicts fairly and without force."

"As a former teacher, Dr. Lickona, I'm impressed by your recommendations for teachers on developing a character education program in each classroom. But I'm a principal. So what is your advice on whole-school character education," said Kim Young.

"Kim, please call me Tom. Many schools lack a positive, cohesive moral culture. Let me demonstrate the whole-school or whole-district approach with a case study of Mt. Lebanon School District." Tom passed his handout to the group. I'll outline a comprehensive approach that calls upon the whole-school to:

- **Provide moral leadership.** It is absolutely essential that leadership sets, models, and consistently enforces high standards of respect and responsibility. Teachers will feel demoralized in their individual efforts to teach good values effectively unless they have a positive school environment;

BEST PRACTICES: CHARACTER EDUCATION

The Mt. Lebanon School District lies just south of Pittsburgh, Pennsylvania.[12] Henry Huffman, assistant superintendent for instruction, describes how the District began in 1988 by holding a PTA workshop for parents. They invited Dr. Tom Lickona, author of a leading book on character education, to speak to the group of 700. The response was so positive that they decided to invite all school staff to join in writing a strategic plan. More than 40 teachers volunteered to work with the planning group.

During the implementation process, the group learned several lessons about getting started. First, be prepared to answer three critical questions about character education: Why, What and How? Second, immediately involve parents, students, faculty and community representatives. And third, develop a communications plan for informing the community and all school employees about the details of your action plan. Dr. Huffman said, "A successful character education plan requires strong leadership at the central office and building level. An "executive champion" is needed, someone who has influence on the school board and in the community; someone who has access to district funds, interpersonal skills necessary to building a critical mass of support, and the authority to make things happen. Our strategic planning process involved more than 200 residents, school staff, and students in developing the character education plan. They communicated the plans effectively several times to the district's staff and the community's 40,000 residents. The group sought visible and substantive support from the school board, which is of critical importance.

The core values adopted by the school district became a statement of belief and a guideline to the school community as it integrated character education into the district's programs. They described a person with core values as one who respects human dignity; shows active responsibility for the welfare of others; integrates individual interests and social responsibilities; demonstrates integrity; applies moral principles when making choices and judgments; and seeks peaceful resolution of conflict. The group learned that it was important to clarify what is meant by values; to define each core value with concrete examples; to follow a process in developing the core values that produces a feeling of ownership—

even though it is slower; to be willing to face controversy because discussing and negotiating value conflicts integrates the community. The group also created a short list of single-word core values; and they learned that core values significantly affect even district operations.

"We shared our character education action plan with school staff," Huffman said, "by making a presentation to all district employees with the support of the superintendent. Then we presented the same plan to the community. Later we expanded a handout into a resource book explaining the history, philosophy, terminology, resources, and bibliography on character education. We also contacted citizens who were critical and set up discussions of the program."

The group's strategy was to integrate character education into existing district academic curriculum rather than adopt a separate curriculum. Core values were translated into behavioral habits by using "user-friendly" materials to supplement daily teaching activities. Ideas were gathered from other successful character education programs. The group learned how important it is to create a context for integrating core values—knowing what's right (the head), caring what is right (the heart) and doing what's right (the hand). They found it essential to place discussions of character education into larger social issues within the curriculum subjects, which presented many opportunities for integrating the core values. They even began integrating values instruction into staff development activities.

Their plans for upgrading the character education environment focused on three strategies: developing a building-level, pro-social code for students that is based on the core values and written by students, teachers, administrators and parents; developing and publishing widely a code of ethics for employees and the School Board; developing "service learning" experiences for elementary and middle school. In high school, these experiences became mandatory for graduation.

- **Foster caring beyond the classroom.** Use positive role models to inspire altruistic behavior and provide service opportunities for both school and community;

- **Create a positive moral culture in the school.** Develop a schoolwide expectation that supports and amplifies the values taught in class-rooms. This is done through leadership of the principal, discipline, a schoolwide sense of community, meaningful student government, a moral community among adults, and making time for moral concerns; and

- **Recruit parents and the community as partners in character education.** Recognize that parents are a child's first and most important moral teacher and give parents specific ways to reinforce the values the school is trying to teach. The school needs to seek the help of the community, churches, businesses, local government, and the media in promoting the core ethical values.

"After two years, we learned three lessons about parent education as a high priority. First, parent education sessions should be offered at two levels—preschool through elementary and middle school through high school. Second, sessions should be offered in the day-time and evening because preschool through elementary draws three or four times as many parents. Third, all series should cover six single-topic sessions.

"We also learned lessons about evaluation design. In the initial planning phase, for instance, plans for evaluation, including an implementation assessment, should be developed. Literature should be reviewed on evaluation of character education programs. And it's especially important that parents, students, all staff, and community agencies be involved in developing evaluation components.

Ray, the Commission chair, couldn't wait to speak up. "Tom, your character education program has certainly opened my eyes. Why isn't every school adopting this right now? How could anyone lose by implementing this approach?"

"Thanks for your positive reactions, Ray. Let me say that whether or not character education takes hold in American schools remains to be seen. But its long-range success will depend on public support for school reform. This means that the religious community will need to get behind character education instead of sniping at public schools for their shortcomings. The character education movement also depends on whether or not college and university education programs start preparing future teachers and equipping present teachers with the knowledge and skills to implement this in their classrooms.[13]   Parents and others may have to demand it as part of nationwide school reform.

"Wendy, I see my time is up. I've enjoyed meeting with you and this fine Commission. Good luck on your mission to reform Jefferson Elementary School."[14]

"Thank you for introducing us to character education, Tom," said Wendy, "Let's take a refreshment break."

****

Nate said, "Our next two guests, Dr. David Brooks and Dr. Eric Schaps are here in Washington, D.C. attending a conference of the Character Education Partnership. We are fortunate to have them appear before our Commission. Our first guest, Dr. David Brooks, is from my part of the country in southern California. He is president of the Jefferson Center for Character Education located in Pasadena. He has an unusual background as an elementary, middle and high school teacher, and also as a counselor and a high school principal. David, your colleague Tom Lickona has introduced us to the history of character education. And I understand that you and Frank Goble are updating his book on *The Case for Character Education.*"

"Yes, we are, Nate," said Dr. Brooks, "and I should briefly mention that Frank Goble was an early pioneer in this field. He was a business executive and engineer who became concerned about character development almost 20 years ago. He's a leading authority on the great psychologist Abraham Maslow whose work in human values provides a scientific foundation for the revival of character education today. I say revival because a concern for teaching youth moral values can be traced to ancient Egypt in the 27th Century B.C., to ancient India, Greece and China, and, of course, to ancient Israel and the Ten Commandments.

"Does this sound familiar? **'Our youth now love luxury, they have bad manners, contempt for authority, show disrespect for their elders, and love to chatter in place of exercise. They no longer rise when elders enter the room. They contradict their parents, they chatter before company, they gobble their food, and terrorize their teachers.'** Socrates said this nearly 24 hundred years ago.

"These youth problems eventually led to the decline and fall of the Greek empire. In ancient China, Confucius said, 'Men possess a moral nature; but if they are well fed, warmly clad, and comfortably lodged without at the same time being instructed, they become like unto beasts.' And commenting on our day, an American philosopher, Andrew Oldenquist said, 'If we found that they (leaders) had ceased to teach, through ritual and other organized means, the moral and other values of their culture, we would take them to be on the way to cultural suicide.'[15]

"For the past two decades, we've been concerned with relatively low-level academic achievement. But we actually have a far more serious problem. I speak of youth character disorders, as measured by such symptoms as suicide, homicide, and drug use among all races and classes. In my judgment, this has become an even more profound challenge than the decline of formal education. In the 1990s, political leaders from both parties seem convinced, however, that the solution for crime and violence is more police, more jails, and longer jail sentences. The first money from the 1994 national crime bill was used to put more police on the street, implying that the cause of crime is insufficient law enforcement. What's wrong with this picture? Do we really know what causes crime? Thirty years of expert advice from behavioral scientists have pointed to poverty, discrimination, unemployment and other injustices.

"Crime and violence have risen to alarming heights, in the very years we've invested the most in welfare and education to reduce poverty. If poverty is the cause of crime, why is crime among affluent youth steadily increasing? And what about such white-collar crime as the Savings and Loan and Wall Street traders scandals? It is finally dawning on people that **the root cause of crime, violence, drug addiction, and other symptoms of irresponsible behavior is inadequate character education of our youth. Responsible behavior must be consciously taught and observed**.

After making this powerful point, David Brooks went on. "In addressing the American Bar Association in 1981, Chief Justice Warren Burger said, 'We have virtually eliminated from the public schools and higher education any effort to teach values…[This has led to a] 'reign of terror in American cities.' Following up on Justice Berger's charges, his Administrative Assistant, Dr. Mark W. Cannon, said,[16]

> Violent crime and juvenile delinquency have been ascending. Attempts to explain and fight crime have been only partially successful. The diminished influence of traditional institutions and our failure to promote ethical standards suggest another explanation for crime. Audiovisual media have

partially replaced the family, church, school, and community in conveying values to the oncoming generation, and these often appear to encourage hedonism and the use of force. We are in jeopardy of becoming a valueless society and of encouraging decision-making by aggression instead of by reason and democratically established law. If this is the case, then possible avenues to pursue in the prevention and elimination of crime are: teach values in our schools; promote law-related education so young people understand both the rights and the responsibilities of our Constitution and the legal system; increase youth activities by constructive organizations; guide children to quality media productions; increase the number of potential bonds or attachments citizens have with pro-social institutions; strengthen families and communities; and educate and constructively counsel delinquents. We must, in short, revitalize and strengthen the moral and ethical foundation of our society.

"Dr. Brooks, what finally triggered the renewed national interest in character education?" Debbie Cohen asked.

"A July 1992 three-day meeting in Aspen, Colorado ignited national efforts, although there were already some character education programs in local schools. Josephson Institute of Ethics brought together educators, youth leaders, ethics scholars and other professionals to develop a common language for advocates of character education. In their Aspen Declaration, they identified six core ethical values that transcend cultural, religious, and socioeconomic differences: respect, responsibility, trustworthiness, caring, fairness and citizenship.[17] These form the basis of a democratic society. Since then the Character Counts Coalition and the Character Education Partnership have become clearinghouses for thousands of local initiatives that introduce character education programs into local schools. It appears that a genuine grassroots movement is underway! Even the federal government officials are interested. Under the 1994 *Improving America's School Act*, California, Iowa, New Mexico and Utah received grants for character education pilot projects. In 1996 there were also some grants to states, including Maryland."

"Dr. Brooks," Paul asked, "I think we'd all agree this is a promising solution for our social problems. I'm excited because it looks like a program that focuses on personal responsibility for changing life conditions, not on more money for social experiments that have failed up to now." *Paul Christopher has his conservative business hat on again,* Maria thought.

"Dr. Brooks, Dave, could you elaborate on the family and the community responsibility for teaching children character education or good moral habits? Schools can't be expected to do it alone!" Christina Peterson from Community Interfaith spoke up.

"That's a critical issue, Christina. Here's a BEST PRACTICES handout to look at. Historically, teaching character and values has been shared by the community.[18] The African proverb, 'It takes a village to raise a child' is even more true today. As we said before, public education from the beginning has had a two-fold mission: to teach children to be smart and to teach them to be good. Actually it's difficult to teach children to be smart *unless* they're taught to be good. This means the individual student cannot cop out on his or her behavior by blaming parents, poverty, or even the peer group. Each has the responsibility for his or her own behavior. The family, community, and schools used to teach language, attitudes, and skills of good character.

"But during the 1960s, '70s and '80s, the mass media has eroded the influence of families and community organizations, such as churches and synagogues. Records, tapes, television shows and advertisements glorify sex and violence and reinforce the prevailing attitude of doing your own thing. It didn't take long for the youth to act out the culture of narcissism, hedonism or selfishness. Today, however, we're finally seeing a community rebellion—not only by the Christian Coalition. All religious faiths are joining with community youth organizations, law enforcement and government agencies, business groups and schools. Educators have our children's attention each day, so they're opening the dialogue. Clearly faith communities and youth organizations can join with parents and educators to advocate effective character education programs that reach children and youth."

"But Dave, I'm Jewish. I don't want my children brainwashed by the Christian Coalition, the Baptists, the Catholics or any other religious group!" said Debbie.

"Fair enough, Debbie. But the question is not whose values, but what values. The character education programs I know of refuse to be missionaries for any given religious group. All great religions hold common principles, however, which they've taught their followers throughout history.

BEST PRACTICES: CHARACTER EDUCATION PROGRAMS

The Jefferson Center for Character Education has implemented its programs in St. Louis, Pittsburgh, Honolulu and Los Angeles. They are convinced that eleven elements are essential if a program is to be carried out effectively in our public schools:[19]

1. *Direct Instruction.* Like arithmetic, the teaching of character values such as responsibility and respect must be purposeful and directly taught through specific curriculum activities. Educators cannot assume that the language, concepts, behaviors and skills of good character are written into the genetic code. They are not absorbed through the invisible hand of the general curriculum, but are learned at home, from television, or in the neighborhood.

2. *Language-based Curriculum.* Children entering the schools today often lack the vocabulary for understanding basic value concepts such as honesty and courage. Successful character education programs focus students' attention on the basic language that expresses core concepts and links the words to explicit behavior. At Newcomb School in Long Beach, California, for example, students in a third grade class learned the meaning of courage by working in cooperative learning groups to identify courageous ways they could act in the classroom.

3. *Positive Language.* Students must know what is expected of them if they are to practice appropriate behavior. Instructions in common negative language, such as "Don't be late"or "Don't forget your pencil," are less effective than using explicit positive language, such as "Be on time" or "Be prepared with a pencil." At Bellerive School in St. Louis County, Missouri, a veteran teacher was overheard telling a new teacher to stop telling the kids, "Don't do this or that." She said to tell them what you want them to do, as in "Sit down." "Complete your homework assignment." To the new teacher's amazement, the students did!

4. *Content and Process.* In addition to teaching the content of consensus and civic values, an effective character education curriculum should provide a process for implementing those values when making decisions. We teach a four step decision-making process

for making ethical choices in practical situations. The STAR method shows students how to (1) Stop what you are doing; (2) Think about what is happening; (3) Act ethically; and (4) Review my actions asking myself, did my actions further my personal responsibility? At Parmalee Elementary School in Los Angeles, students are taught that honesty is better than dishonesty, that being polite is better than being rude through actual experience encounters using the STAR process.

5. *Visual Reinforcement.* Character education is in competition with society's opposing or hostile desires, messages, and pressures, most effectively delivered through the media. The visual presentation of character values is, in effect, an advertising campaign intended to keep students focused on the words, concepts, and behaviors learned in class. The campaign must be illustrated in as colorful a display as possible. In the hallways of the Santa Barbara Junior High School, students encounter 4' x 8' silver and blue character signs hanging from the hallway ceilings.

6. *School Climate Approach.* This approach generates a common culture and language that fosters positive peer recognition and encourages all members of the school community to exemplify and reward behavior consistent with core values and responsible ethical decision making. Effective character education spills over the boundaries of the classroom into the playground, the office, the cafeteria, the bus, and the neighborhood, thus reinforcing the core values taught in the home. During "Be Polite" month at the Bellerive School in St. Louis, for example, students, faculty and visitors are greeted with a large calendar listing the different ways to be polite each day of the month.

7. *Teacher-friendly Materials.* Teachers must see systematic character education as an essential component of their teaching mission. Teachers must be able to implement the character education curriculum with limited training and preparation. They should not have to write lengthy lesson plans, prepare student handouts, search out supplementary materials, or decode impossibly complex instructional manuals. The Thomas Jefferson Center on Character Education has published a colorful set of illustrated materi-

als for students and teachers for each grade level using literature and stories that inspire and teach character values in an exciting way.

8. *Teacher Flexibility and Creativity.* Teachers not only need a basic framework to work with, but they also should be able to adjust character education lessons to individual teaching and learning styles. A successful character education curriculum is sufficiently flexible to allow teachers to exercise creativity in addressing special classroom circumstances, while adhering to school wide standards. Some teachers may integrate character education lessons into ongoing curricular subject areas like history or English, while others may teach it as a separate subject.

9. *Student Participation.* It is almost useless to tell students how to behave. Character education is most effective when students develop a sense of ownership by participating in the process of framing the goals they will achieve. At the Kauluwela School in Honolulu, Hawaii, each fifth-grade student participates in goal setting, such as completing homework, and develops written plans on how best to carry out that character habit.

10. *Parental Involvement and Then Some.* Character education programs are most effective and enduring when the school routinely confers with parents, shares what is being taught, and involves them in the curriculum. Bellerive School helped to sustain and enrich its program, first by keeping parents informed of the theme of the month, and then by providing suggestions for how parents could encourage theme-appropriate behavior at home; and

11. *Evaluation.* Implementation of a character education program must include a pre-assessment of goals, occasional consultation during the program and then a post-evaluation of results. In the planning stages, school staff should clearly articulate their expectations and detail the goals they hope to accomplish. During the 1990-91 school year, the 25 Los Angeles elementary and middle schools completing the Jefferson Center pilot program found that major discipline problems decreased by 25%; minor discipline problems by 39%; suspensions by 16%; tardiness by 40%; and unexcused absences (lost revenue to the district) by 18 %. At the same time, the num-

bers of students on the honor role increased.[20] In 1994 the Learning Research and Development Center at the University of Pittsburgh conducted an evaluation of the STAR program and found it successfully meeting its education goals.

"These are valuing the family, the individual, the community, hard work, delayed gratification and courage. In other words, the six pillars of character I mentioned earlier. I'm going to repeat them. If anyone objects to this list, raise your hands. *Trustworthiness,* which encompasses honesty, integrity, promise keeping and loyalty. So far I don't see any hands raised. I'll keep going: *Respect for Others; Responsibility,* which includes accountability, excellence and self-restraint; *Fairness* or justice; *Caring,* which means sharing, kindness and compassion; and *Citizenship,* which includes civic virtue, play by the rules, obey laws, respect authority, be charitable, be informed and vote, protect neighbors, pay taxes, volunteer service to help community and protect environment. I still don't see any hands raised. Debbie, tell me, are these values all right with you? Can the schools teach your child these values? And, just as important, can you as a parent do the same?"

"It's finally getting through to me what character education is all about. Now I think I'm embarrassed," Debbie said. "I can see that this is a job for everyone. We've got to keep our children from self-destructing."

Nate Johnson agreed. "Between you and Tom Lickona, Dave, we've had our eyes opened to an obvious and very powerful antidote to the destructive behavior patterns of youth and adults. We see these problems everyday when we read the headlines of our newspapers or watch the evening news. We realize that character education is a solution that we have not tried in this country for many years. Its absence left a void that has been filled by the tremendously destructive pop culture we now have."

"David, let's assume we buy your solution," said Paul. "Suppose character education programs were adopted in every school across the nation. Suppose that every family, community organization, business and government agency were to demand it by tomorrow morning. What can a school do now while we are waiting for the results of character education programs. It takes time to shape the habits of students going through the public schools? What can we do in the short run? Does anyone else have this question?"

BEST PRACTICES: SAFE SCHOOLS—[21]
A PLANNING GUIDE FOR ACTION

The Safe Schools program is a joint project of the California Department of Education's School Safety and Violence Prevention Office and the Office of the California Attorney Generals Crime and Violence Prevention Center. It has a description and a "tool kit" for any school to use in putting together an effective safe school program. This is not to be confused with a sound character education program. It's an effective band-aid, a sometimes life saving one, while schools implement a solid character education program. It represents an action step schools can adopt immediately and can be integrated with other models of systemic school reform considered.

Safe Schools: A Planning Guide for Action presents the latest ideas about creating safe school environments. The recommendations come from successful education and law enforcement partners who have tested the strategies in communities as large as Los Angeles and as small as Joshua Tree. Over the past ten years, it has been refined and revised and now represents the wisdom and experience of hundreds of dedicated professionals.

How can safe schools be created? First, recognize that safe schools are *caring schools*. Students in safe schools feel respected and know that the people in that learning community care about their individual needs and expect them to succeed. Each student's cultural heritage is respected, and there is tolerance for racial, language, physical, and ethnic difference in the school. Similarly, staff members in a safe school perceive that they are safe and that their ideas about school improvement are valued. Safe schools welcome parents and community members who share their ideas, talents and resources to improve the school culture and to make the school a valued part of the community.

Second, safe schools are built through the *cooperative efforts* of parents, students, teachers, security staff, classified staff, law enforcement representatives, and community members and leaders. The continued involvement of a broad spectrum of the community in the design and constant revision of a safe school plan ensures that the community stays informed and invested in the endeavor to keep the school a safe and successful learning community. The community's involvement also ensures that there are alternatives in the community to assist students who have difficulties adjusting to the school environment.

Third, safe schools communicate *high standards*. Students and staff know that learning and achievement are encouraged and highly valued and that positive social behaviors are expected. They know that the achievement of each individual is valued regardless of innate academic or physical talents. The consequences for violating the rules and standards are equally clear.

Fourth, safe schools stress *prevention*, and staff and students are *prepared*. Ongoing training opportunities allow students and staff to increase their ability to deal with conflict, anger, and other threats to safety. Safe schools have security checks on a regular basis to identify physical hazards or the school's vulnerability to crime and vandalism. They also institute ongoing programs to prevent gang activity; drug, tobacco, and alcohol abuse; and other negative behaviors. Finally, because it is impossible to prevent all problems, safe schools have crisis response plans in place to deal with unforeseen emergencies.

Why is it absolutely necessary to undertake a safe school plan? Because safe schools create an environment where effective education can take place. Schools also have a legal responsibility to provide equal safe school environments to all students. Safe school planning carries out the school's social responsibility. Every future drug user, suicide victim, gang member, dropout, child abuse victim, and arsonist is at one time a student. A safe school builds public confidence in public education and thus carries out a financial responsibility.

Safe school planning, like all school reform planning and implementation, requires seven specific steps to be successful:

- Identify your safe school planning committee by soliciting broad representation from students, parents, faculty and staff and integrating with other school reform committees and activities;

- Create a vision for your school by brainstorming and coming to an agreement on what your ideal school should look like, compare it with the school's educational mission, compare present conditions with the vision, and obtain vision consensus;

- Gather and analyze information about your school's existing conditions and its' community relationships by involving parents, staff, students, and community members—both qualitative and quantitative information, inventory resources, including people with expertise, and identify areas of pride and strength;

- Identify your school's and community's areas of desired change by identifying needed change and improvement, explore possible causes of safety concerns, identify what needs to change to meet new requirements, and make action priorities;

- Set your major goal by ranking your significant safety concerns and select your goals that must be attained during the coming academic year;

- Select and implement strategies, actions and resources for carrying out each safe school component; assign responsibilities, timelines, and completion dates and develop evaluation criteria and timelines; and

- Evaluate and assess your progress by monitoring the implementation of the plan, determining whether goals are being achieved, reassess the safe school vision, committee membership, and priorities at least quarterly and celebrate your success.[22]

The Safe School process works! A Safe Schools Planning Tool Kit for School-Community Teams for school, school board, parents and community leaders helps them create a safe school environment while implementing a serious preventive character education program. The combination could reverse our climate of destructive culture and behavior.

"I do, Nate," volunteered Dale. *Rush Limbaugh would love these guys,* Dale thought. *This is powerful stuff.*

"I hear you, guys. As I understand it, your question is, how can schools protect students from the violence and lawlessness that surround them now while we take the time to put this program in place? Is that what you're asking?" Heads nodded. The handout about safe schools is from Los Angeles County Office of Education.

"Let me share with you some statistics about the crime surrounding our schools today," David continued. "In or near our 85,000 public schools, more than three million crimes a year are committed. The FBI's Violent Crimes Index indicates that between 1987 and 1991 juvenile arrests increased by 50%—twice the increase for persons 18 years of age or older. But even more alarming during the same period, juvenile arrests for murder increased by 85% compared to a 21% increase for those over 18 years of age. In a survey of tenth- to twelfth-grade students, 55% know that weapons are regularly brought to school; 79% say that violence often occurs from 'stupid' things, like 'bumping into someone.' Some believe that juvenile crime increases when teen population rises.

"If that's true, then over the next decade, we can anticipate an even greater increase in youth murder arrests since youth population increases (ages 15 to 19) are projected to be 23%.[22] But since 1985, murder arrests of youths under 18 jumped 92% as the population of that group remained steady! We'd better start making school safety and character education one of our highest education priorities!

"David, we've kept you longer than you anticipated. But we've really appreciated your remarks. Thanks for meeting with us!" Turning to the group, Nate said, "Take a short break, stretch your legs.

✷✷✷✷✷✷✷✷✷✷✷✷✷✷

"Welcome back," Wendy said enthusiastically. "Our third guest today is Dr. Eric Schaps, president of the Developmental Studies Center in Oakland, California. Dr. Schaps is a social psychologist and a specialist in program evaluation. Eric, thanks for staying over to be with us. Tell us about the Developmental Studies Center."

"Thank you, Wendy. I've enjoyed listening to my colleagues, David Brooks and Tom Lickona. I'm working closely with them in the Character Education Partnership. I'll try not to cover the same ground. I'll focus on the Center's work during the past 16 years. The Developmental Studies Center (DSC) is a nonprofit organization. Its research and development programs foster children's ethical, social, and intellectual development.[24] Our largest and oldest project, the Child Development Project (CDP), helps elementary schools to strengthen children's tendencies to be caring and responsible and their motivation to learn. It also focuses on helping children develop their capacities to think skillfully and critically, so they can continue learning throughout their lives. The overall program is both intensive and comprehensive, including Classroom, Schoolwide, and Family Involvement Programs. The Classroom Program focuses broadly on curriculum content, pedagogy, and classroom climate. The Schoolwide Program focuses on school policies, practices and events. And the Family Involvement Program concentrates on creating, expanding, and maintaining links between school and home."

Lenora leaned over to Delores and whispered, "I like what he says, but what's that word peda...pedagogy?"

Delores whispered back, "It has to do with how you go about teaching." Then, turning back to Dr. Schaps, she asked, "Could you explain your classroom program?"

"We believe that classroom teachers need instructional and curricular materials in the regular subject areas that help them figure out how to do things differently.[25] So we have formulated three approaches to the classroom program:

1. A literature-based reading and language arts program that stimulates children's enjoyment of reading and encourages them to think deeply about what they read, while helping them build empathy for others and values such as loyalty and caring;

2. A cooperative approach to classroom learning that emphasizes the importance of challenging and meaningful learning tasks, the benefits of students collaborating on learning tasks, and the importance of learning to work with others in fair, caring, and responsible ways; and

3. An approach to classroom management and discipline that builds a caring community in which all are treated with respect. It uses problem solving and emphasizes intrinsic motivation (rather than rewards and punishments) to develop student responsibility and competence."

"Have you developed specific materials we can use in the classroom?" asked Delores.

"Yes, we've developed extensive materials for students, teachers and parents at each grade level."

"What about your schoolwide program, Dr. Schaps?" asked Kim.

"It has various activities and events, often planned and carried out by a team of parents and teachers, designed to involve parents in the life of the school and in their children's learning. It includes family events at school and a series of activities for students and their parents (or other significant adults) to do together at home that are closely coordinated with the curriculum. For example, once or twice each month, teachers send home 15- to 20- minute Homeside Activities that the student and a parent can do together (in both English and Spanish).[26] Often, these activities involve children asking their parents about their personal experiences that relate to what the children are learning in their classrooms.

"Our work on the Child Development Project began in 1980, and our approaches and assumptions have been systematically evolving since then as we've tried to learn from our experiences. In our early work, for example, we realized the importance of supportive schoolwide and family-involvement activities. We've gradually expanded these aspects of the program. With respect to the process of making change, we've discovered the critical importance of working with a total school faculty simultaneously and of creating district-level commitment and active support. More recently, we've moved from conducting our own staff development to training cadres of experts within a district. They can then take over the responsibility for training new teachers, supporting and maintaining the program within the initial schools, and extending it to new schools.

"During our years of implementing and refining the CDP program, we've come to see the development of a 'caring community of learners' in the classroom and in the school itself as an essential intermediate goal. We define caring community of learners as one in which faculty, students, and parents are all concerned about one another, are actively involved in learning together, and help and support one another continually to achieve their common goals. Providing a sense of community is an important part of meeting children's basic psychological needs for belonging, competence and autonomy. Students become committed to the norms and values of the school and the larger society when they participate in such a community.

"The CDP program emphasizes four values which the caring community both exemplifies and helps children to adopt and internalize. These include the values of *helpfulness* and *concern for others*—a considerate, kind, and caring attitude that is not limited to concern for members of one's own group; *fairness*—an interest in having everyone treated justly and equitably; and *personal responsibility*—feeling committed to do one's best, to par-

ticipate actively, to do one's fair share. I should add that we believe character education should not be an *indoctrination* program. It is a *teaching* program to encourage children to gradually understand the values being examined and see why positive values are useful to their own lives—an intrinsic motivation rather than a reward or punishment approach.[27]

"How effective is your program, Dr. Schaps?" Ray asked. "Can you share
with us your evaluation of results from schools that have tried your program?"

"Yes, from the beginning, we've been very big on conducting careful assessments of our programs. Our first effort to pilot and evaluate the CDP
program longitudinally occurred in San Ramon, California, beginning in
the 1982-83 school year and continuing through 1988-89. There we worked
closely with teachers in three program schools, one grade level at a time, to
develop and implement the program. We followed a cohort of students
receiving the program from kindergarten through sixth grade, and then into
eighth grade in a two-year followup assessment in intermediate school. The
evaluation also included teachers and students in three comparison schools
that were similar to the program schools in terms of demographic characteristics and scores on a series of assessments conducted the year before the
start of the program.[28]

"We trained observers to use a system specifically designed to assess each
implementation. Data from repeated yearly visits to each participating classroom showed large differences between the program and comparison classrooms, with program teachers scoring higher on all the indicators. We also
assessed effects of the program on students' interpersonal behavior, attitudes, academic and interpersonal motivation, moral reasoning, and academic performance. We did this with interviews, small-group activities,
questionnaires (from third grade up), and achievement tests. Over the seven
years of this longitudinal evaluation, we found consistent, repeated differences that favored the program students:

- Their behavior toward one another in classrooms was more positive and considerate;

- They got along better and worked better with their classmates and
  were less lonely in school;

- They showed better understanding of others and greater ability to
  solve interpersonal problems and conflicts;

- They showed greater commitment to democratic values;
- Although both groups scored at the same high level on standardized achievement tests, the program students scored higher on a performance-based measure of higher-order reading comprehension;
- Program students also were more likely to see their classrooms as *communities*, and this sense of community was itself related to a broad set of other positive characteristics among students like self-esteem, social competence, empathy, achievement motivation, and reading comprehension.

"Follow-up assessments in eighth grade showed program students to have better conflict resolution skills and higher self-esteem, and to be rated as more popular and assertive by their teachers. We concluded that results in San Ramon demonstrated the CDP program could be well-implemented in public schools, and that it was effective in bringing about many of the positive effects for students' social, ethical, and intellectual development.

"We are now completing assessments in six more districts where CDP was gradually introduced beginning in 1991—Louisville, Kentucky; Cupertino, Salinas and San Francisco, California; Dade County, Florida; and White Plains, New York. Preliminary analyses of the data show a positive impact on students' social, ethical and intellectual development where the program was well implemented.[29] These positive outcomes include significant reductions in alcohol and marijuana use and in such delinquent behaviors as carrying weapons and joining gangs. In many cases, disadvantaged students in high-poverty schools showed that a caring school community makes an even greater impact on their positive outcomes."[30]

"I guess I'm still lost, Dr. Schaps," said Maria. "I don't understand how your program is different from the other character education programs."

"Maria, probably the way we differ most strongly from other approaches to character education and from traditional academic improvement programs is by emphasizing that effective reform lies in educators *simultaneously* focusing on the child's intellectual, social, and ethical development. We see these three dimensions of child development as inescapably intertwined within every student, and we believe every schooling decision inescapably affects all three. So our approach aims at *systematic, integrated* attention to all three dimensions of development in every decision about classroom pedagogy, content, and discipline, and in every school policy decision.

"Today, there is a continuing conflict between what parents say they want children to become—able, motivated learners and principled, caring human beings—and our nation's preoccupation with test scores to prove schools are giving us our money's worth. Education that emphasizes memorization and drill and neglects understanding may actually be causing many of the well-publicized failures of American students.[31] **Common classroom and school discipline practice based on teacher-imposed rewards and punishments—assertive discipline—usually turns off most children, especially children who are disadvantaged.** They need to explore learning for its own sake. School improvement strategies must ask whether or not a new curriculum fosters students' intrinsic interest in learning and builds bonds with fellow students as well as increases students' subject-matter knowledge. Schools must become caring communities for all their students. They must provide all of them with an engaging, challenging curriculum to optimize their chances of becoming mature, healthy, knowledgeable and self-actualizing adults.

"I could go on about these issues, but I see that our time is up. Thank you for being such a receptive group today. I wish you well in your Jefferson Elementary School mission."

"Thanks, Eric. You've given us much to think about," Nate said, as he took over again. "Here's a BEST PRACTICES handout on a CDP school."

"I'd like to summarize the major points that have been made today," said Nate.

"Hold on a minute," said Ted Alexander, frustrated. "I think we've been exposed to an afternoon of propaganda. These scare tactics advocate indoctrinating our kids with conservative values. I've heard all this before so I've done some homework. I've discovered there are lots of important people who don't agree with this."

"Tell us about it, Ted!" said Nate."

"I read four articles criticizing character education programs and took notes. They made sense to me.[32] They made these points:

- There is no direct correlation between the values people profess and their behavior. Back in 1928-30, Hartshorne and May studied students in fifth through eighth grade in 23 communities across the United States. The study showed that most children were taught about honesty and service but when they had the opportunity to

BEST PRACTICES: CHILD DEVELOPMENT PROJECT

In 1991 Jefferson County, Kentucky, was selected as one of six districts for expanded testing of the Child Development Project (CDP), which aims to improve children's intellectual, social and ethical learning. Hazelwood Elementary was chosen to be a program school as the state was embarking on what is probably the most sweeping education reform in the nation. Built in 1951, the school lies adjacent to the largest Federal Housing Project in Kentucky. Only a rusted chain-link fence separates the school from this Housing Project, where most students (75%) reside.

Hazelwood has about 40 teachers for their 600 disadvantaged students, who are African American (48%), Caucasian (48%) and Asian or Hispanic (4%). Few enrichment opportunities exist for these children, who live among the ravages of drugs and violence each day. The school receives $1976 per child from the general fund. At this time, 95% of students are eligible for free or reduced meals. Because so many children come from families in poverty, it also gets $400,000 (an additional 34% above the state budget) from the federal Title 1 School-wide Program. Hazelwood has used this extra money to develop a science lab, to hire a full-time computer teacher, instruction assistants for classrooms and more reading teachers who can bring students in the primary years up to grade level.

"When I first came," said Brenda Logan, who became principal barely a year before the Project started, "teachers were lined up at the door trying to find other places to go...It's a high-risk area, and you're dealing with poverty and difficult parents." She found that teachers were having difficulty keeping order in their classes by using assertive-discipline techniques with rewards—checks or stickers—for good behavior.

When the Child Development Project was introduced, teacher reactions ranged from supportive to skeptical, although a large majority of the faculty had voted to adopt it. They soon discovered that CDP provided the "up-close" support that was missing from the Kentucky Education Reform Act (KERA). In training sessions, teachers were taught to revamp their teaching practices and to maintain order with minimal use of extrinsic rewards or punishments. They learned how to create environments that foster learning, to ask the kinds of questions that develop students' critical thinking, to have children work cooperatively in groups, and to help students take responsibility for their own learning. As a result, teachers changed the way they presented academic curriculum; they still gave some lectures but much of the time in class they served as "facilitators of learning."

Ongoing staff development has helped develop a clear vision for the school with strong staff ownership. Workshops are practical and also provide opportunities for teacher networking within the building. Faculty members reconvene regularly to determine successes and needs. The entire staff has focused on developmental discipline, cooperative learning, a Buddy Program and constructivist learning. Hazelwood's dynamic principal, Brenda Logan, says that this next year she hopes to get "more input from the site-based leadership team' in order to continue deepening commitment to the CDP philosophy.

The CDP cooperative learning lessons teach students both academic content and techniques for getting along. For example, students learn skills to resolve problems that arise on the playground or elsewhere. In teaching reading, teachers build character by selecting from the CDP's list of 200 books chosen for their literary quality and for the constructive values they portray.

Gradually other program components were put in place, including making strong home connections with families. Parents and grandparents are encouraged to visit the school. The school holds annual "family nights" where parents and children share supper and academic activities. A "buddy system" brings younger and older students together weekly for mentoring and team building in a variety of ways. Careful attention is paid to "unity building" exercises that promote a sense of caring and community.

After only one year in the CDP, positive changes in teacher and student behavior were evident. Teacher requests for transfers to other schools nearly stopped. They were able to create a warm, caring and stimulating environment for themselves and their students. The number of discipline problems referred to the principal's office dropped from about 50 a month to 12. Over a sustained period of time, based on state assessments, the students' test scores improved. Strong teachers with high expectations and a focus on literature helped Hazelwood surpass its state goals. For example, state assessments of reading initially showed more than half (56%) of Hazelwood's students scored in the lowest quartile, while one year later less than one in five (18%) were reading that poorly. One year ago, Hazelwood qualified as a "reward school" in Kentucky. The school's ongoing improvement shows fundamental changes in delivering its academic and character education program. "We're really using those test scores to diagnose what we need to do to get those students where they need to be," states Brenda Logan, Hazelwood's principal.

cheat, they did.[33] In 1969 Lawrence Kohlberg said, 'Half a dozen studies show no positive correlation between high school or college students' verbal valuing of honesty or badness of cheating and actual honest behavior in experimental situations.'[34]

- When core values come into conflict, as they sometimes do, character educators don't teach children how to choose—and that's one fallacy in their theory.

- Character education indoctrinates youth into core values that transmit the status quo and teach unquestioning acceptance of authority relationships. They become empty vessels that can simply be brainwashed into believing these values.

- Character educators begin with a bad image of youth of today; they see them as self-centered, selfish and destructive.

- Social-psychologists know that the situation often has more to do with influencing behavior than expressed value commitments.

- In 1989 Girl Scouts commissioned a study of the values and beliefs of American youth in grades 4-12. It found that children ranked youth problems—such as teenage pregnancy, physical abuse, violence in schools and alcohol abuse—quite low as compared to adults.

- It also discovered that one-third of the children said teachers and coaches 'really cared' for them, but only 7% would go to them for advice—showing that students won't listen to teachers or coaches telling them about core values.

- Assessments indicate that most character education programs don't show the results their authors claim, including the Jefferson Center on Character Education and the Developmental Studies Center.

- Finally, character education is useless and a waste of money and time. Research on drug and sex education programs in the '60s, '70s and '80s show that 'preaching,' or information sharing and decision-making exercises are ineffective and do not prevent drug abuse and pregnancy.

"Hope I haven't ruined your day, Nate," said Ted smugly.

"Quite the contrary, Ted, you've made my day. This helps us understand why our guests this afternoon have been testifying before this Commission. Surely we should not waste our time and money on character education if it's not working—better to put our money into more prisons to lock up violent youth and drug abusers. But I guess we'd better take these objections one at a time.

Summary

"Let me invite our Commission members to summarize by responding to Ted's charges against character education," said Nate. **"The first is that there's little relationship between values, what people say they believe is important and what they actually do?"**

Kim spoke up. **"I think we've all had enough experience to know that people often violate their own moral preferences. It hardly takes a great study to confirm this observation. But Dr. Lickona has clearly identified the steps a person must go through to link values-understanding and decision-making to actions that can become moral habits. Most of us refuse to pay the price for developing effective moral habits. But I can point to some who have—like honor students, top athletes, Olympians, Nobel Prize winners, accomplished musicians. I don't want to overreact, Ted, but you can hardly expect high moral performance without practice. That's the whole point of our discussion on character education."**

"Thanks, Kim," said Nate. **"Let's take Ted's second point—that character educators don't tell kids how to choose when values conflict—being loyal to a President who is acting illegally, for instance, as in the Watergate scandal."**

"Some of us were young in 1973. But I still remember being glued to the TV as John Dean struggled to serve President Nixon and finally had

to come forward with the truth," said Ray. "But isn't that the whole point of teaching character education? It's to sensitize students to moral issues and to teach them to see the conflicts but to act responsibly with courage. That's hardly a shortcoming of character educators. They're trying to help students become conscious of right and wrong and act morally. What an opportunity to teach the great lessons of history, like Gandhi in India, and Martin Luther King, Jr. in our own Civil Rights Movement. All public school teachers should raise these issues in class and help students to discover moral answers."

"Thank you, Ray," said Nate. "Those were great examples. Let's deal with Ted's next point—that character education is basically a conservative indoctrination program that defends the status quo by brainwashing youth into accepting traditional authority. As a conservative, Paul, would you like to field that one?"

"Let me address you directly, Ted. Can you honestly believe that teaching kids core values would brainwash them? I cite the protests of the Vietnam war, the Civil Rights Revolution led by student sit-in demonstrators. Now I didn't much like these challenges to legal authority, but I'm proud of those students who had the courage to stand up for their beliefs. I happen to think that conscious teaching about core values and their application would help students become more honest attorneys and stockbrokers and politicians someday. Is it brainwashing or indoctrination to teach that certain core values have conserved our culture for the past 400 years and that other values are now at work destroying our freedom and survival? I happen to think this is what education is all about. Should math teachers not teach or indoctrinate, if you will, students in the principles of algebra or geometry? History is a pretty good teacher that certain values promote responsible behavior and other values promote destructive behavior. Is it indoctrination to teach these historical examples and principles and their consequences?"

"Whoa, Paul," said Nate. "You don't sound much like some of the conservatives I know!"

"Nate, I think it's time you got better acquainted with more enlightened conservatives," Paul said.

"Okay, Paul," Nate said with a smile, "you win that one. **Who would like to tackle the objection about character educators not having a good opinion of teenagers today."**

"Are you serious?" Delores came to life. **"Of course teenagers are self-centered, selfish and often don't know what they're doing. Anyone here whose raised a teenager want to fight me on that one? Of course babies are empty vessels who must be filled with the right kind of values and experiences. If you parents don't do it, the neighborhood gangs will. If the schools don't do it, the teenage hoods will. Kids don't suddenly spring full-grown into responsible, mature, well-educated and disciplined adults. It's true that it does take a village to raise a child. Some teenagers seem to grow up just fine and don't get into too much trouble. But, the juvenile crime statistics show that many parents just aren't cutting it today. This character education business offers some promise for turning things around. If it helps in any way to teach my kids right from wrong, you got my vote."**

"Thanks, Delores, we need to hear more from you," Nate said. **"How about Ted's next point—that preaching to the kids about core values is a waste of money because the research on sex and drug education shows preaching and sharing information or decision-making skills does not change destructive behavior."**

"I want that one, Nate," Kathie said. **"We've heard that character educators are smart enough to know and to learn from the failures of the '60s, '70s and '80s. I know that every teacher here, including you, Ted, knows enough not to leave the answers to the next day's test lying around. We need to establish a code of conduct in which all class members participate in making the rules and demonstrate their values by developing good moral habits. Teachers should be fired if we're so naive as to ignore undisciplined and untrained human nature. We usually learn that much after only a week as a new teacher."**

"Thank you, Kathie. What about the next criticism? Ted has cited re-search from social psychology showing that certain environmental factors can influence our behavior and overcome our personal value commitments. What would a character educator say to that?"

"I'll try that one, Nate," Tamar spoke up. **"If the environment of poverty is winning, why are we investing all the taxpayer's money—my**

money—in public education of our disadvantaged children? Of course the situation can shape behavior. Strong families or gangs certainly do influence young children and teenagers. But the whole challenge is to teach academic and moral habits. In time it can become like software programs that condition behavior regardless of the destructive environmental or cultural conditions. That's what we call character."

"Well said, Tamar. I know we could enlarge on each of these comments, and we're not giving Ted rebuttal time, but we've got to adjourn soon. Let's take the findings of the national Girl Scout survey—that youth don't agree with their parents on what issues are crises and that they don't come to parents and teachers for advice."

"Maria," Nate said.

"I can't believe this nonsense! Of course teenagers don't believe that sex, drug and alcohol abuse, and violence are big crises like their parents do. Young people think they're invincible, and that they know everything. That's what being 16 is all about! And we humor them for a few years until it's time to start working and paying the bills. They must become accountable for dumb habits that can destroy them. Parents have usually made enough mistakes to see through this smart-ass behavior. I want to talk with parents about how to prevent crises behavior at Jefferson Elementary—not my 10-year old.

"Next, you wonder why students don't confide and ask counsel. Well, the key here is trust and bonding. Some parents and teachers have earned that trust, and students do seek their help in a crises. Favorite teachers, understanding and loving parents, and special counselors or coaches still play critical roles in the lives of my children."

"Thank you, Maria," Nate said. "What are we to make of the accusation that character education programs either have not been carefully evaluated or have shown little impact?"

"I'd like to try that one out, Nate," said Debbie. "This relates specifically to Jefferson Center and the Developmental Studies Center. I've been doing my homework too, Ted. And whoever you've been reading is behind the times. It's true that in the 1980s reductions in student misbehavior reported by Jefferson Center's first character education models were supported only by anecdotal evidence or teacher testimonials. The Developmental Studies Project also showed little gain in student achievement while complex models linking attitudes and behaviors were being tested. Since then, however, both groups have developed and implemented more carefully controlled models. They've become more sophisticated in their delivery of character education programs and they're better able to assess the impact on students, classroom teachers and whole schools. They've also demonstrated greater power in linking social and psychological development of elementary students with advanced academic thinking and creative skills, together with the traditional indicators of reduced student misbehavior. At least that's what my notes say from the presentations by Drs. Lickona, Brooks and Schaps."

"Thank you, Debbie. Ted, did the group answer some of your objections?"

"Well, I didn't say that I believed all these objections," Ted replied sheepishly. "I just had to raise them before we got carried away. But I'm still skeptical."

"Okay, we haven't heard from Dale, Delores and Christina," said Nate. "Would you three like to comment?"

"This is all kind of new to me," said Dale. "But since I'm pretty conservative—a strong law and order man—I'm all for any program that addresses ways to halt the spread of youth crime."

"What we've heard this afternoon," Lenora said, "is what I thought teachers were teachin' my kids. Now I learn that they're afraid to teach values. No wonder we're goin' to hell in a handbasket."

"I don't agree," said Christina. "I've been working with youth groups, and I'm delighted to see that educators are starting to take an aggressive stand on character education. I'm impressed with what I've heard. It has great potential for healing between parents, teachers and the community."

Nate paused as he looked directly at each person. "Thank you for a great day and for your response. I'll turn the time back to Kim."

"Thank you, Nate. I've enjoyed it too," said Kim. "I've never really been briefed on these character education programs. This really opened my eyes to what I've been missing at my own school.

"Our next month's Hearing will focus on quality education for children who are disadvantaged. I think we're ready! Thanks again to our regulars from the community who were in the audience today. Travel safely. See you next month."

7

Chapter 9
EDUCATING STUDENTS AT RISK
Saturday morning, January 18

Nate's plane touched down at National Airport at 7:30 right on time. He picked up *The Washington Post* and walked to the cab for the 20 minutes ride to Jefferson Elementary. *I'll just have time to catch coffee and a bagel before our kickoff at 8:00 a.m.*, he thought. *Ray's doing a hell of a job keeping the Commission moving — at least he's supporting Wendy and me as we dash through these guest reformers. After today we'll be half-way through, and the real work begins — getting a consensus report for the Board. We've had some impressive people — most have hands-on school experience and are deeply committed. But most reform ideas are not reaching the school and classroom.*

I wonder how this Citizens' Commission will hold up when we get to the tough part — selecting a model or models for Jefferson and then implementing them. Who do we hear from today? Let's see...Levin, Slavin, and the big man, Comer. We finish with Linda Darling-Hammond. Big day and heavy guns. Children at risk — that's a bulls-eye for this Commission!

There's the school. My driver made good time. The gang is going in. Dale and Maria are actually talking. That's a good sign.

"Welcome to the fifth Hearing of the Citizens' Commission on Elementary School Reform," Kim said. "Our guests this morning are Dr. Henry Levin, director of Accelerated Schools Project at Stanford University in Palo Alto, California, and Dr. James Comer of Yale University's Child Study Center in New Haven, Connecticut."

"Before we begin, here's a handout on the controversial Bell Curve MYTH. This myth challenges the basic foundations of our national attitudes toward the education of disadvantaged students. It may cast some light on why our nation is doing such a poor job in this area.

MYTH: Because IQ tests show that minority students are not as intelligent as White students, minority students cannot be expected to perform as well in school and later in life.

In 1994 two conservative social scientists, Richard J. Herrnstein and Charles Murray, authored a controversial book, *The Bell Curve: Intelligence and Class Structure in American Life.* It became the most incendiary social science research in the past few decades. It hit the exposed public nerves of race and social class. *Newsweek* called it "frightening stuff" while the *National Review* described it as "magisterial." The authors claim that race and class differences are largely caused by essentially unchangeable genetic factors. They speculate that inherited lower IQ is largely responsible for high rates of poverty and crime in minority populations, not environmental and cultural factors. The name of the book is taken from the standard Bell Curve shape showing the statistical probabilities that a given score clusters around the median or average score of those in a given test population.

A grading system using the Bell Curve assumes that intelligence or knowledge about a certain course is distributed symmetrically. Test scores are assigned according to the following formula—about 15% of a class get Ds, 35% get Cs, 35% get Bs and 15% get As. If everyone in the class knows the test material well enough to get near 100%, it is usually interpreted as the teacher designing a poor test or the student cheating. The fact that it might be a result of good teaching and learning is ignored.

The Bell Curve myth has devastating implications for national school reform, especially in inner-city schools. According to Herrnstein and Murray's theory, minority students have inherited a lower IQ, so on average they will be poorer students and underachievers when compared with their White counterparts. Social and political policy that attempts to "level the playing field" for minority students, like compensatory education programs, are destined to fail because students are already damaged by genetic inheritance and are forever handicapped by intellectual limitations. The authors suggest that money spent on compensatory education programs should not be wasted on disadvantaged minorities, but spent on gifted students.

Herrnstein and Murray's book created a firestorm because many Americans found justification for their prejudice and discriminatory behavior towards minority citizens in this book. Such attitudes are reflected in the "savage inequalities" that plague schools serving a growing number of disadvantaged American children today. An increasing majority of white citizens resist paying taxes or supporting political candidates who provide funding for education programs that benefit students who are disadvantaged. How objective and scientific, then, is the evidence presented in the *Bell Curve*? What are its policy implications for reform in America's schools?

FINDINGS: The many critics of the *Bell Curve* represent all political views. They adamantly reject its major thesis and interpretations of data. The following eight points summarize criticism of the book's theory, methodology and policy implications:[1]

First, *social scientists doubt that a single IQ score accurately measures an individual's intelligence or effectively ranks different cultural groups.* Some 100 years of research challenge the notion of a single, uniform, innate human intelligence. Intelligence is defined as "the capacity to solve problems or to fashion products that are valued in one or more cultural settings."[2] Research shows that students have at least eight multiple intelligences in varying degrees, including interpersonal, musical, spatial, kinesthetic, linguistic, intrapersonal, logical/mathematical, and naturalist. Intelligence is multi-faceted and developed by each student's unique, integrative learning style.

Second, *social scientists do not believe that intelligence is hereditary* beyond providing a body with a physical brain that has the capacity to be expanded through social experience and intellectual development. Defined as "biopsychological potential," intelligence is expanded through education and training in relevant contexts. There may be exceptions, however, for babies who have been physically damaged by rare diseases or by their pregnant mothers' substance abuse. New research shows that training and effort, rather than inborn talent, account for much of an expert's best performances in chess or with musical instruments.[3] An avalanche of evidence points out the environmental basis of ethnic differences in intelligence. There is every reason to believe that improving the environment in which many minority or disadvantaged children grow up will markedly close the achievement gap.[4]

Third, *social scientists believe that individual and average group intelligence levels can change as* a result of better health, environment, education, social, economic and family conditions and opportunities. Before the 1960s Civil Rights movement, only one-sixth of African Americans were earning enough to be considered middle-class. By the 1990s, 30% were classified as middle-class. The Civil Rights movement opened up political, economic and educational opportunities. It is widely credited with this amazing doubling in socioeconomic status for middle-class African Americans.[5]

Evidence also shows that when poor Black children are adopted into affluent homes, then IQ scores change impressively. In fact, average IQ increases in many nations since World War II are equal to the entire 15-point difference now separating Blacks and Whites in America. Scientists fail to find any cognitive differences between two cohorts of children born out of wedlock to German women, reared in Germany as Germans, but fathered by Black and White American soldiers.[6] Even the authors note that when Blacks move from rural southern to urban northern areas, their intelligence scores also rise. Differences between the performances of Black and White students have declined on tests ranging from the Scholastic Aptitude Test to the National Assessment of Educational Progress. Studies of East Asian students and American students show that Asian and American students begin with approximately the same IQ. By the middle school years, however, there are significant differences in reading and mathematics performances between the two populations! *But genetics, heredity, and measured intelligence play no role in these differences.*

Perhaps the strongest evidence against a genetic basis for intergroup differences in IQ is that the average level of mental test performance has significantly changed for Black and White populations over time. During a period when there was little intermarriage to change the genetic makeup of these groups, ethnic groups within the population have changed their relative positions. Jews, Italian Americans, Polish Americans, as well as WWI soldiers and their GI sons, have all registered dramatic IQ increases over time—greater than the 15 points that now separate Black and White Americans.[7]

Fourth, *social scientist critics believe that Herrnstein and Murray have used sloppy, unscientific methodology* in arriving at their conclusions about inherited IQ differences between African Americans and Whites. The authors have synthesized the work of "disreputable race theorists and eccentric eugenicists." An eminent psychometrician, after examining all existing research on intelligence, finds that *most point to a zero genetic contribution to the Black/White differential in IQ.* He concludes that Murray and Herrnstein's slipshod treatment of this and other vital statistical questions would prohibit their publication in any respectable peer-reviewed journal.[8] The Black/White gap in NAEP scores has been decreasing about 2.5 IQ points per decade. Overall, even with a broader base of participating minority students, SAT scores have been maintained, not by an *increase in White scores but a relative increase in Black scores.*

Fifth, *social scientists believe that IQ test scores of young children have little connection with success later in school or on the job.* Links between genetic inheritance and IQ, and then between IQ and social class, are too weak to infer that genes determine an individual's ultimate status in society. "Nearly all of the reported correlations between measured intelligence and societal outcomes explain at most 20% of the variance. In other words, over 80% (and perhaps over 90%) of the factors contributing to socioeconomic status lie beyond measured intelligence." There is no evidence of a relationship between test scores and later career success. There is no hard link between IQ and job performance; nor does IQ predict income disparities later in life.[9] Income and education of parents positively affect the intelligence of children. But cultural differences, such as the intensity of parental pressure on children to achieve and children's willingness to dutifully comply, explain a good deal more.[10]

Sixth, *social scientists reject The Bell Curve claim that higher crime rates among minorities also demonstrate that intelligence governs behavior.* This theory does not explain the increase in violent crime between the 1960s and 1980s and the decline in adult crime in the 1990s.[11] It does not explain the increase of white-collar crime, like the Savings and Loan scandals, by supposedly high-IQ White executives.[12] The authors own data indicate that IQ is not a major factor in determining variation in nearly all social behaviors they studied. It is not possible to predict what a given person will do from his/her IQ score.[13]

Seventh, *social scientists believe the authors neglect poverty and educational achievement, more accurate determiners of intelligence.* While insulting Blacks for lower IQ scores, the authors do not disclose that IQ tests, cultural and economic performance of poor, rural White southerners is significantly below their northern urban counterparts.[14] They do not disclose that East Asian students learn more and score better on just about every kind of measure because they attend school for more days, work harder in school and at home after school, and have better-prepared teachers and more deeply-engaged parents who encourage and coach them each day. Most Americans believe, like Herrnstein and Murray, that if students do not perform well, it is because they lack talent or ability. By contrast, Asians believe it is because students do not work hard enough![15]

Eighth, *policy analysts believe that the authors do not take responsibility for the public policy implications* of their 'pseudo social science' in a nationally-explosive and racially-sensitive environment. "The text of *The Bell Curve* supports claims associated with conservative think tanks: reduction or elimination of welfare, ending or sharply curtailing affirmative action in schools and workplaces, cutting back Head Start and other forms of preschool education."[16] *The Bell Curve* contributes negatively to the national discussion of how to focus resources on reforming inner-city schools and provide disadvantaged students with quality education. Much recent research documents, however, that early intervention raises performance and intelligence of disadvantaged students in preschool, public school and college.

Accelerated Schools Project

"Dr. Levin," said Nate, "please define 'children at risk' for us. Tell us why you believe these children should be the focus of our reform efforts, not only here at Jefferson Elementary, but throughout the nation."

"Nate, and members of the Citizens' Commission, that's a good place to start.[17] Today children at risk comprise over one-third of all elementary and secondary enrollments, and they will constitute one-of-every-two students by the year 2020—only 23 years from now. In some states, like California and Texas, the minority student populations have already reached over 50%. So the future is now! In many of our largest cities, like New York, Chicago, Los Angeles, Philadelphia, Miami and Detroit, minority students comprise three-out-of-four K-12 students. Minority enrollments are increasing rapidly because of higher birth rates and unprecedented immigration—both legal and undocumented.

"Poverty is also a strong indicator for at-risk populations. In 1970 less than 15% of children under age 18 were living in poverty; by 1992 it had risen to 21% and today it's about 27%.[18] Right now, one-in-two African-American children is living in poverty. By the year 2020, the number of children raised in families where the mother has not completed high school will rise by 56% to over 21 million. Many of these are from rural regions of Latin America."

"What's the difference in learning opportunities between high- and low-poverty schools, Dr. Levin?" Ray, the Commission chair, asked.

"The learning gap between them is alarming. Let me summarize research from the *Final Report of the National Assessment of the Chapter I Program* for the U.S. Department of Education.[19]

- Poor children tend to be concentrated in high-poverty schools—those in which at least 75% of students participate in subsidized lunch. Of the schools in which more than half the students are poor, about 19% of all children but 50% of poor children are served.

- Limited English-proficient (LEP) students are more likely to attend high-poverty schools than are native English-speakers. Almost 25% of the fourth graders in high-poverty schools are LEP, compared with only 2% in low-poverty schools.

- Students in high-poverty schools are less likely than their counterparts in low-poverty schools to have teachers who look forward to each working day, believe that their school administration is supportive, or see their colleagues as continually learning and seeking new ideas.

- Students in high-poverty schools are more likely than their counterparts in low-poverty schools to have teachers whose absenteeism is reportedly a problem or whose performance is rated low by the principal.

- In reading and language arts, students in high-poverty schools are exposed to instruction that relies more heavily on textbooks and basal readers and less on literature and children's books.

- First-graders in high-poverty schools start school at a disadvantage, scoring 27 and 32 percentile points lower in reading and math, respectively, than their peers in low-poverty schools. High-poverty schools appear unable to close the initial gap, which increases by fourth grade and again by eighth grade.

- By fourth grade, about 23% of all students in high-poverty schools have been held back one or more times, compared with only 7% of students in low-poverty schools.

"How big is the population of disadvantaged or children at risk?" asked Tamar.

"When achievement is the criterion," said Dr. Levin, "the number of at-risk students may be as high as 40%. The majority of these is White! The high number of at-risk students who fail in school seriously impacts the labor market. Service and front-line industrial and information workers are crucial to high productivity and maintaining our standard of living. This means increased costs for remedial work in higher education, public services, criminal justice, unemployment and health. **Taxes will go up for all citizens.**"

"Who are these at-risk children?" Dale asked.

"Those who are unlikely to succeed in schools as currently constituted. Their poverty-stricken homes and community seldom provide experiences on which school success is built. In other words, children from backgrounds of poverty, minority, immigrant, non-standard English, and single-parents are far less likely to succeed educationally than students from middle-class and non-minority backgrounds with both parents present and who speak standard English."

"Why should we spend scarce resources on these children?" Paul asked.

"If we don't pay now, we pay far more later in terms of higher taxes for unemployment, welfare and crime. The system is working well for most middle-class students who stay in school and graduate from college or take specialized technical training to become productive. But the growing number of those who do not follow this path will become relatively unproductive and a burden on society. Targeted public investments in high school dropout prevention and preschool intervention show dramatic returns in taxes paid and welfare expenditures saved (2.5 times to as much as 9 times the ratio for benefits received back for each tax dollar spent).[20] Public investments must be targeted on proven strategies for effective learning or combined with major organizational changes in schools. Without basic changes, simply appropriating money for children at risk is ineffective in most cases! Adequate resources are a necessary, but not a sufficient, condition.[21]

"In summary, it's poor public policy to invest increasing tax dollars on education and social programs that show little or negative return. We know that with a targeted investment strategy, we can invest the same public money and get a three-to-seven-fold return."

"Okay, Dr. Levin," said Debbie coolly. "I appreciate the return on our tax dollar arguments here, but I suspect that just makes people like Paul feel better. All children have a right to a quality education. It's not a child's fault that he or she is born into a poor, uneducated family. But I think it's a moral question. Do we value all children equally or do we systematically discriminate against disadvantaged children—White as well as minority? Tell us about how your project on Accelerated Schools came to be organized?"

"The Accelerated Schools Project was established to bring at-risk students into the educational mainstream by the end of elementary school. The ideas for the Accelerated School had their origin in work that I did in the '60s, '70s and '80s on urban schools. Most of the reform reports on schools in the late '80s did not focus on at-risk children. I reviewed the research, interviewed teachers, parents, principals and central office administrators and observed practices in schools around the country with high concentrations of at-risk students. I found that current practices for educating at-risk children were undermining their progress. The children were stigmatized as remedial students or slow learners and were assigned boring and repetitive exercises on worksheets. Parents were not involved. Publishers provided low-level textbooks with dull drills and tedious exercises. At-risk students rarely had opportunities for problem solving, enrichment, or application of knowledge that drew on their experiences and interests.

"The solution seemed obvious. Instead of slowing down these students— who were on average falling two years behind other students—we needed to *accelerate* their progress. Using research on learning and effective organizations, I designed and implemented a process whereby schools could accelerate the learning of students in at-risk situations. It became clear that schools implementing this process could draw on the talents of all their staff, students and parents. They would learn effective approaches to gathering information, making decisions, and building incentives for success at all levels. I used the same approach as that used for gifted and talented students and built on their strengths.

"We began with two elementary schools. We have since discovered that it takes about five or six years to bring all students in the school into the educational mainstream before they go to middle school. As a by-product, this approach reduces the dropout rate, drug use, and teenage pregnancies in secondary school. From our small beginning in 1986-87 with two schools, we have 1000 schools in 41 states that impact over 500,000 at-risk students in 1996-97. The market place of reform ideas and models is clearly working in that school communities are voluntarily requesting to undertake the Accelerated Schools Model."[22]

Ray practically rose out of his chair! "Dr. Levin, what's the secret? How does it work?"

"Accelerated schools are built on a unity of purpose among the entire school community in creating practices and activities that are dedicated toward accelerated progress for all students. They establish a viable school-site decision-making process with responsibility for results, and active participation in decisions by all school staff as well as parents. These schools rely on small-group task forces, a school-wide steering committee and governance groups. Instead of focusing on weaknesses, Accelerated School staff and parents use a pedagogy constructed on the strengths of the children, their culture and the larger community. We rely heavily on relevant applications, problem solving, and active, hands-on learning approaches as well as thematic learning that integrates subjects into a common set of themes. Finally, parent involvement at home and at school is central to the success of an Accelerated School."[23]

"I'm still quite skeptical, Dr. Levin. Exactly what do you do in your program? Bring it down to a practical level," Delores pleaded. "For example, if the staff and parents here at Jefferson wanted to become an Accelerated School, how would we begin the process."

"First, the full staff, which includes administrators, teachers, para-professionals, and support staff, and parent representatives carefully study materials on the Accelerated Schools Project. They organize a series of meetings with all members of the school community to discuss the Accelerated

Schools' philosophy and process, voice concerns and address questions. They invite key district office personnel and school board members to join in this initial exploration phase either at the school site or at board meetings.

"Second, members of the school community call or visit Accelerated Schools to clarify questions or concerns participants have about the philosophy and process. Talking with teachers, principals, support staff, and parents involved in the process, and seeing the philosophy in action, helps school community members decide whether or not to embrace the model. Interested schools can contact the National Center for the Accelerated Schools Project directly or a local regional center for referrals to nearby schools. The school community may also want to invite someone from an existing Accelerated School, the National Center or a regional center to visit the school and to give the entire school community an in-depth presentation with questions and answers. This visit may involve travel costs and consulting fees. Meanwhile, the school community should be considering individuals, preferably from the district (or state education departments or nearby universities), to serve as prospective coaches. After thoroughly exploring the Accelerated Schools model, members of the school community formally vote or come to consensus on whether or not to embrace the Accelerated Schools' philosophy and process. While consensus is optimal, a school will not be accepted unless at least 90% of full-time staff and school community representatives are willing to transform their school into an Accelerated School."

"Whoa, you must be pretty confident about your model to believe that at least 90% of a school community could agree on anything—much less a five- or six-year struggle to transform a troubled elementary school into an Accelerated School," Kathie spoke up. "What's the incentive? Why should a school be turned over to your group to transform itself? How much does it cost? Who pays? How does it work? Sounds like big add-on work for already burned out teachers."

"Accelerated Schools agree to abide by three principles," said Dr. Levin. "First, **unity of purpose**. All members of the school community create a shared dream for the school and work together toward a common set of goals that will benefit all students. Second, **empowerment coupled with responsibility.** Every member of the school community is empowered to participate in shared decision-making, shared responsibility for implementation, and shared accountability for outcomes. Third, **building on**

strengths. In creating their dream school, accelerated schools recognize and utilize the knowledge, talents, and resources of every member of the school community. We have found that Accelerated School communities share a set of values, beliefs and behaviors which create an environment that nurtures innovation and collaboration. As an Accelerated School develops, qualities such as equity, trust, participation, collaboration, reflection, and risk-taking emerge and help guide the actions and interactions of all members of the school community.

"The process of school transformation begins with **taking stock**—assessing the school's strengths and shortcomings. The entire community then forges a **shared vision** of what it wants the school to be—the kind of dream school that everyone would want for their own child. By comparing the vision to its present situation, the school community identifies priority challenge areas. The Accelerated School uses the **inquiry process** to address those **priority challenge areas,** working through its **governance structure.** The inquiry process is a systematic method that helps school communities clearly understand problems, find and implement solutions, and assess their results. A representative school steering committee meets every other week to coordinate and assess progress and task force cadres or work teams and *ad hoc* committees meet weekly. When major policy alternatives are worked out, the entire school community (school as a whole—SAW) holds a townhall-like meeting, with the public notified well in advance, to discuss the policy and vote to accept or reject it as school policy."

Maria's hand shot up. "You mean that parents actually make policy for the school along with the teachers and principal? Is it really that open and democratic? What if we did it? Wouldn't the school district officials be looking over our shoulders? What about the principal who usually makes all the important decisions for the teachers and students?"

"Principals and school district officials should have different roles," said Dr. Levin. "The principal needs to be responsible for coordinating and facilitating the activities of decision bodies, providing logistical support for information gathering, staff development, assessment, implementation, and providing instructional resources. The principal needs to be an instructional leader, coach, and motivator of students, teachers, staff and parents. The principal should be the keeper of the dream—especially during setbacks—and to buffer the school from outside interference. School districts need to serve individual schools rather than simply regulate them with rules, mandates, and policies to ensure compliance with district, state or federal bureaucracies."

Paul was agitated. "Dr. Levin, all this democracy and sweetness and light sounds interesting, but nobody's accountable. There's no strong leader who gives direction or kicks butt when necessary. Where are the challenging academic standards that we heard about from Hirsch and Ravitch. This sounds like the hippie movement when every teacher was doing his or her own thing. How do we know this Accelerated Schools Model will work? This sounds like a very expensive experiment to me. Hell, you're an economist. I thought you'd be a bottom-line man."

"You seem to be asking three questions, Paul. What about content or standards of behavior imposed from some outside source? Will this model actually improve student achievement scores? What will it cost the community in extra money and resources? Am I right?"

Paul smiled. He was sure he'd exposed the weaknesses in this kind-hearted academic's approach. "Yes, those are my questions. If you can answer them, then I'm a believer."

"Let's start with the cost issue," said Dr. Levin. "Our experience shows that the annual cost for creating and implementing the Accelerated Schools Model is between $30-$50 per student. It costs less than 1% of the school budget to bring about the spectacular student achievement gains I will be sharing with you. In return the school gets several hundred thousand dollars in parent and teacher contributions back to the school each year.

"Second question, where do the standards for academic content and student and adult behavior come from? Accelerated Schools are required to make informed decisions that draw upon high standards and expectations in which the school constructs unique curriculum and instructional approaches for all children. We call this the powerful learning approach. This model assumes that we can tap into the rich talent that we're paying for at the school-site level, that is the creativity and productivity of teachers, administrators, students and parents. When we impose regulations from the federal, state, district or even principal level, with no teacher ownership, we have successfully ignored the very workers we have hired to do the job. The Japanese have taught us a hard lesson that quality control in electronics and automobiles is possible only if ownership and creativity comes from the front-line worker—not the manager and certainly not the corporate planners at another location. Yet most school reform is still stuck in the factory school model of low productivity that is failing at-risk students all over America. Talk about wasting resources! We pay teachers who fail to educate disadvantaged students and then pay again for unemployment, welfare, criminal justice and prison costs. Good business practice means to stop doing what we have proved doesn't work. Would you argue with that, Paul?

"Third, we've discovered that children at risk can learn as fast and effectively as middle-class children. We have to expect them to do so, and we challenge them to do it. We build on their strengths. This requires a new approach to learning and teaching. The entire school community must be involved—teachers, administrators, parents and students.

"Can you prove that this strategy of Accelerated Schools works?" Ray asked.

"Before answering that question, we should understand that the typical assessment instruments used by school districts are not sensitive to capturing the change in school culture and outcomes that are unique to Accelerated Schools or high standards that are needed. For example, standardized tests of achievement are designed to sample snapshots of information about a subject. They are not designed to assess the higher-order learning, the quality of student projects, the originality of student oral and written expressions, and the artistic accomplishments and scientific thinking that are expected in powerful learning situations. Accelerated Schools have extremely diverse enrollments—African-American, Hispanic, Native American, and Caucasian students—but the majority come from poverty backgrounds. The geographical settings and levels of district support have also been diverse—from California, Illinois, Massachusetts, Missouri, South Carolina and Texas. Even so, the results have been remarkably consistent. Schools have documented increases in student and teacher attendance, substantial increases in parent participation, higher achievement scores, waiting lists for enrollment, reduced grade repetition and special education placements—all resulting in considerable savings to participating schools."

"Dr. Levin, can you describe what kinds of assessment your teams undertake in the Accelerated Schools?" Kim asked.

"Evaluation and assessment are part of virtually every activity in the Accelerated Schools Project. Since the onset of the project, we've dedicated ourselves to formative evaluations to improve our process and practices and summative evaluations to see what has been accomplished. We've done internal assessments of our work, and we've asked the schools to do similar assessments. We've cooperated with outsiders who have undertaken external evaluations of Accelerated Schools. We've even sponsored qualitative evaluations of schools, such as ethnographies, and undertaken quantitative studies of school change. We've held a conference on evaluation of Accelerated Schools, and we've supported a continuing roundtable by our satellite centers on the subject. The challenge we face is providing assessments and assessment tools that address the needs of stakeholders—teachers, parents, school board members, researchers, other educators—considering the Accelerated Schools Project.[24] Individual schools participating in the project are given the Assessment Toolkit that provides step-by-step assessment procedures and includes a school questionnaire, a coach's log, a school data portfolio, school documents collection guide and Accelerated Schools benchmarks." Let me give you a handout describing one of our inner-city schools."

Dr. Levin," Maria said, "can you tell us about Hispanic students, like those attending Jefferson?"

"Studies comparing Accelerated Schools with matched controls have shown strong effects. Hollibrook Elementary School in Houston, Texas, enrolls over 1,000 students. Many of them are recently arrived immigrants from Central and South America. About 90% are minority students from poverty families. The fifth graders were one and one-half years behind their grade level in student achievement on SRA in 1988 and below the scores of the control school. Three years later, the fifth graders were performing slightly above grade level in overall achievement and one year above grade level in mathematics. Meanwhile, the achievement scores of the matched control school declined over the same period. But even more than the achievements, the Hollibrook Elementary had become a place of joy for its students, staff and parents. Through hands-on activities, research, discourse, imagination, and creativity, the school had been transformed to a place of excitement and high academic standards—a beehive of activity."

Do you have an example of a predominantly African-American school?" Delores asked.

BEST PRACTICES: LEVIN'S ACCELERATED SCHOOLS

Bond Accelerated School is a neighborhood school in Tallahassee, Florida, within walking distance of Florida A&M University. Its principal and staff, which includes a faculty of 29 teachers, serve 439 students (pre K-5). The student population is 98% African American and 2% White. Because Bond is a low-income community, 92% of students receive free or reduced-price lunches. The average per pupil expenditure is $3,512. Its 34% mobility rate contrasts with the stability of 33% third-generation students, those with a grandparent who attended the school.

According to Mrs. Barbara James, principal since 1989, Bond became an Accelerated School in 1993. Her concern at the time was that, "I could not see academic 'leaps and bounds,' and I wanted these children to have experiences that would develop their skills and raise their self-esteem. A colleague shared a video on the Accelerated Program and I knew it was just what we needed to make a difference...I was impressed with the way it involved parents in the education of their children at school and at home."

Because Bond is a site-based school, Mrs. James provided teachers with information on the Accelerated Program, telling them that it would take "lots of hard work" besides that required to meet district requirements. Workshops were held for teachers, then they began getting the support of parents and the larger community. When Mrs. James became ill during the first year, two other principals filled in to help launch the program.

Even though stability in leadership was not reached until last year, the Accelerated Schools process is having a positive impact on faculty, students, families and community. The process has resulted in most teachers now working in teams, sharing ideas and materials and providing inservice workshops for themselves and other teachers, thus deepening their sense of commitment. One teacher commented, "There is open communication among teachers and administrators. We have developed a professional as well as a social bond among ourselves." By working together, one said, "We feel empowered and accepting of the expertise of our colleagues." During the 1995-96 school year, the faculty and staff systemically implemented Peaceworks and Conflict Mediation components, which has drastically reduced student discipline referrals. As one teacher puts it, "More students are taking responsibility for their choices and actions!" A growing sense of community is clearly evident.

The Accelerated Schools build upon children's strengths. The program has stopped remediation and enriches the environment with computers, charts, hands-on manipulatives—all of which have helped raise student performance. The Accelerated Program also helps students to feel a sense of belonging or community. As one student expressed it, "We do more activities together and they are fun." The improved student achievement also reflects the increased involvement of parents. "We feel welcome at Bond. They show us how to help our children so they do better in school." Others talk about how it is easier now to talk to teachers. "They have time to talk with us about our children." This, of course, reflects the priority placed on parent engagement in this accelerated approach.

Most children at Bond are from single-parent families. The adults are especially appreciative of students from Florida A&M University who volunteer to "adopt" a student—a kind of big brother or sister. They spend two to three hours each week with a child, tutoring, asking questions and giving encouragement, which is helping these young students feel more confident and valued.

On June 1, 1996, the Sunshine State Standards were put in place to improve student outcomes. To achieve these standards, new and improved strategies are required—strategies that are holistic with an integrated curriculum focus. Bond is using additional strategies, such as increased on-site peer assistance, improved consensus decision-making, and cross-grade interactions and planning. They are continuing to have the "Principal's Spelling Club" and her "comprehensive story sharing" where they learn to respond to questions about the stories. Team building around academic content occurs across grades as, for example, fifth grade students help kindergartners score the ABCD-choice answers to questions.

In addition to standardized tests, Bond's Accelerated Schools Program encourages the use of alternative assessment tools—student portfolios, interviews and observations—to determine student achievement. They also compare the quality and quantity of student output relative to the respective student's past performance. Attendance rates are now improving and scores are beginning to climb. On the CAT-5, for example, the third grade scores went from 28% (1995) to 37% (1996) in reading, and from 28% (1995) to 53% in math (percent of students scoring above the 50% rank). The improvement was large enough that Bond has now been taken off the state's schools at-risk list.

Bond is assisted in implementing the Accelerated Schools process by volunteers from the community, local churches, Florida A&M University and Florida State University. It is also being served by AmeriCorps. Also, because of its location, Bond Accelerated School has some unique advantages. It is within walking distance from the Walker-Ford Community Center and the Smith/Williams Service Center. The Walker-Ford Community Center provides vital services for students and adults, such as tutoring, recreation, arts & crafts and cultural events. The Smith/Williams Service Center provides health services.

"Yes. The 99th Street School in the Watts section of Los Angeles has about 700 students. Two-thirds are African American and one-third are Hispanic. Prior to the 1990-91 school year, 99th Street was one of the bottom 20 schools in achievement among the 650 schools in Los Angeles School District. Gangs, vandalism, fighting, poor attendance, high teacher turnover, and low achievement. All of these were chronic conditions at 99th Street. By 1992, even after having weathered the worst urban riot in U.S. history, 99th Street's reading scores had jumped from the 18th percentile to the 30th percentile, over six times the average gain for the district. They have continued to climb. When students were involved in artistic projects and research, student behavior problems waned and, for the first time, parents were actively involved in the school.[25]

"Both 99th Street and East Harlem's P.S. 108 are neighborhood schools, but they are not choice schools that draw higher-achieving students through self-selection. P.S. 108 has 100% minority enrollment. Ninety-five percent of students receive free or reduced-cost lunches. In 1993, the year before it became an Accelerated School, its test scores were at the 35th percentile nationally. Since then, scores have risen to the 67th percentile in math and the 58th percentile in reading. This happened even though most students are limited English proficient (LEP)."

Tamar raised her hand. "I still don't see how teachers, principals, staff, and parents in a school like Jefferson could transform it into a community school like you describe and get these amazing results. I heard you say there's a process, a philosophy and a set of guidelines. But what comes next?"

"Without taking too much time, let me just say that the Accelerated Schools Resource Guide explains this process. With the help of a trained coach from your district, a school staff and parents can find their own solutions. The number of schools is growing that are proving this model brings significant change. We now know it can be done. The only question is, do you have the will to do it? We're training coaches now, and we provide continuing technical assistance to faculty who spend about six staff development days going through the transformation process. We give them powerful learning tools to help them transform their school into an innovative and effective one for all students at risk."

"One more question, Hank," said Nate. "Where has this Accelerated Schools process broken down? Do you have some disappointments?"

"I can think of two—inadequate resources and principal turnover. These Accelerated School achievements have been replicated over and over throughout the United States. We've done this without substantial increases in funding or staff. But the problem of insufficient resources means that some inner-city schools are in disrepair. They have poorly equipped libraries and resource centers and crowded classrooms. They have inadequate teachers; language, emotional or physical shortcomings; and lack basic parental support services. No reform program can fully overcome these handicaps without adequate funding.[26]

"The second problems is the turnover of principals. In Accelerated Schools, principals are not only leaders as keepers of the dream and facilitators of change—like an orchestra conductor—but they also grow along with the teachers and parents as the school culture is transformed. This takes five or six years. Principal leadership and school-site decision-making are crucial. Bond Elementary School, our sample Best Practice, had three principals in the first year.

"The growth of a new school can be stopped dead in several ways. For example, superintendents can interfere with the process by imposing top-down regulations. Even when student scores are improving dramatically after two or three years, if the superintendent decides to transfer that principal and put in another, the investment can be lost, especially if that new principal has no training in the new process and has not earned the trust of the staff and parents. Unfortunately, we cannot control superintendents and school board members, some of whom are unpredictable and constantly turning over. We're exploring ways to offset inadequate resources and principal turnover. But overall, we're very positive about the progress we're making."

"Thank you, Hank," said Nate. "You've given us some profound ideas on how to transform Jefferson Elementary School. Now it's time for our break. Dr. Levin has agreed to stay and answer questions. See you in about 20 minutes."

This is a very promising model for Jefferson! thought Delores, the first grade teacher. *I can't wait to get my hands on his Resource Guide. This White guy, Dr. Levin, is really something. I heard that Dr. Levin's wife is Hispanic and they have young children in school. But working in inner-city, at-risk schools can't be a great career enhancer. I wonder why he does it?*

I'm excited about meeting Dr. Comer. He's another pioneer in educating at-risk and minority children. Why haven't we been told how to educate at-risk children? Why didn't the Title I people share this information? I feel like I've been wasting my teaching career. I've got some serious catching up to do.

School Development Model

After the break, Wendy announced a special guest. "Dr. James Comer is perhaps the best known pioneer on the education of minority and poor children. Dr. Comer, why would a child psychiatrist undertake reform?"

"Thanks, Wendy. I took it on because time is running out on this generation of children. Soon more than 50% of our school children will be minority or disadvantaged. When I started back in 1968, the 50% level had already been reached by several of our large cities. Today, these same cities are at least 75%. Remember, there are still more White children who are disadvantaged than minority, although minority children constitute a higher percentage of children in poverty.

"In 1968 my colleagues and I at Yale University's Child Study Center started an intervention project at two inner-city schools in New Haven.[27] Unlike many reforms that focus on teacher credentials and basic skills, our program builds supportive bonds that draw children, parents and educators together. This bonding experience promotes development and learning. It positively affects school performance, and reduces truancy and other disciplinary problems.

"My training in child psychiatry and in public health gives me a natural focus on the kind of social climate in which the disadvantaged child lives, both at home and in school. My own background was rich and rewarding. In contrast to my friends, my parents gave me social skills and confidence that helped me take advantage of educational opportunities.[28] My third grade teacher was a special friend who, along with my parents, introduced me to the exciting world of the library. Some of my friends' parents were afraid to go to the library. They were uncomfortable around White people in general. By the 1960s, I was seeing the contrast between a child's experience in a poverty home and in school. The social and cultural gap was deeply affecting children's psychosocial development, which in turn shaped their academic achievement. If these hunches were correct, then the failure to bridge the gap between home and school may lie at the root of the poor academic performance of many of these children.[29]

"Some educational reforms focus on instruction and curriculum and ignore interpersonal factors. They assume that all children come from mainstream backgrounds and arrive at school equally well prepared. Reading, writing, arithmetic and science are delivered to students in much the same way as tires, windows and doors are attached to an automobile on the assembly line. Yet students do not come in standardized frames. They do not passively receive what is delivered. School staffs lack training in child development and behavior. They believe that intellectual ability and achievement are genetically determined. Most educators do not challenge this assumption. Teachers continue to be trained without researching the assumptions or experimenting with alternative methods. The schools are ill-prepared to modify behavior. They cannot close the developmental gaps of their students, and the staff usually responds with punishment and low expectations."

The sixth-grade teacher, Ted, spoke up. "That's the way I was trained. I believe that children's IQ is pretty well set by the time I get them in the sixth grade. I can tell which way they're headed, usually toward poor grades. They barely graduate from high school or drop out before graduation. So

215

what's your alternative, Dr. Comer? Most of these at-risk kids are wasted before I get them."

"I don't mean to offend you, Ted, but I believe your attitude is one reason at-risk children don't prosper in school. You're suggesting that measured intelligence and test scores alone can predict school and life outcomes. But there is no correlation between them. The major purpose of schooling is to advance the student's social, emotional and academic development toward becoming a good citizen. This can be done for all students by important people in their lives. Our model advocates a consensus-building, no-fault approach to problem solving. It encourages a positive, strong sense of identity among all students.

"At Yale's Child Study Center, Albert J. Solnit and his colleagues believe that educational reformers should develop their theories by directly observing and intervening in schools over long periods.[30] Today you're hearing from school reformers who have gotten their hands dirty by actually going into schools and trying out their models. They then step back to assess their success or failure, and modify them accordingly. They are intent on improving the education of real children, coming often from dysfunctional home environments, who are taught by real teachers. This is where the tire of reform theory meets the road of the classroom of at-risk students.

"From 1968 to 1980, I directed the school intervention project in the New Haven school system. I worked with a social worker, a psychologist and a special education teacher. We immersed ourselves in the schools. We learned how they function, and then, on the basis of our findings, we developed and implemented our model. Our knowledge base was public health, human ecology, history, child development—and common sense.

"Our first year in two high-poverty schools was frustrating for both staff and parents. While we gradually learned that our project needed more structure with goal setting and planning, we saw the gap between home and school—a social-cultural misalignment. We learned that the development of children depends on strong emotional bonds with competent care givers. Many kinds of development are critical to academic learning—social, psychological, emotional, moral, linguistic and cognitive. The attitudes, the values and the behavior of the family and its social network strongly affects the development of all these. We call that social capital. The meshing of home and school builds this capital and fosters development. When teachers consider a child's social skills appropriate, they elicit positive reactions. A bond then develops between the teacher and the child which supports overall development of the child.[31] We early-on formed a program called ' The Social Skills Curriculum for Inner-City Children.' We integrated the teaching of basic academic skills, social skills and appreciation of the arts. This served to channel the aggressive energy of the students into learning and work. It has now been expanded into a social development program that extends from kindergarten through twelfth grade.[32]

"Children from poor, marginal families usually enter school without having learned such social skills as negotiation and compromise. Children expected to read by first grade may come from homes where no one reads. Parents may never have read them bedtime stories. So the children's language skills are underdeveloped or non-standard.[32] Expectations at home and at school may be radically at odds. For example, in some families, a child who does not fight back will be punished. This same behavior will get the child into trouble at school.

"A typical, hierarchical school with an authoritarian structure cannot give the underdeveloped or differently-developed students those skills and experiences they need to succeed. Staff people punish the children, hold low expectations for them, and usually blame the parents or community for their poor socialization. In turn the parents are offended. Mutual distrust develops."

"How does a program overcome these problems, Dr. Comer?" Maria asked.

"We analyzed the two original New Haven schools and found that the key to academic achievement is to create a school system based on knowledge of child development and understanding of relationships that encourages bonding to the school. Positive interaction between parents and school staff is also required—a task for which most staff are not trained. This all promotes psychological development in students. We promoted a strategy that would overcome staff resistance to change. We taught the staff a working understanding of child development and helped them to improve relations with parents. In our first year, we learned that progress could not be made until we reduced destructive interactions among parents, teachers and administrators. We had to develop cohesiveness and give direction to the schools' management and teaching.

"To this end, we created in each school a governance and management team of about a dozen people. This was led by the principal and made up of elected parents and teachers, a mental-health specialist and a nonprofessional support staff person. These were adults with a stake in the outcome. First, we recognized the authority of the principal. Second, we agreed to focus on problem solving and not waste time assigning blame. Third, we made decisions by consensus rather than by vote, which promoted cooperation and not competition.

"Over the years, we've developed nine components that are useful in working collaboratively with parents and staff. Our nine-components model consist of three mechanisms, three operations, and three guidelines. The three mechanisms are a *governance and management team* representative of the parents, teachers, administrators and support staff; a *mental health or student and staff support team*; and a *parent program*. The governance and management team carries out three critical operations. They develop a *Comprehensive School Plan* with specific goals in the social climate and academic areas. The *staff development activities* are based on building-level goals in these areas. *Periodic assessment* allows the staff to adjust the program to meet needs and opportunities.

"Several other important guidelines and agreements are needed. Participants on the governance and management team *should not paralyze* the leader. But the leader should not use the group as a rubber stamp. *Decisions are made by consensus* to avoid winner-loser feelings and behavior. *No-fault problem-solving* is used by all working groups in the school. Eventually these attitudes will permeate the thinking of most individuals in the group.

"This School Development Model (SDP) is now being used in over 650 schools around the country—mostly in elementary schools, but also in several middle and high schools. In comparing schools using the SDP model with similar schools not using the model, we find statistically significant gains, and some spectacular gains, especially in language arts, reading, mathematics, school attendance, suspensions, classroom behavior, group participation, attitude toward authority, self-concept and school climate.[34]

"SDP trains school personnel from various school districts to implement the program in their own schools or districts. The local school district administration, with direct support from the Yale Child Study Center SDP staff, selects these participants to become change agents or facilitators. The

Center's SDP staff trains the facilitators for two weeks to implement SDP and monitors their plans for implementation. They visit the district, and maintain regular telephone contact. Principals attend a one-week Principals' Academy as well. We've developed partnerships with schools of education and other institutions and organizations to conduct SDP orientation for local personnel and college students. We've also developed How-To videotapes and related manuals. We even have for parents a website and a 10-minute video in Spanish.[35]

"The School Development Program is not a quick fix, nor is it an add-on. It is a different way of working with schools. It completely replaces the old bureaucratic-authoritarian leadership and structure. It is a proven, comprehensive, nine-component process model that takes significant time, commitment and energy to implement."

"Dr. Comer, what other challenges do you see when you look ahead?" Wendy asked.

"I believe we have to change schools one at a time, and we know how to do it. But the challenge is to change the system. We need support from the superintendent, district staff and board members. We must work with the district rather than individual schools. District support helps to create stability. Even with a stable environment, it takes three to five years to change a school.

"Another challenge is training of teachers. We need to get better people in the first place and then train them in child development, social interaction skills and parent involvement. We must stop assuming that just anybody can teach! Our biggest challenge is that we have to scale-up and reach more schools. Millions of children need serious education in order to overcome the effects of poverty."

"Well, Dr. Comer, how can a school district start this process?" Wendy asked.

"The superintendent should contact the Director of the Comer Process for Change in Education (CPCE). The director will convene a meeting with district personnel to examine the match between SDP, the overall district direction, and the needs of the schools. Based on this analysis, the district, the schools and SDP create a Memorandum of Understanding that lays out the roles and responsibilities for implementation. One of the district's responsibilities is to appoint a facilitator who will coordinate the change process in the district."

"Dr. Comer," said Wendy, "this has been an honor to have you appear before our Citizens' Commission. As we break for lunch, Dr. Comer will be available for questions. Here is a BEST PRACTICES handout on one of his schools.

BEST PRACTICES: COMER'S SCHOOL DEVELOPMENT PROJECT

Helene W. Grant School is one of 27 elementary schools that feed into seven middle schools and seven high schools in Connecticut's New Haven Public School System. This one-story building, with its broken playground equipment and a bell that was once the signal tower for the fire department, is in the middle of a ghetto. Its neighborhoods are plagued by gangs, drug dealers and shootings. Situated between two housing projects and flanked by two churches, Grant is one block away from the juvenile detention centers, a high school, community shopping plaza and Police Sub-Station. Yet Grant is a "light on a hill"—a public school of choice, not a magnet school—that draws 63% of its students from all across the city. Mrs. Jeffie Frazier, principal, and her staff, including 19 teachers, serve 450 students, 98% of whom are African American. Seventy five percent of students receive free or reduced price lunch. The average per pupil expenditure is $8,350.

The Comer SDP Model, wherever implemented, has improved educational opportunities for poor minority children. Grant began using this model in 1985. Like other Comer schools, Grant has stressed children's holistic development—that children be taught social as well as academic skills. Grant has emphasized putting children's needs first by coordinating all available resources. It involves the total school community—teachers, parents, counselors and others, even students—in school-related decisions that are made by consensus. Grant sees parent and community involvement as critical to the success of this program. For example, it requests that parents give 20 hours of service per school year; many give far more. Some contribute more than 200 hours, with one father volunteering six hours weekly in barber services. Mrs. Frazier explained, "We have a men's mentoring program that provides services during and after school.

The culture at Grant Elementary has developed many unique features. The students, parents, teachers and other school staff are "bubbling with pride" at what they are achieving "with everyone working together." It has an after-school choir that is a tremendous self-esteem builder. Over 90 children from third to fifth grades sing in the group. Grant's curriculum, which is science/math based, has kept phonics as a key part of their reading program.

They began a special "gardening on school grounds" project to introduce the concept of growing your own food in an urban garden to supplement less than adequate nutrition in low-income families. The project helps bring lessons from science class out of the books and into the hands of these inner-city children. By participating in this constructive activity, the children can learn to take care of themselves. They also learn about landscaping shrubs and flowers, as well as a Christmas tree, vegetables and legumes. The garden is a cooperative effort between different groups and costs the school nothing.

Grant students have become pen pals with those at a school in Hartford, Connecticut. They recently had the opportunity to meet during a field trip to the Science Center of Connecticut in West Hartford. At the Science Center, students were paired with their pen pal and went through a small zoo, "touch tank" and saw live animal demonstrations.

Helene Grant Elementary was the first public school in New England to wear uniforms. In 1988 Grant adopted the crisp green and white uniforms the children wear to school each day. The decision was made to eliminate competitiveness over clothing, to encourage self-discipline, and to improve students' self-esteem. The benefits of this choice are clearly evident.

When asked what changes could improve their program, the consortium of School Planning and Management Team (SPMT) suggested moving school hours from 8 a.m. to 7 a.m., from 2 p.m. to 3 p.m. They also want to expand their limited, extended-day program, where the emphasis is on the arts and homework, so that children could be there from 3 p.m. to 6 p.m.

Criteria for tracking improvements include standardized tests, teacher-made tests, student self-assessment, even absences. The number of absentees, for example, dropped from 30 to 40 students daily to between 5 and 7. The Connecticut Mastery Test, a standardized test, measures achievement in reading, writing and math skills. Grant was one of three schools selected for recognition by state education officials because their students' consistently scored higher on portions of the exam than other poverty schools in the state. In some cases, Grant students scored higher than students in schools with much less poverty. More than 63% of all students scored above the state goal in reading on the Mastery Test. These are amazing reading scores, especially when compared with the citywide average of between 15% and 20%.

Grant officials were asked what made the difference in how well their students achieve. They identified a sense of school pride, evident in student uniforms, lots of parent involvement, good, school-based leadership, and everyone working together toward the same clearly understood goals. As Senator J.D. Rockefeller IV said when visiting the school, "…At Helene Grant we found hope at work!"

****

Summary

We are going to try something a little different for our Hearing summary. We asked four Commission members to help us. First, Kim on Dr. Levin."

Kim nodded. "**Dr. Levin has shown that students at risk receive a poorer education than students in low-poverty schools, which puts them at least two years behind middle-class students. He argues for investing scarce education dollars in proven programs for students at risk. His Project is designed to accelerate the education of students at risk, which helps them overcome their limited educational background by the time they complete elementary school. This Project requires a whole-school, site-based decision-making process by school staff and parents. The three principles of Accelerated Schools are unity of purpose, empowerment coupled with responsibility, and building on strengths. The Accelerated School Project model is low-cost intervention—about $30 to $50 per student, or less than 1% of the school budget. The model is now operating in over 1000 schools** in 41 states with 500,000 students. Both qualitative and quantitative assessments show that the Project is an effective reform model for students at risk. And, finally, to be successful, this model must be in place for five or six years with stable leadership by the same principal. They also need adequate resources to run a normal school program."

"Thanks, Kim. Debbie, will you summarize Dr. Comer?"

"Sure. The Comer model focuses on student psychosocial development and learning by building supportive bonds between children, parents and teachers. Academic skills cannot be learned until children overcome the cultural gaps in their homes and schools. Most schools and teachers have not been trained to deal with disadvantaged students, and they are ill-prepared to modify behavior or close developmental gaps. The main purpose of schooling is to advance students' social, emotional and academic development toward good citizenship. This objective is accomplished by a process of goal-setting and planning that builds emotional bonds with competent caregivers. The model has nine components: a governance and management team; a mental health or student and staff support team; and a parent program. It also has a comprehensive school plan; staff development activities; and periodic assessment, and stresses not paralyzing the leader, decisions by consensus and 'no-fault' problem solving. Videotapes and manuals are available. The Comer model is now being used in over 650 schools nationwide—mostly in elementary schools. And, finally, they know how to change individual schools in only three to five years. The main challenge is changing the school district."

"Those are great summaries," Wendy said. "Now we hope you're getting to know your fellow Commissioners during our lunch breaks. In the months to come, these lunches will be helpful in building understanding, perspectives and trust with each other."

****

Chapter 10
STUDENTS AT RISK AND AUTHENTIC ASSESSMENT
Saturday afternoon, January 18

After lunch and small group discussions, Wendy called the Commission to order at 1:00 p.m. "Welcome back. It's my pleasure to introduce another pioneer, Dr. Robert E. Slavin, co-director of the Center for Research on the Education of Students Placed at Risk. Although a relatively young man, Dr. Slavin is the author of 15 books and 180 professional articles and reports."

"Dr. Slavin, I've reviewed much of your recent work. I'd like to start off by asking you to summarize your article, 'Sand, Bricks, and Seeds: School Change Strategies and Readiness for Reform.' As you know, this morning we heard from Dr. Levin. He told us about his rapidly growing Accelerated Schools Project. How does your program for at-risk students differ from his and other reformers?"

Sand, Bricks or Seeds

"Thank you, Wendy, and members of the Jefferson Citizens' Commission. You've clearly got your work cut out for you in recommending a comprehensive reform project for your elementary school. I'd like you to think about what elements you must consider in order to be successful in your mandate. Let's use Jefferson Elementary as an example. Is it a 'Sand, Bricks, or Seeds' school in terms of its readiness for reform? Important changes in student performance only come about if teachers use markedly better methods and materials every day. This requires a lot of high-quality professional development and a process of school change unfolding over a period of years. The change process is difficult, expensive and uncertain. Key changes in personnel, funding or curriculum, or district, state, and national policies, often disrupt or terminate even the most successful reforms. Many reforms are never successful. Some individual schools and pilot projects are compelling examples of what schools could be. But these 'lighthouse' schools are rarely replicated, even in their own districts, much less on a broad scale."[1]

"Would you describe Jefferson Elementary as a 'sand, bricks or seeds' school, Dr. Slavin?" Debbie interrupted.

"That depends. Let's describe each type of school and then see if we can characterize Jefferson. A 'seeds' school is one that has extraordinary capacity to translate a vision into reality. It's a school where the staff is cohesive, excited about teaching, led by a visionary leader who involves the entire staff in decisions, and broadly aware of research trends and ideas being implemented elsewhere. In such schools, a reformer need only introduce a vision and a set of principles and connect the school staff with other staffs undergoing reform to expose the staff to new ideas. A reformer tries to protect the staff from external pressures opposing the reform process. The 'seeds' analogy refers to the idea that the soil is fertile and the seed has within it the capacity to grow and bear fruit. It needs time, nurturing and protection."

A chorus of voices—Maria, Delores, Kathie, Tamar and Ted—all shook their heads and spoke excitedly: "No way, not our school!" "This school is a total disaster!" "No leadership!" "Poor student and teacher morale, and failing student achievement scores." "That's why this Citizens' Commission was formed!"

"Okay, let's look at a 'brick' school. A "brick' school is one in which school staffs would like to do a better job. They're willing and able to engage in a reform process if they're convinced it would work, but unlikely to create their own path to reform, even with external assistance. These are schools with good relations among staff and leadership, a positive orientation toward change, and some stability in the school and its district. Yet the teachers in the school do not perceive the need or have the capability to develop new curricula, instructional methods or organizational forms. Introducing reforms in such schools is like building a structure out of bricks. The bricks must be brought to the building site. Detailed, comprehensive blueprints are needed to put them together into a viable, functional structure. Once built, the structure may stand forever with moderate maintenance."

"Jefferson Elementary is not a 'brick' school," shouted Kathie! "That's why we're meeting as a Citizens' Commission. Maybe we need to completely reorganize this school and start over with a new principal, new teachers who want to be here, and new curriculum, in fact, new everything. I believe Jefferson needs reorganizing from the ground up. We need firm but democratic leadership to get the resources for building an effective school backed by a supportive community."

"Okay, Kathie. Then we have only one type of school left. It has two alternatives. One 'sand' school is a typical suburban school in a middle-class or wealthy community, usually well financed with students who come from educated well-to-do families. The school may be doing pretty well with most of its students going on to college. But the principal and teachers feel very smug about its level of achievement and community support. They see no reason to change the way they are doing things as educators. There's no outside pressure to change from parents, community, school board or state officials. It's a waste of time and resources to try to impose change from the outside, and it would probably fail.

"The second alternative 'sand' school is undergoing major change, and is in turmoil. It's lost funding, has poor relationships among staff and principal, or has conservative, fearful or incompetent leadership as well as poor student achievement. Working with such schools to create a climate for reform is extremely difficult and success is unlikely. Such failing schools are candidates for reconstitution—an increasingly popular negative sanction. It usually means transferring out all staff, except those who apply to remain and are accepted by a new, dynamic principal with effective team and instructional leadership skills."

"Bingo!" Debbie said. "Bingo!" Lenora echoed Debbie.

"Clearly," Dr. Slavin went on, "Jefferson faces a mighty challenge. Or maybe I should say this Citizens' Commission faces a mighty challenge of recommending a complete overhaul or new start with new leadership, staff, faculty, and perhaps, new students and parents. A new school culture must be developed, with systems and habits put in place before student achievement will begin to rise along with student, teacher and parent morale."

"Suppose we make the assumption, Dr. Slavin, that the Citizens' Commission recommends this kind of drastic overhaul, a little like taking over a bankrupt business that's in receivership." Paul had on his business hat. "What are the next steps to get the new organization moving?"

"Well, I understand the mission of the Jefferson Citizens' Commission is to recommend a comprehensive model of school reform. The challenge is to match the school reform model with the school 'readiness' to make the changes necessary to get it moving again.[2] There are three school-by-school reform strategies to consider here. One strategy comes from the organizational development field, or 'seed' school, in which school staffs are engaged in an extended process of formulating a vision, creating work groups to implement that vision, identifying resources (such as external assistance, professional development and instructional materials) to help the school toward its vision, and often locating critical friends to help the school evaluate and continually refine its approaches. Well-known examples of these networks are Sizer's Coalition of Essential Schools, currently approaching 1000 middle and high schools, and Levin's Accelerated Schools network, with 1000 schools, mostly elementary.

"A second widespread model, a comprehensive one, promotes state and district systematic reforms around standards, assessments and accountability. The National Alliance for Reforming Education is one of these, and it's closely affiliated with the New Standards Project. Another is Comer's School Development Project which has more specific guidelines for activities relating to parent participation and integrated approaches to mental health and self-esteem, but it also asks schools to create their own approaches to curriculum, instruction and professional development. Dozens of smaller networks of reforming schools also exist, including the Carnegie Corporation's Middle Grade School State Policy Initiative; the Paedeia Network built around the work of Mortimer Adler; the Foxfire network; and groups of schools working with such organizational development experts as Michael Fullan, Ann Leiberman, Seymour Saranson, and John Goodlad. These projects have in common a philosophy of change that emphasizes teachers and administrators finding their own way to reform. There's some guidance from the national project, but few, if any, student materials, teacher guides or specific instructional approaches."

Christina spoke up. "What reform model do you advocate, Dr. Slavin?"

He smiled as he said, "Well, our own 'Success for All and Roots and Wings' approach, of course. It's another whole-school model. We provide schools with specific student materials, teacher manuals, focused professional development, and relatively prescribed patterns of staffing, governance, internal and external assessment, and other features of school organization—a 'bricks' model. Success for All provides specific curriculum materials for pre-kindergarten, kindergarten, and grades 1-6 reading, writing and language arts. Roots and Wings adds to this material in mathematics, social studies and science. Both programs provide one-to-one tutoring for primary-grade students who are struggling in reading. They provide family support teams to build positive home-school relations and deal with such issues as attendance, behavior, physical and mental health. They have a building facilitator to help teachers implement and coordinate all program elements. The Core Knowledge Curriculum, advocated by E.D. Hirsch, and the Modern Red Schoolhouse, which uses Core Knowledge materials, are two additional approaches increasingly being used in the United States. They're relatively well-specified curriculum, instruction and school organization.[3]

"A third category is made up of programs focusing on a single subject, and, often, a limited grade span. Reading Recovery is a successful example. This one-to-one tutoring program was originally developed by Marie Clay in New Zealand. It's now used in thousands of schools throughout the English-speaking world. The National Diffusion Network (NDN) has identified more than 500 projects that met a minimal standard of effectiveness and replicability. Some of these are in widespread use."

Success For All/Roots and Wings

Wendy raised another question. "Dr. Slavin, describe for us your Success for All program and your Roots and Wings program. I'm a bit confused about them?"

"Our basic approach to designing a program to ensure the success of all children who are disadvantaged begins with two essential principles: prevention and immediate, intensive intervention. Learning problems must be prevented by providing children with the best available classroom programs and by engaging parents in support of their children's education. Success for All does not require significant additional expenditures, but rather shifts existing Title 1, special education, and other dollars from remediation to prevention and early intervention.[4]

"Before I do that, let me give you a BEST PRACTICES handout describing one of our schools in Maryland."

BEST PRACTICES: SLAVIN'S ROOTS AND WINGS DESIGN

Ridge Elementary School is located in rural Ridge, Maryland. The staff of 19 has 11 classroom teachers and eight others for such areas as art, music, special education, Title I and instructional resource. The staff serves nearly 300 students—Pre-kindergarten through fifth grade. The student population is approximately 75% White and 25% minority. Free lunches are received by 33% of students.

In November 1992, Ridge began implementing Success For All Reading as a strategy to raise student achievement. When Janet Kellam became principal three years ago, Ridge continued to strengthen Roots and Wings, which grew out of the Success For All reading program. Roots and Wings is especially effective because it is now integrated into the school improvement plan, which was formulated—and periodically updated—by a team of parents, staff and community leaders.

Roots and Wings guarantees that every child will be successful in elementary school, regardless of family background or disability. To achieve this goal and steer children at risk away from the need for long-term remedial or special education services, the program uses such tools as family literacy, one-on-one tutoring and family support services. Roots and Wings also uses research-based programs for reading, writing, language arts and mathematics. The "roots" are basic literacy and numeracy for each student; the "wings" are creativity, problem-solving ability and broad knowledge.

WorldLab is an approach to "wings" that integrates science, social studies and writing. Students role-play people in history, in other countries or occupations. In these simulations, students work in small cooperative groups. Ridge Elementary students in WorldLab classes recently planned and held a Colonial Fair—complete with spinning wool, making butter and lawn bowling—as part of their unit on the Revolutionary War.

Dr. Kellam uses a "fluid process" to maximize resources by using them where they are most needed. For example, unassigned teachers and paraprofessionals focus on students who have been targeted for additional attention on the basis of assessment feedback. Their staff development is organized around activities that are highlighted on the school improvement plan. In addition, this year they will work with Howard Gardner's dimensions in learning, which will expand their understanding of the variety of intelligences that students possess and how to develop their potential into strengths.

Student achievement is on the rise. Last school year, first graders came out of kindergarten at a readiness level or beginning reading level. By the end of the school year, as a result of the Reading Roots program, 98% of first graders scored on or above grade level on reading—an incredible achievement! As one parent said about the Reading Roots and Wings, "It seems to be very successful. The reading required each night is great because it reinforces what the children do each day. It gets the parents involved with the children more and I feel that it is much needed. It also pushes each family to do more and try harder in a positive way. I am very pleased."

Maryland School Performance Assessment Program (MSPAP) also shows that the third graders are making significant progress. By May of this year (1996), 70% of the students reached the 'satisfactory level' of the MSPAP, scoring above 70% in science and social studies and at 69.2% in math. This is considered extraordinary since Ridge has been in the Math Roots and Wings program only 3 years. Fifth graders showed a 12 point gain in math over the previous year, a 12 point gain in social studies, and a 10 point gain in science.

MathWings program is working well for both students and teachers. One student commented about the program, "What we do is exciting because its not just write down problems and answer them. I like MathWings!" Another student said, "…You don't have to work by your-self and do problems. You also don't have to just work in a book. You get to use rulers, calculators, and other math materials. You didn't get to use those things in the other kind of math." Commenting on MathWings, one teacher said, "I've always wanted to teach math this way…now I have the materials and manipulatives to do it!"

Dr. Kellam and her staff use assessment data to target areas for enrich-ment in their staff development, collegial meetings and teacher one-on-one sharing. This year they have decided to begin primary Math Wings in first and second grades, as well as continue the extended-day program, the during-the-day one-on-one tutorials, and the Partnerships they have formed. From their Partnerships with the Patuxent River Naval Hospital, St. Mary's College, and Spring Ridge Middle School peer tutors, the school benefits from volunteers who focus mostly on tutoring first grade children.

"Let's go on now with the elements of the Success for All program:

"*Reading Tutors.* In grades 1-3, especially trained, certified teachers work one-on-one with any students who are failing to keep up with their classmates. First grade students have priority for tutoring.

"*Eight-Week Assessments.* Students in grades 1-5 are assessed every eight weeks to determine whether they are making adequate progress in reading. This information is used to assign students to tutoring, to suggest alternative teachings strategies, and to make changes in reading group placement, family support interventions, or other ways to meet students' needs. The school facilitator coordinates this process with the active involvement of teachers in grade-level teams.

"*Preschool and Kindergarten.* Whenever possible, a half-day preschool program is provided for all four-year olds. The program emphasizes language development, readiness, and positive self-concept. A half- or full-day kindergarten program continues the emphasis on language, using children's literature and big books, as well as oral and written composition. The activities promote development of concepts about print, alphabet games and math. Peabody Language Development Kits are used to provide additional experience in language.

"*Reading and Writing Programs.* During reading periods for 90 minutes, students are regrouped across age lines so that each reading class contains students reading at one level. This eliminates the need for reading groups within the class, and increases time for direct instruction. Also, by using tutors as reading teachers during reading time, the size of most reading classes are smaller. The reading program in grades K-1 emphasizes the development of language skills by careful instruction that focuses on phonetic awareness, auditory discrimination, and sound blending as well as meaning, context and self-monitoring strategies. Students become fluent as they read and reread to one another in pairs."

"What do you do after the kindergarten and first grade intensive reading program?" Tamar, the third grade teacher, asked.

"In second- through fifth-grade levels, students use reading materials, basals, and trade books selected by school or district. The program carefully structures interactive opportunities to read, discuss and write. It emphasizes cooperative learning built around partner reading, character identification, settings, and problem solutions in narratives, story summarization and writing. It stresses direct instruction in reading comprehension skills. Students read books of their choice for 20 minutes each evening as homework. For this purpose, classroom libraries are developed. Writing is also emphasized. The writing instruction program uses a writer's workshop format. Students plan, draft, revise, edit, and publish compositions, receiving feedback at each stage from teachers and peers. For schools with Spanish bilingual programs, Success for All provides a Spanish reading curriculum for grades one through five.

"Another element is *Cooperative Learning*. Success for All curriculum emphasizes cooperative learning. Students work together in partnerships and teams to become strategic readers and writers. They share common goals, learn individual accountability, and recognize group success.

"Next is *Family Support Team*. The family support team works with parents in ensuring their children's success.[5] The team promotes parent involvement, develops plans to meet the needs of students who are having difficulty. For example, some children need new glasses. They implement attendance plans, and integrate community and school resources. Team members are the principal or assistant principal, facilitator, social worker, and other personnel.

Facilitator. A full-time facilitator works with teachers in each Success for All school to help them implement the reading program and coordinate eight-week assessments. In addition, he/she assists the Family Support Team, plans and implements staff development, and helps teachers make certain that every child is making adequate progress.

"*Staff Support Teams*. Teachers in this program learn to support one another through the training and implementation process in coaching partnerships, grade level teams, and other staff team configurations. These teams become a catalyst for disseminating new material, goal setting, and problem solving. They provide a supportive forum to discuss new instructional strategies.

"Another element is *Professional Development*. Success for All requires three days of professional development for teachers before the program begins and then several visits and in-service workshops throughout the year. After the initial training, building facilitators use classroom visits, coaching, and team meetings to follow up."

"Where is your program now being used, Dr. Slavin?" Tamar asked.

"In 1996-97, Success for All is being implemented in 457 schools in 120 districts in 31 states in all parts of the United States."

"Have you measured your success?" Debbie asked.

"Yes, in several school districts. We matched Success for All schools with control schools and compared them on individually-administered reading scales, district-administered standardized tests and other measures. The results have consistently favored Success for All, both the English and Spanish versions. In average grade equivalents, Success for All students perform approximately three months ahead of comparison students by first grade, and more than a year ahead by fifth grade. Effects are particularly strong for students who are most at risk, those in the lowest 25% of their grade. Success for All has substantially reduced retentions and special education referrals and placements."[6]

"How do schools like Jefferson adopt Success for All, Dr. Slavin?" Maria asked.

"We encourage district and school staff to review program materials, view video tapes, and visit nearby Success for All schools. District and building administrators really need to support the program, and school staff need an opportunity to learn about the program and vote on it. A positive vote of 80% or more of all teachers is required to participate. The costs are typically paid for by reallocations of existing Title I, state compensatory education, and special education funds. Title I teachers generally become tutors. During the first implementation year, other than personnel, typical costs for full-scale implementation average $50,000 for materials and 20 person days of training, plus travel."

"How does the Success for All reading program differ from your Roots and Wings program?" Ted, the sixth grade teacher, asked.

"Roots and Wings," replied Bob Slavin, "essentially adds math, science, and social studies curricula to Success for All. The idea is that we want children to have *roots*—the academic foundation, self-concept, and positive attitudes on which school success depends. We also want our children to have *wings*—the thinking skills, creativity, flexibility, enthusiasm, and the broad world view to soar beyond the commonplace. For example, *MathWings* is based on the National Council of Mathematics Teachers standards. This program involves students in cooperative groups to discover and apply the powerful ideas of mathematics. The curriculum balances problem-solving skills and concept development to make math meaningful and alive for students in grades one through six."[7]

"Can you describe for us your WorldLab program that's part of Roots and Wings?" Kathie asked.

"WorldLab is an integrated approach to science, social studies, writing and other subjects. In this 90-minute daily exercise, students play the role of historical figures or people in various occupations. They become active participants in the scientific discoveries and historical events being studied. These simulations draw on the entire content of grades one through six science and social studies programs, and integrate reading, writing, mathematics, and fine arts skills. For example, in one unit students learn about a local waterway in preparation for a model state legislature, in which they will write, propose, and debate many bills that relate to cleaning up the water. In other WorldLab units, students may play the role of inventors, delegates to the Constitutional Convention, advisors to the pharaohs of ancient Egypt or 15th century explorers. In these simulations, they work in small, cooperative groups. They read books and articles; write broadsides, letters, and proposals; and use fine arts, music and computers, video, and other technology to prepare newspapers and multimedia reports."[8]

"Bob, we can see why you are excited about your programs and why they're rapidly spreading throughout the nation and the world. Do your reform strategies have negatives or weaknesses?" Wendy was now watching the clock and getting ready to wrap up.

"Wendy, our biggest problem is staffing and training a staff to meet the growing demand," Bob Slavin replied.

"Well, thanks for being with us at this Hearing of the Citizens' Commission on Elementary School Reform. We've been well rewarded listening to your programs and reading your background materials. We'll now break for refreshments."

****

Authentic Assessment In Action

Nate welcomed the group back from their refreshment break. "Our last guest this afternoon is Dr. Linda Darling-Hammond, who will also be meeting with us again next month on the subject of Professional Teacher Development. Today she'll be speaking to us and answering questions about alternative student assessment. Dr. Darling-Hammond is currently the William F. Russell Professor of Education at Teachers College, Columbia University, and co-director of the National Center for Restructuring Education, Schools, and Teaching (NCREST). She has just completed a term as president of the American Educational Research Association (AERA), is author or editor of seven books and more than 150 articles. She began her career as a public school teacher and was co-founder of a preschool and day care center. Linda has accomplished this distinguished record in a relatively short time. She's an amazing educator. It is my pleasure to welcome one of the most productive and creative contributors to the field of educational reform—Dr. Linda Darling-Hammond."

As she began to speak, her warmth and enthusiasm seemed to energize the whole group.[9] "Nate, and members of the Citizens' Commission, I applaud the work you're doing here. Today I'd like to review some of the alternatives to classroom assessment of students that are replacing the traditional standardized tests. U.S. schools administer a wide variety of standardized tests to children in all grades. As you know, these tests are used to determine readiness for school and placement in grade and class levels; to assess academic achievement levels and place students in different programs, groups, or tracks; and to diagnose potential learning problems. These multiple choice tests, that we have all experienced in school, do not evaluate student performance on actual tasks, such as reading, writing, or problem-solving in various subject areas, and are poor measures of higher-order thinking skills. These tests do not measure the ability to think deeply, to create, or to perform in any field. They are unable to measure students' abilities to write coherently and persuasively, or to use mathematics in the context of real-life problems, to make meaning from text when reading, to understand and use scientific methods or reasoning, or to grasp and apply social science concepts. In summary, most standardized tests do not reflect current understandings of how students learn. They are based on an outmoded theory of learning that stresses the accumulation and recall of isolated facts and skills. Thinking skills are the foundation for building basic skills and not the other way around.[10]

"Worse, yet, if overused, standardized multiple choice testing can distort teaching and force classroom teachers to narrow their curriculum and teach to the test. Superficial content coverage and rote drill on discrete information bits are favored over in-depth projects and other thought tasks that take more student and teacher time like writing essays, conducting research, experimenting, reading and discussing literature, debating, solving difficult problems and creating products. Standardized tests are also poor diagnostic tools. They are poor predictors of how students will perform in other settings. They are unable to provide information as to why students score or behave as they do. Students not socialized in the dominant culture are often assigned to special education, bilingual or remedial education. This further limits the child's educational opportunities. National and international assessments of American student achievement confirm that higher-order thinking skills have declined in virtually all subject areas."

"Dr. Darling-Hammond," Delores spoke up, "why then do schools continue to assess student performance with these standardized tests that appear to be so useless?"

"Well, they are relatively cheap. They don't cost the school district much money. They are easy to give and easy to correct and assign a grade according to the Bell Curve—I understand you have dealt with the shortcomings of that! One resistance is that moving away from standardized testing requires the teacher to rethink teaching and, often, to learn new skills in curriculum building, coaching and group dynamics. Another pressure on the school is to report achievement scores. This is easily accomplished with standardized tests, although performance assessments are now being used for this purpose in many districts and states. There is also a concern by some policymakers, parents and others that today's students are not being taught the basics, and they want easily understood comparisons before spending more money on schools. Still others want to see schools held more accountable—and low scores are justifications for not giving schools more money if they are viewed as ineffective with the dollars they do have."

"What alternatives do we have for getting serious about real student assessment, Dr. Darling-Hammond? May I call you Linda?" Delores was getting more courageous.

"Please do, Delores. Many educators and researchers are seeking to overcome the problems of standardized testing. They are developing alternative assessment practices that look directly at students' work in ways that can evaluate the performances of students, classes, and whole schools. These alternatives are frequently called authentic assessments because they engage students in real world tasks rather than in multiple choice exercises; they evaluate them according to criteria that are important for actual performance in that field. Such assessments include oral presentations or performances along with collections of students' written products and their solutions to problems, experiments, debates and inquiries. They also include teacher observations and inventories of individual students' work and behavior, as well as of cooperative group projects.

"These kinds of assessment practices directly measure actual performance. They are intended to provide a broad range of continuous, qualitative data that can be used by teachers to inform and shape instruction. They aim to evaluate students' abilities and performances more fully and accurately, and to provide teachers with information that helps them develop strategies to meet real needs of individual children."

"Dr. Darling-Hammond, Linda, how do other countries assess student progress?" Debbie wanted to know.

"Actually, Debbie, the new qualitative assessments I have been describing more closely resemble assessment in many other countries, which is substantially different from the kind of multiple choice testing common in the United States. The Advanced Placement tests are taken by a small number of American high school seniors. High school students in most European countries complete extended essay examinations, often coupled with oral examinations, in a range of subjects requiring serious critical thought. In most of these countries, educators have long been actively involved in assessment development. They have not relied on commercial testing companies to determine content and manage test administration. Faculties convene to develop and score the assessments. Teachers are involved in examining their own students and also those in other schools. In many cases, much of the assessment process is internal. Assessment is under the control of the teacher and directly tied to ongoing instruction. In these ways, the act of assessment improves knowledge, practice, and shared standards across the educational enterprise as a whole, among both the professional faculty and the students."

"I don't mean to be slow in understanding these authentic assessments, but could you describe them in more detail—maybe give some examples?" Tamar asked.

"Authentic assessments have four characteristics. First, they are designed to be truly representative of *performance in the field*. Students actually *do* writing—for real audiences—rather than taking spelling tests or answering questions *about* writing. They *conduct* science experiments, rather than memorizing disconnected facts about science. The tasks are contextualized, complex intellectual challenges involving the student's own research or use of knowledge in tasks requiring the development and use of meta-cognitive skills. They also allow appropriate room for student learning styles, aptitudes, and interests. They serve as a source for developing competence and for the identification of strengths.

"Second, the criteria in the assessment seek to evaluate essentials of performance against well-articulated *performance standards*. They are openly expressed to students and others in the learning community, rather than kept secret in the tradition of fact-based examinations that are kept secure. Knowing the tasks and the standards is not cheating when a task requires an actual performance, and is intrinsically valuable and inherently complex. This is more useful than the recognition of a single right answer from a list. Learning and performance are enhanced when assessment focuses on the students' demonstrated ability to evaluate competing viewpoints and use evidence in a persuasive essay of social importance.

"Performances are based on explicit and shared schoolwide aims. They are mutifaceted rather reduced to a single dimension or grade. The criteria are performance-oriented and they guide teaching, learning, and evaluation. They place teachers in the role of coach and students in the role of performers as well as of self-evaluators.

"Third, *self assessment* plays an important role in authentic tasks. Authentic assessment is to help students evaluate their own work against public standards. Students then revise, modify, and redirect their energies, and then take initiative to assess their own progress. This is a major aspect of self-directed work and of the self-motivated improvement required of all human beings in real world situations. Performance standards take the concept of progress seriously. They make the processes of refinement and improvement of products a central aspect of the task and its evaluation. They also allow students of all initial levels of developed competence the opportunity to see, acknowledge, and receive credit for their own growth.

"Finally, the students are often expected to *present their work publicly and orally to teachers, classmates and parents.* This deepens their learning by requiring that they reflect on what they know and frame it in a way that others can also understand. It also ensures that their apparent mastery of an idea, concept, or topic is genuine. This characteristic of authentic assessment serves other goals as well. It signals to students that their work is important enough to receive public attention and celebration. Authentic assessment also provides opportunities for others in the learning community—students, faculty, and parents—to continually examine, refine, learn from, and appreciate shared goals and achievements. Authentic assessment creates living representations of the purposes and standards of the learning community, so that they remain vital and energizing."

"This all sounds wonderful," Ted Alexander said skeptically. "But how can teachers take the time to develop all these individual assessment tools and exercises? How can teachers grade them all and give each student the ongoing individual attention each needs if this is to work? Our union would never go for this without lots of time off to plan and extra pay for the extra work."

"Let me try to answer you, Ted, with these examples, " Linda replied. "A growing number of states, including Vermont, California, Connecticut, Kentucky, Maryland, New York, and Texas, are developing new approaches to assessment that will transform state-wide testing. Teachers in Vermont have developed student portfolios in writing and mathematics as the basis of their state's assessment system. Connecticut, Kentucky and New York have begun to develop performance-based assessments. These require students to perform a science experiment or solve a real world problem using mathematical and scientific concepts, rather than merely complete a multiple choice test. As part of the examination process, California, Maryland, and several other states have developed writing assessments requiring several days of work, including revisions. Urban, suburban and rural districts create authentic assessments to take the place of standardized testing. For example, these include affluent Shoreham-Wading River, New York; urban Pittsburgh, Pennsylvania; Rochester, New York; and Albuquerque, New Mexico; and rural towns in states as far apart as Vermont and Arizona. So you see, Ted, there are teachers who have decided that authentic assessment is a worthwhile way to re-invent teaching and learning. Initiatives such as these are an attempt to make schools genuinely accountable. Students need to acquire the kinds of complex, integrated skills and abilities for use in the world outside of school."

"Have you actually studied authentic assessment being tried out at a school?" Kathie asked.

"Yes, Kathie. I understand that Debbie Meier was here three months ago and reviewed the story of her Central Park East school. This school is part of the Coalition of Essential Schools, a network of schools who are developing authentic assessments. We also did an in-depth study of authentic assessments in place of standardized testing at three high schools and two elementary schools. The Bronx New School and P.S. 261 were our two elementary schools. They serve typical New York City populations—a multiracial, multiethnic, multi-linguistic mix of students from low-income, working-class, and middle-class neighborhoods.

"P.S. 261 is using the *Primary Language Record* (PLR), an authentic measure of young children's literacy development. PLR was designed in England and is increasingly used in the U.S. It has influenced teaching and learning in over 50 New York City elementary schools. The PLR involves teachers in collecting guided reading and writing samples of student's work. Teachers interview parents and students, and document students' literacy behaviors in a wide range of settings and tasks.[11] The California Learning Record, a PLR adaptation in the U.S., documents student growth and learning across subject areas at the elementary and secondary levels.

"The Bronx New School assessment system was designed to inform instruction and support teaching and learning through the collection of descriptive records of student growth. Teachers and school support staff across grade levels developed a common plan that systematically looked at various forms of learning in meaningful, real-life contexts. The staff borrowed from the work of others and develops tools and instruments of their own. The staff then created a system involving multiple sources of information collected over an extended period. Teacher-kept observations, student-kept records, samples of student work and observations of their families are used to develop a picture of a child's learning.[12] I could go on and on with the details of these assessments, but I believe you see the picture.

"Let me just summarize by saying that authentic learning assessment systems will restructure the learning organization of the school that undertakes them. They help provide a way of creating standards without standardization. Participation by teachers, students, and parents is required and welcomed. Without having to re-invent the wheel every time, it is critical to have supportive networks of schools and teachers who have gone through the drill before."

"Let me just say, in closing, that I commend your Citizens' Commission for undertaking the mission of re-inventing Jefferson Elementary School. I would urge you to recommend authentic assessment in your final reform report. It is a critical element of schoolwide reform that can help guarantee more exciting school teaching and learning for all children, teachers and parents. Thank you."

Nate spoke up. "Linda, you can see by the questions from our Commission teachers that this is an area we could pursue all night. Unfortunately, the time is up. Thank you again, Linda, for traveling from New York to share your knowledge on authentic assessment. Undoubtedly this Citizens' Commission will be recommending these ideas in our final report."

Summary

"This afternoon we're going to try something a little different for our summary. We asked four Commission members to help us. First, Ray will summarize Dr. Slavin."

Ray looked at his notes. "**Dr. Slavin created a metaphor to illustrate the readiness of schools for reform: 'sand' (resisting or in crisis), 'bricks' (adopting tested curriculum or other programs) and 'seeds' (turning vision into action by talented and dedicated staff). He taught us that the difference in developmentally-appropriate reforms depends on where the individual school is in the change process.**

"**He also shared the three comprehensive school change models: an organization-development model that depends on whole-school change by all participants over an extended time period; a model that promotes systematic reforms around standards, assessments and accountability; and** a model that focuses on a single subject, such as reading or limited grade span. Success for All and Roots and Wings is a whole-school change strategy. They provide schools with specific student materials, teacher manuals, and focused professional development. They prescribe patterns of staffing, governance, internal and external assessment, and other features of school organization. His model provides curriculum materials for pre-kindergarten, kindergarten, and first through sixth grade reading, writing, mathematics, social studies and science. It revolves around two essential principles—prevention and immediate, intensive intervention. His model emphasizes cooperative learning, family support teams, facilitators, staff support teams and professional development. It requires a favorable vote by at least 80% of a schools' faculty before Dr. Slavin will help them introduce his programs. The Success for All reading program is being used by 457 schools in 120 districts in 31 states. His programs show powerful academic results with both White and minority student populations."

"Thanks, Ray. Now, Paul, would you summarize Dr. Darling-Hammond?"

"Glad to. Standardized multiple choice tests do not accurately measure learning. They warp teaching and learning in classrooms and distort the opportunity to provide effective educational experiences, especially for students at risk. Many educators use authentic assessment techniques that look directly at students' work and their performances in ways that can evaluate students, classes and whole schools. Authentic assessments are intended to provide a broad range of continuous, qualitative data that teachers can use to shape instruction and to assess student abilities. Many other countries use authentic assessments developed by the teachers themselves, not by textbook publishers. Authentic assessment tools evaluate student performance against well-articulated and publicly-accepted performance standards. Both students and teachers develop the school reform plan and standards. Authentic assessment is widely used and many states are replacing standardized multiple choice testing. Finally, Dr. Darling-Hammond believes that authentic assessment is a powerful tool for restructuring the learning organization of any school."

"It's time to close for another month." said Nate. "This has been the highlight of all our day-long Hearings together. What impressive guests and heroic figures we've heard from. Can anyone in this room doubt that children at risk can learn and even excel, no matter what their color or ethnicity. Well, enough of my speeches! Let's hear a one-line reaction from each one of our group. Paul, I wonder if you could start off?"

"I'm in shock!" said Paul. "I've been out to lunch all my life on this area of educating disadvantaged children. I need to go home and do some serious thinking."

"Much of this still goes over my head," said Lenora. "But today has been the best. I've heard and talked with two of my heroes, Dr. Comer and Dr. Darling-Hammond. They're as good as they come."

Kathie said, "I couldn't agree more. What an eye opener! Why don't teachers and the general public know more about what we've heard today. I know we've got a tough job ahead in creating our final report for Jefferson— but what we could do, if we really wanted to!"

"I'm thrilled about today, but I'm also depressed! I can't believe how our children have been neglected all these years by the public education system just because they are minority or perhaps just disadvantaged. It's criminal!" said Maria.

"This has been great experience for me," said Kim, "just to sit here today and listen to these pioneers in educating real students. I take my hat off to all four of our guests, but I'm especially touched by Dr. Slavin and Dr. Levin. What drives these men to focus their careers on helping children who are disadvantaged?"

"I have much to think about now," said Debbie. "I have been taking notes as fast as I can write. This was exactly what this Citizens' Commission has needed—examples of just how and where disadvantaged children have been helped to succeed—and even better—to excel. Never again will I make the mistake of thinking these kids can't succeed."

"I echo what's been said. I'm getting anxious to draft our recommendations for Jefferson Elementary now that we know what's possible," said Wendy.

"I am dumbfounded!" said Dale. "I just had no idea. I'm pretty confused."

"I'm proud to be a teacher," Delores said. "I'm more hopeful now. This has charged my batteries. I look forward to our report."

"Today was great! I am so excited to be a new teacher with all these new ideas," said Tamar. "Now I'm beginning to see the possibilities. I'll be back."

"I'll admit this has been powerful today," said Ted. "But I still don't think your average teacher will step up to all the work that's required to turn urban schools around in my life-time."

"I'm charged up—again! Today, we've been on hallowed ground," Christina said.

"I agree with everybody," Ray concluded. "This has been the highlight. We now have the tools to put together a great recommendation for reforming Jefferson and saving our children. Thank you, Linda, Nate and Wendy. Again we acknowledge those parents and community members who are in our audience today. We hope you have found this Hearing as valuable as our Commission has. We'll see all of you next month."

Chapter 11
PROFESSIONAL TEACHER DEVELOPMENT
AND SCHOOL REFORM

Saturday, February 22

Deborah Cohen kissed her children, David and Heather, goodbye. After giving instructions to her live-in maid, she drove out of Cathcart Springs, a small community of townhouses near Jefferson Elementary School. She found a parking space and sat quietly thinking. *I wonder what we'll do today? Last month was amazing — Students At Risk. There's real hope after all for changing Jefferson. Drs. Levin, Comer and Slavin showed how to turn these high-poverty schools around. I'm amazed at what they're accomplishing. David is doing pretty well at the middle school, but I don't think Heather can wait that long. I may have to move or send her to private school next year — but where? My kids are Jewish! I don't want them going to Catholic schools, and the others are so elitist and expensive. I don't want to join the White flight. How long can I wait?*

What was it that Dr. Levin said? The real test of reform is to make the school so good that teachers want to send their own children there. It's easy to talk big about school reform, but I can't sacrifice Heather's education. I don't know what to do.

Let's see. What's coming up today? Oh yes, teacher preparation. I wonder if teacher training and development is as bad as when I first went into teaching ten years ago in Los Angeles? No one on the Commission knows I was a teacher for one year. Low salary, low status, isolation — it was awful! That experience convinced me to go to law school.

"Welcome to our sixth Citizens' Commission Hearing," said Ray as he called the group to order. "Nate, will you introduce our first guest?"

"Thank you, Ray. I hope that everyone has had a good month. I understand it is becoming your worst winter on record. I missed it. I was home in sunny Southern California," he smiled. "Today, we have another exciting experience that'll help us write recommendations for Jefferson Elementary. Our subject is teacher development—and we have the nation's Who's Who in this area—Dr. John Goodlad, Dr. James Kelly, and, in the afternoon, Dr. Linda Darling-Hammond."

He turned and read from the whiteboard. "National Education Goal #4 states, '**By the year 2000, the nation's teaching force will have access to programs for the continued improvement of their professional skills and the opportunity to acquire the knowledge and skills needed to instruct and prepare all American students for the next century.**' To kick off, I'd like to summarize the latest poll of teachers' attitudes by *Phi Delta Kappan.*[1] Teachers give their local public schools higher grades than they give other public schools—30% of teachers surveyed give grades of A or B to all public schools, while only 21% of the public do. Teachers report that the biggest problem in their classrooms is lack of parental support. Their second problem is lack of proper financial support. The third is student discipline. The public sees the biggest problem in their local public schools as drug abuse, followed by lack of discipline, then lack of financial support. When teachers were asked why they leave their profession, four reasons emerged: lack of discipline in schools, lack of parental support, lack of student interest and low salaries. The purposes of public schools were identified as preparing students for responsible citizenship (99% teachers and 95% public), economic self-sufficiency (95% and 96%), and happier lives that are culturally and intellectually enriched (83% and 84%).

Professional Teacher Development

"Our first guest is Dr. John Goodlad, director of the Center for Educational Renewal at the University of Washington in Seattle, and president of the Institute for Educational Inquiry. He has authored, co-authored or edited over 30 books, and has chapters in more than 100 other books. He has also written over 200 articles in professional journals and encyclopedias. John Goodlad has been a pioneer in school reform for over 25 years. He has conducted large-scale studies of educational change, schooling and teacher education.

"John has taught at every grade level—including a one-room rural school in Canada. He was born and educated there before taking his doctorate at the University of Chicago. During the 1970s, John directed the UCLA laboratory school where he worked out many of his ideas for improvement of elementary schools. In his 1984 groundbreaking publication, *A Place Called*

School, he focused on national school reform and the need for renewal of each local school as a complex ecosystem.[2] John, welcome!"

"Thank you, Nate, and members of the Citizens' Commission. I'm pleased to share some conclusions I've reached after many years of research and practice looking for ways to improve local schools and better educate all children."

"To get us started, John," said Nate, "tell us the two or three lessons you've learned in those years."

"Well, in the past, we've simply focused on one area, like curricular reform, teaching reform, or restructuring. So the first lesson I've learned is that until we address the entire school as a culture, there will be no significant change in schools. We need to address the school as a total entity. We don't prepare teachers for schools, but for classrooms. The second lesson is that unless reformers have a specific *agenda* that is understood from the outset, educational change will not happen. We have several successful reforms, like Ted Sizer's Coalition of Essential Schools, Howard Gardner's Multiple Intelligence Program, Hank Levin's Accelerated Schools, the Comer Schools, and our National Network for Educational Renewal. All of these have principles, or rules of the game, that educators and parents must follow to get the planned results. In some ways, my third lesson is the most important—without teacher education from the ground up, there will be no systemic school renewal."[3]

Kim raised her hand. "Could you tell us briefly about your Center for Educational Renewal?"

"Yes, Kim. The Center was created in 1985. We're now entering the twelfth year of a 15-year agenda. We've developed a strategy for change based on more than 25 years of research and other experiences. We've even managed to get people to buy into that agenda voluntarily. The network respects each school's uniqueness and is committed to intense training of educators in renewal techniques for schools and teacher education—renewal that must occur simultaneously. The Center's network involves 34 colleges and universities, over 100 school districts, and more than 400 partner schools. We believe that schools in a democratic society must go beyond custodial functions, regulations, and other barriers to creative change.[4]

"A most strange and puzzling fact is that policymakers throughout this whole century have failed to link school reform to teacher education. Reform reports are only now addressing the connection between preparation of teachers and the needs of schools.[5] For several years, my colleagues and I researched the nature of education and the role of schools in defining teacher education. Schools in our society are called upon to perform two distinctive functions: enculturate the young into a social and political democracy,[6] and introduce them to ways of reasoning that lead to intelligent, satisfying participation in the human conversation. Teachers must be thoroughly grounded in understandings, beliefs and pedagogy (ways of teaching) necessary for carrying out these functions.[7] Teachers must possess the knowledge and skills necessary to continually renew the schools. These requirements are the underpinnings of the teaching profession.

"Both the school's purposes and the teacher's preparation contain moral imperatives. In our studies of teacher education programs, we find several problems like lack of prestige; lack of program coherence; separation of theory and practice; and stifling conformity. Let's take the first one—lack of prestige or status. This dates back to the origins of teaching as a low-paid occupation, engaged in mostly by women, that required little educational attainment. Many good teachers find the low status regarded their profession as debilitating to their morale. In many colleges and universities, unlike such fields as law, medicine, and accounting, education is a 'cash cow.' Most institutions don't invest those resources back into making education a serious professional preparation as they do with the other more prestigious professional schools. Salaries, professorships, libraries, and recognition in teacher education all fall at the bottom of the academic pecking order.

"We find a lack of coherence which means that curriculum requirements and standards are scattered or unconnected. This happens when those creating the programs have not collaborated with surrounding schools as equal partners to create and conduct teacher education programs. Professors who contribute to teacher education programs—subject-matter content, pedagogy or philosophy—are on different faculties and have little interaction with each other. The resulting programs are defective and students are commonly exposed to only fragmented, bite-size courses.

"We also find separation of theory and practice. This happens because faculty in schools of education hardly ever coordinate with teachers in local schools who are responsible for clinical student teaching experiences. Usually, practice or applied experience is not guided by theory and research.[8]

As a result, when students practice teach, they often receive conflicting expectations from the theory they study and the practices they carry out.

"And finally we note the stifling effects of conformity. This happens when conformity to teacher education requirements are determined more by bureaucracy and its ongoing regularities of practice than by the knowledge base required for teaching in elementary and secondary schools."[9]

At this point, Maria raised her hand. "As a parent, I'm shocked by your findings! No wonder teachers are transferring and quitting. What can we do?"

"In the past," said Dr. Goodlad, "we've seen neither effective school reform nor a steady supply of high-quality teachers. It's time to do two things—completely redesign teacher education programs and get broad participation in the redesign process. This means involving all policymakers, university presidents, faculties from arts and sciences as well as schools of education. And equally important, it means involving administrators, teachers, parents and community leaders. If teacher education programs are not collaborating with surrounding schools as equal partners, they should be closed. At the college or university level, the professors who contribute to teacher education programs should be colleagues in one faculty. Finally, teachers who direct student teaching in the local schools must be recognized along with the school administrators and practicing teachers as essential partners in the education of future teachers. I am also suggesting that, as in other professional schools, practice or applied experience should guide theory and research. It's also time for university presidents, provosts and other top administrators to get honest about investing resources into their education programs.

"Now the heart of my recommendation is for universities to organize a 'Center of Pedagogy'—for the art and science of teaching—geared to the mission of schooling in a democratic society.[10] These new Centers would draw faculty from the Departments of Arts and Sciences; the school, college, or department of education; and the participating school districts. These Centers should stand between the University and the School District and prepare educators for early childhood educational settings, elementary schools, and secondary schools.

"The mission of these Centers of Pedagogy is two-fold: first is to prepare teachers well with serious foundation courses like ethics, epistemology, aesthetics, comparative religion and literature, political philosophy, history, written and oral communications, and the social, physical, and biological sciences. The second is to address the proper role of schools in a democratic society. Right now schools are merely the servants of our economic and business interests.

"A key development in these new Centers is their active partnerships with schools and school districts. They should have equal say in planning curriculum and clinical teaching experiences for new teacher candidates. This collaboration is important in bringing together the two different cultures in education—higher education professors and practicing school administrators and teachers. Professors often look down on 'lowly' practitioners, whereas most practicing educators believe that education professors know little about what is needed in schools. This cultural clash has undercut the serious development of teaching as a respected profession. Teacher preparation and on-going training go hand in hand with successful school reform!

"This new model of teacher preparation requires seven activities which are summarized here." He handed out a single sheet of paper:

- *recruitment*—Start in junior and senior high schools to motivate students to go into the new profession when they first enter college;

- *general studies*—Carefully design the first two years of general studies to provide breath and depth of preparation, much like pre-med courses carefully prepare students for medical school;

- *socialization*—During the first two years, conduct seminars that expose students to educational leaders and on-site school experiences, such as tutoring children in reading;

- *subject-matter specialization*—During the third and fourth year, give future teachers in-depth preparation in the academic content, teaching process, and research areas on which they will focus. This is when they begin to specialize;

- *professional sequence*—Plan courses in a way that integrates specific subject matter and the development of teaching skills with education and child development research;

- *internship*—Provide student teachers with extended immersion in two different partnership school experiences; and

- *feedback and follow-up*—Master teachers carefully evaluate and tutor teachers who are candidates for licensing and state examinations.

"I have a BEST PRACTICES handout here that describes the establishment of one of these Centers."

BEST PRACTICES: UNIVERSITY-SCHOOL PARTNERSHIP— MONTCLAIR STATE UNIVERSITY'S CENTER OF PEDAGOGY

In November 1995, Montclair State University in New Jersey established the Center of Pedagogy. The Center is among the first in the nation and has attracted considerable attention. The case for such centers has been carefully laid by the work of John Goodlad, particularly in his 1990 book, *Teachers for Our Nation's Schools*, and in his 1994 book, *Educational Renewal*. The idea of centers has been widely discussed in public forums attended by administrators and faculties in public schools and in all major universities.

Working with John Goodlad's Center for Educational Renewal, faculty representatives from Montclair's University's School of Education and School of Arts and Sciences and from collaborating school districts' schools created the new Center of Pedagogy. After conducting a nationwide search, a director was selected. The DeWitt Wallace Reader's Digest Fund awarded an Incentive Grant in Teacher Education (along with other external matches and a match from the University) for 1995-97 funding to plan and initially establish the Center and to engage in ongoing renewal.

The new Center recognizes a key hallmark of excellent teacher education programs—the shared commitment and mutual responsibility of the three participating groups: faculties from education, arts and sciences, and public school districts. All work as equals. The Center of Pedagogy, which is characterized by shared governance and open communication, works in the interest of improved student learning. The three groups developed a working definition of the proposed Center of Pedagogy: (1) Its mission is to conceptualize, plan and carry out the education of educators, encouraged by a wide range of scholarship, especially in the areas of pedagogy and its application; and (2) As it facilitates the education of educators, its goal is to also simultaneously renew both the University's educational program(s) and the schools' educational program. The Center of Pedagogy is to consolidate all the coordinating functions previously carried out by the Office of Teacher Education, bringing together grant programs and community outreach programs with common goals and agendas.

The University and the collaborating school districts have made strengthening the teaching profession a top priority, with the Center established as a vehicle for collaboration. The competence of participating faculty and the personal interest of superintendents of collaborating school districts indicates the high quality of leadership provided by the 'tripartite groups.' Top leadership is important for overcoming the main barriers to the effective planning and coordinating of these three groups—their separate, distinct cultures, structures and physical locations.

The Center of Pedagogy is a loose structure that 'floats above,' without supplanting or replacing existing structures. Membership is informal and does not impinge on responsibilities to their primary affiliation. The following organizations are members or potential members: The Office of Teacher Education and Placement, The Office of Admissions and Post Baccalaureate Program, The Teacher Education Policy Committee, The Curriculum Resource Center, The New Jersey Network for Educational Renewal, Public School Faculty, Staff and Administrators, University Faculty Staff and Administrators, The Agenda for Education in a Democracy (DeWitt Wallace Reader's Digest Project), and Project THISTLE: Thinking Skills in Teaching and Learning.

Officials from university schools of education, school districts, foundations, state and federal leaders throughout the nation all watch with anticipation the new experiment in teacher preparation.

"Dr. Goodlad," Delores said, "my teacher preparation program was nowhere near what you're describing. No wonder I felt like it was sink or swim! I still feel like a pretender sometimes. After four years, I'm supposed to know how to teach. But now I am so busy I don't even know where to turn to get retooled for national standards." *Oh, oh,* thought Delores, *Ted's looking down at the table like he's embarrassed by my confession.*

"Maybe I've just been lucky," said Tamar. "The five-year program I just completed has really been good. George Mason University recruited top students who had majored in other academic subjects to enter their special new Masters Degree in Education. The program takes 15-months. I started teaching in another school at a pretty good level on the pay scale (above most new teachers with a four-year degree). When I came to Jefferson, it was because I actually wanted to! But my internship experiences were great preparation. I feel like I've benefited from a program like the one you describe, Dr. Goodlad."

"You're lucky, Tamar. And you've obviously made good use of your opportunities. **Now, let me close my testimony by restating what I believe is the most significant mission for tomorrow's schools. We must not lose sight of public schools' essential mission—enculturating the young in a social and political democracy. That means to help them understand and commit to democracy and the rights and responsibilities of all citizens. It means to enjoy and participate in all the individual and collective freedoms implied in *e pluribus unum*—from many in our multi-culture society to a social and political democracy embracing us all as one. These proposed reforms in teacher preparation will be wasted if we continue turning out teachers who simply make schooling the preparation of workers in our global economy. Earning a living is an expected correlate of schooling, but it should come out of preparing students for effective citizenship in their families, schools, communities and nation. Only then will they be prepared to enjoy richer, more satisfying and caring lives.** Effective and highly-motivated teachers of tomorrow will seek out schools that have strong, determined principals who are leaders. These schools will also have teachers who actively participate in planning a challenging curriculum that's exciting for themselves and their students.

"The schools of the future are educative communities. I see them sprouting up in every community in America. The work in these new schools is in the conversations, the inquiries, the collaborations about teaching and learning together. It involves every child, every teacher and every parent. Enactment of this vision depends on the production of teachers who are committed to it and who possess the knowledge and skills to implement it. It also requires communities of parents and other citizens who value good schools and demand that their children and grandchildren have nothing less. These schools are conscious of their learning culture. They take care of business and have orderly routines. They value academic achievement and making all kids smart kids. They promote respect and connectedness among students, teachers, administrators; and they are connected to homes and parents in many positive ways. Create this kind of school for the children, educators and parents of Jefferson Elementary School. Thank you for allowing me to come before your Commission. I wish you well in your mission."

"Thank you, Dr. Goodlad. We'll take these lessons seriously! Now it's time for a break. When we come back, Wendy will introduce Dr. James Kelly."

Professional Teaching Standards

Wendy welcomed the group back. "Dr. James A. Kelly is president of the National Board for Professional Teaching Standards, headquartered in Southfield, just outside of Detroit. He will give us a different perspective on teacher development. While Dr. Goodlad focused on the need to restructure university teacher recruitment and preparation programs, Dr. Kelly will deal with advanced training of experienced teachers.

"Jim, could you start by giving us two or three lessons you've learned about school reform in your experience as an educator?"

"Wendy, I suppose the first lesson is that you must have a concrete vision that will hold up through all the battles. And there will be battles if you stand for something of value. Second, you must have a strategy for creating demand for your reform. I'm convinced most reformers don't really understand this. Public education in this country is totally fragmented. No one is in charge—not the President, secretary of education, governors, chief state school officers, or board of education. Neither can superintendents, principals, teachers or parents do anything. Only interest groups can drive change in the status quo. The challenge, or game, is to create demand. Then interest groups that support the demand can create the conditions for change.

"Third, I would say you must have witnesses to the demonstration project who can testify that something good has happened and others should follow that example. Then you must broaden that base to include the whole power structure—Congress, state legislatures, the local boards—so that they can make the demonstration part of public policy—the new rules of the game. The reform can only be sustained if demand is created and demonstrations have witnesses. Reform takes a long time, and it may take a generation before we see its value. It must be systemic, not a one-shot demonstration. Most foundation funders believe it's a three to five year process."[11]

"Jim, why is it necessary to have a National Board for Professional Teaching Standards today?" asked Nate.

"The world around us is changing rapidly. Our schools are falling short in meeting the new, more complex challenges of today. Against the standards of the past, our schools are not failing. But teachers must teach to new, higher standards in order to help young people meet different and more intellectually-demanding needs of tomorrow. Education has always been a cornerstone of our society, but in our harried daily lives, it's become a lower priority. What Thomas Jefferson said is a great reminder: 'A Nation that seeks to be both free and ignorant, never was and never will be.' Schools and colleges need to build on freedom and equality to develop the potential of all our children.[12] America must have a world-class teaching force, if we are to have world-class schools. The two go hand in hand."

"What will it take to redesign an effective school?" Paul asked.

"Paul, as a businessman, you're aware of the re-engineering movement that's causing dislocation or growing pains. American business had to streamline its organizations. In order to be more competitive, business had to re-examine everything it does. They tried mere tinkering and imposing new goals and outcomes on outmoded organizational arrangements and facilities. These approaches failed. Educators desperately need to re-think the school as an organization. We need to get rid of pre-conceived notions like schools must be housed in buildings full of isolated workplaces (classrooms) and schools must be run by top-heavy bureaucratic structures.

"Schools face intense outside pressures today, such as developing national standards, curricula and assessments. They also face demands for more parent and community control of schools, demands for social justice and equality by teaching all children, regardless of background, and professionalism of teachers. Today's youth are growing up surrounded by a flourishing pop culture, today's equivalent of religion. For many of them, the shopping mall has become their temple and school is seen as irrelevant.

"If we are to survive as a nation, every community in America had better start serious school reform. More than half of all school expenditures are used for buildings and equipment, and for management, supervision and technical support; less than half goes directly for teachers. We must design a collaborative learning system that involves parents, teachers, aides, technicians and older students in educative roles. Each school should have at least one National Board Certified Teacher. We must design a learning enterprise which uses modern computers and interactive telecommunications systems to strengthen teaching and learning of students and teachers alike. We must insist that all professional educators teach daily so they keep a hand in the classroom and a connection with kids. We must create roles and career paths, and give incentives and rewards for demonstrated accomplishment in teaching."

Kathie raised her hand. "Dr. Kelly, where does the National Board For Professional Teaching Standards come in? Just how does it expect to make a difference?"

"I thought you'd never ask, Kathie! Let me give you a little background. Three years after *A Nation At Risk* was released, the Carnegie Task Force on Teaching as a Profession published, *A Nation Prepared: Teachers for the 21st Century*. This pivotal report called for a National Board for Professional Teaching Standards. Its mission is to establish high and rigorous standards for what accomplished teachers should know and be able to do. It should develop and operate a national voluntary system to assess and certify teachers who meet these standards. It should advance related educational reforms for the purpose of improving student learning in American schools.

"National Board Certification is designed for experienced teachers whose preparation and experience have enabled them to understand how theory translates into practice. They must be able to ascertain what works and to learn how to judge student behavior and performance, and to practice as mature, professional decision-makers. Let me read the list of fundamental requirements for tomorrow's teachers:

- a broad grounding in the liberal arts and sciences;

- knowledge of the subjects to be taught, of the skills to be developed;

- knowledge of general and subject-specific methods for teaching and for managing and monitoring student learning;

- knowledge of students and human development;

- skills in effectively teaching students from diverse racial, ethnic, and socioeconomic backgrounds; and

- skills, capacities and dispositions to employ such knowledge wisely in the interest of students."[13]

"How does the National Board Certification differ from state systems of mandatory licensure for beginning teachers? I already have a license to teach," said Ted.

"State licensing systems set entry level standards to protect the public interest and to make sure teachers will do no harm, like when doctors take the Hippocratic oath. Professional certification verifies high-quality teaching. Experienced teachers must pass a series of standards-based performance assessments—one at the school site and the other at an assessment center—to receive National Board Certification. Their portfolio includes student work, teacher reflections on the work, and videotapes of classroom activities. At the assessment center, teachers write essay examinations addressing their teaching skills and knowledge of their subjects. In every state, school districts and schools will decide on how to capitalize on National Board Certification. Local leaders can design instructional arrangements that promote student learning and support professional practice. In this way, the National Board serves as a catalyst to improve schools.[14]

"National Board Certification is organized into more than 30 fields, which are categorized into student developmental levels and subject matter. The developmental levels are early childhood (ages 3-8); middle childhood (ages 7-12); early adolescence (ages 11-15); and adolescence and young adulthood (ages 14-18). A teacher may choose to become certified as either a subject-matter specialist, such as music, history/social studies, and English language arts, or as a generalist, which includes all subjects across the curriculum. Each set of standards is grounded in the National Board's policy statement on what teachers should know and be able to do. Let me read the five general propositions about accomplished practice:

1. Teachers are committed to students and their learning;

2. Teachers know the subjects they teach and how to teach those subjects to students;

3. Teachers are responsible for managing and monitoring student learning;

4. Teachers think systematically about their practice and learn from experience; and

5. Teachers are members of learning communities.

"The standards for the individual certification fields are developed by committees composed of teachers, scholars and experts in child development, curriculum development, teacher education and relevant subject disciplines. Teachers comprise a majority of each committee, which are also balanced to represent the diversity of educators in each field. As of October 1996, the National Board has certified 376 teachers from 31 states. About 1500 teachers from across the country have moved through the initial assessments. In 1997 we will begin upscaling and expect 1500 new candidates. Over the next decade, we expect to double each succeeding year."

"Dr. Kelly," Kathie said, "how much would it cost me to go through the National Board Certification process? Who pays? Is there a financial advantage to certification?"

"The cost is $2000. Many states are picking up that cost or returning it to teachers after they pass. For example, in Virginia the legislature has passed an education budget that provides $1,000 for each of 75 teachers (to be matched locally) during the 1996-97 school year.[15] The really good news is that many other states are following suit and paying additional compensation to teachers after they pass the national boards. In some cases, they are raising teachers' salaries several levels higher in recognition of achieving advanced professional competence.

"It's a modest beginning, but now that we've laid the foundation and created the demand, teachers and state legislatures are reaching out. National Board Certification is recognizing good teaching and teaching as a true profession, just like we'd hoped it would do. Kathie, I hope you'll contact our offices for an application. You'll find the process challenging and satisfying. It's well worth the time. Our best witnesses are teachers who are going through the process. Even those who don't succeed the first time are happy with it. But let me quote just two teachers:[16]

National Board Certification lets people see what teaching can be. I think that good teaching is an ability to take subject matter expertise...and transform [it] into the classroom with the students—to make that bridge between your subject and the student's own backgrounds. That's no easy trick.

BRADY KELSO, San Diego

I know I was a good teacher [when I started]. But every teacher has a responsibility to be better tomorrow than they were today. I am a much more deliberate teacher now, more focused. I can never do anything again with my students and not ask, 'Why am I doing this? What are the effects on my kids? What are the benefits to my kids?' It's not that I didn't care about those things before, but it's on such a conscious level now.

SHIRLEY BZDEWAKA, Dayton, New Jersey

Ted Alexander raised his hand. "As a union man, I want to know what my local and state union has to say about your National Board Certification. Doesn't the increased pay violate the seniority rules of most teacher contracts?"

"That's a good question, Ted. We've been working closely with both major teacher unions. Al Shanker first called for national certification in a 1985 speech. Many union leaders see the advantages of supporting National Board Certification and rewarding teachers who achieve it with additional pay, just like seniority. Some union officials are urging state legislatures to help pick up the cost and then to reward those teachers who obtain Board Certification. It's a win-win situation. Public recognition of teaching as a real profession helps everyone. There will be no real school reform in America without improving classroom teaching."

"Jim," Nate said, "we want to thank you for your presentation. Most of us did not know what National Board Certification means. Your goal of having at least one National Board Certified teacher in every school by 2006 has implications for our work here at Jefferson Elementary. You can be sure you'll hear from this Commission about teachers applying for national certification as one strategy for reforming this elementary school.

"Jim will be with us for lunch and can answer further questions. Please check your luncheon partner assignments. When we return at 1:00 p.m., we will summarize our morning's contributions. Our guest will be Dr. Linda Darling-Hammond."

****

Mid-Summary

After lunch, Wendy welcomed the group back. "Our two guests gave us a lot to digest. **Let's summarize our morning and see what we can learn for our report on Jefferson Elementary School."**

Dale called out, **"I want to say how surprised I was when the National Education Goals Report reminded us that Goal #4 talked about the need to recruit and train better teachers! I guess the federal government and Goals 2000 aren't as crazy as I've been led to believe. Who could be against that goal? I'm beginning to see that the federal government is just citizens like us who work at that level instead of the state or local level. But I still worry about powerful education interest groups, like NEA."**

"Many of our guests keep reminding us," said Maria, **"that teaching democracy is the most important purpose of public schools in America. But I see a connection between citizenship in a democracy and good citizenship in the family, the school and the community. It reminded me of last month's character education Hearings. No teachers have ever taught democratic principles to my children, and I never learned about them."**

"I was surprised," said Ted Alexander, **"at how haphazard recruitment and training of teachers still is. Sounds like it hasn't changed since I decided to become a teacher—almost 35 years ago. I'm glad Goodlad wants to tie teacher preparation to school reform."**

"Well, I have a confession to make," Debbie said. **"after graduating from UCLA, I taught for only one year because of the very conditions Dr. Goodlad described today. He discussed the lack of cooperation between the universities' schools of education and the school districts and schools where the teachers have to do student teaching. Anyway, my short teaching career was a disaster! I was forced to sink or swim and I sank. I wonder how teachers here at Jefferson were trained and recruited?"**

"I don't think anything will change until universities become more accountable!" Kim spoke up angrily. **"I blame the university presidents and top administrators for the sorry state of teacher education. They would rather have a winning football or basketball team than train good teachers. But it's really a life or death matter for many of our children! Policymakers are simply not being held accountable by the state legislatures or by the alumni of the schools of education, or by the local school districts. It's time someone started dealing with accountability."**

"I'm not a teacher," said Christina, "but I think Dr. Goodlad is on to something. He wants to organize new Centers of Pedagogy (or Teaching) to stand between the universities and the school districts. These Centers would concentrate on training professional teachers."

"Dr. Goodlad has shown me why the public does not respect teachers!" Delores burst out. "No wonder! We're not a professional group until we pass challenging state examinations that demonstrate we know something special about education that parents don't know—something that sets us apart."

"The public's attitude toward teachers is sobering, isn't it Delores," Wendy said. "Well, let's go on to Dr. Kelly's presentation. How does it relate to this Commission's report on Jefferson Elementary?"

"Dr. Kelly has opened my eyes," Paul said. "If the program is such a standard setter for teaching excellence, let's invest in four or five teachers who want to pass the National Boards. The whole school would benefit. Let's find the good teachers."

Ray was smiling. "It looks like Dr. Kelly's strategy to create a demand for reform is working with you, Paul. But I agree. Let's get the best teachers in here. I'll bet I can sell the board of education on money for National Teacher Certification."

Lenora spoke up. "Why does certification takes so long? I thought teachers were already trained good, and that's why we hired them in the first place."

"Well I know I'm just a beginning teacher," Tamar said excitedly, "but I want to apply for National Certification. And I'll help any teacher who wants to try. Kathie, why don't you apply? You're a great teacher!"

"You've all made some valuable points," Wendy said. "Now let's turn back to Nate."

"I'd like to introduce Dr. Linda Darling-Hammond, who was here last month. She is a professor at Teachers College, Columbia University, and co-director of the National Center for Restructuring Education, Schools, and Teaching (NCREST). She is executive director of the National Commission on Teaching and America's Future. We met Linda last month when she talked about authentic assessment. Welcome back, Linda."

Teaching and America's Future

"Thanks, Nate. Glad to be here again. I've been asked to preview what our National Commission on Teaching is discovering—that teacher preparation and development is the most important strategy for reforming schools in America today. Our Commission proposes a challenging goal for America's future: By the year 2006, we will provide every student in America with what should be his or her educational birthright—access to competent, caring, qualified teaching. The Commission is developing a blueprint for recruiting, preparing, and supporting excellent teachers in all America's schools.

"Qualified teachers are absolutely essential if we want every child to reach high levels of intellectual and social competence.[17] Today, however, at least one of every four teachers lacks even minimal qualifications in the subject areas for which he or she has been hired. In the next decade, because the school population will explode, many teacher will retire. We'll need to recruit and hire two million new teachers. So far the school reform movement has ignored the obvious: what teachers know and can do makes the crucial difference in what children learn. The central strategy for improving our schools should be to recruit, prepare and retain good teachers. School reform cannot succeed until it focuses on conditions that foster good teaching. When the public was asked to name the most important thing public schools need to help students learn, the answer was good teachers.[18]

"The soul of America has been lost, and we must reclaim it. We need an education system that helps people forge shared values. They need to understand and respect one another, learn and work at high levels of competence, and be willing to take risks and persevere against the odds. Education should teach people from diverse backgrounds to work well together, and to learn throughout their lifetime. We should be investing at the front-end in education programs—preschool enrollment and job training. Instead, we are spending money at the back-end—on state penitentiaries, welfare rolls and unemployment checks. We are now leading advanced nations in our high rates of childhood poverty, homelessness, and mortality (under age 25). We lag behind in preschool enrollment. Most children live in a single-parent household at some time while growing up, and many parents are too hurried and harried to attend to their children's needs, especially with fewer community supports to help them. Many children arrive at school hungry. They are frightened because their neighborhoods are racked with crime and violence, drug and alcohol abuse. Their health care is inadequate; some are unvaccinated. Although many teachers are well aware of the stress on their students, most schools are still organized on models that were used a generation ago—ignoring the huge challenges facing teachers from today's children.

"Schools of the 21st century must teach students from more diverse backgrounds. They must help students master more challenging content, more effectively than they have ever done before. This means that teachers need to be multicultural in their approach. Teachers must understand students and their many pathways to learning as deeply as they comprehend subjects and teaching methods. It means that teachers need to understand how students of different cultures and language backgrounds can be supported in learning academic content. Teachers need a variety of teaching strategies to meet students' different ways of learning. It also means that schools must reorganize themselves to enable more intensive kinds of student learning, supported by close, personal relationships, as well as new technologies.

"In other modern nations, teachers are better prepared, highly respected and well compensated. In the United States, teaching has long been viewed as little more than a combination of glorified baby sitting and clerical work. Although some progress has been made, teachers in many school districts are still treated as semi-skilled workers, underpaid and micromanaged.

Paul Christopher aggressively attacked this statement. "Dr. Darling-Hammond, I don't see how you can possibly defend the teaching profession. After all, teachers have an easy time of it compared with other professionals—working nine-month years, half the afternoon free, many long holidays. And, of course, they can't be fired because of tenure. Teacher unions will block the very reforms you advocate. For nine month's work, they're paid well. The poorest graduates go into teaching because they can't compete in the real world. The big thing we need is tougher standards. We don't need to pour big dollars into teacher preparation and staff development. I thought teachers were prepared in college—using my tax dollars. And the students still can't do math or read!"

"Paul, these are serious charges," said Linda. "Let's see if I understand you. I've taken some notes on what you said. Before I respond, however, let me share a fictional want ad:"

WANTED

College graduate with academic major (master's degree preferred). Excellent communication/leadership skills required. Challenging opportunity to serve 150 clients daily on a tight schedule, developing up to five different products each day to meet individual needs, while adhering to multiple-product specifications.

Adaptability helpful, since suppliers cannot always deliver goods on time, incumbent must arrange for own support services, and customers rarely know what they want. Ideal candidate will enjoy working in isolation from colleagues. This diversified position allows employee to exercise typing, clerical, law enforcement, and social work skills between assignments and after hours. Typical work week: 50 hours. Special nature of the work precludes amenities, such as telephones or computers, but work has many intrinsic rewards. Starting salary $24,661, rising to $34,495 after only 15 years.

"Now, Paul, your first objection: **All we need is tougher standards!** At least since *A Nation At Risk* was published fourteen years ago, the nation has been clamoring for higher academic standards. Who could possibly be against them? The rub is no student will learn higher standards until teachers know the standards and are prepared to teach to them. So we fully applaud the standards movement for *both* students and teachers. The work of this Commission is standards for teachers.

"**Can anyone teach?** Students know better. Anyone who's ever tried to teach a lesson to children or adolescents can attest to the fact that not everyone can teach. Being responsible for a room full of children or adolescents, even for a few hours, is difficult and frustrating, even if the goal is merely survival.

"**Training teachers is a waste of time.** Well, no other organization would feel that way about their employees. Certainly nobody I know in the business world would hire people and then not train them to be as effective as possible. Only people in education would assume that any random training is enough that you may bring to the job. The most effective teachers are not only well-prepared in their subject area, but they also understand learning, child development, and teaching methods.

"**Teachers don't work hard enough**. Despite the shorter school year, no nation requires teachers to teach a greater number of hours per day and year than the United States. Our teachers teach more than 1,000 hours per year. Teachers in other industrialized countries teach between 600 and 800 hour per year, depending on grade level. The typical teacher in America works 50 to 55 hours per week and most days over their vacations. Most spend 10 to 15 hours each week outside school preparing lessons and grading homework and papers—usually in isolation. In many other countries, teachers have 15 to 20 hours per week in school to plan and work collaboratively.

"**Teachers are well paid**. Most occupations pay better than teaching (see Table 11.1). Teaching is hardly a well-paid profession (see Table 11.2 for a comparison of earnings by occupation). No wonder we lose so many in the first three years.[19]

"**Tenure is the problem**. The original purpose of tenure was to protect teachers from political pressures, right and left, and to help them teach objectively what they've learned as professionals—to make those judgment calls. There is no such thing as lifetime tenure in public schools. After three years on probation, it is presumed that public school teachers will be rehired for one-year terms—unless cause for not hiring them can be demonstrated. Even then there is no buy-out, no golden parachute. We need to improve evaluations in ways that support teacher learning and to deal with incompetence. I would say, don't eliminate tenure—just evaluate better.

"**Unions block reform**. Yes, some union rules have blocked reform. But, today, many unions and school boards have moderated their conflicts. They're working together to negotiate working conditions, which should contribute to higher productivity for teachers and students. These unions and school boards are also trying to change teacher education programs to turn out better-trained teachers. They participate also in counseling and removing poor teachers."

I think I've been hit by a truck, Paul thought. *I'm embarrassed! Our Commission teachers are sure enjoying me getting clobbered by this woman.*

Dr. Darling-Hammond pressed on. "Our challenge is not to defend the present state of teaching but to improve our overall performance. By contrast with slipshod teacher preparation in the United States, let me give you a handout that describes how teachers are developed in Germany, France and Japan.[20]

Table 11.1
Teacher Salaries Around the World

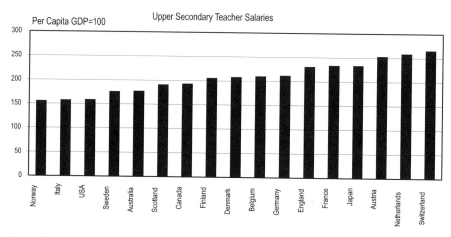

Source: F. Howard Nelson and Timothy O'Brien, Teacher Pay, Training, an Conditions of Service | How U.S. Teachers Measure Up Internationally: A Comparative Sutdy of (Washington, D.C.: American Federation of teachers, 1993), p.99

Table 11.2
Comparisons of Earnings by Occupation

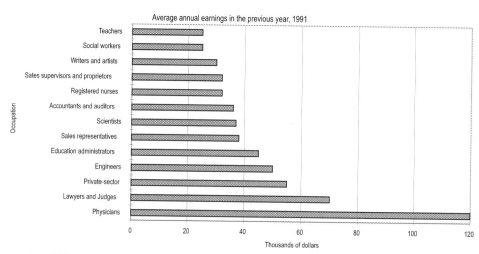

Source: U.S. Department of Education, National Adult Leteracy Servey, 1992. Published in the (Washington, D.C.: National Center for Education Statistics, 1995), p.161 | Condition of Education 1995

BEST PRACTICES: LEARNING TO TEACH IN GERMANY, FRANCE AND JAPAN

Teacher education in the former West Germany has long been considered an international flagship, as one report noted of the system's rigorous standards and training. "In Germany, those who can, teach." Prospective teachers get degrees in two subjects, write a thesis, and pass a series of essay and oral exams before they undertake pedagogical training. Two years of teaching preparation include teaching seminars combined with classroom experience—first observing and then, after four to six weeks, beginning to practice in a classroom with a mentor teacher. Over the two years of internship, college and school-based supervisors observe and grade at least 25 lessons. At the end of this period, candidates prepare and evaluate a series of lessons, prepare a curriculum analysis, and undergo another set of exams before they are finally ready to teach.

In 1989 France undertook a sweeping overhaul of teacher education. The overhaul was motivated by a conviction that both elementary and secondary teachers need to understand subject-matter disciplines and pedagogy more fully if their students are ultimately to succeed at more challenging kinds of learning. Now, after completing an undergraduate degree, would-be teachers apply for a highly-selective, two-year graduate program in a new University Institute for the Preparation of Teachers. There they learn about teaching methods, curriculum design, learning theory, and child development while they conduct research and practice teaching in affiliated schools. Teachers are supported in their studies by government stipends, and they receive a salary in their final year of training, during which they take on a teaching position under supervision.

Japan also launched major reforms of teacher education in 1989. The changes encourage more emphasis on graduate-level teacher education and add an intensive one-year internship to university training in education. After passing a highly-competitive teacher appointment examination, beginning teachers are assigned to a school where they work with a master teacher who is released from his or her classroom to advise and counsel interns. Master teachers observe each intern's class weekly and give the intern the opportunity to observe the classes of other teachers. These observations are especially helpful to beginning teachers, like Kenji Yamota, who observed, "Only after I try what I observe do I begin to think." First-year novices also participate in retreats, seminars, training sessions, and 60 days of in-school professional development on topics such as classroom management, computer use, teaching strategies and counseling methods.

Kenji also values what he learns informally from his colleagues. Each teacher has a desk in a shared staff room, and the desks are grouped to promote interaction. New teachers are placed next to veterans in their grade level. Every morning teachers hold a brief meeting in the staff room and return later in the day to work and relax. Once a week, they share an extended block of time for demonstrations, lesson planning and other joint work. Learning to teach is considered a lifelong task that is well supported throughout the career.

"How can America build an effective teaching workforce, like Japan?" Tamar asked.

"The National Commission has identified seven common barriers that defeat fielding a strong teacher team in most schools. These include:

1. **Low-performance expectations for all students**—Teachers do not have high expectations around which to build strong, cumulative curriculum standards for their students;

2. **Unenforced standards for teachers**—Only about 500 of the nation's 1,200 education schools have met common professional standards. Fewer than 75% of teachers hold a degree in their subject, have studied child development, learning and teaching methods, and have passed tests of teaching, knowledge and skills;

3. **Major flaws in teacher preparation**—With few exceptions, teacher preparation programs—unlike those in law, medicine, accounting, engineering—do not allow teachers adequate time to master subject matter, teaching methods, child development and practice their knowledge and skills under supervision of mentors in clinical (school) settings;

4. **Slipshod teacher recruitment**—College and school district recruit-

ment of future teachers is uncoordinated and haphazard. Too many districts delay hiring decisions until the school year starts and make poor teacher assignments. They also have transfer policies that block teacher mobility, such as salary caps for veteran teachers, lack of licensing reciprocity among states, and inability to transfer pension benefits between states;

5. **Inadequate induction for beginning teachers**—New teachers receive little or no support, particularly in the first two or three years of their careers, and especially in urban school districts. This crude sink-or-swim method results in chronic high rates of teacher replacement;

6. **Poor professional development opportunities**—Most teacher staff development is fragmented—a one shot 'flavor of the month'—not tied to classroom practice. It's not sustained, long-term knowledge and skill oriented, not assessed in relation to individual needs, and not adequately funded (1% to 3% of budgets for in-service training compared with 8% to 10% in high-performance industries);

7. **Old industrial, factory-style model**—Most schools are hierarchically-structured, rigid and centralized. This type of organization provides few incentives for veteran teachers to build teaching careers. Without professional recognition and rewards, they leave teaching for administration. Staff, time, and money are used unproductively. In other countries, 60% to 80% of school personnel directly teach in the classroom, as compared to America's 43.5%, which results in large classes and wasted resources that could be used more effectively. **New site-based schools are flexible, decentralized, high performance learning, professional knowledge and collaborative team organizations where teachers make up at least 70% or more of the staff.**"

Kim spoke up. "I have to agree with your findings, Linda, but I'm appalled by what I'm hearing! You've certainly identified the reasons our teaching profession is strangling on bureaucratic procedures: from state policies to colleges of education, through the school district maze and into the school classrooms. I now see why we waste our time replacing good teachers. I can only imagine the morale of teachers here at Jefferson. School reform will not be successful until we better manage teacher recruitment, preparation, on-the-job training, and career incentives. Most important, we must reorganize their jobs and working environments. What recommendations do you and your National Commission have?"

"Kim, I have a BEST PRACTICES handout here with our core recommendations," Linda said as she passed it out. "The way to begin in each school district and individual school is to reallocate resources, rethink staffing, redirect professional development funds and invest in strategic improvements. I think it's essential to redefine roles so that at least 70% of total staff is in the classrooms. This will reduce class sizes significantly and create time for teachers to work and plan together.[21] For example, Figure 11.1 *Restructuring Elementary Schools* shows how a typical elementary school of 600 students can reorganize its staff so that average class sizes can be reduced from 25 students to 16 or 17 students, while teachers' planning time is increased from less than 4 hours a week to at least 10 hours. This is accomplished by reducing the number of non-teaching staff and by infusing pullout teachers into teaching teams. While keeping key administrative sup-

Figure 11.1

Restructuring Elementary Schools

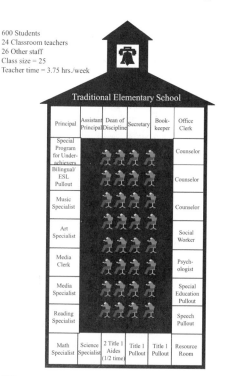

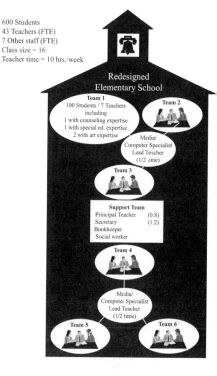

BEST PRACTICES: WHAT MATTERS MOST TEACHING FOR AMERICA'S FUTURE

1. **Get serious about standards, for both students and teachers.**

   - Establish professional standards boards in every state.

   - Insist on accreditation for all schools of education.

   - Close inadequate schools of education.

   - License teachers based on demonstrated performance, including tests of subject-matter knowledge, teaching knowledge, and teaching skill.

   - Use National Board standards as the benchmark for accomplished teaching.

2. **Reinvent teacher preparation and professional development.**

   - Organize teacher education and professional development programs around standards for students and teachers.

   - Develop extended, graduate-level teacher-preparation programs that provide a yearlong internship in a professional development school.

   - Create and fund mentoring programs for beginning teachers, along with evaluation of teaching skills.

   - Create stable, high-quality sources of professional development.

3. **Fix teacher recruitment and put qualified teachers in every classroom.**

   - Increase the ability of low-wealth districts to pay for qualified teachers, and insist that districts hire only qualified teachers.

   - Redesign and streamline district hiring.

   - Eliminate barriers to teacher mobility.

   - Aggressively recruit high-need teachers and provide incentives for teaching in shortage areas like math and science.

   - Develop high-quality pathways to teaching for a wide range of recruits—including older candidates retiring from other fields.

4. **Encourage and reward teacher knowledge and skill.**

- Develop a career continuum for teaching linked to assessments and compensation systems that reward knowledge and skill.

- Remove incompetent teachers through peer review and shared accountability processes.

- Set goals and enact incentives for National Board Certification in every state and district.

- Aim to certify 105,000 teachers in this decade, one for every school in the United States.

5. **Create schools that are organized for student and teacher success.**

- Flatten hierarchies and reallocate resources to send more dollars to the front lines of schools. Invest more in teachers and technology and less in non-teaching personnel.

- Provide venture capital in the form of challenge grants to schools for teacher learning linked to school improvement and rewards for team efforts that lead to improved practice and greater learning;

- Select, prepare, and retain principals who understand teaching and learning and who can lead high-performing schools—any community's best investment.

ports in place—including a principal, secretary, bookkeeper, and social worker—this increases the total number of full-time equivalent classroom teachers from 24 to 43 (from less than 50% of all staff to more than 80%).

"In the redesigned school, each team of seven teachers serves 100 students and includes teachers with expertise in the arts, counseling, and the teaching of special-needs students. The teams can draw upon this expertise in curriculum planning, and they can organize their time and efforts to take advantage of different talents in various ways for different activities. The three primary-grade teams share a media/computer specialist and a lead teacher, who has half of her time released from teaching to facilitate planning and cover classes while other teachers visit and observe one another. The same supports are available to the three upper-grade teams. The result is more personalized education for students, more collegial learning opportunities for teachers, and a system more capable of taking responsibility for student learning.

"We need to rethink school staffing so that all personnel are involved in thinking as well as doing. And we need to revamp spending to invest in the front lines of schools, not the back offices.If most staff in U.S. schools were engaged in teaching, teachers could have both greater time for collaboration and learning and smaller sclass sizes and pupil loads. In the Commission's view, world-class teaching depends on world-class benchmarks. Most nations invest 60% or more of their staff resources in teachers; we should aim for no less

"I see Nate getting nervous about the time," said Linda with a smile. "Our Commission recognizes that good work is going on all across the country. Many successful programs for recruiting, educating, and mentoring new teachers have sprung up. Professional networks and teacher academies have been launched. Many education school programs have been redesigned. Higher standards for licensing teachers and accrediting education schools have been developed. And, of course, the National Board for Professional Teaching Standards is now fully established. We're beginning to define and reward accomplished teaching. All these activities, and many others, form the foundation of this crusade.[22] But, like the work of this Citizens' Commission, what we do about school and teacher reform will determine America's future. Let me borrow two scenarios from our National Commission Report.[23] Here's one more handout.

TWO FUTURES FOR AMERICAN SCHOOL REFORM

The first continues our current course in the face of major demographic and economic changes and expanding expectations of schools. In the year 2006, it looks something like this:

Following a brief and familiar flurry of education reform activity in the 1980s and early 1990s, schools settled back down to business as usual. The education governors had come and gone; educational leaders were relieved to have the waves of commission reports shelved and out of the way. A period of teacher shortages had been addressed by modest salary increases and increased use of emergency and alternative certification.

By 1995 teacher salaries had returned to the levels of the early 1970s and then stagnated, remaining 30% below those of competing occupations. As momentum for reform receded, teacher recruitment remained problematic, especially in fields like mathematics and science, and in cities and the Sunbelt, where enrollments boomed.

As more than 30% of teachers retired over the 1990s, and many new teachers left shortly after they started, continuous shortages led to larger classes, more out-of-field teaching, and more hiring of untrained people. A growing number of teachers serving poor and minority students had formal pedagogical preparation consisting only of a three-week summer course. They desperately wanted to address the learning needs of their students, but their training in such fundamentals as subject matter, learning and development, and teaching methods was too skimpy to provide them with adequate ammunition for the job.

Throughout the 1990s, students in the public education system changed, but schools did not. Great waves of immigration boosted the numbers of poor, minority, and non-English-speaking children to nearly 40% of public school enrollments. Some teachers, who had attended restructured schools of education created in the high tide of reform—and who taught in schools redesigned to focus more intensely on learning—were able to teach these and other students successfully. But their successes could not be replicated in other schools where teachers were less well prepared and schools were not designed to support quality teaching.

The public's periodic concern for low student performance was pacified by the enactment of 'stiffer' requirements; more tests, more course requirements, and more record-keeping procedures. In only a few places, schools staffed by highly skilled teachers were able to respond to these mandates. In most cases, they led to disappointing results! More students were held back and dropped out. More watered-down courses were taught by teachers without adequate training in their fields. More add-on special programs were created to address student failure. And more bureaucracy evolved to manage all of the above, draining more dollars from classrooms to support the administration of all these mandates.

Because many teachers did not know how to get the results sought, student learning was increasingly structured by practice tests and worksheets. Scores in basic skills remained static while scores on higher-order thinking continued to decline. U.S. students continued to rank near the bottom on international tests of more advanced skills.

Earlier enthusiasm for reforms gave way to disillusionment and lower school budgets, as middle-class parents fled to private schools and the general population, made up largely of older citizens without children in schools, voted down tax levies for education. Just as the reforms of the 1960s were replaced in the 1970s by movements to reduce school spending and go "back to the basics," so reform rhetoric of the 1990s gave way to a backlash against innovation and investment in public education. By the year 2006, public frustration with the schools resurfaced with cries from the business community for employees who could function in an information-based, technological economy. New commissions declared the nation, once again, at risk.

Another future—one that envisions different resolutions of the dilemmas described above—is possible. In this future, teaching continues its progress toward becoming a profession. In the year 2006, a different public education system has emerged. It looks something like this:

Much had changed since the last 'crisis' in education during the 1980s. A second wave of reform impelled new coalitions between teachers, administrators, and teacher educators, all of whom began thinking of themselves as members of the same profession with common goals. They developed the first professional definition of teaching knowledge through the National Board for Professional Teaching Standards. This stimulated the creation of state boards that build upon the new vision to create more meaningful standards for teacher preparation and licensing. States worked with colleges to establish internships in professional development schools as part of a master's degree in teaching. Teachers-in-training were coached by expert mentor teachers working in conjunction with university faculty on the reform of schooling and teaching. The new cohort of teachers—more than a million of them—was better prepared than any that had preceded them.

Teacher shortages were met with higher salaries and recruitment incentives. As salaries reached a level comparable with those of other competing occupations, the supply of teachers willing to undergo rigorous preparation programs grew. And as the qualifications of teachers increased, the perceived need to spend large portions of education budgets on massive inspection systems diminished. Long hierarchies that had grown to design, regulate, and monitor teaching flattened out. Teachers took on more professional responsibilities, and schools took on new shapes conducive to professional teaching and intensive learning.

As in other professions, differentiated roles and responsibilities gradually emerged as a means to balancing the requirements of supply and qualifications. Those less extensively trained—such as beginning teaching interns—practiced under the supervision of career professionals, many of whom were engaged in becoming more expert by pursuing National Board Certification. Practitioners worked in teams that jointly assumed responsibility for groups of students. In settings where several teachers and interns were responsible for a group of students over several years, new possibilities emerged for organizing instruction, for collaborating on teaching plans and decisions, and for developing strategies to meet individual children's needs. These structures promoted consultation and peer review of practice that continually improved teaching and learning.

Educators insisted on selecting and inducting their peers based on professional standards of practice and on shared decision-making so they could pool their wisdom about the best use of resources to meet students' needs. Professional knowledge and effectiveness grew as serious induction, sustained professional development, and collaboration replace the sink-or swim, closed-door ethos of an earlier era.

Instructional practices changed too. Schools became more focused on higher standards of performance *and* on the needs of students. As teachers became more skilled, they used more powerful methods of teaching and learning: research projects, experiments, debates, and exhibitions replaced superficial tests and worksheets. Students were encouraged to read great books and engage meaty ideas, to construct and solve intellectual problems, and to demonstrate their learning in challenging performances.

More productive approaches to organizing the school day and the school year gave individual teachers and students more time together, reducing the pullouts, pass-throughs, start-ups, and wind-downs that had stolen teaching time and decreased teachers' capacity to come to know students well. Schools became smaller and more personalized. Fewer students fell through the cracks.

Incentives to attract the most expert teachers to the profession's greatest needs and challenges also emerged. Lead teachers redesigned inner-city schools as exemplars of professional practice where they coached new teachers, put research into practice—and practice into research—and put state-of-the-art knowledge to work for children. Equity and excellence became joined with professionalism.

By the year 2006, a renaissance had occurred in American education. The best American students performed as well as students anywhere in the world. The vast majority of students graduated with not only minimal basic skills, but with the capacity to write, reason, and think analytically. Complaints from the business community about the quality of graduates subsided for the first time since World War II. And for the first time since the beginning of the 20th century, a decade was launched without a chorus of commission reports crying crisis in the American public schools. The road taken, as it turned out, was the one that finally made a difference. Two roads—two futures. Which one will Americans take for our children?

"Linda, once again you've had this Citizens' Commission spellbound. This comes from your report on 'What Matters Most: Teaching for America's Future.' As usual, your presentation is very persuasive. You've given us plenty to think about for our reform report on Jefferson Elementary School. Thank you for coming today."

What a great role model, Delores thought. *Her professional background and experience have inspired me to be a better teacher.*

****

Summary

"Linda has agreed to stay for a few more minutes and answer your questions before we adjourn. But first, Linda, it's our custom to have the members of the Commission summarize the main points in today's Hearing."

"Linda, I'm enthusiastic about the work of your Commission!" Debbie said. "It's bold and courageous to come out with the facts about how badly we recruit, train, place and in-service teachers in this country. And we complain about how poorly our schools are doing. Teaching is mostly considered women's work, and especially teaching minority and disadvantaged children. Is it any wonder that the nation's business and political leaders, mostly men, do not come up with the money to reform education?"

"Well, I'm blown away," said Ray. "If two million new teachers have to be hired over the next decade, what an opportunity to impact school reform—especially if they're well trained and well paid! We need to attract the best and brightest of our college graduates."

"I'm intrigued by the Commission's main goal: every child with a qualified teacher who can help him or her reach high levels of intellectual and social competence. Did I get that right, Linda?" Maria asked. "Why can't we make this goal one of our objectives for Jefferson Elementary School? We need to recruit and hire the very top teachers in the district, perhaps the whole area!"

"Paul," said Tamar, "do you think the business community will help the school board to come up with the money?"

"Well," said Paul, "I'm ready to get behind a campaign to recruit and pay for top teachers for Jefferson Elementary. I didn't know that only 25% of practicing teachers are fully qualified to teach our kids. We have to get serious about developing professionally-qualified teachers."

Kim spoke next. "Linda made her point that the key to school reform is the quality of teacher preparation. She supported that position using solid research and examples that we all can understand. She described the flaws in the present system—or non-system—of teacher recruitment, preparation and hiring. We don't have a serious teaching profession yet. But we have a map of the territory now. We know how to create a demand for good teachers. We need to do our part here at Jefferson."

"One more thing," Paul volunteered. "I was most impressed by Linda's description of the need for restructuring schools to use scarce teaching resources much more effectively. If teaching is the mission of any school, then surely at least 60% to 70% of the workers should be teaching every day. We must reorganize the teaching so that we can reduce the student/ teacher ratios significantly. If we do that, we can get quality teaching at about the same cost to the taxpayers. Ray, you and the School Board should pick up on this recommendation, big time! We can't wait to implement these ideas."

"Thank you, Nate and Wendy, and all our guests," said Kim. "We learned a lot today. Linda, you have shared two scenarios for the future of school reform. I wonder how we get top policymakers to take these predictions seriously?

"We want to recognize the parents and members of the community in our audience today. Thanks again to all of you. Now we stand adjourned until Saturday, March 22."

****

Chapter 12
RESPONSIBLE LEARNING CULTURES
Saturday morning, March 22

Delores was running late. She gave Sabrina, her 10-year-old daughter, the antibiotic, and kissed Michael, her husband of 22 years, goodbye. It took Delores just eight minutes to reach Jefferson from their modest home on Quincy Drive. She drove the same way every morning, but on Saturday there was little traffic. Spring was in the air. Life was good for Delores.

Thank God it's Saturday, she thought. My first-grade class is driving me crazy. But after last month's Commission Hearing on professional development of teachers, I'm wondering if I need training in all the new teaching methods? I'm feeling like a dinosaur. I'm sure Ted does too. Kathie is pretty confident. I can tell she's a good teacher. And Tamar—just out of school and thinks she knows it all. She'll find out how hard it is to teach these kids day after day when they don't want to learn and their parents don't care.

Paul pulled into an empty space next to Delores and waved hello. His mind turned to the Citizens' Commission. *I was really excited at last month's Hearing on teacher development to meet our guests. John Goodlad is practically a legend in school reform. I didn't know much about the National Board for Professional Teaching Standards until Jim Kelly told us what they're doing to certifying teachers. They have a long way to go if they're going to reach every school by 2000. Linda Darling-Hammond's testimony was depressing and, at the same time, hopeful because of the National Commission on Teaching. I had no idea how bad teacher recruitment, education and professional development is. These Hearings have been great! We're facing a big challenge if we're going to do something really big for Jefferson Elementary. It looks pretty futile to me—a really sick school culture. How are we going to turn it around? No wonder so many kids are failing. They face hopeless lives of poverty, crime and even early death. Urban schools are a disaster! It's like the Titanic, nobody in charge as they go down. Is this what local control of schools means? Where the hell are the governors? Where are the President and the Congress?[1] We watch helplessly as our children are destroyed!*

There's Nate and Wendy. Boy, they've been terrific—really keep things moving. The Commission members are even starting to trust one another. Our days are more productive and there's less conflict. We may become a team yet. That would be something to write home about—a Citizens' Commission that actually worked and did some good!

"Good morning," Ray said, calling the group to order. "It's 8:00 a.m., and we have a long way to go. We have only three more monthly sessions before we get our report ready for the County Board of Education. I know that choosing between the good models of effective school reform we've heard about is enough to give you a headache. But we've been keeping good records, and at our June session, we'll put it all together for Jefferson Elementary. Nate, I'll turn the time over to you."

"Thanks, Ray," Nate said. "Before I introduce our experts for today, I want to give you a handout." As the group passed the material, he said, "This MYTH reminds us of the challenges facing today's families. It provides a context for our Hearing on responsible learning cultures.'"

Responsible Family Learning Cultures

Nate was now ready to begin. "Our first two guests this morning are from the Washington D.C. area. We still don't understand very much about the links between values and behavior. Why do some children who grow up in poverty self-destruct, while others achieve a good education, go on to higher education or good jobs, and become successful parents and citizens? Our first guest can help us better understand how cultural values shape our lives and lead to responsible or destructive behavior. I've known Dr. Diane Ramsey for many years. I first worked with her in southern California, where she lived. Diane is now Vice President of *The Terrel H. Bell* KNOWLEDGE NETWORK *for Education Reform,* located in McLean, Virginia. She has been trained as a cultural sociologist specializing in families and education. Diane, I understand you came up with the term *responsible family learning cultures.* What does it mean? Why should we care about it?"

"Nate, I'm really pleased to see you again. My compliments to the Citizens' Commission on Reforming Jefferson Elementary School. I understand you're hearing from the nation's outstanding education reformers. I hope

MYTH: Most American families have healthy, responsible, well-behaved, and well-educated children.

Families provide the critical foundation for children's growth. It is in the home that children first experience the love and discipline that will guide their development. Yet family resources to raise children are not as favorable to educational improvement as in the past. For the last two decades, 60% of our families have incomes that have stagnated or declined and would have been even lower if more mothers had not gone to work. Today, one-out-of-four of our children lives in poverty with its devastating consequences. Two-parent and single-parent households can create strong, healthy families, but single-parent families are more vulnerable to environmental demands. **Single parent families are six times more likely to be poor than two-parent families.**[2] Today 60% of all children will live in a one-parent household at some time during their school years.[3] Children of single-parent families are more likely to drop out of school, exhibit emotional distress, get into trouble with the law, and abuse drugs or alcohol than children who grow up with two biological parents. More than one-third of all two-parent families today would be poor if both parents didn't work—causing more children to be left alone after school. While there are many outstanding exceptions in single- and two-parent households, most families are not adequately preparing children—physically, emotionally, morally and intellectually—for today's challenges.

FINDING A: Many of America's children are in physical danger. They are not born healthy, do not receive adequate nutrition and exercise, do not get preventive health care and do not have safe neighborhoods.

- Ten million of 69 million children had no health insurance in 1994. If current trends continue, between 1992 and 2002, the number of uninsured under 18 will increase nearly 40% to 14 million.[4]

- Twenty percent of our population is covered by health insurance as compared to over 90% in European countries.[5]

- The United States has one of the highest infant mortality rates—8.5 for every 1,000 babies in 1992—among all industrialized nations.[6]

- In spite of improved overall immunization rates from 1992 to 1994, recent rates are not sufficiently high to protect our children from epidemics of measles, polio, whooping cough, diphtheria and other childhood diseases.[7]

- One-in-five children between ages 3 and 17 experiences developmental delays, behavioral problems or learning disabilities due to preventable illnesses.[8]

- For 15- to 19-year-old teenagers, firearm injuries are the second leading cause of death, after automobile crashes. Their risk of dying from a gun injury has increased by 77% since 1985.[9]

- In 1990 the cost of gunshot injuries was about $20.4 billion. That includes the medical treatment, rehabilitation and loss of potential income of those who die. Because many of the wounded are poor, most of the expense is passed onto taxpayers.[10]

FINDING B: The emotional health of American children has deteriorated over the past generation. Many mothers and fathers are too highly stressed by job and other daily demands to properly nurture their children. Failure to develop close, enduring bonds can have severe consequences for children in terms of suicide, alcohol and drug abuse and mental illness.

- Six children in America commit suicide daily. Over the last two decades, the suicide rate has doubled for children (10-14-year olds) and has risen by 31% for youths (15-19 year olds). In 1992, 2,161 youths (10-19-year olds) committed suicide, with 81% being gun-related.[11]

- Between 1994 and 1995, use of cigarettes and most illicit drugs increased among students in all racial/ethnic groups. These changes continued recent trends that began in the early 1990s, reversing a decade of decreases in drug use.[12]

- Between 1992 and 1994, use of marijuana by 12- to 17-year olds nearly doubled.[13] Driven in large part by the rise of marijuana use, the rate of current illicit drug use increased for youth 12- to 17-year old between 1993 and 1994 (from 6.6% to 12.5%), after declining from 18.5% in 1979 to 6.1% in 1992.[14]

- In 1995 alcohol use continued at unacceptably high levels. Notably, daily drinking increased among twelfth graders, and more tenth graders reported having "been drunk" daily in the past month.

- 7.5 million children or 12% of U.S. residents under 18 years of age have a diagnosable mental disorder, and nearly half of these are severely handicapped by their disabilities.[15]

FINDING C: Many parents are not providing character education for their children that encourages moral, responsible, caring and constructive behavior.

Parents influence their children's moral development by what they say and do in their own daily lives. Most children in America of every race, ethnic or income group do not receive the nurturing and discipline that provides motivation for their character development. On average, employed adults are now working longer hours and more days away from home than in the past.[16] Thus, the household has shifted from a focus on productive activities that requires personal habits or traits of industry, responsibility and pride of performance to one in which these habits are learned only if parents act to inculcate them. Parents now have to consciously design and intentionally intervene to instill these traits or personal habits.[17] More is required of parents to be effective in bringing up their children—despite the fact that schools took over the task of teaching reading, writing and arithmetic.

Even when both parents are in the home, they often do not take the time or energy to instill moral values in their children. Many parents do not want to go through the hassle of organizing and assigning their children household tasks. But without regularly sharing household tasks, children often lack the opportunity to gain a sense of "ownership" and responsibility, pride and satisfaction in the family. Either through over-indulging or over-directing, too many parents unintentionally foster destructive dependence or apathy in their children.

Without learning citizenship in the family, children are more likely to engage in or experience high-risk behaviors. During the past two decades, premarital sexual experience among adolescents has steadily increased. Adolescents are at higher risk for acquiring sexually transmitted disease (STD) because they are more likely to have multiple sexual partners rather than single, long-term relationships, engage in unprotected intercourse and select partners at higher risk.

Adolescents who become parents risk lifelong social and economic disadvantages. Adolescent parents, compared to persons who begin childbearing in their 20s, are less likely to complete their education or to be employed and are more likely to have lower incomes, larger families, more marital disruptions, and greater need for welfare assistance. Compared with mothers in their 20s and 30s, children of adolescent mothers have a higher risk of poor intellectual and academic achievement together with social and behavioral problems.

- Each week, the average working parent spends about 30 minutes in conversation with his/her children, while most of these children watch nearly 30 hours of television.[18]

- In 1993, there were almost 11 million victims of violence. One million of these were related to the offender. Violent victimization rates declined with increases in family income. People living in households with a yearly income of under $7,500 were more than twice as likely to fall victim to violence as people in households with incomes of $75,000 or more.[19]

- The total cost of STD prevention and treatment currently exceeds $3.5 billion annually.[20]

- The total cumulative cost of treating all people with HIV infection increased from $10.3 billion in 1992 to $15.2 billion in 1995.[21]

- In 1993 nearly 3 million of our 68 million children were victims of abuse and neglect.[22]

FINDING D: Many families are not preparing their children with the learning attitudes and skills necessary to succeed in school, such as enjoyment of reading, opportunities for self-expression and completion of tasks.

Parents shape a learning environment in their home that fosters or hinders children's educational development. This can be done intentionally rather than ignored and left to chance. A child learns a great deal before entering school.[23] By age three, for example, children have acquired more than half the language they will use in their lifetime as they interact with the adults in their lives.[24] From age 5 to 18, only about 17% of their awake time is spent in school. Research indicates that parents are a critical factor in children's development. Whether children have one parent or two at home, therefore, should make a difference. Studies find that students with two parents in the home score considerably higher on achievement tests than those with one parent, especially if the parent has low income and less education.

Some parents use television as a convenient babysitter. Overexposure to this passive form of entertainment distorts the learning process, reduces reading and contributes to illiteracy. Television watching tends to develop the attitude in children that they will try to learn only if it is easy and fun. Over the past decade, reading materials in the home have declined. Children are reading less today than in the 1980s.

- Excessive television and video watching is associated with a shrinking written vocabulary among children today. For example, in 1945 the average 6-to 14-year-old American child used 25,000 words as compared to 10,000 today.[25]

- The quantity of reading is associated with high achievement, yet children spend 12 times as much time watching television as they do outside reading.[26]

- In 1991, 13-year-old children in the U.S. did less reading for fun than their peers in 11 other countries.[27]

- Reading has not improved but has stagnated. Only one third of our students read at proficient levels.[28]

- By 1995 math and science achievement by our students had improved, but is still low compared to other industrialized countries.[29] Among students in 12 countries, America's advanced science students ranked last in biology, tenth in physics and eleventh in chemistry.[30]

FINDING E: Most self-reliant, academically achieving, well-rounded and healthy children have parents/families who have created a stable, supportive educational environment in the home and are involved at school. When parents value education, they set high but realistic expectations for their children's achievement and future careers. They can intentionally establish family practices that enhance student achievement, such as regular homework time and monitoring, regular bedtime, regular school attendance, quiet study place, and limited television-watching. For older children, the amount of homework completed is associated with a rise in proficiency, as well as development of good work habits and discipline.

- The amount of homework that students do varies considerably among the states, but the U.S. ranks relatively low among 15 countries in the amount of homework done.[31]

- The Keep the Promise Educational Excellence Partnership has 19 suggestions for parents.[32]

- The American Association of School Administrators has 101 ways parent can help.[33]

my message will contribute to your work. Some strategies are more effective than others. Some are less expensive. Some reach more students. But the bottom line is that we must save each child, and only effective parents and skillful teachers can do this. Remember, we raise children within the family, but knowledge and skills are acquired largely through the education system.[34]

"Let me put in perspective how essential parents are to student achievement. Over 30 years of research documents the positive correlation between parental involvement and student success.[35] Nate, you asked why we should care about this connection. We should care because parent participation in their children's education may be the most powerful school reform strategy available.

"We face significant challenges to survive and prosper as a democracy in today's global knowledge society. It will require our best. There are no easy victories. We must declare war on the destructive aspects of our popular culture, which undermine the values that brought America greatness. This will require significant changes of the magnitude comparable to those during the Reformation, the Renaissance and the Industrial Revolution. We now know which values advance learning and improvement and which block individual or group progress.[36] Our key resource, or secret weapon, is quality academic and character education that develops the moral leadership to generate cultural transformation.

"Let's first clarify the meaning of culture. Many of us think of fine arts or enrichment activities when we use the word *culture*. Those are important aspects, but culture is much broader. One of my favorite quotes about culture is from an early French observer of 19th century America. In describing *Democracy in America,* Alexis de Tocqueville said: "I here use the word customs...to what might be termed the habits of the heart...the mass of ideas which constitute the character of mind...the whole moral and intellectual condition of a people."[37] Culture is like a mental map or blueprint of stable ideas—values, attitudes and strategies—that have the power to shape our lives and that of our community, even the larger society. Individuals are carriers of the culture.[38] Culture helps people deal with their daily lives by pointing out what's important and how to achieve it.[39]

"My graduate training in anthropology emphasized the importance of cultural relativism—the idea that all cultures are of equal value and fill about the same functions. Of course, we should be respectful of the cultures of other people! But the notion of cultural relativism has kept us from objectively assessing the consequences of cultural practices—the real costs or benefits to individuals, their families, and their community. Assessing consequences was not politically correct.

"Research shows that when individuals, families, groups or organizations practice progress-prone values, their likelihood of advancing and prospering is increased.[40] When they do not, they tend to set up conditions in which they regress or, at least, fail to improve. Read any newspaper or watch the evening news, and you'll see overwhelming evidence of destructive aspect of our pop culture—aspects that convey or reinforce self-centered, permissive values, attitudes and behaviors. These glamorized behaviors blind us to the real consequences for other people. We act as if the violent, destructive acts we see in the mass media result from mysterious or unknown forces. Let's get real! We know what influences shape individual lives. We know what is likely to result in responsible moral behavior and in destructive immoral behavior.

"We now have enough studies of cultures and organizations throughout the world to show us which values lead to prosperity. Progress-resistant societies are fatalistic, particularistic, ascriptive, passive, individualistic and familistic. They are past or present-oriented, hierarchical and static. By contrast, societies with progress-prone cultures are characterized by ten values:[41]

1. **Future Time Orientation**: Focus on the future (often in the next world) rather than on the past or the present as in traditional societies;

2. **Work Ethic:** Work is a source of satisfaction and self-respect, the foundation structure of daily life, and an individual's obligation to the broader society. Attitudes about work are intimately linked to achievement and entrepreneurship, on which economic development depends;

3. **Frugality and Savings:** Frugality or savings conserves the fruit of work for investment or subsequent consumption;

4. **Quality Education:** Education is the key to progress. This is why leaders in the United States are concerned about the relatively low level of American student performance that poorly prepares them for today's global knowledge economy;

5. **Merit Performance:** As the basis for personal advancement, merit is intimately linked with achievement;[42]

6. **Extended Community:** The sense of community goes beyond the family to the broader society and generates patterns of association, trust, and cooperation that facilitate good governance and economic prosperity;[43]

7. **Rigorous Ethical Codes:** High moral standards increase levels of trust, so important to political pluralism and economic efficiency;

8. **Social Justice:** Justice and fair play for everyone;

9. **Respect for Authority:** The proper respect for authority permits leaders to organize for more efficient operations. This kind of respect for authority also values others' experience, outstanding knowledge, skills and performance. By contrast, authoritarian leadership in a society or organization stifles criticism and dissent, creativity, and entrepreneurship; and

10. **Role of Religion:** Some religious ideas inspire individuals to improve themselves and make contributions to building a better society.

"A family, like other small groups, develops a unique culture of its own, even though it is part of the larger society and is deeply influenced by its values. We need a much better understanding of family culture. More recently, a few researchers have started to study family culture and its impact on home and school. Research in the '70s and early '80s, however, usually focused on sick or dysfunctional families. In the '80s, some researchers described strong or healthy families.

"Family culture gives individuals a road map that influences their development as well as that of the group as a whole.[44] As the foundation that shapes attitudes and behavior, it forms the basis for our self-concept as learners. Although other factors, such as peer pressure, mass media, and the school are influential, the early home environment has the most impact on a child's learning and behavior.[45]

"Parents are the major creators of their family culture just as teachers are the major creators of classroom culture. Parents influence, or even decide, what values will prevail. Their leadership skills, therefore, are crucial to developing *responsible learning cultures*. A family develops patterns of coping with its everyday challenges. If their solutions work well, they may become cultural responses to be passed on to new family members. Culture is transmitted formally through rules and codes, and informally through ideologies and folk beliefs, stories and scripts, jargon and jokes, music and rap. Certain rituals and ceremonies may be created formally and informally. As family members draw from their shared family culture, an environment for learning gradually evolves.[46]

"When the family's responses no longer meet existing challenges, individuals may feel overwhelmed and the group may start to disintegrate. They may develop new behavior patterns that are destructive or someone may offer more effective strategies that become new cultural patterns in the family.[47]

"I had firsthand experience with this in my own life. Twenty five years ago, I married a second time and helped create a blended or stepfamily. We integrated two families into one large unit—or at least tried to—with seven daughters ranging in age from ages 4 through 17," she smiled, "and lived to tell about it. This challenging process of shaping or negotiating a new family culture became the focus of my doctoral dissertation. I could see some adults taking a leadership role in transforming their family's cultural values. I could see this process not only with parents who create successful stepfamilies, but with principals who turn around troubled schools, and coaches who build winning athletic teams. Political leaders have to chart new directions for a nation—as did Churchill during World War II. Most anthropologists have neglected the role of leadership in cultural transformation. We now have research evidence that shows some leaders can do this if they have progress-prone values, correct timing and skills required for effective communication and action.

"Our patterns of behavior are organized around dominant cultural values that are learned, transmitted, and shared within a society.[48] Our values and goals flow from our basic human needs. Abraham Maslow, the noted psychologist, identified universal human needs. You've heard of these: physical survival, safety, love, self-reliance and self-actualization (or leadership contribution). The parents, and other leaders, have to set expectations or standards with rules or ways to achieve them. The family learns to perform these ritual behaviors associated with different roles. These behaviors become habits. Finally, these behaviors achieve some product or some outcome. These are often called artifacts or symbols. The family group can't communicate or cooperate without shared cultural understandings. Differences may be a source of creativity and innovation for adapting to change (to assess the strengths of your family learning culture, see Appendix for the Responsible Family Learning Culture Diagnostic Questionnaire).

Education for Responsible Cultures

"Let's look at Figure 12.1 in your handouts. Column 1 identifies Maslow's hierarchy of basic needs. Column 2 identifies the values and beliefs that follow from each level of need. Column 3 shows the expectations, rules, and strategies flowing from each level of values and beliefs. Column 4 identifies major ritual behaviors or habits that could result from each expectation. Finally, Column 5 reflects the physical evidence that results from behaviors that have become habits. All these relationships are so habitual, we rarely notice them in daily family activities. All together these levels and positive habits make up a *Responsible Family Learning Culture*."

"Wait a minute, Dr. Ramsey, are you saying that if a family, school or community doesn't believe in these progress-prone values, they won't prosper?" Maria asked.

You tell' her, Maria. Who does she think she is? Delores wondered.

"Maria, we know that people tend to succeed when they hold progress-prone values as their highest priorities. Again these values are future time focus, work, thrift, education, merit, community, ethics, justice, and respect for authority.

"What about different groups of immigrants? They bring their cultural values with them," said Paul.

"Throughout American history, Paul, different immigrants have been very successful, like European Jews, Scandinavians, certainly the early Puritans, and Asians generally. But one clear, recent example of the influence of progress-prone cultural values on families is the Southeast Asian Boat People. They came to America over the past two decades. They carry a deep cultural tradition dating back to Confucius. Recent studies of immigrants show that East Asians are doing much better than others with respect to education, income, upward mobility, crime rates and acculturation.[49] (Within groups, people vary even though they carry the same general culture.) In one generation, most children of the Boat People have overcome the barriers in our poor urban public schools to become exceptional students. Many of them go on to college.[50] Researchers found that at night these parents, who were mostly uneducated, would clear the table (instead of turn on the television) and the family would study together. Older children would tutor younger siblings.* Parents would read to children, which, by the way, has a positive impact regardless of the language being read. Those parents had to consistently teach and model the cultural values so their children could learn to succeed in their new country. These progress-prone values help individuals transcend even poverty, discrimination or language barriers."

At last someone said it out loud, thought Kim. *That took some courage. She'll be criticized if people don't look deeper at her message—the power of education can reverse progress-resistant values. This is the whole issue both at home and in schools—creating responsible learning cultures.*

"The good news," Diane said, "is that we can actually add different progress-prone values to our own family culture. We've got to be willing to learn from each other, to search out strengths—to adapt, not just imitate. We have to make the value our own, put our own unique stamp on it. Then we must practice new habits. Over time, we'll learn how."

"A good education can counter some negative cultural patterns that have been handed down from generation to generation. The organizer of the Communitarian Movement, Amitai Etzioni, was correct when he said:[51]

> For too long in the U.S. we have accepted the rights of democracy without the required responsibilities. Now we are

FIGURE 12.1
RESPONSIBLE FAMILY LEARNING CULTURE

Maslow's Hierarchy of Basic Needs	Values / Beliefs	Expectations: Rules / Strategies	Ritual Behavior: Habits	School Artifacts/ Symbols
V. Self-Actualization (Leadership)	Democracy Excellence Accountability Contribution to Family/ Profession, Community	Responsibility Vision Creativity Courage/ Sacrifice Effectiveness Coalition-Bldging	Leading Organizing Managing Contributing Self-Disciplining	Recognition of School/ Community Contribution
IV. Self-Reliance	Life-Long Learning Independence Savings Entrpreneurship	Educ Achievement Share Work in Family; Courage/ Discipline Delayed Gratification	Daily Studying & Practicing to Improve Knowledge & Skills	Graduation Degrees Scholarships Athletic Music/Art Awards
III. Love	Individual Worth Being Together Care & Sacrifice Acceptance	Respect Self & Others Trustworthy Time Together	Sharing Activities Serving Family Nurture/ Bonding Showing Affection	Record of Active Parent/School Participation; Recognition of Student Service
II. Safety	Protection - Life, Property, Individual & Family Rights	Justice/Equity Code of Conduct Safe/Drug Free	Resolving Conflict Peacefully; Healthy Coping; Drug Free Behavior	Good Citizenship Grade
I. Physical Survival	Physical & Emotional Health	Good Nutrition, Exercise, Sleep	Regularly Eating Nutritious Meals, Exercising, Sleeping	Medical & Dental Records for School Admission

paying the price for our neglect. The psychological trait we need to be an effective...moral person has one common denominator—that is, we must learn through education to control our impulses...that's what separates us from the animals. The animals give in to their impulses; we develop self-control and learn to delay gratification.

"Now, of course, not all patterns are negative, but parents can learn to recognize what habits do undermine their children's progress and they can change family patterns or habits. It's hard, but it can and does happen. Look at the **rise of the African-American middle-class** in 30 short years, surely a direct result of the civil rights movement. In 1960 only one-sixth of the Blacks were middle-class. By 1990 the number had doubled to one-third.[52] Parents taught their young children they had to adopt some new cultural habits, which takes personal discipline, to obtain a better education, improve their lives and escape poverty.

"Almost all parents, regardless of income level, love their children and want them to succeed. But love is not enough. Parents spend an average of only 17 minutes per week with each child—and very few minutes of that can be called quality time—compared with 30 minutes in 1965—which is still not enough.[53] Parents have a moral responsibility to the community to spend time with their children."

"You've been pretty blunt with us and sometimes pretty hard on minorities," Delores said.

"Delores, please call me Diane. I guess it could sound that way on the surface. But every individual and every group has within them the potential to grow and improve. Every cultural or racial group has many positive values to build on. As parents, we must eliminate destructive values and behaviors that cripple our children.

"Building a family is one of the most important investments of time, energy and money adults will ever make. A *responsible family learning culture* has social and economic consequences for individual members. By some counts, it costs more than $100,000 to raise a child to age 18.[54] It's time we

---

*In the U.S., the pattern of achievement in larger families generally declines from the oldest to the youngest child. Parents don't usually have as much time to work with the younger children as they did for the older children. In these Asian families, however, the pattern is reversed. This is because the older siblings are taught to tutor their younger siblings and to take pride in their achievement as well as their own.

take a hard look at what it takes to create a successful or well-functioning family. Most of us wouldn't run a small business the way we run our family. We are learning what contributes to creating *responsible family learning cultures*. We see around us the consequences of failure to do so.

"Parenting styles can be learned and shaped through education and training. I recently discovered a study that confirms the research findings on parenting style done over the last two decades. These researchers found that parenting style is a more powerful predictor of student achievement than parent education, ethnicity or even family structure. The three main parenting styles are authoritarian, permissive and authoritative. Authoritarian parenting is associated with the lowest grades, permissive parenting with the next lowest grades, and authoritative or structured styles with the highest grades.[55] Parents cannot control all the influences upon their children, but they can increase the positive life chances for their children. We've no time to lose. Another generation of children is being wasted while people debate politically-correct behavior.

"We now know which values lead to prosperity and freedom. A destructive pop culture is growing in America. The violent, anti-social behavior of young people and their adult role models are ruining us. Over the past 15 years, adolescent violent crime has increased 60%.[56] We see families and other community institutions, including our schools, breaking down. We know which values are critical to our survival and success. We must build cultural capital.

"But, Dr. Ramsey, how can we hope to turn our families, our schools, and our nation around?" asked Maria.

"The fastest way that we can change our cultural values from progress resistant to progress prone is by quality educational experiences at home and at the schools. This is why elementary school reform is so essential for disadvantaged students, their families and the United States. First, we must begin by understanding those values that are essential to building a *responsible family learning culture*.[57] Second, we must develop the attitudes and moral habits that help us practice positive, life-affirming behavior. Third, we must exert leadership and pioneer the way for our family. Fourth, we must demand that public schools support and reinforce these values. Fifth, both parents and educators must build partnerships with other community associations to provide quality character and academic education for all our children.

"Finally, we must build trust relationships between teachers and parents. One practical tool for doing this is a student/parent/teacher compact.[58,59] These are widely used in Utah, where they are called student education plans (SEP). They are now required across America in the new federal Title I legislation.

"Diane, thank you for being here today," said Nate. "You've stimulated our thinking and presented a solid foundation for better understanding culture. During our refreshment break, take a look at the Lawrence Public Schools Home/School Learning Compact and BEST PRACTICES Family Education Plan (FEP) in your notebook. FEP was originally designed by Diane and her colleagues at The Terrel H. Bell *KNOWLEDGE NETWORK* for Education Reform. It has become one of the largest and longest-running statewide parent-involvement programs in the nation.

MegaSkills

"Our next guest," said Wendy, "is Dr. Dorothy Rich, founder and president of the non-profit Home and School Institute in Washington, D.C. The Institute focuses directly on the educational role of the family. For the past 25 years, Dorothy has created programs that assist families in helping children achieve in school and beyond.[60] She is best known as the author of *MegaSkills*.[61] Dorothy, let's begin by asking you to tell us about MegaSkills. What are they and why are they so important for educational reform?"

"Thank you, Wendy, and members of the Citizens' Commission for inviting me. As we all know, many of our children are not acquiring the understandings, the values and skills they need to succeed in life. They can be taught! Through the MegaSkills Program, parents and schools are ensuring that children know what it takes. We can't assume that children already know these things. MegaSkills have been called the 'inner engines of learning'—today I'd call it character education for success in school and in life. The ten MegaSkills include:

1. **Confidence**—feeling able to do it;
2. **Motivation**—wanting to do it;
3. **Effort**—being able to do it;
4. **Responsibility**—doing what's right;
5. **Initiative**—moving into action;

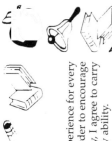

TEACHER

I understand the importance of the educational experience for every student and my role as a teacher and model. In order to encourage learning at home, at school and in the community, I agree to carry out the following responsibilities to the best of my ability.

I will:
1. Have high expectations of success for all students.
2. Address each student's individual needs, encourage individual talents, and respect individual differences.
3. Provide a safe and positive learning environment for each student.
4. Communicate with all parents regarding their child's progress.
5. Help parents to support learning and positive behavior at home.

Teacher's Signature _____ Date _____

STUDENT

I understand that my education is important. I know that I am responsible for my own success. Therefore, I agree to carry out the following responsibilities to the best of my ability.

I will:
1. Attend school on time every day.
2. Do my best in class and complete homework on time.
3. Respect myself, my teachers and classmates, and be a cooperative learner.
4. Keep my parents informed about my progress in school
5. Use my time productively in school, at home, and in the community.

Student's Signature _____ Date _____

Student's Name _____

Home • School
Learning Compact
PARENTS AS PARTNERS

A Program of the Lawrence Public Schools

PARENT

I understand that my involvement in my child's education will help his/her achievement, attitude and behavior. Therefore, I agree to carry out the following responsibilities to the best of my ability.

I will:
1. Provide my child with a healthy home environement.
2. Support homework, discipline and attendance policies.
3. Visit my child's school and participate in school events when ever I can.
4. Communicate with my child's school and teacher as much as I can.
5. Encourage my child's learning at school, at home and in the community.

Parent's Signature _____ Date _____

BEST PRACTICES:
UTAH STATE CENTER FOR FAMILIES IN EDUCATION

The Utah State Office of Education in partnership with the Utah PTA officially opened the Center for Families in Education in 1990. Under the direction of Dr. Gary Lloyd, the **Center's mission is:**

- To provide families with the opportunity to create *responsible learning cultures* that prepare their children for success in lifelong learning as parents, citizens, consumers and workers.

- To provide opportunities for families, schools and communities to become involved more fully in communicating and collaborating with each other.

Programs of the Center:

1. **Pilot Schools:**

   - Five schools have just completed the five-year model on how parents and schools can coordinate more effectively using the Joyce Epstein framework for school-family-community partnerships. Outside assessments show substantial increases in academic performance.

   - Four more elementary schools, two middle schools, and three high schools are in the program.

2. **Family Education Plan (FEP) Training Program:**

   - Over 8,000 parents in 400 elementary and secondary schools throughout the state of Utah have received this three-session parent education program that provides parents with additional skills to strengthen family relationships at home, and between home and school.

   - The FEP parent program consists of training in (1) identification of and meeting basic needs of children pre K-12 and to enhance communication skills and self esteem of both children and parents; (2) assessment of and providing materials for teaching children character education—respect, responsibility, trustworthiness, justice, and citizenship at home; and (3) understanding of and preparing parents and children to design and work with teachers on the state's mandated Student Education Plan to enrich each child's academic achievement in reading and writing, math and science, English and history, humanities and the arts; and assist parents in becoming advocates for their children.

• In January 1994, the two Public Broadcasting Service TV stations broadcast two prime-time hours on successive week nights dramatized the FEP program to Utah parents. The media blitz included a special 8-page insert in all of Utah's newspapers with announcements of the coming TV broadcasts.

2. **Student Education Plan (SEP) Training Program:**

• This unique opportunity for the student, parent, and teacher to meet together up to three times per year for a 20-minute private meeting designed to "celebrate" the child. The student participates with the parent and teacher in planning his/her short- and long-range academic and character education goals for the school year. The written plan identifies responsibilities for each party and promotes better home-school partnerships.

• The Utah State legislature was the first to mandate into law the requirement that every student, parent and teacher should have a SEP to help facilitate each child's successful participation in school. In 1995 The Center for Families in Education was given the responsibility to conduct training for each of Utah's schools by January 1997.

4. **Communication and Coordination with Parents, Schools and Community:**

• **The Edinfo Hotline** provides information on a variety of subjects from how to find good child care to how to help children with their homework, offers a toll-free number and has been accessed by over 100,000 teachers, parents and children seeking information.

• **The Parent-Child Activity Calendar** is published annually and provides tips, trivia, and family activity suggestions—the 45,000 annual printing is exhausted within the first 60 days.

• **Research** is coordinated with other states and the U.S. Department of Education on current practices in strengthening families and committing parents and schools to more formal ways to improve communication and participation with each other.

- **Family Resource Center** is located at the Salt Lake City library system. The Center provides a place for families to come and obtain many free brochures and pamphlets, videotapes, books, family training programs, and computer software.

- **Annual state-wide family conference** attracts over 600 participants to a Friday night workshop on strengthening parenting skills. Saturday morning workshop activities involve the entire family. Activities are instantly translated into five languages. Regional conferences are co-sponsored with Governor Mike Leavitt.

6. **Perseverance**—completing what you start;

7. **Caring**—showing concern for others;

8. **Teamwork**—working well with others;

9. **Common Sense**—using good judgment; and

10. **Problem Solving**—putting what you know and what you can do into action.

"There's been an assumption that children already know the attitudes and behaviors needed for school success—that they somehow learn them somewhere. We can't assume this. I identified the MegaSkills from two sources of data: school report cards and job evaluations. They are truly our Never-Ending Report Card, and we can learn how to raise these grades. The unique dimension of the MegaSkills Process is that it develops the synergistic educational relationship between the school and the home in support of all children's achievement."

"The what kind of relationship?" Lenora asked.

"Synergistic. What I mean by that is that we're stronger together than alone. Good question. I'm so used to the term I forget it's unfamiliar to most people. Well, MegaSkills training programs have been or are now being conducted in over 2,000 schools in 48 states. Parent workshops have reached over 100,000 families from diverse cultural, economic and social backgrounds. More than 10,000 MegaSkills leaders are conducting parent workshops and the classroom programs."

"This sounds a lot like the character education programs we were introduced to last month," Debbie interrupted. "How do you know that it's effective in doing for children what you say it will do? As a parent, why should I take on another time consuming educational task that my school should be providing my children?"

"Debbie, thank you for that bottom-line question. "Let me try to answer it for you.

The Austin, Texas, Independent School District using the MegaSkills Leader Parent Program tracked 1,196 students in grades pre K-6. Students whose parents attended MegaSkills Workshops showed: higher scores on statewide achievement tests, fewer discipline problems, higher attendance rates and higher test scores than the national average. Parents indicated that they now feel more able to become involved in their children's education and have better communication with their children. Principals of the involved schools corroborate these findings and strongly support continuing the program.

"We've had other independent evaluations of the programs' impact. They've also found fewer discipline problems and higher attendance rates. But, in addition, they noted increased homework and parent-child time, and reduced television watching after parents and teachers had been trained.[62]

"Memphis State University researchers evaluated the impact on students and families participating in the MegaSkills Workshop Program in Tennessee. They found a significant extension of learning time beyond the classroom: children spending six hours a week on homework doubled (12% to 24%), while the number spending less than one hour decreased. The average time children spend watching TV during the school week decreased 31 minutes per week. Time not spent on TV was spent on homework. Most important, average time parents spent with children each day increased after the workshop by 12% each day. Finally, the MegaSkills Program at Louisville, Kentucky's Maupin Elementary School shows that: 90% of teachers have integrated the program into their individual class curriculum, more than 90% of teachers using the MegaSkills Essentials found children have more respect for others, work more cooperatively, are more able to concentrate and pay attention, have fewer discipline problems, show greater responsibility in completing assignments, and show more interest in school.[63] A MegaSkills School combines four elements: school environment, parent involvement training, classroom training, and Bond Training. These assessments show that MegaSkills training can be effective both with parents in the home and with teachers in the school." [64]

"Dorothy," Maria spoke up, "are your MegaSkills Programs effective with minorities? I'm skeptical that these programs help disadvantaged students."

"Maria, I'm glad you asked that question. Commercial parent education programs tend to target middle-class students. Middle-class parents are looking for ways to supplement their children's public education, especially where it doesn't take more of their time. That's why new computer games are such hot items. But there's no substitute for personal one-on-one parent time with children. Nothing can replace it—not babysitters, not TV, not the latest computer game. But you asked specifically about how MegaSkills impacts minority children. Workshops have been successfully conducted for over 100,000 families, including African American, Hispanic, Native American and Pacific Americans. Materials are also available in Spanish.[65] Family activities are easy to read, take 15-20 minutes, and cost little or no money. Materials are culturally sensitive and increase positive parent-child interaction in all families. Home-Learning-Activities are provided across the grades from pre-kindergarten to secondary schools."

"Dorothy, I'm impressed with what you're telling us," Paul said. "Could you tell us what benefits we can expect if we adopt a MegaSkills Program at Jefferson Elementary?"

"Yes, Paul. The data we've been gathering point out benefits for students, parents, teachers and principals. For example, students like school more, spend more time on learning, spend more time on homework, are more motivated to learn, receive better 'effort' or 'citizenship' grades, enjoy more quality time with their parents, and experience more success in academics. Parents develop better parenting skills, have a deeper understanding of their children's educational strengths and needs, enjoy a better relationship with their children, and feel empowered to be more active in their children's education. The number of participating parents who report working well with their children increased from 55% to 75%. Teachers have fewer classroom discipline problems, are able to spend more time on tasks, find more children prepared and ready to learn, and experience more positive communication with students and parents. Principals report fewer individual discipline incidents, better attendance, increased parent involvement, better school/parent/community relations, higher effort or citizenship grades, and gains over base-line performance on a number of academic achievement indicators."

"Dorothy, how do you deliver MegaSkills to parents and teachers?" Delores asked.

"We've developed four training programs. The one-day **Leader Training** MegaSkills Workshop for parent involvement is designed for classroom and Title I teachers, social workers, guidance counselors, administrators, parent liaison workers and aides. The two-day **Leader Training** MegaSkills Workshop for parent involvement provides human resource personnel, community and parent leaders with more in-depth training to develop effective presentation skills to help parents help their children achieve academically. **Classroom Training** is a one-day workshop for classroom special education, Title I, Even-Start staff and Head Start teachers and volunteers to show them how to use the classroom program with students for better study skills and higher academic achievement. And **Professional Development** workshops are introducing the new MegaSkills Bond Training that translates National Education Goals and Mandates into practical action for educators and parent leaders working together. It focuses on developing school improvement plans for family/school/community involvement programs, including school-home agreements. It trains in improving communication between school and family, family and student, and school partnerships with community agencies and businesses. MegaSkills training is also available for schools anticipating site-based management and effective schools programs. The U.S. Department of Education has presented MegaSkills its Breaking the Mold Award. I believe MegaSkills are critical to national school reform."

Wendy broke in with a question. "Dorothy, we have asked many of our guests to talk about the two or three lessons about school reform they've learned over the years."

"Well, Wendy, that's a good question. I suppose that my first one is why I created MegaSkills in the first place. Families are very important in the education of kids. When I first said that 30 years ago, and every year since then, I was humored by male educators, most of them former coaches, as the home-learning recipe lady. They would say that's nice, but it's unimportant. Now the research shows that parents and families are not only the first, and very important, teacher of their children, but parent participation can contribute to improving student achievement. Since we've also learned that by high school graduation, students will have spent about 85% of their lives outside of formal school—they must be learning plenty of things in the home, watching TV, playing sports and computer games, relating with friends, and whatever else they do besides sleeping.

"The second lesson I've learned is about learning. I was trained as an English teacher and spent time in the classroom. Then I thought the challenge was to teach reading and academic subjects even if it was boring and difficult. I thought that's how children learn. Over the years, I gradually learned that academic subjects will not be taught or caught unless children first catch the excitement of learning in some way, and it must rest on a moral foundation. In the 1980s, we were having our decade's national fit over the need to start teaching basics again. But families would report to me that the kids couldn't concentrate, just weren't motivated, weren't able to stick to anything, or just don't have common sense today. If this sounds like your teenager, then you know I'm right about this.

"From the very start of our Institute, I've always designed recipes—easy to do lessons that all parents could understand and teach in non-formal settings—using everyday experiences at home and shopping and during community activities. I believe that every family has the ultimate responsibility for helping their children develop, build and practice character. Where do kids get help to do this? They get help from their parents, the church, and the school. Well, in looking around, I didn't see much being done to help parents informally and formally teach their children character education. Children must be prepared to enjoy the challenge of learning. Research is showing that it takes a partnership between families, schools, and the larger community with its varied associations to impact our children— Little League, Girl Scouts, religious group activities, summer camp, etc. These experiences can counter what sometimes become the bloodless drill-and-kill approaches of some teachers. They can also counter the latest academic standards movements of reformers, and the nonsense that educational technology will replace the teacher. Technology is one tool, but it's not enough. People are education's biggest and best bargain.[66] Education at home or at school, on an athletic team or in life, requires enthusiasm, personal effort and caring. It also requires patience to work with one individual at a time until he or she catches the excitement and the vision of what is possible in the world beyond his or her small experience."

"Dorothy," Dale spoke up, "you're concerned with local schools, family values and parent responsibility for character education. You must be a big critic of the federal government's role in the education of our children. Am I right?"

"No, Dale, you're not. Let me explain why I believe we need federal leadership. First take the problem of mobility as it relates to education. Most students will move several times in their lives. Does it make sense for these mobile students to have one standard for math in Mississippi, another standard in California, and still another in Michigan? Two and two are four wherever you go. That's an international standard.

"Medicine knows no boundaries in treating patients; we don't have Mississippi treating smallpox one way and New York treating it another. Engineering knows no boundaries; we don't have engineers building public bridges one way in Russia, another way in Germany and still another way in Texas. We have world-class standards recognized by professionals everywhere. And, as we know from the Olympics, those standards are constantly changing for the better. All humanity benefits from this knowledge.

"Next, we must stop these games about who controls education. Education is first of all the responsibility of parents. They have the responsibility, and the right, to contract out the formal education of their children to the local schools. They have the responsibility to hold local educators and school board members, governors and state legislators, members of Congress and their President accountable for providing resources—human and financial— to educate all of our children with the best education possible today. This requires sensitive school/family/ community partnerships to create and operate public schools worthy of our democratic ideals."

Wendy stepped in. "Dale, what makes us believe that local control of school alone is so much better for our children's education? Did you know, for example, that only 4% of New York City citizens turn out for a school board election? Let's not pretend that local schools are getting the job done. The federal government's 11% financial support for local schools (not just the 6%-7% in the U.S. Department of Education), is not the cause of our education problems. Let's wake up."

"Thank you, Wendy," said Dorothy. "We must all take responsibility for improving our schools. We need to stop bashing teachers, parents, or the federal government. We need to start paying our fair share towards the education of all children. This will better their futures and the future of the United States—not just a local school and a state like Iowa, Utah or California. We are all Americans—and that includes the newest legal immigrants and their children. That's why school/family/community partnerships are essential."

"Dorothy, it's lunch time, and we want to thank you for coming today," said Wendy.

"Thank you, Wendy and members of the Citizens' Commission. I have a BEST PRACTICES handout, although I had a hard time choosing just one from so many schools that fit that category. I hope you can tell from my remarks that I am 'bullish' and very optimistic about education. Good luck with Jefferson."

Summary

"Now it's time for our morning summary. Our first guest today was **Dr. Diane Ramsey.** What do you remember about her testimony before our Commission?"

Maria spoke first. **"She made me think about a** *responsible family learning culture*. **I've never heard about it. What did she call it, a microculture? Now I realize that my husband, Miguel, and I can really make a difference. We set up values, expectations and habits that are the soil for our children's values, attitudes and habits to grow. I've always believed that if we just worked hard, prayed every day, and kept telling our children to be good, they'd turn out all right. Now I'm going to talk with Miguel and our family. I want to assess our family learning culture. I'm not going to leave their future to chance, to the neighborhood or to television. We can do it."**

Paul raised his hand. **"I was most impressed to learn of research on primary values—future time focus, work ethic, savings, quality education, merit, sense of community, rigorous ethics, social justice, respect for authority, and the role of some religious beliefs—that fosters progress and development of individuals, families and nations. I've always wondered why certain immigrant groups prosper more than others. After all, people are people. Now I see that families within any group can carry and practice these progress-prone values. If they do, they are much more likely to advance and prosper. Many immigrant groups, including some disadvantaged Whites and minorities, are held back by progress-resistant values."**

BEST PRACTICES: MEGASKILLS SCHOOL-WIDE PROGRAM

Maupin Elementary in Louisville, Kentucky, is an inner-city school with 500 students in K-5th grades. As a magnet school, Maupin draws students from across the school system to achieve greater racial balance. The school is 44% African American, about 42% White and 14% Asian, Bosnian and other "English as a Second Language" groups (ESL). Most families live at or near the poverty line. Nearly 80% of the students qualify for free or reduced lunches.

The pilot adoption of the MegaSkills School-Wide Program by Maupin Elementary in September 1993 through June 1995 school year was made possible by funding from Jefferson County's Learning Choices grant. Maupin School formed a MegaSkills Committee of staff and parents to work with The Home and School Institute (HSI), which provided the MegaSkills curricula. The HSI staff did initial and follow-up training of teachers in the program components, with on-going monitoring and technical assistance as they worked with others.

Robin M. Dix, Maupin's principal for the last two years, explained that they decided to use The MegaSkills School-Wide Program because, "it is a comprehensive, integrated approach to helping children develop the specific skills and attitudes needed for success in school and later life. We were interested in the MegaSkills that underlie academic and career achievement, such as motivation, responsibility, initiative, perseverance, teamwork and problem solving. We also selected specific school improvement areas, such as discipline, attendance and academics, and developed program strategies and activities that would impact them and lead to higher achievement." The School-Wide Program creates a systematic delivery system that brings together the three HSI programs: (1) **MegaSkills Essentials for the Classroom**, a curriculum for teaching MegaSkills directly to students; (2) **MegaSkills Leader Training for Parent Workshops**, a curriculum for teaching parents to develop their children's MegaSkills at home; and (3) **The New MegaSkills Bond**, a curriculum to build parent and school partnerships in support of academic achievement. This School-Wide Program also provides complementary roles for all school staff and parents so that MegaSkills are consistently taught and reinforced in the classroom, the home and through-out the school.

Maupin's MegaSkills Committee helped implement the program by planning and coordinating activities and by involving staff and parents. Seventeen classroom and resource teachers used the curriculum on a regular basis, and 17 support staff were also involved. A series of six workshops at the school, each with a day and evening session, averaged 23 parents who attended each workshop.

Mrs. Dix said, "We created a school-wide MegaSkills environment by using posters, daily exercises and announcements, and special assemblies and ceremonies. We recognize MegaStar Students, those who demonstrate effort in a special way. For example, one boy finished 100% of his homework during the year. Another student showed responsibility by staying after school regularly to help tutor another child."

In assessing the impact of the program, a high percentage of teachers indicated areas of student improvement: 93% said students were more able to work cooperatively and responsibly; 93% said there were fewer discipline problems; 92% said students were more respectful and considerate of others; 86% said students were more interested in school, more confident and self-reliant. Workshop leaders (teachers trained in MegaSkills) reported that the program's impact on parents seemed to increase their understanding of what their children do in school, their willingness and ability to discuss problems with teachers, their ability to deal with their children's problems and monitor progress, and to make them more confident of their own abilities and strengths, more supportive of each other, and more involved in school activities. Parents confirmed these findings about themselves and their children. Program impact on faculty showed that expectations for student achievement were raised, and their involvement of parents at parent-teacher conferences became more productive. MegaSkills' impact on the whole school was to generate a common language about student attitudes and behaviors and to more clearly define complementary support roles for stakeholders. The program also improved the school climate and developed a greater sense of community.

According to Mrs. Dix, "One of our challenges is to be more creative in seeking funds to continue training new staff and refresh the others. The MegaSkills program has become a part of everything we do...a culture of learning and respect for others. On-going training is critical so the program doesn't die." Parents who have completed the workshops note improved communication with their children. One parent said, "My children are helping me understand what responsible, respectful and cooperative behavior looks like. They're translating these abstract concepts into concrete behavior, so we're able to reinforce these lessons in our home."

"Wait a damn minute, Mr. Christopher," said Lenora. "What are you sayin' about minorities?"

"Lenora," said Paul, "I'm saying that anyone—White or minority—who isn't taught to practice these progress-prone values can end up in destructive behavior. This means everybody, whether they're rich or poor, male or female, Wall Street lawyers, stockbrokers, bankers, politicians, or janitors and clerks. I'm really most interested in how Asian families teach these values and habits to their children. Maybe I can learn something from them that will also help me with my family."

Kathie spoke next. **"I guess I was most interested in seeing the impact on our schools of parents creating** *responsible family learning cultures.* **The research is pretty clear that we've been negligent about these issues. Like Maria, I'm going home to talk with my family. And I'm also looking at my classroom as a** *responsible learning culture.* **I want to see what I'm inadvertently reinforcing. I may be making some serious changes. For one thing, I'll start with the Home-School Compacts with students and their parents. That way we can begin our partnerships without waiting for whole-school reform."**

"Let's move on to Dorothy Rich and MegaSkills," said Maria. **"I didn't realize that MegaSkills was a character education program that parents could use to teach their own children. And now I find that the Home and School Institute is training many teachers in the MegaSkills program to be used in schools."**

Dale cut in. **"Yeah, it's a lot like the character education programs we've been reviewing, only MegaSkills starts with the parents. I believe that parents should be the ones to teach values to their children. Let the schools teach academics."**

"What about the families that are not able to do it. They don't know how, or they won't?" Tamar took Dale on.

"Well, I guess you have me there," said Dale sheepishly.

Tamar went on. "I guess that's the power of the school/family/community partnerships. If everyone pushes character education values—parents, teachers, and all community associations and public leaders—I'm betting that we'll rapidly reduce disruptive and criminal behavior. Just think how much easier it would be to teach if all students came to school with values or MegaSkills like confidence, motivation, effort, responsibility, initiative, perseverance, caring, teamwork, common sense and problem-solving. Then we could reinforce these values through our focus on academic subjects.

"Well done!" Wendy said. "Now it's time now to check for your lunch partner assignments, take a break and be back for our exciting afternoon on Parent Engagement. While you are at lunch please review the Responsible Family Learning Culture Diagnostic Questionnaire in your notebook (see Appendix)?"

****

Chapter 13
PARENT ENGAGEMENT
Saturday afternoon, March 22

"Welcome back," said Wendy. "It's my pleasure to introduce Dr. Joyce Epstein, director of the Center on School, Family, and Community Partnerships at Johns Hopkins University, where she is also professor of Sociology. Joyce is recognized internationally as a founder of partnership programs in the schools. She is the author of more than 100 publications on the effects of school, classroom, family and peer environments on student learning and development. Her latest book is *School, Family, and Community Partnerships: Your Handbook for Action.*[1] Joyce, could you begin by telling us two or three important lessons you've learned in your professional career?"

Family/School/Cummunity Partnerships

"Thank you, Wendy. I have learned that partnerships must focus on students—their development, achievement, attitudes, behaviors, and success not only in school but in their lives after school. The second lesson I've learned is this: while parent or family involvement leads to improvements in student learning, some activities are more effective than others. We must learn which partnership practices are most effective in achieving specific results for students, families and schools. The third lesson is that family / school / community partnerships are most effective when they lead to school improvement.[2]

"Before I discuss each of these points, let me give you a short history of parent involvement. In the past, the amorphous term 'parent involvement' referred to things that parents can do on their own. In the 1960s, when Congress passed the federal Head Start and Follow-Through programs for preschoolers and K-3 students, they legislated for the involvement of low-income parents in the education of their young children. Successful parenting was a major focus to better prepare children for entering school. In the 1970s, the effective schools movement gradually recognized that family involvement is critical to improving schools. By the 1980s, however, research and practice began to show that the term 'school/family/community partnerships' was a better name for the shared responsibilities of parents, teachers, and other community members who educate and influence children's learning and development.[3] It was during the 1980s that I developed a theoretical perspective called 'overlapping spheres of influence' that explains these shared responsibilities.

"In 1990 the federal government created the National Center on Families, Communities, Schools and Children's Learning. The Center conducted an active research and development program on school and family partnerships from birth through high school. We had 20 researchers associated with the Center, where I served as co-director. Over 300 researchers, representing more than 40 nations, including the United States, are sharing their work with us through conferences like the American Educational Research Association meetings. The work continues at the Center on School, Family, and Community Partnerships at Johns Hopkins University in Baltimore, Maryland."

Debbie raised her hand. "I've heard about your work on six types of parent involvement, Dr. Epstein. Would you mind sharing them with us?"

"I'd be glad to, Debbie," said Joyce. "Today, we prefer the term 'partnerships' instead of 'parent involvement.' This recognizes the responsibilities for children that are shared within and across many different contexts. This name change is important because the concept of partnerships places major responsibilities on the schools. They must create permanent and equitable programs that will inform and involve all families. It's no longer left up to parents to figure out how to become involved in their children's education.[4] The framework of these six types of involvement is derived from research on school programs. It directs attention to partnership practices that fall within the six 'overlapping spheres of influence model.' It helps parents, educators and researchers plan activities within the areas of family, school and community."

Reaching for a marker pen, Joyce wrote the names of the six types on the whiteboard. Turning back to the group, she said, "This means that the partnership should do the following:

- Type 1—**Parenting.** Provide activities that assist families with parenting and child-rearing skills, and with understanding child and adolescent development. We also should plan activities that show how to create home conditions for learning at each age and grade level. We should assist schools to understand families;

- Type 2—**Communicating.** Contact families about school programs and student progress with school-to-home communications. We should make sure there are ways to encourage home-to-school communications;

- Type 3—**Volunteering.** Improve recruitment, training, work and schedules to involve families as volunteers and audiences at the school or in other locations to support student and school programs;

- Type 4—**Learning at home.** Involve families with their children in academic learning activities at home, including homework and other curricular-linked activities and decisions;

- Type 5—**Decision making.** Include families as participants in school decisions, governance, and advocacy activities through PTA, committees, councils and other parent organizations;

- Type 6—**Collaborating with community.** Coordinate the work and resources of community businesses, agencies, cultural and civic organizations, colleges or universities, and other groups to strengthen school programs, family practices, and student learning and development. We should also provide services to the community.

"Although schools may use the framework of six types as a guide, each school must tailor its choice of practices to meet the needs of its families and students at various grade levels. Each type of involvement has particular challenges that must be met to have a successful program that engages all families. Each type suggests needed redefinitions of some basic principles of involvement to succeed with today's families. Each type can be fulfilled by many different practices of partnership. And, finally, each type is likely to lead to different results for students, for parents, for teaching practice and for school climate."

"How is connecting with the community linked to school improvement?" asked Kim.

"In the past, researchers have classified communities using such census data as education, income, ethnicity or race. Recent studies, however, show that the strengths of people, programs, and organizations in all communities may better predict and explain the success of students. Good programs of partnerships will mobilize the skills and talents of parents and others. Good programs integrate community services for families. Good programs can focus the connections of schools, families, and community groups on important goals for students."

"What are some specific practices that come out of your research?" Paul asked. "Are there some that teachers can actually use?"

"Yes, Paul. Researchers and educators are designing and studying activities that target student achievement and school improvement. We have designed a program called Teachers Involve Parents in Schoolwork (TIPS).[5] This program of interactive homework helps students complete their homework and it involves their families. TIPS improves the performance of elementary and middle grade students in math, science, health and language arts, regardless of economic or cultural background. We know that as teachers become more comfortable with the participation of parents, they work more effectively with them. This includes single parents and parents in high-poverty schools.[6] We now have research information about family involvement at important transition points—from one grade level to the next, and during the summer or other vacations—and have developed practical guidelines. We now know much more about which activities are effective and how successful school/family/community partnerships actually help improve schools."

"Joyce, talk to us about the best way to start developing a program of school/family/ community partnership here at Jefferson. Can you translate your research into practical, easily understood steps that will be useful for us now?" Christina sounded frustrated.

"Thank you, Christina. It's sometimes frustrating to hear about the results of research while you are 'up to your neck in alligators.' My advice for your Citizens' Commission is that you organize a school Action Team to focus on School/Family/Community Partnerships.[7] This Action Team will link to your overall school improvement council at Jefferson. It can develop a comprehensive program of partnership, including all six types of involvement. This will integrate all family and community connections within a single, unified plan and program. From the trials and errors, efforts and insights of many schools in our projects, we've identified five important steps that schools can take to develop more positive school/family/community connections.[8] I've written them on the board:

1. **Create an Action Team for School, Family, and Community Partnerships**. Teachers, parents, administrators, and others will serve on the Action Team. Their responsibilities will be to assess present partnership practices, organize new practices, and implement selected activities. They will evaluate needed next steps, and continue improving and coordinating practices for all six types of involvement.

2. **Obtain funds and other support for the Action Team and its work**. A modest budget is needed to support the work and expenses of each school's Action Team for School/Family/Community Partnerships. Funds may come from federal, state, and local programs that mandate, request, or support family involvement. Some of these are Title I, Title IV, Title VII, and Goals 2000. This budget will be used for planning, implementation, and revising practices of partnership on all six types of involvement.

3. **Identify each school's starting points on the six types of involvement**. The Action Team needs to inventory present involvement practices and grade levels where families are involved. This information provides 'starting points.' The Team also may conduct surveys, interviews, panels, focus groups, or other discussions, such as a series of principal's breakfasts for representative groups of teachers, parents, students and others. This will provide information about the school's present practices of partnership on the six types, and which practices are presently working well. Then they will know what to add or improve so that all families are reached and school goals are met.

4. **Set a three-year outline and a one-year action plan**. Based on what practices are present or needed, the Action Team can develop a three-year outline for all six types. A detailed one-year action plan will show how the subcommittees for all types of involvement will conduct their work each month over the school year. The plans will show the delegation of responsibilities, will link activities to school goals, and will show how to measure results. The outline and plans

will be shared with the school improvement council, parent organization, faculty, students and community.

5. **Continue planning and working toward good partnerships**. The Action Team schedules an annual presentation of its work and a celebration of progress. This helps all teachers, families, students and the community to know what work is being done to strengthen partnerships. Each year the Action Team will update the school's three-year outline and develop a new one-year action plan. Even if the Action Team adds to or improves only one activity a year for each of the six types, it will lead to 18 improvements over three years."

"Joyce," asked Ray, "what have you learned about the performance of these Action Teams?"

"As schools have implemented these partnership programs, we've found several characteristics of successful partnerships. First, partnerships take time to develop—it's a process not a single event. Second, a partnership program has to focus on children's learning and development. This is important to curricular and instructional reform. A partnership is strengthened by improving the content and conduct of parent/teacher/student conferences and by goal-setting activities. The objective is to move partnerships from peripheral public relations activities about parents to central programs about student learning and development. Third, the Action Team approach to partnerships guides the work of educators by restructuring staff development. Colleagues work together and with parents to develop, implement, evaluate, and continually improve practices of partnership for better teaching and learning. Most principals and district leaders are not prepared to help their staffs develop strong school and classroom programs that inform and involve all families. Most teachers have not had any formal education or in-service training on how to work effectively with families. They do not know how to mobilize parent and community resources to improve student performance and achievement.

"At the Center on School, Family, and Community Partnerships, we have formed the National Network of Partnership 2000 Schools to link and assist state, district, and school leaders. The Network aims to help members improve programs of partnership using Action Teams and the six types of involvement in all elementary, middle, and high schools. Network members evaluate results of specific practices of partnerships each year. Focus on Results, for example, will identify which school/family/community connections improve student attendance.[9] You can see the handout on Longfellow Elementary School in Milwaukee, Wisconsin for a BEST PRACTICES example."

"This would be a good time to explain about government support. Tell us about how your program fits with Secretary Riley's Parent/Family Initiative and federal education legislation, like Goals 2000 or Title I for high-poverty schools?" Ray asked.

"Secretary Riley has been a champion of school/family/community partnerships. He's used his personal and official standing to speak out. He organized the Partnership for Family Involvement in Education and has funded demonstration programs. He's helped focus public attention on the importance of partnerships using departmental publications and bringing political support and legislative action.[10] In 1994 Goals 2000: Educate America Act was enacted by a bi-partisan Congress. It sets eight voluntary national goals. The Eighth Goal states: **Every school will promote partnerships that will increase parental involvement and participation in promoting the social, emotional, and academic growth of children.**"

"In my view, *every school* means all grade levels—preschool through grade 12.[11] *Will promote* means that the states, districts, and schools will take responsibility in developing programs and practices so that all families can be involved. *To increase parent involvement and participation* means that the program will not be casual, but planned. It will include practices for all six major types of involvement. Over time it will show that more families, educators and students are engaged with each other in positive education-related activities. *To promote the social, emotional, and academic growth of children* means that the practices selected to involve families will be those that are most likely to improve and maintain positive student attitudes, behaviors and achievement. This government mandate defines three objectives for Goal Eight:

BEST PRACTICES: FAMILY/SCHOOL/ COMMUNITY PARTNERSHIPS

Longfellow Elementary School is located in the heart of Milwaukee's south side. The school (K-6th) serves a student population of 640, who are drawn from a community that is ethnically and racially diverse— 49% Hispanic, 26% White, 16% African American, and 9% Asian, Native American and other. Most families, many of them single-parent, are economically disadvantaged. Eighty one percent of students receive free or reduced price lunches. The average per pupil expenditure from the state budget is $2,245 plus $442 from the Title I budget. In addition to problems of poverty, the area is plagued by gangs. Yet the majority of parents are deeply concerned about their children's safety and want them to succeed in school and later.

LaBelle Calaway, principal of Longfellow, says, "We realize that teachers, parents, educational assistants, support staff, psychologists and social workers can't provide for the increasingly complex needs of today's students, unless all of us work together collaboratively. The idea of "the village" is essential. We try to bring all parties—school staff, parents, community agencies, and businesses—together for the benefit of our students. We are a team who embrace the philosophy that all students can learn, must learn and will learn, regardless of socioeconomic status or ethnicity. We find ways to facilitate their achievement…innovative teaching strategies and methods to deal with students' particular needs."

After applying for a grant two year ago, Longfellow was one of two schools in Wisconsin to receive state funding to implement the Epstein Model of Family/School/ Community Partnerships. The approach fits well with the school's philosophy and practices. With the focus on collaborative teamwork, Longfellow is now making good progress. Two challenges they faced were to increase parent involvement in decision-making at the school, and to add practices that increased student learning. "We know that certain types of parent involvement help children do better in school. Last year," said Ms. Calaway, "some parents participated in meetings where they learned what their children need to know and how to best help them. Our parents also volunteered over 1,260 hours in such activities as tutoring in classrooms and assisting teachers. The goal this year is to increase these hours by 15%."

Ms. Calaway is justifiably proud of her "strong leadership team." They accept children where they find them, and use a multi-sensory approach. They devote time and energy beyond actual school day hours, clear evidence that they truly care about their students and their families. They are risk-takers, willing to try innovative approaches to raise achievement.

During the 1995-96 school year, the kindergarten and first grade teachers, supported by the administration, parents and other community members, embraced a new program called Student Achievement Guarantee in Education (SAGE). This program provides students in the early grades with rigorous academic curriculum and with two teachers in a classroom, which reduces class size to a ratio of 15 to 1. Longfellow also offers Bilingual Education, English as a Second Language, computer literacy, drug awareness, Title I and Exceptional Education.

The school continues to evaluate and refine its goals and implementation strategies, using several data sources to monitor improvements in its programs for student achievement. On the Writing Proficiency Assessment, 84% of fourth graders scored at or above 4.0, while 95% of fifth graders scored at or above 4.0—both excellent scores. On the Iowa Test of Basic Skills (ITBS), 77% of fifth graders scored at or above the national average, also very good. Ms. Calaway will focus this year on the third graders, "I want 85% of them to read at or above the state standard, not this last year's 70%, and to decrease the achievement gap between Hispanic and White students by at least 10%." Their average student attendance last year was 93%.

Longfellow's adoption of the Epstein Model focuses all activities on improving student learning by strengthening family/community partnerships. They are successfully "partnering," for example, with two local churches whose members hold "homework clubs" from 4 to 6 p.m. every Tuesday and Thursday, picking up 70 children for tutoring. Another innovative community collaboration is with a law firm that sponsors the "Choice Program" to help children learn to make good decisions and to see the consequences of their choices. Once each month, a "role model" (a teenager or professional) shares positive lessons from his/her own experiences, after which a panel of students summarizes what they learned from the presentation.

Longfellow's team has planned and implemented another impressive strategy to counter the problem of gangs. They take sixth grade boys to tour part of a prison and speak to inmates—a real eye-opener for these youngsters. A Masonic Lodge has also been partnering with the school by sponsoring "zoo ambassadors"—a fourth-grade program that provides a field trip where children learn the habits of animals and how to protect them and their environment. Students' families are informed about and involved in all of these activities.

1. Every state will develop policies to assist local schools and LEAs to establish programs for increasing partnerships that respond to varying needs of parents and the home, including parents of children who are disadvantaged or bilingual, or parents of children with disabilities.

2. Every school will actively engage parents and families in a partnership which supports the academic work of children at home and shared educational decision-making at school.

3. Parents and families will help ensure that schools are adequately supported, and will hold schools and teachers to high standards of accountability.

"The other education goals will also benefit from the participation of families. The federal government has been a positive force supporting school/family/community partnerships. Title IV of the Educate America Act establishes Parental Resource Centers that are mandated for every state by 1998.[12] In 1994 the Elementary and Secondary Education Act was reauthorized. It targets federal funds for high-poverty schools, emphasizes high standards for all children and requires participation by parents in the planning and implementation of Title I services. Title I also directs the creation of school/parent compacts. These should be comprehensive plans for how parents, school staff, and students will share responsibility for students reaching high performance standards set by their state, district, or school. The bottom line is that federal funds can be used for partnership activities. Federal, state, district, and school interests are making partnerships a dynamic part of school reform."

"Thank you, Joyce, for being here today," Wendy said. "You can be certain our Citizens' Commission will use the information you've shared."

Turning to Commission members, Wendy said, "Joyce will answer your questions as we break for refreshments."

****

Parent Involvement

Nate welcomed the group back from a lively exchange at the refreshment table. "Our next guest is Joan Dykstra, president of the National PTA, which is celebrating its 100-year anniversary.[13] Joan, welcome to our Citizens' Commission. Can you tell us the two or three most important lessons you've learned about school reform in your tenure as national PTA President?"

"Thank you, Nate. The number one lesson on school reform that I've learned, over and over again, is that there's no serious school reform without the parents. This is a bold statement, but I know it's true. Parents must be involved at the very beginning, not brought in after professional educators have decided what to do. These educators need to hear from those outside the school. This means that informed parents must speak out. The community often has a different view of school reform than local educators do. When outside views are not heard, the public becomes disenchanted with the schools and withdraws its support. Sometimes it leads to protests before the school board or bad press. Educators quite often fail to acknowledge this public frustration. By truly listening, especially to criticism, the educators have a chance to engage the public. When the loving critics fade away, a school is in trouble.

"My second lesson is that successful school reform must follow a clear outline of the goals and objectives. Parents and community must be engaged up front in defining the problem. They must solve the problems through open, informed discussion by all parties. Everyone, or at least a representative group of educators, parents and community members, must go through the whole process. Too often the leaders address the problem only after the whole educational dialogue breaks down or the kids' education. So unfortunately, school reform is often neglected until a smaller issue has turned into a crisis.

"My third lesson is that changing public education is difficult because certain traditions resist change. Most people have attended public schools, so they say to themselves, 'what was fine for me will work for my children.' But the world has changed, and the academic standards must change with it so our children are prepared with the knowledge and skills to be success-ful. How can we make these changes? All the stakeholders, not just profes-sional educators or reformers alone, must be involved. As President of PTA, I have tried to find ways we can help parents by supporting them in their home as well as at school. Some officials in the district office don't want to share their power with the parents. They resist changes that mean delegat-ing authority to school-site councils where parents are full participants with educators in managing local schools. PTA provides excellent training for parents on how to get involved with their schools and how to contribute to school reform, as well as how to strengthen their own parenting skills.

"Our student population has undergone dramatic changes. We are not preparing schools for these changes in the students and their parents. Di-versity is one of our strengths. We can involve parents from every back-ground, and help them feel comfortable participating in the education of their children, both at home and at schools. Research has shown that par-ent involvement leads to greater student success. I'm convinced that school reform will take place only if we involve parents! If we do not, we are wasting our time and money."

"Mrs. Dykstra," said Maria, "why hasn't PTA been more successful with minority parents in urban schools?"

"Not a week goes by that my PTA staff and I don't ask that question. We are trying to find ways of engaging minority parents. There are so many minority parents, especially single mothers, who are forced into the work-place with little time for volunteer activities at night and none during the day. So much of PTA work is carried out by mothers who are at a home with their children. Some parents from certain Latin American countries have learned to fear the government, and they are not accustomed to work-ing with the government in any way. Some governments have terrorized their citizens, so they distrust public officials. So when they come to this country and are invited to participate in the life of a school, they are ex-tremely cautious. Some also lack training in basic parenting skills. The PTA has been offering training programs to help these parents. We've also worked closely with the National Urban League in developing a new set of standards for parent involvement. We still need to find a way to recruit minority parents into PTA."

Paul raised his hand. "Did you say that national PTA has been working on national standards for parent involvement?"

"Yes, I did. The Eighth National Education Goal as enacted by Congress states: **Every school will promote partnerships that will increase parental involvement and participation in promoting the social, emotional and academic growth of children.**

"PTA was a powerful advocate for including this national goal in the six original ones advanced by the governors in 1989. Early this year, the national PTA began distributing a new handbook on standards to encourage parent involvement in their children's education through our state PTAs. This handbook is the result of years of work and careful review with the National Coalition for Parent Involvement (NCPIE) and the National Urban League. Here is a handout on these six standards that I'll read aloud. We believe they are essential for any school or program involving parents and families:[14]

> **Standard I: Communicating**—Communication between home and school is regular, two-way, and meaningful;
>
> **Standard II: Parenting**—Parenting skills are promoted and supported;
>
> **Standard III: Student Learning**—Parents play an integral role in assisting student learning;
>
> **Standard IV: Volunteering**—Parents are welcome in the school, and their support and assistance are sought;
>
> **Standard V: School Decision Making and Advocacy**—Parents are full partners in the decisions that affect children and families;
>
> **Standard VI: Collaborating with Community**—Community resources are used to strengthen schools, families, and student learning.

"These National Standards for Parent/Family Involvement Programs and their quality indicators are research-based and grounded in sound philosophy and practical experience. The purpose of the standards is threefold:

- To promote meaningful parent and family participation (including all adults who play an important role in a child's family life like grandparents, aunts, uncles, stepparents, guardians, who may carry the primary responsibility for child's education, development and well-being);

- To raise awareness regarding the components of effective programs; and

- To provide guidelines for schools that wish to improve their programs.

"The new handbook provides examples of each standard, quality indicators of successful programs, and sample applications. These are to assist parents, teachers and school policy makers and administrators in organizing successful parent involvement programs."

Nate spoke up. "Joan, thanks for coming today. We appreciate hearing about the role PTA is playing in school reform, especially in the development of standards for parent involvement. Let's take a short break before we hear from our final two guests this afternoon."

****

Nate called the Commission into session. "It is now my pleasure to introduce Marilyn Acklin, executive director of the National Coalition of Title I/Chapter 1 Parents.[15] Welcome to our Citizens' Commission. Jefferson is a Title I school, so we're eager to get your views. Could you begin by sharing the most important lessons you've learned about school reform?"

"Thank you, Nate, and members of this Citizens' Commission. Congratulations on including four parents and two community representatives on your Citizens' Commission—that balance is in itself significant. One of the first lessons that I learned about school reform is that people must be aware of exactly what you are trying to do. If you are a superintendent, principal, teacher or community leader, you'd better be very clear about what changes you'd like to see. You should be able to define exactly what they are and how you want to achieve them. This seems obvious, but my experience with Title I parents is that they are skeptical about change. For many years, they've heard about how sweeping these changes are going to be and how their children will benefit from more money and other resources. And then activities are begun, but then you do not see evidence of improvement or the results presented are not understandable. Parents leave frustrated and cynical.

"I'd say second, define the strategies you'll really be using to bring about changes before you start. Changes in Title I mandate that parents partici- pate in making school policies with a voice in how the money will be spent. There are many new requirements in the Title I program, including devel- oping compacts between parents, schools and students that promote the achievement of high standards. By 1997-98, states are supposed to develop or adopt challenging state content standards, in at least reading and math. These standards are to specify what all children are expected to know and be able to do. Challenging performance standards are also required to be developed. These standards show the level children will be expected to attain in mastering the material in the content standards for Title I. In addi- tion to the standards, high quality assessments are to be developed. How- ever, the assessments are not due until 2000-01. Until 2000-01, states may use a transitional assessment system. Many parents are not aware of the compacts, standards or assessments. Parents could use the compacts and standards as vehicles to ask questions about what they can and are expected to do to help their children. And they could use the assessments to gauge whether or not schools are carrying out their responsibilities. If parents are not informed and engaged in the process now, you cannot blame them or the children for low student performance.

"My last point is, you need public support for serious school reform. Support must come from the parents and all school personnel, including principals, teachers, staff, and even bus drivers and custodians. Support must also come from the business community and voluntary organizations that provide family services and youth services. Social service agencies and religious institutions must also be involved.

"Marilyn," said Delores, "I'm a first grade teacher here at Jefferson, and I can really relate to what you are saying. Not much is happening since the old Chapter I funding. What's stopping us?"

"Thanks, Delores, for that question. I think that we haven't worked out our time frame for carrying out the reforms. We haven't worked out strat- egies. We need people who are experienced enough and committed enough to bring about the changes. Parents and community people don't have a great deal of time to participate in defining the problems or developing strategies, but they do want to be consulted. They want to participate in implementing new programs. They want to see results. Parents become frustrated and cynical without this kind of participation."

"Marilyn," Maria raised her hand, "I am a Chapter 1 parent here at Jefferson. I have not been told about the new law or invited to help the principal make policy. I don't even know what Congress has done that would affect us here at Jefferson. Should we invite a member of Congress to come and explain our new rights and responsibilities to us? By the way, exactly what does your Coalition do to help Title I parents?"

"Our Coalition hosts regional and national conferences that give parents information about Title I. We provide information on model programs, and we try to give guidance to parents that help them to help themselves and other parents. We tell them how to form parent groups. We've developed a network of parents who are able to find out what is happening in school districts across the country. We advocate both at the state and local level, as well as in the halls of Congress. Title I parents actually meet with education officials, state and national legislators and local school board members. They are able to share what is going on in their respective schools. We serve as a convener of parents. We want Title I parents to be assertive and well in-formed. Many Title I parents have participated in our training conferences. They receive our newsletter and are more informed than many of the school principals. In some cases, these parents have been purposely ignored by school officials who feel threatened. These parents are ready to take actions outlined in the federal legislation."

"Have you've worked with Title I principals?" asked Kim.

"Many Title I principals attend our regional and national conferences and even present. Many principals are supporters and members of the Coali-tion. I recognize that principals are the key to success in Title I programs. After all the school is governed, literally, by the principal. So parent in-volvement really depends on how qualified, experienced and committed that school principal is. In most elementary schools, the principal is the only professional administrator who is trying to relate to 20 or 30 teachers and staff. As a principal, Kim, you know what happens every day. It's overwhelming. You know how essential federal Title I money is to high-poverty schools. **The law passed in 1994 means that Title I funds are the major resource for reforming the schools. Parents must, by law, be deeply involved in planning and carrying out the schools' educational program.**"

"Marilyn, thank you," said Nate. "We now better understand the vital role of parent participation in schools like Jefferson Elementary.[16] You have reminded us how important federal funding is. With the new law, that federal money can be used for more innovation and change than in the past. Wendy, will you introduce our next guest?"

Parent Engagement

"Our last guest is Ernie Cortes," Wendy said. "I've known Ernie personally for many years, and before that, by reputation. Before I turn the time over to him, I'd like to share some of his background. He is Executive Director, Southwest Region, Industrial Areas Foundation (IAF) with headquarters in Austin, Texas. The IAF was started by labor organizer Saul Alinsky over 50 years ago to form peoples' organizations to improve the social and economic welfare of Chicago's poorest neighborhood residents. When asked if the IAF is a liberal or conservative organization, Ernie usually replies that it is neither, it is 'radical.' Today, IAF has more than 40 community-based organizations across the country, most of them coalitions of religious congregations, representing nearly 1,000 institutions and over one million families. The largest affiliates are in Texas and the Southwest—the region Ernie supervises.

"Ernie left his graduate studies in economics at the University of Texas to work with Cesar Chavez and the farmworkers' movement in California. After that, he organized voter registration in Memphis, organized the first IAF affiliate in Texas (San Antonio COPS), and launched several others in Houston, the Rio Grande Valley and Austin. He now supervises lead organizers of 17 affiliates in Texas, Arizona, New Mexico, Louisiana and Nebraska.[17]

"Ernie is a voracious reader in political theory, economics, sociology and educational reform. Each year he brings in prominent educators from all political persuasions to explain their ideas in clear, jargon-free presentations to parents and teachers. IAF founded the three-year-old Alliance Schools project to help restructure 120 schools in 22 school districts. It focuses on developing parent leadership and making student achievement the focus of school improvement. It builds community relationships around education reform. It's my pleasure to introduce Ernie Cortes."

"Thanks, Wendy, for that introduction. We miss you in Austin Interfaith. I want to recognize also Sister Christina Peterson of Community Interfaith whom I've known for many years and who is a member of your Citizens' Commission. I commend the members of the Commission for taking on the challenge to restructure Jefferson Elementary School. I believe that what you're doing here can become a model for school/family/community partnerships throughout the United States. After many years of trying to break through school bureaucratic resistance, many enlightened school officials are beginning to work with parents as true partners. We are proud of the work we're doing in Texas."

"Ernie, to get us started today," said Wendy, "could you share a couple of lessons you've learned about engaging parents in school reform?"[18]

"Number one I call *The Iron Rule*—'Never do for others what they can do for themselves.' We believe that leaders are made, not born, and that most men and women have the ability to listen, to understand, to speak, to persuade, to confront, and to resolve. We find in our congregations and our blocks, in our public-housing projects and barrios, a vast pool of citizens. They are able-bodied and able-minded men and women, but they are often untrained and untaught. They are ignored by almost everyone. But time and again they have proved their ability to grow and develop. The IAF has won its victories not by speaking for ordinary people but by teaching them how to speak, to act and to engage in politics for themselves. The IAF has found that the potential of ordinary citizens emerges when they engage each other in the serious business of the *polis*. That business is about fundamental issues of family, property and education.

"Following *The Iron Rule*, community organizers have developed thousands of ordinary people into powerful community leaders. Housewives, pastors, bus drivers, secretaries, nurses, and teachers have learned how to participate as partners with businessmen, politicians, and bureaucrats, those who are normally thought of as our society's sole decision-makers. By carefully selecting and training grassroots community leaders, IAF believes that ordinary people can have a voice in the economic, social and political systems that govern their lives. We like to teach people to obtain consent by informing people, and developing their capacity to make judgments and to analyze alternatives. This gives them a kind of power—moral authority—that's different from the kind of power where you obtain consent through force or violence. You have to have a long-term perspective.

"The second is that we can't avoid the power question in school reform. It's central to the culture of any school. We have to know how power works in school reform, before anything much will happen. I go to a fair number of meetings with people in the reform business. They say they understand the importance of power and politics, but we never talk about it in any

sustained way. Mostly we just back away from it, because we all hate conflict. But we must organize and train so that people connect with the real
actions that must be taken. It has to be something people can get hold of,
something they can do.

"Working families in low-income urban areas have become increasingly
disconnected from the power and money they need to rebuild and maintain their communities.[19] Without strong institutions, families living in inner cities are simply unable to provide or arrange for their families' basics
needs, including early care and education for their young children. The
decline in mediating institutions is even more damaging because it's removed an avenue for their participation in public life. Without a connection to neighborhood churches, schools, and civic associations, these families are isolated and rendered powerless to bring about change. Community organizing revitalizes these institutions that support and defend families. To strengthen these mediating institutions, community leaders need
to act collaboratively, not in isolation. Parents, service providers, and community leaders must come together, engage each other in debate and discussion over important issues. Only then can they reach consensus and
make decisions about how to improve their community and act upon them.

"Let me hand out a BEST PRACTICES example of Zavala Elementary
School in Austin, Texas. It shows how to change the culture of a school by
connecting parents, students and teachers to bring about real school reform.
This was the first time the parents had organized around an issue they identified, faced opposition, persisted and won. The morale of parents, students and teachers soared as they learned the basic tools of democracy. While
you are passing that example around, let me go on."

"Politics is really about collective action which is initiated by people who
have engaged in this kind of public discourse. It's about relationships which
enable people to disagree, argue, interrupt in order to clarify, confront, negotiate.[20] Through this process of debate and conversation, they forge a
compromise and a consensus that will enable them to act. A proper understanding of politics means that people join together to confront public officials. This is the way to improve their schools and neighborhoods. Ordinary citizens learn how to participate and achieve not just short-term results, but long-lasting changes. Focusing on the least important elements
of political action like voting, elections and turnout really trivializes our
citizenship. It disconnects them from the real debate and real power in

BEST PRACTICES: ZAVALA ELEMENTARY SCHOOL, LEARNING THE TOOLS OF DEMOCRACY

Like many urban schools, Zavala Elementary was experiencing problems related to poverty and ethnic tensions associated with rapid changes from a predominantly Black to Hispanic population. In December 1990, Al Mindiz-Melton was made principal of Zavala Elementary. Of its 440 students, nearly 95% were eligible for free or reduced lunches. Most students lived in two public housing projects adjacent to school where average family income was under $5,200 per year. One third of Zavala's students were in bilingual education classes. Sixty four percent of all students were taught in 18 portable classrooms outside the main building. Teacher turnover was 50%. PTA attendance was often under 12.

Melton, proud of his Sephardic Jewish background, eagerly embraced the values of his school's Mexican-American and Catholic community. He felt the school had been "just a holding institution for children." Zavala scored poorly on the state's criterion-referenced test, even though most students were on the principal's honor roll and were earning As and Bs. He wanted to find ways to raise academic achievement. Melton wanted to highlight the discrepancy between the teachers' high evaluations of their students and the state's low assessment of their skills. He invited Austin Interfaith to help him engage parents in reforming the dying elementary school.

In December 1991, a pivotal PTA meeting was held. A disgruntled father, Albert Soto, was asked to read aloud Zavala's poor test results. Soto accused teachers of deceiving parents about how weak the student and school test scores really were. He demanded greater accountability from the teachers. The anger of Soto and other parents shocked most teachers.

Melton worked with Austin Interfaith (AI) to create an opportunity for people to change the school and improve parental engagement. Organizers asked teachers which parents could most likely develop into leaders. They used home visits to have one-on-one conversations to find out why parents were reluctant to collaborate with the school. They learned that parents felt overwhelmed by problems, such as low academic achievement, flagrant drug dealing and children's poor health. (Texas ranked 49th of all 50 states in immunizing preschoolers). They invited parents to become more engaged in the school.

One parent that responded was Tona Vasques (TA), a mother of four who had grown up in the area. She had graduated from high school, had a strong and happy marriage, and was a tireless advocate of her children's right to a high-quality education. TA's participation at Zavala increased her knowledge and skills so that she now mentors parents in east Austin to improve their schools and neighborhoods. Her growth into citizenship inspires other parents.

The dramatic transformation of Zavala's culture began with home visits by the principal, teachers, and AI organizers. They continued to hold house and individual meetings to ask what could be done to improve the school. By Spring 1992, Zavala held its first "Walk for Success," followed by more home visits to get parents' help in shaping a new school culture. On May 25, Zavala held its first "Rally for Success," which was attended by Mayor Bruce Todd, and others from the Texas Education Agency, the Austin School Board and the Police Department.

Melton, his teachers and parents worked with AI to advocate the creation of a school clinic that would provide comprehensive, preventive health care for children, including an immunization program. Eventually, Zavala's low-income parents achieved this objective by resolving an impasse between the City Council, the Department of Health and the School Board. Their children are now fully immunized. In 1993 Zavala won an "Award for Excellence" from the Texas Health Foundation and the Texas Department of Health for its new clinic.

Focusing next on academic achievement, parents and teachers attended workshops to address the test scores on the Texas Assessment of Academic Skills. Parental interest led teachers to reexamine their instructional styles and curricula, and to develop new attitudes and techniques for teaching their students better. Parents also began a tutoring program. In the next year, both academic scores and teacher retention rates—crucial indicators of school improvement—rose dramatically. The scores of third and fourth graders climbed from 23% in reading to 43%; 40% in writing to 92%; and 17% in math to 50%. Zavala's teacher turnover went from 50% in 1991 to 0% in 1993.

Parents have also been concerned about the safety of their children after school. Most parents are at work until after 6:00 p.m. Working with Austin Interfaith, Zavala parents and teachers, meeting with city council members, identified funds to support free after-school programs that accelerate their intellectual and social development in a safe environment.

There are other indices of cultural changes at Zavala. By 1993 all communication to parents was in both English and Spanish. Students began perceiving themselves more positively as they read good news about themselves in papers and saw visitors coming to take notes on what had happened. Melton and his teachers began creating new programs to counter tracking by preparing children for opportunities that develop their curiosities and thinking skills, such as the Zavala Young Scientists program. In addition, Zavala teachers began using discretionary funds to transform their curricula by focusing on interdisciplinary topics which emphasize conceptual development rather than memorization alone.

Ms. Loretta Caro became the new principal in August 1996. The work continues to progress under her leadership.

public life. It renders them incompetent. They become mere passive viewers of an electronic display.

"Two people, or even 10 people, may not be able to do very much. But as they build coalitions and learn the rules of politics, relational power and reciprocity, they can make real changes. The value and strength of these public relationships are what economists and social scientists now call social capital. This is a measure of how much collaborative time and energy people have for each other, how much time parents have for their children. It also includes time for PTAs or other civic organizations like scout troops, churches and voluntary associations that contribute to community building. We must revitalize the civic culture in America by teaching people how to be citizens. This will strengthen community institutions."

"Ernie," Ray said. "How does IAF organize? How do you reach and train these grassroots community leaders? In other words, how do you build social capital?"

"That's a good question, Ray," said Ernie. "Our community organizers begin serious, one-on-one conversations where citizens exchange views, judgments and commitments. These one-on-one meetings are held with administrators, teachers, pastors, community leaders and parents. They are not surveys. They involve true dialogue between parties. The organizer identifies a leader's concerns, and his or her willingness to participate in reform efforts along with each one's ability to teach others. The organizers see themselves as teachers, mentors and agitators who cultivate leadership that sustains broad-based organizations. These individual meetings create the foundation of personal relationships upon which collective work around school issues can be built.

"As individual meetings continue, organizers and leaders also begin a process of holding small group or community meetings, or house meetings. These will be neighbors and parents who express interest in school reform. Networks of relationships are established, and actions are strategized. As key leaders emerge, they will convene a team of parents, teachers, principals, administrators, and other leaders to address their concerns in an organized way. The team will assess the school's strengths and weaknesses, will deliberate, and will hold strategic planning sessions. Out of these sessions, they will develop a step-by-step plan of action for their school, and they will constantly reevaluate their plan.

"As IAF recognizes, all successful organizing is constant reorganizing. The core leadership team then presents their plan to the larger community in a neighborhood meeting. This includes community organizations, churches and businesses, elected officials, school officials and personnel, and parents. After the community ratifies the plan, or a version of it, all of these stakeholders make a public commitment to implement it."

"Ernie, how do you develop these leadership skills?" asked Maria.

"Organizers develop community leadership through training sessions. They hold regular training sessions for parents and community leaders to explain the education system. Parents and community leaders discuss their ideas about how to improve the school and how to become involved in new ways. They learn to act collaboratively and to negotiate compromises whenever differences arise. As they strengthen their leadership skills, they will plan neighborhood meetings around issues that affect the entire community. This means organizing door-to-door, reach-out campaigns to speak individually with each parent, and implementing their plans for school and community improvement.

"Leaders will develop their own abilities and will build the power base of their organization. This will happened when they begin to tackle small, winnable issues, like repairing streetlights and putting up stop signs. This will build confidence as they move into larger concerns, like curriculum reform and school safety. Soon these new leaders will have developed the capacity to set agendas for capital improvement budgets. They will learn how to strategize with corporate leaders and members of city councils on issues like bond and tax policies. They will then be able to tackle larger issues, like community growth, health, public safety and drug and alcohol abuse. This will create positive economic and social environments that all civic cultures need in order to promote effective community schools."

"Ernie," Tamar asked, "could you tell us a little more about your Alliance Schools?"

"Yes, Tamar, the Alliance Schools Initiative is dedicated to developing a strong, community-based constituency of parents, teachers, and leaders working to improve student achievement in low-income communities all through Texas.[21] The Alliance Schools Initiative includes 120 schools in a partnership with the Interfaith Education Fund, the Texas Industrial Areas Foundation Network, campus staff and parents, school district officials, Regional Education Service Centers, and the Texas Education Agency.

"The Alliance implements strategies that stress local solutions to local needs. This means developing schools that are committed to the deregulation of campuses and restructuring that involves all stakeholders—parents, teachers, school administrators, students, community and business leaders and public officials. The Alliance is committed to improving the education of all students. The Alliance operates under the assumption that the process of reform is self-directed, not imposed from above. We judge its effectiveness by increases in the level of parent involvement, improvements in student academic achievement, and increases in the number of institutions that want to become involved. Many Alliance Schools have received competitive Investment Capital Fund Grants through the Texas Education Agency to support their work in deregulating and restructuring their schools."

Wendy stood up. "Ernie, we're nearing the adjournment hour. Thank you for coming to share this exciting dimension of parent/community engagement in schools. We'll wind up this great day on parent and community engagement by asking you, the Commission members, to help summarize what we've heard from our afternoon guests.

Summary

"Now we come to our summary segment," said Wendy. "Who'd like to begin?"

Debbie spoke up. **"I'm impressed with Joyce Epstein's research on parent involvement. Now volunteering for PTA activities was only one kind of participation. The school must take a leadership role in inviting parents to become part of a program of school/family/community partnerships. I think we've been using parents as window dressing. After all parents do own the school and pay teacher salaries, and parents have to keep working with their children year after year. We should be equal partners in our children's education."**

"But parents are not trained educators," Ted Alexander said. **"I don't want them telling me what to do in my classroom. That's what I'm paid to decide."**[22]

"What we're learning about parent engagement in schools is that educators need to open up their schools if they want the support of parents and grandparents who do pay the taxes, and do love their children," said Debbie. **"Public educators have been 'out to lunch' where serious parent involvement is concerned. At Jefferson Elementary the administrators have been violating the federal law by not involving Title I parents in the design, planning and operations of all Title I activities every year. I do think that parents must respect teachers' right and authority to plan curriculum and teach the children in the ways they've been trained. But, as a parent, you should seek the right kind of help. We have a new day of accountability coming. The old game of 'keep the parents out of the school' is over. School/family/community partnerships are here."**

"I was most fascinated to learn about the new Action Team concept," Ray said. **"Joyce told us that Action Teams are the way to jump start serious school reform. We need to do that in our Citizens' Commission. I hope we can be an effective Action Team that will resurrect Jefferson.**

And I'm also impressed that the federal government is giving local schools money. I'm in favor of Goals 2000 and Title I legislation."

"Are you putting us on again, Ray?" Delores asked. "Our Governor turned down Goals 2000 money —with the 'cock-an-bull' story that he didn't want the U.S. Department of Education messing with his local schools. But he does want their Title I money, their Special Ed money, their Bilingual money, their student financial aid money for his colleges. He accepts the Department of Defense support to educate children of our military service families in Europe. What's with our governor, Ray? Why would he want to stop us from getting Goals 2000 money to use in helping Jefferson? Aren't those federal tax dollars partly our money to spend on school reform?

Kathie spoke up. "As both a parent and a teacher with three children in public schools, I was impressed by the testimony of Joan Dykstra, president of the National PTA. She stated, 'there will be no serious school reform without parent participation.' She also spoke about the importance of clear school reform goals and objectives in terms that parents understand and buy into. She pointed out that resistance to changing schools is often the result of not consulting with all stakeholders. She also called our attention to the changing student populations coming into our nation's schools—and the challenge PTA faces to involve minority parents in school activities. What is most exciting to me, however, is the National PTA's new handbook on parent involvement standards. It shows parents and schools how to launch an effective parent involvement program. This handbook will be a great resource for teachers, parents and principals."

Maria raised her hand. "I would like to summarize Marilyn Acklin's testimony," she said. "I didn't know there was a National Coalition of Title I/Chapter 1 Parents. I agree with Marilyn's experience with Title I parents—they are skeptical about reform. They have heard it all before, about how the federal funds will shape up schools for disadvantaged students—then the money is so thin, not much happens and our children still get the newest, least experienced teachers, and the worst school buildings. Nothing much changes. I was very surprised to hear that the new Title I law requires that parents participate in planning and helping to carry out educational programs in high-poverty schools that get federal money. And what's this about requiring 'parent compacts' where parents must work with the teachers on individual education plans for their children. Whatever our Citizens' Commission decides to do about Jefferson, from now on, I'm going to insist that the new principal start involving parents in their children's education by spending these federal funds for serious school reform. I'm going to get hold of our member of Congress and invite her to come and explain why she voted for these federal education funds. Why hasn't someone been held accountable for this money?"

"I'd like to highlight Ernie Cortes' contributions," Christina said. "I can't say enough about him. He's reaching parents that the schools and everyone else has forgotten—disadvantaged Latinos and African Americans. By his leadership training, he has empowered poor parents across the southwestern part of the United States. He's also bringing the churches into support activities."

"But I don't like the sound of his radical political ideas," said Paul.

"Wait a minute, Paul. What do you mean?" Christina asked. "Are you against leadership training of citizens? Are you against empowering community parents to fight for better schools? Or is it un-American to teach democracy and active citizen participation to minority parents? The people Ernie works with are not wild-eyed radicals—the Catholic Church, the Texas Education Agency, elected public officials, and corporate foundations.""I guess you're right," Paul said. "His methods seem radical because we don't expect much from the community of parents and citizens. Maybe we do need lessons in grassroots politics. I suppose I just don't feel comfortable with conflict or with minority leaders organizing parents to protest for their rights. It's a whole other world for me."

Nate stepped in again. "On that note, we'll call for adjournment. Kim, it's all yours."

"Thank you for participating today. Each session seems to open up new perspectives for me. These guests on parent engagement were exciting. Each was very different and gave us much to think about in our own personal lives with our families and with our work at Jefferson. Now we know more of what can be done.

"During the next two months, we've invited a number of distinguished practitioners—superintendents, journalists, technology people, heads of national teacher organizations, business association executives, a state school board member, a U.S. Senator and the U.S. Secretary of Education. See you on April 19."

Chapter 14
EMPOWERING YOUR COMMUNITY SCHOOL, PART I
Saturday morning, April 19

Wendy got up from the breakfast table. John, her husband, didn't look too happy that she was leaving for another Commission Hearing. Saturday was usually a big day to fix up the townhouse together and run errands.

As she drove toward Jefferson Elementary, she thought: *What a year this has been! It's almost a relief for me to spend one Saturday a month with the Citizens' Commission at Community Interfaith. We've been working hard to find housing, health services and jobs for the 'downsizing refugees' and immigrants coming into our community. County services are overloaded. Churches and private charities are overwhelmed.*

Last month's hearing on parent and community engagement was one of the best. It was good to see Ernie again—he's still so inspiring and down to earth. I'm grateful to him for training me in neighborhood organizing. Our Commission members are coming together nicely. In two months, we'll have to put together our final report and recommendations. Then the really tough part will come—confronting the Board.

Today, we'll have the real experienced practitioners that I've only read about up 'til now. I'm excited to hear from Ray Cortines, David Hornbeck, Tom Payzant, Sam Sava, Anne Bryant and Howard Mehlinger. What a lineup!

She pulled into a parking space, and hurried to the room. Kim Su Young, the impressive vice chair, was ready to welcome the group. "Today, our Citizens' Commission Hearing will take a different format. In our other Hearings, we've invited school reformers to give separate testimonies. This morning we are fortunate to have six distinguished practitioners to share their experiences on the firing line. They will present different perspectives than the school reformers we've heard. Collectively they have been responsible for thousands of schools and school districts, state offices of education, thousands of teachers or school board members, and millions of students. Our subject is empowering your community school. As you listen, please think about how what you hear will help with our final report and recommendations. Nate Johnson will introduce the first panel."

Empowering the School Site: School Superintendents

"Thank you, Kim," said Nate. "Our first panel is three nationally-recognized superintendents of urban school districts—Ramon Cortines, former chancellor of New York City Schools; David Hornbeck, superintendent of schools in Philadelphia; and Thomas Payzant, superintendent of Boston Schools. I'll ask each to give us two or three lessons they've learned about school reform. Let's start with Ray Cortines. Ray holds the record for the number of superintendencies in major urban school districts. He's been superintendent in Pasadena, in San Jose, and in San Francisco. He recently retired as chancellor of the New York City School System. Ray, we really appreciate your being with us today."

"Thank you, Nate, for inviting me to appear before this Citizens' Commission. Let me get right to the point.[1] The first lesson is this—the name of the game is school improvement. I don't like the term reform. For me, reform implies that a school is bad. We need to identify those things that are good within the school community and work from there. At times I've been too far out front, too enthusiastic, and too impatient—the reforms were mine rather than the community's. I'm still old fashioned enough to believe that the mission of the school is to improve teaching and learning—not putting it on the kids, but helping the teacher. The first teacher may be a parent, a guardian, a grandparent, even a business person, but helping these teachers understand the complexity of the job of teaching is everybody's business.

"I believe all kids can learn. But they must take the right courses with tough standards, and the standards have to be the same for all. Our responsibility is to help each child meet those standards. It takes all of us—the chief administrator, the principal, the teacher, the parent and the student. If we want children to be motivated and challenged to meet the standards, we have to provide leadership. Staff development must focus on teaching and learning. Leadership starts in the classroom. Someone asked me what it was like to be chancellor. I said it wasn't much different from teaching my first sixth grade class—only the scale is different. If you want to lead, you must motivate and challenge. Children must have standards and priorities.

"Let me give you a couple of examples. In San Francisco, we had many students from Hunter's Point and other areas who were mostly poor children of color. The reading scores for these kids were two years below grade level, so I established a Saturday reading program that involved parents. Very quickly we saw that as parent involvement increased, school attendance improved and discipline problems decreased. There was even a slight increase in standardized test scores.

"I learned over and over again that keeping our focus on teaching and learning every day is hard work. It's not just feeling good about kids. It takes skill, knowledge, practice and time. Teaching is an art and a science. It's complex. I believe our teacher training institutions just haven't stepped up to the plate and become accountable for turning out well-trained, qualified teachers. In New York City, we made it clear to all students that they would not be able to walk across the stage unless they had actually passed the courses. Summer school attendance then went up, from 72% to 92%. We were no longer just playing school.

"A superintendent must take the responsibility for communicating priorities and then providing incentives to carry them out. We did this in New York—not just raising test scores, because many times the upper quartile can carry a school. I put about $500,000 out for elementary schools. The only way they could get grants of $10,000 was for the school community to decide how they could make improvements in the lowest quartile, the middle two and then the upper. If just one quartile moved, they only got a third of the money. The important thing was that the community became involved in helping to solve the academic and discipline problems.

"The second lesson I learned is the importance of building civic capacity and linking it to education. During my first year in New York, I held 38 community meetings with not fewer than 300 people each. We used interpreters and everything to make it work. The schools weren't happy about it because they'd been keeping the parents out. Parents had to make an appointment before they could visit the school. I told them that parents own the school, and I encouraged parents to go to the school any time they want to. Parents, including those who don't speak English, can see what is happening and what is not happening in a classroom. Administrators, teachers and unions use the lack of parent involvement as a cop-out. We [the school staff] want to complain. We just don't want to deal with those parents 'cause they're different from us.

"We talk about a level playing field for kids. It's got to be level for the whole community, too, which has the responsibility for children's education. This means paying attention to adult education. We need literacy and English classes for parents so they can help children with homework. In Pasadena, we brought Mexican-American mothers back to the school for an hour and a half and tutored them in English related to their children's homework. After that, those parents were no longer afraid of the school. We made the school a friendly place for both parents and students.

"What I mean by building civic capacity is that we must teach citizenship both in the classroom and in the community. I believe in community service. We can't have a democratic society if we don't teach citizenship. If people don't understand their role and responsibilities as an individual citizen and in a collective citizenry, then all this focus on higher academic standards doesn't mean a thing. We found that out from the Nazis in World War II. No wonder we're becoming more racist today. The seeds of prejudice are deeper than ever before. We have to take democracy seriously. One place to start is by building a civic culture around every public school and invite the community to become part of that school community. If we fail—public education fails."

"Well, thank you, Ray," said Nate. "We'll follow up on this during our Q & A period. Next, let's hear from David Hornbeck, superintendent of Philadelphia Schools.[2] Mr. Hornbeck was the main architect of Kentucky's sweeping 1990 reform legislation. Before that, he was Maryland's State Superintendent of Schools. He was trained in history, divinity and law. David, you bring an unusual background to the superintendency. Please start by sharing two or three important lessons you've learned about school reform or, as Ray put it, school improvement."

"Thank you, Nate," said David. "Let's see. The first lesson I have learned is the necessity for comprehensive reform of the whole system. I've worked with states like Kentucky and Maryland, and Dick Riley in South Carolina, even an urban system like Philadelphia. I've found that mere pilots or demonstrations don't bring reform to scale. Most pilots or demonstrations don't work in the long run because they have unusual things—great leaders, big foundation money, and long gestation periods—without dramatic improvements on a broad basis. The forces against change are powerful. If you go about it incrementally, you get eaten alive before you get a critical mass going in another direction. You can get stopped by interest groups who are against change. They'll always wait you out, and then reinstate the old ways. When I came to Philadelphia, I made an agreement with the board that we'd implement a reform model with ten components which later became *The Children Achieving Action Design* agenda.[3] Here's a handout prepared for our School Board. Let me talk you through it:

1. **Set high expectations for everyone.** Rigorous, challenging graduation standards, with appropriate benchmarks at the fourth and eighth and eleventh grades are essential. This must be made possible by opportunity-to-learn standards and a flexible and innovative school culture. Underlying the high standards must be a belief that all students will achieve;

2. **Design accurate performance indicators to hold everyone accountable for results.** The performance-based assessments should be tied to new standards. This task will be under the direction of a new Office of Standards, Assessment and Accountability to develop and implement strategies for accountability;

3. **Shrink the central bureaucracy and let local schools make more decisions.** Schools should be organized into small learning communities (200 to 500 students) with school-site councils. These schools could be organized into feeder patterns of 22 clusters with six to ten elementary schools feeding into two to four middle schools and one comprehensive high school. The central office should be restructured and downsized to become more service oriented and accountable. Decision-making and budgeting should be site-based with a system of client-centered services and supports;

4. **Provide intensive and sustained professional development for all staff.** Twenty days or its budgetary equivalent should be devoted to site-based staff development. A central Professional Development Office should assist schools with resources, give feedback on effective teaching and learning practices, and encourage teacher networks. It should also broker with outside service providers to meet priority needs of new and experienced classroom teachers;

5. **Make sure that all students are really ready for school.** Provide all eligible children with full-day kindergarten programs that are developmentally appropriate. A full-services office should be created to coordinate health, educational and social services for children and their families;

6. **Provide students with the community supports and services they need to succeed in school.** Link students with health and social services agencies. School officials should ensure that each school has an ongoing relationship with at least one community-based organization. Staff should recruit and match 10,000 new volunteers with the schools. They should conduct a campaign to prevent pregnancy or provide adequate services to students who are pregnant;

7. **Provide up-to-date technology and instructional materials.** Provide schools with a computer for every six students, transforming libraries into technology resource centers. Responsibility for technology should be under a single office. It should conduct comprehensive analysis and make five-year recommendations for technology services;

8. **Engage the public in shaping, understanding, supporting and participating in school reform.** School staff should listen closely to what the community wants and expects from its schools. They should develop accountability tools to help the public access the district's performance data. They should develop messages and strategies that clearly explain what the schools are doing and why. Community efforts to mobilize and organize support for high-quality public education should also be supported. The school staff should build the capacity of all district staff to be better ambassadors for educational excellence;

9. **Ensure adequate resources and use them effectively.** School staff should aggressively improve efficiency and effectiveness in non-instructional areas. They should investigate alternative financing opportunities from foundations, state and federal government, and other private sources. They should ensure the best use of present and future space requirements. They should ensure the district is drawing on all available time and money resources to teach more effectively and improve student achievement; and

10. Be prepared to address all of these priorities together and for the long term—starting now!

"My second lesson is the importance of a system of hard-edged accountability for student performance with consequences attached. Standards and education mean very little without fairly immediate consequences for students, and educators, administrators and superintendent. If a school team significantly improves the student performance using explicit assessment measures, then the team of teachers should be rewarded. When student performance doesn't improve, educators should receive help. If the school persistently fails to improve student achievement, school staff should face penalties, including reconstitution of schools.

"There is a third lesson. We must take seriously the practice of driving decisions down to the school site. This means setting up school-site councils with authority over all the operational questions, money, personnel, instructional materials and strategies, teacher assignments, discipline, staff development, parent and community engagement. Our councils are made up of 51% teachers, who were selected by other teachers, and 35% parent representatives, who were chosen by parents and the principal."

"Thank you, David," Nate said. "We'll move right along now to Dr. Thomas Payzant, superintendent of the Boston Public Schools.[4] He moved there from Washington, D.C., where he was assistant secretary for Elementary and Secondary Education at the U.S. Department of Education. Prior to that, he was superintendent of the San Diego City Schools.

"Tom, you've seen public education from the top where you worked with Secretary Riley and President Clinton to fashion a more effective *Goals 2000 Educate America Act,* and the latest reauthorization of the Elementary and Secondary Education Act, especially the Title I focus on high-poverty schools. With your varied experience, what are the two or three lessons you've learned about how to implement school reform successfully?"

"Nate, and members of the Citizens' Commission, I appreciate being asked to testify on ways to empower the community school. The first lesson is that there is not just one way to go about school reform. The second is that we often try to do too many things with reform, so we lose our focus on teaching and learning. Third is that reform strategies often ignore the changing demographics of our students, parents and communities. Let me enlarge on these lessons by reaching back to my experiences in San Diego where I managed a district-wide restructuring process.

"I'll start with the third lesson about the changing context of reform—the demographics of school populations. In 1978-79 the student population in San Diego was about two-thirds (62%) White and one-third (38%) African American, Asian and Hispanic. Ten years later, San Diego was the fastest growing city among the nation's 25 largest cities. With 124,000 students, it was the eighth largest urban school district in America.[5] By 1992, the makeup of the student population had reversed to one-third White (35%), and about two-thirds minority (16% African American, 19% Asian and 30% Hispanic).

"Students speak over 60 languages, and 30,000 students are limited English speaking. This is an increase of over 300% in ten years. Almost 60% of the children qualify for free or reduced price lunch. Despite increasing enrollments of about 2,500 students per year, the percentage of households with children in San Diego is declining. Other institutions that have traditionally provided for the physical, social, emotional, and economic needs of children have been overwhelmed. This has left the schools with a role that is no longer limited to meeting the academic needs of children. Just as our new restructuring program got underway, our depressed economy required a 4% cutback in the schools' budgets. Trends show less parent support for public schools and lower grades for schools by the general public.

"Let me illustrate the other two lessons learned in a case study of San Diego School District's attempts to restructure and change the school culture. The progress of our five-year San Diego restructuring process was uneven, slow in some areas, and more encouraging in others. We met resistance to changing practices. Our restructuring process focused on several components. I've listed them on the board:

- **academic standards**—The California Curriculum frameworks provided a benchmark for what students should know and be able to do;

- **assessment**—Multiple forms of assessment and multiple indicators were used in addition to standardized testing;

- **accountability**—Every school was held accountable for student achievement, not just schools with low-scoring students where intervention occurs. (The mere mention of the word accountability unleashes a wide range of emotions);

- **curriculum, instruction, and equity**—All tracks were eliminated and all students receive the common curriculum, with the exception of Gifted and Talented Education (GATE) and special education programs;

- **human resources**—For all teachers, all classified employees and administrators, professional development was linked to improved classroom performance and to extended, not reduced, instructional time with students;

- **governance and decentralization**—The central office was downsized by 21% and its function was changed to a resource and service center for its clients (the schools). Principals shifted their roles from plant manager to instructional leader. Schools accepted the responsibility for many decisions about staffing, curriculum, organization, assessment and allocation of resources;

- **integrated services for children, youth and families.** The district established new collaborative relationships among the major public agencies to provide services for children, youth, and families who live in the school district;

- **parents and community engagement and support**—Governance teams at schools, which included parent and community representatives, provided new opportunities and incentives for engagement in decision-making. They should include parent compacts, and parent information centers; and

- **resources and infrastructure support**—Additional financial resources (not the net reductions we experienced in the 1991-93 school years) were required to prevent overcrowding. Maintenance will be deferred until public support is built for meeting the additional costs of restructuring, reforming, decentralizing and rebuilding a modern urban school system.

"Overall, we made great strides in restructuring, but I'm sobered by how long it takes and how difficult it is to overcome the resistance to change and renewal. Restructuring the system required school-site decision-making and serious parent and community engagement. This is hard work and requires constant, unrelenting attention to teaching and learning before students can achieve high standards."

"Thank you, Tom," said Nate. "We'll take questions from the Commission."

Paul Christopher raised his hand. "As a businessman, I've been listening carefully to what you top education executives have been saying about managing the change process in big organizations. I realize you've been dealing with big budgets ranging from $500 million to $1.5 billion dollar operations, and 75% or more of the budget is labor. That's an incredible management challenge under normal operating circumstances, let alone carrying out dramatic reforms at the same time. Do you have any advice for empowering our small Jefferson Elementary School? In a nutshell, what would you focus on if you were on our Commission?"

"I'll take that question," said Ray Cortines. "You start with your comparative advantages. You have a small school here—that's the best unit and the best size for culture change. You must insist on high-quality standards for every student and for all teachers and administrators. I think local control is a plain cop-out in today's nonsensical discussions of school reform. That's why we probably need national curriculum standards. Third, priorities must be established—so that every action or reform must be shown to improve teaching and learning for all children. And finally, make what you have right here a laboratory for citizenship! Your students, teachers and parents are a good example of an integrated American suburban school. Build on this strength. Don't try to escape from it! That will take tolerance, collaboration, respect, patience and leadership. Everyone must be challenged."

"I'd like to add to Ray's list," soft-spoken David Hornbeck said. "You must demand accountability from all parties—from the school board and superintendent, the principal, teachers, classified staff, students and parents—no exceptions! Have regular reports on student performance and make them public. Then insist on creating a powerful school-site council that really represents teachers, who were chosen by their peers, the principal, and elected parents. This school-site team must exercise authority over all aspects of the school's operation. This includes budget, personnel recruiting and assignments, annual assessments of performance, student and faculty discipline, curriculum materials, professional development, and parent and community engagement."

"I second all that's been said by my two colleagues," said Tom Payzant. "I'd like to add just two additional items. Create a collaborative multi-service center at the school so that children and families can get support services first. Then the children can concentrate on school work.

"Next, watch your back! School reform, improvement or restructuring, whatever you call it, is hard and threatening work. There'll be opposition by all the special interests that want to maintain the status quo. Identify them early. Then remember that people are not the enemies, but traditional practices that limit people and keep them from moving beyond their own experience. Your most difficult challenge is to win and keep the support of your school board and superintendent. They both have a legitimate role and responsibility in Jefferson's reform process and operation. They are legally accountable. But, having said that, you can't let them sabotage your plans. The bottom line is dramatically improving student performance. You have the right and responsibility to fight for this claim on the community's money, talent and attention. You have been given the moral right to make that judgment for Jefferson Elementary. Don't give it away! Don't be compromised!"

"With those words of wisdom," said Nate, "from you three successful superintendents, we'd like to thank you for sharing your perspectives today. We'll take a refreshment break."

Empowering the School Site: State Education Officers

"Our second panel," began Wendy, "is also on empowering the community school. Reform models seem to have forgotten two major players—the principal and the school board member. We'll hear first from Dr. Sam Sava, executive director of the National Association of Elementary School Principals (NAESP). Our second guest is Dr. Anne Bryant, executive director of the National School Boards Association (NSBA). Both associations are located in Alexandria, Virginia. Our third guest is Dr. Howard Mehlinger, director of the Center for Excellence in Education, and professor of Education at Indiana University. He will introduce us to the exciting world of educational technology and education reform.

"Dr. Sava," said Wendy, "in your 15 years representing grassroots school principals all over the United States, you've watched school reform up close. What are the two or three lessons you've learned?"[6]

"Thank you, Wendy, and members of the Citizens' Commission. My views on school reform may be somewhat different from those who've appeared so far. My first lesson is that school reform must help young children to succeed in school. Many of the reforms have been downright destructive by distorting the learning that should be going on in the classroom. For example, if you insist that standardized achievement scores are the only measure of success, then teachers will spend time drilling children on the answers to these tests, even though the needs of the children may be entirely different. Teachers have to meet the needs of students on many different levels. Some children live in poverty. Some have physical or learning disabilities. Some just have different learning styles. We also have many new immigrants with limited English proficiency. And some aren't even in school because their migrant parents are moving around. For example, some schools located near our southern borders have a 90% student turn-over rate in a given year.

"The second lesson is that this nation's focus has been on standards, and not on providing the resources to meet these standards. When *A Nation At Risk* was released, the Commission spelled out a set of standards. These were certainly long overdue, but they failed to discuss how the resources would flow to schools so that standards could be achieved by all children.

"The third lesson is that the federal government must become a serious partner in school reform. It is irresponsible for Congress to pass legislation for education programs without providing new funding sources and then expect states and local schools to carry out the regulations. We call these unfunded mandates. Significant programs, like special education, bilingual education, Title I students, Head Start (and I could go on) help children! So Congress should also provide the funds so that principals and teachers can carry them out."

Kim Su Young raised her hand. "Dr. Sava, I'm an elementary school principal in this county. Is the NAESP helping to solve the problems you've defined?"

"Kim, NAESP has been helping to define the qualities of an effective elementary school. We have to know what a quality school and an effective principal look like before we can transform American education. Because principals have the key leadership role, we've produced a workbook that identifies the basic knowledge and skills that principals need for effective leadership. For example, this tool assesses advanced teaching and learning; practical application of child development; curriculum development and instructional strategies. Principals also need a solid background in liberal arts, and a deep commitment to children's welfare and progress. It is widely used as a standard for judging performance of elementary and middle school principals.[7] With this basic foundation, effective principals must be trained in such leadership skills as communication; group process; team performance; organizational, fiscal and political management; and evaluation. Principals also need skills in curriculum and instruction.

"Our national association has also produced a workbook that identifies the characteristics of high-quality elementary and middle schools. It combines the findings of effective schooling with the practical, on-site experience of K-8 principals.[8] Let me go over the highlights of what quality schools include:

1. **Organization**—A quality school has a written statement of its mission and goals that is disseminated widely at least annually. The statement should be developed cooperatively by the staff and school community, and it should guide planning and assessment of the school's educational objectives and activities. The underlying philosophy should be reflected in both instructional and non-instructional practices;

2. **Leadership**—The principal is directly involved in every aspect of the school's operations, and is the primary figure in determining the school's quality and character. The principal's values, beliefs, and personal characteristics inspire people to accomplish the school's mission. The principal demonstrates leadership skills that help the school to reach its goals and accomplish its mission. The principal shares responsibility with all members of the school community;

3. **Curriculum and Instruction**—The principal in a quality school guides the instructional program toward the achievement of clearly-defined curricular goals and objectives. An established curriculum framework provides direction for teaching and learning. A common core of learning provides children with knowledge, skills, and understanding to function effectively in a global society. That core is supported by adequate financial and material resources. Effective instructional practices are essential to accomplishing the school's mission;

4. **Staff Development**—Staff development in a quality school is the key to effective teaching and improved student performance. An

effective staff development program is designed to further the school's mission and goals. The staff recognizes the need for continuing professional development activities that promote personal growth;

5. **School Climate**—School climate is made up of school qualities that affect the attitudes, behavior, and achievement of the people involved in its operation—students, staff, parents, and members of the community. The school's environment emphasizes the worth of individuals and encourages development of their capabilities; and

6. **Assessment**—A quality school continually assesses its programs, student achievement and staff performance. It uses assessment data to improve school programs. It assesses students based on their achievement of objectives defined by the common core of learning. It assesses all staff members using a fair and systematic procedure."

"Dr. Sava," Paul asked, "how do you feel about school-site councils?"

"Paul, we should transfer resources to the school site because that's where the students are being educated. We haven't figured out how to do this efficiently yet. State and federal regulations show a lack of trust in local educators and parents. The result is that most reform activities end up failing. This demoralizes school-site educators—principals and teachers. When educators become discouraged and quit trying, it's the students who suffer."

"You've given us much to think about today, Sam," said Wendy. "Thanks for coming.

"Our next guest is Dr. Anne L. Bryant, executive director of the National School Boards Association (NSBA).[9] She was recruited from the American Association of University Women, where she was Executive Director for 10 years. NSBA, a 57-year-old organization, is a federation of 53 state and territorial school boards' associations. Welcome to our Hearings, Anne. Could you begin by telling us two or three lessons you've been learning about school reform since you joined NSBA?"

"Thank you, Wendy. I'm new to the school reform business. We decided to rethink and redefine the roles, objectives, priorities, and vision for NSBA in the 21st century. What we've discovered is consistent with your theme— empowering your community school. First, we must engage the public in figuring out what their schools should be. We need a vision for each school district and its schools. We should make schools the centerpiece of the community. Second, we must become effective advocates in bringing together business and community people, teachers, administrators, parents, and students—and then align the power of the community on behalf of raising the performance of all students. Third, NSBA must continue our leadership role in the use of technology for improving teaching and learning and in making education decision-makers more effective.[10] Finally, NSBA will become a primary source for reliable educational research and information."

"What do you see as obstacles to reaching these new goals?" Debbie asked.

"We've been slow to learn that one model doesn't fit all communities," said Anne. "Reformers have not measured a program's impact on students and schools. We haven't been very effective in helping the public understand the challenges of school reform. It makes parents nervous when educators and school board members don't know if a reform model is going to work. Good research which measures the results of a reform is what parents and school boards need. Parents don't want us experimenting with their children. School boards represent parents.

"Our student bodies are very different from those 30 or more years ago. There's more poverty, more broken homes, and more single parents, with far more multi-cultural and multi-lingual backgrounds along with special education challenges. We face more violence, and serious drug and abuse problems. With these tidal waves sweeping over our schools, it's a very impressive accomplishment that we've been able to keep student achievement scores stable. But clearly we have new challenges if we are to improve student performance. We have to implement high academic standards, prepare a better-trained teaching force, and recruit and train more effective school boards. Reforming schools takes time. Boards must communicate that message to community parents, and other citizens, who are the taxpayers."

"Well, as a teacher, I don't see the value of school boards," said Ted Alexander. "They seem to be just one more layer of bureaucracy that adds more rules to make a teacher's life more miserable."

"I'm sure some boards do overstep their responsibilities, but the majority are mindful of their role as governors, not managers, of the district," said Dr. Bryant. "They interfere with management of the school district. School boards should stay out of the business of managing. School boards are part of our American democracy. They were designed originally to act as trustees in overseeing the work of professional educators. They look at the big picture and ask the right questions: How does a new education practice affect the school, the educators, the parents, the students? Will it benefit the whole school community? State school board associations provide training which helps focus on their primary roles. Boards need to lead, set policy, hire superintendents to manage, and hold schools accountable. They should help create a vision for what schools should be for the community and provide the resources. Then they should get out of the way so that the education professionals and parents can educate the children."

"But, Dr. Bryant," said Dale, "I hear that school boards are the greatest obstacle to the school-cite council movement. They don't want to delegate their authority."

"I think this is an old stereotype, Dale. School board members are responsible for making sure that local schools have the talent and skills to make school policy. They are responsible to manage their resources effectively, and to demonstrate through objective assessments that all students are learning at high levels. The local school board is responsible to collaborate in meeting these educational challenges. But it takes trusted and skilled people at all levels to find just the right balance of roles, responsibilities and accountability to make school-site councils work for the benefit of students, teachers and parents.

"School boards should become leaders in decentralizing authority and they will when they can be shown that this model is a practical alternative to our present struggling system. Then school boards—as district-wide, policy-making trustees of the community—will focus their time and energy on holding school-site officials responsible for day-to-day management of more effective public schools."

"Dr. Bryant," said Ray, "I'm curious. How does the National School Boards Association provide reliable education research and information?" Ray Gonzales, chair of the Commission, spoke from his experience as vice-chair of the county school board.

"Thanks, Ray, I appreciate that question. I'm impressed that your County School Board initiated leadership of this Citizens' Commission. First, through our 53 state and territorial associations, we deliver literally thousands of training and outreach programs to local school boards all year long.

At the national level, we do original research and publications which will augment these activities. Now let me suggest an example—NSBA has just published, *Character Education in the Classroom: How America's School Boards Are Promoting Values and Virtues.* We believe this kind of information is a useful tool to bring communities together around significant educational issues that have divided them in the past.

"Thank you for listening and good luck. We'll be looking for your final report on elementary school reform."[11]

"Thank you for coming, Dr. Bryant," said Wendy. "We appreciate you sharing your views on how a national association can help empower a community school.

"We'll turn now to our next topic—educational technology.[12] Dr. Howard Mehlinger is Director of the Center for Excellence in Education at Indiana University, where he is also Professor of Education and History. Howard, welcome to the Citizens' Commission.[13] In addition, you wrote *School Reform in the Information Age.* You've also designed and built a state of the art technology center at Indiana University for training teachers and school district personnel."[14] Turning to the group, he said, "Here's another BEST PRACTICES handout that describes his University's Center."

"Howard, tell us what school reform lessons you've learned as they relate to technology."

"Thank you, Wendy, and members of the Commission. My first lesson is this—school reform takes time. It's slow. It's hard to turn a system around when you're changing the way people think, the way they approach their job, even their culture. Schools serve a conservation function rather than a transforming one. That's why our visions of school are so limited, and why schools find it so hard to change. Schools change as society changes. The Information Age technology is having a profound effect on the ways we live; it cannot help but alter the way we conduct schooling. We need to imagine just what kind of a school would take full advantage of technology. Then we should take the necessary steps to create such schools. Technology is the key to a new school vision. It's not that we should worship technology, but we should use it to get where we want to go. Technology will help us permit students to work at their own pace, learn far greater knowledge, and enjoy the process more. We need a new vision of technology to make that possible. We need money to implement the vision. In the process, technology will change the total operation, structure and culture of the school.

"After 15 years and a massive investment in computers and other technology, relatively few schools are really equipped for the job. We are preparing teachers without the knowledge and skills they need to use technology. Teachers who lack this training will continue to instruct, and they are already employed in the schools.[15] That is the bad news. The good news is that about half of the teachers are using computers at home. This will help them see the possibilities for classroom teaching and student learning. Then they'll press for the latest technology.

"My second lesson is that we have been too optimistic in thinking that pilot school demonstrations are easily transferable to other schools. This is the cookie-cutter approach. The pilots' range of adaptations in American schools is almost limitless. A big barrier is our motivation and ability to adapt. If it doesn't deal with teacher/student interaction, the reform will fail. Reforms that outsiders and superintendents and principals put on teachers usually fail. The local teachers know that outside reformers and mobile superintendents will leave, and that principals will be transferred. The resister only needs to wait it out, and the reform will go away. Local teachers have to be involved right from the start.

"Not many new reforms are actually implemented. The community, as well as all district personnel, must be sold on the proposed change. Most school reforms offer 'cheap' solutions that cost little money to adopt and have little impact. In contrast, enormous amounts of money will have to be spent on rewiring and equipping schools, and additional money must be devoted to staff training.

"American culture is being rapidly transformed by technology, and schools need to catch up. President Clinton has launched his technology initiative and, at the most recent Summit in New York, the governors committed themselves to connecting schools to the internet. The money is actually not that much—estimated at about $120 billion over the next ten years—about one-fifth of the cost of bailing out our Savings and Loans institutions. It's not yet clear that Americans want new kinds of schools badly enough to pay for them."

BEST PRACTICES: TECHNOLOGY FOR TEACHING CENTER[16]

The Indiana University Center for Excellence in Education (CEE) was founded in the belief that information-age technologies will have a profound impact on teaching and learning. When used properly, these technologies can make instruction more powerful, more accessible and more adaptable. They also will change the institutions that provide instruction. In September 1992, CEE opened with a focused mission: to explore the appropriateness of technology for teaching and learning at all levels of education. Its goals:

- Operating a national demonstration program that enables visitors to view and discuss existing applications of technology in a variety of education settings from preschool to corporate training;

- Developing and testing new instructional applications of technology, based upon demands from teachers, administrators and students;

- Providing training, mainly through distance learning, to increase the knowledge and competence of faculty, staff and administrators in the use of instructional technology.

The Center is housed in the new education building and is served by AT&T's SYSTIMAX Premises Distribution System, an integrated, comprehensive cabling system that handles all communications—voice, video and data—within the building as well as between it and other locations. The wiring system supports a video classroom, video conference room and two audio graphics suites, lighting and TV studios, computer labs, classrooms, offices and electronic information kiosks—all of which advance the transmission and reception of interactive voice, video and data to support educational research and training. The facility is wholly dedicated to the use of technology in education and training educators about how to use the technology.

In its first five months of operation, CEE received more than 1,000 visitors. A typical visit includes demonstrations focused on questions visitors have raised prior to their arrival, as well as "brainstorming" sessions which help the groups establish priorities and construct plans. The demonstration program encompasses visitor observations in classrooms, laboratories and the library; watching various technologies in use; consultations between visitors and individual faculty and staff; and interactive teleconferencing with experts from all over the United States.

"Dr. Mehlinger, just how could technology really drive school reform?" asked Ted Alexander.

"My school reform strategy, Ted, is to use technology as the carrot. We tell school district officials who see our Center to rethink what they really want to do. What kind of school do they want to be? What kind of learning opportunities do they really want to provide their students? We help to facilitate that discussion. After two days, they come up with a clearer vision of what's possible. Then they go back to their school and discuss it with their colleagues. In two or three months, they return and report. In the meantime, they develop team support and put together a needs assessment plan that tells their school how technology will improve their teaching and learning. Each plan will be different because each school is different.

"Then they have to design a tight proposal with budget requests for the superintendent and the board. The cultural change is a big one. They have to move concepts of teaching and learning from a print-based learning environment to a digital-based one. Printed books as the sole basis of instruction are passing away. Publishers now provide CD ROMS, video tapes, slides and games. The use of these will depend on how fast teachers adapt these new tools to their teaching practices. In the hands of a good teacher, they are so powerful."

"Thank you, Howard, for your insightful remarks." Looking at the group, Wendy said, "We also have for you another BEST PRACTICE—this one illustrates federal leadership in technology.

BEST PRACTICE: FEDERAL LEADERSHIP IN TECHNOLOGY EDUCATION[17]

Technology literacy—computing skills and the ability to use computers and other technology to improve learning, productivity, and performance—is the nation's 'new basic.' It is as fundamental to a person's ability to navigate through society as traditional skills like reading, writing, and arithmetic. Research shows that computers can enhance student achievement by improving basic skills; provide a more interesting, wide-variety of advanced multi-media interactive education; regularly assess student progress; prepare students for later job opportunities; provide individual student motivation; improve teacher skills; improve school administration and management; and increase family involvement in their children's education.

Yet, for the most part, these new technologies are not found in the nation's schools. Students make minimal use of new technologies for learning, typically employing them for only a few minutes a day. Indeed, the hard realities are that only 4% of schools have a computer for every five students (a ratio deemed adequate to allow regular use) and only 9% of classrooms are connected to the internet. *In schools with large concentrations of low-income students, the number is often lower.* Research and the experiences of schools in the forefront of the digital revolution underscore the enormous learning opportunities available through technology.

The federal investments in research and development in technology have paid huge dividends to education. The development of the microcomputer grew in part out of NASA's space exploration program in the 1960s and 1970s. The Department of Defense's Advanced Research Projects Agency began experimenting with computer networks in the 1950s, which led to the development of the Internet. The National Science Foundation enabled the Internet to form by expanding its reach and supporting research and development on networks. The Kurzweil machine, which converts written words into speech, was developed in part with the support of the U.S. Department of Education.

In his State of the Union address in January 1996, President Clinton called for a national partnership to ensure that every classroom is "connected to the information superhighway with computers and good software and well-trained teachers." On February 8, 1996, the President signed the Telecommunications Act of 1996, which will help ensure that every child in every classroom in America will be connected to the information superhighway—opening up worlds of knowledge and opportunities. And on February 15, 1996, President Clinton and Vice President Gore announced the Technology Literacy Challenge, including a $2 billion five-year federal contribution, that is designed to help states and private enterprise energize the nation to make young Americans technologically literate by the turn of the century. The challenge is for communities, private companies, state leaders, and individuals—including students and their families—to work together to reach the four technology goals:

Goal 1: All teachers in the nation will have the training and support they need to help students learn to use computers and the information superhighway. *Upgrading teacher training is key to integrating technology into classrooms and to increasing student learning.*

Goal 2: All teachers and students will have modern multimedia computers in their classrooms. *Computers become effective instructional tools only if they are readily accessible by students and teachers.*

Goal 3: Every classroom will be connected to the information superhighway.

Connections to networks, especially the Internet, multiply the power and usefulness of computers as learning tools by putting the best libraries, museums, and other research and cultural resources at our students' and teachers' fingertips.

Goal 4: Effective software and on-line learning resources will be an integral part of every school's curriculum. *Software and on-line learning resources can increase students' learning opportunities, but they must be high quality, engaging, and directly related to the school's curriculum.*

Estimates to carry out activities by state and local education agencies and individual schools to meet these goals amount to between $10 and $12 billion each year for the next 10 years. Schools alone cannot meet their needs for technology education. It will take a partnership of the private sector, states and local communities, higher education and foundations and the federal government to shoulder the financial burden of meeting these goals. The federal government's role is to provide the momentum to support state and local efforts by providing leadership, targeted funding, and support for activities that will catalyze national action. Our children's future, the future economic health of the nation, and the competence of America's future workforce depend on our meeting this challenge.

Summary

Wendy took over again. "We've had an impressive morning with our high-powered guests sharing their perspectives on how school reform can empower the school. Now we need to summarize their lessons learned and adapt them as we prepare our Reform Blueprint for one small school in our community—Jefferson Elementary. I need your help in this exercise. Who'd like to start with Ray Cortines?"

"I'll start," said Christina. "**I was impressed with Ray's comment that we should build on the school community's strengths. At Jefferson, we should draw strength from our ethnically-varied community. We should teach democracy and citizenship as we strive to teach high academic standards. We must invite all parents and community leaders to school. The school must recognize that parents need to feel accepted too. They may also need adult education to more effectively assist in the education of their children. We must build a school/ family/community partnership.**"

"**I'll take David Hornbeck's testimony?**" Paul said. "**He told us that school reform must be done boldly and should address all priorities at once. It's like a war against bureaucracy, cultural resistance and entrenched interest groups. His main point is that the bottom line is accountability for improving student performance. It should drive the enterprise and rewards should follow those teachers and schools who meet high-performance standards. I was also impressed with his 10-point model for improving system-wide school performance. He's an advocate of school-site decision-making, which he called school councils or school-improvement teams—with principals, teachers, parents and community representatives making the policy decisions. I believe his model provides guidelines for our final report and recommendations for Jefferson.**"

"I'd like to talk about Tom Payzant's testimony," said Maria. "Tom talked about becoming sensitive to our changing, diverse population. We've been acting like Jefferson should be run as it was 30 years ago when the student body and the teachers were mostly Caucasian. He thinks we should go for high academic standards for all children. He says that strict accountability for results is important, and parents have to be involved in decision-making. Dr. Payzant also called for creating multi-service facilities for students on campus. "

Kim spoke up next. "Dr. Sava was concerned for how our reforms are distorting children's learning opportunities. We're overloading our teachers. We are not facing up to the challenges of our multicultural students. He's right when he says that it won't help if Congress or state legislators or the governor mandates another reform program but don't provide the money to carry it out. His national association focuses on the leadership role of the principal and the characteristics of a quality elementary school."

"I'll try to summarize Dr. Bryant's testimony, " Ray said. "I was impressed at how well Anne identified with school board members, even though she's been with NSBA less than a year. She started her tenure conducting a needs assessment of school board members. With that information, they designed a strategic plan with a new mission, goals and priorities for the national association. That's what we're doing right now with our Citizens' Commission on Reform of Jefferson Elementary School. She certainly made a case for keeping district school boards because they are the only ones who can bring together the whole community. I was pleased that NSBA is introducing character education to its membership."

"I was most impressed," said Ted, "by the way Dr. Mehlinger approached technology. First, he asked about the vision of teaching and learning we had for Jefferson. Most teachers aren't computer literate and haven't tried to work the new technology into the daily curriculum plans or teaching methods. President Clinton and Secretary Riley are trying to get money appropriated to help schools get on-line and students connected to the internet. We need to train all our teachers at Jefferson to use the new technology. Perhaps we need to send a team to meet with Dr. Mehlinger's Center at Indiana University."

"What a team!" said Wendy. "Those were good summaries. We'll feed the information directly into our final report and recommendations. Before we dismiss for lunch, Ray and Kim would like to make some Action Team assignments for our June Commission Meeting. During our final June meeting, we'll review Action Team proposals before finalizing recommendations to the County School Board on June 18."

Ray spoke up. "We have spent eight Commission Hearings listening to nationally-recognized school reformers who have carried out elementary school reform in local schools. It's clear that these experts know how to do it and that we can benefit from their experience. In order to draft recommendations for our final report, we've divided the Commission members into eight three-member teams. We'll call these Action Teams. This means that each of you will serve on two Action Teams. The first one will meet at lunch today, and the second one at lunch next month.

"We've appointed chairs of each Action Team, and the chairs will draft the Action Team's recommendations for presentation and discussion at our June 14 executive work session. Because we will have heard from our 44 experts, we believe that this Citizens' Commission can now produce a great Reform Blueprint for Jefferson. Kim, will you please announce the Action Team assignments?"

"Thank you, Ray," said Kim. "It's time for our own performance test. It'll take hard work and courage to get our recommendations enacted into policy. Be BOLD in your recommendations. Our Citizens' Commission Reform Blueprint will be the action plan for educators, parents and community members. We want to reclaim Jefferson Elementary School. Any questions?"

"I have a question," said Ted. "Just how were these assignments made?"

"Well," Kim replied, "it wasn't quite random. Ray and I listened carefully to the interests you have expressed in various topics of school reform. Of course, there are many tasks no one likes to do. So each of you gets a major assignment and a less interesting secondary one. We selected chairs who have strong motivation and skills. We tried to be sensitive to racial, ethnic and gender issues. But we can't please everybody. We tried to balance teachers, parents, and community representatives. We have more women than men on this Commission, so men have only two chair positions. We also tried to balance political perspectives as best we could.

"Our objective is to produce a final report that every Commissioner can approve." She slowly scanned the group, then continued, "If this Citizens'

Commission doesn't come through with a politically and educationally practical report that can be sold to the County Board and the community—Jefferson School will have to close. We are the last and best hope!

"Please take your work seriously and put aside petty differences. Be prepared to negotiate any clashes that might happen—for the good of all our children. We've differed among ourselves, but we're confident that when our unanimous recommendations reach the Board and public, the support we need will be there. This goes beyond conservatism or liberalism, progressive education or back-to-the-basics, phonics or whole language. It's time to stop experimenting on our children. We know what works and now it's time to act!"

"I'm sorry for the lecture, Ted. Did I answer your question?' Kim asked.

"Yes, and I appreciate your candor and openness," Ted replied. "I guess it's time to get serious and stop holding back. I do have some sharp differences with some of you. But I'll work constructively with everyone here to produce a consensus report. Ray, I hope your friends on the County Board will take this report seriously."

Ray nodded slowly. "If there are no further questions, the following Action Teams will meet today:—School Reform Council, Challenging Academic Standards, Character Education, and Professional Development to Improve Classroom Teaching. Ray Gonzales is Chair of the School Reform Council with Co-Chairs Maria Morales and Debbie Cohen. Our Academic Standards Action Team (ASAT) has Kim Su Young as Chair, Tamar Espinosa and Lenora Brown as Co-Chairs. The Character Education Action Team (CEAT) has Christina Peterson as Chair, with Dale Jones and Delores Williams as Co-Chairs. Our Professional Development Action Team (PDAT) has Kathie Sorenson as Chair, with Co-Chairs Tamar Espinosa and Dale Jones.

"During the next month, the Teams will draft their recommendations using the research we've reviewed and the testimonies from our expert witnesses. In our May meeting, the lunch hour will be devoted to the four remaining Action Teams: Parent and Community Engagement, Comprehensive Technology Services, Administrative Support Services, and Student Assessment and School Accountability. So let's get to work! See you all back by 1:30 p.m. today."

Chapter 15
EMPOWERING YOUR COMMUNITY SCHOOL, PART II
Saturday afternoon, April 19

"Welcome back. I hope you and your new Action Teams had a good lunch and a great planning session," said Wendy, as she called the group together. "This afternoon we have a distinguished panel of teacher union leaders—Al Shanker, president of the American Federation of Teachers (AFT);* Bob Chase, president of the National Education Association (NEA); and Helen Bernstein, former president of the United Teachers of Los Angeles.

Empowering the School Site: Classroom Teachers

"We'll hear first from Mr. Albert Shanker. He leads a 900,000-member teacher union where he's been elected president every two years since 1974. He founded Education International, a federation of some 20 million teachers from democratic countries around the world. His weekly article in the Sunday *New York Times*, 'Where We Stand,' and his advocacy activities make Al Shanker a household name. Al, start by telling us the two or three lessons you've learned about school reform."

"Thanks, Wendy, and members of the Citizens' Commission on School Reform.[1] Before I answer that question, let me say that I believe public education is the glue that has held this country together...[It] brought together

---

*On February 22, 1997, Al Shanker died after a long struggle with cancer—one of the few battles he ever lost. Many are calling Shanker the most dominant and influential force in public education over the past two decades. He will be remembered for his intellectual brilliance and tough-minded approach. He called for challenging national standards and honest public engagement over the future of public schools. Most of all, Al Shanker was a model of moral integrity in his support for unpopular causes like children's rights, civil rights and teacher professionalism. Following our interview with Shanker for this study, he personally edited his section of the final text—patiently answering our questions. All three authors are grateful to have know this giant of American public school reform.

children of different races, languages, religions and cultures and gave them a common language and a sense of common purpose. We have not outgrown our need for this; far from it.

"Today, Americans come from more different countries and speak more different languages than ever before. Whenever the problems connected with school reform seem especially tough, I think about this. I think about what public education gave me—a kid who couldn't even speak English when I entered first grade.

"I think about what it...can give to countless numbers of kids like me. And I know that keeping public education together is worth whatever effort it takes.[2]

"Everybody is trying to save public education these days. Voucher and privatization supporters say that they have the answer. The public education establishment is trying to save schools by saying that nothing is wrong, that it's a manufactured crisis and can be solved by better public relations.[3] Some reformers are pushing a 'do your own thing' approach with charter schools, and others are advocating innovations like de-tracking, interdisciplinary studies, restructured schools, and so forth. There is little evidence any of these things really work. Most parents and the public aren't buying this. The American people still support public schools, but they want to fix them so they won't have to abandon them. Parents, teachers, and the general public have different ideas from most reformers about what's wrong with the schools and how to fix them. They are frustrated that the schools are not delivering on their most legitimate and fundamental expectations—an orderly, disciplined environment for learning and high academic standards. Their patience is wearing thin. Their support of vouchers is increasing because public officials aren't listening to them.

"If we really want to save public schools, we need to look at what's troubling the public. In a democracy, if we think the public's right, we ought to give them what they want. If we think they're wrong, we need to convince them that they're wrong. We think the public is right about what our schools need, and we think they should get what they want. For that reason, the AFT has launched a national campaign which focuses on standards of conduct and standards for achievement. It's called *Lessons for Life: Responsibility, Respect, Results,* and it aims to make safe, orderly classrooms and higher academic standards a reality in all American schools.[4]

"Now let's talk about what lessons I've learned. The first is that we often try any idea that comes along, and they're often politically motivated, and then continue doing it even though the model program hasn't worked. Most reforms have actually never been implemented. Reformers, by and large, have not always been honest about how effective their programs are. They rarely acknowledge that what they're doing is still in the experimental stage. Most of them don't do careful evaluations. Sometimes these reformers don't really understand change and how schools and systems work. They've never taught in public schools, and they use models that have not been widely implemented. This leads to public cynicism that hurts genuine efforts to improve schools.

"Vouchers are a good example of this. Has this market-will-save-us, private-enterprise scheme been tried? The voucher experiment in Milwaukee involved about 1,000 children a year for five years. It's the largest one so far. It has done nothing to improve either achievement of individual students or of the whole system.[5] Four schools in its voucher program for low-income students have shut their doors—about a 25% market failure rate. Was this because of competition? No, it was bad financial management, and sometimes even corruption. When a small business fails, it's the owner who picks up the tab. When a voucher or charter school goes out of business, the taxpayer's money is thrown away. And, of course, the chief victims are the students. They are the ones who lose school time that cannot be replaced.[6] **The truth is that vouchers have never been shown to improve student achievement or school performance either in the U.S. or in any other successful system abroad. But voucher supporters have talked up their scheme for so long that some people think vouchers have been a big success. They haven't!**

"Let's spend our school reform energy on proven best practices that have already been tried, and we know will work in real schools with real principals, teachers and parents. We will not be dazzled by the stars that bring in foundation money and publicity. Even after a long period of trial, they usually result in very marginal improvements that can't be replicated. If we're serious about reform, why don't we adapt the best practices of other countries who seem to be educating students at higher levels than we are.

"My second lesson has to do with national academic standards. If you don't know where you're going, you're not going to get there. The goal of public education at the end of the 20th century is to ensure that children of all backgrounds can master a demanding core curriculum. We want to prepare them to assume their civic and social responsibilities in a democratic society. They will have to compete in the global economy, and they must be able to benefit from higher education.[7] We must be able to say what students graduating from high school should have mastered—a certain level of reading, mathematics, writing, history, geography and so forth. Then you can map backwards and see what the youngster should be doing when he's 5, 6, 7, 8 and 9.

"Education is made up of building blocks. Where we don't realize this, we are destroying the education of our children. Schools or districts can't expect to educate children to high academic standards when teachers are allowed to do their own thing. We are the only country that believes in this educational anarchy. Other advanced industrial countries have systems that do, on average, a much better job with their students than ours. They all have four essential elements: discipline, rigorous state or national academic standards and curriculum, external assessments based on the curriculum, and incentives for students to work hard and achieve in school. How well their students do in school counts for getting into college or getting a good job. I'm not suggesting that we just copy these systems, we just need to adapt them to our circumstances. If they work, we have a moral obligation to do what we know works. There is no reason why a youngster should learn different English in California than in New York or Utah. The recent Summit of the Governors and CEOs in New York underscored our nation's need for high-quality academic standards and student incentives. We should honor the public's demands for standards, discipline, and improved student achievement, because they're right, and because we must restore public confidence in our schools. It's a slow process, but it has to happen."

"Thank you, Al," said Wendy. "As usual, we are impressed with your command of the school reform field and your talent for cutting to the bottom line. Now we are going to hear from Bob Chase, president of NEA with its 2.2 million members. Before being elected last summer, Bob served three terms as vice-president of NEA. He began as a social studies teacher in Danbury, Connecticut. Welcome to our Citizens' Commission. Our lead question is: What are two or three lessons that you've learned about school reform?"[8]

"Thank you, Wendy. It's a pleasure to meet with you today," said Bob. "I have the greatest respect for Al Shanker who is an internationally-recognized teacher union leader. I find it especially interesting that you are focusing on the local elementary school. Let me start with one absolute essential: Without meaningful community and parent involvement from the very beginning, school reform will not work.

"The second lesson I have learned is that school staff members must be part of the decision-making process in their own school. The power can't be imposed from the top down; it must be generated within guidelines by the school itself—the staff, community, administrators, teachers—all working collaboratively.

"My third lesson is that these things take time. People need to allow time before assessing school reform. Too often a plan is put into place and people want quantifiable results in six months or even six weeks. This just will not happen. If we are going to change a bureaucratic system, it takes time. People must be able to stay for the long haul. We have to take time planning, time for results to come in, and time for staff and community to learn to work together on things that will make the difference."

"Bob, besides taking time, what will keep us from carrying out activities learned from your three lessons?" asked Paul.

"Probably the greatest barrier is that we live in a culture that doesn't allow educators to take risks. But to make changes, people must be willing to do things differently—to take risks and make mistakes. Another problem is that we don't have the resources to do what we need to do. Sometimes more funding is needed, but sometimes we just need to reallocate or redirect funding and resources that are already there. We are spending lots of money on layers of bureaucracy. Those monies can be spent in activities that will directly enhance the learning opportunities for students rather than keep that bureaucracy in place. We need to take a hard look at how dollars are allocated and expended, before we seek additional funding sources.

"Sometimes those in authority are unwilling to give up or even to share some of that authority. This means that people give a lot of lip service to the idea of shared authority. But when it comes right down to it, they resent giving it up. They have worked too hard to get it. People don't understand that successful school reform depends on shared authority."

"I've always believed that unions are the biggest obstacles to school reform," Dale said. "Is NEA doing anything to contribute to school reform across the nation?"

"Dale, NEA has spent approximately $70 million at the local level plus technical assistance to local school districts in renewal efforts over the past 10 years. But very few people know what were doing in school reform. We haven't told the story very well."

"Bob, what are your personal priorities as NEA President for school reform?" asked Debbie.

"I think, Debbie, that NEA needs to focus on professional teacher development. The public sees NEA as an industrial-type union concerned only about collective bargaining over economic issues. Teachers have had the right to bargain collectively for about 30 years. Much time and energy has gone into traditional union-type activities. But now we also realize that we must become involved in producing a product or service that represents our best—issues that craft unions have traditionally advocated. We have a responsibility to be the best teachers that we can be. This means that we must develop the professional side of our work. We must be more like a craft union, where the workers have to get retooled periodically. We need higher academic standards to help us actually improve our teaching performance."

"Do you support the school-site councils?" asked Kathie.

"Yes. We think they're a natural outgrowth of charter schools, which we favor if they can become accountable to the public.[9] You know from our NEA newsletters that we want our teachers to become equal partners in school reforms, like school-site councils, as long as people don't try to pay for that reform by cutting teachers' salaries. Many school districts right now have waivers to decentralize to school sites within certain parameters. Local union leaders, like Roger Urstin, executive director of our affiliate in Seattle, are experimenting with a contract that is only five or six pages rather than 40-100 pages as in some jurisdictions. In Columbus, Ohio, John Grossman is pioneering a program of peer assessment that will become a model to help teachers become better prepared and trained to teach in our new schools.

"I'd simply like to point out that many NEA local leaders are active participants in school reform. We want to make certain that these reforms are fair to teachers and include them as full partners from the beginning. We're working very hard within our own headquarters to reorganize ourselves to provide more effective technical assistance for our local affiliates. Effective school reform must include teachers as full partners with administrators and parents. We're proud of the Teacher Union Reform Network (TURN) of progressive union leaders from 21 teacher unions in urban areas."

"Thank you, Bob, for giving us a better picture of NEA participation in reform activities. Good luck on your new leadership role with NEA."

Nate introduced the third member of the teacher union panel. "Helen Bernstein is a teacher organizer at the grassroots level in Los Angeles School District, where I was a high school science teacher.[10] She is Director of the TURN Project at UCLA that brings together progressive union leaders who are charting a new leadership course for teacher unions in school districts throughout the United States.* Helen was a teacher and counselor, and President of the United Teachers Association of Los Angeles from 1990-96. Could you begin by telling us two or three lessons you've learned from your work in the teachers' union?"

"Thank you, Nate. The first lesson is that reform is far harder and more time consuming than I ever imagined. Without adequate time and money, it's impossible. You don't necessarily need new time and money, but you have to be able to reallocate the resources you already have. Teachers must be able to collaborate, or it will never happen! The second lesson is that adults must move beyond the adult issues to the real issues of children. If they can't do that, nothing will happen. Teachers must represent the children's best interests. Teacher unions have been organized around an industrial model of collective bargaining because schools are organized around a factory model. Until schools can be reorganized around productive learning models, teacher unions are frozen in place.

"We are a relatively new union. Teacher union collective bargaining is only about 25 years old in Los Angeles. Before then, working conditions for many teachers were intolerable. Now teacher unions must expand their involvement beyond traditional trade union issues. For example, take professional development. We can now rapidly communicate with every

---

*Helen Bernstein was killed in an automobile accident on April 3, 1997. Helen's heart, passion and vision were always inspired by what was best for children and their teachers. We will miss her courageous spirit.

teacher. In about 10 days, we can talk with 32,000 teachers. Once each month, we make tapes to communicate with all classroom teachers. School districts and superintendents can't do that because of all the layers of bureaucracy."

"I have two questions," said Paul. "My business friends in Los Angeles were surprised at the role you played in the LEARN Project. Could you describe it for us? My second question is this—is it true that teacher unions are against school-site management because it weakens the general contract?"

"Well, Paul, I can only speak from my own experience. When Los Angeles Educational Alliance for Restructuring Now (LEARN) was getting organized in Los Angeles, teachers were asked by the district to cut their wages by 17.5%! This led to protracted negotiations over wages. With all that coverage, I felt that we also needed to show the public that teachers care about teaching and learning. We needed to take an aggressive stand in favor of school reform. We spoke to hundreds of school faculties and gathered information which has contributed to organizing 300 LEARN schools. Today LEARN schools are becoming a success in Los Angeles because of the teacher union.

"I was part of the three-member teacher union team back in 1989 that negotiated agreements calling for school-site management which included teachers as full partners with administrators. We recognized, however, that school reform is dead without the money and time for professional development of teachers so that they can learn new skills and collaborate with fellow teachers. The auto industry learned that participation of front-line workers in all decisions made for better products. I know some people are turned off by associating high-quality products and high student performance. The principle is still the same. So why would school reform at the school site be any different? Our union leadership in Los Angeles pushed state legislation calling for peer review with strong accountability measures, but we insisted on due process! We have a vested interest in making sure that good teaching is going on in every classroom."

"Helen," said Ray, "I'm getting a very different picture of union leadership from you than I had before."

"Any group—whether parents, administrators, board members, or governors—have entirely different leadership objectives. Many union leaders are still stuck in the idea that their only role is to protect jobs and to bargain only on economic issues. Because of this attitude, the public image of unions is one of defending the status quo. It's a self-serving image. Of course, the same thing could be said of administrators, board members and parents. You may be surprised to learn that a new teacher union leadership cadre is now emerging across the nation. It is helping to organize high-performing schools. It is pushing for active and positive contributions from teachers in grassroots, school-site management. It is also advocating professional teacher development, parent involvement and collaborative decision-making by administrators and teachers. I am speaking of TURN, a loose association of 21 teacher unions that represents a significant number of teachers and students in urban areas. A grant from Pew Charitable Trusts helped us form this association to demonstrate a new style of teacher union leadership. We wanted to change our public image from one of blocking local school and classroom reform to one of contributing to reform. So far, TURN has been working in such urban centers as Seattle, Washington; Rochester, New York; Dade County, Florida; and New York City."

Nate stepped in. "Thanks, Helen, you've given us much to ponder. Your comments are very encouraging for our work here at Jefferson Elementary School.

Empowering the School Site: State Education Officers

"What a great time we're having today!" said Nate. "Our guests have been insightful. They're giving us some real-world reality checks. Now I'd like to introduce a man I've known for some time—a former superintendent of a school district in New York and two school districts in southern California. He was superintendent of the San Diego County Schools before being selected to implement the first comprehensive state reform in Kentucky. Please welcome Dr. Thomas Boysen to our Commission."

"Thank you, Nate. I haven't seen you for a long time. I'll start by responding to the question you've asked the other guests—what lessons have I learned about reform.[11]

"The first lesson is this—we have no hope of preparing our children for the 21st century if we don't have clear standards, effective assessment and meaningful accountability. My first teaching experience was in Kenya in 1964. The students in this rural high school knew they had to study hard to pass the Cambridge School Certification Examination, and it was tough. At the end of the year, they took the exam and shipped it back to England for grading. Nearly every student passed! The students, their parents and their new teacher were all convinced that education is serious business with standards, assessment and consequences. In the United States, we haven't learned that lesson yet. Kentucky is an exception since they passed school reform legislation in 1990. The Kentucky Education Reform Act (KERA) was a comprehensive strategy to change the total education culture through standards, assessments and accountability. It's still intact, and it's working! Virtually nothing has been taken out. So you see, we do know how to do it!

"The second lesson I've learned is that you can't implement serious reform without the voluntary participation of all administrators, teachers and parents. This seems to fly in the face of what was mandated by the Kentucky courts in 1989 and then passed by the state legislature in 1990. The enacted legislation was a general strategy with incentives for local schools to figure out how to carry out reform in their community. The key leverage point in bringing about community participation is the local school councils. These councils consist of three teachers, two parents and the principal—the people in the best position to know the needs of the students. The legislation shifted the decision-making authority and responsibility from state government, school boards, and school district offices to local school councils. The school councils humanize and counterbalance the strong state standards-assessment-accountability program. You must have both levels involved. The state reform package provided the propulsion system, and the local councils provided the guidance system. We invited school districts to apply for the federal Goals 2000 money and tell us how they were going to involve parents. Most of this money was used for parent involvement.

"We also involved teachers by rewarding them for improving total school performance. Some 40% of our teachers got rewards averaging $1,500. But, much to my surprise, 50 schools actually went backwards. Their student scores fell. That would seem almost impossible to do. What we learned from that shows the importance of involvement. Schools that went backwards did not accept ownership of the problem. They blamed it on everyone else but the teachers. They refused responsibility for discussions about making improvements. They complained and moaned. In successful schools, teachers and parents took charge of their school and worked together to implement KERA. A promising start has been made by courageous legislators, educators, teachers and parents, but much yet needs to be done. They are actually changing the culture and improving education for all students in Kentucky. I enjoyed being a part of that experience."

"Dr. Boysen," said Tamar. "What do you say to critics who claim your reform experience is not typical? They say the state supreme court forced the legislature to completely design a new school system from the ground up."

"Well, I'm always puzzled by this. If the court forces a state to completely reform its education system, then somehow that experience is discounted because it's too easy or not as challenging as in some places. I'll answer with two points. Yes, it's a great help if the court forces a state to start over. I believe that state courts all over the U.S. will be declaring education systems unconstitutional because of unequal financing and expenditures between districts. In that respect, Kentucky should be a model. The next point is this. Totally organizing and launching a new state education system from the ground up is a challenge that more people should try before judging how easy it is."

"Thanks, Tom, for sharing your provocative views," said Nate. "We've described the Kentucky experience in our next BEST PRACTICES.

"Our next guest this afternoon is Dr. Nancy Grasmick, Maryland State Superintendent of Schools since 1991. She was Special Secretary for Children, Youth, and Families until 1995. She is the first woman and the only person to ever hold two cabinet positions at the same time in Maryland state government. Nancy has been a special education teacher for deaf children, a principal, and an associate Superintendent in the Baltimore County Public School System. Maryland and Kentucky are the only two states that have implemented statewide school reform for at least five years and have had dramatic results. Before we get into the nationally-recognized Maryland School Performance Assessment Program (MSPAP), Nancy, please give us the two or three most important lessons you've learned about school reform."[12]

"Nate, Chairman Gonzales and members of the Citizens' Commission. I'll start by saying that in Maryland we are carrying out a new renaissance in our public schools. We're proud of our students, teachers, administrators and parents. They are our state treasures, as precious to us as our Chesapeake Bay. But, like all states and communities, we face major challenges.

BEST PRACTICES: KENTUCKY EDUCATION REFORM[13]

In 1989 the Kentucky Supreme Court declared the whole state system of public schools unconstitutional and ordered the General Assembly to create an "efficient system of common schools" as required by the Kentucky Constitution. The governor and General Assembly formed a 22-member Task Force on Education Reform. In 1990 the Kentucky General Assembly enacted the Kentucky Education Reform Act (KERA). In January 1991 Dr. Thomas C. Boysen was selected as the state's first appointed Commissioner of Education, responsible for implementing the new reform act. The State Department of Education was first abolished and then totally reorganized in July 1991. By 1994-95 it was downsized with three bureaus: Management and Support Services, Learning Results Services and Learning Support Services. Two independent agencies, the Education Professional Standards Board and the Office of Education Accountability, were established. The State Board of Education was also given authority to remove school district board members and superintendents who were not performing effectively and to provide financial and leadership assistance for their recovery. The legislature also established a financial program (SEEK) designed to equalize funding for all students between the state's 176 school districts. Kentucky's school budget from all sources for the 1994-95 school year was $3.3 billion.

The Kentucky Education Reform was designed to challenge those responsible for improving the performance of schools: the state department of education, local schools boards, school administrators, teachers, parents and students. The new Act provided a new system of performance-based tests for students and held teachers, administrators, and local school districts responsible for steadily improving student performance on those tests. For those who succeeded the accountability system provided rewards; for those who failed, immediate state assistance and eventually sanctions were provided. Three new programs were introduced—a statewide preschool program for at-risk four-year-old children, extended school services for students needing extra help, and family resource/youth services centers to provide families access to social and health services—that targeted new resources toward students who needed them most. Extra funding was provided for special-needs children and at-risk students of all ages. From 1990 to 1994, state and local revenue was increased by 39%.

Schools were given important new tools. Through school-based decision making, the authority and responsibility for the most important decisions affecting learning was shifted away from state government, school boards, and school district offices to school councils consisting of teachers, parents, and the principal, the people in the best position to know the needs of students. In October 1994 a survey was conducted that found 62.5% of teachers, 70.2% of parents and 81.2% of principals rated school-based decision making as "excellent" or "good."

Professional development opportunities available to teachers were greatly expanded, and teachers were given a greater voice in selecting the training that would benefit their students the most. A statewide technology program is rapidly bringing state-of-the-art, worldwide educational resources into classrooms for the benefit of students and teachers. Primary schools removed artificial barriers to learning for some youngsters while giving others additional time to succeed. The state assessment system provided writing and mathematics portfolio programs and reading from real literature that have focused attention on the 3 Rs. In five years, this re-created Kentucky public school system has begun to produce the results envisioned by the Kentucky General Assembly in 1990. To accomplish these results Kentucky focused on: What do our youngsters need to know and be able to do by the time they graduate from high school? What resources and tools does state government need to provide to districts and schools to ensure achievement? What changes do the schools, teachers, and parents need to make to become more effective in preparing all students to become successful adults? How can districts and schools be held accountable for improving student achievement?

Between 1992 and 1994, student academic achievement in reading, writing, mathematics, science, and social studies increased by 19%. The percent of students performing at the two highest levels (proficient and distinguished) nearly doubled, while the proportion performing at the lowest level (novice) declined from nearly half (48%) to one third (34.8%). Fully 95% of the schools raised the level of their students' academic performance, and 38% of all schools and 24 % of all districts improved enough to earn state rewards. The high school graduation rate reached 70% for the first time in the state's history. And, in 1994 the number of graduates who successfully entered college or the work force increased to 93.9%.

We need to reform each of our 1200 local schools for the benefit of every child.

This well groomed, confident and attractive blond woman is obviously experienced in appearing before public groups, Debbie thought.

"The first lesson I'd like to mention is that whatever the reform initiative is, it must be linked to real children in real classrooms. That's the only way that teachers, parents, local superintendents, local central offices, or local school boards will take it seriously. Many researchers or critics of public education sound as though they're talking about schools with no children. They're more concerned with benefits for the adults. You hear about taxpayers, teachers, reformers or politicians. But we don't deal with the real circumstances our young people face in the workplace. That's why I insisted on building the strong alliance with the corporate community. Education is the single most important factor that will enable students to be productive in the world of work. This applies equally to whether they are high school, community college or college graduates.

"The second lesson I've learned is that you have to build strong political support, or hard won victories will be swept away with every change in leadership of governors and legislators. The leaders change frequently in and out of the political arena. For example, 50% of the nation's state superintendents were turned out of office in the Republican Revolution. Each new leader needs to have ownership of the successful programs. Again the lesson here is that unless you pay attention to building a broad base of political support—even the very best school reform program cannot survive the realities of changing leadership.

"That has happened in Maryland. Governor Schaeffer laid a great foundation. When our new Governor Glendenning came to office, he was helped to understand the value of our education reform program by the persuasive leaders of our state Business Roundtable who'd supported our serious reform progress over the years. This governor is now a strong advocate for school reform. We also had the benefit of stability in the legislative leadership. They let political candidates know of their united bipartisan support for Maryland's reforms. This support also includes local superintendents, boards of education and parents.

"My third lesson is that high academic standards and assessments are the heart and soul of the accountability system. When we began developing our academic programs, we tried to set world class standards. I went to Taiwan and Germany to be certain that we were doing real international bench-marking. We designed developmentally-appropriate assessments of these academic standards targeted to what a student should know and be able to do in grades 3, 5, and 8. We wanted them to think critically, solve problems, and work both independently and in groups. We wanted them to be able to combine knowledge and skills from different subjects, and to communicate clearly both orally and in writing. This focus on educational excellence is paying off. A recent study showed that Maryland now ranks thirteenth in SAT scores; another study ranks Maryland fourth among states in the number of students taking and passing the Advanced Placement tests.[14]

"The final lesson I've learned is that we must involve teachers in scoring the statewide assessment tests. This encourages their ownership of the program and improvement of their own teaching. Last summer about 500 teachers participated in this professional development opportunity. As paid scorers, they were supervised by an expert contractor. We found that teachers as scorers had the highest validation of any scoring practice in the country. These teachers became our disciples and were determined to improve their practices and to spread the word to their colleagues.

"As a result of this experience, we have looked very hard at professional development for teachers. Now every teacher in the state of Maryland is required to have professional development plans, which must relate to daily responsibilities in the classroom. We redid our re-certification requirements. We now have an alternative route for certification for teachers, where specialists from other fields in the Washington, D.C. area can enter a master's program in teaching at several participating universities. We are also working closely with our State Secretary of Higher Education to redesign teacher education in the colleges and universities and require that future teachers major in a content specialty as an undergraduate. We are also trying to impress our local school districts that we expect every school to teach to high standards. We've set up a Student Outcome Achievement Report to trace back to their high school when any student requires remedial work to attend college. The report helps the school to understand how their students are doing in college."

"Dr. Grasmick," said Paul. "I'm very impressed with your sweeping statewide school reform program. It seems that you've tied together the annual assessment, challenging academic standards and professional teacher development activities. I wish we'd had your reforms working in our state. If we had, this Citizens' Reform Commission would not be sitting here, would we? What happens to schools in Maryland that don't improve? I read something in *The Washington Post* about some schools in Baltimore where 60% of students never graduate. They have been placed on a reconstitution list. Can you tell us about this?"

"Yes, Paul, an important part of accountability is that all children must receive high-quality education in our state. We make no exceptions! The State Board of Education has adopted a policy for non-performing schools called reconstitution. The possibility of state intervention is one motivator for school improvement. By each January 15, the State Superintendent must notify school systems which of their local schools are distant from state standards or declining. These schools are eligible for reconstitution.[15] By March 15, the school system will respond with a local reconstitution proposal which sets forth the framework in which the school needs to make major improvements. The Maryland Board of Education must approve this proposal, and the local system then must submit a transition plan with specific activities and deadlines for the coming year. By the following February 1, a long-term plan for the school is due to the State Board. The plan may include changes in administrators, staff, organization and instructional program."

"What is the role of the school improvement team then in your reform program?" Ray asked.

"MSPAP requires each school to have a school improvement team in place. It's composed of at least school staff, parents and business and community representatives. It's responsible for studying the school's report card and crafting a measurable and reasonable plan. Maryland has enlisted the support of local school systems by setting up local Technical Assistance Support Teams to monitor and support school planning.

"In low-performing schools, where problems are compounded and all the more intractable, the challenges of planning are often magnified. Also in low-performing schools, the State Department of Education has provided leadership training to hundreds of teachers, administrators, school improvement team members, and local school district personnel. The training helps them set improvement goals, use data to identify performance problems, and find strategies to turn the school around.[16]

"Dr. Grasmick," Maria asked, "where do parents fit into your strategy for school reform?"

"We believe deeply in parent partnerships with our schools, Maria. We will not approve a local school improvement program without the active participation of parents. This year we're making parent participation a major goal. We've made special efforts to keep our parents informed about the MSPAP. We've been able to avoid the destructive debates on school reform that occurred in Pennsylvania and Virginia over outcome-based education. In Maryland we talk about results-oriented education and performance assessment. We have prototypes of all the assessments now. We have a very sophisticated group of parents, so we've been learning about them through focus groups and by visiting local schools. We sit down with parents and actually go through the assessments with them and with their children. We've spent time with real parents in real schools with real children, and we've tried to build a level of confidence. We're using community groups like the Urban League to train trainers in helping parents. They even go into their homes when necessary. We've developed a strong partnership with the National Council of Jewish Women focusing on the parents of young children in a program called Maryland Cares. We are working with private foundations to develop programs of public engagement."[17]

"Nancy, where do you stand on the question of charter schools?" asked Dale. "I'm sure you wouldn't entertain the voucher concept that I favor— or at least I did before we talked about it. But now I'm an advocate of charter schools, because I still don't trust public educators. No offense."

"Well, first, let me say that our Maryland school reform includes all public schools. Each one must show evidence that they are getting better every year. Our goal is to raise 70% of our students to satisfactory standards by the year 2000. Last year we were more than half-way there with about 40%. But the tough work is still ahead—especially with our disadvantaged students concentrated in urban and rural schools. Our Legislature has not yet passed charter school legislation, probably because the energy of the legislature and State Board of Education has been focused on our revolutionary state assessment program. But my position is that if there is a sound proposal, this Board would probably endorse it, and we would work in conjunction with the local board of education. There hasn't been a lot of motivation for charter schools in Maryland. We don't prohibit them, but we just believe that reforming a whole state is more powerful than one-at-a-time, small experiments here and there.

"I see that my time is up. Thank you so much for letting me share our progress on school reform. We are interested in looking at your final recommendations. You're considering some of the nation's most impressive models for reform. If I can assist, please call on me. In the meantime, I've brought a BEST PRACTICES handout for you describing MSPAP."

Wendy stepped in. "Thank you, Nancy, for sharing your exciting reforms in Maryland, I had no idea how far you've come.

"Our next guest, Christopher Cross, works closely with Dr. Grasmick. I'll introduce him next. He is President of the Maryland State School Board. Chris is also the President of the Council for Basic Education. He is the former Director of the Education Initiative for the Business Roundtable, and was Assistant Secretary of Education Research and Improvement, U.S. Department of Education. Welcome, Chris."

BEST PRACTICES: MARYLAND SCHOOL PERFORMANCE ASSESSMENT PROGRAM (MSPAP)

In 1991 Maryland rejected the traditional approach to testing and launched MSPAP, keystone of the state's broader plan to improve student and school performance. The assessment is based on academic standards that spell out what is expected of students. The underlying belief is that assessment against high achievement levels will elevate curriculum and instruction for all students. Dr. Richard Bavaria of the Baltimore County Public Schools said, "For years, testing students has been like driving to a destination by looking out the back window of the car to see how far we've come. MSPAP is like looking ahead, through the windshield, to see how far we must go before we reach our destination."

The Maryland performance assessments are a new breed of measures. They typically ask students to answer questions in writing and do tasks individually and in groups. Instead of multiple choice, students are expected to write extended answers. Instead of repeating memorized historical facts or mathematical formulas, students are expected to explain events, analyze situations and solve problems. They are tested in reading, writing, language usage, mathematics, science and social studies. Tasks may focus on one subject or integrate disciplines.

In the past, most tests used in this country have been multiple-choice or fill-in-the-blank. Almost all tests were norm-referenced, meaning that scores showed how a student's effort compared with others. Because these "minimum competency" tests were norm-referenced, it was possible for every state to be "above the national average."

Teacher participation and professional development is critical to MSPAP. Teachers work as teams to create assessments, devise scoring guidelines, and score tests in consultation with education department personnel. When teachers are involved in the process, they begin to think differently and to assess the strengths and weaknesses of their own teaching. They see achievement trends across the state and become less defensive about their students' performance. They have an opportunity to buy into the process, rather than initially reject it.

Students in third, fifth and eighth grades are assigned randomly to groups in their schools. These are performance-based "criterion-referenced" tests, meaning that scores reflect the number of right answers rather than how the individual student's effort compared with that of someone else. The assessment measures school performance not individual student performance. The state is piloting a plan to determine the most accurate way of presenting parents with meaningful information on how individual children are progressing.

In the first two years, the program resulted in great resistance. Some teachers were frustrated by the poor fit between their beliefs and practices and the new model of instruction and assessment. Many complained of inadequate training to administer tests, unfamiliarity with materials received just prior to testing, and, in some cases, faulty test questions. Some feared that this type of assessment would lead to standardization of the curriculum and "teaching to the test." Early results were poor. Nearly every school in the state failed to reach satisfactory scores. Critics charged that tests were too hard, or not age-appropriate—anything but admit that the old "feel-good" tests had concealed a generation of educational mediocrity.

Teachers' support for the assessments increased markedly in 1994 and 1995 after the state corrected early problems with test administration, provided more training related to the assessments, and gave teachers earlier access to the test materials each year. From 1994 through 1996, isolated improvements in test performance spread to statewide improvements. For example, improvements in the percentage of fifth grade students scoring at "satisfactory" have moved from 32.1% in 1993 and 35.3% in 1994 to 38.4% in 1995 and 42.8% in 1996. Eighth graders moved from 31.9% in 1993 and 37.3% in 1994 to 41.0% in 1995 and 41.8% in 1996.

Maryland continues advancing steadily to meet the high standards of the new assessments. The 1996 Report Card reveals significant progress over 1994 and 1995 performance both on the state level and among Maryland's 24 school systems. Most schools are becoming successful. For example, in 1993, 38 elementary schools approached or met the fifth grade reading standard. By 1996, 180 elementary schools reached that status. In every district, some schools have reached satisfactory performance levels. Maryland is now more than half way toward meeting its 70% MSPAP standard. This progress shows that what were once called "impossibly high expectations" can be reached by Maryland school children.

Maryland is learning that teaching to a good test tailored to state [and national] education goals can be a great help. Good instruction can be modeled through assessment, although assessment alone cannot do the job. Assessment is the bedrock. It provides data on whether or not students are making progress and, therefore, whether or not instructional strategies are working.

"Thank you, Wendy, and members of the Citizens' Commission. I'm glad to be here with Nancy Grasmick. We're fortunate that she is an effective executive and communicator. She's built confidence with the 24 county superintendents and she meets monthly to review policy and practice. She has also reached out to develop a strong system of business support—70 companies of the Business Roundtable. Unlike what happens in most states, she's also developed a partnership with our legislators to the point where they back Maryland's State Assessment Program. Our governors have also become strong advocates of the reform program."

"Chris, let's begin by asking you to define the mission and major activities of the Council for Basic Education."

"Wendy, the Council is an independent, nonprofit advocate for national education reform.[18] Its mission is to strengthen teaching and learning of the basic subjects. This includes English, history, government, geography, mathematics, the sciences, foreign languages, and the arts. We're trying to develop the capacity for lifelong learning and responsible citizenship. We carry out this mission by promoting high academic standards for all elementary and secondary school students. We want to provide educators with intellectually challenging professional development opportunities, which are designed to make them academic leaders in their schools and districts. We believe that high academic standards promote a healthy democracy.[19]

Debbie asked. "Didn't I hear that your organization helped get the history standards back on track?"

"Yes, Debbie, at the request of several of the leading foundations, we convened two blue-ribbon panels of historians and teachers—one for U.S. History, the other for World History. They conducted a balanced review of the standards and prepared recommendations to guide revisions, which were done by the UCLA Center for History in the Schools.[20] We've begun a multi-year project to provide clarity and coherence to the content standards prepared in several academic disciplines. We are producing a series of documents that clearly and succinctly present the standards. We want everyone—policymakers, school district officials, teachers, parents and students—to understand them and use them. We convened an international symposium on Criteria for a World Class Education at the Rockefeller Foundation Conference Center at Bellagio, Italy. We had representatives from Australia, France, Germany, Japan, Norway, the United Kingdom, and the United States.

"We're also doing things at the local level. We've been working with educators in the Los Angeles Unified School District and public schools in

Milwaukee, Wisconsin; Cleveland, Ohio; and Jackson, Mississippi. We're also working with business leaders in Virginia to develop high academic standards for students and teachers. We publish *Basic Education* and *Perspective* and give examples of rigorous academic standards and good teaching practices"(see Appendix B).

"Chris," said Wendy, "let me shift to the question we've been asking each guest reformer. What are two or three important lessons you've learned about reforming the nation's schools?"

"The first is that we need to have high academic standards for all children if we are going to have serious school reform. At the Council for Basic Education, we are committed to this strategy. The second lesson is that we have to reach out and really involve teachers, principals and parents. They've been neglected in the past. Most reforms have tried to change schools without really communicating with the teachers. Principals too have been forgotten. We talk to the superintendents, and we take teachers away for a workshop occasionally, but we forget the one leader who will make reform happen—the principal.

"I see that Sam Sava testified before your Commission this morning about the leadership role of the principal in school reform. Everything we know about leadership says that if the first-level manager is not committed to reform, it won't happen, or if it does happen, it's unlikely to last.

"As important as it is to involve teachers and principals, we'll fail if we don't engage parents. Educators often intimidate and confuse parents. We use jargon that means nothing to parents. Parents can help their children meet challenging academic standards if they know that kids are also being taught the fundamentals at school. Otherwise, parents just become suspicious of educators."

"Government can also be a barrier to school reform. There's still much confusion about who has the governing responsibility for the schools. Is it an independent, but highly political school board as in New York City, or perhaps the mayor's office as in Chicago? Or the Financial Control Board in Washington D.C.? Who is really in charge? Lack of clarity on this issue leads to paralysis, overreaching or meddling by the school board. Boards should remain in the policy oversight role, not interfere in management."

"Chris, what you're saying is true," Tamar said. "But tell us how you've been applying these ideas in Maryland?"

"In Maryland we have a very effective State School Board that meets one or two days each month. We work hard to review the policy and the actions of the state superintendent's office, but we're not in competition with the superintendent or the state legislature. We're not paid. No one has an office. We are true citizen, public-policy advocates. I'm told that we're among the most powerful boards in the country in terms of authority. Over the past three years, we've identified 42 schools for the reconstitution process. We plan to turn these schools around and to require that educators assist all of Maryland's students to meet challenging academic standards. We have standards already in grades three, five, and eight. We're now working on challenging standards for high school graduation. Students will have to pass certain examinations before they can graduate.

"My third lesson about school reform is the necessity of providing serious classroom-based professional development for teachers. We have upgraded their skills to teach the more demanding academic standards that teachers will have to master. We are effectively using the new educational technology now flooding the classrooms. When a school district announces it is going to invest in technology, the budget should include up-front, 20% for teacher training. For the past 30 years, teachers have seen too many promises. They have a right to be skeptical about the wonders of technology. You can't create a new standards program without training the teachers to meet them. Teachers must be retooled with new software. We've learned hard lessons from the American automobile industry about training front-line workers to be competitive. Why should education be any different?"

"Thanks for meeting with us today, Chris," said Wendy. "Now, I want to turn the time back to Nate to lead our Commission members in summarizing what they've heard from our guests this afternoon. Nate?"

Summary

"Thank you, Wendy. What have we learned this afternoon that applies to empowering our school? Who'll start?"

"I know you'll think it kinda' strange," Dale volunteered, **"but I was totally blown away by Al Shanker's testimony. I'll have to admit that I've never met a teacher union official. I'm now wondering if my hero, Rush Limbaugh, has ever met one either. Mr. Shanker destroyed all the arguments I've ever heard about vouchers. He calls for a plan to fix pub-**

lic schools by implementing no-nonsense national standards. He sort of demolishes the objections I've been carrying around. I think I'm finally convinced we do need academic standards for math, science, English and social studies. We can't have it one way in Mississippi and another way in Virginia. He's very tough on insisting that teachers get trained and take responsibility for teaching high standards and be held accountable for results. I'm blown away!" he said, shaking his head.

"Bob Chase is my man," said Delores. "He stressed the importance of meaningful teacher and staff, community and parent involvement. He pointed out that you need to reform bureaucracies and change our cultural mindset. I was surprised at how many school reform activities NEA is doing, like advocating strong charter schools and school-site decision-making. Bob's interest in craft unionism should make NEA a real leader."

"I'll try to summarize Helen's testimony," said Tamar. "I was surprised to learn that a cadre of new teacher union leaders is interested in promoting school reform. They will strengthen local school-site management. They're in favor of professional development, peer review of all teachers, and they want teachers to be accountable. I'm glad teacher unions will support merit pay. But I'm going to find out more about the TURN group of 21 teacher unions. These progressive union leaders are going beyond traditional economic, collective-bargaining issues."

"Since I grew up in San Diego," said Kathie, "that's where Dr. Boysen was superintendent of the county schools, I'd like to summarize his testimony. The Kentucky Education Reform was really comprehensive. I think it's our first state example of clear standards and the idea of assessment tied to accountability. As a teacher, I'm glad to see incentives tied to improved performance. I learned that one state actually has operating school-site councils, and students across the state seem to be learning more. I'm impressed."

Debbie offered to summarize Dr. Grasmick's testimony. "I learned that Maryland has a five-year start on reforming its schools. Two governors, the legislature and the State Department of Education have all cooperated in this. They have a solid state assessment model on-line. They're half-way to their goal: Maryland wants to have 70% of the students meeting demanding academic standards. This shows what can be done with good political leadership. Teachers are gradually accepting ownership of the standards and assessment program. Much needs to be done still. We need more parent understanding and community partnership involvement, more functioning school-site councils—but at least now someone's showing that what we've been learning this past year about school reform can be done in a planned professional way. We need to develop ways to report individual student achievement in the assessments. I was also impressed that Maryland has taken its obligation seriously in the reconstitution process. It's what we're trying to do on this Commission with Jefferson Elementary!"

"I'll take Christopher Cross," said Christina. "Chris described the work of the Council for Basic Education. He emphasizes teaching and learning of basic subjects through development and promotion of high academic standards. He emphasizes the importance of a healthy democracy, and the effective use of technology in schools. He focuses on the principal, along with teacher development and parent participation. His leadership of the Maryland State Board of Education supports the pioneering work of statewide comprehensive school reform. Along with Kentucky, Maryland has the most comprehensive state reform in the nation today.

The Commission Chair, Ray Gonzales, spoke next. "This was an excellent summary! Thank you. I hope you saw the differences between these practitioners' approaches compared with the school reformers we've heard. For the past seven months, we heard about designing and implementing reform models from those who demonstrate them in schools across America. Next month, we'll look at how education impacts personal and family income and life style and how national education policy affects school reform. That will be our last Hearing before we prepare our final report. See you next month."

Chapter 16
EDUCATIONAL ACHIEVEMENT AND ECONOMIC CONSEQUENCES

Saturday morning, May 24

Kathie Sorensen pulled into a parking space in front of Jefferson Elementary School. *It seems longer than four weeks since we last met, she thought. I thought about the Commission a lot. I didn't know that economics and education were so related. But now that we're becoming a global knowledge economy, I can see that education will become far more important to everyone!*

The other Jefferson teachers are quizzing me like crazy about what's going on. They have real anxiety. They're even afraid of losing their jobs. I wonder how it will affect me? I guess I can always go back to teaching a fifth-grade gifted class as I did before volunteering to teach here. I thought dealing with parents at the other school was hard. But I had quite a few interested and informed parents to deal with, even if some were a pain. What a contrast! Most of these parents don't know and don't seem to care what's happening to their children. I'm starting to feel like a failure as a teacher!

"Please take your coffee or juice to your seats," Ray Gonzales was speaking. "Let's start our ninth Hearing of the Citizens' Commission on School Reform. I hope you survived the past four weeks. The Spring flowers are everywhere and it looks like the garden spot of America. I hope you enjoyed your reading. I feel like I'm in school again. I'm looking forward to today's discussion. Nate Johnson, our able consultant-leader, will overview our subject—the contribution of education to economic productivity. Nate?"

"Thanks, Ray. This morning I hope to convince you that the key to personal and family economic survival is quality education for all children. We're trying to understand how a malfunctioning school like Jefferson is a microcosm of the larger society and its problems. We need to fully grasp what failing schools mean to our national economic productivity and future economic growth. Until we understand the global knowledge economic competition that America faces, we won't know the kind of education our children need for the 21st Century. That's just three years from now. Some women define economics and business as men's work! As long as you believe this, men will continue to control society's rewards—the serious money and power of American society.

Education and Economic Productivity: Personal Consequences

"We don't realize this, but an earthquake has swept the entire world. Within the last 10 years, our lifestyle has been transformed. We now live in an information-based global knowledge economy. This means that in every community throughout America, 80% of what we produce—our goods and services—has competition internationally. In advanced nations, knowledge now drives productivity. For most of this century, oil and money powered the world's industrial economy. We are no longer an industrial economy, but a global knowledge economy. Knowledge drives hi-tech agriculture, manufacturing, financial, health and most other service sectors. **In America today, knowledge represents the main cost, the most valuable investment, and the key service.**[1]

"Knowledge knows no boundaries. It is portable, and it's not tied to any country. It can be created anywhere, anytime, any place. Knowledge is different from the resources traditionally measured by economists: land, labor and capital. Knowledge is by definition always changing. We're now dealing with the market forces of the world economy, rather than national economy. In the future, individuals and nations will have to acquire and apply knowledge resources to keep their competitive standing.

"The largest workforce of professional, managerial and technical people ever employed in the U.S. and other modern nations now make their living by providing knowledge services. Information workers grew from 42% to almost 60% of the workforce during the last 30 years (see Figure 16.1 on *Employment by Major Economic Sector: 1800-1993, The Rise of the Knowledge Economy*). In the next five years, over half of the new jobs will be knowledge-based. The fastest growing occupations will bring higher pay and will require employees with advanced math, language and reasoning capabilities. This will be far greater than what most of our sons and daughters

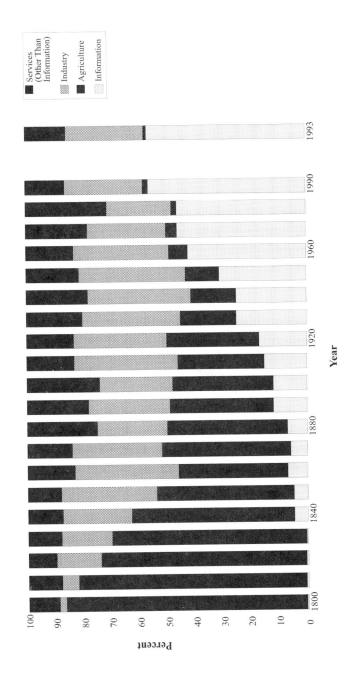

Figure 16.1

Employment By Major Economic Sector: 1900-1993

Source: Adapted from James R. Beniger (1986) and Baumol, Blackman and Wolff (1989) and updated by Knowledge Network

are now learning in public schools. Most of them won't have competitive knowledge."

"Just what does that mean?" asked Ted. "I'm confused."

"Well, I think the best definition of **competitive knowledge is, 'informa-tion disciplined by responsible personal and civic values, then skillfully applied to improving the quality of life for self, family and others.'** If we acquire competitive knowledge through our education, we are preparing ourselves to become life-long learners, responsible parents, accountable citizens, informed consumers and productive workers."

"That's still a little abstract," said Ted.

"Well, I'm really saying, Ted, that our children **who are failing in public schools today are victims of an undeclared war against ignorance. For whatever reasons, they are not being educated with the knowledge and skills necessary to be competitive in this new national and world economy. They are the neglected social and economic casualties of tomorrow.**

Educational Achievement and Personal Economic Rewards

"Unlike the past, knowledge can be acquired only through formal schooling, and not always in the school building. Our global competitors are nations with strong public education systems. Their national governments invest their scarce public dollars in the race to develop knowledge workers. They see their workers as their national wealth. Peter Drucker says, 'Education will become the center of the knowledge society, and the school its key institution...' The performance of the schools and their basic values will increasingly concern society as a whole. Everyone will have to be concerned. We can't leave it to the educators alone.[2] Research consistently shows that the higher the number of knowledge workers, the higher an industry's rate of technological progress.

"Competitive knowledge is becoming the capital upon which tomorrow's investments depend. In other words, the educated person with competitive knowledge will be at the core of our society. That person carries, creates, improves knowledge, uses or misuses it, teaches and passes it on. Competitive knowledge is more than just technical or professional training; it is based on social values and basic academic skills learned through an integrated education in the humanities, arts and sciences. Building on this foundation, an individual must develop the perspective and strategic thinking abilities necessary to earn a good living.

"We know now that investment in education leads to greater economic productivity and a higher standard of living for individuals and the nation.[3] **In 1992 the average annual earnings for those with a bachelor's degree were almost twice those with only a high school diploma, and more than two-and-a-half times greater than those who had not graduated from high school (see Figure 16.2** *Average Annual Earnings by Level of Education).* **Those who completed a graduate professional degree earned six times as much as a high school dropout, and four times as much as a high school graduate. In the 1990s, nine-out-of-ten new jobs (89 %) will require some form of post secondary education."**

Nate's really getting warmed up now, thought Ray.

Maria spoke up. "I'm not following you, Nate. Can you simplify this so I can explain it to my teenage son? Why should he graduate from high school, let alone go on to college?"

"Perhaps this example will help, Maria," said Nate. "By quitting after high school graduation, your son will likely make $50 per day (in 1995 dollars) the rest of his life. Or he can stay in school four more years, graduate from college and make about $100 per day. But by going on to get a professional degree, your son is likely to earn $225 per day. The average lifetime earnings of a college graduate is $1,420,000 as compared to $3,010,000 earned by a graduate with a professional degree—more than twice as much.[4] This means that highly educated people with competitive knowledge are earning far more than those with a high school education because of our hi-tech workplace."

"Wait a minute, Nate!" Maria Morales was agitated. "Are you telling me that my kid can't support a family without a college education?"

"Yes, that's exactly what I'm saying. It's economic survival. Of course, it's up to you and your children to make these decisions. But you understand that a high school diploma is really not enough preparation to support a family. In 1973, 60% of young men under age 24 were earning enough to support a family of three above the poverty level. By 1990, only 34% could do the same.* In 1991 real entry wages paid to male high school

---

*Current economic analysis cannot measure the quality of education, individual motivation, discipline and responsibility that affect individual performance in school and the workplace and gradually develop a competitive workforce. These are averages only—remember half the population actually will do worse.

Figure 16.2

Average Annual Earnings by Level of Education
1992

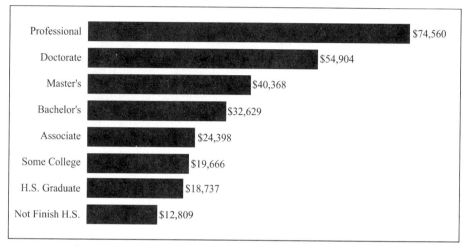

Professional	$74,560
Doctorate	$54,904
Master's	$40,368
Bachelor's	$32,629
Associate	$24,398
Some College	$19,666
H.S. Graduate	$18,737
Not Finish H.S.	$12,809

Source: U.S. Bureau of the Census (1994)

graduates were 26.5% lower than their counterparts received in 1979, even though the number of low-skill jobs has expanded dramatically.

"One other fact, Maria," Nate said, "is that Hispanic immigrants arriving in the late 1970s received wages half the level of Native Americans; and by 1990, their wages were still about half, while the wages of Asian and European immigrants were catching up or exceeding American-born workers.[5] Second generation Hispanic immigrants have a higher dropout rate than first generation.[6] If you want your children to escape poverty and get better jobs, they need to get a college education and, if possible, postgraduate training. What do you think about this, Ray?"

"Nate, you're absolutely right. My family are immigrants to Texas. My parents were fanatic about education. They made us learn fluent English. They helped set my sights on becoming a lawyer so I would have the respect of my own people, as well as Anglos. So my family would never go hungry! The formula worked for me, and it will work for my children. I think a top education is the only way out for minorities. Just look closely at the poorest Asians—the boat people. They arrived in this country in the 1970s and 1980s without being able to speak English.[7] Their children have gone right through the terrible urban public school systems and become the strongest students. Many have become the best of the college and professional school graduates. Their children won't live in poverty under the crippling effects of discrimination. These Asian parents bring with them a culture that highly values education. They instill that drive for education in their children. Until Hispanics and African-American families discover this, our people are going to continue to cry racism and discrimination— while living wasted lives in poverty and rage."

"But I want my children to keep the old culture and the old language!" Maria said.

"Yes," said Ray, "but they can still be taught to respect the Mexican culture and speak Spanish. But that is a private family decision. I'm simply saying that they won't escape poverty until they learn English and get a high-quality education. This is their new birthright—that's why you immigrated to America, isn't it?

"Maria, I can see that this is a very emotional issue for you," said Nate. "But the link between education and earning power is clear. According to the government's Current Population Survey, the family income of a typical American with a college diploma increased 28% in inflation-adjusted dollars from 1975 to 1994, while incomes of high school graduates increased just 3%. Meanwhile, the incomes of those without a high school diploma shrank by more than 10%. In the last 20 years, 60% of families have seen their incomes fall."[8]

"We have been in the 'vicious cycle,'" Nate continued, "where poor education performance leads to lower worker productivity, less income, and reduced tax receipts. This leads to cutbacks in education investment. We need to move into the 'virtuous cycle,' where quality education leads to higher skills and productivity, and greater income. The more people earn, the more taxes they pay, and the greater funding for education of our children. One Nobel Prize economist has said, '…growth requires an educated and trained labor force, since production of computers, other electronics, and most manufactured goods and services needs knowledgeable workers. An economy grows faster when rates of return on investments in human capital [people] increases, or when the amount invested expands.'[9]

"It's time to break," Nate said. "When we come back we'll look at the effect of education on our everyday standard of living. Can we afford to spend more money on education or are we already spending too much? You might also want to look at this handout on Myth: American taxpayers spend more money educating public school students than our competitors."

MYTH: American taxpayers spend more money educating public school students than our competitors.

All American taxpayers support public schools by paying individual federal, state and local income, corporate, property or sales taxes. Voters and elected public officials decide the spending priorities. If adequately financed and properly managed, public school investments can offer the greatest economic return for all American taxpayers—individually and nationally. Three barriers, however, are preventing us from achieving the maximum economic and educational returns from our investments.

FINDING A: *All American students do not receive the same level of financial support because of differences in state and local expenditures.* For example, in the 1989-90 school year, per pupil expenditures ranged from $8,000 in New Jersey to less than $3,000 in Utah. Nationwide, expenditures also vary substantially between districts, ranging from less than $2,000 per pupil to more than $20,000. On average, the wealthiest districts, in terms of household income, contribute 16% more revenue per student than the poorest districts after adjustment for cost-of-living. In addition, low-poverty school districts receive 20% more revenue for schools than high-poverty districts.[10] In the next five years, by the year 2000, 40 % of the public school population will be children of immigrant, minority or poor families, who attend increasingly segregated high-poverty schools. Inequitable education financial support results in 50% or more of our future citizens not acquiring the knowledge and skills to be responsible citizens and productive workers. The economic bottom line is that if they do not receive an equal education, they will be dependents of the state, not productive taxpayers.

FINDING B: *Present expenditures for public elementary and secondary education for our heterogeneous population of students—those who are immigrants, with disabilities or disruptive—are inadequate to bring them up to the achievement levels of our competitor nation's students.* Ninety percent of all Americans have attended K-12 public schools. The academic achievement scores of U.S. high school graduates are consistently below those of international competitors. In 1992 the U.S. spent 4.1 % of its Gross Domestic Product (GDP) on public elementary and secondary schooling (approximately $6,000 on average per student each year). Other modern nations spending a higher percentage than the U.S. are Denmark, Norway, Portugal and Sweden—nations with relatively homogeneous student populations. England, New Zealand and Ireland have about the same GDP expenditures for public education as the U.S.

Our objective is to prepare our students to achieve equal or greater performance than those in competitor nations. We want them to be individually and nationally competitive. This will require an investment strategy for reforming our primary and secondary schools that exceeds the expenditures of other countries. In addition to years of neglect; we have a more diverse population, with growing numbers of disadvantaged children and students with disabilities. Students with disabilities, for example, represent 12% of our student population with an average per pupil expenditure of $14,000. This means that the other 88% of our students have almost one-fifth less to spend on their education. We also spend more for student disruptions. For example, the New York City school security force is the second largest police force in New York state.

FINDING C: *Competitor nations' elementary and secondary investments are more effective than U.S. public school investments.* It will take additional investment, beyond what other competitor nations are spending per student, to bring our greater number of disadvantaged and immigrant students up to acceptable academic performance. This is because we have permitted our inner-city schools to deteriorate physically and because these schools have greater numbers of high-poverty students' who are performing poorly.

FINDING D: *Only by investing money in more productive schools can the gap between performance of American students and those of our competitors be closed.* Investing more money in poorly performing public schools will not produce better students. Most American schools should undertake major reform programs to significantly improve all students academic performance and character education.

FINDING E: *Some have argued that Americans cannot afford to invest more money in reforming their public schools today because of their heavy tax burden.* Since 1973 the total tax burden of American taxpayers has held constant at between 29% and 31%. In 1994 the average person paid a 30.7% tax rate (19.9% federal and 10.8% state and local). As a percentage of GDP, U.S. taxpayers had the fourth *lowest* burden of 24 modern nations. We can afford it!

****

Educational Investment and National Economic Growth:
Family Consequences

Nate called the group to order. "Welcome back. Contrary to what some say, the U.S. is not losing its industrial competitiveness. Between 1970 and 1987, the United States actually increased its share of manufacturing output by 1% compared to other advanced countries.[11] But **evidence shows that other competitors are catching up**. In countries with comparable levels of education, productivity is converging. By 1990, for example, Japan achieved 77% of U.S. productivity and Germany 79%.[12] Then, for the next five years, the world-wide recession slowed the productivity growth of all modern nations, masking the impact of education on productivity.

"The foundation of economic competitiveness is investment in human capital or people. Every citizen has a direct stake in our nation's economic productivity. Between 1948 and 1973, productivity (GDP) improved about 3.25% each year. From 1973 through the 1980s, however, our national productivity declined to about 2.25% each year. This means that each American lost about $28,000 in potential earnings.[13] Historically, human capital investment has grown relatively faster than physical capital investment. Between 1929 and 1990, at least 60% of the business sector's productivity growth can be traced to investments in education, training, health and mobility. Today, we find that investments in human capital—people who demonstrate **competitive knowledge**—account for greater productivity increases than all other public or private investment strategies combined (see Figure 16.3 *Components Fueling U.S. Domestic Economic Growth*)![14]

"After WWII, Japan recognized that investment in human capital or its citizens is the foundation of economic competitiveness. So with no other natural resources, they built a K-12 education system that now graduates 92% of its children, prepares high school graduates to meet world-class knowledge standards, and to be bilingual in Japanese and English.

"Between 1970 and 1990, American productivity suffered. Our traditional U.S. markets were seized by foreign competitors who produced better products at lower prices. Our 500 largest industrial companies created no additional jobs. Today companies are downsizing and laying off obsolete employees. By the year 2000, semiskilled, blue-collar manufacturing workers will be only 10% of our workforce. Those with agricultural jobs will dwindle

Figure 16.3

Components Fueling U.S. Domestic Economic Growth

1929 to 1998

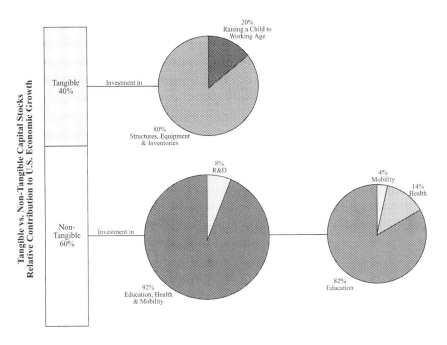

Source: Adapted from recent work by John W. Kendrick, Total Capital and Economic Growth (March 1994)

to 3%. Workers are looking at two new types of employment that have emerged—stagnant, labor-intensive personal services and highly-productive, information services. Meanwhile, both men and women work longer hours and more days each year just to maintain their eroding standard of living.[15] In 1989 the average wife worked 36% more hours than in 1979.[16] More women are employed at higher levels than ever before.

"Our public education system in the United States functions as a gatekeeper. It decides who, how, and how many of our children will become competitive in the new global economy. Do any of you have questions before we look at components fueling U.S. domestic economic growth?" asked Nate.

Ted Alexander was frustrated. "As a teacher at Jefferson, I've never really seen a clear relationship between education and standard of living. I've always believed that a good education was its own reward, a good civilized life. I resent the idea that the main purpose of education is to create workers in the global knowledge economy!

"All we hear these days is the middle-class complaining about job insecurity and declining standard of living. Our political leaders tell us that the economy looks strong, inflation is down, and the stock market has never been better. But my wife, Jan, and I both work full-time. It seems the harder we work, the behinder we get. Now it looks like our married children will be back on our doorstep because they can't make a decent living. One son was just downsized from a middle-management job at IBM. How can this happen?"

"Ted, you're caught in a middle-class squeeze," said Nate. "Between 1973 and 1993, the value of real wages corrected for inflation declined for men of all ages, industries, occupations and education groups.[17] For example, if full-time, year-round working men earned $34,048 in 1973, by 1993, it was only worth $30,407, a 11% drop. At the same time, the real per capita GDP was rising 29%.[18] Let's look at Table 16.4 which shows the value of wages of White men declined even more (14 %). It gets worse in your age category, Ted. Male college graduates between 45 and 54 years old, their peak earning years, endured almost **one-third reduction in median earnings. For the past two years, their wages have gotten steadily worse**. The bottom line is that, during these 20 years, everyone's wages actually declined in value, except for the top 20% of the workforce. It was these individuals with the highest skills and frequently the most postgraduate professional degrees whose incomes rose by 10%.

"During that same 20 years, from 1973 to 1993, the young and less educated experienced the biggest hits. Those workers 25 to 34 years old took a 25% decline in real earnings. The percentage of men (ages 18 to 24), mostly high school graduates, earning less than $12,195 (1990s dollars) rose from 18% in 1979 to 40% in 1989. Real wages fell consistently while real productivity went up. In other words, America's real per capita GDP rose 33%, while real hourly wages fell 14%. If current trends continue, by the turn of the century, real wages will be below where they were in 1950, while the stock market and profits in many industries are at an all time high! **Many companies that are making large profits are also downsizing. Employees with highly-marketable knowledge and skills make the transition to new jobs and careers. But those with limited education and skills—without** marketable competitive knowledge—experience lower wages in their next job or unemployment in the global information-knowledge economy. The Committee on Economic Development concludes:[19]

> In a highly integrated global economy, a nation that falls behind in the education and training of its labor force will not remain a leading economic power. If the United States is to remain competitive while achieving satisfactory economic progress for its people, the reality of global integration requires that improvement in our education and training programs be given high priority in both government and private planning.

"Even though we think that the United States is a highly-educated country, only about one in four working Americans has a college degree. The ones with degrees were the only group to enjoy rising earnings during the 1980s. The wages fell for the other 75% of the population without college degrees. The gap between college graduates and everybody else is widening sharply.[20] In 1964 only 29% of the population said the country was run for the rich. By 1992, 80% were saying they thought the country was run for the rich.[21] Although most Americans are beginning to understand this reality, they have not yet tied their economic situation to their level of education.

"At the top of America's economic ladder are those with wealth and high skills—the greatest advantage in today's economy. The next level is an upper echelon of highly-skilled, highly-educated professionals who are doing quite well. Semiskilled and unskilled workers are experiencing falling wages, declining living standards, and increasing economic uncertainty. Those with no wealth and low skills are joining a growing American underclass."

Now Ray was frustrated. "This is a pretty scary story! I thought the income decline was limited to high school dropouts and high school graduates. Now I hear we all are affected except those in that upper 20% with competitive knowledge gained by earning graduate or professional degrees. I thought when wives went to work, most of our families could at least hold their own."

"During the past 20 years, Ray, the decline of men's income was partially offset by wives going to work (see Table 16.4)," said Nate. "But in the fu-

Table 16.4
CHANGES IN REAL WAGES AND INCOMES
1973-1992

Quintiles	Males Year-Round Full-Time Workers (Wages)	Household (Incomes)
Bottom	-23%	-3%
Two	-21%	-3%
Three	-15%	-0.5%
Four	-10%	-6%
Top	+10%	+16%

Source: U.S. Bureau of the Census, *Current Population Reports, Consumer Income* (Washington, D.C.: Government Printing Office, 1973, 1992), pp.137, 148.

ture, a wife is unlikely to be able to offset her husband's declining wages, especially those in the bottom 60% of the earnings distribution. This is because most women are already working full-time.

"We are steadily dividing into haves and have nots. Let me show you how bad this really is. In 1979 the richest 5% of American families earned, on average, $137,482. By 1993 their income had risen to $177,518, an increase of 29.1%. The top 1% increased their income by 78%! The only way to counter this division is to increase the knowledge and skills of have nots through advanced educational opportunities.

"The reason that our European and Asian competitors have almost caught up with us is that for decades they have required high standards for all high school graduates. We have not. They have motivated students to excel in school by clearly connecting school curriculum with personal life and job requirements. We have not. They have learned that competitive knowledge in the marketplace comes from a good education. We have not. They have invested heavily in training and technology and have demanded high-level skills and productivity from their workers. We have not. From 1973 to 1993, our public education has failed to properly educate one half or more of our students. Most Americans are suffering the economic consequences."

National Education Policy: Business Expectations
of American Schools

Wendy took over. "Thanks, Nate. Your figures are sobering! Now we'd like to introduce Dr. Milton Goldberg, executive vice president of the National Alliance of Business (NAB).[22] Before coming to NAB, Milt had a distinguished career at the U.S. Department of Education. He served as Director of the staff that produced *A Nation At Risk*. He also was the Executive Director of the National Education Commission on Time and Learning, and was a principal and associate superintendent of schools. Could we begin by asking you, Dr. Goldberg, what are the two or three lessons you've learned about school reform."

"Chairman Gonzales, Wendy and members of the Citizens' Commission, I'm pleased to be here today. This takes me back almost fourteen years to the publication of *A Nation At Risk*. Education Secretary Terrel H. Bell asked our National Commission on Educational Excellence to bring to the public's attention the challenges we face in improving American schools. That report had such an impact.

"The first lesson I've learned is that nothing much will happen unless we have local ownership of reform. By this I mean the professionals who work in schools, the families of the children who attend the school, and the civic, business and political leadership in the community. They must coalesce and agree that change is necessary and what these changes are. Only then is improvement likely to happen. It's not who controls the change, but who owns the change. It takes more than a few people for an innovation to survive. Reform must be shared by a fairly large number of people inside and outside the school for it to endure after a dynamic leader has gone. School reform cannot be left to the educators alone. It's really a challenge for the whole community. Public school graduates are the community's workers, parents and taxpayers.

"The second lesson is that we're reaching national consensus on the need for challenging academic standards for all students, including those who are disadvantaged. We expect all children to learn, to know, and to do. Every school should be a demonstration school that challenges all students to higher standards. We cannot leave the developing and teaching of standards to each of 85,000 schools, or we'll have the wide range of academic performance we have today. It's our hope that all students will enter the world of work after high school, community college, graduate or professional school. The world of work is changing so rapidly that nobody will be successful without competitive knowledge. This is a life-long learning situation. We're committed to supporting those national grassroots reforms that prepare young people to be life-long students, responsible citizens and productive workers."

"Dr. Goldberg," said Dale, "how does the business community feel about the federal government interfering in our local schools? Surely you don't support a federal role in education!"

"Well, Dale, another lesson I learned is that there are very important leadership roles in education for the federal government, for business, and for national associations. Ted Bell at the U.S. Department of Education showed remarkable leadership when he formed the National Commission that authored A *Nation At Risk.* I know because I was the director of that Commission. The National Education Goals Panel and the National Assessment of Educational Progress have also contributed to the improvement of the nation's schools by providing research, information, financial resources and presidential-level leadership. National business, civic and educational association leadership is essential too. The governors' leadership has also moved reform ahead. We have a delicate balance in this country between local, state and national initiatives. Each level must boldly carry out its leadership functions. Each must overcome sometimes crippling local interests and provide every child in America with a quality education."

"What is the Business Coalition for Educational Reform?" Paul asked.

"NAB has convened major business groups like U.S. Chamber of Commerce, the Business Roundtable, the Committee for Economic Development, the National Association of Manufacturers, the Black Business Bureau, the Hispanic Chamber of Commerce, and many more. We meet monthly and speak with one voice about education reform. We represent 218,000 employers, and we provide support for a growing network of local and state coalitions that are helping schools and communities with school reform activities."

"Dr. Goldberg," Kathie spoke up. "You were also the director of the National Commission on Time and Learning. What did this Commission have to say?

"In our 1994 report, *Prisoners of Time,* we found five ingredients or myths that we call a recipe for 'slow motion social suicide' that we are experiencing today."[23] These myths contribute to the nation's continuing poor academic performance that the National Education Goals Panel report highlighted last Fall. The first myth is that all students arrive at school equally prepared to learn the same way, on the same schedule. This is simply not true. We recommend that every child in the United States be helped to achieve world-class standards in core academic subjects. The second myth is that time for extra-curricular and non-academic activities can be taken from academic time with no negative consequences. We recommend that schools reclaim the school day for academic instruction, at least 5.5 hours per day. The third myth is a nine-month school year that was designed for an agrarian economy is good enough for today's global economy. We recommend that schools stay open longer every day and that some schools in every district stay open throughout the year.

"The fourth myth is that schools can be transformed without giving teachers the time to retool, to reorganize and to prepare. We recommend that teachers be provided with professional time and opportunity to do their job. The final myth is that American students will be able to overcome their academic handicaps and surpass our competitor nations in the time allowed within the existing system. We recommend that schools seize on new technologies for increasing productivity, enhancing student achievement, and expanding learning time. We also recommend that all Americans take responsibility for transforming their schools and expanding student learning time and opportunities."

"Dr. Goldberg," Paul asked, "In the early 1990s, I heard that The Business Roundtable had identified nine essential components of a successful education system. Could you tell us what they are?"

"Yes, Paul. The BRT has committed to a 10-year effort to work with state policymakers and educators on restructuring state education systems and ensuring that all students achieve at high levels.[24] The first component is that a successful education system operates with these assumptions: (1) Every student can learn at significantly higher levels; (2) Every student can be taught successfully; (3) Every student and every preschool child needs an advocate—preferably a parent; and (4) high expectations for every student are reflected in curriculum content, though instructional strategies may vary.

"The next components of a successful system deal with a system being performance or outcome based, and using assessment strategies as strong and rich as the outcomes. They reward schools for success, help schools in trouble, and penalize schools for persistent or dramatic failure. Other components emphasize staff development and give staff a major role in making instructional decisions. The last points are providing high-quality prekindergarten programs, at least for every disadvantaged child, and providing health and other social services to reduce significant learning barriers. Finally, a successful system uses technology to raise student and teacher productivity and expand access to learning.

"Thank you so much, Milt, for your remarks today," said Nate. "I would like to hand out a BEST PRACTICES in school reform that illustrates some of the points you just made. It shows how business and community leadership can help reform urban schools. It is taking place in Los Angeles and is called LEARN.

BEST PRACTICES: LOS ANGELES EDUCATIONAL ALLIANCE FOR RESTRUCTURING NOW (LEARN) SCHOOL

James A. Foshay Learning Center, one of 650 schools in Los Angeles Unified School District, is located in south-central Los Angeles. The surrounding neighborhood reveals scars from the 1992 Los Angeles riots: bars and gates cover windows and doors of nearly every home, business and church. But Foshay has been dramatically transformed into a real "community school"—an oasis of safety—committed to providing a "world-class education" for 3200 inner-city students in K-12. Built in 1994, the elementary school that serves 200 children was built across from the original structure. Ninety-two percent receive free or reduced lunch. The student population is two-thirds Hispanic and one-third African American. The per pupil expenditure from the district is $2,900 with an additional $500 from federal Compensatory Education Programs, such as Title 1 and Bilingual.

In 1989 Principal Howard Lappin arrived to find test scores in reading and writing near the bottom of the state, and the school in danger of being taken over. "Our first step in turning this school around," Mr.

Lappin said, "was school-based management, which emphasizes joint decision making. It's effective, but not always smooth. Our 'School-Based Management Leadership Council' is made up of nine teachers, nine parents, two classified representatives, two clerks, two students, a bilingual coordinator, the union chapter chair and the principal. We meet two times a month to make policy decisions. That's where our school uniforms for elementary and middle school kids came from." For the first time, teachers and parents are involved and they've developed ownership of the change process. The Council has full authority over the budget, curriculum, teacher development, class size and mixing. (Although they do not have the authority to decide on teacher assignments, which is a contractual issue.)

Foshay's basic philosophy is that all children can learn, regardless of poverty, race or ability to speak English. The school emphasizes the basics—reading, writing, and arithmetic—and enriches the learning process with 'constructivist' hands-on activities and discovery. They are experimenting with a "seamless approach" to see the impact of having K-12 students in one functional setting.

Foshay's transformation into a Learning Center could not have happened without the groundwork laid by the Los Angeles Educational Partnership (LAEP), a nonprofit organization of good corporate citizens. In 1993 Foshay became part of the LEARN alliance of 89 innovative, courageous school communities. LEARN is a large-business-community coalition of private and public sector groups committed to improving Los Angeles City Schools.

As a LEARN campus, Foshay exemplifies a flexible, student-centered organization with a passion for results. It emphasizes team teaching of theme-based curriculum, which is infused with technology. This appeals to many innovative teachers. When Foshay expanded to K-12, one of the new arrivals was a sixth-grade teacher who had taught for 10 years. Angela Dotson explained, "I liked the technology, the fact that it was supposed to be an integral part of the curriculum, the school's commitment to the idea that all students can learn, … the focus on staff development." Staff and parent training provides "school community members" with the tools and skills to develop collaboratively their vision, mission, goals, objectives, performance measures, and action timelines.

Also in 1993 Foshay was selected as a model site for school reform and the New American Schools Development Corporation underwrote a collaborative project—between the Los Angeles Unified School District, its teachers' union and business sponsors—developed by the Los Angeles Learning Centers. Since then the Learning Centers pumped more than $1 million into the school for computer equipment and training. In 1994 Foshay invested money to send its teachers through an intensive 13-day technology training workshop. "We could have bought a lot of other things," said Lappin, "but it would have been a waste without staff development..." The purpose [of technology training] is not just to learn technology, [but] to develop an interdisciplinary curriculum and teams."

Inner-city kids come to school significantly behind. But they can and do succeed. Foshay supplements the learning process by tutoring after school on Mondays, Tuesdays, and Wednesdays until 7 p.m. All Saturday, they hold tutoring, remedial and enrichment classes for both students and parents. Foshay is partnering with social service providers to have a school-based health clinic to help families. They have created an active Parent Center to more effectively involve parents.

In 1996 Foshay was taken off the state's "at risk" schools. There is a genuine focus on meaningful measurement and understanding of student learning by using portfolios and tests where they must write as well as read. Standardized tests, however, are more difficult for these children, one third of whom are limited English proficient (LEP). In response, the school has developed an active, one-on-one tutoring program to help these children move ahead.

"The kids are doing better this year," stated Lappin. "In two years, scores on the California Test of Basic Skills have gone from the 15th percentile in reading, math, and language to the 30th percentile. Attendance is 97% and transcience has dropped from 80% to 60%." This multitrack, 'year-round' program is filled with active, involved, well-behaved students. "Next year we're expecting to become a 'Blue Ribbon School.' All our students will be winners." Howard Lappin was named California's 1997 Principal of the Year.

Summary

"We've now reached our noon hour," said Nate. "You've worked hard this morning. Sometimes the information has been mind-boggling.

"Let me start the wrap-up by summarizing your great presentation, Nate," Wendy said. **"In today's American economy, two out of every three workers are in knowledge occupations, rather than in industrial, service or agricultural jobs. Eighty percent of our goods and services are now facing international competition. The occupational literacy in this knowledge-based economy requires at least two years of postsecondary education. There are 20% of us who have postgraduate professional training, and we will make the most money. This means that education and training are the biggest factors in economic productivity. Our international competitors learned this before we did.**

"We also learned that the U.S. does not spend more money educating public school students than our competitors, when we take into account students with disabilities, our heterogeneous population, unequal financing and the educational gap experienced by our disadvantaged students. Finally, the standard of living is declining for all of us except the top 20% of our population. This means that the gap between haves and have-nots is widening in our country. Our nation's educational investments will not be adequate to sustain the high productivity, growth and standard of living that most Americans want."

I had no idea that education was so related to economic productivity, Paul Christopher thought. *I didn't realize the national education picture is such a disaster! The country is headed over the cliff, and we're asleep at the wheel. How can we possibly absorb the 50% of our students who are not prepared to make a decent living? That's about 20 million students who are headed for trouble. Unless we wake up soon, it'll be too late! Where are the president and the media?*

Debbie volunteered next. **"Dr. Goldberg said that to be successful, school reform must be owned by all parties in the school and civic community. Challenging academic standards must be expected of all students—not just those in the middle and upper classes. The national leadership, which includes federal, business, civic and educational associations, must join with governors and state officials. The new Business Coalition for Educational Reform provides a strong voice for 218,000 of the nation's businesses. Finally, the National Commission on Time and Learning recom-**

mends that state and local schools restructure their use of time in a way that supports greater learning.

Kim took over. "Thank you, Wendy and Debbie, for that summary. It was great.

"Last month each of us on the Commission was assigned to an Action team that met over lunch. We worked to draft recommendations that we'll consider at our June 18 Commission meeting. Today at lunch we'll turn to our final four Action Teams and ask you to begin your discussions. Those Action Team are Parent and Community Engagement, Comprehensive Technology, Administrative Support Services, and Student Assessment and School Accountability. These are the assignments: (1) The Parent and Community Engagement Action Team (PCEAT) is chaired by Maria Morales, and co-chaired by Paul Christopher and Christina Peterson; (2) The Comprehensive Technology Action Team (CTAT) has Debbie Cohen as Chair, with Lenora Brown and Ted Alexander as Co-Chairs; (3) The Administrative Support Services Action Team (ASSAT) is chaired by Delores Williams with co-chairs Kim Su Young and Ray Gonzales; and (4) The Student Assessment and School Accountability Action Team (SAAAT) is chaired by Paul Christopher and co-chaired by Ted Alexander and Kathie Sorenson.

"Good luck today! See you back here at 1:30 p.m when we'll listen to another group of distinguished guests."

Chapter 17
NATIONAL EDUCATION POLICY: MEDIA, STATE AND FEDERAL
Saturday afternoon, May 24

Nate welcomed the group back. "Our first panel this afternoon represents the print media: Tom Toch of *U.S. News and World Report;* Chris Pipho of *Phi Delta Kappan;* Virginia Edwards of *Education Week*. Let me introduce our first guest, Tom Toch, senior education editor for *U.S. News*. Tom, welcome to our Citizens' Commission on Elementary School Reform. You have an unusual background for a nationally-recognized journalist. You've been a teacher and have visited schools all over the United States for your award winning book, *In the Name of Excellence*. This book looks at the school reform battles of the Reagan years.[1] Let's start by asking you the two or three lessons you've learned about school reform."

National Education Policy—National Media Reporting

"Thank you, Nate, and members of the Citizens' Commission. I understand you have heard from top school reformers during your Hearings. I hope I will add something of value.[2] I'm looking forward to your report which should help all of us—teachers, principals, parents and community leaders—in reforming our local schools.

"My first lesson is illustrated by your Commission. Successful reform requires that educators and parents and students *own* the school's policies and operations. They must all have a stake in the success or failure of school reform. When you permit parents (students) to select the schools where their children attend, when you permit teachers to work at a school of their own choosing, and when you permit schools to develop distinctive curriculum or instruction, you get people who are vested in its success. There is a sense of shared and mutual obligation on the part of teachers and students, and teachers and parents. They push each other to work harder. The schools are more successful. One of the clearest lessons I learned in the 1980s is that a sense of *ownership* can have a dramatic effect on the quality and success of schools.

"A second lesson is even more subtle. Many educators simply do not believe that a majority of their students have the capacity to use their minds well.[3] There's a long legacy of utilitarianism that has driven our philosophy of schooling. Early in this century, we were satisfied that only 5% to 7% of kids graduated from high school. They represented those capable of learning higher-order skills. The rest could be taught enough to get good jobs in industry or services. By the 1980s, we realized that the rules of the game had been changing. Now, for the first time in history, educators are beginning to believe that most kids can be taught to use their mind well. Unless we come to grips with this belief, we can never seriously address the issue of high standards. In Japan, a very high percentage of teachers—80% to 90%—are convinced that high achievement in math is a function of hard work. This expectation shows up in international comparisons of American students and those of our other competitors. About half of their students take the Advanced Placement exams and about a third pass them. In the U.S., only about 6% take them and about 4% of those pass them. Somehow we've failed to show that education enriches our lives and pays dividends."

"Tom," Kathie Sorenson spoke up. "Why have local schools failed so badly to raise standards?"

"Well, Kathie, we've been saddled with a cultural handicap in this country. It's a belief that education should be a local function and that elected school boards should set standards. Our kids aren't learning as they should and they're now required to master much more to compete in the workplace than ever before. Many school systems cannot clearly define their standards, and they have nothing to do with core knowledge recognized by well-educated individuals throughout history. The irony is that our Constitution guarantees educational opportunities for all children, and it gives ultimate authority to state government. Local politicians gain favor by appealing to conservative and anti-Washington sentiments.

"Another major barrier to raising standards and reforming schools is teacher unions. In fact, teacher unions are the single, most influential force in American education today. They cling to traditional, industrial-style union policies of the industrial economy of 30 years ago.[4] Ironically, much of the labor force in auto and other industries has moved away from the old-style industrial system where people were paid for seniority not performance. I think that until the teaching profession is improved, it will not achieve the status it needs to meet the higher academic standards that reformers have set for the schools. To be attractive as an occupation to the nation's best and brightest, teaching will have to reward performance, be stimulating intellectually, and permit relevant professional development. Unions must relinquish some of their policies. They must pay people on the basis of their performance rather than seniority. They should let schools hire and fire their own faculties. They should permit school systems to remove poorly-performing teachers without spending thousands of dollars over several years on legal fees for due process. We will not attract our top young people into teaching until it becomes a true profession where they are paid according to their knowledge and skills."

"Tom," Debbie asked, "doesn't your description of the union's traditional resistance to reform fly in the face of what we've just heard? In charter schools and school-site councils, parents, teachers and principals are making decisions for their community schools."

"Yes, Debbie, this is the central issue today. It's the struggle between the reformers and the absentee owners at the central school district or local teacher union office. Reformers want to open up the public schools and give them back to the people. The absentee owners or officials now make the key decisions about the operations of a local school. I am encouraged, however, about the formation of TURN, the new Teacher Union Reform Network. I understand that NEA President Bob Chase told you a little about these 21 teacher union presidents across the country. They are attempting to redesign teachers' unions as active participants in school reform by partnering with management to improve education."[5]

As a teacher union advocate, Ted Alexander was disturbed. "Mr. Toch, you sound like many reporters who run down the schools and bash the teachers."

"Well, I'm sorry you feel that way. I have great respect for today's qualified, dedicated teachers. I've spent a good deal of my professional life covering public education, visiting local schools and interviewing teachers. My two young children will enter school shortly. I'm very impressed with the new teachers I meet nearly every week. There is a lot of good learning going on, but there's just not enough of it. I believe we must organize schools not only for the benefit of the adults, some of whom may not be the best leaders for the children, but for the children themselves. I've been a classroom teacher, and I know that most good teachers would prefer to be hired and paid according to their merits. Good teachers are the ones who suffer most from poor teaching because they must then do double duty. They have to teach what they're paid to teach, and then they must do remedial work for colleagues who failed to do their job in previous years. I believe in grassroots accountability. Teaching is a demanding profession, and there are a lot of good teachers now teaching in our public schools. Qualified teachers deserve to be paid and treated like true professionals. They should also be given professional development opportunities to improve their classroom performance.

"The best model for teacher development in the country is at the Yale/ New Haven Teacher Institute. Yale University professors teach subject matter to New Haven teachers. The program gives teachers a very strong sense of professionalism. It gives them a sense that they are not just low-level instructors who must teach assigned subjects to keep a job, but historians, scientists, and scholars of literature. The turnover rate in the New Haven School District has dropped dramatically since this program was developed a decade ago. It's one of the unheralded successes in American education."

"Do you see any changes in teacher union attitudes and practices in the 1990s?" Chairman Gonzales asked.

"Al Shanker warned his members that the survival of teacher unions are at risk. Even though they're working to improve public schools, if classroom teaching does not improve, the unions will wither. Shanker wants to safeguard union members, but he advocates that union leaders take more responsibility for the quality of teaching. He calls for higher teacher entrance standards, the training and retraining of teachers, and performance-based pay. He also wants to streamline due-process protections. Teacher unions can either reform themselves, or they can preside over the demise of public education.

"Unions are watching the charter school movement with ambivalence. This movement could bring fundamental structural reforms that rapidly pen up serious site-based decision-making. Union leaders must seize the opportunity to become constructive participants in the transformation of he public school system. Al Shanker said that teachers must participate in lecisions affecting the whole school: budget, hiring, curriculum, student placement, assessment, and instructional strategies."[6]

Nate spoke up. "You've opened some interesting issues, Tom. Thanks o much for being here. We look forward to your continuing reports on the eform wars."

"Thanks, Nate. I'll watch with interest what your final report says about lementary school reform. Be bold! Perhaps this Commission can light a ire under the reform movement."

Wendy took over from Nate. "Our next guest, Dr. Chris Pipho, is from he national education media. He writes a monthly column called 'Stateline' or *Kappan* magazine. Chris is recognized as an expert in reporting state nd local school reform. He's a former history and music teacher and a igh school administrator. He served in the Colorado Department of Education, and is now Director of the State Relations/Clearinghouse for the ducation Commission of the States (ECS), headquartered in Denver. Let's egin with our question: What two or three lessons have you learned about chool reform, Chris?"

"Thank you, Wendy, and members of the Commission for this opportu-ity. First, we must learn how to engage the public in the whole issue of chool reform. It's difficult for us to get our story out. Hearing the chal-enge from school reform gurus doesn't cut it with the public. One-third of he people understand what you're talking about and are ready to march or change, one-third in the middle could be convinced to go either way but re waiting to be sold, and one-third are digging in their heels. Our chal-enge is the middle third. How do we effectively mobilize them for serious chool reform? We speak too much 'edu-babble' jargon that fails to reach rassroots parents, teachers, principals, and the general public. We don't sten. The Public Agenda Foundation is trying to remedy this. According o the surveys, most parents are concerned about keeping their kids safe nd teaching them basic skills.

"The other day I was in Laramie, Wyoming talking to the editor of the ocal paper about his coverage of education. I discovered that 80% of his aper is made up of wire service stories. This means that they're not usually covering local education stories. And besides, if they are, reporters won't be assigned to education long enough to learn about it. So most reporters don't try to understand the complexity of school finance or other topics. My point is that you need to educate your local newspaper editor and his reporters about what you are doing with the Citizens' Commission. Otherwise, the public in this county will never know you existed. They won't know you held Hearings and made a report with recommendations for Jefferson Elementary.

"The second lesson is about communicating the importance of high academic standards to the public, especially parents and students. I have chronicled school reform in the United States since I began writing 'Stateline for the *Kappan* in September 1983. With all the energy generated by *A Nation at Risk* 14 years ago, we still haven't communicated with the public well about school reform. In every decade, we've tried to reform education. In the 1950s, reforms in science education followed Sputnik. In the 1960s, equity reforms came about with Lyndon Johnson's War on Poverty. In the 1970s, education was part of the new Civil Rights movement. In the 1980s, we began to focus reform on quality and excellence.

"In the 1990s, we're still trying to figure out how to communicate the value of teaching international academic standards to American students. The Goals 2000 controversy shows that we are not yet able to tell the American people what is at stake—that only with high academic standards can we prepare their children for the 21st century. At least 15 academic groups are putting together curriculum standards in every field. But without coordinating and simplifying them, no teacher would have enough time to cover all the knowledge recommended for a given year. Whose responsibility is it to translate these complex education issues into plain, simple English that can be disseminated to parents and the general public? If we don't do this soon, we could lose our national struggle for challenging academic standards."

"Wait a minute, Chris," said Kim. "Are you saying that we educators are to blame for not communicating with the public about the need for school reform? We're too busy educating the children!"

"I'm sympathetic about how hard a job educating our students can be. I remember my days as a teacher, and it's even harder now. But my point is that unless we communicate and engage parents and the wider public, we won't have their support. We need their money and time. The whole community, not just educators, shares the responsibility for school reform and education of all America's children. We educators have the most to gain by public engagement. It's our story. If we don't tell it, who will? School reform depends on our ability to tell it to the community."

"Chris, I haven't seen your columns. Could you give us an idea of what topics you've written about?" Christina asked.

"In December 1986, I reviewed three years of national education reform. I described early stages of reform in states like Mississippi, California and Arkansas, and emerging themes of more rigorous academic standards for students as well as more recognition and higher standards for teachers. I described the debate about whether or not the reform movement was dead or just taking off. There was even talk about choice and vouchers, local control of schools and the growing influence of conservatives on the reform movement.[7] Ten years later, in 1996, my 'Stateline' column is covering the same reforms plus a few others like higher education on-line and charter schools. I've also followed up on the March Education Summit's new resource center Achieve for higher academic standards, assessments, accountability and effective use of technology.[8] I wonder what the author of 'Stateline' will be writing about national school reform in the year 2006? Will we still be tinkering with school reform or will we have finally reinvented public education?"

"Chris, thanks for appearing before our Citizens' Commission," said Wendy. "You have a broad picture of school reform as it unfolds in our 50 states. Nate will now introduce our final media guest."

"Thank you, Wendy," Nate said. "It's my pleasure to introduce Virginia Edwards, editor of *Education Week*, since 1989. *Ed Week* has demonstrated that there is an audience for an independent, credible weekly publication devoted to education news. We've been asking all our guests, what are the two or three lessons you have learned about education reform?"

"Thank you, Nate. It's strange being on the other end of an interview for a change. My first lesson is that school reform is very difficult. People have not really been willing to be tough enough to get it done. If you don't make the commitment to do the hard work, you're going to come up short.

"Another lesson I've learned is that we must engage the public again. Since *A Nation At Risk* was released, many pockets of excellence have developed, but there's still so much mediocrity. This is because people at all levels haven't really committed to reform. Fundamental reform has to come from the federal and state government, the district, the school and the teachers. And, of course, parents may be the most significant players in bringing about change because they have the greatest interest—their children are at stake!

"There's another lesson you might expect from a journalist. Clear communication is lacking among all of these reform levels. The standards debate is a perfect example. Everyone talks about setting high expectations for all kids, ensuring that resources are available to help them meet those standards, and then finding a way to assess progress. The whole notion of standards, especially if they are called 'outcome-based education,' has caused a kind of hysteria. Even education reformers are not talking much among themselves, and so discovering ways to communicate at each level, and between each stakeholder, is absolutely critical to school reform. We need to agree on what must be changed. We journalists believe that when people have the right information, they can act responsibly. But school reform is difficult. Most politicians don't take the time to dig in and master the necessary understanding that leads to significant changes. Legislators, state school people and local school districts must be accountable for state funds.

"Much discussion of school reform simply stops because it threatens the vested bureaucratic interests. In some state offices of education, vocational educators and curriculum people don't talk, or in some districts, the professional staff haven't been inside a school for years. It's hard to start a serious discussion about school reform because it means that someone will have to change jobs. It's much easier to blame the kids, their disadvantaged background, the violence, society breaking down, drugs or welfare. Any excuse will do."

Ted Alexander broke in with a question. "How do you feel about school-site management? Last month, we heard from David Hornbeck, superintendent in Philadelphia, and Tom Boysen, former commissioner of education in Kentucky. They were high on school-site management. Is it a reform we should take seriously?"

"Thanks, Ted, for that question. Our perspective at *Ed Week* is that any school-site reform must have an effective principal. In reporting about school-site councils, we have found that the really great success stories have

a strong principal, talented teachers and committed parents who participate in all policy decisions and accept ownership. We need more examples
where district boards and superintendents delegate the full responsibility
for policy, budgets, personnel, etc., to the local site and then hold the principal and the school-site council accountable. It really is happening."

Kim spoke next. "I read *Education Week* faithfully, and I want to commend you and your staff for your objective reporting. Your coverage of
national policy and education activities in the states and districts is just
amazing. In January, *Ed Week* published a massive state-by-state report card
on progress toward academic standards. How can we best use this resource
to help our Commission?"

"Kim, I'm pleased that as a principal you are taking time to read our
weekly. The special 240-page report you're referring to is called *Quality
Counts*. We described five factors that help states progress toward school
reform. Here's a one-page handout for you:

1) **Standards and assessments**—In most states, challenging standards
   have not reached the classroom and teachers are not prepared to
   teach them. The assessments of student progress are not in place,
   and few states are ready to hold schools or students accountable
   (overall rating for the states = B);

2) **Teaching quality**—At the national level, a policy consensus is emerging about the need for higher standards for training public school
   teachers and for more rigorous licensing requirements. In 1995,
   teacher salaries averaged $36,744. Four-out-of-ten secondary teach-
   ers have no degrees in the subject they teach, and there are too many
   unlicensed teachers in classrooms. Quality teacher education is a
   major problem, and on-the-job education for teachers is a goal rather
   than a reality (overall grade for the states = C);

3) **School climate**—A clear, shared mission that focuses on student
   learning, with classes small enough that teachers come to know their
   students, and a safe, orderly school. Half of our elementary teachers have classes of 25 or more pupils, and more than half of high
   school English teachers teach 80 or more students a day. There is
   not enough parent and community involvement, and school facilities need serious maintenance and repair (overall grade for the states
   = C-);

4) **Resources**—Most states are spending more money for education now than they did 10 years ago, but too few dollars are reaching the classroom. Most funding is spent on increasing special education student costs, trying to keep up with enrollment growth, and on rising salaries for an aging teaching force. State spending on education ranges from an average of $8,100 per student in New Jersey to $3,500 in Utah (states get a B- on spending for school equity). States do not concentrate enough funding in the classroom on teaching and learning, with teachers only 52% of total school staff (states get a C- on how effectively they spend their money), and (overall grade for states on spending for education = C+);

6) **Student achievement**—Most states do not yet have good measures for student achievement, course-taking, dropout rates, and attendance rates. The only comparable measures of student performance are the National Assessment of Educational Progress (NAEP) scores. They are discouraging. In every state, at least half the students perform below the 'proficiency' level in reading and math.

"Thank you, Nate, and members of this Citizens' Commission, for the opportunity to share this information. I've left copies of *Quality Counts* for each of you. Good luck on your reform study of Jefferson Elementary School."

"Thanks, Ginny. We'll take a short break before turning to our panel on the role of state associations and private foundations in national policy formation."

****

National State Associations and Private Foundations

Wendy welcomed the Commission back. "Our next guest is Gordon Ambach, executive director of the Council of Chief State School Officers since 1987.[9] He has also been the New York State Commissioner of Education and President of the University of the State of New York. While at the University, he developed and implemented the nation's most comprehensive school reform act, the Regents Action Plan. The Council's work focuses on building state capacity for early childhood and family education, and on developing standards, assessments and accountability for students, teachers and administrators. The Council also works to expand use of learning technologies, to prepare students for employment, and to link educaion, health and social services. It compares education practices and student achievement across the states, and strengthens international comparisons of American education. Gordon, please tell us two or three important lessons that you've learned about school reform in your distinguished career?"

"My first lesson is the importance of taking substantial time to review current practices you are intending to change and to project exactly what practices would be in place after the change. Too often reformers start with somebody's bright idea and immediately launch activities and reports on desired results. The reformers often neglect the hard work of analyzing what it takes to transform the system into something new and better for children. You must have a clear statement of what is going to change for students at the end and a careful design strategy of how to get there.

"In New York, I was active in this kind of system transformation. We spent a full <u>three years</u> of careful design and building consensus by holding meetings and traveling around the state. We discussed what we thought ought to be changed, how long it would take, and how to do it. The result was the 1984 Regent's Action Plan.

"The second lesson is that widespread education reform requires a substantial time frame. Schools must have carefully designed sequences of learning with high academic standards, sound assessments and public accountability for results. In New York, we programmed the changes for student requirements for each year from kindergarten through graduation in the twelfth grade. The scope of changes was over 13 grade levels, and the time frame for implementation was 13 years! Students who started kindergarten in 1984 are now taking the Regent's examinations and graduating in 1997. I congratulate your Citizens' Commission for taking the time this year to interview the top school reformers and practitioners, carefully inventory your school, and design a five-year Reform Blueprint. I urge you to consider a longer frame."

Paul said, "I'm listening carefully to what you're saying about managing large system school reform. We've just a small school here, so my question is, what are the barriers we should watch out for in trying to launch whole school reform."

"Paul, I would counsel you," said Gordon, "to look very carefully at the reform models already out there. Parents don't want you to experiment on their children. They know their youngsters have only one chance to go to school and get prepared for college and a good job. They expect reforms to be sound. Look at other successful practices.

"Too often administrators and board members resist trying what somebody else is doing successfully. If it is not their own, it is discounted, even if it's proving successful in a neighboring school district or a state. Do not resist adoption of other's successes."

"How would your Council of Chief State School Officers advise us on empowering local schools through site-level decision-making and management?" Debbie asked.

"Debbie, the first issue to be decided on school-level decision-making is exactly what is being decentralized. Local officials must have the authority and the resources to get the job done. The board or the superintendent has to be able to support school-site activities, even when things aren't always going smoothly. You have got to know when to keep hands off and let the local leaders struggle, learn and become successful, and when to pull the plug because the site operation is failing and won't turn around. Just as with charter schools, school-site authority must be accountable for meeting high academic standards and using powerful assessment to assure public accountability. When school boards decentralize authority, they must retain the residual power to call the authority back if the school is not working effectively."

"Mr. Ambach," Dale said. "Do you oppose federal interference with local control of education?"

"I support strong state and local initiatives that are the locus of school authority in the U.S. My association membership comes from the state level. The state chiefs expect us to be strong advocates for federal leadership in school reform too. And, they expect to learn from our international competitors. The Council of Chief State School Officers strongly advocates such legislation as the *Goals 2000: Educate America Act, the Improving America's Schools Act, the 1996 Telecommunications Act for Universal Service for Schools and Libraries,* the National Assessment of Educational Progress, and *The School to Work Opportunities Act.* These Acts all help states and localities to innovate and improve student achievement. We support a strong U.S. Department of Education and believe in greater, but carefully targeted, federal education investments to help state and local educators, parents and community leaders reform American schools.[10] The bottom line is our entire nation has a stake in the strength of education. We must use resources from all levels—local, state and federal—to get the job done."

Thank you, Gordon, for meeting with us today," said Wendy.

"Now, it is my pleasure to introduce our second panel member who represents state policymakers. Since 1985 Dr. Frank Newman has served as President of the Education Commission of the States (ECS). The mission of ECS is to help state leaders develop and carry out policies that improve performance and increase learning by all citizens. ECS conducts policy research, surveys and special studies, and maintains an information clearinghouse. It organizes state, regional and national forums and provides technical assistance to states and their education agencies. It also helps states to implement changes in education and fosters nationwide leadership and cooperation. Our leadoff question for you today is, what are the two or three lessons you have learned about school reform?"

"Wendy, Chairman Gonzales, and members of this Citizens' Commission, I'm pleased to meet with you here at Jefferson Elementary School to discuss this critical subject.[11] My first lesson is about the difficulty in scaling up reform—we can't depend on the big stars to do it. We've identified about 20 very good reform networks that are working on whole-school reform or on specific programs that deal with reading, math or writing. They are getting impressive results and good evaluations of their positive impact on all kinds of students in all kinds of schools. The problem is that successful reform takes enormous effort on the part of the network creators and staff—their time and money. It's clear that our school system is too large and diversified to expect that a Ted Sizer, Jim Comer or Hank Levin can personally supervise the reform process in each school. When the reform networks leave the school and take away their talent and resources, most schools revert back to their old cultures. Upscaling is a big challenge that we have not mastered yet in American schools.

"The second lesson is that you need to have the public with you before you begin on any reform program. Principals usually can and do engage parents to support what they are doing. But the minute you start to scale up, people start coming out of the woodwork to complain. We've seen this happen all over the country with such issues as higher academic standards and Goals 2000. Most state and local school boards and most schools aren't very good at engaging the public, explaining what their trying to do, and building support for the reform.

"Well, what's the problem? Why aren't we educators successful at public engagement?" Kathie asked.

"That's a tough question," said Frank. "I believe we just naturally underestimate the force of the status quo, which is really vested interests in traditional ways of schooling. We have gradually built up a regulatory system for operating our schools. We have added more rules and regulations until, like Gulliver, the small strands that bind us now make it impossible to move. When reformers come to the rescue, the system reacts defensively and may be unintentionally hostile to change. When we started granting waivers from regulations, most people thought reform would just naturally follow. We learned that rules and regulations were based on traditions and on old operating and training habits. Our incentive systems are geared to putting in work time but not to improve performance. Status quo is based on learned educational culture that resists change. Of course the public has become frustrated with our failures to reform schools and threatens to walk away. They then support vouchers for private school alternatives or charter schools.

"Another problem is that we tend to shoot from the hip when making policy. We do not require serious evaluation to demonstrate that school reform actually works on real students in real classrooms with real teachers. Some networks are gathering evaluation data to prove their case, but they've often been too slow and defensive. Schools have not been held accountable like other institutions in our society, and the public is out of patience.

"Finally, educators must do a better job of professional development if we are going to reach our 110,000 public and private schools. Right now the best professional development is coming out of the reform networks and programs. But this affects only about 2,500 schools where they are working. In the other 98%, professional development is fractured and ineffective."

"As a school board member," said Ray, "I wrestle with the decision to decentralize—to give authority to the school site. What is your advice about this? Should we push for it at Jefferson?"

"The more emphasis you place on decision-making by school-site councils," answered Frank, "the more you need to implement clear-cut standards and assessments. At ECS we advocate state academic standards because we believe that, if properly motivated, states are natural laboratories for experimentation. States are making great strides in developing challenging academic standards and sharing their success with each other. Colorado, Kentucky and Maryland have successful state programs. Preliminary results in these cutting-edge states and districts show that clear and rigorous standards lead to improved student performance.[12] They must be supported by good teacher preparation, instructional materials and assessments. Our research on site-based management shows that unless it is accompanied by these serious reforms, there is little improvement in student achievement."

Wendy spoke up. "We appreciate you taking the time to meet with us, Frank. Best wishes on your reform mission. We enjoyed having your colleague, Chris Pipho, earlier today.

"Now I'm happy to introduce Robert Schwartz, former director of Education Programs for the Pew Charitable Trusts," said Wendy. "Bob is now teaching at Harvard University. He is recognized as one of the top private foundation leaders in support grants to non-profit groups for education reform throughout the United States. He has been a high school teacher in northern California, and the principal of an experimental high school in Portland, Oregon. He also served in the Mayor's office in Boston. Bob, you've been in a position to both carry out promising reform projects and provide funding for reform projects of nationwide significance. Could you start by describing the two or three lessons you have learned?"

"Thank you, Wendy. I have two competing views of school reform that reflect approaches that are now being carried forward. The first lesson is from my experience as a high school principal in Portland. I learned that reform must occur one school at a time by dedicated principals, teachers, parents and community leaders. They all have a stake in an individual school. I identify with Debbie Meiers and Ted Sizer who maintain that each school has a culture of its own, and the cookie-cutter approach will not work to reform all schools.

"On the other hand, we can't let each individual school find its way entirely on its own. We don't have time for that. We must figure out system strategies that can really accelerate reform. We can't only depend on individual heroes to provide leadership. This means we must have challenging academic standards established by the states or school districts which include assessments and accountability systems.

"As a grant-maker, I have focused principally on the issue that the country needs a national strategy. Education standards are too important to leave to the individual states, school districts or schools. The problem is complicated, I know, by the deep suspicion people have about the federal government. I believe we need the federal government in the business of education. But I also believe that we need other national organizations to provide guidance, leadership and direction."

"How have grants helped in upscaling?" Paul asked.

"We've tried to focus on the role of the school district. We've supported seven medium-school districts for a four-year period in which they would try to significantly transform all the schools within their district. That meant they'd spread good practices from one school to another. They'd also move the central office from a compliance organization to a technical assistance group. We picked medium-sized school districts because we thought they'd have better success in a short four-year period. These leadership districts within states would have standards projects in motion, and common assessment systems based on new standards. Then we'd have something people could actually look at.

"Restructuring public education is a big priority with us. We've been heavy backers of the Philadelphia reforms, the clusters or networks of schools; they are almost like charters with school-site decision-making. We've also supported the LEARN strategy in Los Angeles to reform the whole system. We've funded the project called TURN, the organization and networking of 21 teacher unions. The project is housed at UCLA and appears very progressive in working to become contributing partners in local school-site decision-making in several lighthouse urban districts."

"Another foundation strategy for national upscaling is grants to develop challenging academic standards. We need to establish benchmarks for each subject at each grade level. So we've invested $25 million in the New Standards Project over the past five years. The New Standards Project has moved from nice general statements to content standards that define what children should know and be able to do. The Project then illustrates performance standards with examples of student work that have been internationally bench-marked. The new edition is a state-of-the-art standards document. They have a lot of work to do to boil these down into a form that is useful and integrated. They will have to develop assessments to measure progress against those standards. Finally, teachers will have to be prepared to know and be able to effectively teach all these new standards.

"This does not even address the problems of opportunity-to-learn standards and inequitable financial support. We also need an integrated educational policy system built around challenging academic standards, assessment, professional development and accountability. Some states like Maryland, Colorado, Oregon, Delaware, and Vermont are leading out. Where strong education governors or chief state school officers work to carry out serious reform, there is a chance.

"Mr. Schwartz, I'm a new third-grade teacher and I've got my hands full just surviving," said Tamar. "Even though I've recently graduated, I'm not prepared to teach new academic curriculums with world-class standards and assessments. How do I get retooled on these standards and when do I have time to collaborate with my colleagues about learning to teach these standards?"

"That's a good question, Tamar. Without massive teacher inservice re-training, standards-based reform will never get off the ground. Not only does every teacher need to be retooled for the coming standards revolution, but for the technology that's sweeping the schools. Good professional development involves teams of teachers who are working together, who have a voice in determining their own learning, and who expect to be life-long learners. We need to create new models for professional development and how to pay for it. Where will the time and money come from? Money is available for professional development, but it's being poorly used. The biggest pot of money is mostly wasted paying for credits from outside college courses that do little to better prepare teachers for classroom teaching. We asked RAND to do a study in Los Angeles. They discovered that the district spent $250 million a year on university credits for their teachers without much improvement in skills. Virtually no teachers were taking courses to improve their classroom performance. Why should they? The system does not hold them accountable."

Maria had a question. "Mr. Schwartz, what about parent engagement?"

"We have supported the work of Ernie Cortes in Texas," answered Bob. "Ernie's Industrial Areas Foundation trains parent organizers to build community support for school reform. They engage in adult education with a vengeance. They bring in top educators to expose parents to the latest reform ideas. Parents hear from experts like Ted Sizer, James Comer and Howard Gardner.

"But Public Agenda shows us a great gap between opinion leaders and the ordinary public about the value of education and economic productivity, and about the value of challenging academic standards. It's hard to build and sustain public support for short-term pain while we ratchet up the whole public education system. Kids must be held accountable for what they are learning. Educators are not very good at communicating with the public about what they do and why more money is needed to do it even better. We must discover how to engage parents and the public in this national school reform movement. All citizens are stakeholders in the future education of our children. I see my time is gone. Thank you for your questions."

"Thank you, Bob, for that overview of reform from the national private foundation perspective," Wendy concluded. "Now it's time for our break."

****

Programs in the U.S. Department of Education

Wendy took over again. "Our next guest is Jack Jennings, who has a distinguished 27-year career as General Counsel for the Education Committee in the U.S. House of Representatives. He is now Director of the Center on National Education Policy in Washington, D.C. Welcome, Jack. Your career with the Congress has spanned most of the federal education legislation enacted since the 1960s. You have a unique view of what federal education is designed to accomplish.[13] Could you describe two or three lessons you have learned from your experience?"

"Thank you, Wendy. Chairman Gonzales and members of the Commission, I'm pleased to testify before you this afternoon. I'd like to start with a little background on the federal education role. It has a long history in this country. Under the Articles of Confederation, Congress permitted the Northwest Territory to come into the Union under the condition that they set aside land for public schools. For the next 125 years, every territory that came into the union met that requirement. The Supreme Court has ruled that the Congress can adopt roles for the federal government that are not explicitly given to states in the Constitution. This policy is based on the use of spending powers, regulation of commerce and the 14th Amendment extending equal protection of the law to all citizens. I think most people understand that if we do not strengthen our educational system, we are going to be in big trouble as individuals, families and as a nation.

"Now the first lesson that I've learned is that our elected representatives must identify the problem that needs the most public attention. The Congress has traditionally seen the federal education role as providing equal opportunity for all children, especially the disadvantaged. When states have failed to provide that opportunity, the federal government has stepped in and granted additional money for the education of disadvantaged children and college students at risk. This has been authorized by such major legislation as the *Elementary and Secondary Education Act—now The Improving America's Schools Act; Head Start; and IDEA*—the special education act for children who are disabled; and Pell grants for college students.[14]

"Second, there has been a historic shift in the role of the federal government in education from a traditional concern with equity and meeting the needs of disadvantaged children to a concern for the quality of the nation's schools for *all* America's children. The *Goals 2000: Educate America Act* funds states to develop challenging academic standards. We are attempting to raise the educational achievement of *all* the nation's students. In the reauthorized elementary and secondary education act of 1994, Title I calls for high standards for all children and comprehensive schoolwide reform strategies to help *all* children to achieve these standards. It specifically addresses overall improvement of teaching and learning in schools with the highest levels of poverty.[15]

"Third, to successfully enact federal legislation, you have to be bipartisan and obtain broad support. In the past few years in Congress, first the Democrats and now the Republicans have made education a partisan issue. In 1995 I toured the United States to investigate the emerging widespread public dissatisfaction with public schools.[16] Wherever I went, I heard constant criticism from governors, state legislators, business leaders and the news media. Later in the year, Public Agenda Foundation, using polling and focus groups, reported that, 'American support for public education is fragile and porous. Although many people voice initial approval of their own local public schools, this support disintegrates at the slightest probing.'[17] In my travels, I identified four causes of the public's skeptical attitude toward public education. First, the news media paints an unbalanced picture of public education. Second, teachers and other educators have not clearly explained what they are doing and have not engaged the public in conversation. Third, we have lost civility in public discourse. The unsubstantiated claims of some Far Right groups must be rebutted even as we address their legitimate concerns. And fourth, we have not agreed as a nation on what we want from our schools. We must take action to deal with each of these. Then we must dedicate ourselves to reaching the objectives.

"Public schools are better than they get credit for, but this does not mean they cannot and must not improve. Important reform efforts are being jeopardized by increasingly negative public attitudes toward the schools.[18] We need to commit to improving public schools. This means all citizens, including leaders and members of both major political parties. Leaders must work with parents and teachers to change attitudes toward school reform. Parents and teachers must buy into reform soon or we could lose the whole 200-year concept of public schools in America. That would pose a serious threat to democracy itself. As Thomas Jefferson said, 'Above all things, I hope the education of the common people will be attended to; [I am] convinced that on this ...[lies] the most security for the preservation of ... liberty.'"

"Mr. Jennings," said Dale. "I'm surprised at what you've been saying about the federal role in education. All I've ever heard is how bad the federal education programs are."

"It's true, Dale, that at times the federal education programs have been intrusive. There are too many regulations for the little money they give to the schools. The various interest groups influence federal legislation so there are too many little programs, at least 150, where there should be only five or ten. Another 100 or more education programs are scattered throughout the federal government. On the one hand, we want the money and recognize the need for programs like Head Start, college loans, and National Science Foundation programs in math and science teacher education. On the other hand, we want the money with no strings attached. That means no accountability to the taxpayers. The federal government has to respect state and local responsibilities for education. But as I said earlier, the founders of our Republic and the Supreme Court have given the federal government the authority to fund and, where necessary, to regulate educational equity. And now, increasingly, to promote educational quality for all America's children. The real issue is not whether the federal government will be involved in education. It's whether or not the public schools for our grandchildren will survive!"

"Thank you, Jack, for being with us today and for sharing lessons from your many years of experience," said Wendy.

"Now I'd like to welcome U.S. Senator James M. Jeffords (R-Vt).[19] He is Chairman of the U.S. Senate Committee on Labor and Human Resources that authorizes all the federal education programs, and he heads the congressional committee that oversees the education policy for the District of Columbia Schools. He has been a courageous protector of education against threatened cuts by conservative congressional Republicans from his own party. Welcome to our Commission Hearing. Please describe what troubles you most about American education."

"Thank you, Wendy, Chairman Gonzales and members of the Citizens' Commission. As a parent, a grandparent, a citizen and a U.S. Senator, I am troubled about education today. In almost every case, the high school diploma doesn't mean much anymore. Educators continue to promote students on the basis of attendance, not academic achievement. Employers are troubled about the lack of knowledge and skills of high school graduates who are seeking jobs. Literacy Council studies verify that about one-half of our young adults are functionally illiterate. We call them the 'forgotten half.' Without a first-class education, heads of families will continue to lose ground as they have been doing over the past 20 years. Do young Americans have time to study and excel in school? According to recent studies, 13-year olds and 17-year olds in the United States watch between seven and five times more hours of TV than they put in on homework. These tragic statistics point to a weak educational foundation.

"How did these young people leave the third grade without knowing how to read and do math? My office is promoting the volunteer reading program called 'Everybody Wins!' Each week I join Senate and House members and their staffs, about 800 people, to donate a lunch hour. We read aloud and mentor children in seven elementary schools in Washington D.C. This is more symbolic than anything else, but some real learning is taking place—not just with the children, but especially among the adults participating in the program. We hope to attract 14,000 volunteers and to demonstrate the value of reading well by the third grade. Hillary Clinton and

Tipper Gore have participated with us, and they are big boosters. If all America's children can master reading before they leave the third grade, the nation's schools will have come a long way in improving all student achievement.

"I am also troubled about the opposition to designing and implementing challenging national or international academic standards in every American school. I know the standards movement has frightened some of my conservative colleagues in the Congress. They believe that national standards will lead to a federally-imposed curriculum and control over our lives. But, I think this is an unfortunate misconception. Educators have got to know what the goals are, and what information and skills young people need to get good jobs. I don't care if you call them world-class, national, state or challenging standards. But change has to start with school boards and teachers. They have to own standards, or we won't get any reform."

"But Senator Jeffords," Paul said. "What are we going to do about the rise in school crime and disruptive student behavior?"

"You may know that, at my urging, Congress has increased funding for the *Safe and Drug Free Schools Act.* We are alarmed at the increase of drug and tobacco use among teenagers. We see increases in school dropouts in urban centers, along with substantial lack of discipline and lack of respect for teachers. We see rising rates of juvenile crime and teenage pregnancy. We see an increase in TV watching, less parental supervision after school and less homework time. We must turn all this around in every school, and it will take everybody to do it. Educators and families must channel the energies of our children and youth into positive educational activities. Schools cannot do it alone."

Delores raised her hand. "Senator Jeffords, I have relatives in the District, and I have many friends teaching in the D.C. school system. They say it's a disaster for most of the 75,000 students who go to school there. I've heard that Congress works with the new Control Board that recently fired the school superintendent and hired retired General Julius W. Becton, Jr. as the new administrator. The General has promised safe schools, healthy lunches, and clean buildings. He promised to start managing the school's personnel and financial resources and support systems so that teachers and principals can devote themselves to serious teaching and learning again. My question is, how is Congress helping?"

"You have your facts straight. Delores. I'm encouraged by the actions of the Control Board. Congress established the Board to take dramatic and bold actions so that students can begin to learn at high levels in D.C. schools.[20] I'm also encouraged by the wide spectrum of community support for the actions of the Control Board. Parents, business leaders, elected officials, ministers and community volunteers need to form dynamic partnerships to help the schools improve for the benefit of all the District's children.[21] The Congress is working closely with the Control Board on all these changes. Congress just made available $52.7 million to carry out repairs and capital improvement in consultation with the General Services Administration. The appropriations act passed in September 1996 increased the number of charter schools that can be approved in a given year from 10 to 20. I think that charter schools hold great promise as a catalyst for innovation and choice within the public education system. The D.C. schools must also have state-of-the-art technology if students are to acquire the skills that employers are demanding from today's high school and college graduates. I intend to take this up with the 105th Congress. The whole country is engaged in education reform, and the District must follow. Working together, I am confident that the District's public schools and the students who attend them will have a bright future."

"How can you be a true Republican and promote the federal government role in education?" asked Dale. *He is at it again,* thought Debbie.

"I've been elected as a Republican and served my state of Vermont in both the House and Senate. I've always fought to increase funding for the federal leadership role in education. I would agree with my conservative colleagues that no reform is going anywhere unless we get people at the local level to create that reform and move it along. But I disagree with them when they say the federal government should stay out of education. We're in global competition now, and education is the key to survival. If people at the local level don't know this, we won't be able to meet the competition, and the future of our nation will be at risk.

"Federal leadership in programs like Goals 2000, the National Education Goals Panel, and the National Assessment of Educational Progress, to mention only three, shows us what the federal government can contribute to education reform. By establishing goals and standards, we can assess our state and local school progress. We've got to take our head out of the sand and work together to make Americans competitive into the next century.

Polls for this past election showed that 80% of the American people wanted to balance the budget, but 80% said they don't want to cut education. In addition, 85% recognized that we must spend more money on education, not less, if we're going to upgrade our educational system. This is a vote of public confidence for public education reform and for a federal role.

"I see that my time is up. Thank you for inviting me to testify. I look forward to reading your reform report on Jefferson Elementary School. Perhaps it will be a model for reforming public schools throughout the U.S."

"Thank you, Senator Jeffords," said Wendy. "I have another education myth to handout."

MYTH: Goals 2000, like other federal education programs, makes our public schools worse.

The passage of the *Goals 2000: Educate America Act* in March of 1994 will lead to a federal government takeover of local education because it is still one more burdensome federal program with a multitude of rules and regulations, the result of the liberal establishment's philosophy of 'Outcome-Based Education, and shows that the bureaucrats in Washington still don't understand that parents want public schools that: teach children character development based on honesty, integrity, selflessness, compassion, and self-discipline; curriculum focused on the basics, including math, science, literature, linguistic skills, music, art and history; and recognition that parents are the child's first teacher, with good schools as a supportive partner.

Answer #1: GOALS 2000: Educate America Act became law in March of 1994. Legally it make absolutely clear that there are **no mandates, and that there will be no federal takeover.** Section 318 states, "Nothing in this Act shall be construed to authorize an officer of employee of the Federal Government to mandate, direct, or control a State, local educational agency, or school's curriculum, program of instruction, or allocation of State or local resources or mandate a State or any subdivision thereof to spend any funds or incur any costs not paid for under this Act...the responsibility for control of education is reserved to the States and local school systems." GOALS 2000 is a responsible "block grant" that goes to states. It sets broad objectives and goals, **there are no federal regula-**

---

tions for Goals 2000, but allows the states to determine the means to reach them if they voluntarily decide to apply for the federal funds.

GOALS 2000 passed the Congress with strong bipartisan support, and has been endorsed by national business organizations, including the U.S. Chamber of Commerce, the National Alliance of Business, the Business Roundtable, and the National Association of Manufactures. The GOALS 2000 Act supports an education agenda that was spearheaded by presidents, members of congress, and governors of both parties.

The primary goal of the GOALS 2000: Educate America Act is to encourage local community-based actions that meet pressing educational needs, help more students achieve to higher standards, increase parental participation, and improve teaching. GOALS 2000 provides federal support for local and state reforms. To educate all children, the Act provides great flexibility in how states and communities develop and implement their bottom-up grassroots reform plans.

Answer #2: GOALS 2000 has nothing to say or to do with 'Outcome-Based Education. The legislation doesn't promote any particular education philosophy or approach; that is strictly a local decision. GOALS 2000 focuses on upgrading academic achievement and preparing students for the world of work. Each state, school district, and school determines what content it wants students to learn, and whether that content should focus strictly on core academic and basic skills or should also include other areas. The federal government will not be involved in these decisions.

Academic achievement, responsible citizenship, and parental involvement are essential features of the GOALS 2000 Act. There is strong consensus that citizenship, knowledge of core academic subject matter, and parent-teacher cooperation are critical if this country is going to reach the National Education Goals—first supported by both Republican and Democratic presidents and members of congress. For example the third goal states: "By the year 2000, all students will leave grades 4, 8, and 12 having demonstrated competency in challenging subject matter, including English math, science, foreign languages, civics and government, economics, arts, history, and geography, and every school in American will ensure that all students learn to use their minds well, so that they may be prepared for responsible citizenship, further learning, and productive employment in our Nation's modern economy." *Does any parent not want this quality education for their children?*

Under GOALS 2000, states and school districts determine their own academic standards that outline what they want their children to learn. If they choose, states and communities can use voluntary national standards developed by professional organizations as models to design their own challenging standards. Standards represent what teachers and the public believe students should know in subject areas such as math, geography, civics, and the arts by certain points in their education—or they will be left behind. Several states are adopting parts of the model national standards while others are developing their own standards. National standards are voluntary, but are supported by governors, parents, business people, and educators from both political parties. No GOALS 2000 funds are tied to the use of these standards. No federal law requires their use in any way. This is a state and local education decision. **All fifty states are now voluntarily participating in GOALS 2000 funded educational activities.**

Education Policy in the U.S. Department of Education

Commission members were still talking with Senator Jeffords and Jack Jennings about the role of Congress in making education policy, when Nate called them to order. "It is now my pleasure to introduce our final guest to appear before this Citizens' Commission, U.S. Secretary of Education Richard Riley. He has served in that position since 1993. When President Clinton was re-elected for a second term, he asked Richard Riley to continue as Secretary. He is charged with carrying out the President's top domestic priority—improvement of the nation's public education system. Before coming to Washington, Secretary Riley served as governor of South Carolina. He was known as an 'education governor.' His reputation as a builder of bipartisan coalitions has made him one of the most successful U.S. Secretaries.

"Secretary Riley, under your leadership, the Clinton Administration and the Congress have reauthorized and enacted major federal education legislation. You have personally introduced some powerful Secretarial Initiatives that are improving the education of students throughout the United States. Could you begin by describing those legislative and Secretarial Initiatives that you believe have most powerfully effected American public education during your tenure as Secretary?"

"Thank you, Nate, and members of this Citizens' Commission. I visit local schools whenever I can throughout this great land of ours. I'm amazed at how parents, teachers and principals are seizing the opportunity to take school reform into their own hands and together discuss ways of improving their community schools. So I congratulate you all for the efforts you are making. This Reform Commission is an example of public engagement and grassroots democracy in action. Let me begin by saying that I am optimistic about American education. I believe that we are, at long last, turning the corner...moving from being a nation at risk to a nation with a hopeful future. In many schools, we are starting to win the battle for excellence and good citizenship in American education. I also believe that the Clinton Administration, with the support of a bipartisan leaders from across America, is helping to lead the way. For the first time in history, the public ranks education as the highest priority for the federal government, ahead of reducing the deficit, protecting social security and medicare, and reducing crime. Just about half of adults surveyed worry the federal government won't be involved enough in doing what's necessary to improve schools.[23]

"Every four or five years, the Congress and the Department of Education assess the effectiveness of federal education programs. We usually evaluate the program's impact on state and local educational agencies and students attending public schools. When it is time for reauthorization, Congress holds public hearings so that all parties can voice their opinions about how it's being carried out and how federal funds can be better spent. The year 1994 became historic for the enactment of federal education legislation. For example, the old 1965 Elementary and Secondary Education Act was reauthorized as the *Improving America's Schools Act*. It reaches down to almost every school district in America and impacts some 50,000 schools. This Act was changed in 1994 to strengthen schoolwide programs for schools serving low-income students. It offers support for helping all students reach high academic standards by making all schools safe, disciplined and drug-free, and by providing high-quality professional development for teachers. It provides bilingual education to help students learn English rapidly, and encourages the use of technology to improve teaching and learning. It also encourages low-income parents to participate in planning and assessing schoolwide improvement programs for their children.

"After reauthorization, Congress appropriates funds each year for the education programs. Most federal money (98%) goes directly to states and school districts where the programs are actually carried out in local schools. The U.S. Department of Education is required to monitor the states and local school districts to make certain the federal funds are used for purposes specified by the Congress. We strive to locate best practices and share what works. Reuathorization gives the U.S. Department of Education more opportunity to cut red tape, and we've been doing just that.

"New legislation is often initiated by the President and the Congress in response to the public's demand for better education. In the 1990s, across America there is great interest in higher academic standards for all America's students. *In 1994 Goals 2000: Educate America Act* provides federal assistance to school, school districts and states that want to raise the education standards. This legislation is the least intrusive federal education law possible. It has no red tape. States can voluntarily participate if they want federal funding to plan for and implement tougher standards for teaching and learning. During the past four years, Congress has enacted several other legislative programs that also benefits high school students, like the new *School-to Work Opportunities Act* and better college loan and grants programs to help families pay for college. This is important because between 1992 and the year 2000, 89% of the jobs created in the U.S. will require postsecondary levels of literacy and numeracy."

"Mr. Secretary, can you explain to us the difference between the education legislation that is passed by the Congress and signed by the President, and a Secretarial Initiative? Are they both legal? Are they binding on the schools?" asked Ted Alexander.

"Ted, let me try and answer your good questions. Secretarial initiatives are different than congressionally-enacted laws. When a secretary believes that some additional initiative or program would be effective in addressing issues facing America's students, he or she can issue guidelines and create programs that assist in carrying out actions to address these problems. For example, acting on behalf of the President, I've launched four initiatives. All four have been well received by the American people. The first is *Partnership for Family Involvement in Education*. The second is the *Educational Technology Initiative and Net Days* for connecting technology to improve teach-

444

ing and learning. A third initiative, *America Goes Back to School,* encourages every caring adult—parents, grandparents, community leaders, employers and employees, members of the arts community, religious leaders—to play a more active role in education in their communities. A fourth initiative is encouraging children to read during the summer and challenging caring adults, college work-study students and families to start reading with their children."

"Secretary Riley, I have heard good things about your Family Involvement Initiative. Would you describe that program in more detail?" Maria asked.

"Maria, I have a strong belief that active parental participation in their children's education is one of the most essential elements in successful schools. In my first annual 'State of American Education' address in 1994, I said that we adults must help family members reconnect with their children. I defined this as a 'moral urgency.'[24] Thirty years of research tells us that the starting point of American education is parental expectations and involvement with their children's education.[25] This consistent finding applies to every family regardless of the parent's station in life, their income or their educational background. Parents exercise authority over three critical factors in a child's educational success—daily attendance in school, reading materials and literature in the home, and the amount of television a young person watches. A child who grows up reading for fun is a child who is on the road to success when it comes to learning. As Secretary I took several steps to advance this initiative. First, I announced the formation of a broad-based partnership of parent, school, business, community-based, and religious organizations to encourage and support American families as they seek to prepare their children for the Information Age that is now upon us. Each partner in this coalition contributes in its own best way. This common effort includes such organizations as the National PTA, the National Alliance of Business, the U.S. Catholic Conference, the National Association of Elementary School Principals, Girl Scouts, and Boys and Girls Clubs of America. Today, over 2,700 groups have joined with us in this partnership.

"Second, the Department of Education has published several handbooks for parents. *Strong Families, Strong Schools: Building Community Partnerships for Learning* provides a research base for family involvement in learning. Another is *Team Up for Kids! How Schools Can Support Family Involvement in*

Education. Employers, Families, and Education: Promoting Family Involvement in Learning shows how employers can encourage their employees in their children's learning. *Reaching All Families: Creating Family-Friendly Schools* presents fresh ideas on school outreach strategies to all families. These and other departmental publications have helped partners see how local parent-involvement partnerships function.

"Third, our initiative *America Goes Back To School* encourages everyone to work together with schools and colleges to make education better and support learning inside and outside the schools, especially during back-to-school time in August through October of each year. As a result, teachers, employers, principals, and community groups have rallied the broader community."

"Our fourth initiative is to help children read well and independently by the end of the third grade. As the President says, 'This is America's reading challenge.'"

"Mr. Secretary," Dale said slyly. "How can you defend the U.S. Department of Education and the federal education role. I understand from my sources that your cabinet department is an unnecessary, big, expensive federal agency. Wouldn't the money be better spent on our children's education at the state and local level?"

"Dale, I'm glad to answer that question. The vast majority of our investment in education by the U.S. Department of Education is used for pre K-12 education at local schools and for student financial aid. Less than 2% of our budget is spent on administrative costs, and most of that is for accountability and financial oversight. Everyone I know from President Clinton on down agrees that education is a state and local responsibility nearest the people whose children are being educated. We've learned, however, that the bipartisan Congress was right in 1979 when they recognized that American education has also become a national priority. The President of the United States, through his cabinet level U.S. Department of Education, should keep the nation's attention on the need to improve education if our students are going to be economically competitive with the students around the world, if we are to have a strong and educated military force, and if our citizens are to be productive. Having a national leadership role in education isn't something new as some uninformed critics contend. The Supreme Court has consistently upheld the federal authority."

"Historically, the federal government has provided educational leadership by launching grammar schools with the Northwest Ordinance of 1787, and by starting the land-grant colleges and universities with the Morrill Act of 1862. In this century, it initiated pioneering programs in vocational education, special education, international education, early childhood education and college student financial aid. The President and congressional leaders have designated the U.S. Department of Education as a partner in providing educational opportunity, conducting educational research on best practices and assessment, funding education for the disadvantaged, and improving educational competitiveness for all Americans in our global economy. *Goals 2000: Educate America Act* now recognizes federal leadership in developing challenging academic goals, standards and assessments leading to a quality education for all children.

"Now let's deal with the U.S. Department of Education—the smallest cabinet agency in the federal government. Its purpose is to ensure equal access to education and to promote educational excellence throughout the nation's 85,000 public schools. Since the department became an cabinet agency, the number of employees has been reduced one-third from 7,700 to less than 5,000.[26] This reduction has been accomplished even though both our budget and the number of our programs have doubled over the same 15-year period. As a result, our administrative costs absorb just 2% of our budget, and we deliver 98% on the dollar in education assistance to states, school districts, postsecondary institutions, and students (more dollars per employee—about $6 million annually—than any other Cabinet agency).[27] Much of that 2% is spent on improving accountability and making sure that taxpayer dollars are used appropriately. For example, the federal government provides about two-thirds of all student aid for postsecondary education. We have made these loans less expensive through the direct student loan program.

"During the past four years, our department has accomplished much. We've clearly defined our mission and proposed comprehensive education reform legislation. We've reduced paperwork and regulation, increased flexibility for states and local school districts, eliminated outdated programs, downsized and streamlined bureaucracy. These changes are helping America's students to learn the basics and reach high academic standards in safe, disciplined, and drug-free environments. These changes are also improving teaching; promoting parental involvement; getting more com-

447

puters into the classroom; and improving access to higher education for deserving students."[28]

"Wait a minute, Mr. Secretary." Paul said. "I'm a businessman. I don't know anyone who can boast of running their business with only 2% for overhead. You must run a tight ship!"

"Thank you, Paul, for that compliment. I believe it's time to get the facts out about the cabinet leadership by the U.S. Department of Education if we are to survive and prosper as a nation. We are no longer an agricultural society or even an industrial society, when it made more sense to think of schools as strictly a state and local concern. We are entering a competitive global economy. Every American child must be given an opportunity to become all that he or she can be. Education is now the great 'fault line' that determines who is part of the American Dream. Today more than ever before, education is the engine that drives our economy. The earnings gap between the educated and the less educated is growing. It will continue to grow unless we educate all of our people to high standards. An average education is just not good enough anymore.[29] I believe that by working together—local, state, and federal policymakers, community leaders, educators, parents and students—we can achieve that dream for all our children, including the disadvantaged. Thank you for letting me share these ideas with you."[30]

****

Summary

"We've heard from an impressive group of national education leaders," Nate said. "Before we adjourn, let's summarize their testimonies. Who'd like to start?"

"I'll summarize **Mr. Toch's remarks**," said Debbie. **"He was very persuasive about the need for the whole school community to own the reform process. This means students, teachers and parents. They should choose the school, and then they should form partnerships to invest in improving and maintaining high performance. They should believe strongly that all children can learn at high levels. Tom was critical of some past teacher union officials who blocked school reform. Some of the new union leaders, however, are supporting site-based decision-making, charter schools, teacher merit pay, and accountability for teaching challenging national academic standards. He quotes Al Shanker, presi-**

dent of the AFT, who calls for unions to take a leadership role in helping to train teachers for their new challenges. Unions should become real advocates of site-based management."

"I'd like to summarize **Mr. Pipho,**" said Lenora. "**He said the educators were talkin' right by us parents and community folk. He said you educators don't listen to the parents and community, so you don't really know what we want. Mr. Pipho made it clear that we've been talking about the same things for over 10 years now.**

"We all seem to be slow learners. By being on this Commission, I'm just now beginnin' to see why Jefferson needs to be teachin' my kids those world-class standards. They want to get good jobs when they graduate or go on to college. Ray, why hasn't the damn School Board told the parents and the community how awful this school has become?"

Tamar raised her hand. "I'd like to review **Virginia Edwards' testimony. She said that school reform is difficult, and I'm beginning to believe her. She agreed with a number of our guests that parent engagement is a pressing need if school reform is ever going to be 'scaled up' on a nationwide basis. Stakeholders must communicate better if we're going to successfully carry out grassroots school reform. I had not realized that one way to avoid school reform, and the threat to your own job, is to blame poor achievement on the students themselves—because they are disadvantaged, minority, sick or lack parental support. She sees effective school-site councils as an important tool in promoting grassroots ownership of reform. *Ed Week's* new publication, *Quality Counts,* will really help us to compare Jefferson with schools in other states as we put academic standards in place.**"

"I'd like to summarize **Gordon Ambach,**" Ray said. "**I was not aware of the work of the Council of Chief State School Officers (CCSSO). It's a powerful association.**

These state education executives represent the children of our nation. This national association is involved in state, federal and national education projects. Gordon told us that reform takes careful planning, and that it takes time to implement reforms in large systems like a state or a whole district. He said that both authority and resources must accompany the delegation of responsibility to the local school-site council. He stressed high standards, sound assessments and public accountability. I

was surprised to learn CCSSO advocates effective federal education programs. CCSSO also takes a leadership role in developing policy for international student assessments."

Paul spoke next. "Frank Newman described the work of the Education Commission of the States (ECS). They report developments in school reform which Chris Pipho writes about each month in *Kappan.* He recognizes that the interests of the status quo work against ongoing school reform. Over the years, we have created a regulatory school culture in the states. ECS is a leader in coordinating the work of states on developing challenging academic standards. Frank said we need to move faster in order to scale up the school reform movement. He is impressed with several school reform networks now emerging. Their assessments show improved student performance—proof of the networks' impact. Frank also calls for more public accountability, professional development and decentralization to school site councils."

"I'll try to summarize **Bob Schwartz**," said Maria. "He talked about the role of national private foundations. He expressed the same ambivalence that most of our guest reformers have experienced. On the one hand, we must reform one school at a time. It will take heroic educators and parents. On the other hand, we must increase the pace of reform to reach all public schools before it's too late. The case for national academic standards for all children and a system of assessment and accountability must be put in place. Mr. Schwartz described the priorities of the Pew Charitable Trusts. They give grants to local school districts in order to encourage school-site decision-making. Their grants also target the development of a new teacher union association of progressive leaders who support school reform, teacher participation and accountability. They also support the development of national academic standards, the need to tie professional teacher development to improving classroom practices, and the need to engage parents and the general public in school reform."

"I'm next," said Christina. "I'll take **Jack Jennings'** testimony. He made three points. He described the federal role in education, and its legal authority and responsibility. He showed how the federal role expanded from educational equity to educational quality and challenging academic standards for all America's children. And most troublesome, he documented the danger we face from public confusion and skepticism about the value of public education. Because of our negative attitudes, we've failed to support public school reform. He warns us that unless we reach out to the general public, which means parents and the community too, we stand in danger of losing this legacy for our grandchildren."

Kim spoke next. "I'd like to summarize **Senator Jeffords' testimony.** He expressed great alarm for the state of American education. He also states that only about one-half of our students are functionally literate. He is concerned that our students cannot compete internationally and that our high school and college graduates are not prepared for careers in the global economy. I was impressed that he personally tutors disadvantaged students in Washington D.C., and that he's been helping the D.C. Control Board to reform the District's troubled school system. He defends federal education programs, and he is the new Chair of the U.S. Senate Committee on Labor and Human Resources."

Kathie spoke up. "I'll try to summarize **Secretary Riley's** testimony. He is optimistic about improving education today. He cited the historic amount of federal education legislation that has been enacted by the Congress during President Clinton's first term including such Acts as *Improving America's Schools Act* targeted for disadvantaged students and *Goals 2000: Educate America Act* designed to support states in their drive for higher standards, assessments to improve teaching and learning within safe and drug-free schools. Secretary Riley has developed some special projects or initiatives to help education, including his family/school/ community partnerships, more technology in the schools, and his 'America goes back to school' initiative to get wide public participation in the education of all our children.

"Secretary Riley gave us his reasons for why the federal government should place education as a national priority. First, all citizens have a right to a quality education without being discriminated against, as many states have done in the past. Second, standards must be nationwide because most students will move to other states during their lifetimes. Third, students must be well educated to overcome poverty and compete in the global knowledge economy. Fourth, the federal government conducts research and assessment to measure the nation's educational progress. Finally, the nation must have a well educated military force. Historically, the Secretary reminds us that the federal government has funded education programs since the beginning of our country's history. It has pioneered educational programs that have since been adopted over time by most states. Finally, the U.S. Department of Education, the smallest federal department, is a well-run, highly-efficient agency that has reduced personnel, paperwork regulations and eliminated outdated programs since he became Secretary of Education. Secretary Riley believes that because education has a cabinet-level department, improving American education is a high priority leadership role of the President of the United States. Recent polls show that the American public agrees!

"What an incredible day we've had," said Ray. "We've had the Who's Who of education media reps, and state and federal policymakers! The lessons they've learned compliment those of the national school reformers who we've heard these past six months. I am impressed by their knowledge, experience and dedication to our children's future.

"Now the responsibility is on our collective shoulders!" said Ray. "You've met with your Action Teams. This coming month, you'll want to meet again to draft recommendations for your reports to the full Commission next month. It's a heavy responsibility. We are the last hope for the children at Jefferson. Good luck."

Chapter 18
RECLAIMING JEFFERSON ELEMENTARY SCHOOL:
THE CITIZENS' COMMISSION REPORTS, PART I
Saturday morning, June 14

Tamar Espinosa locked the door of her apartment on a beautiful Summer morning just after 7:30. She climbed into her new red Mazda Miata and drove left on Highway 50 for the 10 minute drive to Jefferson Elementary School. *After nine months of Citizens' Commission Hearings, we're now getting to the bottom line,* she thought. *I wonder how the Commission members will come through on their Action Team reports today? I spent two extra Saturday mornings in April and May working with both my action teams. It was pretty hectic trying to come up with our model and recommendations. I'm glad I'm not a chairperson. They have to make some sense out of our heated discussions.*

What an experience! We've heard from the Who's Who of national reform. We've also heard from influential urban superintendents, media representatives, and national association leaders who could help disseminate these reforms throughout the nation. I used to read about these heavyweights in graduate seminars. My master's program prepared me well for my first year as a third grade teacher. I had no way to know how exciting and rewarding this first year would be. It's tons of work, but I've really found my mission in life. My 'Dream Team' kids are so precious. I've really learned a lot from them this year. My special parent program has worked really well. The parent feedback made us all feel like we accomplished miracles this year. When the state performance tests came out last month, my class scored at the 36th percentile for third graders. But it's still not good enough. Their portfolios were amazing too. Now I know it can be done. Heck! These students were only achieving at the 24th percentile last year.

It'll take major reform of the whole school before dramatic turnarounds can be made—what they're calling whole-school reform. That could take years! I guess

Jefferson Elementary School's future depends on what happens today and next week when we present our final report to the County Board. I'm feeling pretty close to most of the Commission members now. We've become friends. I'm kind of sorry it's coming to an end.

My fellow teachers at Jefferson are almost frantic wondering what's going to happen next. This is unlike my graduate seminars. It's not like doing a term paper. This is the real world! After next week, my professional life could be turned upside down. I wonder where I'll be teaching next year?

Executive Session

Ray, the Commission Chair, called the group to order. "Welcome to our final Citizens' Commission meeting. Unlike our monthly public hearings, today is an 'executive session' that's closed to the public. This is an internal work meeting to prepare for our public presentation of recommendations to the county board of education next Wednesday night. Today, we hear from our Action Teams. I want to stress that this is **not** our final report and recommendations. We're preparing first drafts to be submitted to our full Commission. After today, the chairpersons will redraft the reports, clear the recommendations with their Action Teams and then polish the final draft. They will get the final version to you for your sign-off. I think you'll be pleased with the product. Now it is again my pleasure to turn the time over to Nate."

"Thank you, Ray. Before we turn to the Action Team reports, we have two items to share—a portrait of a model elementary school; and a short summary of lessons learned by our 44 guest experts. We need to analyze these messages and interpret the lessons for Jefferson. We also need to identify the central reform principles that will guide our final recommendations. This is a tall order, but we've been tutored by the finest group of experts in school reform in the United States today. In addition, we have had the benefit of many of our nation's top education policymakers and practitioners. We have finished our discovery journey. It's time for our Commission to stand up and be counted.

"One giant of school reform, Dr. Ernest L. Boyer, anticipated the major findings of our Citizens' Commission. In his final book, which was on reform of elementary schools, he identified the most essential ingredients for an effective school.[1] According to Boyer, '...*community, coherence, climate, and character* are the building blocks for the basic school...An effective school connects people to create *community*—through a shared vision, teachers as leaders and parents as partners. An effective school connects the curriculum to achieve *coherence*—through centrality of language, the core commonalities of science and history, literature, civics and geography—and we must measure the results. An effective school connects classrooms and resources to enrich the *climate*...resources to enrich learning and services to develop the whole child. An effective school builds *character*(by connecting learning to life)—core virtues of honesty, respect, responsibility, compassion, self-discipline, perseverance, giving and living with moral purpose...Sometimes as school reformers, we forget to integrate our strategies and models into essential guidelines that make up that model school to which we would want to send our own children.' And this must be the final test for this Citizens' Commission." Nate was somber as he shared Boyer's last contributions to school reform before his death in 1995.

"Now, we turn to a summary of the experts' testimonies. The question asked each witness—both reformers and practitioners—was, 'what are the two or three most important lessons you have learned about school reform?' Wendy and I have reviewed the testimonies. We found that the lessons of national reformers differed somewhat from those of the practitioners. These lessons were described qualitatively and are not easily quantified like the answers on a multiple choice test. The expert responses read like short essays drawn from their experiences in carrying out reform in different settings and school cultures. Here goes.

"We ranked by frequency the main lessons shared by our 22 reformers: (1) the need for high academic standards for all children; (2) character education, including citizenship training; (3) ongoing professional development for teachers; and (4) significant parent involvement through family / school / community partnerships, including school-site councils. The national reformers also emphasized the need for better student assessment tools and accountability for all parties—students, teachers, administrators and parents. They mentioned less frequently educational technology, federal programs, school choice, charter schools, and multi-health services at school sites."

Paul raised his hand. "Nate, how did the practitioners' priorities compare?"

"Well, our 22 nationally-recognized practitioners were made up of policymakers, school administrators, media reps, and association executives. Most appeared in our last two Hearings. Their lessons in successful school reform were also collectively ranked by frequency: (1) school/parent/community engagement, including school-site councils; (2) challenging academic standards for all children; and (3) better student assessment and accountability for all parties. These priorities were also listed most frequently by reformers as well. The practitioners, however, had lower rankings for professional teacher development and the federal leadership role. Practitioners seldom mentioned the need for character education-citizenship training, and use of educational technology in the schools. In summary, both groups then ranked as high priorities the need for challenging academic standards for all children, better student assessments and accountability for all stakeholders, and more effective family/school/community partnerships."

The School Reform Public Engagement Process

Paul raised his hand. "Now we know about the priorities of our 44 guests, Nate. And we have ample evidence that they know how to reform schools like Jefferson. You've even shared the model Ernie Boyer advocated for elementary schools. I was also impressed by the quality elementary school model that the National Association of Elementary School Principals have developed. But where do we go from here? How do we get started?"

Nate responded, "Paul, we need to be absolutely clear about the principles to carry out reform before we start. If these principles are compromised, whole school reform always fails. From our experienced guest reformers and practitioners, together with our assigned background reading, we've identified five key principles of public engagement that must guide any new school reform vision. Remember that the reform process must be driven at the grassroots level by citizens.[2] You must begin with a new vision of the school you are hoping to create with your reform activities. Let me read from our written draft:

Our new school reform vision statement is 'to create a quality public school in which our teachers and our community's parents will enthusiastically enroll their own children.

First, the District Board of Education must initiate a public engagement process beginning with a two-day school reform 'discovery workshop' to review best models and practices from among those successful whole-school reform strategies for all children in schools throughout the United States;

Second, the District Board of Education must appoint an official Citizens' Commission representing teachers, parents, principals and community leaders. The new Commission must undertake a systematic 'discovery journey' to review the leading models and best practices in school reform. This reform group will conduct an inventory to establish baseline data that profiles their local school's knowledge gap. (See Appendix for Inventory Questionnaire. This, of course, is what our Citizens' Commission has been doing, and we'll report our results on Jefferson in just a few minutes.) 'The Citizens' Commission must then design a Reform Blueprint that describes the new vision, goals, priorities, roles, action steps, funding and a timetable for whole-school reform for their elementary school (We will complete this step by next week.);

Third, the School Reform Council must be given a five-year public charter or alternative independent school status by the state or district school board. It must give the reform team full authority and the resources to reconstitute the community school. The policies of the new governing school site-council would be exempted from most federal, state, district, and union contract regulations. The exceptions would be civil rights protections, teaching conditions and open student admissions. The school reform team will have complete authority over budget, personnel hiring, compensation, teaching assignments, curriculum, assessment, and professional development. (This reform step will be hard to achieve. It requires the County School Board to delegate authority to a body, such as our Citizens' Commission, to undertake whole-school reform. If this is not done, citizens can apply to a higher authority for independent school status.);

Fourth, the School Reform Council must have the authority and funding to implement the reform blueprint with full and active participation of representative teachers, parents and community leaders in all major policy decisions at the school site. The Council will purchase technical assistance and support services from the district office and outside contractors. (We can't emphasize this enough. This step requires public engagement from the very beginning—in the needs assessment, and in the design, implementation, and evaluation of the Reform Blueprint's impact.); and

Fifth, at least once each year, the School Reform Council must conduct a management audit by assessing student achievement—individual, class and school levels. The Council must also survey parent and community support for school reform. Accountability requires them to annually report a financial audit, student achievement, and survey findings of community support to a public meeting of parents and other taxpayers. (Public reports show citizens what they are getting in exchange for paying school taxes and trusting educators with their children.) **The school charter can be renewed in five years only if the stated new school vision, goals and timetables have been achieved. In the interim, satisfactory progress must be reported annually to the public, and financial accountability certified by outside auditors.'"**

"But, Nate," Ted said. "As a teacher, I don't want some Citizens' Commission telling me what I can teach and how to teach it and then standing around judging my performance."

Nate smiled. "That is the whole idea of accountability, Ted. The taxpayers own the schools, pay your salary, and entrust their children to your care. They have every right to judge the results of their public investment. Teachers will sit on the school-site council. Parent and community representatives will defer to educators on such issues as curriculum selection, assessment measures and teaching techniques. Teachers will no longer have to work in isolation or beg parents to support their children's education. Accountability goes both ways. Parents should send children to school ready to learn and set high expectations for their behavior. They should support homework assignments and participate in school/home activities. We've learned that active parents can be the most significant factor in motivating student achievement."

"Kim, you're a principal," said Ted. "How do you feel about handing your school over to an outside committee?" Ted was still nervous.

"First, Ted," Kim replied. "I don't regard a school-site council as outsiders. This council would serve much as a lay district school board does in directing the work of the district superintendent. A wise board respects the professional training and experience of the superintendent. They work together to build trust for the good of the school district. In the case of the local school-based council, professional educators are more than represented. In this arrangement, we can benefit by the parent and community perspectives. In some ways, the local school is the perfect model for democracy through this public engagement process.

"I believe effective educators have nothing to fear from a strong school-based policy council. Let me summarize Dr. Comer's guidelines for these councils from my notes." Kim shuffled through her papers until she found the page that read, 'The council cannot paralyze the leader, and decisions should be made by consensus. We don't want to create winners and losers. We must build trust between educators and the outside public. But some administrators and school board members will resist sharing their authority. Perhaps they have good reason.'

"All our guests have agreed that genuine public participation is the basic requirement for successful school reform. Either we believe in and begin to practice serious public engagement and accountability or, I believe, public schools will not survive. The key issue then becomes, 'who controls local school reform.' If it's some regulatory authority at the district level, or even a teacher union leader enforcing a district-negotiated contract, the hands of the school-site council are tied. This is simply another example of refusing to carry out site-based reform. We will destroy public education if we aren't smart enough to get the message the public is sending us. If we listen, we can hear calls for vouchers and charter schools. We educators had better take responsibility for improving public education!"

"Let's shift now," said Nate, "from the five action steps to identifying the eight components that must be included in any effective reform model.* In this country, we have about 60,000 public elementary schools, so there's plenty of work for all of us if reform is to reach all these schools in this decade. Remember also the counsel of Bob Slavin. He taught us that 'sand' schools are resistant or not ready for change; 'brick' schools adopt one or more components, like a new curriculum; 'seed' schools change all components into a new school vision—whole school reform.

Paul refused to give up. "Nate, it looks like we'd better find ways to shortcut the long process we've gone through this past year. We've got to ignite the reform process in each school community throughout our district. And almost more important, each reform group cannot re-invent the wheel by having to discover their own school reform components. We are persuaded by the New American Schools' Commitment to whole-school

---

*Other components may be appropriate for high schools, such as 'school-to-work.'

reform. I guess this means that we must first reach agreement on what components are necessary for comprehensive school reform."[3]

"Paul," Nate replied, "our Citizens' Commission has identified **eight components that can be adapted to the needs of each school culture. These reform models, programs and best practices would include** (see Figure 18.1 *Eight Essential Components of Comprehensive School Reform*):

1. a school reform council with authority to implement school-wide policy;

2. a curriculum that integrates challenging academic standards;

3. a school-wide character education program;

4. professional staff development;

5. school support services;

6. technology support;

7. parent and community engagement; and

8. school assessment and accountability.

Figure 18.1

Eight Essential Components of Comprehensive School Reform

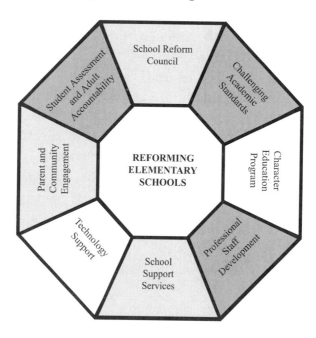

"This brings us down to our school. Kim, could I ask you to pass out the background profile of Jefferson Elementary for the 1996-97 school year?

PROFILE OF JEFFERSON ELEMENTARY SCHOOL
ANY WHERE COUNTY, USA

The student body totals 473, with 31% Whites, 28% African-Americans, 24% Hispanic, 14% Asian, and 3% Native American. LEP students speaking limited English are 26%. Children with disabilities are 14%. Some 68% of the students qualify for the full or reduced federal lunch program. Student mobility is 31%. Absenteeism averages 17% on any given day. Per pupil expenditure is $5,545 each year. Only 37% of sixth grade students score above the national average on the Comprehensive Test of Basic Skills. There is no character education program. Over the past five years, only 22% of Jefferson fourth-grade students consistently scored at or above basic reading levels on NAEP state trial assessments (compared with Northeast and National averages of 55% and 56% respectively). Jefferson spends a smaller part (57%) of its budget on instruction than neighboring districts (64%). Some 45% of Jefferson Elementary alumni fail to graduate from high school.

There are 32 teachers, including 16% African-Americans, 9% Hispanic and 75% White. Teacher absenteeism averages 15% on any given day. Teaching experience averages 7 years. Teacher turnover averages 40%. Teachers with Master's degrees total 16%. Morale is very low.

The Jefferson Elementary School building is 43-years old and in disrepair. Inadequate features include exterior walls, windows and roof. There are problems in some rooms with heating, air conditioning; plumbing, electrical lighting and electrical power. We are not meeting the Life-Safety Codes."

Assessed against the high-performance, independent elementary school inventory (see Appendix), Jefferson rates an "F" (3 points out of 100 possible). It should be closed or reconsituted.

"I'd like to make a comment here," said Kim when she finished reading aloud. "When the educational foundation is not laid in elementary school, most students never recover. It's not the students of Jefferson who have failed, it is the educators, parents and larger community who have failed these students."

"Thanks, Kim, you've set the stage for our Action Team reports," Nate said. "Let's take a short refreshment break. When we return, you'll see how our work is all coming together."

****

Action Team Reports

Wendy welcomed the group back. "Ray Gonzales will present our first Action Team report. He is Chair and Marie Morales and Debbie Cohen are Co-Chairs."

"Thank you, Wendy," said Ray. "Public trust in our community's schools is built on shared authority. The school board and superintendent must delegate authority to teachers and parents on the local school-site council for reforming and operating the new community school. This will be the key issue when our Citizens' Commission makes its recommendations to the County School Board! Make no mistake about it! As Vice Chair of the County Board, I believe we can convince them to accept the principle of shared authority—but don't take anything for granted. I've had to change my mind several times this past year because of our experiences on this Commission's 'discovery journey.'"

1. School Reform Council

Ray went on. "I've asked Debbie Cohen to report the initial recommendations of the School Reform Council's Action Team, also known at SRCAT," he smiled.

"Thank you, Ray," said Debbie. "Our recommendations of this 12-member group define what is essential to any successful school reform. We believe that a new political relationship must be established between the school board, teachers, parents and community. The symbol of this new relationship is the legal delegation of full authority to a representative school-site council. This is our draft:

'This School Reform Council will design the Reform Blueprint, operations and accountability for a new Jefferson Community Learning Center (see Appendix for Introduction to High-Performance Independent Elementary School Inventory). Other areas for which SRCAT will make policy include:

1. designing the new organization;
2. hiring and firing teachers and classified staff;
3. professional staff development;
4. selecting curriculum and teaching materials;
5. selecting a character education program;
6. administrative support systems; including personnel rewards (above standard teacher and other staff salaries) for outstanding performance;
7. full-site operating and school reform investment budgets;
8. building repairs;
9. purchase of educational technology;
10. selection of student and staff assessments;
11. homework and after-school and Saturday tutoring activities;
12. multi-center health services for all children;
13. parent and community engagement activities; and
14. responsibility for annual public reporting of student achievement, school performance and financial accountability.'

"Of course, we'll be guided by the recommendations of the other Action Teams.

Let me read the rest of our draft:

'The School Reform Council will be chaired by the new principal at Jefferson Community Learning Center. The Council will also include a new Vice Chair for parent engagement, and a new Vice Chair for Professional Development. The remaining nine members will include chairs of the other Action Teams and other at-large members selected according to the required balance of community, parent and teacher representatives. The SRCAT will begin taking applications and recruiting an entire new teaching and classified staff for the next school year. We expect to be training new staff by July 14.

'The student/teacher ratio at Jefferson will be 20 to 1. This goal will be reached by requiring all staff to teach at least part time, with staff ratio being two-thirds teachers and one-third classified.

'Jefferson Community Learning Center, its library, multi-media laboratories and gymnasium will meet the expanding needs for working parents and students by offering supplemental activities. Jefferson will stay open from 7:00 a.m. until 9:00 p.m. every day for academic tutoring; recreational, arts and music enrichment. We encourage all age groups to participate in the education of the Jefferson children. For example, we will welcome grandparents and other seniors to help us with literacy programs.'

"But you don't know what you're getting into!" Ted almost shouted. "You can't trust the County Board. They'll never buy into these recommendations. They won't share authority with the School Reform Council at Jefferson. Wait until our superintendent Tom Doolley hears about this power grab. He'll put a stop to all this site based decision-making talk. If other schools in the district started acting like this Citizens' Commission—why we would have a revolution!"

"Ted, that's what we hope," said Ray. "But why don't you like what we're proposing? Why shouldn't we get to work and reform Jefferson? Isn't this our mission?"

Ted was steamed! "You just can't trust this Board to give you the authority. Hell, you're the vice chairman of the Board, have you ever seen them do anything for kids this radical? All this talk about hiring new teachers and holding them accountable for what the children are learning and then rewarding them on the basis of improved performance. That's what they are doing in Kentucky, but our union contract will never permit that here in this district. And what's is all this talk about new academic standards— that means teachers will have to learn to teach all over again. It'll never happen!"

Wendy, broke in. "Ted, we need to move on. What the County decides to do about our request for independent status will be the key issue at next Wednesday's Board meeting."

2. Challenging Academic Standards

"Now," said Wendy, "it's time to hear from our Academic Standards Action Team (ASAT)—Kim Su Young, chair, Tamar Espinosa and Lenora Brown, co-chairs."

"Thank you, Wendy," Kim spoke up. "I'm going to ask Tamar to share our recommendations for academic standards. We wrestled with some tough curriculum choices, but came out with a synthesis. One of our biggest concerns is how poorly Jefferson children are reading—and we don't have years to discover a new curriculum that will fix this. Tamar?"

Thank you, Kim. The Academic Standards Action Team will implement tough academic standards for all children who attend Jefferson beginning next September.

"Our recommendations are the following: **'All Jefferson students will be reading up to grade-level proficiency by the sixth grade or they will not be promoted into middle school. Everyone in the school will know this policy. Every June each student will know where he or she stands. Some students will want to schedule special tutoring sessions or spend their vacations in summer school catching up or learning English.**

'Because we believe small schools are more effective, we suggest that Jefferson's student body be divided into two smaller schools of approximately 250 students each. We believe that this action will attract more students, but we will limit enrollment to 500. We believe that two standards programs are exceptional. Half of our students will follow the Roots and Wings curriculum of Dr. Robert Slavin. We believe its focus on reading and the broader program of math and social studies will prove beneficial. At the same time, we'll invite Dr. E.D. Hirsch to help us implement his Core Curriculum for the other half of our student body. We are not experimenting here because both have demonstrated strong positive results. By using these two models over the next five years, we will be able to assess their impact. We may even work up a bit of healthy competition to see how our students perform. Children using either curriculum will be enriched. We will also look to such New American Schools designs a Outward Bound and Audrey Cohen College to go beyond the core curriculum with special field experiences and service projects in the community.

'We should adopt the philosophy and school development process of models like Dr. Levin's Accelerated Schools that will strengthen interpersonal and group relationships for all our Jefferson students. It will also guide teacher professional development and will help create a more responsible school learning culture.

'We should have all teachers in place by July 14 and spend the rest of July and August in intensive professional development. The teachers will learn about the strength of these curricular programs and be able to integrate them for the benefit of all our children.'

"Wait a damn minute, Tamar," said Dale Jones. "Are you telling me that you're borrowing from these curriculum models to come up with a mix that will be superior to any one of them alone? The creators of these models have spent years field testing their curriculums. They would never permit them to be used in the same school like this. And what makes you think you can get teachers to give up their summer vacations to tool up for this?"

"Let me handle Dale," Lenora spoke up. "First off, we've spent a lot of time examinin' these programs. Most of them work better than lettin' each teacher discover his or her own way. Besides, we don't have any more time to experiment! We're goin' to bring their people back to see how we can integrate the best they have to offer without short changin' the best of each program. We're not afraid to try. Nothin' could be worse than what we've been doin.' And who says teachers won't spend their summer vacations gettin' tooled up. If we can get some professional development money to pay them for one or two extra months, I'll bet they'd be happy about it. Have some faith, man!"

"Your points are well taken, Dale," said Kim. "But we've discussed this strategy with our Professional Development Action Team. You'll hear from them this afternoon. We'll work carefully with the reformers to see how these programs can be integrated into our core curriculum, which we'll enrich with field experience and community service opportunities. Will it work? Not unless we carefully design it for predictable outcomes and then assess our efforts every step of the way. We have to know if it's working for each student. But we're confident that we can mix and match these impressive curricular models and implement an enriched program for all Jefferson children."

3. Character Education

"Thanks, Kim. Let's move now to our next report," said Wendy. "The Character Education Action Team (CEAT) has Christina Peterson as Chair, with Dale Jones and Delores Williams as Co-Chairs. Christina?"

"Thank you, Wendy. Dale and Delores have asked me to share our work," said Christina. "We believe that character education is an essential component of the whole school culture. I'll read our recommendation: **Character education should be part of overall curriculum, not a separate program. All teachers should be trained to integrate character education and cooperative learning into their curriculum during an intensive, two-week sessions. We will ask Dr. Tom Lickona's Center for the 4th and 5th Rs to conduct in-service summer workshops for all of Jefferson's teachers and staff. We will purchase books and materials for teachers, students and parents from those being developed by Dr. David Brooks at the Thomas Jefferson Center on Character Education. We will ask Dr. Eric Schaps and Dr. James Comer to hold teacher workshops targeted specifically for child development and upgrading teaching and counseling skills. We will ask Dr. Shapps, Dr. Comer and Dr. Rich to design monthly training sessions for parents (whom we recognize as the first teachers of character education), to understand and reinforce the school's character education curriculum. We will ask these specialists to design an ongoing series of school-wide character education activities and recognitions that involve students, parents, community representatives, including law enforcement officers and community religious leaders. We are leaning toward requiring all Jefferson students to wear standard school uniforms."**

"Whoa!" shouted Ray. "Aren't we getting a little carried away? I know it's important and I was very impressed with our Hearing on the subject. But won't your recommendations take valuable time away from teaching academic subjects as well as be expensive?"

"I'd like to answer that, Christina," said Dale. "You remember, Ray, our Hearing on education and destructive student behavior? We learned that the Seventh National Education Goal states, 'By the year 2000, every school in the United States will be free of drugs, violence, and the unauthorized presence of firearms and alcohol and will offer a disciplined environment conductive to learning.'

"We can't wait until these kids are in middle or high school, are pregnant, join gangs, are hooked on tobacco, alcohol or drugs, and are dropouts before we attack these destructive behaviors. I should know! That's what happened to me. I wasn't pregnant, of course, but I had to get married as a senior. My single mom didn't have the time or know-how to stop me from joining a gang and getting into trouble. No wonder I was a zero in school!

"And what about student disruption of classes while teachers are trying to teach academic subjects? But it was Nate's presentation on the profile of

467

prison inmates—both Whites and minorities—that really got my attention. By then it's too late."

"We all worry about our kids," said Maria, "especial with the bad influences they're exposed to every day—the destructive effects of glamorized sex and violence in movies, or on television and videos, not to mention the lyrics of pop music. We can't watch them all the time, but we can help prepare them.

"Character education is as important to their future as a strong academic education! And these programs are not expensive to implement. I'll bet every parent at Jefferson will get behind us on this one. They'll probably end up volunteering to help us provide this program. This is the way to build our parent support! These kids at Jefferson, must—how shall I put it—be vaccinated with 'character-education serum' early."

Debbie raised her hand. "But I'm teaching my kids at home the values I want them to have, like honesty, respect, responsibility. I forget the others."

"Debbie, for once I agree with Dale," said Paul. You may be doing a great job teaching your children the core values around respect and responsibility. But what about the other children your kids meet in school and in the community? Your family is already suffering from our failure to teach all children the values most of us were taught growing up. There's a moral deficit in our education system. We can correct that deficit now for Jefferson's children. Let's not leave it to chance when we know what to do and how to do it most effectively. The programs will have long-lasting payoffs in our children's futures."

"Thanks, Paul, for your comments," said Wendy. "And I especially want to thank Christina, Delores and Dale for their good work and recommendations.

4. Professional Development

"Now moving right along," continued Wendy, "our next report is from the Professional Development Action Team (PDAT). Kathie Sorenson is Chair, with Co-Chairs Tamar Espinosa and Dale Jones. Kathie?"

"Thank you, Wendy," said Kathie. "I'll begin with what Dr. Linda Darling-Hammond said, something like, 'school reform is impossible without professional staff development of teachers.' Almost every guest gave the same message. It's the same lesson our failing automobile industry finally got from the Japanese. They learned it from management experts like Deming, Likert, and Drucker when American auto executives wouldn't listen. That lesson is that a school must retrain its worker/teachers and give them full responsibility for operating the production-line/classrooms to become a high-performance organization. In schools that means training every worker—classified and certified. Let me read this for you:

'Our recommendation is that the principal, teachers and other staff at Jefferson undergo a new training program to prepare them for supporting the whole-school reform process. They will also receive regular in-service training. On July 14, all Jefferson teachers and staff will begin retooling to teach the new academic standards and character education curriculum.

'All professional development will focus directly on improving the teaching of knowledge and skills within the classroom. The PDAT will consult with reform network trainers before making its funding recommendations to the School Reform Council, which will allocate funds for professional and classified development. The training of each teacher at Jefferson will be evaluated continuously to determine if their classroom teaching improves. Teachers will no longer receive merit pay for seniority or additional higher education credits. Merit pay will be based on improved performance of their students. During the coming school year, and each year thereafter, the PDAT will select seven or more teachers from different grade levels to be given financial support for the process of certification by the National Board of Professional Teaching Standards.

'Classified personnel will also be trained for their new roles beginning July 14th. Inasmuch as about 70% of the personnel working at Jefferson will be teachers, the number of classified staff will be sharply reduced. Teachers and students will need to work closely with fewer non-teaching staff. (See Figure 18.1 *Eight Essential Components of Whole School Reform* for a model of how we intend to reorganize the teaching staff).[4]

'The Professional Staff Development Action Team will conduct interviews for recruitment of teachers and classified workers and make final recommendations to the School Reform Council. The personnel now serving at Jefferson will not be automatically hired. All positions will be open for applicants who wish to be considered. The startup time for professional development will be significantly reduced by recruiting outstanding, experienced personnel who will be highly motivated to come to Jefferson.'"

"Kathie?" Delores asked, "Are you saying that you, Tamar, Ted and I don't have secure positions next year at Jefferson? I didn't participate on this Commission all year just to see my job eliminated!"

"Delores," said Kathie, "you've hit the nail right on the head. None of us has a reserved position at Jefferson for next year. But I'm certain the County School District will find positions for us at other schools. Or we may choose to apply for one of the new teaching positions at Jefferson and take our chances with the selection committee. You already know some of them from your work on the Commission this year. But clearly this will be a merit selection process based on qualifications."

"Kathie, I'm really mad! Just who gave you the right to determine where I'm going to teach," said Ted. "I'll file a grievance with the union over this. I have seniority rights."

"Ted, I know this is a tough one," Kathie said. "The County Board will make that call, not me, if they buy our report and recommendations. As I said earlier, this is where the tire meets the road. High-performance schools are possible only with high-performance teachers. Our work this past year was not a charade! Now we must show the Board, the community, the parents and other educators that this Citizens' Commission means business by acting with integrity. The 'buck stops here!' But have some faith in yourself, Ted. If you really value the work of this Commission and want to play by the new rules at Jefferson and be judged on your performance as a teacher, you should definitely apply. Your experience on this Citizens' Commission would be a big asset to other teachers who need to catch the vision we are developing here."

"Thanks, Kathie for sharing your team's recommendations," said Wendy. "And, Ted, I hope you'll think about what she's said to you. I think all of us can see ways you could make a significant contribution. Unless there are urgent questions that can't wait, we need to adjourn for lunch. Our objective is to keep improving our draft recommendations until we unveil them to the County Board next week. During lunch, keep discussing what you've heard this morning. See you back at 1:00 p.m."

Chapter 19
RECLAIMING JEFFERSON ELEMENTARY SCHOOL:
THE CITIZENS' COMMISSION REPORTS, PART II

Saturday afternoon, June 14

Wendy took over for the rest of the afternoon. "We have four Action Team reports remaining before we have our final discussion. I'm impressed by the good work that each team has put into its recommendations. I can't imagine that we'd have come to these recommendations without the inputs of our distinguished guests and having examined the best school reform models and practices. Yet as we're now discovering, each school Citizens' Commission must select the components from among the reform models that can be adapted their unique education culture, politics and operations.

Action Team Reports

1. Parent and Community Engagement

"We'll now hear from the Parent and Community Engagement Action Team (PCEAT)," said Wendy. "It's chaired by Maria Morales, and the co-chairs are Paul Christopher and Christina Peterson. Maria?"

"Thank you, Wendy. Paul and Christina speak so well, they should be giving our Action Team report. But they selected me, so here goes. We carefully examined the parent programs available today and found that most have been developed for preschool children, like Head Start, and Parents as Teachers. We looked at the work of our Commission guests—Dr. Diane Ramsey's *Responsible Learning Culture*, Family Education Plan with student/parent/teacher compacts, Dr. Dorothy Rich's MegaSkills program, Dr. Joyce Epstein's family/school/community partnerships." Maria paused to look at her notes before continuing. "We also studied national parent action programs like Marilyn Acklin's Federal Title I Parent Coalition, Joan

Dykstra's National PTA, Ernie Cortes' parent advocacy, and Secretary Riley's parent initiative.

"In the 1990s, we've moved from the traditional approach—parent involvement characterized by occasional attendance at PTA back-to-school nights—to more active parent participation. This means that parents are engaged at school and at home. They prepare their children for school by providing better health care, reading with them daily, and monitoring homework and television viewing. Parents also form a parent/school/partnership where they actively participate at school, serving as tutors, aides, members of school site councils or district school boards.

"The Eighth National Education Goal states: '**By the year 2000, every school will promote partnerships that will increase parental involvement and participation in promoting the social, emotional, and academic growth of children.**' We also learned that the new Title I legislation requires that parents help design and oversee federal expenditures in their schools. U.S. Secretary of Education Richard Riley officially recognized in his family involvement initiative the essential role of parents as their children's first teachers and as essential partners in local school reform.

"Now how does all this information help us reform Jefferson Community Learning Center? Well, we are critical of the way most school administrators and teachers have systematically kept parents out of schools. But they can't educate our children alone. We now realize that without serious, sustained parent engagement, school reform will fail here or anywhere else. Therefore, '**We recommend hiring a full-time Vice-Chair for Parent and Community Engagement on the School Reform Council to coordinate Jefferson's expanded parent engagement program. We also recommend that parents be invited into the school building and into classrooms any time of the day when they've notified the teacher ahead of time. Organizations like PTA and Title I parents should have a parent room or separate area in the library where they can meet and easily access parent education and training materials—printed and audio-visual.**

'**(We've noted how important professional development of teachers is to successful school reform. The same goes for parents.) Parents need ongoing training programs of activities from basic parenting skills to family literacy after school and Saturdays. We recommend programs like MegaSkills that teach parents ways to better support their children's for-**

mal education. We recommend a student/parent/teacher compact. When parents and teachers learn to draft a compact together, with clear goals and responsibilities, the results are impressive. Interested parents should receive systematic training for participation on school-site councils. We should also provide counseling and coordination of parent adult literacy and adult education programs leading to completion of high school diplomas, GEDs, and college degrees. This will help them model the value of continuing education for their children. Classroom teachers need regular training on how to work effectively with all parents, and how to use voice mail and parent/teacher conferences to inform parents about how their children are doing in school.

'We will ask the U.S. Secretary of Education to send in a federal team to see how well we are complying with the new Title I law. It requires parents to help design and monitor all federal education funds—about 23% of Jefferson's annual operating budget. This legislation emphasizes that all parents must become equal partners with classroom teachers in the education of their children. The expenditure of these federal funds for parent engagement activities should be monitored and reported by the Vice-Chair for Parent and Community Engagement.

'Parent volunteer 'time dollars' are the largest untapped resource in school reform today.[1] Each parent whose child attends Jefferson will be required to contribute the equivalent of one-half day per month to parent/school/community partnership activities. Fathers, as well as mothers, will be expected to contribute their share of the family's voluntary time dollars. This can be as tutors or teacher aides in math and science, bilingual instruction, computers or as consultants in legal, financial, building and grounds.' (By the way, with about 250 families that would mean contributions of 1000 additional hours of adult voluntary time or an estimated $10,000 or more in value each month ($60,000 each year) to the Jefferson Community Learning Center)."

"This policy," said Maria, "will quickly send some important messages: (1) Parents who pay taxes, own the schools. They pay teachers' salaries, and entrust them with their children. But the education of our children is no longer the sole responsibility of professional educators, we must become full partners; (2) People who work together on a common cause develop a sense of ownership and community, so often lacking in America today; and (3) People who work together can build coalitions of grassroots support to demonstrate the value of a working democracy in a local school.

'The Vice Chair for Parent and Community Engagement will monitor all parent participation activities. We expect these activities to be managed as effectively as other administrative support services.

'We anticipate involving the whole community in these activities—grandparents, voluntary association members, civic and government employees and private business employees. This proposed parent and community participation will provide needed balance with activities by professional educators for the education of all Jefferson students.'

"We think this recommendation is consistent with our mission statement: 'We will create a high-quality public school in which all teachers and parents are willing to enroll their children.' Are there any questions?"

"Yes, Maria," said Deborah Cohen. "I've never heard of such a thing as parents being forced to give one-half day per month or four hours of contributed time to their public elementary school. I'm appalled! How can you expect them to do this on top of everything else?"

"Glad you asked that question, Debbie!" Maria was on a roll. "Most private schools require parent participation in addition to the steep tuition they pay. If you have several children attending that school, it often means contributing a day or more, sometimes double that. Is it a hardship? Yes, it is. That's the whole idea! It helps guarantee their concern and active support.

"Now the children who will be selected to attend Jefferson will qualify partly because their families will agree to contribute four hours per child per month to the school community. This commitment will be stated in their initial student/parent/teacher compact. In order to do this, we may have to give up one night of television or get up an hour earlier on weekends.

"We need lots of help in figuring out how we can make this work, especially from you single mothers, Debbie. For example, maybe we should modify our parent policy so that single parents only need contribute half that time to the school. Maybe some two-parent families could contribute one day between them. In some cases, community hours could be pooled and given back to help those with special family needs. Whatever is worked out, we all need to share the load so not one child or parent gets left behind."

"I was just thinking," said Paul, "how quickly Jefferson could attract funds to buy computers for every classroom. If we had the participation of the top executives in this community who want their children to attend the new Jefferson Community Learning Center, this would be a piece of cake. Maria, could you explain more about time dollars? Haven't I heard that concept somewhere before?"

"Paul, let me answer that question," said Christina Peterson. "You probably have heard the concept. It's gaining some interest all over the country. The author of a book by that name reports that people in communities are now bartering voluntary services to help provide special assistance. That kind of positive networking used to be common among members of religious and communal associations in early American history. We've almost forgotten the concept except for participation in PTA, or civic or service clubs and religious communities. Individuals who contribute voluntary time-dollars end up meeting new neighbors, helping each others' children, and getting out of their narrow professional ghettoes. It makes for a much healthier community. It also brings a massive pool of talent to the table on behalf of our new community learning center."

"We need to move on now. But this report has really sparked interest," said Wendy. "It's redefined a whole new approach to the role of parents participating in school reform

2. Comprehensive Technology Services

"Our next report," Nate continued, "is from the Technology Services Action Team (TSAT). Debbie Cohen is chair, with Lenora Brown and Ted Alexander as co-chairs. Debbie, you're on."

"Thanks, Nate. I've asked Ted Alexander to present our report. He may be the only one who understands what we're trying to do here. Ted, the time is yours."

"We started by walking around Jefferson to survey the state of computers in each classroom and in the multi-media center. We found that all computers in the office and classrooms were the old Apple II model. They're not really powerful enough for getting to the Internet and running new CD-Roms. The multi-media center does have one good Texas

Instruments Computer that can put students on the Internet—but only one at a time. This means that most students at Jefferson will never be exposed to the opportunities that are routine for most middle-class students at home or in good suburban schools.

"With that in mind, we recommend completely rewiring Jefferson. Then we can put several computers in each room and still have the capacity for continuing expansion. Each classroom needs at least two computers right now. Then each year, for the next five years, we'll add computers until there is one for every three students.

"Second, in the next two weeks, if the County Board approves our report, we will meet with Dr. Howard Mehlinger at Indiana University and have his people help us create a technology design that's consistent with our new curriculum.

"Third, we recommend raising outside money from businesses and foundations in our community to install 55 computers by August—two in each classroom, two in the library, and three in the office.

"Fourth, we recommend installing a more effective computer-assisted system with voice-mail boxes so parents can get the homework assignments each day, and the principal, administrator and teachers can contact parents.

"Fifth, during August we recommend conducting training sessions for teachers. In September we'll begin training sessions to show all parents how to use the voice mail system. Also in September, teachers and the librarian will begin teaching students how to use their classroom computers.'"

"Ted," Paul said, "I'd like to help raise some funds for your 'computers-in-every- classroom' program. After you've met with Dr. Mehlinger and have a proposal with hard numbers, let's meet and develop a strategy. I want to talk with the Kiwanis Club about taking on Jefferson as a project. I'll also talk to the Ballston Compact—that's our Chamber of Commerce. This is a concrete project that we can sell to business people. Maybe a business could adopt a classroom. I'm up for this one!"

Looks like Ted has been put between a rock and a hard place by Debbie and now by Paul, Dale thought. *It's going to be pretty hard for him to get off this reform train now. After all his moaning and groaning, he seems to have discovered a positive role for himself—leading the troops to provide a new state-of-the-art instruc-*

tional technology system for Jefferson. I think he's finally taken some ownership for this program.

"Thank you for that Technology Services Action Report," said Nate. "Now it's time for our refreshment break. See you back in about 15 minutes."

****

3. Administrative Support Services

The Commission members were still talking excitedly about the two Action Team reports as Nate called them to order. "Let's take our next report. The Support Services Action Team (SSAT) is chaired by Delores Williams with co-chairs Kim Su Young and Ray Gonzales. I'm sure this report will be less controversial than some of our other topics," Nate said with a smile. "The time is yours, Delores."

"Well, my experience has been limited to the classroom so I've learned a lot on this Action Team about how a school is run. I've asked Kim to share our work since she has served as principal of Lawndale Elementary for the past seven years."

"Thank you," said Kim. "The three of us brought different perspectives to this task. Delores represented the needs of teachers, Ray represents the Board members, and I represent the principals. Delores and Ray were surprised by some items since they don't directly deal with them. So we decided to first present this list of all the administrative support services that schools perform, to support classroom teaching and the learning processes. I'll go over the 17 system we identified:

"I'm exhausted just listing these," Kim said. "Can you think of anything we might have forgotten?"

"I had no idea," said Debbie. "What an overwhelming job!" Does our principal here at Jefferson Elementary administer all these services?"

"The County School System administers many of these services now, like transportation, financial services, purchasing, and personnel payroll. But if the County Board cuts us loose with some kind of independent school, we'd be responsible for delivering these services. If that happens, the first task would be to find how these services could be contracted out for the highest quality and least expense. If that turned out to be the county, then we could contract with them. Otherwise, it might be another school district or private vendor."

"Kim," Ray asked, "tell the group about our recommendation to 'shrink' the administrative services or classified staff so we can hire more teachers and reduce class size."

"Well, we're concerned about what it takes for high quality teaching and learning. We want to provide that kind of support. One problem we see is that principals are now the school's 'fire marshals,' so to speak. They spend their day generally putting out 'fires'—or crisis management—so teachers

ADMINISTRATIVE SUPPORT SERVICES

1. Transportation—busing contracts and coordination and crossing guard coordination with the local police;

2. Food services—feeding up to 500 people at lunch and perhaps opening our cafeteria for breakfast and dinner under the new plan;

3. Student and employee personnel records, tracking attendance and notifying parents;

4. Student counseling services;

5. Health services—school nurse and supplies and emergency services;

6. School security services and relationships with law enforcement and juvenile authorities; relationships with county social services—coordination with social workers, families and children outside of school;

7. Building services—janitorial, utilities, school grounds, and repair;

8. Low-tech communication maintenance services like mail delivery and sorting, telephones, audio-visual equipment;

9. High-tech communication services like the multi-media center, computer purchases and maintenance;

10. Library services like ordering and maintaining books and learning materials;

11. Relationships with civic, community, district, state and federal officials;

12. Reporting services to district, state and federal representatives;

13. Media relations services—newspaper, radio and TV coverage and response;

14. Legal services;

15. Purchasing services—teaching supplies, textbooks and special materials;

16. Financial services—budgeting, payroll, accounting services, insurance, and tracking multi-year school capital investment, new staff development, training and incentive programs, and funding technology infrastructure upgrade; and

17. Parent engagement activities and records.

can focus on teaching. The net result is that the school's most experienced educator ends up on the teaching sidelines. So we've got to design and operate this new community learning center effectively, otherwise the instructional support will suffer.

"We recommend that the School Reform Council allocate federal funds for *school reform only* educational activities. State and district funds will continue to be used for direct operating expenses, such as teacher salaries, transportation, textbooks, and school overhead. Federal funding for reform, parent engagement and academic enrichment will be used for merit awards for outstanding teaching.

'We recommend changing the ratio and make-up of school staff. We need to achieve a 70 to 30 ratio between teaching and classified personnel by reducing the number of people providing support services. We recommend keeping the building operating from 7:00 a.m. to 9:00 p.m. every day of the week, which will add expenses for janitorial and administrative help. We recommend hiring a vice principal for administration and contracting out some routine services. This would free up the principal to start spending significant time as instructional leader and perhaps doing some teaching again.'"

"That's almost unheard of in American schools today!" Nate said. "I sense that most of you are just as happy to have the Support Services Action Team develop these administrative policies and operations." He smiled. "You just hope they survive long enough to redesign the roles and responsibilities for next September. Right?"

4. Student Assessment and School Accountability

"Our next report is from the Student Assessment and School Account-ability Action Team (SAAAT). It is chaired by Paul Christopher and co-chaired by Ted Alexander and Kathie Sorenson. Paul, it's your turn."

"Thank you, Wendy," Paul said. "Ted and Kathie have asked me to make our presentation. We're very excited about it. Our Action Team is respon-sible for two related activities that make up an essential component of our reform model—assessment and accountability. We define assessment as any test, instrument or method that indicates the level of a student's perfor-mance in school.

"During our Hearings, we've heard a great deal about assessing student performance. We've reviewed Dr. Linda Darling-Hammond's remarks on authentic assessment. She told us that most standardized tests are based on an outmoded theory of learning that stresses the accumulation and recall of isolated facts. They do not reflect current understandings of how students learn or that thinking skills are the foundation for building basic skills, not the other way around.[2] The multiple choice tests that we've all experienced in school do not evaluate a student's ability to think deeply, to create, or to perform in any field. They are unable to measure a student's ability to write coherently and persuasively, to use mathematics for solving real-life prob-lems, to make meaning when reading texts, to understand and use scien-tific methods or reasoning, or to grasp and apply social science concepts. These tests are poor measures of higher order thinking skills.

"The present standardized tests are almost wholly inadequate for mea-suring knowledge of high academic content. One exception is the Advanced Placement Test which does measure content knowledge. A small number of American students take this essay exam to demonstrate their knowledge of a given subject. This approach is used most frequently in Europe. Teach-ers, not commercial testing companies, construct and administer student assessments."

"Can you define for us again what authentic assessment is?" said Lenora.

"Sure," Paul said. "Authentic assessment is the actual performance of knowledge or skills in a given field, such as writing essays or conducting science experiments. Teachers build their teaching and learning experiences around well-defined performance standards. Students know what these standards are in advance, and they are measured against them. Authentic assessment frequently requires students to present their work publicly and orally to teachers, classmates and parents.

"Portfolios, one type of assessment, provide qualitative or descriptive data that are often more useful and authentic than quantitative measures. Qualitative data alone, however, makes comparative analysis almost impossible. To overcome this drawback, Vermont recently adopted both a voluntary portfolio-assessment program along with a new mandatory standardized testing program to determine how well students stack up against the state's new academic standards. We believe this approach has merit. Maryland's State Performance Assessment Program (MSPAP) is showing that standardized testing can be tied to knowledge clusters, as demonstrated by Hirsch's Core Curriculum and Slavin's Roots and Wings. Several states, including Vermont, California, Connecticut, Kentucky, Maryland, New York and Texas, are developing assessment approaches that will transform statewide testing.

"Our Action Team believes that adult accountability requires periodic testing of individual student achievement," said Paul. "This reminds me of what my favorite football 'philosopher,' Vince Lombardi, said, 'If you don't keep score, you're just practicing.' I'll read this aloud: **'We recommend that the Academic Standards Action Team and the Character Education Action Team work together to approve only curricular programs—academic and character education—that include specific norm-referenced testing. The school community should use scores—individual and class averages—to publicly judge the academic progress of Jefferson students and to compare that progress to students nationally and internationally. Jefferson teachers will be deeply involved in selecting assessment instruments and in grading student performance. These activities will help build meaningful professional teacher development activities around classroom teaching and learning assessments. '"**

"Paul, let me get this straight," said Delores. "You mean that all teachers, the principal and classified staff are going to be in a 'fish bowl' where their performance will be measured? Does that mean that teachers will receive additional merit pay, above their union-negotiated salary level, depending on the increased performance of their students?

"That's exactly right, Delores," said Paul. "As our Parent and Community Action Team said before, we intend to use some of our federal program funds for these merit awards. In Kentucky we're learning that when teachers are given merit awards for improving student performance, it counters their traditional culture where salary increases have been given only for seniority and additional college credits. **We recommend providing incentive pay for outstanding performance, while also recognizing comparative professional salary levels for teachers and staff from the school district's negotiated schedule. If necessary, we will also supplement the standard schedule to attract highly-qualified people into teaching math and science, rather than assign unqualified teachers. Our volunteer program will draw scientists and others from high-tech companies in our community, giving us powerful supplemental resources. In every academic subject, Jefferson will attract professionals and volunteers to help all our children achieve high standards. We believe that adults in the Jefferson community are capable of creating a world-class educational opportunity for all students who are willing to work hard. We saw this in the Olympic games held in Atlanta last summer, where committed coaches help athletes achieve world-class standards. Transferring this example to schools, excellence is fostered by high standards, measurement of performance and recognition for outstanding teaching."**

"Paul, how does your Action Team distinguish between student assessment and school accountability?" Dale asked.

"Let me answer that, Paul," said Kathie. "Assessment focuses on student learning while accountability focuses on adult stewardship. In other words, assessment relates directly to how well students are learning academic and character education knowledge and applying it to their performance in real life situations. School accountability, by contrast, relates to those activities of adults—educators, staff, parents, or community representatives—who are responsible for teaching academic and character education of students.

"Professionally certified and classified personnel are paid to help our students learn. Their impact on students will be evaluated on how well that happens. Effective teachers, administrators, and staff should be well compensated for exceptional performance. We also expect students, parents and community volunteers to demonstrate high performance standards. We will develop leadership training programs for all volunteers. We can learn a lot from civic, religious and political associations about training volunteers to make outstanding contributions. Jefferson Community Learning Center will become a community asset and a national laboratory to show what professionals and volunteers can accomplish together on behalf of our children."

Wendy cut in. "Thank you, Paul, Kathie and Ted for your good work on the Student Assessment and School Accountability Action Team. I'm impressed by your clear expectations for both professionals and volunteers. You can see by the positive reactions of our Commission that we are serious about undertaking a new adventure here at the Jefferson Community Learning Center. Now before we begin our final discussion, let's take a 15 minute break."

****

The School Reform Paradox

Nate was smiling when he welcomed the Commission back. "Why are you smilin,' Nate?" Lenora asked.

"Because Wendy and I can see that, as a Citizens' Commission, you're now taking real ownership for carrying out the vision you are creating for Jefferson. Last September when we began as your facilitators, we carried the burden. Its gradually shifted from us to you–members of the Commission's Action Teams. Your chances to pull off this school reform project have just gone up. We're impressed with the work you've all done. Your recommendations are bold. Tomorrow afternoon the Action Team chairs will meet with co-chairs to polish their draft sections and make final recommendations. Tomorrow night Ray, Kim, Wendy and I will meet for final drafting. Monday morning the confidential report will be delivered to you. Your challenge is to get it back to Ray's office by 6:00 p.m. Monday evening. Our final drafting team will negotiate and integrate any remaining issues. On Tuesday and Wednesday, Ray and Kim will brief each of the six other County School Board members. Ray has asked that Board rules be suspended for Wednesday night's Board Meeting. Ray's called for a final decision by the Board on our total package. By the time the Board adjourns Wednesday night, the future of Jefferson Elementary School will be decided.

"This year we've been struggling with the school reform paradox. On the one hand, we must get out the information on school reform to all interested citizens so that we can rapidly upscale by improving schools nationwide. On the other hand, each school must undertake a 'discovery journey' through the participation of a Citizens' Commission made up of the principal, teachers, parents and community representatives.

"The first step for any representative group who's responsible for reforming a local public school is what we are calling a 'discovery journey.' Our Commission has struggled with the reform issues and then created a model for changing Jefferson. Public engagement involves getting to know each other and accepting ownership for the reform process.

"This requires patience and enough time for the group to explore national reform models and best practices and discover which components would be worth implementing in their particular school. Reforming a single school is not a quick fix. Deborah Meier and Central Park East is our prime example.

"Can you possibly imagine this Commission making these informed reports and recommendations without having gone through our 'discovery journey'? During this past year, we heard about the challenges of school reform from 44 expert reformers and practitioners."

"I'm not an educator," said Paul. "I don't normally read much about school reform, so this was an in-depth education for me. It's taken several months for me to learn the terminology and concepts—to get through the educational jargon and learn to discriminate between what's real and what's just 'smoke and mirrors.' We've heard from dedicated reformers and practitioners—and I've been deeply impressed with their personal commitment to helping children! But just by reading about a program with its strengths and weaknesses, I could not possibly have selected between them with any confidence. But by learning about them directly from their creators and then discussing them with all of you, especially those who are educators, I'm better able to make informed contributions and to explain our recommendations to the community."

"Nate, I agree with Paul!" said Debbie. "I thought I knew what was best for my children without some outsiders telling me about educational reform. Was I ever wrong! What I've learned this year could not have been duplicated in any graduate seminar. But my experience of working with each Commissioner this past year has been even more important. When we first met together last September, I worried that I was going to waste my time listening to a bunch of eggheads tell me what a bad parent I was. Later I feared that I'd spend a year listening to each of you tell your sorry troubles. Was I ever mistaken! As impressive as the national reformers and practitioners have been, my hero awards go to every member of this Commission for hanging in there and coming up with courageous recommendations for saving Jefferson. If the Board buys our plan, you can count me in. I'll be the first parent in line to apply to have my children educated at Jefferson. I'll stack up our proposed academic and character education program next to any elite private school's. I believe we're proving that good people—no matter how they differ on some values—can learn to trust each other and come up with a reasonable reform program that will work for all of Jefferson's children. We've all witnessed grassroots democracy in action, at least to this point. Next Wednesday night at the County School Board Meeting, we'll see how it plays out."

"I also have a confession to make," said Ted. *Oh, no! Don't tell me Ted's got religion now!* Lenora muttered to herself. "As you might have noticed, I've been the skunk at this picnic most of the time. I don't mind saying that I've resented spending Saturdays with this damn Commission. I had absolutely no faith that we'd ever agree on anything, let alone a solid reform model for Jefferson. And I didn't like most of you at first. I thought you were crazy do-gooders! I'm finally realizing that you've been serious from the beginning about school reform for all children at Jefferson.

"I guess many years ago, I sort of closed down and quit trying to change things. I've just been holding on until retirement in a few more years. Then I'd go fishing and forget that I was ever a good teacher. You've all taken your turns putting me in my place, and I admit that I deserved it most of the time. Nate, you and Wendy have been fair, and you've kept our work focused on the mission. Hell, I can even have a civil lunch conversation now with Dale over there, or even with Lenora—if she doesn't keep beating me up! At first I resented our lunch assignments—but gradually I got better acquainted on a personal level. Guess what?" he smiled. "You people aren't so crazy after all! I couldn't have said that when we started last September. Years ago I stopped listening to people that didn't agree with me. But after this experience, I may start believing in people again. Maybe I have enough faith in education to give it another try. I used to love to teach! I don't know when I gave up—but that's not right or fair to the kids and parents who expect me to give my best." Ted sounded a little choked up. "Some of you are smiling! Yeah, I'm getting hooked on the possibility of setting up a decent technology capability at Jefferson next year. But, Paul, you'd better damn well help deliver those computers if the County Board gives us the green light. But wait a minute! What am I saying here? The County Board will never let go of Jefferson!"

Ray spoke up. "Don't be so sure about that, Ted. I've been keeping our County Board Chairman, Jack Clayton, informed of our progress. He's not anxious to get the state superintendent and the governor to come in here and take over Jefferson. Of course, he doesn't know about our proposal to set up a kind of charter or alternative school either. But I'm now personally behind this Commission. The recommendations I've heard today are sound. I'll go to bat with the other County Board members and try and convince them to approve our plan next Wednesday night. Kim and I will brief each Board member one-by-one before next Wednesday night's meeting. I don't want our work to just be another agenda item that's ignored. I know how overwhelmed the Board is by the information overload we face each week. But I think briefing the Board members individually will help. We've no time to waste on taking action if we are to pull off the miracle of getting Jefferson up and running by September."

"Ray," said Kim, "it'll be a pleasure to brief each Board member with you. It's the least I can do to say thanks to all you Commission members for doing such good work on this final report. It's really solid. I know we face a difficult challenge in convincing the Board, but I'm beginning to believe that we might pull this off!"

"Nate," Kim asked. "You talked about the nationwide school reform paradox—that every school must undertake a 'discovery journey,' similar to the one our Citizens' Commission has gone through this year. It takes time to digest the reform models and best practices.[3] If you don't take time, you don't understand the reform model options or you don't work together long enough to build trust with each other. But tell us more about rapid, nationwide upscaling?"

"Kim, I believe that effectively communicating the information on proven school reform strategies we have today is a critical part of rapid upscaling. That's a big challenge. At the rate that we're reforming one public school at a time, it'll take another 475 years to reach our 85,000 schools. Suppose we move almost five times as fast in the next 100 years. By the year 2100, we'll have lost another three or four generations of children by the time we've finished. So the question is this: In the next few years, how do we reform schools one at a time, and, at the same time, carry out national school reform in 85,000 public schools? This is the paradox we face" (see Figure 19.1 *Must All 60,000 Elementary Schools Reinvent the Reform Wheel?*).

Figure 19.1

Nationwide Public Engagement Campaign

Must 60,000 Elementary Schools "Reinvent the Wheel"?

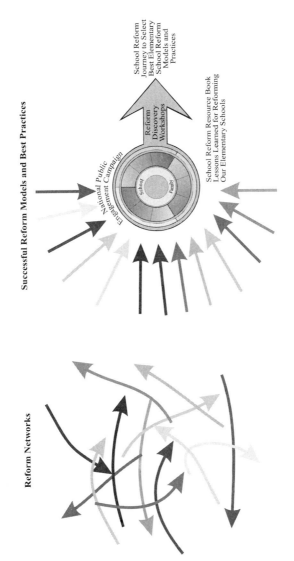

Without knowledge of elementary school reform networks district board members, educators, parents, students waste resources re-inventing the "reform wheel" searching for best models and practices.

With knowledge of successful reform models and best practices district board members, educators, parents & community representatives can undertake a successful discovery journey together to reform our elementary schools & provide quality education for all children.

The Moral Imperative

"But our Commission has spent a whole year just discovering the most effective school reform models," Maria said excitedly. "We know there are people reforming schools like Jefferson within five years. But just knowing how to reform schools doesn't do it! It takes more. What is it you say, 'necessary but not sufficient?' How's that for fancy talk? School reform won't take place in our community just because we know that schools are being reformed in some other communities. What is required to ignite the community's interest so they'll face up to the critical need of their schools to improve? How will they decide to carry out serious whole-school re-form before it is too late to save the futures of these children?"

"Let me answer that one, Nate," said Christina. "Wendy and Nate know that school reform or any reform doesn't just happen one day because some citizens get an idea. Reform goes against embedded interests of the status quo. We all agree the first step is having a vision, or even better, a more detailed Reform Blueprint. Our Citizens' Commission now has a blueprint with eight reform components. We've even specified strategies and pro-grams within the components that we want to try out at Jefferson. But the next step is creating the awareness and building the energy that reform in our school requires—in a big way, and right now! That awareness usually takes a crisis. We confronted one when Jefferson was placed on the state's reconstitution list and our Citizens' Commission was formed. We've spent a year gathering data on best practices and trying to see if they'd work here at Jefferson where current conditions are unacceptable for the children. But we didn't feel that way before we made our best practices survey and com-pared what we found going on in other schools with the tragedy we now see at Jefferson. Still, all our year long efforts will fail if we can't get the attention of the School Board and present a compelling case for them to officially support our recommendations. We need dramatic—even revolu-tionary—reform of Jefferson starting next week! It all comes down to what Martin Luther King or Ernie Cortes called 'creative social tension.' Usually leaders must, in some dramatic way, be encouraged to do what they know is right. Tension is released by changing the unjust status quo situation for our children—regardless of conflicting adult interests."

"Wait a minute, Christina," said Tamar. "Are you saying that even if our process of discovering the best ways to reform Jefferson is perfectly sound, we could lose? All our good work will be lost if we can't convince the Board to act on our recommendations next Wednesday night? This sounds very unfair to the people that matter most—the children and parents at Jefferson."

"Congratulations, and welcome to the world of direct community action, Tamar!" replied Christina. "This is our next and only step. If we fail here, our Citizens' Commission fails the children and parents at Jefferson. No one else knows how bad things are now and how crippling another year of indecision can be to the lives of those children. But we do! It's up to us. We now face a moral challenge. No one else will take the time to find out what we've learned. Yes, the 'buck stops here.'"

"I think I'm beginning to see where you're heading, Christina," said Kathie, who'd been pretty quiet until now. "You're saying that the community has given us the moral responsibility of searching out the best reform models and best practices to reform Jefferson Elementary School. That responsibility now requires us to convince the County School Board to take the action we recommend—not because we're so smart—but because we've paid the price. We've grappled with the information given by our 44 guest experts—national reformers and practitioners. They all expect us now to make tough choices and act on behalf of our children. To do anything else is socially and educationally immoral. Wow!"

"Right, Kathie. It's the situation we now find ourselves in as members of this Citizens' Commission. I suppose that's what makes up the stories we tell about heroes—moral choices against tough obstacles. I'm haunted by Sir Thomas More, 'a man for all seasons.' Maybe we've been cast into a modern morality play as the 'Commission for all seasons.' Isn't this the lessons we teach children, to take bold action when it's required rather than to take the easy or popular way out? But before we can take effective moral action and recommend our plan for reforming Jefferson to the School Board, each of us has his or her own moral challenge.

"Stop me if I'm wrong, Ray, but I believe that our report and recommendations have absolutely no chance of being accepted if our report does not have the full and unanimous support of every last one of us! NO EXCEPTIONS! If we do not see the importance of united and dramatic action now, after all we've been through, then we'll be unable to convince the County School Board to accept our reform plan!"

Paul was stunned. *Christina, the former nun, has been the most retiring of all the Commission members, but she's just cut to the chase and left us morally naked,* Paul thought. *I underestimated this powerful woman!*

"I'll have to agree with your analysis, Christina," said Kathie quietly. "I know this is a politically-controversial decision. We won't win unless the Board, the media, the parents, and the whole community know that we're united at this key moral crossroads. You've suddenly clarified the issues for me. It's not about the fine points of what reform strategy we use or about fine tuning an academic standard. It's about what we believe as a Citizens' Commission. We've paid the price to learn. Nothing but total revolutionary reform will save the lives and futures of 473 students and the thousands of other students who will come through Jefferson in the future. Someone said, 'If not now, when? If not me, who? Ray, you can put me down as fully committed to our Citizens' Commission report and recommendations! I'm proud to stand up for the work of this Commission. I'm may even become fond of you strange Commissioners."

"Ray," said Dale. "You know I'm not an educated man, and I consider myself pretty conservative. I've made my share of mistakes, but I don't run out on a fight. Count me in!"

Ray's now taken over the leadership role from Christina, thought Maria. *This is a dramatic, tense moment. Will we unanimously support our Commission recommendations?*

"Yeah, Ray," Lenora shouted, "Let's kick some butt! I'm with you. *And it won't hurt our cause,* thought Lenora, *if Maria and I get the word out to minority parents that they've got to show up in mass at next Wednesday night's County Board meetin' — Ernie Cortes style.*

Ray spoke up. "Because Christina has clearly stated the moral issue, I believe it's imperative that each member of the Citizens' Commission gets a final opportunity to vote his or her conscience on our report recommendations. I'll not go through each recommendation separately. Today we've heard from our Action Teams. You each have a final opportunity to address any differences you have with the chairs of the Action Teams or again in writing Monday when you approve the final draft. We'll take your objections seriously and then make the final call. Each Commissioner must decide if you're confident enough about what you've heard today and trust us enough, after you've read our final draft tomorrow, to leave the final decision to us. Then you must sign our final report. Now, after a year of Saturdays, we've come down to the bottom line. It's time to vote our conscience. I'll go around the room now and ask each of you for your final vote.

"Paul?" asked Ray.

"I support the Commission's report."

"Debbie?"

"You have my support."

"Ted?"

"I am a reluctant convert, but I still reserve the right to hold my vote until Monday."

Kim?" Ray asked.

"Ray, you have my enthusiastic support."

"Maria?"

"Yes!"

"Lenora?"

"You can count on me, and I'll bring some folks to the meetin' Wednesday.

"Dale?" he continued.

"I'm behind you, Ray. Let me know how I can help."

"Delores?"

"What a trip! I've never seen the likes of this. But, yes, I'm in."

"Kathie?"

"Count me in, Ray. I'd strongly recommend taking Christina along with you and Kim to brief the other County Board members."

"Kim, are you okay with Kathie's suggestion? Kim nodded. "Christina, would you join us?"

Christina smiled, "Sure, I'd be happy too!"

"Tamar?"

"I'm proud to be a member of this Commission. I'm experiencing grassroots democracy in action—just like I tell my third grade 'Dream Team.. Yes, I'm in!"

"Well, Christina, you've become our Commission's moral conscience—nice job!"

"Ray, I couldn't be more impressed with our bottom line. I'm proud to cast my vote for the children of Jefferson Community Learning Center. Amen, brother!" said Christina smiling.

Chapter 20
SCHOOL REFORM THROUGH PUBLIC ENGAGEMENT:
GRASSROOTS DEMOCRACY IN ACTION
Wednesday, June 18

Jack Clayton pulled into a reserved parking space at the County School District offices at 7:10 p.m. It was the big night of the Citizens' Commission report to the board. *Can't believe it was nine months ago that we established this Commission,* Jack thought. *Another school year gone, and things at Jefferson couldn't be worse. The principal resigned last week, teachers are petitioning to be transferred. Parents are pounding on the doors of School Board members and threatening to stage a demonstration tonight if we don't do something. They're calling their state reps. They even talked our fair-haired Congressman Steve Roco into coming tonight.*

Our phones have been ringing off the hook with requests for media interviews. Hell, while I was at lunch, ABC and CNN called. Even the governor's getting into the act. Cole Green, his assistant, called me at home, saying that he 'just happens to be in town tonight' and thought he would wander over to our School Board meeting!

Tom Dooley sure left us holding the bag after he resigned last month—just before we fired him. He let things at Jefferson completely fall apart. He never wanted us to appoint the Citizens' Commission. Thank God for Ray Gonzales. He sure gave us an impressive briefing at breakfast Tuesday. Kim Su Young and Sister Christina Peterson are certainly impressive spokespersons for the Commission. It looks like they've done their homework and by now briefed all Board members.

Ray gave me a heads up last week that they're ready. I agreed to make their report the only item of Board business tonight and reschedule everything else for next week. I hope our executive search firm has set up final interviews for a new superintendent. We've got to get someone in charge of the county office of educa-

tion. I want Tom Dooley out of there, and on his way to that small district he's been lusting after in the Florida sunshine. Oh well, he's their problem now. Superintendents come and go—Board members just hang on like old soldiers and then just fade away. But we still have to live with our mistakes and face the parents after the superintendent is long gone. Maybe I should step down next year. This district may be going no where fast! Tonight could be a circus.

Jack slipped into the back door of the old building that serves as the school district's education palace avoiding the media and crowd that were gathering in front. Jack wondered what else was going on that would cause such a commotion. He took the elevator to the second floor and moved past the security guards into the auditorium. He was stunned by the noise! It was packed with spectators. TV camera crews were setting up in four different locations. *What's going on here,* thought Jack. *Guess I should have brought my best blue shirt and red tie for TV interviews.*

Jack took the Chairman's seat at the head of the large oak Board table with its microphones. Other members of the Board were arriving. Only about four minutes now, before Jack would gavel the County School Board meeting to order. *Look at this audience,* Jack thought! *Not a vacant seat. Must be 2000 here. People are even standing in the aisles. I wonder what they think is going on here tonight? I see some district teachers sitting together in the audience. There's Kathryn Jones and her Christian Coalition group. This crowd must be at least half Black and Hispanic parents, and there are some new Asians parents I've never seen before. Where did all these people come from tonight?*

Members of the Citizens' Commission sat on the first row. Ray, vice chair of the Board, sat next to Jack. "You're looking pretty pleased with yourself, Ray. You've done a hell of a job with this Commission," Jack whispered. "Did you know about this turnout tonight? I've never seen anything like it for a County School Board meeting! We've got media reporters and camera crews." He glanced around the auditorium. "There's Cole Green from the Governor's office." Jack waved to Cole, then to Steve Rocco and his congressional entourage.

Dr. Dooley and his top three assistants finally arrived, looking quite bored by it all—in fact, a little pompous. They took their reserved seats in front of the other Board members—Joyce Green, Lola Gomez, Joy Christiansen, Jake Washington, and Wayne Burnston.

Reporting To The County School Board

Jack Clayton called the Board meeting to order. "Good evening. I'm Jack Clayton, chair of the County School Board. I'd like to recognize our board members and welcome our large audience tonight. We also acknowledge the large number of print, radio and TV journalists. We'll stand for the pledge of allegiance led by Gail Swift, a fourth-grade student from Jefferson Elementary School."

"Thank you, Gail. Last September, the County School Board appointed 12 members of this special Citizens' Commission. We gave them authority to search for new reform strategies and best practices and to do an in-depth assessment of Jefferson Elementary School. They were to use all required resources—community, private, state and federal government. Then on June 18, they were to recommend a plan for reforming Jefferson. Our Citizens' Commission is right on schedule. We've scheduled tonight's entire Board meeting to consider their final report.

"It's my pleasure to call on Ramon Gonzales, our county Board Vice-Chair, who also served as Chair of the Citizens' Commission. I want to commend Ray for his leadership of this fine Commission over the last nine months. Tonight you'll see the impressive results of their work. Ray, the time is yours."

"Thank you, Chairman Clayton. I will begin by introducing the members of the Citizens' Commission and our consultants. Each one has contributed almost 100 hours of community service to this school reform project. Please hold your applause until everyone has been introduced. Serving as our able Vice-Chair is Kim Su Young, principal at Woodlawn Elementary School. The other members in alphabetical order are Ted Alexander (teacher), Lenora Brown (parent), Deborah Cohen (parent), Paul Christopher (community), Tamar Espinosa (teacher), Dale Jones (parent), Maria Morales (parent), Christina Peterson (community), Kathie Sorenson (teacher), and Delores Williams (teacher). Serving as our invaluable coaches and consultants were Nate Johnson and Wendy Swenson. Let's all give this Citizens' Commission a big round of applause!" Loud applause erupted from the audience.

"Now," said Ray, "I'll begin with a short profile of Jefferson Elementary School. Then I've asked the chairpersons representing our eight Action Teams to present five minute reports. They will also include our recommendations for totally reforming Jefferson Elementary School. When they have finished, we'll take a break for 15 minutes before turning to our board members for their questions."

****

During the break, reporters furiously interviewed members of the Citizens' Commission. Cameras panned people in the audience who were talking excitedly in small groups.

"May I have your attention, please!" Jack Clayton gaveled the County School Board meeting back to order. Looking directly at the Commission members he said, "Ray, each chairpersons has made an excellent report here tonight! We are impressed with your collective knowledge of national school reform and your specific recommendations for carrying out a whole school reform project here at Jefferson. That's an interesting new name you've proposed for the school—the Jefferson Community Learning Center!" The audience burst into loud applause!

"Please hold your applause," said Jack. "We turn now to questions from our County Board. I recognize first Mrs. Joyce Green. We'll proceed around the table according to seniority—I ask each of you board member to restrict your remarks to questions about the Commission's report and recommendations. When we have answered their questions, the Board will begin its deliberations. We hope to vote on these recommendations before the night is out. Mrs. Green."

"Thank you, Chairman Clayton. I too would like to commend all members of the Citizens' Commission for taking on the thankless job of trying to figure out what this community is going to do about the deplorable conditions at Jefferson. Are you saying, Mr. Gonzales, that your Citizens' Commission is actually recommending that we close Jefferson and turn the entire school over to some outside School Reform Council? Don't you think that's quite extreme?" The audience began to clap.

Jack Clayton spoke into the microphone, "I must caution the audience NOT to applaud! Ray, do you want to respond to this?"

"Yes, I would," said Ray. "Mrs. Green has cut directly to the bottom line. We Commission members have taken nine months to arrive at this unanimous recommendation. We believe that no other step can save the students at Jefferson from further failure. Since we began our work last September, conditions have become nothing short of tragic! Continuing to tinker with half measures will not put us on the road to recovery.

"The problem is not really with the people—the administrators, teachers, parents and students. They've suffered enough and have demonstrated over the years that they cannot turn the school around by themselves. The problem is not just committing enough resources. A complete turnaround will require additional investment funds—just as in any failing business. You can't do it on 'the cheap.' But it's not a financial issue. The core problems at Jefferson are political and structural. Whoever is given the sorry task of reforming that school must have complete authority to lead and manage the entire reform project for the next three to five years. They must have the resources to get the job done, and they must be held accountable for providing a quality education. Somehow Jefferson students have got to start meeting demanding standards at each grade level—and they must begin next year!

"We know from our interviews with the top school reformers, policymakers and practitioners that, with the proper conditions, even children who are disadvantaged, like most of those at Jefferson, can be well educated. Either we provide a new reform team with the authority and tools to do the job, or the children of Jefferson are back to square one, and our year's work has been simply wasted. The whole Commission is united on this recommendation. I might add there are at least 500 other communities all across America that are taking this step. It's known as the Charter School Movement."

Joy Christiansen spoke up aggressively. "Are you saying, Ray, this Board of Education, is now being asked to simply turn over their responsibility to any group who happens to want to try out their reform ideas on our children? Why we were elected to protect the public from using public funds for 'half-baked' education reforms?"

If our Commission believed that, Joy, we would vote against such a plan ourselves. No, we've spent the past nine months talking with nationally recognized experts on school reform throughout the United States. These reformers are not sitting in their university ivory towers theorizing about how to experiment on our children. The reformers that appeared before our Commission have spent the past 10 to 20 years actually working with thousands of principals, teachers and parents in schools just like Jefferson. They have field-tested these proven reforms and their evaluations show positive results with all kinds of children. Members of the Commission have done their homework. We've examined reform models and best practices. We are now making unanimous recommendations about how to bring new tools and resources to all educators, students and parents here at Jefferson.

Joy was now listening intently. "What are you recommending?"

The Anti-Ignorance Vaccine

Ray nodded and said, "Let me give you an analogy, Joy. When my parents were young many children died of polio. But after years of careful research and development, Dr. Salk and others, discovered a vaccine that would prevent children from getting polio. In a similar way, students at Jefferson have been suffering from the fatal disease of ignorance. Suppose that a preventive medicine or vaccine has been found to cure the ignorance disease in all those children. Suppose this Board sent a special team to check out this new 'wonder drug.' Suppose further that our team returns to report that they've witnessed the cure with their own eyes, and that this miracle drug really does work. Every member of the team recommends that the County Board order the new vaccine immediately and have it administered to each child at Jefferson. Of course, we must watch the treatment very carefully and report back to the parents and community about how effectively it works with each student at the school at least twice each year. If the treatment doesn't work after a fair trial, we can stop. But if it works, we will have gone a long way toward eliminating ignorance at Jefferson. One thing is certain. Just as we can't be telling the doctors and nurses how to administer the cure, we can't tell educators how to do their job."

"Ray," Lola Gomez said. "I see where you're going with this story. But it seems to me we've heard most of this before from education experts. Ten years ago, we were asked to trust them on the new math. Then it was trust our professional judgment on whole language! Both of these crashed and burned and our children were the victims—but the educators still got paid! Now we're being asked to turn the entire school over to experts we haven't even met?"

"Kim Su Young, I see you'd like to respond," said Chair Jack Clayton.

"Yes, I would. Most of you Board members know me as the principal of Lawndale Elementary here in our County. I too feel strongly about not harming the children under my stewardship. I am surely as skeptical as you are about untested theories of education. And we've all made some mistakes. Education is not a science, but an applied art based on the science of learning. But I think we've reached the place in this discussion where we need to define the role of professionals as compared to clients or customers. I guess it was Aristotle who talked about the classic conflict between the professional and the customer. He said that the customer doesn't tell the shoemaker how to make shoes, but the customer does have to feel comfortable wearing the shoes, or the shoemaker doesn't get paid.

"In today's world," Kim continued, "when I decide to fly to see my children and grandchildren in San Francisco, I give my trust and my future to the pilot and his professional crew. I trust that they've been trained and will maintain high standards of safety. Sometimes, those standards are violated and planes crash, bringing tragedy. But we don't quit flying. And we don't stop wearing shoes if the first pair we try on doesn't fit. But we, the customers, must give professionals the feedback they need for correction and hold them accountable for services they deliver. It should be the same in education. But too often parents and community members leave the education of their children entirely to educators. This is a mistake—it takes us all.

"I've served on this Citizens' Commission one full Saturday each month for the past school year. When we began, I hardly trusted anyone on the Commission, including the facilitator-consultants. Now they have earned my trust—11 good teachers, parents and community representatives—to carry out our mission, which is to discover the cure for ignorance among Jefferson students. Don't misunderstand. This isn't a one shot deal. It is a long, hard journey that will take at least three to five years, if we're fortunate, have the authority and work very effectively. We've read the evaluations of school children just like ours at Jefferson who are now benefiting from these education reform models. We suggest that you listen to our recommendations. We didn't know where we were going when we started out together. But we were fortunate to have hired some very good guides in Nate and Wendy. Some of us bitched and complained along the way—just human nature. But remember, we didn't ask for this journey—you asked us to voluntarily go in your place.

"Now the hard work begins. Our Commissioners have no vested interest except for wanting the best future possible for the children of Jefferson and their families. The bottom line is, who's going to be responsible and accountable for providing the 'anti-ignorance vaccine' for the children at

Jefferson. This is the key policy decision here tonight that will affect every child at Jefferson now and in the years to come. Make no mistake 'the buck stops here tonight!' Thank you."

Wayne raised his hand. "Yes, Mr. Burnston. Do you have a question for the Citizens' Commission?" said Jack.

"Yes, I do, Mr. Chairman. I am impressed with what this Commission of ours has done. But it's my understanding that the County School Board had been given the authority by the voters to administer the new anti-ignorance vaccine and to keep very close control over any educator we hire to do the job. Clearly the people—I include Dr. Dooley and his staff, here—the administrators and teachers who've been employed at Jefferson have not been performing—providing the right anti-ignorance vaccine. Maybe we need a whole new medical (educational) team to come and do the job under our closer supervision. What's wrong with that idea, Ray?"

Jack watched the exchange between Ray and the Board members. *I'm fascinated,* he thought. *The Board appointed Ray as Chair of the Citizens' Commission. They know they can count on Ray's Commission because they trust his objectivity and ties to the community. They know he won't sell them out! They're struggling to find a responsible way to support the Commission recommendations. I'm glad the discussion is on the big issue of who's responsible for the reform and not degenerating into our usual debates on financial, program or personnel details. This principal, Kim, is really something. How do you argue with her logic?*

The New *District* Charter or Independent School Model

Ray responded to Wayne's question. "Let me try another analogy. Every year we decide which bus company will get our district's transportation business, right? And every year we decide which textbooks to buy, and which teachers to hire. We decide which security people to hire for the high schools. And we hire an accounting firm to keep our books. Now the district contracts out almost everything except educational services. But we still insist on making policy and on seeing to it that the district office manages the education program for 14 schools in our small district. Isn't it time we started subcontracting education services to local schools, as we do with other professional services? And when we sign a contract with a business to provide a service for the district, we don't tell contractors how to manage their operations. We have confidence in their professional judgment and performance—or we damn well better get a new contractor. By the way, a school charter is a legal contract for services.

"The question is," Ray continued, "why don't we trust a school-site council to provide education services for their own children and then hold them accountable, as we do our accountants or bus drivers? We could exchange control for accountability and, at the same time, provide a quality education for children in this district. Why should this be such a radical idea? I will admit, I didn't think this way until just recently. But this Commission has been a life changing experience for me.

"We all think we know about public education because we went to school. We know we can't fly a jumbo jet unless we've been trained, so we are more than happy to trust the skill of a pilot we don't know—but not Mrs. Jones, the third grade teacher we do know. Why don't we trust the principals and teachers in our local schools? As a board, why can't we delegate the authority and responsibility for providing educational services where it should be—the local school site? We have an historic opportunity to try out a new model here.

"Successful organizations in America are going through the quality revolution by decentralizing and downsizing—except for public education. If we don't try out a better model soon, the public will force us into a full-out voucher or charter school revolution. We may lose our best and brightest teachers, principals, parents and students. Don't forget we also lose the public funding that goes with the students. And if those schools fail because they don't have the support they need to make their charters work effectively, we get to educate the kids all over—again at additional public expense—and we surely don't want that to happen."

"Ray, what do you mean by a charter school?" asked Jake Washington. "I didn't know we had those schools in our state as they do in California and Colorado."

"I'll take that question," said Jack, president of the School Board. "Let's give Ray a breather."

"I've learned from Ray's report that the charter school movement is sweeping across the country. It's now in 25 states and about 500 schools in just three years. It works this way. Any group of parents, teachers or other citizens can petition the school district, the state office or another outside group for the authority to open a public school using the equivalent tax dollars the district now spends to educate each child. When a binding legal agreement is negotiated, the charter waives most federal, state and district regulations in exchange for the school's meeting its stated educational objectives. Periodic financial reports and academic assessments assure that high standards of accountability and student achievement are being reached. The charter school must admit any student who applies and can't discriminate against teachers or parents. I read somewhere that most union rules can also be waived. Even the NEA and the AFT are establishing charter schools. So this is a dramatic, new development in reforming American schools. We don't know all the downsides yet, but we do know that the charter school movement is forcing us to rethink the relationship between districts offices and their local schools."

"Are you suggesting, Jack, that we let Jefferson become a charter school? Seems like we'd be abandoning our responsibility to those children and parents?" said Jake. "I still don't understand how this would work?"

"I think I see where the Citizens' Commission recommendation is headed," Jack said. "Jefferson could be granted independent charter school status if we can't negotiate a mutually acceptable policy here tonight. The Commission hasn't threatened to do this, but just suppose they got together as private citizens and petitioned the governor for a charter to run an independent school—let's say in the Jefferson neighborhood. Suppose the Governor said yes. The chartered group then forms a school-site council—a type of Reform Council—and opens for business. This means that the district loses those who go to the new charter school—talented principal, teachers, students and parents—not to mention the money. The funds follow the new school, depending on the number of students who enroll. And, when the charter comes up for renewal in five years, the Governor is long gone. In the meantime, if the school leadership fails to reach its objectives because they didn't have backup technical support from the district, the school could close. The money will have been wasted, and the students as victims are back on our doorstep having lost some valuable years of their education. All this because we can't negotiate a better policy alternative."

"Jack, what is a better alternative to an independent charter like that?" Jake asked. "If the latest state achievement results are any indication, we are continuing to fail the students at Jefferson as well as the rest of our County's students. With our traditional district bureaucracy, we've made a sorry mess of things. We spend most of our county board meetings regulating personnel, finances, student expulsions, and other management issues that should probably be handled at the school site.

"As a District Board, we have the legal responsibility for providing a quality education for all students in our County. How do we fulfill our public trust to the voters that elected us? The key question is how do we do that and still empower local schools as high-performance learning centers? Every private business and more government agencies are coming to realize that they must turn the corporate office into a technical support service center and delegate operations to the local plant or office, and then hold them accountable for their performance. In our case, the superintendent's office must learn to provide technical support for local schools that should be responsible for daily operations. This delegation requires creating a new school community culture—by setting up some new expectations and some new standards."

"Jake, my key question is quite different," said Joyce Green. "Who are we turning Jefferson over to? The Board has always assumed the superintendent and his staff knew what they were doing. We had the illusion that we knew the principals and teachers at Jefferson, and they were 'our' people. We were accountable for their performance. We paid their salaries! This is our community. I'm not turning my public responsibility over to some outside reformers from who knows where. These are our babies we're talking about!"

"You're right on, Joyce," said Ray. "I feel the same way and so does our Commission. Each member has a personal interest in Jefferson—especially after working hard this year to find answers and make recommendations to this County Board. Your question really goes to the next step—who will administer the 'vaccine'? Should we find a new superintendent, bring in a new district office team and go through the same motions we've gone through for five more years. Should we just hope things at Jefferson will magically improve in the meantime?—that somehow the teachers and students at Jefferson, in their spare time, will discover the anti-ignorance vaccine on their own? Or is it time to adopt a different strategy? Is this a people problem or an organizational problem?"

Ray paused, "Let's go back to what our Commission is recommending. We have identified the eight components and specific action steps that will deliver the new anti-ignorance vaccine. This Commission represents every conceivable point of view from our parents, teachers and community interests. They've done their homework and we trust their judgment. After all, we've chosen them for this 'mission impossible.' Let's not shoot the messengers before they deliver the message. The Commission says we need a new reform model (the vaccine), a new reform strategy (method of administering the vaccine), and a team of specialists to accomplish the mission. Tonight, I believe this board will fail our final exam, if we don't delegate the authority and resources to get the job done to a new leadership team at Jefferson. But I recognize why many of my fellow Board members resist delegating authority to an unknown school-site council. I believe your main concern is not delegating the public responsibility given you by the voters you represent without someone to hold publicly accountable. Fair enough! Before my experience with this Citizens' Commission, I felt just the way you do tonight. Before we make our recommendation on who should operate the new Jefferson Community Learning Center next year, let me just summarize our position."

Grassroots School Reform: Eight Components and Five Action Steps

Jack spoke up again. "Ray, let me see if I understand what your Commission is recommending? I will read aloud the eight components of your detailed model, so that everyone hears them one last time. I have a copy of your report right here. Your Commission has found from their research that the new anti-ignorance vaccine is made up of eight components:

1. **A School Reform Council, with the Principal as the responsible executive;**
2. **A Challenging Academic Standards Curriculum;**
3. **A Character Education Program;**
4. **Professional Staff Development;**
5. **Parent and Community Engagement;**
6. **Comprehensive Technology Services;**
7. **Administrative Support Services; and**
8. **Student Assessment and School Accountability.**

"I believe these components and the educational programs your Commission has recommended are sound. Since my main concern is for the children at Jefferson, **I am impressed by your mission statement: to create a quality public school in which our teachers and the parents in this com-**

munity will enthusiastically enroll their own children. You create that kind of a school and I will enroll my own children!

"Now let me read the five action steps in your public engagement strategy," said Jack. "These steps must be undertaken to administer the 'vaccine' most effectively and to bring about the desired cure—knowledgeable students at Jefferson:

1. **The District Board of Education** must initiate a school reform 'discovery journey' to review best practice models from among those successful whole-school reform strategies that are improving educational performance for all children in schools throughout the United States." (Sounds like the Board will need to do this if we agree to undertake this strategy with the rest of our district schools," Jack said to the board.)

2. **A Citizens' Commission**, appointed by the District Board of Education, representing teachers, parents, principals and community leaders must undertake a systematic 'discovery journey' in which they review for themselves the leading models and best practices in school reform. The Commission must then conduct an inventory of the school's reform knowledge gap. Finally, the Commission must then design a Reform Blueprint (the eight components) showing the mission, goals, organization, staffing, strategies, action steps and timetables necessary to accomplish a new vision for the school.' ("This, of course, is what our Citizens' Commission has done with flying colors," Jack smiled with pride.);

3. **A District Charter** or alternative school status must be granted by the Board to a qualified School Reform Council made up of representative educators, parents and citizens. The five year Charter transfers funding and responsibilities, to reconstitute the school and implement the Reform Blueprint conditional only upon following civil rights laws, due process protection for teachers, and annual reporting of educational progress and financial accountability. ("Of course, this is what we're here tonight to decide," Jack said. "This is the key political issue—who has the authority to carry out the reform?");

4. **The School-Site Reform Council** is responsible for implementing the Reform Blueprint with teachers, parents and community representatives fully participating in all major policy decisions. The School

Reform Council must conduct a management audit, at least once a year assessing student performance by individual and by class average. The Council must survey parent and community support for the ongoing reform and report publicly all results.' ("This will help us know how effective the Reform Council has been each year. This democratic process also provides the energy, ownership and accountability we all seek. I certainly buy that principle," Jack said."); and

5. **The District Charter** can be renewed for five years only if all financial, management and educational objectives have been met.' ("This is the essential cornerstone of public accountability for me," stated Jack.)

"So we're down to two last issues—steps three and four: Who is the proposed Jefferson School Reform Council? And will this Board grant them a *District* Charter—an alternative school status, if you will, so they can carry out their school reform here as part of our district? With this model, the board can hold them publicly accountable for their performance. Right? I want to stop right here and find out how all board members are feeling about where we've come tonight thus far. Are you comfortable that we are asking the right questions, Joy?" Jack had every board member's attention.

"I believe we have narrowed the issues to the critical questions—now the hard work starts," Joy replied.

"Wayne, are we okay?" said Jack.

"I believe we're on target, Jack."

"How do you feel about our discussion, Lola?"

"It's been pretty heavy, but I'm thrilled with the Commission report. It's given me new hope for Jefferson. Let's not lose this opportunity."

"Still with us, Jake?

"Yeah, Jack. Your explanation of the charter school movement has opened up my mind to some interesting possibilities. I'm cool!"

Jack turned to Ray and said, "Perhaps we haven't been ready to address the 'who question' until now. Does your Commission have a recommendation about who this new team is that should get the charter authority for reforming Jefferson? You have our undivided attention. From the commotion among the TV crews and our large audience here tonight, they are also interested in what you have to say. After we discuss your recommendation, we'll be ready for the final policy question: Will this board grant them *district* charter school status? This recommendation had better be a good one Ray! Your whole case rests upon our comfort level with the team we are asked to trust to take over the reform of Jefferson—this is pretty heavy."

"Thank you, Jack," said Ray. "Our Citizens' Commission has worked very hard all year, but the past two months we've really struggled to come up first with the recommended eight-component model, and then with the five action steps necessary to implement the reform strategy. In our research, we've drawn from the experience of all 44 reformers and practitioners who have appeared before us—and some giants like Ted Bell, Ernie Boyer and Al Shanker who are no longer with us. When we finally organized into eight Action Teams to draft final recommendations, it became clear that each Action Team—its Chair and two Vice-Chairs—were taking personal ownership of the new reform model and the reform strategy. We could see leaders emerging from the Commission who were just the kind of individuals we all hoped would make up a reform team for Jefferson. In our final work session last Saturday, we talked about leadership roles and who might fill them—on the possibility that the Board discussion might go this well and end up at this point. The audience suddenly stirred at Ray's statement. Board members also came to attention!

Jefferson's New School Reform Council

"As a Citizens' Commission we unanimously recommend that Kim Su Young be asked tonight by this Board to become the new Principal at Jefferson Community Learning Center and **Chair of the Jefferson School Reform Council**," said Ray. The audience broke into thunderous applause! "Kim Su Young, who is now **Chair of the Academic Standards Action Team**, will continue as Chair and spend most of her time as the instructional leader when she assumes the principalship. We recommend that Kathie Sorenson, a fifth-grade teacher at Jefferson, be appointed Vice Chair of the School Reform Council and **Chair for Professional Development** and that Maria Morales, a Jefferson parent, be hired as a full-time Vice Chair of the School Reform Council and **Chair for Parent and Community Engagement**.

"We recommend that the Chairs of the remaining four action teams be appointed members of the School Reform Council, including:

- **Character Education Action** Chair Christina Peterson, an organizer for Community Interfaith;

- **Technology Services Action Team** Chair Ted Alexander, a sixth grade teacher at Jefferson;

- **Student Assessment and School Accountability Action Team** Chair Paul Christopher, a local business executive; and

- **Support Service Action Team** Chair Delores Williams, a first grade teacher at Jefferson, will serve until we are able to recruit an Administrative Vice Principal for school support services. We have our eye on a top services administrator from the County District office of education and will announce that selection next week—provided the Board gives us the district charter authority tonight." The media began snapping photos. Lights flashed everywhere.

Looking at his report, Ray went on. "The Commission recommends that the 12 member School Reform Council consist of the Principal Kim Su Young, as Chair, and two Vice Chairs—a teacher—Kathie Sorenson, and a parent—Maria Morales; three other teachers; three other parents and two community representatives. In order to take advantage of the experience gained by our Citizens' Commission, we recommend that eight additional members of the Council be appointed from the Commission and the Vice Principal for Administrative Services. I'd better read the names of initial members so I don't leave someone out: Lenora Brown, parent; Deborah Cohen, parent; Dale Jones, parent; Ted Alexander, sixth-grade teacher; Delores Williams, first-grade teacher; and Tamar Espinosa, third-grade teacher; with Christina Peterson and Paul Christopher as community representatives. The School Reform Council needs to get organized and prepared this summer, beginning July 14. This team builds on the experience of members of the Citizens' Commission—10 of whom are now well known members of the Jefferson school community. We are starting out by appointing experienced and dedicated Commission members who have designed our Reform Blueprint. We recommend that beginning in 1998, one-third of the School Reform Council be replaced each year by elected parent and teacher representatives and appointed community representatives. We recommend that this leadership team take over Jefferson Community Learning Center immediately. All other teachers and classified personnel positions will be filled from the most qualified applicants who apply in writing by July 5th and who will be interviewed by members of the School Reform Council. July and August will be spent in intensive staff development. Any questions?"

"Ray, it looks like you're the only Commission member left off the new Reform Team, Jack said. "What about you?"

Kathie Sorenson spoke up. "Our Commission felt that Ray can be more help to us as Vice Chair of the County School Board, where he can use his influence to help you create district charters for all county schools by creating 13 new Citizens' Commissions that, along with the Board, can start the discovery process this summer. Our Citizens' Commission believes that the Board cannot by-pass the need for each school community to take ownership of their reform process. Each School Reform Commission must undertake the discovery process. They must adapt the best reform programs and best practices to the special needs of their specific school culture. Finally, they must hold their own School Reform Council responsible for providing a quality education for their children. We believe that to be successful the eight components of an effective school reform model and the five action steps must be followed by every school community. I speak for the whole Commission when I say how much we have appreciated Ray and Kim's leadership. And we have a special thank you for Wendy Swenson and Nate Johnson. Without them, there would have been no unanimous Commission report. It takes everyone participating to make democracy work."

"Thank you, Kathie," Ray responded. "If this Board goes along with the Commission recommendations for remaking this district into a series of *district* charter or independent public schools, this has implications for the kind of new superintendent we will recruit. He or she must be hired to streamline the county office and provide technical assistance to our new local district charter schools when they request help. This model means that we Board members can focus on what we were elected to do—hold local schools accountable for providing better education services for all children in our community. And that means keeping our 'feet to the fire'—all of us—students, teachers, parents and this community."

The Moral Imperative

Ray continued. "Mr. Chairman and members of the County Board, this has been a productive and inspiring evening. Now, I don't want to spoil the party. Tonight, we have identified for you the members of the new Jefferson team who have agreed to serve on the School Reform Council and to implement the Commission's Reform Blueprint—on one condition. That condition is that the County Board votes tonight to grant Jefferson a *district*

509

charter or independent public school status. The board must guarantee the School Reform Council absolute independence in carrying out its mission for the next five years. The School Reform Council will decide how funds are to be allocated and spent, with state and district waivers from all regulations except for normal civil rights and financial accountability requirements. The full budget must be based on the average daily attendance by Jefferson students. All other expenditures for students or for building repairs among district schools, should be pro-rated and allocated to the School Reform Council to be spent for improving performance of students at Jefferson. In other words, Jefferson's students will receive equal financial resources.

"Independent *district* charter status is the bottom line for our Citizens' Commission members. It's not a political preference for us. It's a matter of personal principle if they are to serve as the School Reform Council. Without full authority, they cannot be held accountable for reforming Jefferson. As Chair of the Citizens' Commission, I believe each member has earned the right to make this request. This is our moral imperative!" The crowd exploded in loud applause!

There was a long pause before Wayne Burnston spoke. "Tonight we have seen a magnificent performance by a talented Citizens' Commission. Jack, I think we should hereby officially commend Ray and this group for their outstanding service to the County Schools and this community." The audience broke into thunderous applause lasting almost two minutes.

Wayne continued, "But even as we appreciate their service to our community, we've got to be reasonable. We can't just grant what you call a district charter status to Jefferson just because the Commission tells us to do so! I, for one, will not be given an ultimatum! We are accountable to the voters. You know that, Ray, you were elected too. This scheme takes away tax dollars from an already shaky county school budget. I don't feel comfortable turning over that kind of money to a new untried group—without the financial, accounting and legal safeguards we have built into the County office."

"I agree with Wayne," Joy said. "We can't be rushing to judgment here. We need more time to study this proposal and to discuss it thoroughly. Then we can carefully consider all the options before us. This decision has lasting consequences, not only financially in the district, but in the lives of the Jefferson students and their families."

510

"Excuse me!" Lola Gomez grabbed her microphone. "I thought this Citizens' Commission has been working on this for nine damn months! They've accomplished their mission faithfully, objectively and effectively. Now they have a right to call on this Board to perform our policy making responsibility with equal courage. I received a personal briefing on this report and recommendations at lunch today. I've been given ample chance to question or object. It's a rare County School Board meeting when we get two hours in depth to consider anything having this kind of impact. This may be our new five-year strategy, for heaven's sakes. This may be a road map on how we transform our district over the next few years—but that's a discussion for another board meeting! Tonight is the time to act on the Citizens' Commission recommendation about saving Jefferson and those children! I for one am prepared to stay in session until we have all our questions answered. I'll spend all night and as long as it takes into tomorrow. Then we can take a public vote on our Citizens' Commission recommendations—preferably with the TV cameras rolling. Why do you think all these folks in the audience showed up here tonight? Not just to watch us study this to death and schedule more meetings!" Again the audience broke into loud applause. "It's really not very complicated," Lola said. "Is this what you Commission members mean by a moral imperative—putting politics aside and voting our conscience? I'm up for this vote tonight!"

"I agree with you, Lola," Joyce Green said. "We've all had extensive briefing on this report. We've now spent more board time on this proposal than any we've ever considered—except for selecting a new superintendent or passing the annual school district budget. It's pretty exciting for me to think we might undertake the transformation of this school system in a series of district charters over the next three to five years! And Jefferson Community Learning Center is our lead horse. I'm not willing to chuck all the great work this Commission has done and start over for what? I don't want the members of this talented and dedicated Commission to walk away just because we're too damn stubborn to let go of a failed central office bureaucracy and force them to go to the governor for relief. I'd be too embarrassed to explain it to my constituency who are watching our little drama tonight in the audience or on television. I'm sure they're wondering about now if they should ever vote for us again!"

"I guess I'm done too," said a tired Jake Washington. "What's to decide here after all? We gave them a mission. They were wildly successful, even reporting back on the appointed day—and with unanimous recommendations. Would anyone have guessed this result nine months ago? Give me a break! It's the miracle of democracy that a representative Citizens' Commission made up of teachers and parents and community leaders of all races and ethnic backgrounds could have succeeded with the mission we gave them. It gives me hope that maybe, just maybe, they can turn Jefferson around and save those kids. Do any of us want the job? This Commission is committed to moving forward and reforming Jefferson from the ground up. And they'll probably succeed because they've now earned the moral authority from this community to implement their recommendations.

"I'm just proud to be here tonight. This Commission shows everyone that average citizens can put aside their differences and learn to work together for our children. But, having said all this, I'm struck by one thing Wayne said. How do we know this new Jefferson School Reform Council can run a school? If we vote to give them a new district charter but they don't have to see us again for five years, we're taking a mighty big risk, aren't we? Why don't we bring this Reform Council back twice each year—in February and September—to publicly account for their progress in reforming Jefferson. If they're on track, they keep right on going without our interference. If they're falling short, then we have a right to step in and renegotiate. This way we are still accountable for our stewardship to our voters. So, if we can make this small exception to the district charter idea, I'm ready to vote. It's not everyday we can change history. Remember we don't have great alternatives—and nobody else is volunteering to take Jefferson off our hands."

Grassroots Democracy: The County School Board Decides

"Are there further Board questions for the Commission? Are there further questions for any Board members?" Seeing no takers, Jack Clayton called for the vote. "All those who can vote to grant the new leaders of the Jefferson Community Learning Center a district charter to implement the Reform Blueprint developed by the Citizens' Commission on Reform of Jefferson Elementary School, provided they give the County Board a progress report twice each year—vote 'Aye.' "Joyce Green?"

"Aye."

"Lola Gomez?"

"Aye," she said. Jack Washington, Ray Gonzales and Jack Clayton also voted Aye.

"Those who vote against the motion, say 'Nay.' Joy Christiansen?"

"Nay," she said.

"Wayne Burnston?"

"Reluctantly, I vote Nay," he said.

"The motion is carried 5 votes to 2," Jack said. "We will instruct district counsel to prepare legal charter papers for final sign off and consult with our district teachers union to obtain waivers. Official approval will come at next week's Board meeting. Congratulations Ray, Kim and all members of the Citizens' Commission. I hereby declare the Commission disbanded and instruct the Board secretary to prepare a special commendation for each member. This meeting of the County School Board is adjourned!"

The crowd's applause was deafening! TV reporters rushed to interview Ray and Kim and members of the new School Reform Council for Jefferson Community Learning Center. *Here comes Jerri Rilley, CNN's TV anchor,* Jack thought. *I guess we made big news tonight. Tomorrow the war against ignorance begins all over again by courageous teachers in classrooms throughout the county. But tonight one community won a moral victory for its children. Sometimes—just sometimes—after all, we do make a difference for our children and our grandchildren!*

APPENDICES

A. High-Performance Independent Elementary School Inventory

B. Council for Basic Education: Student [Academic] Learning Standards

C. Figure C.1 *The Elementary School Reform Blueprint*

D. Responsible Family Learning Culture Diagnostic Questionnaire

E. Model District Charter [or Independent Public] School Compact

F. Supporters: Corporate and Private Foundations and Individuals

G. Endnotes

H. Authors' Professional Resumés

Appendix A
High-Performance Independent Elementary School Inventory[1]

Rate your elementary school in eight categories with six questions each as:
"not present" (0); "partially present" (1 point) and "fully operating" (2 points).

1. **School-Site Councils:** High-performance elementary schools have a School-Site Council that is responsible and accountable and can be characterized as having:

A. A written vision statement; mission with outcome goals and strategies to achieve them; and performance budgets that define results expected for expenditures for long (3-5 years) and short (annual) budgets;
___(0);___(1);___(2).

B. A qualified principal who is the instructional leader and chief executive officer of the School-Site Council;
___(0);___(1);___(2).

C. A principal shares various leadership roles with professional and classified staff and trains individuals and groups in leadership skills like team-building, problem-solving, consensus-building to implement school reform;
___(0);___(1);___(2).

D. A School-Site Council with full authority to make policy decisions about money, administrative support systems, personnel, instructional materials and strategies, staff development, teacher assignments, character education programs, discipline, student assessment, parent and community engagement;
___(0);___(1);___(2).

E. A School-Site Council whose representatives are elected teachers, parents, community leaders that meets at least weekly as a group with the principal;
___(0);___(1);___(2).

517

F. A School-Site Council who is responsible for operating the high-performance school according to the principles agreed to in the School Reform Charter;

___(0);___(1);___(2).

2. **Challenging Academic Standards for All Children:** High-performance elementary schools have challenging academic standards for all children with a core curriculum framework that:

A. Provides direction for teaching and learning, is written and is bench-marked to high-quality, standards-based teaching and learning examples;

___(0);___(1);___(2).

B. Is used in planning and modifying the instructional program annually;

___(0);___(1);___(2).

C. Is developed collaboratively by and communicated to the school community on a regular basis,

___(0);___(1);___(2).

D. Correlates all student and teacher materials and professional development with academic standards;

___(0);___(1);___(2).

E. Enables teachers and students to build cumulative core knowledge, skills, and understanding from grade to grade against standard's benchmarks;

___(0);___(1);___(2).

F. Is enriched by interdisciplinary field projects and community experiences.

___(0);___(1);___(2).

3. **Character Education Programs:** High-performance elementary schools have challenging character education programs within the academic curriculum, through extra-curricular activities, and through example of teachers, administrators, parents and students by:

A. Having a School-Site Council appoint a representative Action Team that consults with experts and makes field visits to review successful programs and assess the character education needs of your elementary school;

___(0);___(1);___(2).

B. Having the Action Team design a comprehensive character education program;

___(0);___(1);___(2).

C. Conducting professional development training programs for teachers, classified staff, parents, community members and media;

___(0);___(1);___(2).

D. Implementing psychosocial and multicultural program education to build emotional, knowledge and skill base of all children;

___(0);___(1);___(2).

E. Requiring all students to participate in community service projects each year with voluntary associations working in the neighborhood;

___(0);___(1);___(2).

F. Developing classroom cultures where students and teachers use cooperative learning and practice democratic principles based on respect for others;

___(0);___(1);___(2).

4. **Staff Development:** High-performance elementary schools invest time and money into professional and classified staff development and parent adult education by:

A. Focusing all professional development on preparation to teach new standards and improve classroom teaching performance;

___(0);___(1);___(2).

B. Reorganizing so that 70% of staff are teaching, student-teacher ratios are reduced, and day-time preparation and teacher collaboration periods are provided;

___(0);___(1);___(2).

C. Selecting and assisting at least two teachers each year to begin qualifying for National Teacher Certification;

___(0);___(1);___(2).

D. Involving Action Team of representative teachers, parents and community representatives in assessing needs and designing a school-wide staff development and assessment plan with suggested annual budgets

___(0);___(1);___(2).

E. Providing all teachers with 20 days of professional staff development (not taken away from regular student attendance days each year) to retool themselves on teaching the new academic standards, to receive special training on working with parents, and to integrate new computer software packages into curriculum;

___(0);___(1);___(2).

F. Involving Action Team of representative teachers, parents and community representatives in assessing needs and designing a parent adult education program to support the teaching and learning program at both home and school;

___(0);___(1);___(2).

5. **School Support Services:** High-performance elementary schools provide school support services to advance the teaching and learning mission of the organization by providing effective:

A. Professional administrative leadership by appointing a qualified vice principal as director of school support services;

___(0);___(1);___(2).

B. Student personnel services like transportation, health services, food services, student records;

___(0);___(1);___(2).

C. Building and grounds services, security services, development of good working relationships with law enforcement agencies, maintenance of telephone services, computers, equipment, voice mail;

___(0);___(1);___(2).

D. Information services, multi-media center, library services;

___(0);___(1);___(2).

E. Financial and legal services—budgeting, payroll, accounting, purchasing, contracting, insurance, capital investment; state, federal and foundation grants, and merit payments;

___(0);___(1);___(2).

F. Parent participation support networks, provide separate parent room in the school, publish parent newsletters, and provide adult education programs in parenting and literacy.

___(0);___(1);___(2).

6. **Educational Technology:** High-performance elementary schools design, purchase and use the latest high-tech learning tools and train all teachers and students to use them by:

A. Conducting a technical needs assessment of present facilities, equipment, budget for new resources, and prepare a five-year plan for equipping the school;

___(0);___(1);___(2).

B. Working with parents, business representatives, foundations and federal government agencies to raise funds for fully equipping the school with high-tech equipment;

___(0);___(1);___(2).

C. Training all teachers and administrators to effectively integrate proven educational software programming into the classroom teaching;

___(0);___(1);___(2).

D. Introducing all students to computer software programs that enhance learning through student interaction with new information sources, such as the internet;

___(0);___(1);___(2).

E. Implementing "low-tech" systems of communication between teachers and parents such as voice mail and automated calls to homes to check on student absenteeism;

___(0);___(1);___(2).

F. Providing evening computer courses for parents in the multi-media center to improve their employment skills and to enhance their abilities assisting their children and sharing educational experiences with the families.

___(0);___(1);___(2).

7. **Student Assessment and Adult Accountability:** High-performance elementary schools make regular assessments of student and adult performance by:

A. Annually assessing every student's knowledge and skills against high national or state academic standards;

___(0);___(1);___(2).

B. Supplementing student academic assessment with "authentic assessment" tools, such as portfolios, scientific experiments, community-based experiences and community service projects;

___(0);___(1);___(2).

C. Annually assessing character education activities to determine student progress in applying universal moral values, such as honesty, respect for others;

___(0);___(1);___(2).

D. Annually assessing teachers and the principal in improving classroom and school leadership knowledge and skills;

___(0);___(1);___(2).

E. Annually assessing classified staff performance in terms of contribution to the teaching and learning mission of the school;

___(0);___(1);___(2).

F. Reporting annually the improvements on student performance to the parents, media, the school and larger community and comparing with other state, national and international student achievement.

___(0);___(1);___(2).

8. **Public Engagement: High-performance elementary schools design and carry out parent and community engagement activities to improve student performance by:**

A. Inviting parents to visit the school regularly as welcome guests and to participate in all school activities;

___(0);___(1);___(2).

B. Expecting parents to prepare children to come to school physically, emotionally, and intellectually ready to learn; and providing parenting and literacy classes, where necessary;

___(0);___(1);___(2).

C. Expecting parents to support homework assignments, provide home-study environment, control TV watching, and read with small children;

___(0);___(1);___(2).

D. Inviting parents to participate in a written parent/student/teacher compact that describes expectations and reviews progress at least twice each year;

___(0);___(1);___(2).

E. Inviting parents, grandparents, and community members to become school volunteers that supplement school services by meaningful school/family/partnerships;

___(0);___(1);___(2).

F. Engaging the public by developing supportive relationships with media, social service providers, relationships with civic, neighborhood community groups .

___(0);___(1);___(2).

SCORING

1. Add up the number of points for each section, 1-8. (For example, section 1: A=1; B=2; C=0; D=2; E=1; F=0;

2. Total for Section 1= 8 (possible points = 8 per section and 96 total);

3. If you receive 8 points in a section, add one-half point bonus;

4. To reach 100 points, your school would need to score a 2 on each question=96 plus 8 x 1/2=4, for 100 points.

A. 86-100 points = This is a high-performance independent elementary school where student achievement and morale should be outstanding.

B. 71-85 points = Some improvements should be made to become a high performance school.

C. 66-70 points = Discussions should be held with district officials about improving your school.

D. 51-65 points = School board members and superintendent's top staff should participate in a "Reform Discovery Workshop" to determine the future of school reform in that district.

E. Below 50 points = Without delay participate in organizing a Citizens' Commission on reforming your elementary school and begin a "School Reform Discovery Journey."

---

[1] David Osborne and Peter Plastrick, *Banishing Bureaucracy: The Five Strategies For Reinventing Government* (1997). Many guest reformers interviewed for this study also represent whole-school reform models including John Anderson, New American Schools; The Business Roundtable, *The Essential Components of a Successful Education System: Putting Policy Into Practice* (1992); Thomas Boysen, *Kentuck Education Reform: The First*

Five Years—1990-1995 (1995); Viginia Edwards, Education Week, *Quality Counts* (1997); Nancy Grasmick, Maryland State Department of Education, "Improving Learning for All Children Through School Reform: Education Reform in Maryland: 1977-1996 (1996); David Hornbeck, *Children Achieving Action Agenda*; Henry Levin, Accelerated Schools; Ken Nelson, National Education Goals Panel; Thomas Payzant, Model for restructuring San Diego Schools; Sam Sava, National Association of Elementary School Principals, *Standards for Quality Elementary & Middle Schools Kindergarten Through Eighth Grade* (1996); and Robert Slavin, Roots and Wings; U.S. Department of Education Blue Ribbon Schools have these features: challenging academic standards and rigorous curriculum for students; a disciplined, supportive, safe and drug-free environment; participatory leadership and a strong partnership among family, school and community; excellent teaching and an environment that strengths teacher skills and improvement; and low dropout rates and documented student achievement. The Effective Schools model calls for: clear and specific purposes; strong educational leadership; high expectations for students; frequent monitoring of student progress; positive climate for learning; partnerships with parents and community. School-Based Reform—Lessons From A National Study-1995 calls for: setting high expectations for all students; developing a challenging curriculum; considering alternative configurations of students and teachers; and tracking student progress with a range of outcome measures. U.S. Department of Education, Office of Education Research and Improvement, "Reform Studies (1995).

Appendix B

Council for Basic Education: Student Learning Standards
Los Angeles Unified School District—Elementary Schools

History and Social Science

Upon completion of grade four, students will be able to:

Describe how California's physical environment influenced where people lived, their beliefs, their social organizations, and their work.

Compare and contrast the cultural characteristics and contributions of the American Indians of California with diverse immigrant groups who came to California.

Describe why different groups of people have come and continue to come to California and the influence they have had and continue to have on California.

Identify human and natural resources available to different people in California at different times and describe how these resources have influenced the choices people have made and continue to make, especially about the work that they do.

Evaluate historical information reflecting a diversity of ideas, values, behaviors, and institutions, using multiple sources, in order to better understand history from different points of view.

Analyze and explain events, trends, issues, historical figures, and movements that have shaped the history of California.

Explain how the people of California have attempted to resolve the issues of justice, fairness, equity, personal responsibility, and civic responsibility.

Evaluate the role of representative government in school, community, and state organizations.

Language Arts

Upon completing grade three in the LAUSD, students will be able to:

Listen actively to gather information and respond appropriately.

Demonstrate oral language skills of pace, volume, emphasis, pronunciation, audibility, and appropriate choice of words.

Use various reading strategies such as phonics, pictorial context, grammatical, and context clues to read with accuracy, fluency, and comprehension.

Retell, make predictions, make inferences, and evaluate passages from culturally diverse literature and other reading materials.

Use correct spelling, grammar usage, sentence structure, capitalization, and punctuation for clarity in finished written products.

Use a variety of writing processes—including prewriting, drafting, evaluating, revising, editing, and publishing, with teacher assistance—to develop and express ideas.

Write in simple paragraph form, supporting a central idea with relevant facts and details for various purposes and audiences.

Gather information for a report using sources such as interviews, questionnaires, computers, and library/multimedia centers.

Identify conflicts and points of view in grade-appropriate literature and suggest solutions to similar problems in everyday situations.

Note: Students who are not proficient in English will receive instruction in English Language Development (ELD) on the basis of California ELD standards until they are able to participate in classes taught in English. While they are acquiring English, access to the above language arts standards and to the standards in other core disciplines will be provided in the student's primary language when required.

Language Arts

Upon completing grade three in LAUSAD, students will be able to:

Apply the basic operations (addition, subtraction, multiplication, and division) using whole numbers and simple fractions (halves, fourths); use rounding to the tens, hundreds, and thousands as an estimation strategy to check the reasonableness of results.

Use appropriate non-standard and standard measurement systems and measurement tools (rulers, scales, thermometers, clocks, money, etc.) to estimate or directly measure length, capacity, weight, mass, area, volume, time, temperature, and monetary value.

Express the appropriate operation symbols $(+, -, \times, \div, =, >, <)$ and find missing numbers to make a true mathematical sentence; show how the basic arithmetic operations are related.

Use the geometric concepts of space and form to construct, describe, and compare the properties of one-, two-, and three- dimensional figures such as line segments, circles, simple polygons, and solids.

Create and use discrete structures such as sets, graphs, tables, and diagrams to find possible combinations and arrangements of countable items (for example, how many combinations of outfits are possible given three different shirts and three pairs of pants?)

Predict outcomes and perform simple experiments (such as with dice and spinners) to check if predicted outcomes are reasonable; identify possible strategies in increase or decrease the likelihood of a predicted outcome (such as a raffle drawing).

Collect, organize and interpret statistical data in charts, tables, and bar graphs; formulate and solve problems using data to make appropriate and useful decisions.

Select and use appropriate technology, such as calculators and computers with software models to solve problems; develop and apply strategies to solve problems and explain solutions using hand-on materials, trial and error, analysis of patterns and sequences, and arithmetic reasoning.

Interpret and use logical statements that contain expressions, such as and, or, if…then, all, some, none, not, and out of, to make reasonable inferences.

Make connections among mathematical concepts and relate them to concepts in other in daily life.

Compare the use of various number systems (for example, Hindu-Arabic, Roman, tally, etc.) from different historical periods.

Use oral and written language, drawings, and mathematical symbols and terms to communicate understanding of mathematics.

Science

Upon completing grade four in the LAUSD, students will be able to:

Make observations of weather, seasons, the sky, and physical features of the earth; describe how some events in nature have patterns, sequences, and relationships. (Earth Science)

Identify and describe physical concepts of force, motion, and energy as demonstrated by the use of objects such as playground equipment and toys. (Physical Science)

Observe and describe the properties of matter and its changes in form; classify its forms into solid, liquid, and gas. (Chemistry)

Identify the characteristics of living things, including humans, and how they interact with each other, and the ways they adapt to their changing environment. (Life Science)

Ask questions and give reasonable explanations after observing, comparing and classifying objects, living things, and events in the world. (Scientific Thinking)

Communicate predictions, data, and conclusions about the natural and physical world using language, pictures, and graphs. (Communication)

Explore, observe, and classify living and nonliving things through both independent and team investigations. (Investigation)

Use various tools to order, count, observe, and measure objects and events in the world. (Science Tools)

Use concepts learned in life science, earth science, and physical science to make decisions about a school or local environmental issues such as preventing erosion, recycling, or air quality. (Applications and Connections)

Appendix C

Figure C.1
The Elementary School Reform Blueprint

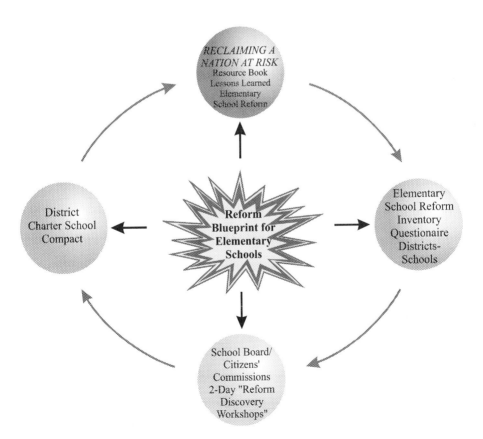

Appendix D

The Terrel H. Bell KNOWLEDGE NETWORK for Education Reform
Responsible Family Learning Culture Diagnostic Questionnaire
By Kent Lloyd, Ph.D. and Diane Ramsey, Ph.D.

Name _____

This questionnaire attempts to assess the strength of your family's responsible learning culture. It is to be used as a diagnostic tool only. It has not been carefully validated as a reliable scientific research instrument, but is now being developed for the KNOWLEDGE NETWORK'S parent projects.

Instructions:

The questionnaire is composed of two parts: **Part I** is a brief question. **Part II** is a series of 20 questions.

Part I

Read the question, then circle the letter that best describes your parental style.

In your judgment, when compared with the people with whom you associate, how would you judge your parental leadership style?

Authoritarian Strict Discipline Parental Authority	Authoritative Structure Shared Responsibility	Laize Faire Permissive/Full Freedom
X	Y	Z

Part II

Now turn to the additional questions. After reading each question, please circle the number which most nearly describes your family. Each question answered is a matter of personal judgment. There are no "right" answers, but the information may be helpful to you in discussions with your family.

The Terrel H. Bell KNOWLEDGE NETWORK for Education Reform

Characteristics:			
	Circle the number best describing your family.		
1. Would you describe the amount of time your family spends obtaining basic needs (food, shelter, clothes, health) as:	Most of Time 1	About ½ Time 3	About 1/3 Time 5
2. Does your family expect all members to be responsible, honest, and trustworthy at all times?	Very Seldom 1	Sometimes 3	Regularly 5
3. Except for young children, do all your family members contribute time working to support your family?	Very Seldom 1	Sometimes 3	Regularly 5
4. Do most members receive recognition by family members for their contributions to the family?	Very Seldom 1	Sometimes 3	Usually 5
5. Would you describe the value your family places on protection of life, property, individual rights as:	Low Value 1	Somewhat Valued 3	High Value 5
6. Does your family expect their members to be just, equitable, fair and accountable to all members?	Very Seldom 1	Sometimes 3	Regularly 5
7. Except for very young children, do all your family members learn to save resources for the future, such as time, money and energy?	Very Seldom 1	Sometimes 3	Regularly 5
8. Are most family members rewarded for self-control and delaying gratification?	Very Seldom 1	Sometimes 3	Usually 5
9. Would you describe the value your family places on the worth and uniqueness of each family member as:	Low Value 1	Somewhat Valued 3	High Value 5
10. Does your family expect each members to be respectful, kind and giving to all other members?	Very Seldom 1	Sometimes 3	Regularly 5
11. Do all your family members learn to give and receive special time, affection and bonding from each other?	Very Seldom 1	Sometimes 3	Regularly 5
12. Do most family members want to spend time when possible with each other and with the whole Family	Very Seldom 1	Sometimes 3	Usually 5
13. Would you describe the value your family places on life-long improvement and self reliance as: as:	Low Value 1	Somewhat Valued 3	High Value 5

14. Does your family expect all their members to achieve their goals with courage and discipline?	Very Seldom 1	Somewhat Expected 3	Always Expected 5
15. Does your family expect that all members will be life-long students of new knowledge and learn new skills?	Very Seldom 1	Somewhat Expected 3	Always Expected 5
16. Are all family members encouraged by positive reinforcement to improve themselves?	Very Seldom 1	Sometimes 3	Usually 5
17. Would you describe the value your family places on making contributions to the larger community as:	Low Value 1	Somewhat Valued 3	High Value 5
18. Does your family expect their members to learn how to perform their talents with excellence and creativity?	Very Seldom 1	Somewhat Expected 3	Always Expected 5
19. Except for very young children, do all your family members contribute time effectively to the larger community?	Very Seldom 1	Sometimes 3	Regularly 5
20. Do most family members receive recognition by the larger community for their contributions?	Very Seldom 1	Sometimes 3	Usually 5

Scoring Instructions:

Add the scores for each of the 20 questions to obtain the total. The highest possible score is 100; the lowest possible score is 20. Please note your total score in the box below

Total Score: [   ]

Appendix E
Model District Charter [or Independent Public] School Compact

Section 1. Background. This compact charters public school districts to approve the establishment of a new class of public schools called "District Charter Schools", which are a part of the school district and state program of public education.

Section 2. Purpose. The purpose of this compact is to:

(a) Improve pupil learning;

(b) Encourage the use of different and innovative learning methods;

(c) Increase *choice* of learning opportunities for pupils;

(d) Establish a new form of accountability for schools;

(e) Require the measurement of learning outcomes and create innovative measurement tools;

(f) Make the school the unit for improvement; and

(g) Create new professional opportunities for teachers, including the opportunity to own the learning program at the school site.

Section 3. Sponsor. Existing schools, new schools. A board of education on its own may convert all or some of its schools to charter status:

(a) By converting an existing school to charter status. In the case of an existing public school, the proposers will be the principal, teachers and parents at the school.

(b) By creating a new school. A proposal for a new charter school may be made by an individual, a group of individuals or an organization. Individuals are most commonly teachers or parents. Organizations could be, for example, community groups, universities, community colleges, hospitals, zoos or museums or other recognized educational organization. The chartering group must show that the governing group includes both professional educators and parent and community representatives.

Section 5. Number of schools. The number of district charter schools shall not be limited.

Section 6. Eligible pupils.

(a) Charter schools shall be open to any student residing in the district;

(b) The school shall enroll an eligible pupil who submits a timely application, unless the number of applications exceeds the capacity of a program, class, grade level or building. Priority will be given to those students who reside within the school boundaries. Additional students who meet the standard requirements shall have an equal chance of being admitted by lot.

(c) A district charter school may elect to specialize in:

(1) granting a charter to an existing neighborhood school pupils within an age group or age level;

(2) pupils considered "at risk;" and

(3) residents of a specific geographic area where the percentage of the population of people of color of that area is greater than the percentage of people of color in the congressional district in which the geographic area is located, as long as the school reflects the racial and ethnic diversity oft the specific area.

Section 7. The school is a legal entity.

(a) The charter school, new or existing, shall organize under one of the forms of organization available under the laws of the state, e.g., nonprofit, cooperative, partnership, public benefit corporation, etc. Or a new form may be established for a charter school.

Section 8. Requirements for public education.

(a) The school must not be affiliated with a nonpublic sectarian school or religious institution. The school must be nonsectarian in its programs, admission policies,employment practices and all other operations.

(b) The school must admit students as provided in Section 6 above;

(c) The school is accountable to public authority for performance as provided in Section 9 below;

(d) The school may not charge tuition fees beyond those allowed in the regular K-12 system;

(e) The school must meet all applicable state and local health, safety and civil rights requirements;

(f) The school may not discriminate;

(g) A district charter school will conform to the uniform financial accounting and reporting standards and processes that govern school districts generally. The governing entity of the charter school must contract for an annual financial audit by a certified public accountant, in accordance with Generally Accepted Accounting Principles. Said audit shall also examine the validity and integrity of data reported to the state for revenue purposes (e.g., average daily attendance, enrollment, etc., that drive the calculations of the school's entitlements) and internal controls of the charter school.

Section 9. The Charter document. The district will simply require that the major issues involving the operation of the school be thought through in advance and written into the charter document, which must be signed by the responsible school executive.

(a) The school and the district must come to a written agreement on the following:

(1) The education program: the school's mission, the students to be served, the ages and grades to be included and the focus of the curriculum;

(2) The outcomes to be achieved and the method of measurement that will be used, including how the school will meet state-required outcomes;

(3) The admissions procedures and dismissal procedures;

(4) The ways by which the school will achieve a racial/ethnic balance reflective of the community it serves;

(5) The manner in which the program and fiscal audit will be conducted;

(6) The term of the agreement—three to five years; and

(7) The qualifications to be required of the teachers;

(8) The governance structure of the school must include an equal balance of representative teachers and the principal, and parents and community representatives.

(b) In addition, the sponsor must require that the school include as an addendum to the charter document a plan covering the following items, although the school and the district need not reach agreement on the terms of the plan for these items:

(1) The management and administration of the school;

(2) Alternative arrangements for current students who choose not to attend the school and for current teachers who choose not to teach in the school after conversion;

(3) The learning methods and teaching technology to be used;

(4) Any distinctive learning techniques to be employed;

(5) Internal financial controls;

(6) How the school will be insured;

(7) The facilities to be used and their location;

(8)   The arrangements for covering teachers and other staff for health, retirement and other benefits; and

(9)   The whole-school reform model that will be used to reach the learning objectives.

Section 10. Causes for nonrenewal or termination.

(a)   At the end of the term, the school district may choose not to renew the agreement on any of the following grounds:

(1)   Failure to meet the requirements for student performance stated in the agreement;

(2)   Failure to meet generally accepted standards of fiscal management;

(3)   Violation of law; or

(4)   Other good causes shown following public due process.

(b)   During the term of the agreement, the sponsor may act to terminate the agreement on any of the grounds listed above. At least 60 days before not renewing or terminating a contract, the district shall notify the board of directors of the school of the proposed action in writing. The notice shall state the grounds for the proposed action in reasonable detail and that the school's board of directors may request in writing an informal school's hearing before the board of education within 14 days of receiving the notice. A termination shall be effective only at the conclusion of a school year, unless continued operation of the school presents a clear and immediate threat to health and safety.

(c) The school may appeal the district's decision to terminate or not renew the agreement to the state board of education.

(d) When an agreement is not renewed or is terminated, the school shall be dissolved, as provided by state law governing nonprofit organizations.

(e) If an agreement is not renewed or is terminated, a student who attended the school may apply to and shall be enrolled in another public school.

Section 11. Exemption from statutes and rules. Except as provided in this section, a charter school is exempt from all statutes and rules applicable to a school board or school district, although it may elect to comply with one or more provisions of statutes or rules.

Section 12. Teachers.

(a)   The charter school will select its teachers and the teachers will select the school.

(b)   If the teachers choose to be employees of the school, they shall have the rights of teachers in public education to organize and bargain collectively. Bargaining units at the school will be separate from other units, such as the district unit. Staff at existing schools converting to district charter status may continue perquisites or benefits granted by the district as specified in a district charter, without regard to potential conflict with existing collective bargaining agreements.

(c) Alternatively, the teachers may chose to be part of a professional group that operates the instructional program under an agreement with the school, forming a partnership or producer cooperative that they collectively own.

(d) Teachers leaving a current position in a public school district to teach in a charter school may take leave to teach. While on leave, they retain their seniority position and continue to be covered by the benefit programs of the district in which they had been working. A school district must also grant service credit to such teachers for teaching experiences at a charter school, provided their service at a charter school is reasonably comparable to service in a school district.

(f) Teachers not previously teaching in a public school district may be made eligible for the state teacher retirement program. Alternatively, the state may add to the financing of the school an amount equal to the employer contribution for teacher retirement so that the school may establish or enroll teachers in its own program.

Section 13. Revenue. The state will provide the charter school with the full amount of revenue for each student that would be available if the student were enrolled in a regular school.

(a) The state will pay directly to the school the average amount per pupil spent statewide for operating purposes, plus weightings and categoricals.

(b) District charter schools are exempt from the restrictions normally associated with any state funded categorical education funding programs.

(c) A district charter school may receive other state and federal aids, grants and revenue as though it were a district.

(d) The school may receive gifts and grants from private sources in whatever manner is available to districts.

(e) Special education will be, as now, an obligation of the district of residence.

Section 14. Immunity.

(a) The district charter school may sue and be sued.

(b) Members of the board of education as sponsors of a district charter school in their official capacity and employees of the district are immune from civil or criminal liability with respect to all activities related to a district charter school they approve or sponsor.

Section 15. Length of school year. The district charter school shall provide instruction for at least the number of days required by state law. It may provide instruction for more days.

Section 16. Leased space. A school district may lease space or sell services to a district charter school. A charter school may lease space or secure services from another public body, nonprofit organization or private organization or individual.

Section 17. Transportation. Transportation for pupils enrolled at a charter school shall be provided by the district in which the school is located for students residing in the district in which the school is located, or to and from the border of the district for nonresident students. Districts may provide transportation for nonresident students. Or the charter school, at its option, may receive a proportionate share of any state or local transportation funds and arrange for its own transportation service.

Section 18. Initial costs. A school district may authorize a school before the applicant has secured space, equipment, personnel, etc., if the applicant indicates authorization is necessary for it to raise working capital.

Section 19. Information. The state department of education and the school district must disseminate information to the public directly, both on how to form and operate a district charter school and on how to enroll in charter schools once they are created.

Section 20. General Authority. A charter school may not levy taxes or issue bonds secured by tax revenues.

---

*Patterned after Ted Kolderie's "Model Bill: Chartering Sponsors That May Charter Schools," 9/25/96.

Appendix F
Sponsors and Special Contributors

Private Foundations
Hewlette Foundation
Freddie Mac Foundation
Kellogg Foundation
Ford Motor Fund
Exxon Education Fund
Union Carbide Foundation
MCI Foundation
Rockwell International

Corporate Contributions
Better Impressions
Jenner & Block
John Behrens Associates

Individual Contributors
Nolan and Margaret Archibald
V.J. and Kathleen Adduci
John T. and Linda Alexander
Dan and Susan Alexander
Ramon and Jeanne Alvarez
Lori Annaheim
Anthony and Betsy Antonelli
Temple Ashbrook II and
Loretta Hyatt-Ashbook
Dixie Barlow
John and Tyra Behrens
John Bowman
Mary L. Bradford
Wayne M. and Dorothy Burnette
Kent and Winnie Burton
Mark and Betty Cannon
Kent and Janice Christensen
Lenora Cox
Christopher and Diane Cross
Arthur Dee and
Catherine Barbara Decker
Francis and Pauline Eichbush
Jeanne Forrest

Morris and Lori Gordon
Stuart E. Gothold
Pamela Greene
Sven and Suzanne Groennings
David and Leslie Guido
Ray and Claire Ehler
Rob and Laurie Friend
Pat Henry
Allan Howe
Jerry and Edith Hymas
Scot and Jeralie Hymas
Lorie Flemming Josephson
Gary and Donna Lloyd
Zane and Louise Mason
Ladd and Susan McNamara
Carolyn and Eric Miller
Thomas F. and Heidi Mosher
Morris and Lynne Musig
Kathie and Peter Nielsen
Samantha L. O'Neill
David and Kellie Persinger
Velda Pirtle
Lewis and Evelyn Ramsey
Steven and Christine Ramsey
Tamar Ridenour
Virginia C. Riedy
Boyd and Jill Smith
Carlos and Mona Smith
Wendall M. and Monetta Smoot
Rudi S. Southerland
Lillian Stark
Dwayne and Carolyn Stevenson
Brian and Sue Swinton
Jennifer Tepper
Leslie Vartanian
Richard and Donna Welch
Woodrow and Virginia Williams
Richard and Jeralie Wirthlin

Appendix G
END NOTES

Chapter 2

1. National Commission on Excellence, *A Nation At Risk: The Imperative for Educational Reform* (U.S. Government Printing Office, 1983).

2. In his well-reasoned and written *Final Exam: A study of the Perpetual Scrutiny of American Education* (Technos Press, 1995), Gerald Bracey presents a strong case for recognizing that (1) American schools are perpetually being criticized for their shortcomings—even given the steady progress they are making; (2) reform efforts are usually based on poor assumptions about education; (3) the present push for national academic standards will likely mean that fewer students will actually reach the standards; (4) the condition of American education is much better than the media or the reformers portray it; and (5) that the financial inequities between public schools are the major educational challenge facing reformers.

3. *Time for Results: The Governor' 1991 Report on Education* (National Governors Association, 1986).

4. Edmonds, Ronald. *A Discussion of the Literature and Issues Related to Effective Schooling (CEMREL 1979).*

5. GOALS 2000: Educate America Act, Section 318 (1994)

6. *U.S. News Poll,* March 1996.

7. Princeton Survey Research Associates, 17 January 1996.

8. *U.S. News Poll,* March 1996.

9. Nevertheless, a recent USA Today/CNN/Gallup survey shows, "quality of public education will be the number one concern of voters in the 1996 presidential election." Broad support exists for higher academic standards and for students not being promoted or given a high school diploma unless they demonstrate mastery over required materials.

10. Much of this information is taken from four sources: National Education Goals Panel (1995 and 1996 Reports), and the U.S. Department of Education's *Condition of Education* (1995) and *Digest of Educational Statistics* (1995). These documents give snapshots of the public schools' effectiveness in educating some 51 million students to meet our ambitious national education goals.

11. Office of Educational Research and Improvement, *Projections of Education Statistics to 2005* (U.S. Department of Education, 1995).

12. National Center on Education Statistics, *Adult Literacy in America: A First Look at the Results of the National Adult Literacy Survey* (U.S. Department of Education, 1993). Three new assessments of adult literacy were administered to a national sample of adults ages 19-24. The two lowest levels of "functional" literacy meant that individuals were operating at or below a high school level of competency in prose reading 48%; understanding simple documents 51%; and qualitative analysis 47%. The third level of literacy proficiency is the lowest level to negotiate entry level jobs in the information-knowledge economy and make an income that would support a family at a lower working class life-style includes 31-32% more Americans (roughly some college through college graduation). Competitive well paying jobs in today's economy require literacy levels 4 and 5 or advanced technical, graduate or professional education where roughly 20% of the adult population qualify by virtue of their educational achievement. See also Organization for Economic Co-Operation and Development's

13. Center for Educational Research and Innovation, Indicators of Education Systems, *Education at a Glance: Analysis* (1996).

14. Educational Testing Service *A World of Differences: An International Assessment of Mathematics and Science* (1989).

15. Report of the National Education Commission on Time and Learning, *Prisoners of Time* (1994).

16. *Economic Report of the President 1995.*

17. National Center for Education Statistics *NAEP 1994 Trends in Academic Progress: Achievement of U.S. Students in Science, 1969-1994; Mathematics, 1973 to 1994; Reading, 1971 to 1994; Writing, 1984 to 1994* (November 1996).

18. National Center For Education Statistics. *The Condition of Education 1995*, (U.S. Department of Education, 1995).

19. National Center for Education Statistics, Office of Educational Research and Improvement, U.S. Department of Education *Pursuing Excellence: A Study of U.S. Eighth-Grade Mathematics and Science Teaching, Learning, Curriculum, and Achievement in International Context: Initial Finds from the Third International Mathematics and Science Study* (November 1996).

20. The Organization for Economic Co-Operation and Development, *Education At A Glance: OECD Indicators*, R6 Tables (1996).

21. William H. Schmidt, *A Splintered Vision: An Investigation of U.S. Mathematics and Science Education* (National Science Foundation, 1965).

22. Jean Johnson and Steve Farkas with Ali Bers *Getting By: What American Teenagers Really Think About Their Schools* (Public Agenda, 1997).

23. The National Education Goals Panel, *The National Education Goals Report: Building A Nation of Learners: 1966.* See Dennis P. Doyle and S. Pimental *Setting Standards, Meeting Standards: Creating High Performance Schools* (forthcoming in 1997).

24. GOAL LINE can be contacted by telephone 202-835-2000 and E-mail: connect @ goalline.org.

25. The 1995 National Education Goals Report, *Building A Nation of Learners*

Chapter 3

1. Deborah Meier, *The Power of Their Ideas* (1996). Also taken from personal interview with author on May 21, 1996.
2. The 28th Annual Phi Delta Kappa/Gallup Poll, *Phi Delta Kappan*, September 1996.
3. Nathan Tarcov, "The Meanings of Democracy," *Democracy, Education, and the Schools*, Roger Soder, Ed.(1996).
4. Adam Smith, *Wealth of Nations* (1776). Smith believed that "the public good" results from free exchange of goods and services ("the invisible hand") and specialization for greater efficiency. In this market exchange, an individual's self-interests are best servEd. See also Adam Smith, *The Theory of Moral Sentiments* (1776) and Jerry Z. Muller, *Adam Smith: In His Time and Ours* (1993).
5. Ibid.
6. Robert D. Putnam, *Making Democracy Work: Civic Traditions in Modern Italy* (1993).
7. Donna H. Kerr, "Democracy, Nurturance, and Community," *Democracy, Education, and the Schools* Roger Soder, Ed. (1996). Alan Wolfe, *Whose Keeper? Social Science and Moral Obligation* (1989); Herbert I. Schiller, *Culture, Inc.: The Corporate Takeover of Public Expression* (1991); John McDermott, *Corporate Society: Class, Property and Contemporary Capitalism* (1991).
8. Letter to John Adams, 28 October 1813, in M.D. Peterson, Ed., *The Portable Jefferson* (1975).
9. John I. Goodlad, "Common Schools for the Common Weal: Reconciling Self-Interest with the Common Good," in J.I. Goodlad and P. Keating, Eds., *Access to Knowledge: An Agenda for Our Nation's Schools* (1990).
10. Gordon C. Lee, "Learning and Liberty: The Jefferson Tradition in Education," in G.C.Less, Ed., *Crusade Against Ignorance: Thomas Jefferson on Education (*1961).
11. We are indebted to John I. Goodlad for his review of Erik Erikson's work on individual development and John Dewey in Robert B. Westbrook, *John Dewey and American Democracy* (1991) and recently Benjamin Barber, *An Aristocracy of Everyone: The Politics of Education and the Future of America* (1992), and "America Skips School," *Harper's Magazine,* November 1993.
12. Merle Curti, *The Social Ideas of American Educators* (1959).
13. We are indebted to Linda Darling-Hammond and Jacqueline Ancess, "Democracy and Access to Education," in Roger Soder, Ed., *Democracy, Education, and the Schools* (1996), for their brilliant essay on the disadvantaged's access to public education.
14. Ronald F. Ferguson, "Paying for Public Education: New Evidence on How and Why Money Matters," *Harvard Journal on Legislation,* 1991, vol. 28, no. 2; William T. Hartman, "District Spending Disparaties: What Do the Dollars Buy? *Journal of Education Finance,* 1988, vol. 13, no. 4; Jonathan Kozol *Savage Inequalities* (1991)*;* Eleanor Armour-Thomas and others, *An Outline Study of Elementary and Middle Schools in New York City: Final Report* (New York Cit y Board of Education: 1989)*;* Jeannie Oakes, *Multiplying Inequalities: The Effects of Race, Social Class, and Tracking on Opportunities to Learn Mathematics and Science* (RAND Corporation, 1990)

15. Julie E. Kaufman and James E. Rosenbaum, "Education and Employment of Low-Income Black Youth in White Suburbs," *Educational Evaluation and Policy Analysis*, 1992, vol.14, no. 3.

16. E. P. Cubberly, *Public Education in the United States* (1934).

17. One expert identified seven principles that characterize such an approach to teaching: having a moral purpose; showing knowledge-in-use (discuss public problems and citizen action to correct them); discussing face-to-face (involve all parties); reflecting on citizen action (carry out and negotiate action steps); respecting diverse perspectives (show how others experience their lives); forging majority agreement around ideas and planned action steps (open discussion, negotiation, problem solving); and exploring and reconciling tensions and conflicts between multiple associations (many parties) without resorting to force, exclusion or violence.

18. Also see Barbara A. Lewis, *The Kid's Guide to Social Action: How to Solve the Social Problems You Choose—And Turn Creative Thinking Into Positive Action* (1991).

19. Barbara A. Lewis, *The Kid's Guide to Social Action: How to solve the social problems you choose—and turn creative thinking into positive action* (1991).

Chapter 4

1. See *Phi Delta Kappan* Special Issue on Charter Schools, Joe Nathan, Guest Ed., September 1996; in the same issue, see Ray Budde, "The Evolution of the Charter Concept." Budde first published a book on the charter concept in 1988.

2. Ted Kolderie, "Charter Schools: The State Begins to Withdraw the 'Exclusive,' *Public Service Redesign Project Newsletter*, Center for Policy Studies, 1993.

3. Jeanne Allen and Angela Hulsey, *School Choice Programs: What's Happening in the States* (1992). John E. Chubb and Terry M. Moe believe that systemic reform will come only by overturning the present public educaton institutions and opening the competitive market model to parent consumers financed through tax-subsidized vouchers. See their *Politics, Markets, and America's Schools (1990)*.

4. David Osborne and Peter Plastrik, *Banishing Bureaucracy: The Five Strategies for Reinventing Government* (1997).

5. The Carnegie Foundation for the Advancement of Teaching, *School Choice* (1992).

6. Thomas Toch with Warren Cohen, "Why Vouchers Won't Work," *U.S. News and World Report*, 7 October 1996.

7. Ibid.; and see *Education Week*, 6 March 1996; see the continuing studies of John F. Witte, Troy D. Sterr, and Christopher A. Thorn, *Fifth-Year Report: Milwaukee Parental Choice Program* (University of Wisconsin, 1995).

8. Ibid.

9. Kathryn Stearns, *School Reform: Lessons from England* (The Carnegie Foundation for the Advance of Teaching, 1996).

10. Albert Shanker, "Bush's New Voucher Program: G.I. Bull," *The New Republic*, 27 July 1992, vol. 207, no. 30.

11. Jerome J. Hanas and Peter W. Cookson, Jr., *Choosing Schools: Vouchers and American Education* (1996). Although some believe that if vouchers are given to parents, not to the religious school as with student financial aid grants, it would be constitutional.

12. Ted Kolderie, "The Charter Idea: Update and Prospects, Fall '95" (Center for Policy Studies, St. Paul, MN, 1995).

13. *Phi Delta Kappan,* June 1993; see also 28th Annual Poll, *Phi Delta Kappan,* September 1996.

14. Joe Freedman, M.D. *The Charter School Idea: Breaking Educational Deadlock,* Society for Advancing Educational Research (1995); also see Louann A.Bierle in, *Existing Charter School Laws: Analysis of 'Stronger' Components,* Louisiana Education Policy Research Center (1995).

15. Marc Dean Millot, *Autonomy, Accountability, and the Values of Public Education (RAND, 1995).*

16. Ann Bradley, "NEA Seeks To Help Start Five Charter Schools" *Education Week* April 24, 1996; and "Charter School Laws: Do They Measure Up," American Federation of Teachers (1996)

17. Wellford W. Wilms, "Laboring Toward a New Compact on Schools: Why Teachers' Unions Should Not Be A Political Scapegoal," *Education Week,* 2 October 1996. This article describes the new Teacher Union Reform Network (TURN).

18. Marc Dean Millot, Paul T. Hill, and Robin Lake "Commentary: Charter Schools: Escape or Reform?" *Education Week,* 6 June 1996.

19. Terrel H. Bell, "Commentary: The Charter School Plus," *Education Week,* 15 March 1995.

20. Mary Anne Raywid, "The Struggles and Joys of Trailblazing," *Phi Delta Kappan,* March 1995; William Windler, "Colorado's Charter Schools: A Spark for Change and a Catalyst for Reform," *Phi Delta Kappan* September 1996.

21. Ted Kolderie *A Guide To Charter Activity* (Center for Policy Studies. St. Paul, MN: August 1996). Kolderie has drafted a "Model Charter Schools Bill" that can serve as a guide to legislation.

22. Joe Nathan, *Charter Schools* (1996).

23. Chester E. Finn Jr., Bruno V. Manno and Louann Bierlein *Charter Schools in Action: What Have We Learned?* (Hudson Institute: Educational Excellence Network: 1996); Hudson Institute headquarters in Indianapolis also publishes a helpful briefing packet. The Internet has a busy forum on charter schools.

24. Howard Fuller, "Develop Alternatives to Existing School System," *Minnesota Journal,* 18 July 1995.

25. Joe Nathan, "Possibilities, Problems, and Progress: Early Lessons from the Charter Movement," and Ray Budde, "The Evolution of the Charter Concept," *Phi Delta Kappan,* September 1996.

26. Joe Freedman, M.D., *The Charter School Idea: Breaking Educational Gridlock* (Society for Advancing Education Research: 1995); see also the Southwest Educational Development Laboratory's review of three reports on charter schools in *R &D Watch,* May 1996.

Chapter 5

1. Diane Ravitch, *National Standards in American Education: A Citizens Guide* (Brookings, 1995).

2. Diane Ravitch, "Schools That Specialize: Are They Democratic?" *The Washington Post Education Review,* 28 July 1996.

3. Diane Ravitch, "Why We Need A Literate Core Curriculum," *Common Knowledge* (Core Knowledge Newsletter) vol. 9, Winter/Spring 1996.
4. Diane Ravitch, "50 Ways to Teach Them Grammar," *The Washington Post, 3* April 1996.
5. Council for Basic Education, "Special Report: History in the Making: An Independent Review of the Voluntary National History Standards," January 1996.
6. Diane Ravitch, "The New, Improved History Standards," *The Wall Street Journal,* 3 April 1996; George Will, *The Washington Post,* 4 April 1996.
7. Karen Diegmueller, "AFT Report" *Education Week,* 7 August 1996; American Federal of Teachers, *Making Standards Matter,* 1996.
8. David C. Berliner and Bruce J. Biddle *The Manufactured Crises: Myths, Fraud, and the Attack on America's Schools* (1995).
9. The National Education Goals Report, *Building A Nation of Learners 1995;* U.S. Department of Education, Office of educational Research and Improvement, *The Condition of Education, 1995.*
10. E. D. Hirsch, Jr. *The Schools We Need and Why We Don't Have Them* (1996).
11. E.D. Hirsch, Jr. "The Core Knowledge Curriculum—What's Behind Its Success" (Core Curriculum Foundation, May 1993), quoted extensively here.
12. E.D. Hirsch, Jr. *The Schools We Need and Why We Don't Have Them* (1996).
13. W. C. Bagley, *Education and Emergent Man: A Theory of Education with Particular Application to Public Education in the United States* (1934); also see General Accounting Office, *Elementary School Children: Many Change School Frequently, Harming Their Education* (1994).
14. Gail Owen Schubnell, "Hawthorne Elementary School: The Evaluator's Perspective," *Journal of Education for Students Placed At Risk,* vol. 1, no. 1, 1996.
15. H. Stevenson and J. Stigler, *The Learning Gap* (1992).

Chapter 6

1. Personal interview with John Anderson, 6 June 1996.
2. New American School Development Corporation, *Bringing Success To Scale: Sharing the Vision of New American Schools* (September, 1995); and see *Annual Report 1994-95: A Thousand Actions—And A Single Purpose.*
3. Lynn Olson, "Designs for Learning," *Education Week,* 12 February 1997.
4. Susan Bodilly, *Lessons From New American Schools Development Corporation's Demonstration Phase* (RAND Institute on Education and Training, 1996); see also Susan Bodilly, et al., *Designing New American Schools: Baseline Observations on Nine Design Teams* (RAND, 1995).

Chapter 7

1. The National Education Goals Panel, *Building A Nation Of Learners,* (1995); most information taken from the Goals Report, but additional data taken from reports cited below.

2. Substance Abuse and Mental Health Services Administration Office of Applied Studies, U.S. Department of Health and Human Services, *Preliminary Estimates from the 1995 National Household Survey on Drug Abuse* (August 1996); and the U.S. Department of Education, *A Parent's Guide to Prevention: Growing Up Drug Free* (no date).

3. Much of the information for this Myth has been taken from Kent Lloyd, Diane Ramsey and Sven Groennings, *KNOWLEDGE REVOLUTION For All Americans: Winning the War Against Ignorance—Empowering the Public Schools* (1992).

4. Associated Press poll, cited by Pierce O'Donnell, "Killing the Golden Goose: Hollywood's Death Wish," *Beverly Hills Bar Journal*, Summer 1992.

5. "TV Violence: More Objectionable in Entertainment Than in Newscasts," *Times Mirror Media Monitor*, 24 March 1993.

6. A.C. Hustorn, E. Donnerstein, H. Fairchild, et al., Eds., *Big World, Small Screen: The Role of Television in American Society* (U. of Nebraska, 1992); E. Donnerstein, R. Slaby, L. Eron, *Violence and Youth: The Mass Media and Youth Aggression* (American Psychological Association: in press, 1996).

7. Joel Federman, *Media Ratings: Design, Use and Consequences* (Mediascope, Inc., 1996).

8. James B. Twitchell, *Carnival Culture: The Trashing of Taste in America* (1992); Deborah Baldwin, "The Hard Sell," *The Utne Reader*, January/February 1992.

9. Mediascope, Inc. *National Television Violence Study: Executive Summary, 1994-95.*

10. Brendon S. Centerwell, "Television and Violence," *Journal of American Medical Association*, vol. 267, no.2, 1992.

11. George R. Kaplan, *Images of Education: The Mass Media's Version of America's Schools* (1992).

12. U.S. Department of Education, "Crime and Violence in Our Schools: an Overview of Statistics," (1996).

13. *U.S. News and World Report*, 8 November 1993.

14. Children's Defense Fund, *The State of America's Children* (1996); also see Norman Randolph *Gangs, My Town and the Nation* (1996), for a discussion of gang formation and activities in Pittsburgh.

15. Mary Jordan, "Japan Clamors for Stricter Gun Laws Though Shooting Deaths Still Rare by U.S. Standards, Citizens Concerned," *The Washington Post*, 16 March 1997.

16. Metropolitan Life, "*Violence in America's Public Schools*, The Metropolitan Life Survey of The American Teacher 1994," 1995.

17. National School Boards Association (NSBA), "Violence in the Schools" (1993).

18. Stanley M. Elam, et al., "The 28th Annual Phil Delta Kappa/Gallup Poll Of the Public's Attitudes Toward the Public Schools."

19. Josephson Institute of Ethics, *The Ethics of American Youth: A Warning and a Call to Action* (Marina Del Rey, California:1990) and *Ethics, Values, Attitudes and Behavior in American Schools* (1992).

20. Josephson Institute of Ethics, *1996 Report Card on American Integrity* (1996).

21. Rene Sanchez, "Blacks, Whites Finish High School at Same Pace,' *The Washington Post*, 6 September 1996.

22. Educational Testing Service, *Dreams Deferred: High School Dropouts in the United States* (1995).

23. The Conference Board, *Corporate Support of Dropout Prevention and Work Readiness* (1963).

24. Centers for Disease Control and Prevention, "Sexual Behavior Among High School Students,"*Morbidity and Mortality Weekly Report,* vol. 40, 1992; see also Thomas Lickona, "Where Sex Education Went Wrong," *Educational Leadership,* November 1993.

25. Barbara Dafoe Whitehead, "The Failure of Sex Education," *Atlantic Monthly,* October, 1994 (Data is from The 1988 National Survey of Family Growth and 1988 National Survey of Young Men).

26. Thomas Lickona, "Where Sex Education Went Wrong," *Educational Leadership,* November 1993.

27. Barbara Dafoe Whitehead, "The Failure of Sex Education."

28. National Center for Health Statistics, "Birth Rate for Unmarried Teens:1965-1994"; see also Suzanne Chazin, "Teen Pregancy: Let's Get Real," *Reader's Digest,* September 1996; William Raspberry, "Strip the Myths From Teen Pregnancy, " *The Washington Post,* 6 September 1996.

29. Barbara Dafoe Whitehead, "The Failure of Sex Education."

30. Charles Murray, "Bad News About Illegitimacy," *The Weekly Standard,* 5 August 1996.

31. Ibid.; William Raspberry, "Strip the Myths From Teen Pregnancy."

32. Family Impact Seminar, *Disconnected Dads: Strategies for Promoting Responsible Fatherhood* (1995).

33. Louis Harris, "American Teens Speak: Sex, Myth, TV, and Birth Control," (Planned Parenthood Federation of America: 1986).

34. Peggy Brick and Deborah M. Roffman, "'Abstinence, No Buts' Is Simplistic," *Educational Leadership,* November 1993.

35. Jon Jeter, "For $20 Million, the Birth of a Notion," *The Washington Post,* 7 September 1996.

36. "Who's Who Among American High School Students, *Eleventh National Opinion Survey: Attitudes and Opinions from the Nation's High Achieving Teens* (Educational Communications, Inc., Northbrook, IL: 1980).

37. Dr. Christensen drew upon two models of discipline, in addition to *Three Strikes Discipline. See* Cristine Hopkins, *Three Strikes Discipline: A Model Prevention/ Intervention Program for Violent, Disruptive and Non-Compliant Students.* (1996). For further information about the *Three Strikes Discipline Training Manual* (1997) with record forms, contact Hopkins at (801) 484-5251; see also Ginger Rhode, Ph.D., William R. Jenson, Ph.D., and H. Kenton Reavis, Ed.D., *The Tough Kid Book* (1992).

38. Don Oldenburg, "A Real Doll, but Not So Cuddly or Cute: A Baby Simulator Deglamorizes Teen Pregnancy," *The Washington Post,* 13 September 1996. The infant simulator sells for $250. Between 16,000 and 20,000 have been sold to high schools and social service organizations. Fewer than 50 of them have been used in the Washington, D.C. area where they are most needed.

39. Marc Mauer, *Americans Behind Bars: A Comparison of International Rates of Incarceration* (The Sentencing Project, January 1991).

40. Steven Donziger, "The Prison-Industrial Complex," *The Washington Post,* 17 March 1996.

41. National Center for Education Statistics, U.S. Department of Education *Literacy, Behind Prison Walls: Profiles of the Prison Population from the National Adult Literacy Survey* (1994).
42. *The Washington Post*, 30 July 1996.

Chapter 8

1. Stanley M. Elam, Lowell C. Rose, and Alec M. Gallup, "The 28th Annual Phi Delta Kappa/Gallup Poll of the Public's Attitudes Toward the Public Schools," *Phi Delta Kappan*, September 1996.
2. "How to Raise a Moral Child," *U.S. News & World Report*, 3 June 1996.
3. Public Agenda, *Given the Circumstances: Teachers Talk About Public Education Today* (1996).
4. Thomas Lickona, "Combating Violence with Values: The Character Education Solution," *Law Studies*, Fall 1994.
5. National Research Council (1992).
6. Thomas Lickona, "The Return of Character Education," *Educational Leadership*, November 1993; and Personal Interview on 9 June 1996.
7. Josephson Institute of Ethics, *Making Ethical Decisions: Using the Six Pillars of Character* ; and their *Ethics, Values, Attitudes, and Behavior in American Schools*.
8. Thomas Lickona, Eric Schaps and Catherine Lewis, "Eleven Principles of Effective Character Education," (The Character education Partnership, no date).
9. Jack Frymier, Luvern Cunningham, Willard Duckett, Bruce Gansneder, Frances Link, June Rimmer, and James Scholz, *Values On Which We Agree* (1995).
10. William Kilpatrick, *Why Can't Johnny Tell Right From Wrong: Moral Illiteracy and the Case for Character education* (1991).
11. For documentation of these youth trends, see T. Lickona, *Educating for Character: How Our Schools Can Teach Respect and Responsibility* (1991).
12. Henry A. Huffman, *Developing A CharacterEducation Program: One School District's Experience* (1994).
13. The Center for the 4th and 5th Rs teaches summer institutes for teachers at the New York State University at Cortland, New York.
14. Thomas Lickona, "A Comprehensive Approach to Character Education," in Don E. Eberly, ed., *America's Character : Recovering Civic Virtue* (1995).
15. B. David Brooks and Frank G. Goble, *The Case for Character Education* (1983, revised 1996); also Personal Interview, 8 January 1996.
16. Mark W. Cannon, "Crime and the Decline of Values," *Phi Alpha Delta Law Fraternity*, An Address to the Southwestern Judicial Conference, Santa Fe, New Mexico, 4 June 1981.
17. Michael Josephson, *Making Ethical Decisions: Using the Six Pillars of Character* (Marina Del Ray, California, 1992).
18. B. David Brooks, "Strengthening Character Through Community-Based Organizations," Don E. Eberly, Ed., *The Content of America's Character* (1995).
19. B. David Brooks and Mark E. Kann, "What Makes Character Education Programs Work?" *Educational Leadership*, November 1993.

20. Richard D. Satnick, California Survey Research, *The Thomas Jefferson Center Values Education Project: A Survey of Administrators in The Los Angeles Unified School District* (1991).

21. Ibid.

22. Ibid.; and *Safe Schools: A Planning Tool Kit for School-Community Teams* (1995).

23. California Department of Education's Office of School Safety and Violence Prevention and the Office of the California Attorney General's Crime and Violence Prevention Center, *Safe Schools: A Planning Guide for Action* (1995).

24. Developmental Studies Center, Brochure (1993); see also DSC, "The Child Development Project: Summary of Findings in Two Initial Districts and the First Phase of An Expansion to Six Additional Districts Nationally (August 1994).

25. Personal Interview, 9 May 1996.

26. Developmental Studies Center, *Homeside Activities: Conversations and Activities That Bring Parents Into Children's Schoolside Learning.* (1995).

27. Marilyn Watson, Daniel Solomon, Victor Battistich, Eric Schaps and Judith Solomon, "The Child Development Project: Combining Traditional and Developmental Approaches to Values Education," in Larry P. Nucci, Ed., *Moral; Development and Character Education: A Dialogue* (1989); and Daniel Solomon, *et al.,* "Creating a Caring Community: Educational Practices That Promote Children's Prosocial Development," in Fritz K. Oser, *et al., Effective and Responsible Teaching: The New Synthesis* (1992).

28. Developmental Studies Center, "The Child Development Project: Summary of Findings in Two Initial Districts and the First Phase of an Expansion to Six Additional Districts Nationally"(August 1994); Victor Battistich. Daniel Solomon, Don-il Kim, Marilyn Watson, and Eric Schaps, "Effects of an Elementary School Program to Enhance Prosocial Behavior on Children's Cognitive Social Problem-Solving Skills and Strategies,"*Journal of Applied Developmental Psychology, vol. 10,* 1989; Daniel Solomon, Marilyn S. Watson, Kevin L. Delucchi, Eric Schaps and Victor Battistich, "Enhancing Children's Prosocial Behavior in the Classroom," *American Educational Research Journal,* Winter 1988.

29. Debra Viadero, "Learning to Care," *Education Week,* 26 October 1994.

30. Victor Battistich, *et al.,* "Schools as Communities, Poverty Levels of Student Populations, and Students' Attitudes, Motives, and Performance: A Multilevel Analysis," *American Educational Research Journal,* Fall 1995.

31. Catherine C. Lewis, Eric Schaps, and Marilyn Watson, "Beyond the Pendulum: Creating Challenging and Caring Schools,' *Phi Delta Kappan,* March 1995.

32. James S. Leming, "In Search of Effective Character Education," and Alan L. Lockwood, " A Letter to Character Educators," *Educational Leadership,* November 1993; Alfie Kohn, "What's Wrong With Character Education," *Association for Supervision and Curriculum Development Newsletter,* May 1996; and Alfie Kohn "How Not to Teach Character Education: A Critical Look at Character Education," in *Phi Delta Kappan,* February 1997.

33. H.M. Hartshorne and J.B. Maller, *Studies in Service and Self-Control* (1929).

34. Lawrence Kohlberg, "Stage and Sequence: The Cognitive-Developmental Approach to Socialization," in D.A. Goslin, ed., *Handbook of Socialization Theory and Research* (1969).

Chapter 9

1. Critics of *The Bell Curve* have been taken from Steven Fraser, Ed., *The Bell Curve Wars: Race, Intelligence, and the Future of America* (1995); see also R. Jacoby and N. Glauberman, *The Bell Curve Debate: History, Documents, Opinions* (1995); and Joe L. Kincheloe, Shirley R. Steinberg and Aaron D. Gresson III, *Measured Lies: The Bell Curve Examined* (1996).
2. Howard Gardner, "Cracking Open the IQ Box," in Fraser, Ed. *The Bell Curve Wars; Multiple Intelligences: The Theory in Practice, A Reader* (1993).
3. Gardner, "Cracking Open the IQ Box."
4. Mickey Kaus, "The 'It Matter-Little' Gambit," in Fraser, Ed., *The Bell Curve Wars.*
5. Gerald David Jaynes and Robin M. Williams, Jr.,. Eds., *A Common Destiny: Blacks and American Society* (1989).
6. Stephen Jay Gould, "*Curveball,,*" in Fraser, Ed., *The Bell Curve Wars.*
7. Thomas Sowell, "Ethnicity and IQ," in Fraser, Ed., *The Bell Curve Wars.*
8. Jeffery Rosen and Charles Lane, "The Sources of The Bell Curve," in Fraser, Ed., *The Bell Curve Wars*; see Dante Ramos, "Paradise Miscalculated" in Fraser, Ed., *The Bell Curve Wars,* where he claims there is 'too much counter-evidence relegated to endnotes, too much tendentious data interpretation, and too many not-quite-credible studies.
9. Alan Wolfe, "Has There Been A Cognitive Revolution in America? The Flawed Sociology of *The Bell Curve,*" in Fraser, Ed., *The Bell Curve Wars.*
10. Nathan Glazer, "Scientific Truth and the American Dilemma," in Fraser, Ed., *The Bell Curve Wars.*
11. Richard Nisbett, "Race, IQ, and Scientism," in Fraser, Ed., *The Bell Curve Wars.*
12. Andrew Hecker, "Caste, Crime, and Precocity," in Fraser, Ed., *The Bell Curve Wars.*
13. Stephen Jay Gould, "Curveball" in Fraser, Ed., *The Bell Curve Wars; see also* Wolfe, "Has There Been A Cognitive Revolution in America?."
14. Orlando Patterson, "For Whom the Bell Curves," in Fraser, Ed., *The Bell Curve Wars.*
15. Harold Stevenson and James Stigler, *The Learning Gap: Why Our Schools Are Failing and What We Can Learn from Japanese and Chinese Education* (1992).
16. Gould, "Curveball."
17. Personal Interview with Henry Levin, 4 August 1996.
18. Aaron Pallas, Gary Natriello, and Edward L. McDill, "The Changing Nature of the Disadvantaged Population: Current Dimensions and Future Trends," *Educational Researcher, vol ?.,*1989.
19. U.S. Department of Education, *Reinventing Chapter I: The Current Chapter 1 Program and New Directions. Final Report of the National Assessment of the Chapter 1 Program,* 1993.
20. Henry M. Levin, *The Costs to the Nation of Inadequate Education,* Report prepared for the Select Senate Committee on Equal Educational Opportunity, 92nd

Congress (1972); David Ramirez and Maria del Refugio Robledo, *Texas School Dropout Survey Project: A Summary of Findings* (San Antonio: Intercultural Development Research Association (1986); see Lawrence J. Schweinhart and David P. Weikart, Ed., *Significant Benefits: the High/Scope Perry Preschool Study Through Age 27* (High/Scope Press, 1994) that shows pre-school investments and returns on the Perry Preschool Project continue to demonstrate a 7:1 return for investment.

21. Henry M. Levin, *Economics of School Reform for At-Risk Students* (Unpublished paper, 1994).

22. Henry M. Levin, "Accelerated Schools: The Background," in Christine Finnan, Jane McCarthy, Ed St. John, and Simeon Slovack, Eds., *Accelerated School in Action: Lessons from the Field* (1995).

23. Wendy S. Hopfenberg, Henry M. Levin, and Associates, *The Accelerated Schools Guide* (1993).

24. Henry M. Levin, "Assessing Accelerated Schools," *Accelerated Schools* (Winter 1995-96); and Christine Finnan, et al., *Accelerated Schools in Action: Lessons from the Field.*

25. Henry M. Levin, "Learning from Accelerated Schools;" James H. Block, Susan Toft Everson and Thomas R. Guskey, *School Improvement Programs: A Handbook for Educational Leaders* (Scholastic, Inc.,1995).

26. Henry M. Levin, "Accelerated Schools After Eight Years," in L. Schauble and R. Glaser, eds., *Innovations in Learning: New Environments for Education* (1995).

27. Personal interview with James Comer, 9 August 1996.

28. James P. Comer, *Maggie's American Dream* (1989).

29. James P. Comer, *James P. Comer, M.D., on the School Development Program: Making a Difference for Children* (1993).

30. James P. Comer, *School Power* (1980); and J.P. Comer, N.M. Haynes, and M. Hamilton-Lee, "School Power: A Model for Improving Black Student Achievement," in W.D. Smith and W.E. Chun, Eds., *Black Education: A Quest for Equity and Excellence* (1989).

31. Comer follows Abraham Maslow's hierarchy of needs by insisting on focusing on safety, belongingness, love and self-esteem, see R.F. Biehler and J. Snowman, *Psychology Applied to Teaching* (1993).

32. James P. Comer, "Educating Poor Minority Children," *Scientific American*, November 1988; Christina Ramirez-Smith, "Stopping the Cycle of Failure: The Comer Model," *Educational Leadership*, February 1995.

33. For a discussion of differences in children's intellectual development, see Paul Chance, "Speaking of Differences," *Phi Delta Kappan*, March 1997.

34. James P. Comer and Norris M Haynes, "Summary of School Development Program (SDP) Effects," (No date).

35. The Yale Child Study Center has a website—http://info.med.yale.educ/comer.

Chapter 10

1. Robert E. Slavin, "Sand, Bricks, and Seeds: School Change Strategies and Readiness for Reform," a Policy Paper for the Center for Research on the Education of Students Placed At Risk (April 1995).

2. Personal interview with Robert Slavin, 26 April 1996.
3. Richard F. Elmore, "Getting to Scale With Good Educational Practice," *Harvard Educational Review*, Spring 1996. Elmore recommends four proposals for core changes in education necessary for upscaling: (1) Develop strong external normative structures for practice to build incentives beyond individual motivations of teachers and school leaders; (2) Develop organizational structures that intensify and focus, rather than dissipate and scatter, intrinsic motivation to engage in challenging practice; (3) Create intentional processes for reproduction of successes; and (4) Create structures that promote learning of new practices and incentive systems that support them.
4. Robert E. Slavin, Nancy A Madden, Lawrence J. Dolan, Barbara A. Wasik, Steven M. Ross, and Lana J. Smith, "Whenever and Wherever We Choose: The Replication of Success for All," *Phi Delta Kappan*, April 1994.
5. Barbara Haxby, Maggie Lasaga-Flister, Nancy Madden, Robert Slavin, Laurence Dolan, *Success for All Family Support Manual* (Johns Hopkins University, 1995).
6. Robert Slavin, Nancy A. Madden, Lawrence J. Dolan, and Barbara A. Wasik, Steven Ross, Lana Smith, and Marcella Dianda, "Success for All: A Summary of Research," *Journal of Education for Students Placed At Risk*, vol. 1, no. 1, 1996; Steven M. Ross, Lana J. Smith, Jason Casey, and Robert E. Slavin, "Increasing the Academic Success of Disadvantaged Children: An Examination of Alternative Early Intervention Programs," *American Educational Research Journal*, Winter 1995; Robert J. Stevens and Robert E. Slavin, "Effects of a Cooperative Learning Approach in Reading and Writing on Academically Handicapped and Non-Handicapped Students," *The Elementary School Journal*, vol. 95, no. 3, 1995; Robert E. Slavin, "A Model of Effective Instruction," *The Educational Forum*, Winter 1995.
7. Lynn Olson, "Roots & Wings: Designing a Break the Mold School," *Education Week*, 15 December 1993.
8. Robert E. Slavin, Nancy A. Madden, Lawrence J. Dolan, and Barbara A. Wasik, "Roots and Wings: Inspiring Academic Excellence," *Educational Leadership*, November 1994; and Robert E. Slavin, "Cooperative Learning: Applying Contact Theory in Desegregated Schools," *Journal of Social Issues*, vol. 41, no. 3, 1985.
9. Personal interview with Linda Darling-Hammond, 20 May 1996.
10. See "Authentic Assessment in Context: The Motivation for Change," in Linda Darling-Hammond, Jacqueline Ancess and Beverly Falk, Eds., *Authentic Assessment in Action: Studies of Schools and Students at Work* (1995).
11. "The Primary Language Record At P.S. 261," in Darling-Hammond, et al., Ibid..
12. "The Bronx New School: Weaving Assessment into the Fabric of Teaching and Learning," in Darling-Hammond, et al., Ibid.

Chapter 11

1. Carol A. Langdon, "The Third Phi Delta Kappa Poll of Teachers' Attitudes Toward the Public Schools," *Phi Delta Kappan*, November 1996.
2. John I. Goodlad, *A Place Called School* (1984).
3. Personal Interview, 7 May 1996.

4. Mark F. Goldberg, "A Portrait of John Goodlad," *Educational Leadership,* March 1995.

5. See, for example, Carnegie Forum on Education and the Economy, *A Nation Prepared: Teachers for the 21st Century* (1986); and Holmes Group, *Tomorrow's Teachers: A Report of the Holmes Group* (1986).

6. John I. Goodlad, "Democracy, Education, and Community," in Roger Soder, ed., *Democracy, Education and The Schools* (1996); and see Robert B. Westbrook, *John Dewey and American Democracy* (1991).

7. John I. Goodlad, Roger Soder, and Kenneth A. Sirotnik, Eds., *The Moral Dimensions of Teaching* (1990); Goodlad, et al., *Places Where Teachers Are Taught* (1990); Goodlad, et al., *Teachers for Our Nation's Schools* (1990).

8. Ron Brandt, "On Teacher Education," *Educational Leadership,* November 1991.

9. John I.Goodlad, "Why We Need a Complete Redesign of Teacher Education," *Educational Leadership,* November 1991.

10. John I. Goodlad, *Educational Renewal: Better Teachers, Better Schools* (1994).

11. James A. Kelly, "National Certification in the New Context of Educational Policy," an address to the Peabody College of Education, Vanderbilt University, 16 March 1995.

12. National Board For Professional Teaching Standards, "What Teachers Should Know And Be Able To Do," (1994); for case studies of teachers going through the board certification process, see Ann Bradley, "Pioneers in Professionalism," *Education Week,* 20 April 1994.

13. National Board For Professional Teaching Standards, "What Teachers Should Know and Be Able To Do," (1994); for case studies of teachers going through the board certification process, see Ann Bradley, "Pioneers in Professionalism," *Education Week,* 20 April 1994.

14. James A. Kelly, "National Board Certification in the Arts," an address at the Getty Center for Education in the Arts, Fifth National Conference, 12 January 1995.

15. National Board for Professional Teaching Standards, "State and Local Action Supporting National Board Certification," April 1996 Report.

16. Teachers' statements taken from The National Commission on Teaching & America's Future, *What Matters Most: Teaching for America's Future* (1996).

17. Testimony taken from The National Commission on Teaching & America's Future, *What Matters Most*; Personal Interview, 20 May 1996, and Background Paper prepared for the National Commission on Teaching and America's Future, "The Current Status of Teaching and Teacher Development in the United States," (November 1994).

18. Jean Johnson and John Immerwahr, *First Things First: What Americans Expect from the Public Schools* (Public Agenda: 1994).

19. National Commission on Teaching & America's Future, *What Matters Most*.

20. Ibid.; John Holyoake, "Initial Teacher Training: The French View," *Journal of Education for Teaching,* vol. 19, 1993; Nancy Sato and Milbrey W. McLaughlin, "Context Matters: Teaching in Japan and in the United States," *Phi Delta Kappan,* vol. 66, 1992; Nobuo K. Shimahara and Akira Sakai, *Learning to Teach in Two Cultures: Japan and the United States* (Garland Publishing: 1995); and T. Waldrop,

"Before You Lead a German Class, You Really Must Know Your Stuff," *Newsweek*, December 1991.

21. Linda Darling-Hammond, "Restructuring Schools for High Performance," in Susan H. Fuhrman and Jennifer A. O'Day, eds., *Rewards and Reform: Creating Educational Incentives That Work* (1996).

22. Linda Darling-Hammond, *Professional Development Schools: Schools for Developing a Profession* (In Press); Linda Darling-Hammond and Milbrey W. McLaughlin, "Policies that Support Professional Development in an Era of Reform," in Milbrey W. McLaughlin and Ida Oberman, Eds., *Teacher Learnings: New Policies, New Practices* (1996); and Linda Darling-Hammond, "The Quiet Revolution: Rethinking Teacher Development," *Educational Leadership*, March 1996; and Linda Darling-Hammond and Milbrey W. McLaughlin, "Policies That Support Professional Development in an Era of Reform," *Phi Delta Kappan*, April 1995.

23. National Commission on Teaching & America's Future, *What Matters Most*.

Chapter 12

1. National Commission on Teaching & America's Future, *What Matters Most*.

2. Stephanie Coontz, "The American Family and the Nostalgia Trap," *Kappan Special Report*, March 1995; see also National Commission on Children, "Speaking of Kids: A National Survey of Children and Parents" (1991); "Parents As Partners: Special Report," *Education Week*, 4 April, 9 May, 1 August, 21 November 1990.

3. The Commonwealth Fund 1995 Annual Report: U.S. House of Representatives (Committee on Ways and Means, 1994 Green Book).

4. Children's Defense Fund, *The State of America's Children* (1996); see also "Kids Count Data Book," The Annie E. Casey Foundation, 1995; Children's Defense Fund, "Child Poverty in America," 1991; Children's Defense Fund, *Report on the Costs of Child Poverty* (1994).

5. Kent Lloyd, Diane Ramsey and Sven Groennings, *KNOWLEDGE REVOLUTION FOR ALL AMERICANS — Winning The War Against Ignorance: Empowering Public Schools* (Knowledge Network, 1992).

6. Children's Defense Fund, *The State of America's Children* (1996).

7. Ibid.

8. Lloyd, *et al.*, *KNOWLEDGE REVOLUTION FOR ALL AMERICANS*.

9. Angelique Chengelis, "Medical Authorities Measure Toll of Firearm Violence," *Gannett News Service*, 31 March 1994.

10. Ibid.

11. Children's Defense Fund, *The State of America's Children* (1996).

12. Clearinghouse for Alcohol and Drug Information, Summary of Findings through 1995)

13. Children's Defense Fund, *The State of America's Children* (1996).

14. Trends in Substance Use, 1979-1994.

15. Congressional Office of Technology Assessment (1986).

16. Juliet B. Schor, *The Overworked American: The Unexpected Decline of Leisure* (1991).

17. Arlie R. Hochschild, *The Time Bind* (1997)

18. Lloyd, et al, *KNOWLEDGE REVOLUTION FOR ALL AMERICANS*.

19. Department of Justice, Press Release, 31 May 1995.
20. A.E. Washington, P.S. Arno and M.A. Brooks, "The Economic Cost of Pelvic Inflammatory Disease," *JAMA*, 4 April 1986.
21. F.J. Hellinger, "Forecasts of the Costs of Medical Care for Persons with HIV: 1992-1995," *Inquiry*, vol. 29, 1992.
22. Children's Defense Fund, *The State of America's Children*.
23. See Sharon Begley, *Newsweek*, 19 February 1996; for simple activities designed to enhance cognitive, language, social and motor development; see also Joseph Sparling and Isabelle Lewis, *Learningames* (1996).
24. B.L. White, "Education Begins at Birth," *Principal*, vol. 66, no. 5, 1987.
25. Lloyd, et al., *KNOWLEDGE REVOLUTION FOR ALL AMERICANS*.
26. Educational Testing Service, *America's Smallest School: The Family* (1992).
27. Ibid.
28. An Initiative of the Family Involvement Partnership for Learning, *America Goes Back to School: A Place for Families and the Community* (1995).
29. Ibid.
30. Lloyd, et al., *KNOWLEDGE REVOLUTION FOR ALL AMERICANS*.
31. Educational Testing Service, *America's Smallest School: The Family*.
32. Keep the Promise: Educational Excellence Partnership, "Moving America to the Head of the Class—50 Simple Things You Can Do. (no date); Center for the Revitalization of Urban Education, "Parent /School/Community Partnerships," (National Education Association, 1996).
33. American Association of School Administrators, "101 Ways Parents Can Help Students Achieve," 1992.
34. Lloyd, et al., *KNOWLEDGE REVOLUTION FOR ALL AMERICANS*.
35. Anne T. Henderson and Nancy Berla, *A New Generation of Evidence: The Family is Critical to Student Achievement* (Center for Law and Education, 1995).
36. Lawrence E. Harrison, *Who Prospers? How Cultural Values Shape Economic and Political Success* (1992).
37. Alexis de Tocqueville, *Democracy in America* (London: David Campbell Publishers, 1994).
38. See Coleman, *Parental Involvement in Education.*, for definition of 'cultural capital.'
39. Jerome Bruner, *The Culture of Education* (1996), In this collection Bruner explores nine "tenets" that mark the intersection of mind, culture, and education. "Culture...provides the tools for organizing and understanding and understanding our worlds in communicable ways," culture both "forms and makes possible the workings of a distincly human mind." Culture, Bruner asserts, is always implicated in teaching and learning.
40. Harrison, *Who Prospers? How Cultural Values Shape Economic and Political Success;* see also Edgar H. Schein, *Organizational Culture and Leadership* (1985); Warren Bennis, *On Becoming a Leader,* (1989); Steven Covey, *The Seven Habits for Effective People: Powerful Lessons in Personal Change* (1990).
41. Lawrence E. Harrison, *Pan American Dream: Do Latin America's Cultural Values Discourage True Partnership With The United States and Canada?* (1997).
42. David McClelland, *The Achieving Society* (1961).
43. Robert Putnam, *Making Democracy Work—Civic Traditions in Modern Italy* (1993).

44. Diane Ramsey, *The Social World of Remarriage Families* (University of California, San Diego: Unpublished Doctoral Dissertation, 1990).

45. Anne T. Henderson and Nancy Berla, Eds., *The Family Is Critical To Student Achievement: A New Generation of Evidence* (Center for Law and Education, 1995); Sau-Fong Siu and Jay Feldman, "How Chinese-American Parents Support Their Children's Success in School," *Research and Development REPORT*, Center on Families, Communities, Schools & Children's Learning, no. 6, September 1995.

46. Edgar H. Schein, "On Dialogue, Culture, and Organizational Learning, *Organizational Dynamics*, Autumn 1993.

47. For three types of parental leadership—*authoritative or* shared responsibilities; *authoritarian or* strict discipline parental authority; *laissez faire or* permissive— see Sanford Dornbush, Phillip Ritter, P. Herbert Leiderman, Donald F. Roberts, and Michael Fraleigh, "The Relation of Parenting Styles to Adolescent School Performance," *Child Development*, vol. 58, no. 5, October 1987.

48. Talcott Parsons, *Toward a General Theory of Action* (1957), p. 15; also see Max Weber's differentiation of cultures according to religious teaching in which he links the ration/ascetic/ethical features of Calvinist Protestantism to capitalism and economic prosperity. Max Weber, *The Protestant Ethic and the Spirit of Capitalism* (Scribner,1950).

49. Harrison, *Pan American Dream.* "The vast majority of Mexican immigrants, particularly those who enter illegally, come from the lower strata of Mexican society, which suggests that for many, *the average number of years of education may be four or less.* A RAND study of Mexican immigrants in California show that 70% had not completed high school and that the third generation were slightly less likely to finish than the second generation. In terms of income, Japanese, Koreans, and Chinese upon immigrating to the U.S. were making 76% of the wages of native earnings and 103% ten years later. Mexicans start at 52% of native earnings and have *declined* to 47% ten years later (see Robert F. Schoeni, Kevin F. McCarthy, and Georges Vernez, *Pursuing the American Dream: The Progress of Immigrant Men in California and the United States* (June 1996). Harrison cites additional studies that show East Asian immigrants have lower welfare payments and frequency, lower crime rates and higher voting participation rates than immigrants from Mexico, Central and South America. These findings support Harrison's thesis that cultural roots play a great role in influencing individual behavior. He also shows in the example of post-Franco Spain that cultural values can be altered over time to promote progress prone values that result in improved political and economic consequences.

50. Nathan Caplan, Marcella H. Choy, and John K. Whitmore, "Indochinese Refugee Families and Academic Achievement," *Scientific American*, February 1992.

51. Amitai Etzioni, *The Spirit of Community: Rights, Responsibilities, and the Communitarian Agenda* (1993); see also Diane Berreth and Marge Scherer, "On Transmitting Values: A Conversation With Amitai Etzioni," *Educational Leadership*, November 1993.

52. Gerald David Jaynes and Robin M. Williams, Jr., eds., *A Common Destiny: Blacks and American Society* (National Research Council, 1989).

53. William R. Mattox, Jr., "The Parent Trap," *Policy Review*, Winter 1991.

54. Center for Nutrition Policy and Promotion's Annual Report, "Expenditures on Children by Families," (U.S. Department of Agriculture, 1994.

55. Ibid.

56. *Washington Post,* 12 October 1996.

57. See Appendix for sample "Responsible Family Learning Culture Diagnostic Questionnaire."

58. Terrel H. Bell and Donna L. Elmquist, *How To Shape Up Our Nation's Schools: Three Crucial Steps for Renewing American Education* (1991).

59. See Joyce Epstein's Type 2 Communications activities. A compact or pledge is not a whole partnership.

60. Personal interview with Dorothy Rich, 3 June 1996; see also *Phi Delta Kappan,* "Schools of Thought" Interview, 30 December 1992.

61. Dorothy Rich, *MegaSkills: In School and in Life—The Best Gift You Can Give Your Child* (1992).

62. See Ann Bradley, "The Recipes of Dorothy Rich," *Education Week,* 5 March 1997.

63. Denzil Edge, "Executive Summary—Final Evaluation of MegaSkill Program adopted by Maupin Elementary School-1994-95," (University of Louisville, Spring 1996).

64. MegaSkills Education Center publications (1996).

65. Dorothy Rich and Harriett Stonehill, *The MegaSkills Parent Handbook* (1992).

66. Dorothy Rich, "People Are Education's Biggest Bargain," *Education Week,* 9 September 1992.

Chapter 13

1. Joyce L. Epstein, Lucretia Coates, Karen Clark Salinas, Mavis G. Sanders, and Beth S. Simon, *School, Family, and Community Partnerships: Your Handbook for Action* (Thousand Oaks, California: Corwin Press, 1997).

2. Personal Interview with Joyce Epstein, 26 April 1996.

3. Joyce Epstein, "Perspectives and Previews on Research and Policy for School, Family, and Community Partnerships," *Family-School Links: How Do They Affect Educational Outcomes?* 1995.

4. Joyce Epstein, "Advances in Family, Community, and School Partnerships," *New Schools, New Communities,* Spring 1996.

5. Joyce L. Epstein, "New Connections For Sociology and Education: Contributing to School Reform,' *Sociology of Education,* vol. 69, 1996. See discussion on multilingualism and the differing cultures of researchers, policymakers and practiners.

6. Joyce L. Epstein, "Single Parents and the Schools: Effects of Marital Status of Parent and Teacher Interactions," in Maureen T. Hallinan, David M. Klein and Jennifer Glass, Eds., *Change in Societal Institutions* (1990).

7. Joyce L. Epstein, "School/Family/Community Partnerships: Caring for the Children We Share," *Phi Delta Kappan,* May 1995; see also Joyce L. Epstein, guest Ed., "Special Section on Parent Involvement," *Phi Delta Kappan,* January 1991.

8. Ibid., May 1995.

9. Epstein, et al., *School, Family, Community Partnerships*; see also Joyce L. Epstein, "Network Goals and Activities for 1996-97," *Type 2: National Network of Partnership-2000 Schools*, no. 1, Fall 1996..

10. U.S. Department of Education, *Strong Families, Strong Schools: Building Community Partnerships for Learning* (1994) and *An Invitation To Your Community: Building Community Partnerships for Learning* (1995).

11. Joyce L. Epstein, "Goals 2000, Title I, and School-to-Work Legislation: Implications for School, Family, and Community Connections," June 1995.

12. Goals 2000:Educate America Act, "Parent Information And Resource Centers," Grant Abstracts FY 1995.

13. Personal interview with Joan Dykstra, 18 December 1996.

14. National PTA *National Standards for Parent Involvement Programs* (1997).

15. Personal interview with Marilyn Acklin, 9 December 1996.

16. Anne T. Henderson, Carl L. Marburger and Theodora Ooms, *Beyond The Bake Sale: An Educator's Guide To Working With Parents* (1986; 1995).

17. Meg Sommerfeld, "Ordinary People," *Education Week*, 25 January 1995.

18. Personal interview with Ernesto Cortes, Jr., 24 June 1996.

19. Ernesto Cortes, Jr., "The IAF and Education Reform: Organizing Citizens for Change," in Sharon Lynn Kagan, Ed., *American Early Care and Education: Responding to the Crisis of Quality*, 1996.

20. Ernesto Cortes, Jr. "Reweaving the Fabric: The Iron Rule and the IAF Strategy for Power and Politics," in Henry Cisneros, Ed., *Interwoven Destinies: Cities and the Nation* (1993).

21. The Texas I.A.F. Vision For Public Schools: Communities of Learners (1990).

22. "Should All Parents Be Involved In All School Decisions?" *NEA Today*, April 1996.

Chapter 14

1. Personal Interview with Ramon Cortines, 10 May 1996.

2. Personal Interview with David Hornbeck, 30 April 1996.

3. The School District of Philadelphia, "Action Design: Children Achieving," 6 February 1995.

4. Personal Interview with Thomas Payzant, 24 May 1996.

5. Thomas W. Payzant, "Restructuring San Diego City Schools: The Myths and Realities of Systemic Change," (The Claremont Graduate School, April 1992).

6. Personal Interview with Sam Sava, 16 December 1996.

7. National Association of Elementary School Principals, *Proficiencies for Principals: Elementary and Middle Schools* (Revised, 1991).

8. National Association of Elementary School Principals *Standards for Quality Elementary & Middle Schools Kindergarten Through Eighth Grade* (Third Edition, 1996).

9. Personal Interview with Anne Bryant, 3 December 1996; Anne L. Bryant, "NSBA is Engaging in an Extensive Strategic Planning Process to Set a Clear Vision for the 21st Century,' *School Board News*, 29 October 1996; Ann Bradley, "With Bryant At Helm, NSBA Eyes New Role," *Education Week*, 5 June 1996; "Joint Communique," 19-22 September 1996.

10. Dr. Anne L. Bryant, executive director of NSBA, and Don Cameron, executive director of NEA, were elected to be co-chairs of the 15-member Forum on Education and Technology. These 15 CEOs pledged to work together to bring technology to the nation's schools and classrooms. See Andrew Trotter, "CEOs, Educators Unite With a Strong Promise To Promote Technology," *Education Week*, 12 March 1997.

11. Judith B. Saks, *Character Education in the Classroom: How America's School Boards Are Promoting Values and Virtues* (1996).

12. For using technology as a catalyst for restructuring our schools, see Terrel H. Bell and Donna L. Elmquist, *How To Shape Up Our Nation's Schools: Three Crucial Steps for Renewing American Education* (1991).

13. Personal Interview with Howard D. Mehlinger, 16 May 1996.

14. Howard D. Mehlinger, *School Reform in the Information Age* (1995).

15. Jerry W. Willis and Howard D. Mehlinger, "Information Technology and Teacher Education," in *Handbook of Research on Teacher Education* (Second Edition, 1995).

16. Howard D. Mehlinger, "Technology For Teaching: Center Explores Issues," *Phone +*, July 1993.

17. U.S. Department of Education, *Getting America's Students Ready for the 21st Century: Meeting the Technology Literacy Challenge* (June 1996).

Chapter 15

1. Personal Interview with Albert Shanker, 29 April 1996.

2. This quote is taken from Albert Shanker's last column published in the *New York Times*, 2 March 1997.

3. Albert Shanker, "Why Schools Need Standards And Innovation," *Education Week*, 1 January 1996.

4. Ann Bradley, "AFT Project To Push Order and Basics," *Education Week*, 6 September 1995.

5. Albert Shanker, "Where We Stand A Battle in D.C.," *New York Times*, 21 January 1996.

6. Albert Shanker, "Where We Stand: Risky Business," *New York Times*, 18 February 1996.

7. Albert Shanker, "Quality Assurance: What Must Be Done to Strengthen the Teaching Profession," *Phi Delta Kappan*, October 1996.

8. Personal Interview with Bob Chase, 12 December 1996.

9. Bob Chase, "Commentary:Which Charters Are Smarter?" *Education Week*, 4 December 1996.

10. Personal interview with Helen Bernstein, 26 November 1996.

11. Personal interview with Thomas C. Boysen, 14 May 1996.

12. Personal interview with Nancy Grasmick, 24 April 1996.

13. Kentucky Department of Education, *Kentucky Education Reform: The First Five Years—1990-1995* (June 1995).

14. Maryland State Department of Education, "Maryland Education: Connections," March/April 1996.

15. Maryland State Department of Education, "School Reconstruction: State Intervention Procedures for Schools Not Progressing Toward State Standards," Fact Sheet #5, Revised December 1995.
16. Maryland State Department of Education, "Improving Learning for All Children Through School Reform: Education Reform in Maryland: 1977-1996," April 1996.
17. Maryland State Department of Education, "Raising Expectations for Maryland Students: MSPAP Parent Handbook," (no date).
18. Personal Interview with Christopher Cross, 24 April 1996.
19. *1995 Annual Report: Council For Basic Education.*
20. Council for Basic Education, "Special Report: History in the Making: An Independent Review of the Voluntary National History Standards," January 1996.

Chapter 16
1. Peter Drucker, "The Age of Social Transformation," *Atlantic Monthly*, November 1994; "The Rise of the Knowledge Society," *The Wilson Quarterly*, Spring 1993; Peter Drucker, *Post-Industrial Society* (1993); and see also Robert Reich, *The Work of Nations: Preparing Ourselves for 21ˢᵗ Century Capitalism* (1991).
2. Drucker, Ibid.
3. Linkages between education and economic productivity are multiple, complex and causal in both directions—educational investment increases productivity and higher productivity increases investment in education. Investment in a college education is still one of the most significant an individual can make—a return of 11 percent. *Economic Report of the President* (February 1996).
4. Condition of Education, 1995; Nathan Caplan, Marcella H. Choy and John K. Whitmore, "Indochinese Refugee Families and Academic Achievement," *Scientific American*, February 1992; Gary S. Becker, "Economic Viewpoint," *Business Week*, 6 February 1995; See William J. Beeman and Isaiah Frank, *New Dynamics in the Global Economy* (CEC 1988).
5. Roland Sturm, *How Do Education and Training Affect a Country's Economic Performance? A Literature Survey* (Rand Institute on Education and Training, 1994).
6. *Condition of Education*, 1995.
7. Nathan Caplan, Marcella H. Choy and John K. Whitmore, "Indochinese Refugee Families and Academic Achievement," *Scientific American*, February 1992.
8. *Washington Post* (October 14, 1996), and the 1992 Survey of Consumer Finances, Congressional Budget Office.
9. Gary S. Becker, "Economic Viewpoint," *Business Week*, 6 February 1995.
10. Information taken from U.S. Department of Education, Office of Educational Research *The Condition of Education 1995*; U.S. Department of Education, Office of Educational Research and Improvement *Digest of Educational Statistics 1995*; and Linda Darling-Hammond "Democracy and Access to Education," *Democracy, Education, and the Schools* edited by Roger Soder (1996). Economic Policy Institute, *The State of Working America 1996-97*. Also see U.S. General Accounting Office, "School Finance: State Efforts to Reduce Gaps between Poor and Wealthy District," 1997.

11. Sturm, *How Do Education and Training Affect a Country's Economic Performance?* (1994).

12. U.S. Bureau of Labor Statistics, "Comparative Real Gross Domestic Product, Real GDP Per Capita, and Real GDP Per Employed Person: Fourteen Countries, 1950-1990,: Memorandum, 1991.

13. Sven Groennings, Kent Lloyd, Jack Carlson and Diane Ramsey, "Education Reform and Investment, New England's Economic Stake," *Connection,* Winter 1992. The *1995 Economic Report of the President* states, "If real compensation had continued to grow at the same rate after 1973 as it had in the previous 25 years, the average compensation of a full-time worker in the United States would have been $62,400 instead of $40,000." Workers would have lost $22,400.

14. Official estimates of gross private domestic investments are badly flawed, failing to accurately account for the tangible and nontangible human knowledge investments by all sectors of the U.S. economy. See John W. Kendrick, "Total Capital and Economic Growth," *Atlantic Economic Journal,* March 1994, presidential address. Baumol has concluded that only about one-fourth of the productivity gain since 1948 came through an increase in education (26%) and on-the-job training over one-half (55%). Baumol, W.J., S.A. Blackman, and E.N. Wolff, *Productivity and American Leadership* (1989).

15. Juliet B. Schor, *The Overworked American: The Unexpected Decline of Leisure* (1991).

16. Lawrence Mishel, Jared Bernstein and John Schmitt *The State of Working America 1996-97*, Economic Policy Institute (1996).

17. See Lester Thurow, *The Future of Capitalism: How Today's Economic Forces Shape Tomorrow's World* (1996). Thurow cites research by a wide-range of economists on falling real wages.

18. U.S. Bureau of the Census (1993) and Council of Economic Advisors, *Economic Report of the President 1995.*

19. See William J. Beeman and Isaiah Frank, *New Dynamics in the Global Economy* (CEC 1988).

20. John Cassidy, "Who Killed the Middle Class?" *New Yorker,* October 1995.

21. Kevin Phillips, *Boiling Point: The Decline of Middle Class Prosperity* (1993).

22. Personal Interview with Milton Goldberg, 29 October 1996.

23. *Prisoners of Time* (National Commission on Time and Learning (1994).

24. Terri Bergman, "The Essential Components of a Successful Education System: Putting Policy into Practice," (Education Task Force of The Business Roundtable, December 1992).

Chapter 17

1. Thomas Toch, *In The Name of Excellence: The Struggle to Reform the Nation's Schools, Why It's Failing and What Should Be Done* (1991).

2. Personal Interview with Thomas Toch, 29 April 1996.

3. Thomas Toch, "Schools That Work," *U.S. News & World Report,* 7 October 1996.

4. Thomas Toch, "Why Teachers Don't Teach: How Teacher Unions Are Wrecking Our Schools," *U.S. News & World Report,* 26 February 1996.

5. Wellford W. Wilms, "Laboring Toward a New Compact on Schools: Why Teachers' Unions Should Not Be A Political Scapegoal," *Education Week,* 2

October 1996. This article describes the new Teacher Union Reform Network (TURN).

6. Albert Shanker, "Quality Assurance: What Must Be Done to Strengthen the Teaching Profession," *Phi Delta Kappan,* October 1996.

7. Chris Pipho, "States Move Reform Closer to Reality," *Phi Delta Kappan,* December 1986.

8. Chris Pipho, "Stateline," *Phi Delta Kappan,* June, September, October, November, December 1996.

9. Personal Interview with Gordon Ambach, 27 November 1996.

10. Gordon Ambach, Testimony Before The House Committee on Economics and Educational Opportunties June 7, 1995; also see Council of Chief State School Officers, *1997 Federal Education Policy and Funding Recommendations* (November 15, 1996); and Gordon M. Ambach, "Federal Action Essential for Education Reform," in John F. Jennings, Ed. *National Issues in Education: The Past is Prologue* (1993); and Gordon M. Ambach, " Goals 2000: A New Partnership for Student Achievement," in John F. Jennings, Ed. *National Issues in Education: Goals 2000 and School to Work* (1995).

11. Personal Interview with Frank Newman, 9 December 1996.

12. Education Commission of the States *Standards & Education: A Roadmap for State Policymakers* (March 1996); also see *Bending Without Breaking: Improving Education Through Flexibility & Choise* (June 1996); and *Bridging the Gap: School Reform and Student Achievement* (December 1995).

13. Personal Interview with Jack Jennings, 25 April 1996.

14. See newsletters by Jack Jennings and Diane Stark, "A View From the Capital," Phi Delta Kappan Wasington Newsletter, Center on National Education Policy.

15. Thomas W. Payzant and Jessica Levin, "Improving America's Schools for Children in Greatest Need," in John F. Jennings, Ed., *National Issues in Education* (1995).

16. John F. Jennings, "Travels Without Charlie," *Phi Delta Kappan* (September 1996).

17. Jean Johnson, et al., *Assignment Incomplete: The Unfinished Business of Education Reform,* Public Agenda Foundation, 1995.

18. Nancy Kober, "Do We Still Need Public Schools?" Center on National Education Policy and Phi Delta Kappa (1996).

19. Personal Interview with Senator James Jeffords, 30 October 1996.

20. The District of Columbia Financial Responsibility and Management Assistance Authority, *Children in Crises: A Report on the Failure of D.C.'s Public Schools* (November 1996)

21. James M. Jeffords, "What Congress Is Doing And What We want the District to Do in Return," *Washington Post* (27 October 1996).

22. Richard W. Riley, *Second Annual State of American Education Address,* 1 February 1995.

23. Albert R. Hunt, "Education Becomes Top Issue, and Consensus may Emerge for Significant Change," *The Wall Street Journal,* 14 March 1997.

24. Richard W. Riley, *First Annual State of American Education Address,* 15 February 1994.

25. Testimony of Richard W. Riley, U.S. Secretary of Education, before the Senate Committee On Labor and Human Resources Subcommittee on Education, arts and Humanities, Friday, 7 October 1994.
26. Testimony of Richard W. Riley, Secretary, U.S. Department of Education before the Committee on Economic and Educational Opportunities, U.S. House of Representatives, 29 June 1995.
27. Richard W. Riley, "We Do More With Less," *The Washington Post*, 3 July 1995.
28. Richard W. Riley, *Third Annual State of American Education Address*, 28 February 1996.
29. Richard W. Riley, *Fourth Annual State of American Education Address*, 18 February 1997
30. Secretary Riley's simulated interview was taken from his public "State of American Education" address and testimony before Congress, found on the U.S. Department of Education web site.

Chapter 18

1. Ernest L. Boyer, *The Basic School: A Community for Learning* (1995).
2. See such process tools as Wendy S. Hopfenberg, Henry M. Levin, and Associates, *The Accelerated Schools Resource Guide* (1993); and The National Goals Panel, *Community Action Tool Kit — A Do It Yourself Kit for Education Renewal* (No date).
3. A comprehensive 10-component school reform model is presented in David Hornbeck's *Children Achieving*, An Action Design for the School District of Philadelphia (6 February 1995). See also Chapter 14 in this book. Henry M. Levin, Wendy S. Hopfenberg and Associates identify organization development perspectives and steps for school reform in *The Accelerated Schools Resource Guide* (1993). See Boyer, *The Basic School* (1995). National Association of Elementary School Principals, *Standards for Quality Elementary & Middle Schools* (3rd edition, 1996). New American Schools and RAND are developing a school district assessment instrument comparing attributes of a traditional system with attributes of a supportive operating environment (in press, 1997). Dennis Doyle and S. Pimental of the Hudson Institute have defined a nine-point process to create high-performance schools, in *Setting Standards, Meeting Standards: Creating High Performance Schools* (Hudson Institute, 1997); the nine points are also listed in The National Education Goals Report, Executive Summary for 1996. The nine points combine elements of the five reform principles and eight components of a reform model: 1) Build demand for standards and reform; 2) Set high academic standards; 3) Conduct an 'educational inventory' to identify the school system's strengths and weaknesses; 4) Build community consensus; 5) Reorganize for change; 6) Develop new student assessments; 7) Build staff capacity; 8) Create an accountability system; and 9) Set checkpoints and make adjustments as needed.
4. Linda Darling-Hammond, et al., "Restructuring Schools For High Performance," in Susan H. Fuhrman and Jennifer A. O'Day, Eds., *Rewards and Reform: Creating Educational Incentives That Work* (1996).

Chapter 19

1. Edgar Cahn and Jonathan Rowe, *Time Dollars* (1992).
2. See Chapter 10 testimony by Linda Darling-Hammond take from her article, "Authentic Assessment in Context: The Motivation for Change," in Linda Darling-Hammond, Jacqueline Ancess and Beverly Falk, Eds., *Authentic Assessment in Action: Studies of Schools and Students At Work* (1995).
3. For an excellent overview of various reform models, see Paul T. Hill, Lawrence C. Pierce and James W. Guthrie, *Reinventing Public Education: How Contracting Can Transform America's Schools* (1997).

Appendix H
AUTHORS' PROFESSIONAL RESUMES

Kent Lloyd, Ph.D. (Stanford University), is Chairman of The Terrel H. Bell KNOWLEDGE NETWORK for Education Reform, a private, non-profit organization. The NETWORK'S mission is to carry out nationwide school reform through education policy research, publication and coalition building. In 1981 Dr. Lloyd was a presidential appointee serving as Deputy Undersecretary for Management in the U.S. Department of Education. Under the direction of former U.S. Secretary of Education Terrel H. Bell, current U.S. Secretary Richard W. Riley and Senator James M. Jeffords, he served as Director of the April 1995 *Key to the Future: National Summit on World-Class Education for All America's Children* in Washington, D.C. He has been Management Counselor to the President of Public Broadcasting Services; Professor of Business Management at Pepperdine University and Assistant Professor of Public Administration at the University of Southern California, where he was named Professor of the Year. While in California, Dr. Lloyd was Co-Founder and President of the Center for Leadership Development, and Director of Advanced Leadership Training Programs for 3600 school superintendents, principals, women, and bilingual administrators. He was also Co-Director of The Rockefeller Advanced Leadership Programs for 100 minority educators. Dr. Lloyd has authored four books on public education, and over 50 professional articles and reports on education, law enforcement and race relations and is cited in *Who's Who in America.*

Diane Ramsey, Ph.D. (University of California/San Diego), is President of The Terrel H. Bell KNOWLEDGE NETWORK for Education Reform. She is a specialist in education and the family, and in creating "responsible learning cultures." Dr. Ramsey was co-designer of the *Family Education Plan (FEP)*, the nation's largest, statewide parent-involvement program. She served as Project Director of the NETWORK'S study of the formation and functioning of effective small groups, and Research Supervisor of a study of the U.S. Department of Education's Regional Laboratories and National Centers. As a cultural sociologist, she has taught courses in Anthropology and Sociology at the University of California/San Diego and Northern Virginia Community College. Dr. Ramsey co-authored with Lloyd and Groennings, *KNOWLEDGE REVOLUTION for All Americans: Winning The War Against Ignorance — Empowering Public Schools* (1992). She is lead author of *RECLAIMING OUR NATION AT RISK: Reforming Our Schools Through Parent Engagement* (1998, in press).

Terrel (Ted) H. Bell, Ed.D. (University of Utah), served as U.S. Secretary of Education from 1981-85 and appointed the National Commission on Excellence in Education that produced *A Nation At Risk*, igniting a decade of school reform in the United States. Dr. Bell is a life-long educator who has served as a classroom science teacher, a principal and a local superintendent in Wyoming, Professor of Educational Administration at University of Utah and Utah State, Weber County Superintendent of Schools, and Superintendent of Granite School District, Utah State Superintendent of Education, Utah Commissioner of Higher Education, and U.S. Commissioner of Education. He was a nationally-known lecturer, author, and consultant. He was the Co-Founder of T.H. Bell Education Alliance in Salt Lake City, Utah. Dr. Bell is the author of eight other books and has been awarded 37 honorary doctor's degrees. He is cited in *Who's Who in America*. With Secretary of Education Richard W. Riley and Senator James M. Jefford, Ted Bell was a convenor of the 1995 *Key to the Future: National Summit on World-Class Education for All America's Children*.